RELIGIONS
IN ANTIQUITY

STUDIES

IN THE HISTORY OF RELIGIONS

(SUPPLEMENTS TO *NUMEN*)

XIV

RELIGIONS IN ANTIQUITY

RELIGIONS IN ANTIQUITY

ESSAYS IN MEMORY OF
ERWIN RAMSDELL GOODENOUGH

EDITED BY

JACOB NEUSNER

Professor of Religious Studies
Brown University

With a portrait, 5 plates and 6 figures

PUBLISHERS
Eugene, Oregon

Wipf and Stock Publishers
199 W 8th Ave, Suite 3
Eugene, OR 97401

Religions in Antiquity
Essays in Memory of Erwin Ramsdell Goodenough
By Neusner, Jacob
Copyright©1968 by Neusner, Jacob
ISBN: 1-59244-743-0
Publication date 7/9/2004
Previously published by E. J. Brill, 1968

TABLE OF CONTENTS

	Page
Foreword	ix
In Memoriam	1
MORTON SMITH, Columbia University	
An Appreciation	3
SAMUEL SANDMEL, Hebrew Union College Jewish Institute of Religion, Cincinnati	
Memoir	18
ALAN MENDELSON, University of Chicago	

I. A POSTHUMOUS PAPER

Paul and the Hellenization of Christianity 23
   ERWIN R. GOODENOUGH with A. THOMAS KRAABEL

II. BIBLICAL STUDIES

On the Presence of God in Biblical Religion 71
   BARUCH A. LEVINE, Brandeis University

The Celebration of the Feast of Booths according to Zech. xiv 16-21 88
   WALTER HARRELSON, Vanderbilt University

Psalm 118: The Song of the Citadel 97
   HARRY S. MAY, University of Tennessee, Nashville

Psychological Study of the Bible 107
   FREDERICK C. GRANT, Union Theological Seminary, New York

Rome in the East 125
   MORTON S. ENSLIN, Bryn Mawr College

God's Agent in the Fourth Gospel 137
   PEDER BORGEN, University of Bergen, Norway

The Samaritan Origin of the Gospel of John 149
   GEORGE WESLEY BUCHANAN, Wesley Theological Seminary

	Page
The Earliest Hellenistic Christianity	176

ROBIN SCROGGS, Dartmouth College

The Purpose of the Hellenistic Patterns in the Epistle to the Hebrews 207
ROBERT S. ECCLES, De Pauw University

New Testament and Gnostic Christology 227
CARSTEN COLPÉ, Göttingen University

Jewish Influences on the "Heliand" 244
GILLES QUISPEL, Utrecht University

III. APOCRYPHA AND PSEUDEPIGRAPHA

The Prayer of Joseph 253
JONATHAN Z. SMITH, University of California, Santa Barbara

The Concept of the Messiah in IV Ezra 295
MICHAEL STONE, Hebrew University, Jerusalem

IV. HISTORY OF JUDAISM

On the Shape of God and the Humanity of Gentiles 315
MORTON SMITH, Columbia University

The Facade of Herod's Temple, an attempted Reconstruction . 327
M. AVI-YONAH, Hebrew University, Jerusalem

Hellenizations in Josephus' Portrayal of Man's Decline 336
LOUIS H. FELDMAN, Yeshiva College

Moses as God and King 354
WAYNE A. MEEKS, Indiana University

Studies in Cynicism and the Ancient Near East: the Transformations of a *Chria*
HENRY A. FISCHEL, Indiana University 372

"Not by Means of an Angel and not by Means of a Messenger" 412
JUDAH GOLDIN, Yale University

Freedom within Obedience to the Torah 425
ROBERT M. MONTGOMERY, Ohio Wesleyan University

Rabbis and Community in Third-Century Babylonia 438
  JACOB NEUSNER, Brown University

V. SYMBOLISM AND HISTORY OF RELIGIONS

Notes on the Symbolism of the Arrow 463
  MIRCEA ELIADE, University of Chicago

The "Significance" of Symbols: A Hypothesis Tested with
  Relation to Egyptian Symbols 476
  BEATRICE L. GOFF, Yale University

The Waters of Life: Some Reflections on Zionist Water Symbolism 506
  V. W. TURNER, Cornell University

ΝΟΜΟΣ ΦΥΣΕΩΣ: The Concept of Natural Law in Greek
  Thought 521
  HELMUT KOESTER, Harvard University

A Sabazios Inscription from Sardis 542
  SHERMAN E. JOHNSON, Church Divinity School of the Pacific

Heavenly Enthronement and Baptism, Studies in Mandaean
  Baptism 551
  GEO WIDENGREN, Uppsala University

Problems in the Study of Iranian Religions 583
  RICHARD N. FRYE, Harvard University.

Religionswissenschaft revisited 590
  WILLARD GURDON OXTOBY, Yale University

On the Universality of Symbols 609
  PAUL FRIEDMAN, M.D., PhD., New York City

VI. BIBLIOGRAPHY

A Bibliography of the Writings of Erwin Ramsdell Goodenough 621
  A. THOMAS KRAABEL, University of Minnesota

Biblical Index 633
General Index 641

Grace Goldin

Erwin Ramsdell Goodenough
1893-1965

FOREWORD

These essays were originally intended for presentation to Professor Erwin Ramsdell Goodenough on the occasion of his seventy-fifth birthday. Before his death, in March, 1965, he knew of our plans for this volume and was gladdened by them.

Special thanks are due to Mrs. Grace Goldin, Hamden, Connecticut, for the portrait which appears at the frontispiece.

The subsidy for this volume was provided by four institutions: Yale University, where Goodenough taught History of Religions from 1923 to his retirement in 1962; the National Foundation for Jewish Culture, as a memorial tribute in behalf of the Jewish community to Goodenough's scholarly contributions to the study of the history of Judaism; the American Council of Learned Societies; and the Dartmouth College Comparative Studies Center. The support of the National Foundation for Jewish Culture was made possible by Dr. Ralph Halbert, Mr. Harold Green, Mr. Wayne Tannenbaum, Mr. Herbert Solway, Mr. Abbey Lipson, Mr. Ray Wolfe, Mr. Mark Tanz, and Mr. Donald Carr, all of Toronto, Canada. Goodenough was closely associated with the American Council of Learned Societies for many years. He was a delegate to the Council from the Society of Biblical Literature and Exegesis from 1956 to 1963, and served on the ACLS Committee on the History of Religions from 1953 to 1965, and on the Committee of Scholarly Publication from 1958 to 1959. The ACLS grant toward the publication of this volume is a result of a contribution from the United States Steel Foundation. The Dartmouth College Comparative Studies Center expresses, through its support, its gratitude for Goodenough's assistance in the formation of its Seminar on Religions in Antiquity, held from March, 1965, to June, 1966. He presided over the planning sessions in January, 1965, despite the onset of his final illness. The paper read at the seminar by Professor Richard N. Frye is included in this volume. Professors Gilles Quispel and Morton Smith, who conducted several sessions, and Wayne A. Meeks, Robin Scroggs, Jonathan Z. Smith, and the editor, who participated in them, are herein represented. It was therefore found appropriate to participate in the publication of this memorial volume, in significant measure a byproduct of the Comparative Studies Center seminar which Goodenough helped to shape.

The extra costs of setting type in Greek and Hebrew alphabets and of preparing tables for Professor Henry A. Fischel's essay have been shared by Indiana University. The Dartmouth College Committee on Research made a generous grant toward the editor's expenses. To both institutions the editor expresses warm gratitude.

The editor hopes that these papers, many of which fruitfully utilize Goodenough's scholarship, may contribute to the critical discussion of some problems of concern to him during his lifetime. He can conceive no higher, nor more appropriate, act of reverence for the memory of a beloved teacher and friend.

JACOB NEUSNER

Comparative Studies Center
Dartmouth College
Hanover, New Hampshire

October 24, 1966.

IN MEMORIAM

BY

MORTON SMITH
Columbia University

Erwin Ramsdell Goodenough was born in Brooklyn, New York, in 1893. After attending Hamilton College he went for two years to Drew Theological Seminary and then to Garrett Biblical Institute, from which he received the bachelor's degree in theology in 1917. He then studied for three years at Harvard, where he was much influenced by the teaching of George Foot Moore, and for three years at Oxford, from which he received the D.Phil. in 1923. In that year he returned to the United States as instructor in history at Yale, where he remained, becoming Assistant Professor of History in 1926 and Associate Professor in 1931, then Professor of the History of Religion in 1934, and John A. Hoober Professor of Religion in 1959. On his retirement from Yale in 1962 he spent a year at Brandeis University, and settled in Cambridge, where Harvard placed at his disposal an office in Widener Library. Here he continued his research until his final illness.

During his work for his first published book, *The Theology of Justin Martyr*, 1923, he came to the conclusion that many hellenistic elements of early Christianity were probably derived, not directly from the pagan world, but from the already hellenized Judaism through which Christianity first spread abroad. Almost all the rest of his scholarly work was devoted to the study of this hellenized Judaism, which figured largely in all his works and was the primary concern of *The Jurisprudence of the Jewish Courts in Egypt*, 1929, *By Light, Light: The Mystic Gospel of Hellenistic Judaism*, 1935, *The Politics of Philo Judaeus, with a General Bibliography of Philo*, 1938, *An Introduction to Philo Judaeus*, 1940, and the monumental *Jewish Symbols in the Greco-Roman Period*, of which the publication has continued since 1953 and which will be completed, by publication of the thirteenth volume, this year. In these works Goodenough set forth a picture of hellenized Judaism which may be seen as complement and counterpart to Moore's classic picture of rabbinic Judaism. But while Moore's work was the careful analysis and description of a well-recognized body of written sources, Goodenough's work required the collection of a vast body of archaeological material hitherto scattered through thousands of publications, museums, and private collections, some of it unrecognized, most of it neglected, and almost all of it misinterpreted. With the presentation of this material, the volumes of *Jewish Symbols* necessitated a profound revision of previous notions of hellenistic, and also of rabbinic, Judaism. From now on, wherever the Judaism of the Greco-Roman world is seriously studied, Goodenough's work must be used as one of the major sources.

This great scholarly achievement was recognized by grants from the Bollingen Foundation (whose magnificent publication of *Jewish Symbols* is a credit to our country), by degrees from Garrett, Yale, the Hebrew Union College, and the University of Uppsala, and by membership in the American Academy of Arts and Sciences. It was, however, only one aspect of Goodenough's career. He was always an active participant in many scholarly organizations in this country and abroad. From 1934-42 he edited the Journal of Biblical Literature and he was long the representative of the Society of Biblical Literature to the American Council of Learned Societies; from 1947-58 he was President of the Connecticut Academy of Arts and Sciences; he was a member of the councils of the I.A.H.R. and the World Union for Jewish Studies, and of the Committee on the History of Religion of the A.C.L.S. In this last role he played a large part in the organization of The American Society for the Study of Religion and was its first President. He was also deeply concerned with contemporary religious problems, a concern which derived from his upbringing in a household of intense Protestant piety. Because of this he was always anxious to determine the valid and enduring elements of religion and to redefine the religious life in the light of scientific discoveries, particularly in the fields of physics, psychoanalysis, anthropology and sociology. He was much involved in the Institute for Religion in an Age of Science, and was a member of its advisory board from 1956 on. At Yale he gave generously of his time in counseling students with religious problems, his home was always a center for discussion of religious questions, and his own beliefs were summed up in his book, *Toward a Mature Faith*, 1955.

All these achievements live on. What is lost to us, and what we mourn, is the personality—the wide learning, the extraordinary combination of clarity and profundity, the candid recognition of the limitations of his learning and of the suppositions required for his theories, the warmth and intensity of his life.

AN APPRECIATION

BY

SAMUEL SANDMEL

Hebrew Union College, Jewish Institute of Religion, Cincinnati

I

Among the cluster of recollections of Erwin Goodenough, over the past twenty years, many are vivid because of what to me is their piquant character. But just as many recollections are relatively flat and unspicy, and yet seem to me to shed more colorful light on his essential character than do the exotic ones. For two years he allowed me the privilege of working in the large room at the Yale library that was assigned to him. My chore was my doctoral dissertation, under him. Normally we spent the day without communication beyond the casual greetings. At that time he had just embarked on the writing of his *Jewish Symbols*, using yellow typewriter second sheets on which he wrote in pencil in his illegible handwriting. From time to time he would get up to consult one of the books shelved in the room, or else he would go to the stacks for some volume he needed. Occasionally he would interrupt me when some Hebrew passage was beyond his competency and occasionally I would interrupt him for his help in some aspect of Philo or of Hellenistics. Normally, however, we sat and worked in silence, but with the common bond that scholarship offers. It was never clear to me why he invited me to use the room. Perhaps he liked the sense of company which can dispel a certain loneliness; I suspect that this was the reason. But it came about in a matter of fact way; he simply mentioned that since we were using the same books, I might find it convenient to work in the same room with him.

Since I found little reason while working to interrupt him, and he little to interrupt me, neither of us used the other as an excuse for wasting time. The pure pursuit of scholarship was not only his deep conviction, but it was a highly personal, highly private, highly individualistic matter and it took on in its manner an undramatic and almost hundrum form. When occasionally we had lunch together—normally he lunched at Jonathan Edwards College where he was a fellow—we would talk of all kinds of matters; a used car—how old his was!—was a better buy than a new one, for a professor could not afford the depreciation; an apartment, or two family flat, was a better buy than a house, for the tenant's rent could help meet much or all of the mortgage payment. Or else, he would comment that he worked only in the daytime, and devoted the evenings to various forms of pleasure, whether of music, which he often composed, or simply of the reading of poetry. Not only was he too tired in the evening to continue his research and writing, but he felt, after spending a good part of the day in his labors, that the law of diminishing returns would set in.

In the room in the library, he was uncommunicative. In his study at Jonathan Edwards College he was a different person, for there he was talkative, gossipy, and inclined to occasional periods of self revelation. Thus, and quite objectively, he was in a situation of some remarkable paradoxes. He was the professor of the History of Religion at Yale, and taught in the College and the Graduate School, but not in the Divinity School. He had been ordained a Methodist minister, but he had no hesitation in professing himself to be "ex-Christian." It was his contention that the study of religion must be objective and impersonal, and yet at the same time, he was one of the most mystic of men I have ever known. It was never clear to me whether his estrangement from the Divinity School was a cause or effect, whether he was an ex-Christian first, and then estranged, or first estranged and then an ex-Christian. Though he insisted over and over again that he had not been reared in that orthodoxy against which his students often rebelled, I always suspected that unresolved rebellion had something to do with it; I never knew how much his first divorce occasioned or accentuated that estrangement; and while there was no doubt that he was relatively more unorthodox than many of the people at the Divinity School, the Divinity School was scarcely itself a center of orthodoxy. When in a course of his, with three other graduate students, the question arose as to the frequency and extent to which a mystic communes with God, Erwin seemed to me to be speaking for himself in saying that there are scattered and sporadic high moments when a sense of being united with ultimate reality is a vivid experience, but the mystic does not exist in constant communion; he rises only occasionally to the high moment. There never was any doubt in my mind that Erwin had that sense of communion, for when he spoke of ultimate reality, or used the Platonic phrase *To On*, he was no longer the academician immersed in research, but the involved person attesting to that which he had personally experienced. Hence, here he was, a sensitive, a deeply religious man, and at war with organized religion, and by his own proclamation, outside it.

At times he took delight in making clear, and even over-explicit, how much he was an outsider. Since most of his graduate students were ordained ministers or rabbis, he occasionally said shocking things, or things deliberately couched so as to shock, and he occasionally said irreverent things so as to witness the effect of them. Sometimes these were of theological nature, in which he scorned orthodox tenets, or sometimes of a historical nature, in which he challenged the orthodox contentions, or sometimes it was simply an almost juvenile sense of mischief. Once at the Society of Biblical Literature, there was a panel discussion on Greek ethics versus Judaeo-Christian ethics. A series of speakers had made emphatic the viewpoint that the Judaeo-Christian ethics was infinitely superior to that of the Greek tradition. I took the floor to make the comment that I was a little disturbed at the facile assumption of this superiority, in view of the effort in IV Maccabees and very recurrently in Philo, to make the case that Jewish ethics and Stoic ethics were one and the same thing. I suggested that possibly the contention of the superiority of the Judaeo-Christian ethics was a product of the circumstance that all of us in that assembly hall were Jews and Christians. As I walked back towards my place next to Erwin, he kept shaking his head and, so I thought, in disapproval of my comment. When I got back to my place, I said, "What's wrong?" He said, "You should not have included me among the Jews and Christians."

A professed pagan and by his own description an unreconstructed pedant, from time to time he would mention casually that he had recently prayed; and, unless I am now mistaken, he then gave us an impression, which we did not query him about, that he prayed regularly. Perhaps one might put it this way, that he had a quarrel with traditional religion but not with God.

II

I have never known a scholar quite so content with scholarship as Erwin. He would, of course, leave the study room to go to a committee meeting, or to a faculty meeting, or to go somewhere else on the rather infrequent occasions when he was invited to lecture. Student groups occasionally sought him out, and to my knowledge, he always responded with alacrity. I sensed every now and then that he would have relished more invitations than he got, and he ascribed the lack of them to his being *persona non grata* in orthodox circles. But he was very, very content to spend each day in the minute and everdeepening scholarship that had come to be part of his life. His favorite piece of writing by his own statement was a very small piece of work, "The Mystical Value of Scholarship," (*Crozier Quarterly*, XXII, 1945, pp. 221-225) which is, as its title would indicate, a highly personal statement of the nature of that satisfaction that scholarship gave him. I heard him on more than one occasion say privately, but also assert in a public lecture, that in Judaism study was but a half-step removed from prayer, and he always said this as if his own study was his form of religious devotion.

He had a way, however, of dividing scholarship into the picayune and the grandiose. By picayune he had in mind the short items which dot the professional journals, in which someone struggles with some pinpoint of scholarship. He often seemed ambivalent about these, for on the one hand he scorned them, and on the other hand he insisted that these were the warp and woof of the important scholarship. He could, however, be equally scornful of works which pretended to be of major consequence, and which dealt exhaustively with large segments of ancient literature. On more than one occasion I heard him allude to certain works as marked by "footnotes that were always right and ideas that never were." He had nevertheless an unwavering confidence in scholarship, especially for its own sake. At no time did I ever hear him describe scholarship, as many academicians do, as the impartial search for truth; such a description I think he never would have articulated. He, however, lived it. It was his code that one must always probe the more deeply, and probe the more accurately, and probe the more broadly.

Partly because of his own special interest, to which we will revert, but partially because of his commitment to a combination of breadth and depth, he was often scornful of New Testament scholarship, especially of that kind of exegesis which is almost entirely internal and which avoids a confrontation of illustrative and illuminating literature outside the New Testament. Since his own work was ultimately designed to express a particular conviction about early Christianity, the evidence for which is outside the New Testament, he may well have been guilty here of special pleading. Indeed, so thoroughly had he immersed himself in materials outside the New Testament that in inner New Testament problems he often seemed to me either a quasi-Fundamentalist or else even a tyro, for he was not *au courant* with the material which finds its way into introductions. He knew primarily the older introductions. While I recall his expressing opinions on Bultmann in the realm of demythologizing, I believe that it is neither unfair nor an exaggeration to state that he was not only not familiar, but almost unacquainted with Bultmann's work in "form criticism." One of my books which I dedicated to him, *The Genius of Paul*, set forth the theory that all New Testament writings, whether the Gospels or Acts or James or the Johannine Epistles, were all in some way reflections of issues that arose out of the influence of Paul. In conformity with this viewpoint, I proposed a modification of the old Baur theory of *Tendenz* as it related to the Gospels, and I contended there that *Tendenz*, rather than history, shaped the Gospel materials. I had rather expected that this display of historical scepticism, buttressed as it was with certain "evidence," would find a resounding echo in him; to my surprise, it did not. While he was, I know, touched by the dedication of the book to him, and while he was pleased by the reflection of his own influence on me in the book, he was troubled by what he called my overcertainty about the historical uncertainties. It was almost as if he, in his own iconoclasm, found my own a little abrupt or too new or too strange or too extreme. He told me once that my conclusions ran athwart of his own presuppositions; and when I tried to find out what his presuppositions were respecting the New Testament, it seemed to me that he had scarcely moved beyond the proposed solutions of the "synoptic problem" at the turn of the century. The New Testament scholarship was for him a challenge for the future, to be met at that time with all his thoroughness.

The fact is that Erwin often worked with intuition. I never heard him discuss this. I did hear him discuss what he called "accident" in scholarship. His own career he described to me several times as the result of accident. His doctoral work was on the theology of Justin Martyr, and as part of his study and preparation, he traveled in Europe. He had already come to sense what to him was the crucial problem of early Christianity, namely, that the theology of Justin was to his mind a hellenization that came too soon; it seemed to him reasonable that such an advanced hellenization should have come much later in Christianity than in the middle of the second century. While in Rome he visited the catacombs, and there he saw the mural art, and he immersed himself in the literature of it and in the datings proposed in the scholarly literature. It seemed to him that there was something askew in the standard chronology, for he doubted that the murals of Old Testament scenes could have begin *de novo* and have flowered into such advanced Christian art in so relatively short a time. The only explanation that he could give himself was that this Christian art was dependent upon an antecedent flourishing Jewish art, and that the Christian had borrowed from the Jewish, and only thereby was it able to flower in the short period of time. But on all sides it was contended that there had never been any Jewish pictorial art. His recourse to Josephus and Philo and to rabbinic literature, the latter in translation, seemed to negate for him, as for others, the possibility that there ever was a pre-Christian Jewish art, and yet he recurrently had the hunch that there must have been. He discussed the matter with both Jewish and Christian scholars and received the assurance on all sides that there had never been any Jewish pictorial art, and that Philo, Josephus, and the rabbinic literature had to be trusted. But the Yale expedition at Dura Europos, 1932-1935, uncovered the synagogue there with its murals of Old Testament scenes, and Erwin promptly saw in this Dura synagogue a partial confirmation of his hunch.

By now he had begun to formulate his life's work, which was to be a history of early Christianity. More specifically, he wanted to address himself to the problem, that was already a century old, of how it was that Christianity had become so rapidly hellenized. The tentative answer which Erwin gave to himself was that there had existed a hellenistic Judaism, thoroughly hellenized, which served as the precursor to hellenized Christianity, and that this hellenized Judaism included such manifestations as theology, and as the mural art at Dura Europos and the precursors of the murals in the catacombs at Rome. Though Erwin knew barely enough Hebrew to make his way through the Old Testament, he had absolutely no first hand competency (something which he repeatedly lamented!) in rabbinic literature. Moreover, the terminology of George Foot Moore, which spoke of a "normative" Judaism, with the implication that there was an "unnormative", began to appeal to him. He was quite content to hold that in *normative* Judaism, there were profound and immovable objections to pictorial art, but by first supposing there had existed an unnormative Judaism, expressed outside rabbinic literature, from which, among other deviations, mural art could be discovered, and even assembled and given exposition, one could then proceed towards the final objective, the history of early Christianity. The first chore that he had to do, then, was to master this deviant Judaism. He turned to this hellenistic Judaism, the chief literature representative of which is Philo. It must be clearly understood that his many works on Philo and even the great monument to his learning, *Jewish Symbols in the Graeco-Roman Period*, were designed by him as prolegomena to his chosen life's work. His first work on Philo was *By Light, Light*, to which he gave the subtitle *The Mystic Gospel of Hellenistic Judaism*. In it he gave expression to the conviction of the existence of a mystic Judaism, organized in *thiasoi*, replete with sacred rites, including sacred meals, and distinct from rabbinic Judaism in the same way that subjective mystical religion is distinct from objective non-mystical religion. Not only did he write *By Light, Light* at a feverish haste, but his haste brought him into insignificant errors of fact and errors of interpretation. Respecting the errors of fact, his chapters on Abraham, Isaac and Jacob are culled almost entirely from Philo's "Exposition of the Law," and Erwin did not take the time to check these citations against the more abundant material to be found in the "Allegory of the Laws." His assumption that he had the complete material was wrong, and hence certain statements about the materials in Philo are incorrect. On a more serious level, however, he went well beyond the evidence in interpreting the Philonic passages. At that time (in the 1930s), so little were scholars interested in Philo that, as it were, one could write about Philo without much fear of contradiction, for there were few, if any, to contradict. The principal objections by scholars to *By Light, Light*, were not those of incorrectness or misinterpretation, but they aggregated in the realm of scholarly presupposition. There existed, and there still exists, a line of reasoning which Erwin used to describe as follows: People reason that Philo was a Jew, and therefore they start with *their* conclusions as to what Philo must have believed; the proper way, though, is to see what Philo believed, and then to discover how this was consistent with our suppositions about Judaism. In the reviewing literature, as I read it years ago, I found little direct confrontation of Erwin's position, but mostly the indignant denial that there was any substance at all in any theory that posited an unnormative Judaism. I recall reviews which took pains to point out that Erwin was not a rabbinist, and, hence, implicitly "ignorant," and one wretched review (how it hurt him!) which asserted that like "all Christian scholars," Erwin had an implacable bias against Judaism.

Erwin was unquestionably handicapped in making his case by his insufficiency in rabbinics, a handicap increased by his awareness that the rabbinic literature is much too complicated to be approached either in translation or, least of all, in excerpt. He constantly belittled his

·comprehension of rabbinic Judaism, and he considerably exaggerated his lack of acquaintance with it; the fact is that while he had no technical competency in that literature, he had absorbed a tremendous amount of its quantity, and quite a bit of its quality. Never to my knowledge has he dared to offer any first-hand opinion on anything in rabbinic literature.

Philo remained his principal preoccupation for a number of years in such studies as *The Politics of Philo* and *Jewish Jurisprudence*, always in pursuit of a non-normative Judaism, thoroughly hellenized, which paved the way for the rapid hellenization of early Christianity.

As his disciple, naturally I read and reread everything that he wrote. What I chanced to find neither clear nor convincing I raised with him in discussions. The conviction began to dawn on me, even then, that so preoccupied was he with his theory of a pre-Christian hellenized Judaism, that he had not taken the time to set forth in simple and plain English what it was that he was about in his scholarship. As a consequence, his studies seemed both to Christians and to Jews to be exotic and irrelevant, as if Philo was an end in itself. Moreover, in his exposition of Philo, he utilized the resources of the hellenistic philosophers and literateurs, both before and after Philo, as for example, in his essay on hellenistic conceptions of kingship. He appeared to a number of pedestrian reviewers capricious both in chronology and also in coupling Philo with pagan writers and not with Jewish or Christian writers.

So preoccupied was he with his thesis, of which he had as yet not set forth a clear exposition, that I believe he never did justice to those precursors of his in the first half of the 19th century scholarship who also conceived of Philo as a source for understanding a hellenized Judaism which paved the way for Christianity. In particular, he surprised me by lacking a real grasp of the heft of Ferdinand Christian Baur, whose conclusion that much of the New Testament writings were pseud-epigraphs was based on Baur's conviction that Christianity could not have become hellenized so quickly as to yield hellenized literature in the first century; that is to say, Baur solved the problem of the rapid hellenization of Christianity by denying that it was rapidly hellenized. I don't think Erwin really ever studied this literature, nor do I think he was ever aware of the great bubble in the early 19th century that all rabbinic tradition and all Christology stemmed from Alexandria; nor was he deeply acquainted with theories such as those of Bruno Bauer, which supposed that Christianity began as an abstract logos-doctrine in Alexandria and moved to a concrete Jesus who, according to Bruno Bauer, had never existed. That is to say, that while there is no doubt that Erwin knew the contents of the New Testament, he was not immersed in it, nor profoundly a master of the problems of "introduction," nor even cognizant of those who had preceded him in the view of a hellenized Judaism antecedent to hellenized Christianity. Not only was he not a rabbinist, but he was also not a New Testament specialist. One might put it this way, that whenever there was a passage in the New Testament that he encountered, no one exceeded him in the care in which he looked up the passage in the best commentaries; but he seemed to me not to have an organic grasp of the heft of New Testament problems. He knew a great deal that was outside the New Testament; he did not know comparably what was inside it.

But how could he? The hellenistic Roman literature is so vast and the interpretive literature so voluminous, and his own bibliography of the writings of Philo, assembled with Howard K. Goodhart, so lengthy a list, that the two fields—Philo plus hellenistic literature—could be a life-time job for any person. The New Testament literature was to him something to which some day he would get to, when he would have finished his preliminary studies. But most of all, Erwin needed to be a pioneer, the founder of a field of scholarship, and not a purveyor in altered form of what had gone before. There can be no question but that he knew his predecessors, but he had no feeling of relevancy in knowing them thoroughly.

III

The murals at Dura Europos had been carefully copied for the Yale Museum, and it was inevitable that Erwin had to give these synagogue paintings his attention. Especially as sporadic publications appeared, explaining the non-biblical material in the murals on the basis of the rabbinic Midrash, did Erwin feel the necessity of protesting. Not only did he feel that much of the exposition of the murals on the basis of the rabbinic Midrash was quite incorrect, but that the error emerged from an improper methodology, in that it assumed that the non-biblical materials at Dura were explicable only or primarily from rabbinic literature; Erwin preferred to believe that the explanation needed to come from the Hellenistic-Roman literature, pagan and Jewish.

He was, accordingly, led from the murals of Dura Europos to the various synagogue remains of the Roman period, and especially to their mosaics and their signs of the zodiac. Some of these synagogues were described in literature published only in modern Hebrew, and Erwin could not make his way in this literature. On a number of occasions he had important references to look up, and on these occasions, I used to read to him the translation of the relevant articles.

But he moved from the murals into the symbols, the menorah, the fish, the rosette, and the like. While on principle he was willing to believe that these symbols could in part be explained on the basis of rabbinic literature, he was inclined to view these symbols as expressive of mysticism. But more significant was his belief that the symbols were more than merely decorative. Convinced that the symbols were mystic, he set about to explain them and to justify his explanation. He had no idea of the immensity of the task he had undertaken for himself when he began on *Jewish Symbols in the Graeco-Roman Period*. He knew that it would be a work of many volumes, but of how many he had no clear idea. By and large, what he was trying to do here was to supplement and counter-balance through a study of the symbols, that is, the non-literary remains, that evidence which he had earlier assembled from the literary sources, such as Philo. Not only did he face the challenge of interpreting the symbols, but prior to that, he had to assemble them, from wherever they chanced to be, and from whatever publications, in whatever language, located in whatever library.

After Erwin had published the first three volumes of his *Jewish Symbols*, I met him for dinner in New York. These volumes had elicited reviews which praised Erwin's tirelessness and which by and large rejected what he was doing. During dinner he expressed the wish (he expressed it to me a number of times later) that I should myself immerse myself in his books, and make them my own major interest. He found it hard to accept that I could be his loyal disciple and not share in exactly the same scholarly preoccupation that he himself had chosen. He then asked me to speak candidly as to my opinion of what it was that prompted certain reviews, especially by Jewish reviewers, which were both harsh and abrupt. I expressed the opinion that Erwin, in the three volumes, had put before his peers a cart without a horse, in that he had plunged right into the symbols and their meanings, but without giving his readers any indication of what he was trying to do and why he was going about it in the way he was. I ventured to say to him that *Jewish Symbols* had up to that point some of the same fault that I had had to find with *By Light, Light* in that Erwin was so full of what he himself was doing that he never bothered to tell anybody else of the whys and wherefores of it. At first he resisted what I was saying, but since a number of reviews of his book were still fresh in my mind, I managed to make some impression on him that evening. About a month later, he wrote to me that he had gone over the first three volumes and the reviews and had come to the conclusion that there was something in what I had said, and that consequently he was devoting a large part of the fourth volume to an exposition of both his intentions and also his methodology. In the preface of Volume Four he states, respecting the long chapter on methodology, that "I have rewritten that chapter too many times to have any feeling of satisfaction with it in its present form." In many ways I personally find this long section one of the most satisfying of all that Erwin has written. I could only wish that he had written this as part of Volume One, for I continue to have the feeling that the high importance of what he was doing never impressed itself on those who looked at only the first two or three volumes, and that very few of the reviewers who damned One through Three ever directly confronted his long exposition in Volume Four. Moreover, as I wrote elsewhere, his books began to appear at about the same time that the Dead Sea Scrolls were exciting the biblical world, and possibly his work was a casualty of the mania that then developed over the Scrolls. I believe the truth is that Erwin's work has been very, very slow in gaining readers, and undeservedly ineffectual in influencing the readers that he has gained. I think that all of this might have been averted had the long essay in Volume Four appeared as the first essay of Volume One, for the issue would have been drawn clearly and the scholarly battles fought directly on the central thesis that Erwin had put forward.

As it is, his books have made their way through the sheer weight of the scholarship that they embody, without respect to his thesis. Like works of genuine, profound, tremendous scholarship, they can appeal only to those scholars who will take the time and who will have the patience for working through the infinite, painstaking details of text and pictures. The fact is that even if Erwin's interpretation should never gain acceptance, his achievement merely in the assembling of the material is one that any scholar could be proud of.

IV

I do not find it hard to account for this blind spot in Erwin of abstaining from telling the reader what he was about. It stems from a fallacious assumption but a noble one, for Erwin was always so dedicated to scholarship that he assumed that mere dedication would be sufficient to entice fellow researchers. Carefully as he wrote and ardently as he polished what he wrote, he seemed to be without the sense of needing to carry a reader along with him. It is not that he lacked the ability to do so, but only that he lacked the recognition of the necessity, even in a work by a major scholar designed for scholars. He overestimated scholars, for he assessed them by reference to himself.

V

It would not be right to omit mention of one aspect of Goodenough's work, which many have challenged and probably more are destined to challenge, and which in my mind exhibits the tremendous range that he possessed. In connection with the interpretation of symbols, he felt it urgent to call upon the resources of the psychology of religion, and hence he immersed himself in Freudianism and even more deeply in Jungian psychology. For his evaluation of symbols, for which evaluation there is often no literary record, he intended to appeal to psychology for illumination. I am profoundly impressed by the extent to which he penetrated that discipline. I am by no means sure that he has mastered that field in the requisite depth and I lack a basis for judgment. I am only saying that once the necessity of entering it occurred to him, he did not evade the responsibility but did the best that an alert pair of eyes and an intelligent mind could do.

VI

The quantity of scholarship which has come from Erwin Goodenough is staggering in its immensity. His was the lifetime of a scholar, and it was to scholarship that he gave his life. The paradox that the work that he did was the prolegomena to the work that he intended to do, is best illumined for me by my last meeting with him in his home in Cambridge, two weeks before he passed away. We had a half hour together; for perhaps five minutes we brought each other up to date on the ordinary amenities. Next he turned to tell me about the nature of his illness. He knew that he had cancer; either he did not know that the doctors had given him only a matter of months to survive, or else the information was kept from him, or else it was disclosed to him and he did not accept it. He told me that though he had moments of pain, he had moments free from it, and that it was quite possible that he would be spared for two or three years, and now he was beginning to get ready to start on the primary chore, the history of early Christianity.

I hope I listened to him in such a way that he had some sense of my giving full attention. The fact is that I could not do that. He looked to me like a very sick man, and it did not seem to me that it was realistic that he had a long time in which to work. It was not alone the pathos, of being with my beloved teacher and friend, now on the verge of death, that disturbed me, but that, tragically, he had now completed all the prolegomena, and was just beginning to move from his digression and return to the major task—and the conviction that he would never accomplish it upset me.

I think also that I was impressed by this, that it was my opinion, and still is, that what he took for the major chore was not nearly as important as he thought it was. The "prolegomena" seemed to me, and still seems, to be more significant for scholarship than still another theory, and not a new one at that, on the rapid hellenization of Christianity. As we were speaking, it seemed to me that I was catching overtones of his discontent that he had dallied too long on the preliminaries. To me these were by no means preliminaries, but as worthy as what he had expected would ensue. No, in a lifetime of scholarship he carved out for himself his own niche. He had devised his own field, and had penetrated it with comprehension, depth, and thoroughness. He had accomplished something so signal that it worried me that he seemed to feel that he might be prevented from what to his mind was the major task incumbent upon him.

I cannot be sure that I reflect his mood correctly. Possibly I reflect my own subjective reaction to what to me was a very tense situation. I was sure that I was calling for the last time on my mentor. I wanted to say to him that he had accomplished so much more than many men that he had no reason to yearn for additional accomplishment. I could not say that, nor even think of saying it. Not when he spoke of the task which still lay ahead.

I left his home with considerable heartbreak. He was, of course, proud of what he had done; but he was unhappy about what he had left undone, and I was unhappy that he was unhappy about it. Yet I could not feel that I could say that to him, as if transmitting a premature eulogy and the admonition to be content. No, I wanted him to remain discontended, and I wanted him to continue, for as long as he had time vouchsafed to him, to work and to write. I only thought to myself that I could have wished there was some way to tell him that I saw no tragedy in his leaving unfulfilled his wish to write the history of early Christianity, and that his accomplishments in hellenistic Judaism were a monument of his own creation to his own spirit.

VII

Even in that last visit, there were reflections of his dry humor. Essentially, though, he was a humorless man. Occasionally he was witty, but more often he was only sharp in what he said. He was greatly opposed to the intrusion of "theology" into biblical scholarship, but he was sure, as he said, that "it's too phony to last." In a conflict in the faculty at Yale, he did not hesitate to describe one man as a "psalm-singing s.o.b.," but Erwin did not use simply the initials. Once at a meeting of scholars who did not know or my relationship to him, I was considerably surprised to hear him described by the adjective cantankerous. I have no idea of whether that description was just or not. Certainly in academic matters he was stubborn and unyielding and combative. Whether or not he was that way in other personal relationships I have no way of knowing, for I myself never saw such a side to him. I know, to the contrary, that graduate students in New Testament, who on the one hand were offended by his sporadic outspokenness, wanted to write theses under him because he was that rare academician who felt that his obligation to his students was greater than his obligation to his own scholarship. He liked to pretend otherwise; he was overheard in the Yale Library early one September to lament the reopening of school and the need to resume teaching for so he was quoted, "teaching undergraduates was like writing on water." My relationship with him was such that I was able to quote this to him; he admitted saying it; he even smiled sheepishly. "I guess I feel that way some of the time," he said, "but after all, if you're a scholar, it's because you have people to teach." Yes, he said it; he didn't mean it. Not at all.

He was not an effusive person, nor did he make a fuss over his students. He worked with them with fidelity and with thoroughness. I know for a fact that he was not one of that modern breed of scholars who lets the draft of the Ph.D. thesis lie untouched on the desk for months. Once when he had three students writing dissertations at the same time, he said to me, at dinner in New York, casually, "I've got these three boys and I've got to see them through their dissertations."

To "see his students through their dissertations" is an exact description of the kind of teacher that he was. He could be merciless, and he could be cruel. He could be sympathetic to a personal plight, but withhold that sympathy from any academic assessment of his students.

In his view, scholarship is kindred to religion, and its function is "to make sense out of the senseless world of ordinary experience... Scholarship is also a sacrament." A scholar, he said, "discovers a good bit of the pattern of man and the universe." He went on to say, "This is the religious quest and the scholar himself who had the experience of perception and validation about the universe has had, whether he likes it or not, a religious experience."[1]

Erwin was, of course, describing himself.

---

[1] "The Mystical Value of Scholarship," pp. 223-4.

MEMOIR

BY

ALAN MENDELSON
University of Chicago

I remember the first class which he taught at Brandeis University in the autumn of 1962. "This," he began, "will be a course in Goodenough." My initial reaction, I admit, was negative—a strangely presumptuous way for a professor to open a dialogue with graduate students. Only a year later, when I had completed the last volume of *Symbols* and when I knew the man better, was I able to understand the mixture of pride and humility with which he made such startling statements. For here was an historian whose theses did in fact require no less than a major reconsideration of Judaism in the Diaspora and of Christianity at its roots. Here also was a man whose rare honesty permitted no other subject than his own intellectual and spiritual sojourn.

To be a sojourner one must endure a certain amount of discomfort. It requires not only the willingness to break one's own idols; it also demands living without their familiar presence. Iconoclasm is pain. What Dr. Goodenough communicated, however, was not a martyr's tale of leaving one's household gods. Rather he communicated—by implication as much as by words—a youthful faith in values which lie behind the search. This faith allowed him to speak directly to members of my generation who were separated from him by almost half-a-century. In the following paragraphs I would like to indicate some of the things which I learned from his "direct speaking." In so doing I shall perhaps begin to repay an old debt incurred by all students of gifted teachers.

I might begin, as Dr. Goodenough's course did, with Plato's *Euthyphro*. Socrates, we recall, encounters Euthyphro while the latter, in moral indignation and blindness, is determined to prosecute his father for homicide. "Good heavens!" says Socrates, "is your knowledge of religion and of things pious and impious so very exact that... you are not afraid lest you may be doing an impious thing in bringing an action against your father?" And so the Platonic questioning begins: What is piety? As it turned out, of course, neither Euthyphro nor Dr. Goodenough's students had a very clear idea about the nature of piety.

In Dr. Goodenough's classroom Socrates was more than a model of the questioning man. He was the ideal philosopher who combined in his life both striving toward the goal and on a deeper level the goal itself, wisdom. Despite Socrates' relentless questioning, the ancient philosopher had a certainty which expressed itself not in logical propositions, but in moral action. The inspiration Dr. Goodenough drew from this interpretation of Socrates' mission was very clear to his students. I remember, for instance, the deep emotion which marked our teacher's face as he read the concluding passages of the *Phaedo* to the class. Socrates, in Dr. Goodenough's view, could not have accepted his fate so tranquilly if he had not already *possessed* certain fundamental truths about the nature of life. That deep emotion betrayed a yearning for non-cognitive knowledge which was the crown of Socrates' philosophizing and the direction of Dr. Goodenough's struggle.

As Dr. Goodenough's very presence at Brandeis indicated, he sought neither retirement nor repose. Long years earlier, I believe, he had chosen his path. As Emerson has written, "God offers to every mind its choice between truth and repose. Take which you please—you can never have both. Between these, as a pendulum, man oscillates. He in whom the love of repose predominates will accept the first creed, the first philosophy, the first political party he meets.... He gets rest, commodity and reputation; but he shuts the door of truth. He in whom the love of truth predominates will keep himself aloof from all moorings, and afloat. He will abstain from dogmatism, and recognize all the opposite negations between which, as walls, his being is swung. He submits to the inconvenience of suspense and imperfect opinion, but he is a candidate for truth, as the other is not, and respects the highest law of his being."

Dr. Goodenough infused life and meaning into texts which are usually shrouded in the mantle of "paganism." It is no exaggeration to say that Dr. Goodenough served as his students' hierophant in this area. Through his unfailing sense for different modes of religious expression, we entered such texts as Apuleius' *Golden Ass*. Through his eyes, Lucius' Prayer to the Moon became a monotheistic hymn of rare beauty: "Queen of Heaven... by whatever name, and by whatever rites, and in whatever form, it is permitted to invoke you, come now and succour me in the hour of my calamity... Let there be an end to the toils that weary me... Remove from me the hateful shape of a beast, and restore me to the sight of those that love me. Restore me to Lucius, my lost self...." Dr. Goodenough understood these words because he had the heart of a mystic. Always the quest for the lost self. Always the hope that man would be answered as Lucius was: "I, the natural mother of all life, the mistress of the elements, the first child of time, the supreme divinity, the queen of those in hell, the first among those in heaven, the uniform manifestation of all the gods and goddesses... I am come with solace and aid...."

Some students, embarrassed by the all-too-human quality of these lines would protest vigorously against "paganism." Dr. Goodenough would reply simply: "You are a snob...."

Perhaps the most beautiful part of Dr. Goodenough's faith as a teacher was his adherence to the original meaning of "philosophy." Philosophy, he affirmed again and again, is more than the study of words. It is the passionate pursuit of something which has substance— wisdom. To hold such an outrageous belief and to act on it in the Age of Analysis is a rare phenomenon. It is also somewhat of a danger; those who pursue the substantial are more likely to go astray than those who desire repose. That is why Dr. Goodenough remained open to all who continued to question in good faith. And that is why I can picture him concluding with his Socratic mentor: "Reflect well and like a man... for you are young and of an age to learn. And when you have found the truth, come and tell me."

I

A POSTHUMOUS PAPER

PAUL AND THE HELLENIZATION OF CHRISTIANITY*)

BY

ERWIN R. GOODENOUGH with A. T. KRAABEL

1. The "Paul" of the Book of Acts

Understanding of Paul and his message has from the beginning been thrown into confusion by many factors. The Book of Acts gives a beautifully written, straight account of Paul and his preaching, the various journeys, the first trial with its autobiographical speeches—and

---

*) [Dr. Goodenough had long intended that his last major work would be a multi-volumed study of "the hellenization of Christianity"; in the winter of 1964-65, when he learned that he had only a short time to live, he determined to carry the project through, as far as he could. As his research assistant, I was responsible for investigating and summarizing the work done by New Testament scholars on the texts and issues with which he was concerned.

When it became clear that there was not time to complete a book, Dr. Goodenough deliberately began to rework his notes and preliminary material into a long article on Paul; he reasoned that in an essay on this seminal and very early Christian writer he could clarify the methodology and indicate many of the conclusions of the larger work.

At the time of his death, March 20, 1965, Dr. Goodenough had written or dictated the material which is contained in the body of this article; as he requested, I have rewritten and edited it, and supplied such footnotes or parts of footnotes as are enclosed in brackets. I have attempted to carry out his wishes and instructions to the best of my ability, but it should be made clear that he had read little of the rewriting and none of my footnotes at the time of his death.

Three of my teachers have assisted me in this work: Krister Stendahl first brought me into contact with Dr. Goodenough and, at the latter's request, assumed final responsibility for this article and its publication; Helmut Koster and Dieter Georgi advised me in the preparation of the manuscript. A grant from the Bollingen Foundation provided financial support both while I worked with Dr. Goodenough and while I completed the article after his death. With gratitude I acknowledge all this assistance.—A.T.K.

Dr. Goodenough's books which are often cited in the notes are abbreviated as follows:

Light—By Light, Light: The Mystic Gospel of Hellenistic Judaism, New Haven, Yale University Press, 1935.
Introduction—An Introduction to Philo Judaeus, 2nd ed., Oxford, Basil Blackwell, 1962; New York, Barnes and Noble, 1963.
Symbols—Jewish Symbols in the Greco-Roman Period, New York, Pantheon Books, vol. 1-3, 1953; vol. 4, 1954; vol. 5-6, 1956; vol. 7-8, 1958; vol. 9-11, 1964; vol. 12, 1965. (Bollingen Series XXXVII).
Psychology—The Psychology of Religious Experiences, New York, Basic Books, 1965.
In the footnotes, "G." is the abbreviation for Erwin R. Goodenough.]

these seem completely plausible.[1]) His message as Acts presents it—about Christ and salvation and about the coming Great Event—is quite identical with the ideas attributed to Peter and James in the same book.[2]) In practically all the older lives of Paul, and in many present-day popular accounts, the authors approached Paul primarily through Acts. The youth of the Church are commonly trained to outline the missionary journeys on maps. Kirsopp Lake said to a graduate class years ago that if Acts is not an historically reliable account of the beginnings of Christianity, we know nothing of that beginning, and so he and Foakes Jackson compiled their great work called The Beginnings of Christianity, which was almost exclusively a study of Acts.[3])

At the same time it is widely recognized that Paul's own letters reveal a man presenting a scheme of salvation which calls not just for belief that Christ was the son of God who rose from the dead and was soon to return, but a belief *in* Christ, a death of the self and a union with the savior which Acts never suggests.[4]) To take a specific example:

---

[1]) [In his article "The Perspective of Acts" (in *Studies in Luke-Acts*. Essays Presented in Honor of Paul Schubert, ed. L. E. Keck and J. L. Martyn, Nashville, Abingdon Press, 1966, 51-59, G. argues 1) that Acts presents a "largely fictional Paul", 55, with an over-simplified and thoroughly Jewish-Christian theology; and 2) that, for the most part, it is deceptively and deliberately silent about the true nature of the Church's developing theology and organization. On the basis of the way Acts ends, G. concludes that "it was written while Paul was still preaching in Rome", 57.]

[2]) [M. Dibelius delineates some of these similarities in From Tradition to Gospel, 1935, 16ff. In his Studies in the Acts of the Apostles, 1956 (hereafter abbreviated Studies), 165ff, 184, he points out that the repetition of the same themes in the speeches of different men is due in part to Luke's didactic purpose, cf. H. Conzelmann, Die Apostelgeschichte (HNT), 1963, 8: "wollen die Reden nicht die individuelle Art des Redners verfuhren, sondern die substantielle Einheit der urchristlichen, dh normativen Predigt."]

[3]) [The Beginnings of Christianity, I (five volumes, 1920-33, hereafter abbreviated Beginnings) turned out to be just what G. calls it here. However, in a letter dated April 5, 1965, H. J. Cadbury, who collaborated with Lake on the final two volumes, says that the work on Acts was originally planned as the beginning of a much larger study; this is indicated in the prefaces to volume 1, page vii, and volume 2, page v-vi, and by the method of numbering the volumes i.e. the five books on Acts together form only part I of Beginnings.]

[4]) [G.'s understanding of Paul in the epistles is elaborated below, 33 ff. in the major section of this article—but not only there. He often found occasion to refer to Paul at length in his studies of Judaism in the Roman Imperial period, e.g. in Light and in Symbols; so also, when he turned his attention to the modern world and its religions, e.g. in Toward a Mature Faith, 1955, and in Psychology (see the indices to these volumes). Thus, long before he began this article, G. had approached Paul from a number of sides and published some preliminary conclusions; for this reason many of G.'s earlier writings have been brought in to amplify and illuminate the present article.]

there has recently been much dispute about the validity of Paul's speech at Athens[1]) as Acts reports it, with the final judgment that there is nothing in it that Paul could not have said. But this does not establish the validity of the speech, since Paul writes in his letters much that would indeed have instructed the Athenian pundits, but which does not appear in the sermon.[2])

The point is that it is sheer perversity to go from Acts to Paul's letters, from a second-hand account to a man's own exposition of his thought. We must work the other way: first look for Paul in his own writings, and then go to the narrative in Acts; be fully prepared (if necessary) to find discrepancies, and to let the first-hand sources have complete right of way in case of disagreements. We can thus judge the value of the secondary work as a historical source, and read with greater or less credulousness the incidents and speeches for which there is no comparable report from Paul himself.

In a study of the hellenization of Christianity as effected in Paul's work, we are under no obligation to make so complete an analysis of Acts as the preceding paragraphs would suggest. But it is so common to read the letters with Acts in mind that we must at the outset raise a few points to show why Acts seems to be a tendentious document written to exaggerate Paul's Jewish conservatism and the unity of the early Christian preaching.[3])

---

[1]) [Cf. B. Gartner, The Areopagus Speech and Natural Revelation, 1955, 249. G. had read Gartner carefully and critically; many parts of the book he considered excellent, but he also felt that it defined "Greek philosophy" much too narrowly along Stoic lines, cf. his comment in footnote 1, p. 38 below and in Symbols 12 : 187 note 1. Gartner would also minimize the distinctions G. makes between the "Paul" of Acts and the Paul of the Pauline letters; see Gartner's concluding chapter, "The Areopagus Speech and Paul", 248-52.]

[2]) [Conzelmann, op. cit. 103, lists the Pauline theologoumena missing in this speech: the "wrath of God" (cf. Rom. 1), the contrast between faith and law, the theologia crucis, the dialectical relationship between "present" and "future", and the idea of an imminent Parousia. In Studies, 58, Dibelius calls it "a hellenistic speech with a Christian ending" (17:31); for the non-Pauline elements, see 57-64.]

[3]) [Most scholars would agree that Acts has a Tendenz which becomes clear in what the auther chooses to stress or play down, to include or omit. In "Le plan des Actes des Apôtres", NTS 1 (1954-55), 44-51, Ph. Menoud finds the pattern of Acts in the missionary command of the risen Lord, Acts 1 : 8. This command is fulfilled "theologically speaking" by the time of the Jerusalem Council, Acts 15, when both Jews and non-Jews have heard the gospel, and the council's action assures that the Church will include both groups. "Geographically speaking" the command is fulfilled when Paul reaches the center of the Roman Empire, Rome, from which the gospel will penetrate "to the ends of the earth." According to Menoud, Paul is emphasized in the latter part of Acts because of this mission, i.e.

Begin with Paul's early life, before his conversion; the most famous passages are Gal. 1 : 13-5 and Phil. 3 : 4-6.[1]) The first passage says that he "advanced in Judaism beyond many of my own age among my people, so extremely zealous was I for the traditions of my fathers (or, my father, αἱ πατρικαί μου παραδόσεις)"[2]). This continued as he persecuted the Church, but he was suddenly changed when God, who had elected him, "was pleased to reveal his Son within me (ἐν ἐμοί)," vs. 16. The RSV makes this conform to Acts by rendering "reveal to me", precisely the sort of reading Paul *through Acts* which I am deploring.[3]) The RSV translation presupposes the vision on the road to Damascus

because he is the one designated and qualified to carry it out, not because Luke is writing tendentious biography.

B. S. Easten, in Early Christianity: The Purpose of Acts and Other Papers, 1954, holds that Acts portrays Christianity in Jewish terms because Luke's purpose is to show Christianity as "nothing more nor less than Judaism" and thus entitled to recognition as a religio licita, 43. This attempt failed: Luke "could not persuade the Roman government because he could not convince his fellow Christians. Paul had done his work too well" 114f. Conzelmann's understanding differs widely from Easton's, e.g. his summary, op. cit. 10.]

[1]) In 2 Cor. 11 : 22, Paul simply asserts that he was a Hebrew, an Israelite, a descendant of Abraham. We must not look for shades of meaning in this pleonasm, but note that he seems to be dragging in every word he can think of to establish his Jewish character.

[2]) [G.'s good friend, M. Enslin, takes this text as clear evidence of Paul's orthodox and unhellenized background, "Paul—What Manner of Jew" in In the Time of Harvest: Essays in Honor of Abba Hillel Silver, 1963, 158f. G.'s vigorous notations in his offprint of this essay reflect the divergences in their views, cf. also the article of Enslin discussed in note 3, p. 28 below.]

[3]) [G.'s remarks here would probably extend to the NEB's elaborate translation "to me and through me" and to F. Blass and A. Debrunner, A Greek Grammar of the New Testament, 1961, which says that *en* here "appears... to stand for the customary dative proper" and suggests the translation "to me" or "in my case" because "'in me' i.e. 'in my spirit' would be unnatural" (para. 220 : 1). W. Bauer, A Greek-English Lexicon of the New Testament, 1957, takes the same position (s.v. *en* IV : 4,a). However, in all but one of the "parallels" which these authorities offer from Paul, the object of the preposition is plural (Rom. 1: 19, 10: 20; 2 Cor. 4: 3, 8 : 1); an examination will show that the "local" translation "among" for these plurals, and the "local" translation "in" with a singular object (as in Gal. 1 : 16), are just as plausible as "to" or "for". But, further, are these "parallels" with plural objects really germane to Gal. 1: 16? The translation for which G. is arguing here is neatly excluded when plural objects of prepositions are alleged to be similar to the singular *emoi* in the Galatians text. (The one example cited with a singular object is 1 Cor. 14: 11, ὁ λαλῶν ἐν ἐμοὶ βάρβαρος; Blass-Debrunner seems correct in saying that *en* is used here to prevent taking *emoi* as the indirect object of the participle. The difficulty of the reading is obvious, cf. such manuscripts as p 46 and Codex Bezae, which omit *en*.) G. P. Wetter suggests a translation in line with G.'s; he asks, „Ware hier von einer visionaren Erfahrung in erster Linie die Rede, wie konnte Paulus von einer Offenbarung *in* ihm reden?" ("Die Damaskusvision und das paulinische Evangelium," in Festgabe fur A. Julicher, 1927, 82).]

(Acts, chs. 9, 22 and 26), a story I think Paul himself had never heard;[1])
I prefer to follow Paul,[2]) both on historical principles and because this
inward mystical experience, implied by his "revealed (with)in me", will
prove to be the heart of Paul's message.[3]) The zealous early years can

---

[1]) [Lake suggests, Beginnings 5:190, that Paul knew of this story in a version or versions told by his detractors and is deliberately opposing them in, e.g. Gal. 1:1, where the phrase "an apostle not from men or through a man" cannot be reconciled with the figure of Ananias in the Acts account, 9:10ff. See also Conzelmann's summary, op. cit. 59; and, for a defense of the historicity of the Damascus vision, J. Munck, Paul and the Salvation of Mankind, 1959, 11-35, where an attempt is made to reconcile the accounts in Acts with those of Paul.]

[2]) [Wetter, art. cit., draws the following conclusions regarding the Damascus vision: 1) Paul's letters reveal that he was conscious of having received direct commands from the Lord, who often spoke directly to him and sometimes appeared to him. In this way Paul's life and mission were guided; this is the source of his sense of election and of apostolic authority, and the reason for his stubborn attacks on opponents—in matters about which the will of the Lord has been clearly revealed, there can be no compromise. 2) But Paul does not mention a "Damascus vision" in the texts where it would greatly strengthen his argument e.g. where he feels compelled to refer to, or "boast of", his own ecstatic experiences, as in 2 Cor. 12. Had it been possible, surely he would have brought in this vision in such cases. The event thus did not happen to Paul as Luke tells it, but Paul was known to be the kind of man who could and did experience such things, i.e. the kind of man about whom such a story could easily have been told.

G.'s own understanding is similar to Wetter's. In "John a Primitive Gospel", JBL 64 (1945) 176f., he argues strongly that Paul's "tremendous revelation of the institution at the Last Supper" must have come in a vision. In Symbols 5:53 note 106, he quotes A. D. Nock's assertion that "certainly Paul's account of the Last Supper was what he had been taught by early disciples;" G.'s reply: "Since Paul denied that he had received anything from them, and says directly that he received this 'from the Lord,' the certainty of Nock is strange to say the least." Nock's statement is now available in Early Gentile Christianity and its Hellenistic Background, 1964, 125.]

[3]) [G. constantly used the terms "mystery" and "mystic", e.g. in Light, which is subtitled "The Mystic Gospel of Hellenistic Judaism"; he realized, however, that they were often misunderstood, see his comments below, page 59. One attempt at clarification was his article "Literal Mystery in Hellenistic Judaism" in Quantulacumque: Studies Presented to Kirsopp Lake, 1937, 227-41. There he indicates that "mystery" may refer to the Greek mysteries or to the mystery religions, which offer *lusis* in their initiation rites. However, for Plato and later Greeks, philosophy also offers *lusis*, and on a higher level; "this λύσις consists in philosophy's teaching that reality lies not in things perceived by the senses, but in the invisible things perceived by the soul," 230. Further, Plato commonly used terms from the vocabulary of the mysteries and "the question of whether these terms in Plato were intended literally or figuratively turns on the existence not of an initiation rite, but of a belief that the process of learning the higher truths was a real purgation and means of salvation," 229. Thus G. could call philosophy a "mystery" without requiring it to have mystery rites, rites of initiation. He then called hellenistic Judaism a "mystery" in the same sense, but argued at the same time that there may have been rites of some sort in the Jewish cult (for his evidence, chiefly from Philo, see Light, 259-64). When a heavy, altar-like table was found to be a focus of worship in the

be taken as no more than they say, namely that Paul was a completely observant Jew until convicted by a great revelation of Christ within himself.[1])

The passage in Philippians builds up a ponderous pleonasm for Paul's Jewishness: circumcised on the eighth day, of the people of Israel, of the tribe of Benjamin, a Hebrew born of Hebrews,[2]) in his attitude to the law a Pharisee, a persecutor of the Church and blameless before the Law (Phil. 3: 4-6). This passage adds nothing to the other except the allusion to the Pharisees. Much as it would have added to his argument to say that he was himself a Pharisee, he does *not* say it—only that he followed the Pharisees (as did most of the Jews, apparently), rather than, e.g. the Sadducees or Essenes, in his understanding of the Law.

In contrast, the Paul of Acts states, "According to the strictest party of our religion I lived as a Pharisee" (Acts 26 : 5); "Brethren, I am a Pharisee, a son of Pharisees" (23 : 6); and even "I am a Jew born at Tarsus in Cilicia, but brought up in this city at the feet of Gamaliel,[3])

---

huge ancient synagogue at Sardis in Asia Minor, G. considered it strong evidence for his position, see Symbols 12 : 195.—For a description of the mystic who influenced G.'s own youth, his "Uncle Charlie", see Toward a Mature Faith, 1955, 15ff.]

[1]) [On the basis of Paul's involvement in the death of Stephen, Acts 7 : 58f, Enslin suggests that Paul my have been much more conservative and orthodox than the average Palestinian Jew. As an equally plausible alternative to the view "so easily noised about today, that all Jews of the Diaspora must of necessity have been far less Jewish than their fellows in Judea," he suggests that these Hellenists (Acts 6 : 9), may be "'diaspora Jews' who had settled in Zion for the precise purpose of getting free from the contaminating danger of the larger world. In a word... we are free to wonder if these synagogues of 'hellenistic Jews' were not of the most untraorthodoxy, composed of those who had at last been enabled to return to Zion, and that their reason for disputing with Stephen was due to a feeling of outrage that some of their own members had become infected with a sorry heresy," art. cit. 157. G.'s reaction to this hypothesis (and Enslin insists that it is only an hypothesis) might well have been that, were it true to the evidence *in Acts*, it would be but another example of how the author has "Judaized" Paul.]

[2]) The NEB suggests that this could mean "a Hebrew-speaking Jew of a Hebrew-speaking family." I can see this only as another attempt at "Judaizing' Paul.

[3]) [In "Paul and Gamaliel," Jour. of Rel. 7 (1927), 360-75, Enslin has summarized what can be determined about this account of Paul's training in Jerusalem by Gamaliel, *if* the Pauline letters are used as sources and Acts discounted. His verdict is that Paul's "rabbinic exegesis" is what anyone who attended synagogue services regularly might acquire, but that "there is not the slightest trace... of any technical halakic training," 370, such as might be expected from a student of Gamaliel. Further, "there is no trace of any connection with Jerusalem prior to his conversion," 372. Enslin is not arguing here for a "hellenized" view of Paul (see notes 2, p. 26 and 1, p. 28 above); rather he is questioning the reliability of the Lukan picture of Paul, much as G. himself is doing.]

educated according to the strict manner of the law of our fathers" (22 : 3). These passages state that, while his opponents might be Jews, Paul was all of that, and in addition had received the highest rabbinic training, that under the great Gamaliel himself, and had even been a member of the closely guarded ranks of the Pharisaic party, where his ancestors had preceded him. Such references to his background could have been used to great advantage in the letters, as Paul defends himself and answers his Jewish detractors; but he says nothing which corresponds to these texts from Acts. An argument from silence may be weak when used to support an unwelcome judgment, but the natural inference is that Paul would have said the more if he could have done so, and that Acts is expanding Paul's remarks for him. In that case, we should suppose that Acts was interested to pull Paul closer to Judaism than he actually was. Thus far we have grounds only for suspicion that such may be the general purpose of Acts, but unless these grounds of suspicion are removed, we have no right to assume that Paul had been a member of the Pharisaic party and a pupil of Gamaliel merely on the basis of the statements in Acts.[1])

There is much other evidence in Acts for questioning the Lukan versian of Paul. Paul himself says that he did not return to Jerusalem after his conversion until he had spent three years in Arabia, and even then he stayed privately with Peter and consulted no other Jerusalem Christians except James. Then he went to Syria and Cilicia where he began a preaching campaign on his own (Gal. 1 : 18-24). But Acts 9 : 26-30 says on the contrary that when he left Damascus he came to Jerusalem,[2]) where Barnabas brought him to the apostles, and told them of his conversion. According to Acts, Paul did considerable preaching in Jerusalem until the Hellenists wanted to kill him; then he was taken away to Tarsus (which is in Cilicia).[3]) The interesting main points here are that he was for an unspecified time preaching along with the apostles in Jerusalem, and that it was the Hellenists who

---

[1]) [Lake considers it highly unlikely that a "pupil of Gamaliel" could have prodiced " so gross a caricature" of the Jewish law as does Paul, Beginnings 4 : 278f.]

[2]) [„Nach dem Plan der Act kann sich Paulus noch nicht an die Heiden wenden, denn die Heidenmission ist noch nicht sanktioniert; andererseites soll er nicht untatig bleiben: die Wirkung seiner Bekehrung muss demonstriert werden." Luke's solution is to have Paul preach in the synagogue of Damascus (Acts 9 : 19ff.) and then go to Jerusalem, Conzelmann, op. cit. 59. The differences between these accounts in Galatians and Acts are discussed by Lake in Beginnings 5 : 192-94.]

[3]) [Acts 9 : 30 and Gal. 1 : 21 may be in agreement at this point, one giving the name of the city, the other the name of the larger district in which the city is located.]

wanted to kill him. He was apparently fully acceptable to the "Hebrews" in the Jerusalem congregation, but the Hellenists rejected him.[1]) The author is indeed laying it on thick, that Paul's gospel, far from being hellenistic, especially turned the "Hellenists" to murderous fury.

The accounts of the great conference in Jerusalem, which Paul says occured fourteen years later (Gal. 2: 1), show discrepancies in exactly the same direction. Possibly the two accounts refer to different incidents, but I agree with the overwhelming majority of scholars who hold that they report the same Jerusalem meeting. Acts 15 : 1ff. says that some Judean brethren (who had come to Antioch when Paul and Barnabas were preaching) had insisted that without circumcision a Christian could not be saved. Paul and Barnabas opposed this, until the group sent them with some others to Jerusalem to have the point out with the "apostles and elders" there. A group of believers from the Pharisaic party upheld the requirement of circumcision (15 : 5ff.), but Peter, Barnabas and Paul successfully opposed them, and required only that the converts accept the "Noachite law," i.e. that they "abstain from idolatry, from unchastity, from things strangled, and from blood" (15 : 28f.).[2]) To this Paul and Barnabas agreed, and they separated to go on different missions. But Paul had no sooner come to Derbe and Lystra when he at once circumcised Timothy so as not to offend the Jews of that region (16 : 1-3). Paul opposes circumcision at Antioch,

---

[1]) [Acts 6 : 1ff. describes an argument in which the Jerusalem congregation is divided into "Hebrews" and "Hellenist". G. assumes that the "Hellenists" are the hellenized Christians of Jerusalem, i.e. the group whose position is close to that of Paul, and that 9 : 29f. is an attempt to conceal Paul's "Hellenism" by having this group attack him. Cadbury argues that the "Hellenists" are gentiles, Beginnings 5 : 59-74, but most scholars consider them Jews whose native language is Greek rather than Aramaic. Conzelmann states: "Sie mussen mit der Gesetzeshaltung des Judentums in Konflikt gekommen sein, dh sie durften die Linie Jesu klarer als die Zwolf fortgefuhrt haben;" they were driven out of Jerusalem (8 : 1) after the martyrdom of the "Hellenist" Stephen, op. cit., 43, cf. 52. Nock agrees (St Paul, 1937, 61ff.), but Munck holds that while the "Hellenists" and the "Hebrews" differed in language and perhaps in place of birth, "we know nothing of any dogmatic or ethical differences between the two groups," op. cit., 221, cf. 219. Enslin suggests that the "Hellenists" may in fact be ultra-orthodox, see note 1, p. 28 above.]

[2]) [Problems connected with this "apostolic decree" have been widely discussed. Conzelmann, op. cit., 84f., concludes that 1) originally the decree embodied a "concession by the gentile Christians" to facilitate social intercourse with Jewish Christians. But 2) Luke's understanding is „heilsgeschichtlich": "das Dekret stellt die Kontinuitat zwischen Israel und der gesetzesfreien Kirche dar." Finally 3) the Western text shortens the decree and turns it into timeless moral commands, adding the Golden Rule. See also Lake, Beginnings 5 : 204ff.]

then his view prevails in Jerusalem, then he circumcises a gentile as soon as he reaches Asia Minor—a story of incredible contradictions.

Paul's own account of the Jerusalem council (Gal. 2 : 1-10) is that he had a revelation that he should go to Jerusalem; accordingly he went to talk his gospel over privately with the leaders there, taking along Titus and Barnabas.[1]) Titus, a Greek, was uncircumcised and, in spite of protest, remained so; the only thing asked, as the leaders gave Paul and his party the right hand of fellowship, was that they remember the poor (presumably the poor in Jerusalem). That is, not a single trace of legalism intruded into the settlement.

The differences are indeed considerable. The Acts account, even without the Timothy incident, contradicts Paul's repeated insistence that the legal approach in any form cancelled the approach through grace and faith. James in Acts does not explicitly say that it was necessary to be circumcised to be a Christian, but such is the clear implication.[2]) The incident of Timothy's circumcision comes in after the

---

[1]) [Lake's solution of the discrepancies between Acts and Galatians posits a certain amount of confusion or differences of emphasis among the participants and in the later written accounts: 1) Galatians 2 brings out the *theological* questions: Is circumcision necessary for Christians? How does the Law apply to gentile Christians? 2) The actual decree was intended to "facilitate the *social intercourse* of Jewish and gentile Christians by establishing rules of conduct for gentiles which would remove the possibility of offense in Jewish circles," Beginnings 5 : 209f., (emphasis supplied). But since Christians were soon rejected by Jewish society, "social intercourse" was soon no longer a problem; by the time Luke wrote, although he knew the content of the decree itself, "he did not quite know what the exact controversy was", loc. cit.

In Studies 94-7, Dibelius shows that the council speeches in Acts 15 presuppose things known not to the men of the council, but only to the reader of Acts. Peter's speech, vs. 7-9, refers to the story of the conversion of Cornelius not as it occured in more common tradition but as it had been reworked and amplified by Luke in Acts 10 : 1ff., cf. Studies 108ff. The important speeches of Paul and Barnabas are barely mentioned, vs. 12, "because God's acts in the mission to the Gentiles have already been related, not in this gathering of the apostles, but in the Book of Acts." James' speech, vs. 13ff., is surprisingly out of character and also refers to the *Lucan* version of the Cornelius story. Dibelius' conclusion, 99-101, is that Luke has composed the story of the Jerusalem Council to fit the plan of his book. "We thus have only one account of the meeting... that of Paul in Gal. 2. We are not justified in correcting it according to the account in Acts."

Conzelmann, op. cit. 89, suggests that Paul's co-workers (including Titus?, Gal. 2 : 3) must be circumcised so that they may enter the synagogues where (according to Luke's presuppositions) Paul's work always begins. See also the preceding note.]

[2]) [On the basis of investigations by, e.g. Dibelius, Menoud and Conzelmann, many scholars would hold that the pictures of James and Paul have both been softened to suit the purposes of the writer of Acts.]

narrative about the council is closed, as though the author of Acts is saying, "...but Paul was not really so rabid about circumcision as he is reported to be."[1])

Since Paul himself says that even a commandment like "Thou shalt not covet" destroys one when it is presented as law (Rom. 7 : 7ff.), I cannot believe that he would have meekly accepted the law of kosher meat as Acts 15 : 28f. implies; indeed this rule was one he openly flouted in his missions (e.g. Gal. 2 : 11-21). Paul, as we shall see, just did not like what Philo called "specific laws".

On less secure grounds, Paul's Roman citizenship (Acts 22 : 25ff.) also seems dubious.[2]) At one time, under Ptolemy and Caesar, citizenship was given rather freely in the East to those who would help in the army, either in service or by contribution. It is conceivable that Paul's great-grandfather had had such an honor, and that is why I consider it a possibility. But it is by no means a probability, for in that case Paul would have come from a great and probably rich family, and of this there is no indication whatever. The only argument for the truth of the tradition is the name Paul; this is the sort of *gentilicum*[3]) one would have taken over on being made citizen (usually by adoption). The story of Paul's various travels and his trip to Rome are so brilliantly told that it seems utterly perverse to doubt their veracity, but if Paul was not a Roman citizen, there could have been no "appeal to Caesar" (Acts 25 : 9-12) and we must regard that part of Acts as romance or propaganda, wonderfully disguised as history.[4])

---

[1]) [Nock, op. cit., suggests an explanation for the contradiction: "Timothy was the son of a Jewish mother, and on Rabbinic theory obliged to be circumcised, and Paul emphatically held that except in matters of tablefellowship... a convert should abide by the status which was his by birth... So he might fairly hold that Timothy was by birth in the category of circumcision," 108. Nock also points out that a strong emphasis on circumcision might well have resulted in a lower status for uncircumcised Christians; for Paul, however, "you were 'in Christ' or you were not 'in Christ': there was no half-way house, and there were no second-best Christians," 103, cf. 109, 149.]

[2]) [On the question of Paul's citizenship, see G.'s "The Perspective of Acts", 55f. (see note 1, p. 24 above). Lake and Cadbury appear to accept Paul's citizenship at face value; see Beginnings 4 : 283ff.; Cadbury's note "Roman Law and the Trial of Paul," Beginnings 5 : 297-338; and his 1955 book, The Book of Acts in History, 65-82.]

[3]) [See Cadbury, The Book of Acts in History, 76.]

[4]) [Conzelmann, op. cit., points out that, when the specific references to Paul are omitted, the account of the sea journey in Acts 27 becomes a unified narrative and is "in hoherem Grade literarisch als irgend ein anderer Teil des Buches," 146; he quotes similar texts from Lucian and Achilles Tatius, 151-54. His conclusion is that

My chief objection to using Acts *alongside* Paul's letters as a source for his ideas is that the essential preaching of Paul in Acts is a Jewish-Christian message practically identical with that of Peter and James, one which asked of converts only that they believe in the resurrection of Jesus and the coming resurrection of men. Paul could use such language himself, as when he said, "If you confess with your lips that Jesus is Lord, and believe in your heart that God raised him from the dead, you will be saved" (Rom. 10 : 9)—and this after the long explanation in that letter than much more indeed was involved. While much can be found in Paul's letters that resembles his speeches in Acts (e.g. I Thessalonians as a whole is very similar in tone), what appears in *most* of the letters to be the *essential* Paul is not there.[1])

I am not concerned with Acts as such, but only to recover that essential Paul, and to see what his manner of thinking was. For this I consider it extremely dangerous to use Acts as a primary source, implicitly or explicitly.[2]) When we have the Paul of the letters more clearly in mind (we shall never have him clearly so, since his writings are often far from clear), then perhaps we may evaluate the historical reliability of Acts. In this article, however, our problem is to ascertain what Paul contributed to the hellenizing of Christianity, once we have seen what Paul was trying to teach.

II. The letter to the Romans

Method or plan is the first problem in trying to reconstruct the "essential Paul". None of Paul's letters conveys exactly the impression of any other, especially in details, and some seem quite different in kind. Perhaps this diversity stems from Paul's wish to speak to each church

---

the chapter is neither an eyewitness account nor an elaboration thereof, but a literary composition with clear parallels in the pagan literature of the time. E. Haenschen has recently tested Conzelmann's arguments and evidence in his article "Acta 27" in Zeit und Geschichte: Dankesgabe an R. Bultmann, 1964, 235-54.]

[1]) [In "The Perspective of Acts," (see note 1, p. 24 above) G.'s criticism of the "Lucan" Paul is more severe, witness the final paragraph: "One wonders if it was someone thinking like the author of Acts whom Paul had in mind when he wrote to the Galatians: 'Even if we, or an angel from heaven, should preach to you a gospel at variance with the one we preached to you, let him be anathema.' For no one in the 'Galatian' or Corinthian churches would have recognized in the pages of Acts the Paul they had heard preach or had read in his letters."]

[2]) [G.'s doubts about the objectivity of the writer of Acts have the support of many New Testament scholars, cf. the summary opinion of Conzelmann, op. cit., 9f.]

on its own terms (cf. 1 Cor. 9 : 19-22). In 1 Thessalonians, for example, he says that the Thessalonians "became imitators of the churches of God in Christ Jesus which are in Judea" (2 : 14); I strongly suspect that the Thessalonian church was made up largely of Jews and their church "imitated" the churches in Judea. Accordingly, when Paul writes to this particular church, he uses the word "faith" as the Judean church might define it, i.e. much more along the lines of Acts than of Galatians or Romans. In 1 Thess. 3 : 5-10 he is anxious to know about their faith, and that they "stand fast in the Lord", which seems to be what he means here by "faith"; he even hopes to supply what is lacking in their faith if he can come to them. He appears to mean: "Hold the faith" in Christ until those events occur which are related soon after in what we might call Paul's "little apocalypse", (3 : 13, 4 : 13-5 : 11, 23). As he uses it in this letter, faith is acknowledging that a body of statements of external facts is true—facts such as that Christ is Lord, that he rose from the dead, and that he will return for the final judgment. When Paul defines faith differently in other letters, it is due in part to his concern to "speak the language" of the particular congregation to which he writes.

In view of these apparent fluctuations, is it legitimate to attempt to extract from a single letter what we take to be the essential message of Paul? I believe it is, since in this letter, Romans, he is provoked by no outside vagaries or problems; he is expounding the message of Christ, the theme of which is salvation. He does this quietly and as systematically as I think his mind ever could work. He becomes deeply emotional in places, but the gospel was a very deeply emotional message and he a deeply emotional person. Nevertheless, his intent in this letter is clear; he is simply telling to the Romans the gospel of Christ as he understands it.

Our approach in this essay is thus akin to that of the text critic, who strives to establish a single critical text, the text which seems to him the most accurate, then he considers the variants as variants from this. We must have a ποῦ στῶ and Romans seems quite the safest one.[1])

---

[1]) [G.'s view of Romans as a general summary of Pauline thought is supported by T. W. Manson's article, "St. Paul's Letter to the Romans—and Others," now reprinted in Studies in the Gospels and Epistles, 1962, 225-41. Manson concludes: "We should think of our document primarily as the summing up of the positions reached by Paul and his friends at the end of the long controversy whose beginnings appear in I Corinthians and... in Philippians iii. Having got this statement worked out to his own satisfaction, Paul then decided to send a copy of it to his friends in Ephesus... At the same time he conceived the idea of sending a copy to

Romans, Ch. 1

The letter opens with Paul's greeting to "God's beloved in Rome" (cf. vs. 7). He states his qualifications as an apostle, one set apart for the gospel of God (vs. 1). In verses 3 and 4 he makes the puzzling statement that the Son was "descended from David according to the flesh, and designated son of God in power according to the spirit of holiness by his resurrection from the dead." Many have felt that this text manifests an adoptionist conception of the divinity of Christ, one that would contradict other passages in Paul's letters. I think the passage too brief to allow taking a stand, thus I pass it by completely.[1]

Paul's commission was to bring about "the obedience of faith for the sake of his name among all the gentiles" (vs. 5). It should be noted that the word "obedience" implies a legalistic conception of faith or, at least, includes in "faith" some kind of acquiescense;[2] this is echoed in chapter eight, where Paul speaks of the law of the spirit in Christ Jesus. One thing we may say surely: this is not an obedience to the law of Moses; of that there is no hint whatever.

Paul begins his great exposition of the gospel in verse 16. He first speaks of the gospel as the power, δύναμις, of God for salvation to everyone who has faith; the sentence states that the gospel brings salvation, but words are otherwise unclear. We are not in a position to bring Philo[3] at once into the picture as a criterion of interpretation,

---

Rome with a statement of his future plans... Looked at in this way Romans... becomes a manifesto setting forth his deepest convictions on central issues, a manifesto calling for the widest publicity, which the Apostle did his best—not without success—to give it," 241. Munck summarizes the Manson article and agrees with its conclusions, op. cit., 197-200.]

[1] [Many scholars explain this "contradiction" by indentifying vs. 3f. as Christological tradition of the pre-Pauline community; see G. Bornkamm, Studien zu Antike und Urchristentum, 1959, 199, note 25. G. points out that Philo ascribes a "similar double birth" to Moses, see Symbols 9 : 118f, where the passage (QE ii, 46) is printed.]

[2] [The relation between obedience and faith in 1 : 5 is explained by A. Schlatter as follows: "Der Glaubende untergibt sich dem gnädigen Willen Gottes und stellt sich unter Christus. Weil er bewusst und wollend in die Stellung eintritt, die Gott ihm bereitet hat, erhalt das Glauben den Charakter der Gehorsamsbetatigung. Darum sah Paulus fur das, was das Gesetz uber die Statte des gottlichen Gebots und seine Einwohnung im Menschen sagte, im Glauben die Erfüllung," Der Glaube im Neuen Testament [5], 1963, 363. (G. commended an earlier edition of Schlatter's book for its definition of the idea of *pistis* in Philo, Light, 400 note 212.) Cf. R. Bultmann: "Paul understands faith primarily as obedience; he understands the act of faith as an act of obedience... Thus, he can combine the two in the expression ὑπακοὴ πίστεως ('the obedience which faith is,' Rom. 1 : 5)," Theology of the New Testament, 1 : 314 (1951).]

[3] [G. will often refer to Philo because this older contemporary of Paul is the

major figure in the hellenistic Judaism which G. sees behind the hellenization of Christianity. He once stated his argument as follows ("New Light on Hellenistic Judaism," Journal of Bible and Religion 5 [1937] 21f.): "First, there is the fact that Christianity grew out of Judaism, and never lost the sense of its Jewish roots... Second, it is equally well recognized that Christianity was steadily hellenized, even though we disagree on the extent of this hellenization... Third, it is equally evident that at every stage in the development of their religion Christians felt themselves bitterly opposed to paganism, especially to the Mystery Religions toward which in many ideas they seemed steadily tending... There is a fourth fact... which is the most perplexing of all, the crux of the problem of the origin of hellenistic Christianity, namely, that Christianity, in the process of hellenization, never disintegrated into a thousand sects... Only after this process of the hellenization of Christianity was completed did the great controversies arise which ended in a number of separate Christian Churches .. Why, if Christians were in *any* sense borrowing pagan notions, taking them directly from the pagans about them, were there not as many hellenistic Christianities as there were Christians under pagan influence? .. Why hellenization, but at the same time a solid front against *acute* hellenization?"

G. finds the answer in the Judaism behind early Christianity, a Judaism exemplified by Philo and manifesting three important characteristics: 1) It is already heavily hellenized, has already drawn much from mystery religions and the religious philosophies of the time. 2) It is Jewish, and so escapes Christian attacks on "paganism". 3) It is a unity in the sense that it possesses a normative text, the Old Testament, and a standard method of interpretation (see below); drawing on this common tradition, not on "paganism" directly, early Christianity resists fragmentation while it becomes steadily more hellenized.

This hellenistic Judaism has two important similarities to early Christianity: "First (in both)... the Old Testament is made into a mystic document, in which literal adventures of Abraham and Sarah, for example, have much less significance than their typological meaning... Second (in both)... salvation is made available to men by the great struggles of the Patriarchs whose lives are our patterns as they fought down the cloying power of matter and received the crown of victory, union with supra-material reality."

Philo furnishes the clearest evidence for this kind of hellenistic Judaism, but he is himself no innovator; he stands within a well-developed tradition. G. explicates this most thoroughly in his book Light, the thesis of which he once defined as follows: "Philo is directly in line with this tradition (i.e. the combination of religious philosophy and mystery religion which presents the "true philosophy" as the "true mystery"), and the Old Testament was for him a guide to the true philosophy by which man was though saved by association with the immaterial," art. cit. (note 3, p. 27 above), 235 with footnote 31.

If G. was to prove his hypothesis, he had to show that hellenistic Judaism as he defined it was wide-spread in the ancient world. Some of his strongest evidence here is the Jewish art remains assembled and published in the monumental Symbols; in this series (especially volumes 7-8, "Pagan Symbols in Judaism"), many of the references to early Christian writings and art are intended to show how the Greco-Roman world influenced Christianity *not directly*, but via hellenistic Judaism. At the beginning of Symbols 12, G. states explicitly that this hellenistic Jewish background to the New Testament has been his major scholarly preoccupation, beginning with his doctoral dissertation, (The Theology of Justin Martyr, 1923); his "approach to hellenized Judaism has been from two directions, as dictated by the data," i.e. from Philo and from Jewish art, 3. He also lists here six kinds of sources for determining "what impact Greek religion and thought had upon Jews of the ancient world," 184. The first three are covered in Symbols:

but we do recall that he regarded the extension of God's power as a series of powers, which collectively was the Logos;[1]) thus, to say that the gospel is "the Logos of God which works salvation" is by no means a poor guess at what this passage means, for in this gospel "the righteousness of God is revealed" (vs. 17). Here we first meet the term δικαιοσύνη, righteousness, a word whose importance greatly increases as we go on.[2]) We shall see that righteousness is a fixed and absolutely stabilized organization of all one's parts, and that the righteousness of God means his absolutely stable reliability, his unchanging character. Here it is hard to see how a mere conception of this righteousness, a mere revelation of it, would bring salvation.

It is revealed "out of faith into faith" (vs. 17) and commentators have long failed to agree as to what this might mean.[3]) I would suggest that it harmonizes with what follows if we recognize that "righteousness' and "faith" have meanings very similar; faith is really "fidelity, stability", so that Paul is saying that out of the faithfulness, fidelity, righteousness of God we ourselves come into faith.[4]) This explanation gives an active meaning to the sentence, something very much needed if it is to be regarded as the theme of the letter to follow.

---

1) the literary evidence, chiefly from Philo; 2) the archaeological remains; 3) "the biblical paintings of Dura". The others are 4) the rabbinical writings and 5) the Septuagint as these manifest Greek influences, and 6) "the new mystic-gnostic material... from the early rabbis" as studied e.g. by Gershom Scholem.]

[1]) [On the "Logos-Stream" and its powers, see Light, chapter one, "The God of the Mystery," and, more briefly, Introduction, 100-10.]

[2]) [On *dikaiosune* in Paul, see the recent discussion carried on between E. Kasemann, "Gottesgerechtigkeit bei Paulus," (reprinted in his Exegetische Versuche und Besinnungen II, 1964, 181-93) and R. Bultmann, ΔΙΚΑΙΟΣΥΝΗ ΘΕΟΥ, JBL 83 (1964), 12-6. The second article is a critique of the first; when the first was reprinted, Kasemann included new footnotes in reply to Bultmann's criticisms. For the distinctive stamp put on *dikaiosune* by the translators of the Septuagint, and its relation to the use of the word by Paul, see C. H. Dodd, The Bible and the Greeks, 1935, 42-59.]

[3]) [W. Bauer says that this phrase "merely expresses in a rhetorical way the thought that πίστις is the beginning and the end," op. cit. s.v. πίστις 2,d,α. However, his explanation neither suits the verb *apokaluptai* (as it is used in vs. 17f.), nor explains the repetition of *ek pisteos*, i.e. of only half the "rhetorical" phrase in the Old Testament text which ends vs. 17. G.'s interpretation suggests that this vexing phrase in a brief but crucial verse deserves more attention than Bauer would allow.]

[4]) [This interrelation of *dikaiosune*, *nomos* (law) and *pistis* is brought out clearly in G.'s essay "Law in the Subjective Realm," printed as an appendix to Light, 370-413. The relation of *dikaiosune* and *nomos* becomes clear in this sentence: "That blessed state which a man achieves when he turns from sin to a life in harmony

"For the wrath of God has been revealed..." (vs. 18). Here Paul continues to speak along exactly the same lines. There should have been no need for this revelation of wrath, since God had fully revealed himself in nature. He has not been shifting and changing through the varieties of revelation; he is the same faithful, reliable, identical God in whom we may come to the reliability and steadfastness of *pistis* (faith) and *dikaiosune* ourselves. Paul parallels Philo when he says that the nature of God has been revealed in the created world, that his eternal power and deity could have clearly been perceived in the things have been made.[1]) We are thus "without excuse" (vs. 20); we have not come into the faith of God, because we have blinded ourselves to the revelation already given. Men wanted something more immediate, could not take anything so abstract; they exchanged the great God for

---

with God's Spirit or Law is the state of δικαιοσύνη, specifically explained as the voluntary following of the Laws of Nature. To say that a man has acted unjustly, has broken the higher Law, or has committed impiety, these are but three ways of saying the same thing, according to Philo and Paul alike," 398. *Pistis* is "in brief that ultimate trust and dependence upon God that marked the achievement of the life completely oriented in God," 400. God is not simply the God of the Old Testament here, but the God whose law is in a sense co-terminous with the laws of nature, as indicated by the first quotation. G. goes on to point out the differences between *pistis* defined by Philo and that defined by Paul, but then concludes: "In any case it is clear that to Philo as to Paul the association of *dikaiosune* and *pistis* was very close," 401.]

[1]) The Old Testament would say, "The heavens declare the glory of God," etc., but to say that the invisible nature of God has been made known in its *dunamis* and *theiotes* (1 : 20) is to use the hellenistic approach. [For Philo see the discussion of Moses' vision of the "back" of God, Ex. 33 : 17-23, in Light, 213f. and the references to Philo given there. For Plutarch, see *de Iside* 71-75. B. Gartner concludes that 1 : 20-23 has little in common with hellenistic philosophical thought; he understands these verses on the basis of Old Testament—Jewish tradition, although he acknowledges that "what really makes Rom. 1 : 20 ...so difficult to interpret is the number of terms familiar to us from Greek philosophy"! (op. cit. 82, cf. 133-44). G. wrote the following note in his copy of Gartner's book: "In the paragraphs on Greek philosophy and hellenistic Judaism, Gartner considers only Stoicism. His argument is that Paul's thinking in Rom. 1 must *either* follow Old Testament-Jewish tradition *or* Stoicism, and while he finds traces of the latter, he says this is only a small addition to the former." See also footnote 1, p. 25 above. On the other hand, M. Pohlenz finds that 1 : 19f. has perhaps its closest parallels in Philo e.g. "die platonische Scheidung der ὁρατά und νοητά, die fur Philon den Eckpfeiler seiner Welterklarung bildet, und vollends die Worte τὸ γνωστὸν τοῦ θεοῦ die doch voraussetzen, dass Gott in seinem innersten Wesen unfassbar bleibt," "Paulus und die Stoa," ZNW 42 (1949), 71. Pohlenz' section on Philo and Paul, 69-82, buttresses G.'s interpretation of Paul at a number of places, in spite of the fact that Pohlenz would see much more Stoicism in Philo than does G. The Pohlenz article has been reprinted in Das Paulusbild in der Neueren Deutschen Forschung, ed. K. H. Rengstorf, 1964, 522-64.]

"images that resembled mortal men or birds or animals or reptiles" (vs. 23).¹)

Romans, Ch. 2

The result of men's failure to recognize God as revealed in nature is that God has abandoned them to the lusts of the flesh, given them up entirely and will condemn them in the last day of judgment; he will render to every man according to his works (vs. 6), to the Jew first and also to the Greek, whether of reward or of punishment (vs. 9f.). Men were to be obedient to the power and glory of God as revealed in nature, but Paul does not say that this revelation in nature is a revelation of God's *law*; he calls it the revelation of *God himself* and his grace, and it amounts (as we shall see) to a law that is higher.

In verses 14ff. *nomos* (law) clearly has two meanings, so that I would paraphrase: When the gentiles do by nature what the *Jewish* law requires, they are a law to themselves, even though they do not have the Jewish law. For what the *universal* law requires is written on their hearts, "while their conscience also bears witness and their conflicting thoughts accuse or perhaps excuse them..." (vs. 15).²) Clearly a gentile never had the *Jewish* law, the Mosaic code, "written in his heart", but a few righteous gentiles have known the *natural* law, the real law, the law of the spirit, and have obeyed it. Such people become a "law to themselves", because they are guided by the true law; even though they

---

¹) This could easily have come from a hellenistic Jewish treatise in Egypt; certainly God in the form of birds, animals and reptiles is a way of speaking which would be unusual elsewhere. [In Symbols 9 : 6 G. suggests that "Paul might have drawn from either Philo or Gamaliel" for 1 : 22f.; he refers to Philo, Decal. 66-81, and to Introduction, 83ff.]

²) [Gartner again stresses the "Old Testament-Jewish" evidence, citing Test. Judah 20 and the Qumran Manual of Discipline, 1QS 3 : 18-4 : 26 as parallels to Rom. 2: 14-16; see his excursus, op. cit. 83-5. However, in "Gesetz und Natur: Rom. 2 : 14-16" in Studien zu Antike und Urchristentum, 1959, 93-118, G. Bornkamm points out four elements of 2 : 14f. which are clearly hellenistic: "1. das durchaus unbiblische, spezifisch griechische Begriffspaar φύσις/νόμος, 2. die ebenfalls dezidiert unjudische, aber umsomehr griechische Wendung ἑαυτοῖς εἰσιν νόμος, 3. das unverkennbar griechische Motiv des ἄγραφος νόμος in 2 : 15 und 4. der wieder nur aus griechischen Voraussetzungen verstandliche Verweis auf die συνείδησις der Heiden (v. 15)," 101f. The idea of personal self-examination in 2 : 15 (quoted here by G.) has its nearest parallels in Philo and Seneca, 113. Bornkamm concludes, "dass Paulus in Rom. 2 : 14f. nicht nur Einzelheiten des Vokabulars, sondern ein in sich zusammengehorendes Gedankenfuge aus der Tradition der heidnischen theologia naturalis positiv aufnimmt, ihm aber durch die Beziehung auf Gottesgesetz und Gericht eine neue, vollig ungriechische Deutung und Ausrichtung gibt," 117.]

have never heard of the Jewish law, they can be fully acceptable to God.

In addition to this natural law available to all men, the Jews have had the Jewish law, which is a wonderful revelation but which they have not kept (vs. 12f., 17ff.).

The summary in verse 29 makes the contrast clear: the real law is in the spirit, not in the written code, ἐν πνεύματι, οὐ γράμματι. The gentile who has neither the *gramma* nor fleshly circumcision (vs. 25ff.) but still fulfills *the law* will condemn the Jew who for all his *gramma* and circumcision still breaks the law. Clearly there are two laws, the law of the spirit and the law of the letter, i.e. the law written down, the law in nouns and verbs. Of these the law of the spirit is the only true law.[1])

Philo also makes a great point of this contrast between the written law and the universal law (what Paul here and later calls the spirit-law or the law of the spirit); I explicated his understanding of it at great length in my book By Light, Light (1935). Philo was a loyal Jew; he kept the law, he did not abandon it as Paul did.[2]) But he was presented with a great difficulty in that he was looking for a law higher than anything which could be put in writing.[3]) The approach to this higher law, he says, is a matter of allegorizing, of really coming to understand what is implied by the text of the Torah; only those who are in a special,

---

[1]) Cf. Gal. 2:18: "If I build up again these things which I tore down, then I prove myself a transgressor." Paul is very cryptic here—How would he have been a transgressor, a lawbreaker in establishing the law? The next verse suggests the answer: "Through (the) law I died to (the) law." Translators may twice insert the "the" which I parenthesize, but διὰ νόμου νόμῳ ἀπέθανον is purposely vague and is most reasonably understood to refer to the paradox that, by rising to the new law in Christ, Paul destroyed or died to (what are a few mixtures of figure?) the old law of Mosaic precept. To bring back the old laws, or to have any hope in them, denies the whole meaning of the higher law. [See pages 30-32 above on the Jerusalem Council, Acts 15.]

[2]) [Philo found it necessary to attack fellow Jews who looked for the "higher meaning" of the law but neglected the "letter" of it; G. suggests Paul himself as an example of this kind of "reform" Judaism which Philo repudiates, see Introduction 79f. In Symbols 12: 9ff. he discusses the agreements and disagreements between Philonic and rabbinic views of the law.]

[3]) [In Symbols 12: 13f. G. briefly describes the four levels of "law" in Philo: 1) "At the top is the nomos-logos, the metaphysical law (with the true Being above it, of course). God used this as the formal principle in creating the universe, as Plato described the Creator doing in the Timaeus." 2) Next come the "incarnations of the nomos-logos, the metaphysical law become vocal (*logikos*). Such a person was the philosopher-king in Plato's and Aristotle's terminology... the *nomos empsuchos*, the *lex animata*, the law become alive (in a person)." Then, for "the great majority of people" God gave verbal laws, the 3) Decalog and 4) "the positive and negative commands, the 'Specific Laws'."]

spiritual frame of mind can come through to this understanding.

The spirit-law, according to Philo, is revealed also in the great patriarchs, from Enos to Moses, who lived righteous, i.e. *law-abiding* lives before the existence of any written code. They offered the Jews access to the higher law, since the spirit-law was also revealed in the Torah, in the stories about these patriarchs.[1]) Their victory was so great, their power of salvation for other men so mighty, because they had revealed the higher law directly and before there was any written code. This is the very heart of Philo's message. He describes these men as νόμοι ἔμψυχοι, incarnations of the law.

I discussed the *nomoi empsuchoi* at considerable length, with parallels from contemporary hellenistic writers, and showed that the phrase does not mean an incarnation of a written code; both for the Greeks and for the hellenized Jews it rather means the incarnation of the higher general law, what the Stoics call the law of nature, a law which by its very nature could not have been a code.[2]) In theistic circles this law became the way, the will, the nature of God himself; the word "nature" came to mean "God" and the law of nature, the law of God. This is the law which was revealed to everyone and which could become *incarnate*, could become written into the hearts of the few great men of old. The idea was carried on at least through Justin Martyr, who was convinced that Socrates and Plato likewise were incarnations of the Logos;[3]) it was so popular in early Christianity that they came near to being canonized as Christian saints.

The background and atmosphere here are platonic: the law, the true law, was a source of platonic reality which could never adequately represent itself in matter. The written law was *ipso facto* inferior to the law of the spirit (to use Paul's word for it). The *nomos empsuchos*, he who was the incarnation of law, had it as his function to formulate law, or rather, to formulate law*s* in writing. It was essential to have a king who

---

[1]) [In a section entitled „Teilhaber Gottes (θεῖοι ἄνδρες) in der jüdischen Tradition," D. Georgi describes this "divinizing" of Old Testament heroes, Die Gegner des Paulus im 2. Korintherbrief, 1964, 145ff. The evidence he gives from other hellenistic Jewish writers shows that their approach is much the same as that of Philo. G. was impressed with what he knew of this book, but had to break off writing before he could make use of it in this article.]

[2]) [The summary in Introduction, 68-71, is perhaps the most succinct; for further bibliography see notes 3 p. 40 above and 1 p. 42 below. See also the forthcoming article of H. Köster in Theologisches Wörterbuch zum Neuen Testament s.v. φύσις and his "Natural Law in Greek Thought" in the present volume.]

[3]) [See G.'s The Theology of Justin Martyr, 1923, especially chapter 5, "The Logos".]

was an incarnation of law, of the spirit-law, so that he could make it vocal, make it λογικός, verbalize it; he himself stands above all the codes, which periodically turn out in new circumstances to be fallible and unjust.[3]) The only true justice was in the law of the spirit. According to Philo the great advantage of the Jew with his Jewish tradition and scripture was not that the letter of the law was revealed to him, but that Moses, the supreme incarnation of law, had made verbal the true law and that the Jew had access to it in the persons of these great patriarchs.

This understanding of the true law as a kind of platonic Real, a basic thesis of Philo's whole writing, is carried over directly in Paul's contrast between the law of the letter and the higher law of the spirit. It is this latter law which, in the sphere of ethics, issues in the higher principles of morality which Paul is everywhere and throughout his letters exhorting the Christians to follow. It is not at all an antinomianism which allows one to do whatever one pleases; one follows the higher principles of morality, but as *principles* and not as specific commands.

It is this approach to morality which appears behind much of what is said in chapter two of Romans. For example, verse 10: "Glory and honor and peace for everyone who does the good, the Jew first and also the Greek." *The* good, τὸ ἀγαθόν which Jew and Greek may do, is a Greek philosophical term, not a Jewish expression; it reflects the universal good and, with it, the universal law discussed above. Whoever practices this higher law, whoever reflects it in his character, brings into effect what Plato or a later Platonist might have called *to*

---

[1]) [In his lengthy essay, "The Political Philosophy of Hellenistic Kingship," Yale Classical Studies I (1928), 55-102, G. argues that this is "the official political philosophy of the Hellenistic age," 102, and "the philosophy of state which thrust itself irresistibly upon the Roman imperator," 100; "νόμος ἔμψυχος was... a by-word for royalty of great antiquity in the second century of our era," 94 ("*second* century..." is a correction written into G.'s copy of the essay). G. found much of his evidence in neo-Pythagorian texts contained in the Stobaean fragments; his summary of the view of kingship stated there clarifies the present article at this point: "The supreme function of the king is by virtue of his own relationship with deity... to infuse into a man a new power, which is a new recognition by man of his own potential nature... until the logos of the king... like leaven, has transformed man's lumpishness into the divine existence God meant him to be. Thus transformed in his spiritual nature, man will be an imitation of the king as the king imitates God, each in turn self-ruled and subject to no external compulsion. So man will at last have achieved the dream... of all Greek ethical thinking, he will be able to live spontaneously by divine law and dispense with the seriatim compulsion and injustice of the written codes," 90f.]

agathon, just as Philo did.¹) Some gentiles have put *to agathon* before themselves as their model; they have "done" *to agathon*, says Paul. Such gentiles, who have no Jewish law, have the true law written in their hearts (vs. 15). Paul here shows that he is using "law" in two senses, that revealed by Moses in the Torah and that which can become *empsuchos*.

Again in verse 13 Paul contrasts those who are hearers of law with those Jews and gentiles (cf. vs. 9f.) who are doers of law, οἱ ποιηταὶ νόμου. "Law" in both cases is singular; "doers of law" does not mean that these wonderful people are doers of *Jewish* law. If they are a "law to themselves", clearly they do have a law; just as clearly, it need not be a written law.

Romans, Ch. 3

Paul has shown that the keeping of the higher law is a matter of the heart, not something external which can be measured by precepts of the written law. The higher moral good which people should practice has of course been reflected in the written law: avoidance of adultery, of stealing, of blasphemy against God—these are all mentioned in the Mosaic code. If however the gentile avoids these, the question is: What advantage has the Jew in having the Mosaic code? What is the value of circumcision? (vs. 1). Because of the way the previous chapter ends, these questions must arise. Though the written law cannot bring the Jew *dikaiosune*, it does at least bring him knowledge of sin—thus verse 20 finally answers verse 1. But verse 2, always mistranslated because literally untranslatable, answers in a deeper way. The Jews were given a share in that great *pistis*²) (of God) by being given the formu-

---

¹) For example, in *de Posteritate Caini* 85: "(Moses) in a thoroughly philosophical way makes a three-fold division; he says, 'it is in your mouth and heart and hands' (Deut. 30 : 14 LXX), that is, in words, in plans, in actions. For these are the parts of *to agathon*, and of those it is compacted, and the lack of but one not only renders it imperfect but absolutely destroys it." Philo omits the references to the Old Testament covenant and to the commandments which abound in Deut. 30. He talks instead, para. 86f., of the sophists who do not keep the three parts of *to agathon* united. Then, in para. 88f., he mentions "the boundaries of the good and the beautiful... (which) were fixed not by the creation to which we belong, but on principles which are divine and are older than we and all that belongs to earth." We have left the Old Testament thought-world; *to agathon* here is an object of philosophical speculation. [In his article in Kittel's Theological Dictionary of the New Testament I, 1964, s.v. ἀγαθός, W. Grundmann discusses both Philo and Paul but makes no particular reference to the use of *agathon* with the definite article, the point which concerns G. here.]

²) According to vs. 4, God is "true" and "just", words apparently synonymous with *pistos*. [See following note.]

lated laws of God, *ta logia*. Most Jews were false to this *pistis*, but this by no means impugns the *pistis* of God (vs. 3ff.).[1]) The few who did not betray this *pistis* will in the next chapter be presented in the person of Abraham who, because he had *pistis* was also *dikaios* like God.[2])

Thus the Jewish law is itself a great revelation of the righteousness of God, and of his faithfulness, his *pistis*, his stability, which stands out all the more clearly revealed in contrast to the people who break the law and so becloud everything. While the primary revelation, the higher law, is available to all men, the Mosaic code, a second gift of God, was specifically given to the Jews; *this* is their great advantage (vs. 2).

But now (*nuni de*, vs. 21) still a third revelation of the righteousness, the resolute "law-abidingness" of God has been granted; in Christ it has been made freshly available quite beyond anything that men have had before. From this point on indeed no one has any excuse. Now we leave the law of the Jews entirely behind, since through this law comes only knowledge of sin (vs. 20).

Actually all men have been and still are sinners (vs. 23); only as they come into the *dikaiosune* of God can they hope to become righteous themselves (vs. 24). God's *dikaiosune* is available only as a gift, only through Jesus Christ; in his sacrifice he manifested God's *dikaiosune* (vs. 25) by his own faith (vs. 22 & 26). We are made righteous because this faith *of* Christ is given us.

---

[1]) The word *pistis* is one of the most difficult in the New Testament, because it appears in a great variety of meanings. I suggest 1) that the noun, like so many abstractions, is secondary to the adjective *pistis*, which means trustworthy, reliable or trusting; 2) that "to have *pistis*" and "to be *pistos*" are absolutely identical in meaning. [In his Kittel article on *pistis*, Bultmann agress that the noun *pistis* and the verb *pisteuo* are secondary to the adjective *pistis*, although both noun and verb are quite early, the verb being in use from the seventh century BC, (English translation in Bible Key Words III, s.v. *pistis* 34ff.). As *pistos* is sometimes more active in meaning ("trusting"), sometimes passive ("trustworthy"), so the noun "can mean the trust that a man feels as well as the trust that he inspires, that is to say, trustworthiness," 36. Bultmann also indicates that neither the adjective nor the noun are religious terms in classical Greek; it is not until the hellenistic period that they become part of the religious vocabulary. At that time *pistis* "became the key word in the propaganda of the proselytising religions, not only Christianity", 41. There is perhaps an indication of the distance between Paul and Qumran in the understanding of Hab. 2 : 4 in Rom. 1 : 17 and in 1QpHab viii,1; in the latter "the saying is made to refer to the 'doers of the Law'... the exact opposite to what Paul finds in the same prophecy," H. Ringgren, The Faith of Qumran, 1963, 247—but see his discussion there.]

[2]) [Here G. finds the same parallels between the adjective *dikaios* and *pistos* which he drew earlier (page 37f. above) between the nouns *dikaiosune* and *pistis*.]

It is crucial to note that "faith" in this passage (vs. 22 & 26) is not faith *in* Jesus Christ but the faith *of* Jesus Christ, πίστις ('Ιησοῦ) Χριστοῦ.[1]) There have been many attempts to make this phrase conform to the traditional idea of Christian faith; I see no possible way to do so. Rather, as the parallels between the faith *of* Abraham and the faith *of* Christ in the next chapter will make clear, this faith *of* Christ is simply his trusting that the cross would not be the end, and that God would save him from death because God is *pistos*, God is the righteous one who is absolutely supreme in that he is beyond life and death. As we identify with Christ, become one with him, we ourselves are given the faith *of* Christ. It is not our faith, it is no goodness of ours; it is a free gift. By this faith *of* Christ, transferred to us, we have hope of immortality ourselves.[2])

---

[1]) [See now the arguments of G. M. Taylor for the translation "faith of Christ," 75f. in the article treated in the following note.]

[2]) [Here G. states most clearly his understanding of "faith" in Paul as the faith which Christ himself possessed and demonstrated and gives to Christians; while G.'s may be a unique understanding of faith, it is quite in line with the rest of his interpretation of Romans and with his thesis that the key to Paul is to see him against the background of the hellenistic Judaism best known from Philo. G. interprets three major Pauline terms in similar ways: *dikaiosune* (see page 37f. above), *nomos* (see page 39ff. above) and *pistis*. (In an article discussed just below, G. M. Taylor gives useful details regarding the interrelation of these three words in the Pauline letters, 59ff.). Just as *dikaiosune* is primarily the stability and trustworthiness *of God*, and just as *nomos* is embodied *in Christ*, the *nomos empsuchos*, so *pistis* is first of all *Christ's pistis*, his own trust in God, a trust which has a preliminary manifestation in the larger-than-life patriarchs of the Old Testament (cf. the discussion of *nomoi empsuchoi*, page 41ff. above). Once G. has said this about the source of faith, he can go on to describe the faith of Christians in a number of ways, e.g. as gift (page 49ff. below) and as obedience (page. 34f. above). In the traditional Pauline corpus similar or identical expressions occur in Gal. 2 : 16 bis, 20 ("the faith of the Son of God"); 3 : 22; Eph. 3 : 12; Phil. 3 : 9.

G.'s "philonic" understanding of *pistis* in Paul might appear so much his own that no other scholar's work bears directly on it; nevertheless, certain references can be given:

1) In the standard reference works: W. Bauer, op. cit. s.v. πίστις, 2,b, β on "the *pistis Christou* in Paul"; F. Blass and A. Debrunner, op. cit. para. 163 entitled, "objective genitive".

2) A detailed study of „die mit *pistis* verbundenen Christus-Genetiv" is given in O. Schmitz, Die Christusgemeinschaft des Paulus im Lichte seines Genetivgebrauchs, 1924, 91-134. Reviewing the debate on the subject, Schmitz points out certain dangers: 1) that of forcing this genitive into any one grammatical category, e.g. the "objective" or the "subjective" genitives; 2) that of defining *pistis* too narrowly, i.e. equating it either with acceptance of historical data, or with the believer's (mystical) union with Christ, cf. 131. He concludes: „Alle diese Schwierigkeiten fallen mit einem Schlage weg, wenn man sich entschliesst, die mit *pistis* verbundenen Christus-Genetiv im Sinne einer ganz allgemeinen Naherbestimmung dieses 'Glaubens' als 'Christus-Glauben', 'Christus-Jesus-Glauben', 'Jesus-

Glauben' zu verstehen, ohne irgend ein konkretes verbales Verhaltnis zwischen den beiden Nomina, sei es nach Art des Gen. obj., sei es nach Art des Gen. subj. durch den Genetiv als solchen ausgedruckt zu finden.. So versteht es sich von selber, dass Christus 'Gegenstand' des 'Christus-Glaubens' ist (vgl. Gal. 2 : 16); aber das ist nicht die einzige Beziehung, die zwischen diesen beiden Grössen obwaltet, vielmehr wird Christus (wie Gott) fur Paulus nie in der Weise Objekt, dass er nicht zugleich ihn selber (Paulus) zum Objekt machte und zwar so, dass er (Paulus) mit seiner Subjektivitat dadurch an der Objektivitat dieses Subjekts (Christus) beteiligt wurde... Daher bestehen bei Paulus die objektiv-historischen Aussagen und die subjektiv-mystischen Aussagen immer zusammen wie die Wasserbestande in zwei kommunizierenden Rohren. Dieser gesamte, in vollem Gleichgewicht befindliche historisch-mystische, objektiv-subjektive Sachverhalt liegt den mit *pistis* verbundenen Christus-Genetiven zugrunde," 132f. Schmitz's work is evaluated by A. Deissmann (who argues for his own brand of "mystical genitive") in Paul: A Study in Social and Religious History[2], 1927, 162ff. with footnotes; and by R. Bultmann in "Zur Geschichte der Paulus-Forschung," now reprinted in Das Paulusbild in der Neueren Deutschen Forschung, ed. K. H. Rengstorf, 1964, 331ff.

3. In an important article "The Function of πίστις Χριστοῦ in Galatians," JBL 85 (1966), 58-76, G. M. Taylor argues that in this letter this phrase is "the *fidei commissum* of Roman law; and that Paul uses this concept to explain, in juristic terms, how the inheritance of Abraham is transmitted, through Jesus Christ, both to Jews and gentiles," 58. According to Taylor, *diatheke* in Galatians is not the equivalent of the Hebrew *berith*, but of *testamentum*, the Latin term for "will", 63 note 8. *Fidei commissum* (which is translated *pistis* in Roman legal documents written in Greek) is the only variety of *testamentum* by which a testator could name two successive heirs (the first-named heir being obliged, if he accepts the benefits of the legacy, also to accept the second-named as, in effect, his own heir), or by which a national alien could be named the heir of a Roman citizen, 66. Applied to Galatians, this means that "Abraham and Christ are successive testamentary heirs, who receive the inheritance in πίστις—*fidei commissum*—because that device is necessary to constitute Christ as successive heir, and because the testament is intended to benefit gentiles as well as Jews (i.e. people of another nation) and to adopt them all as equal heirs through Christ's heirship. The testament can not take effect until Christ, as successive testamentary heir, accepts the inheritance, including its obligations, with the consent of his father, God (4 : 4f.). Until then the intended beneficiaries are subject to tutelage," 67. While Taylor applies his explanation to the Galatian letter generally, it should be restricted to one section, 3 : 15-4 : 7, where Paul is making use of this Roman legal terminology in an explanatory analogy, beginning with κατὰ ἄνθρωπον λέγω (cf. RSV's paraphrase: "to give a human example..."). In 3 : 26ff. there appear the different and more familiar phrases "baptized into Christ", "put on Christ", and "one in Christ"; these are here paralleled with and "geared into" the legal metaphor, which comes to the fore again at 3 : 29. Taylor's explanation fits well with the use of *pistis Iesou Christou* (3 : 22) and *diatheke* (3 : 15 & 17) within the verses of this metaphor, but not otherwise. Thus, *pistis* in 2 : 16, 20 would not be taken to mean *fidei commissum* without the "help" of 3 : 15ff., and *diatheke* is used later in another analogy (4 : 22-31) in a very different, non-legal way (this in spite of Taylor's denial, 63 note 8). Also, the "entirely new and different juristic personality" effected among the Romans by adoption is quite a distance from the ideas "death to self" and "new life in Christ" in 2 : 20 and "putting on Christ" and being "baptized into Christ" in 3 : 27 (compare these verses with the legal text refered to in note 20; see also 66f.). Nevertheless, Taylor's explanation of *fidei commissum*, 65-74, is a valuable commentary on the use of *pistis*

Before Paul can go on to illuminate this understanding of faith and righteousness from the Old Testament story of Abraham, he must make clear its implications for "law"; the philonic distinction between the higher law and the written law is again essential for the argument. On the basis of "law" our boasting is "excluded" (vs. 27), but "excluded" is the equivalent of the German "verboten"; it implies a law that forbids. By what law is humility enjoined and personal boasting, self-righteousness, excluded? The Mosaic law by no means does so, for there is great satisfaction in obedience, in the law of legal acts, ἔργα. God commands, I obey, and the righteousness is my own. The supreme sin of pride, spiritual pride, is here "boasting" (vs. 27), the inevitable result of an approach to righteousness by deeds, acts, obedience. Psychologically Paul is entirely right. Legalism does bring satisfaction the satisfaction of self-approval; we are sure that God likes an obedient child.

But now, for the Christian, boasting is "excluded". By what law, by what *nomos*? The Jewish law, the law of works? No, but by the law of faith (vs. 27). No more clear statement could be made of the difference between the two laws: one is the higher law, which manifests itself and is achieved through faith; the other is the law of precepts, observed only by human effort and thus never really, thoroughly fulfilled.

The contrast continues: according to verse 27b we are justified "through the *law* of faith", according to verse 28 we are justified "apart from the works of *law*". Again two laws, two entirely different laws, the law of the Jews and the law of faith. In verse 29f. this contrast between two laws in linked to the theme of the inclusion of the gentiles, just as it was in 2 : 10ff., 2 : 25ff. and 3 : 21ff. (πάντες).

"On the contrary, we uphold the law..." (vs. 31). By going beyond the law of Moses to the law of faith, we are not overthrowing the idea of God's law, God's way, but we are coming into a higher version of it;

Christou in 3 : 15-4 : 7; in this "human example" Paul again (cf. page 34 above) appears to be fitting his words carefully to his readers, here the Galatians, since, as Taylor points out, "the Galatian was the only non-Roman legal system" to make use of just this kind of testamentary law, 70. (For an attempt to explain the Galatians passage on the basis of rabbinic law, see E. Bammel, "Gottes ΔΙΑΘΗΚΗ (Gal. iii. 15-17) und das judische Rechtsdenken," NTS 6 (1959/60) 313-19.).

4) The genitive might be explained as a Semitism whose closest parallel is the "construct state" of the Hebrew or Aramaic substantive. This explanation would find some support in K. G. Kuhn's article, "Der Epheserbrief im Lichte der Qumrantexte"; here Kuhn shows that "die Vorliebe... fur Ketten von Genetivverbindungen" in Ephesians is a characteristic of its "semitizing" Greek and has close parallels in the Dead Sea Scrolls, NTS 7 (1960/61), 335f.]

through faith we are able to vindicate the law of God, to live it, to *be* it,[1]) once we have realized the incompleteness of the law of precepts and individual commands. When we go on to the law of faith revealed in Jesus Christ, do we then vitiate the old law? Not at all! We are simply going beyond it to a law that is more potent and real, but in essence the same.

Romans Ch. 4

Paul goes to the Old Testament to prove that justification by (the law of) faith was the only principle of justification from the time of Abraham; his interpretation is philonic as he uses Abraham as the great example of the man who is saved by faith.[2]) His text is Gen. 15 : 6. The faith was very simple: God made Abraham a promise and Abraham believed it. This was all that Abraham had to do (vs. 4f.); God did the rest, God reckoned it (ἐλογίσθη) to him as righteousness, *dikaiosune*, i.e. God pronounced him just, gave him righteousness, quite apart from any knowledge of written law, simply because he had believed God.

Paul very much wanted further Old Testament support for this, so Ps. 32 : 1ff. is made to fit (vs. 6ff.). This text has nothing to do with God's "reckoning" *dikaiosune*; it manifests a traditionally Jewish idea of forgiveness, i.e. God's forgiving a failure to keep the law. But the verb used in the Abraham story also appears here (λογίσηται, vs. 8); following Jewish proof-text methods, this connection was enough.[3])

Afterward came the law and the enjoinment of circumcision (vs. 9f). The faith that made God ascribe righteousness to Abraham was a relation between him and God on a level any pagan could experience

---

[1]) According to 2 Cor. 5 : 21, we "*become* the *dikaiosune* of God" by the fact that God put our sin upon him who knew no sin.

[2]) [On the relationship between Old Testament and New Testament which is implied in Paul's use of Abraham here, see U. Wilckens, "Die Rechtfertigung Abrahams nach Römer 4" in Festschrift G. von Rad, 1961, 111-27; more generally on the use of the Abraham-story, S. Sandmel, Philo's Place in Judaism: A Study of Conceptions of Abraham in Jewish Literature, 1956, and M. Dibelius' excursus "Das Abraham-Beispiel" in Der Brief des Jakobus¹¹ (HNT), 1964, 206-14.]

[3]) [J. Jeremias has shown that Paul's repeated use of the verb *logizesthai* in this chapter is an argument by analogy along the lines of the *gezera šawa*, the second of the seven interpretative rules ascribed to Hillel (cf. H. Strack, Introduction to the Talmud and Midrash, 1959, 94, and G. F. Moore, Judaism, 3 : 73 note 14). Jeremias gives the rule thus: "dass identische (oder gleichbedeutende) Worter, die an zwei verschiedenen Schriftstellen vorkommen, sich gegenseitig erlautern," "Zur Gedankenfuhrung in den paulinischen Briefen" in Studia Paulina, in honorem Johannis de Zwaan septuagenarii, 1953, 149.]

(though few ever did)—no laws, no circumcision, and yet God declared him *dikaios*, just.

God's purpose in this was to make Abraham the father of *all* the faithful, of all who believed (vs. 11f.). Descent from Abraham and inheritance of the blessing have nothing to do with the flesh; the descendants of Abraham are those who have such a faith that *dikaiosune* is reckoned to them, imputed to them, whether they have been circumcised or not. The promise was made to Abraham not through law, διὰ νόμου but διὰ δικαιοσύνης πίστεως (vs. 13); this last phrase is puzzling, but I think it should be translated "through the faith that brings *dikaiosune*" since, throughout, Paul has been contrasting *nomos* and *pistis* as means toward *dikaiosune*.[1])

Paul begins to define this faith. It is a gift—this we must not forget—a gift of trust in God, who can make the dead alive and treat what does not exist (because dead) as though it existed (vs. 17). Abraham believed in the steady rule of God, in his reliability, in his existing beyond life and death. He trusted in God's promise of descendants even though he knew that both his and Sarah's bodies were dead in so far as their power of reproduction was concerned. He was as good as dead, being a centenarian, and there had long been νέκρωσις in Sarah's womb (vs. 19), so that the miracle worked by God would have to be no less than a "resurrection of the body". Nevertheless, Abraham was fully convinced that God was able to do what he had promised (vs. 21); that is why his faith was reckoned to him as *dikaiosune* (vs. 22).

Paul has drawn his parallels clearly. *Abraham* believed that God was to be trusted even to effect a resurrection; this was the faith *of* Abraham, and it "was reckoned to him for righteousness" (vs. 22). *Christ* believed in his own resurrection—the passage takes that for granted; this is the πίστις Ἰησοῦ, the faith *of* Jesus, which brings righteousness. "But (the words) 'it was reckoned to him' were written not for his sake only, but for our sakes too"—righteousness "*was* reckoned" to Abraham and "*would be* reckoned" to us, for "we" are described as "those who trust in the one who *raised* Jesus our lord *from the dead*" (vs. 24). And God raised him for "our righteousness," ἡ δικαίωσις ἡμῶν (vs. 25). To make his point clear, Paul brings our faith, the faith *of* Christ and the faith *of* Abraham together (cf. vs. 17 & 23ff.): each is a faith in

---

[1]) [In his article "Philo Judaeus," Interpreter's Dictionary of the Bible, 3 : 798, (1962), G. says: "The heart of Philo's message is exactly expressed in Rom. 4 : 13: 'The promise to Abraham and his descendants, that they should inherit the world, did not come through the (written) law but through the righteousness of faith.'"]

the God who raises the dead, and the result of each is righteousness.

Clearly Paul has had a great experience and discovery; he has found a new life in the crucified Christ—and all this is strangely identified with a gift of *pistis-dikaiosune*, first given to Abraham, then made available to all men through Christ, the Seed of Promise, as we identify ourselves with Christ.

It is inconceivable that the raw experience of Christ should have suggested to Paul this extraordinary rationalization through Abraham, unless he had had considerable association of religious experience with Abraham already. It could not have come simply from the Genesis story of Abraham. How could he have come to think of a *faith of Abraham* which became the *faith of Christ* and so the *faith of Paul*? It would be too much to say that Paul has simply taken over that tradition of hellenistic Judaism, known from Philo, which saw the patriarchs as *nomoi empsuchoi*, possessing great power of salvation for other men. Indeed Paul seldom deals with patriarchs other than Abraham, but (so far as I can see) this is just because Christ, as revealed in the resurrection, was so supremely the *nomos empsuchos*, the incarnation of the higher law, that he had no need of the others and so passed them by. The presence of Christ has made a great change in Paul's theology, but clear traces of the hellenistic Judaism we know from Philo are everywhere to be seen.

Romans Ch. 5

This chapter adds that *dikaiosune ek pisteos*, righteousness *out of* faith, brings us peace with God. It is through Christ that we have had access to this gift and hope to share in the glory of God (this last is my overtranslation of verse 2, "we have hope of the glory of God"). This is all a free gift; Christ died for us while we were sinners. We contribute nothing, our good deeds purchase us nothing (vs. 8). He atoned for our sins by his blood, indeed we are made righteous by it (vs. 9). This seems at first a contradiction of "righteousness ἐκ πίστεως" righteousness that comes out of faith, Paul's more usual expression; the fact is that the wrath of God had to be appeased before he could begin to give righteousness to us (vs. 9f.). We must be crucified with him before we can have the resurrection in which righteousness is bestowed (6 : 1-11, see below).

In verse 12ff. a whole new problem opens up. How could the righteousness of *one* be the salvation of the human race? This Paul argues quite after an old Jewish way. The world had always been united in Adam; all men are descended from Adam and all men have to die, because of Adam's sin.[1]) Paul leaves the Jewish tradition when he insists that "sin came into the world through one man, and death through sin, so death spread to all men because all men sinned" (vs. 12). The fact of the universality of sin was by no means Paul's invention, but the suggestion that the sin of Adam vitiated Adam's character in such a way that "original sin" came to all men as guilt,[2]) and that all men shared in Adam's sin—so far as I know, this is a contribution of Paul himself.[3]) I can find no parallels in Philo, or in any other writings; the Jewish rabbinical teachings definitely steer away from such a conclusion. The rabbis believed that man had indeed become a mortal

---

[1]) This basic framework is typically Jewish and will be found worked out in G. F. Moore, Judaism 1 : 460-96. [For a summary of the Pauline understanding of sin and the Jewish background of his thought here, see K. Stendahl, "Sunde und Schuld IV. Im NT," in Die Religion in Geschichte und Gegenwart³, 6 : 485f. (1962).]

[2]) [See Psychology 152ff. on the connection Paul makes between human guilt and the death of Christ.]

[3]) [The manner in which Paul goes beyond his "sources" to a "unique" idea of original has been approached in various ways. A. Dubarle, The Biblical Doctrine of Original Sin, 1964, concentrates on Rom. 5 : 12-21 in discussing "original sin in St. Paul," 142-200. He concludes: "Paul does not form any systematic theory on the origin of sin. According to the object that he has in mind at the time, he draws attention to this or that aspect of the reality. He is not unaware that there remains in every man a personal responsibility (e.g.)... Rom. 1-2... But there is also a collective downfall in mankind... (cf.) Rom. 5 : 12-19... There is an element of artificiality in these descriptions, which in each case show only one side of the reality," 166. "In conclusion, Paul teaches a handing on of sin from Adam to all men without explaining how it operates. He is content to take up the thought of Genesis, making explicit the idea that the heritage of the first man contains not only death but also sin," 195, cf. 172, where it is suggested that "perhaps Paul simply brought out and gave abstract formulation to what Genesis described in a concrete way." G. Bornkamm finds in Rom. 5 : 12-21 a mythological understanding of history containing both Jewish and gnostic elements; its "judische Elemente in der Lehre von Erbfluch und Erbtod und im Schema der beiden Äonen erkennbar sind, wahrend die Lehre vom ersten und zweiten Menschen offensichtlich der Gnosis entstammt," "Paulinische Anakoluthe im Rômerbrief," in Das Ende des Gesetzes², 1958, 89, cf. 80-90. However, Paul adds two elements of his own: 1) the fact that sin is an action for which the sinner is responsible, the function of the law being to make that responsibility clear and explicit (vs. 13f.); 2) the superiority of grace, whose relation to sin is expressed not by ὡς but by πολλῷ μᾶλλον (vs. 15-7). The effect of these two "Pauline" additions is to break down the mythological view of history and to go beyond it to an understanding of sin and grace which can be traced neither to Jewish nor to gnostic sources. The anacoluthon in vs. 12-21 reflects the intrusion of this new Pauline element: the comparison between Adam and Christ which begins in vs. 12 is broken off by vs. 13-7 and then continued in vs. 18ff.]

creature through the fall of Adam, but they make no suggestion of a doctrine of original sin.[1])

The purpose of bringing Adam in at this point is stated in verse 14: Adam was a type of the "one who was to come," i.e. in Adam all men were united into a single unit, in Adam all men were represented; his deed accounted for the deeds of all subsequent men. So Christ, the "one who was to come," can gather to himself a new "body", a new community or group whose members are "one in him".[2]) As the sin of

---

[1]) [Paul's Adam-allegory "was in all probability a pure *tour de force* whose consistency with his general thinking had little importance. Philo has scores of such allegories of the moment. But, to the Christian fathers, all that Paul wrote was literally and ponderously true, and so out of this allegory of the fall grew the momentous doctrine of original sin," Psychology, 61. Rom. 5 : 12-21 is a text often investigated, because of what it suggests about the origin of sin (see above note), or because of its use of the figure of Adam; for a recent, detailed examination of the latter, see E. Brandenburger, Adam und Christus, 1962. G. will remark that only a Jew could have used *Adam* at this point, but the question remains: What kind of Judaism is the source here, i.e. how heavily penetrated by other influences? Rabbinic elaboration of the Adam-story is summarized by J. Jervell, Imago Dei, 1960, 96ff., and by W. D. Davies, Paul and Rabbinic Judaism[2], 1955, 44ff.; according to Davies, Paul is familiar both with this speculation (which Davies holds is devoid of hellenistic influence and which results in a glorification of Adam) and with hellenistic Judaism's "distinction between a Celestial and an earthly Adam", 49, a conception which owes much to Greek thought and which occurs, e.g. in the hermetic literature and especially in Philo. But C. K. Barrett holds that Jewish tradition is more unified at this point; he uses Philonic passages to illustrate the tradition "simply because Philo is both more quotable and more intelligible than the Rabbis, and yet proceeds from the same convictions," From First Adam to Last, 1962, 7. On O. Cullmann's interpretation, this text contains the two major Christological conceptions of the early Church, Son of Man and Servant of God, which Paul unites "exactly as Jesus united them," The Christology of the New Testament, 1959, 171, cf. 170-74. This union solves "the Adam-Son of Man problem which Judaism was actually unable to solve either by tracing man's sin to the fall of the angels rather than to the fall of Adam (the Book of Enoch), or by denying the fall of Adam altogether (the Jewish Christians) or by seeking a middle way in presupposing two first men (Philo)," 170. According to Bultmann, "Rom. 5 : 12ff. interprets Adam's fall quite in keeping with Gnosticism, as bringing (sin and) death upon mankind," Theology of the New Testament 1 : 174 (1951), cf. 164ff., 251ff.; for a brief summary of gnostic and other speculation about the Anthropos or (heavenly) Man, see S. E. Johnson, Interpreter's Dictionary of the Bible, 4 : 416ff. (1962). It appears that, for this topic at least, it is quite difficult to be precise about what is Jewish, what gnostic, and what from "Greek thought" in general; and it is nearly impossible to separate the "Jewish" themes according to whether they come from "orthodox" or "Palestinian" or "Old Testament-Rabbinic" Judaism on the one hand, or from "hellenistic" or "Philonic" Judaism on the other.]

[2]) This new group appears in 1 Corinthians very importantly and in various other parts of Paul's writings. [Cf. the Pauline uses of *soma Christou* to mean the *ekklesia*, e.g. 1 Cor. 12, and the development of this idea in Colossians, where

Adam brought condemnation and death for all, so the atoning death and resurrection of Christ brought *dikaiosune* and *zoe* (life) for all (vs. 17f.).[1]) Thus we are now in a new dispensation, a whole new order of existence; now we must live by the grace of Jesus Christ.

Romans Ch. 6

"Are we to continue in sin that grace may abound? By no means!" (vs. 1). We have died to sin, we cannot live in it still (vs. 2). In baptism we partook of the death of Jesus Christ; "we were buried... with him by baptism into death" (vs. 4),[2]) and the result is that we may therefore hope to live with him in the life of glory.

No one can deny that only a Jew could have written such an allegory of Adam (5 : 12ff.); no gentile would have thought in terms of Adam to explain the power and glory of Jesus Christ. But with 6 : 5 we begin to swing into the problem in its Greek sense: "For if we have been united with him in a death like his, we shall certainly be united with him in a resurrection like his. We know that our old *anthropos* was crucified with him, so that the sinful body might be destroyed, and we might no longer be enslaved to sin" (vs. 5f.). This passage opens the whole problem of the identification of sin with the body, something as recognizably hellenistic as it is foreign to essential Jewish thought. We are still in our "mortal bodies" even after baptism, and there is always the great danger that sin will run rampant as a result of the body's influence. Paul appears to be introducing a whole new criterion here, a criterion of the corruptability of the flesh, of the subversiveness of the

---

Christ the head (*kephale*) and the Church, the Body, are joined in mutual dependence, Col. 1 : 18a. For recent summary articles, with bibliography, see H. Schlier, "Corpus Christi" in Reallexikon fur Antike and Christentum 3 : 437-53 (1957) and E. Schweizer in Theologisches Worterbuch zum Neuen Testament 7 : 1064ff. (1964). Explanations of the Body-image and of Paul's use of Adam (see note above) are usually closely related e.g. Bultmann refers both to gnosticism, op. cit. 177ff., 298ff., while Davies links both to rabbinic speculation about Adam, op. cit. 57. For a brief categorization of sources for the Body-image, see J. A. T. Robinson, The Body, 1952 (Studies in Biblical Theology 5), 55.]

[1]) [In an allegory of Noah's ark, Philo says, "because of one righteous and worthy man (Noah), many men were saved" (*QG* ii, 11, p. 83 of the Marcus translation in supplement volume 2 of the Loeb edition of Philo). G. discusses this allegory in Symbols 8 : 162ff. and notes that "reminiscences, or premonitions, of Pauline phraseology in Romans are striking" throughout it, note 323.]

[2]) [Behind this connection of death with the water of baptism, G. finds a widespread ancient (and modern) equasion of water with death; thus the ark or ship becomes a symbol of salvation e.g. in Philo and in the ancient Church. See Symbols 8 : 157-65 for texts and bibliography; this Romans passage is mentioned in note 301.]

flesh over against the spirit. We are indeed free from the Mosaic law of statutes, no longer does the hoped-for *dikaiosune* come from that law, but we can still yield our members to sin as instruments of wickedness (vs. 13f.)—and this is fatal. It is the old problem brought out in Plato's Allegory of the Cave (Rep. vii : 514ff.): those who have gone outside the cave and seen the glory, seen the truth, seen reality, must still return to the cave and sit on its inner bench again, seeing only the shadows and living the life of the shadows.

Romans Ch. 7[1])

We have gone through a real death, a death to the Mosaic law and that whole network of theology and ethics which goes with it. The many references to "death" and "mortal" in chapter six are summed up in 7 : 1-3 in an argument which turns the Mosaic code back upon itself: once a death has occured, the obligations of a marriage contract are annulled. We owe nothing to the law any longer, we are free of it and must stop thinking about it: "My brothers, you have died to the law through the body of Christ, so that you may belong to another, to him who has been raised from the dead in order that we may bear fruit for God" (vs. 4). Paul speaks again in terms of the new community, the common existence of all the faithful in Christ.

What has the Mosaic law been doing to us? "What shall we say? That the law is sin? By no means! But had it not been for the law I should not have known sin; I should not have known what it is to covet, had the law not said 'You shall not covet'. Sin, finding opportunity in the commandment, wrought in me all kinds of covetousness" (vs. 7f.). Paul hinted earlier that the law came in to increase the trespass (5 : 20), but here he makes one of the most extraordinary analyses of the effects of commands upon the human psyche. Every wise parent knows that if children are to be obedient and comply with the wishes and criteria of their parents, they must be given as few actual laws as possible. To give a homely illustration: in the back farms of early New

---

[1]) [This chapter has been the subject of countless studies for the light it throws on e.g. Paul's anthropology or on his view of the law. It has been seen by some as autobiography describing Paul's Christian (*or* pre-Christian) life, and by others as a typical description of a Christian (*or* non-Christian) under the law. Major studies of the chapter include W. Kummel, Römer 7 und die Bekehrung des Paulus, 1929; R. Bultmann, "Romans 7 and the Anthropology of Paul," Existence and Faith, 1960, 147-57; and G. Bornkamm, "Sunde, Gesetz und Tod," Das Ende des Gesetzes[2], 1958, 51-69. For a recent treatment with which G. strongly disagreed, see K. Stendahl, "The Apostle Paul and the Introspective Conscience of the West," HTR 56 (1963), 199-215.]

England, toys were almost non-existent, and a handful of dried beans could be a welcome plaything; but wise mothers knew that to give a two-year-old child some beans to play with, while telling him not to put them up his nose, was to invite him to do precisely that. The parent made the suggestion by making the law and prohibition. This is just Paul's point (vs. 7f.): the law, in setting up prohibitions, sets up desires. It is a common saying that the *id* knows no negatives, that every negative command is for the *id* a suggestion; we are coming pretty close to Freud's *id* in this matter of the members and their special life.[1])

"The very commandment which promised life proved to be death to me; for sin, finding opportunity in the commandment, deceived me and by it killed me" (vs. 10f.). The commandment is perfectly all right (the child should *not* put beans in his nose); it is simply that the giving of the command stimulated the desire to rebellion. There is no difficulty about the law itself; it is "holy, just and good" (vs. 12), but it brings death to me because (while the law is spiritual) I am carnal, fleshly, sold under sin.

Is the self the person Paul knows he ought to be, the person he feels he should be? Or is the self the person he actually is, the one who sins with or without the law's promptings? "The law is spiritual, but *I* am carnal, sold under sin. *I* do not understand my own actions. *I* do not do what *I* want, but *I* do the very thing *I* hate. Now if *I* do what *I* do not want, *I* agree that the law is good, so then it is no longer *I* that do it, but sin that dwells in me, for *I* know that nothing good dwells within me, that is, in my flesh. *I* can will what is right, but *I* cannot do it, for *I* do not do the good *I* want, but the evil *I* do not want is what *I* do. Now if *I* do what *I* do not want, it is no longer *I* that do it but sin that dwells in me" (vs. 14-20). Paul is lost in the problem of finding his own *ego*, split as it is between idealism on the one hand and the flesh with its desires on the other. What is he, Paul? What am I, Erwin Goodenough? This is the great question we all have been asking ourselves all the centuries since, and we still have no answer.[2])

---

[1]) I have no intention of reducing Paul to Freud's categories, but both of them said the truth many times, and one who says the truth is apt to say what others have already said. [In Toward a Mature Faith, 1955, G. called this discussion of the *ego* in Romans 7 "one of the most amazing premonitions of later Freudianism," 119, cf. the pages following. For a further discussion of Romans 7-8 in this context, see Psychology, 58-63.]

[2]) It is true that the Freudians can tell you what the *ego* is, but they do so in their own terms and do not satisfy the rest of us; *ego* is a very mixed-up affair. Philo en-

The array of *nomoi* mentioned in the following verses (vs. 21ff.) will always be the despair of anyone who tries to understand "law" in Paul solely on the basis of the Old Testament and later Judaism. There is an overall law, i.e. that he has a divided *ego*: "I find it to be a *nomos* that when I want to do right, evil lies close at hand" (vs. 21). While Paul calls this a law, it is certainly no part of the code of Moses; it is a law of nature, and we are talking from a Greek point of view which has nothing to do with "codes". "I delight in the law of God in my inmost self" (vs. 22); this could be the law of Moses, but it is more probably the law of the spirit as in verse 25 below. Then "I see in my members another *nomos* at war with the *nomos* of my mind and making me captive to the *nomos* of sin which dwells in my members" (vs. 23);[1] at least one law is introduced here which has not been mentioned in vs. 21f., an evil law which is in the members or in the flesh. Finally Paul closes this extraordinary passage by saying, "I myself serve the *nomos* of God with my mind, but with my flesh I serve the *nomos* of sin" (vs. 25), a condition of conflict which seems to be according to the first law mentioned, the "law that when I want to do right, evil lies close at hand" (vs. 21).

I read with incredulity the arguments of modern commentators which identify this division of the law of the flesh and the law of the spirit with the *yetzer ha ra* and the *yetzer tob* in rabbinic thought. The sense of inner conflict between an impulse to do right and an impulse to do wrong is universal, and the Jews did express it in this latter form. They did not, in rabbinic circles, express it as the war between flesh and spirit; they did not urge us to get away from the flesh, to die to the flesh in order to escape this conflict. The Jew lived with the conflict, he lived with it nobly, and fought his battle out as best he could. But for Paul, this was not enough. He wanted to be free of the conflict altogether and so turned to the Greek identification of sin with the fleshly element in one's constitution.

In his great work *Judaism*, George Foote Moore has a masterful section on the *yetzer ha ra* and the *yetzer tob*, the evil impulse and the good impulse in man;[2] he makes it clear that this conception is quite

---

countered the same difficulty Paul expresses here, see Spec. iii, 1-6, a passage I have often quoted (e.g. in Introduction, 5f.).

[1]) [In Rom. 7 : 21-3 "Paul assumes a knowledge of the sort of treatment of law in the inner man preserved to us only by Philo, a knowledge which his readers most probably had, but whose absence has obscured his remarks ever since for later readers," Light, 394.]

[2]) [In pages 479-96 of volume 1 and the notes thereto in 3: 146-51, especially note

different from the hellenistic idea widely held in the time of Paul, i.e. that these two impulses were centered, one in a superior part of man like the soul, and the other in the body. Later, after the publication of Moore's work, I wrote an appendix to my *By Light, Light* in which I elaborately spelled out this Greek idea of the body as the corrupting agent.¹) The theory originally goes back to the Orphics who saw the soul as a fallen particle from God imprisoned in the body (σῶμα-σῆμα, the body is a tomb). The particle struggled to free itself from the body and those struggles were aided by the Orphic mysteries, the mystic exercises themselves. The idea continues in Plato's *Phaedrus* (246ff.) in the well-known myth of the Charioteer: here the evil horse is the desire for physical pleasure; it pulls the chariot downward, i.e. forces the rest of the soul into an incarnation in the body, where all is lost until man begins to discover the truth again and so orients himself that reason can become master. I will not here review all this material from my book,²) but I can state positively that the doctrine that sin is a product

209. The major study of *yetzer* cited by Moore is F. C. Porter, "The Yeçer Hara: a Study in the Jewish Doctrine of Sin," Biblical and Semitic Studies, 1902, 93-156. Porter concludes: "The result of our review is that in rabbinical usage the *yeçer* is hardly other than a name for man's evil tendencies or inclinations, the evil disposition which as a matter of experience exists in man, and which it is his moral task to subdue or control. It does not contain a metaphysical explanation of the fact, a theory as to its source or nature... All this, it is evident, has nothing to do with a dualistic contrast of body and soul... It must, moreover, be evident, apart from any positive explanation of Paul's doctrine, that the parallelism between his contrast of spirit and flesh and the rabbinical contrast between the good and evil impulses is remote and insignificant. Of course Paul in Rom. 7 is describing the same experience of struggle between two opposing forces in man upon which the Jewish doctrine rests, but his way of expressing the struggle as a war between the law (of sin) in his members, and the law of his mind (νοῦς), or between that which he possesses and does in his flesh and in his mind, is widely different from the Jewish conception, and seems to rest on a different view of the world and of man," 132-34. The rabbinic evidence is categorized and summarized in the excursus, "Der gute u. der bose Trieb" in H. L. Strack and P. Billerbeck, Kommentar zum Neuen Testament aus Talmud und Midrasch IV, 1, 466-83 (1928).]

¹) ["Law in the Subjective Realm," 370-443; much of the material in Light which is most relevant to the present article will be found in this appendix.]

²) [In Light 395, note 160, G. suggests the following passages as examples of Philo's view of the sinfulness of the flesh: *Gig.*, 12-15; *Immut.*, 142f.; *Agr.*, 89; *Heres*, 239f. In "Philo on Immortality," HTR 39 (1946), 96f., he writes: "Often as Philo refers to the 'soul' as the prisoner in the body in the Orphic-Platonic sense, it is strictly (the) higher mind which he means .. It is which this correction that we should read all the passages of Philo where he more loosely speaks of the 'soul' as being confined to the prison, the tomb, of the body (*L.A.* i, 107f.; cf. *Q.G.* iv, 152), or where, in terms which alone make Paul's seventh chapter of Romans intelligible, he speaks of the body as a corpse to which we are bound, and of ourselves as 'corpse-bearers': 'The body is wicked and a plotter against the soul, and is always

of the body, that the law of sin is a part of the body, is quite hellenistic. Perhaps its most striking ancient image is the story of the death of Socrates: Socrates' death means that finally he is to escape the body and come at last into the true realm of being; mortal things will trouble him no longer.

Plato and the other Greeks stop short of the iron-clad dualism of the Persians and later Manichees. These are not eternal principles so much as factual descriptions of man's problem. The various members *do* have their own law. It is the law of the sexual organ that it should seek gratification. It is the law of the stomach that it should want food, the law of the body in its weariness that it wants repose. All the parts of our bodies have a law that they should perform their functions, but they are utterly incorrelated, unorganized, and can (any of them) become obsessions, as when the craving for drink takes over a man's reason and he becomes a dipsomaniac. The law of the mind knows better, but the law of the mind is not strong enough to control our impulses, and we have all sinned, as we all know.[1] The law of the mind is not a matter of precepts, but of the perception of the true religious values; somehow we must have access to a greater realization and acceptance of this higher law.

With their deep hellenistic coloring, Philo's writings run along these same lines: here incarnation in the body is the great tragedy, one is trying always to free oneself from the body, e.g. by ascetic practices or by study. The Greek mysteries were presenting a savior in a Hercules or an Isis; savior-gods were springing up all over. This appealed to Philo and he turned the great patriarchs into incarnations of the higher law; they become his *nomoi empsuchoi*, through whom we could come into the higher law and live lives of value and virtue. He was convinced that the Mosaic law was but a shadow of the higher law; the

---

a corpse and a dead thing. For you must understand that each of us does nothing but carry a corpse about, since the soul lifts up and bears without effort the body which is in itself a corpse' (*L.A.* iii, 68, cf. 72, 74). Philo has in this connection the same confusion of figures as Paul, for with both of them the body is simultaneously a corpse tied to the soul, and an active schemer for the soul's destruction." For a brief summary of this point from the New Testament point of view, with relevant texts, see H. Lietzmann's excursus, "Das Fleisch und die Sunde," An die Romer[4], (HNT) 1933, 75-77. Lietzmann finds Philo to be the ancient writer whose ideas on "flesh and sin" most closely resemble Paul's, and says that this connection of sin with flesh is, for Philo, "das Fundament der Ethik", 75.]

[1] [For a description of human nature in these same terms, but in a discussion of Philonic ethics, see Introduction, 116f. For an earlier discussion of Paul's "law of the members," see Light, 391ff.]

business of man was indeed to live by the law, but we are not to stop with the precepts and the written law, but go on to the higher law. This higher law was made accessible to man in the patriarchs who had been law-abiding and pleasing to God before, and thus without, the Mosaic code.

In a lengthy discussion in *By Light, Light* I called this the "mystery" of hellenistic Judaism.[1]) The term received more attention than the idea behind it, an idea which was very familiar to Paul himself, for he has left us a most masterful summary of the real meaning of this mystery: "I want you to know, brothers, that our fathers were all under the cloud and all passed through the sea and all were baptized into Moses in the cloud and in the sea, and all ate the same 'pneumatic' food and all drank the same 'pneumatic' drink, for they drank from the 'pneumatic'[2]) rock which followed them, and the rock was Christ" (1 Cor. 10 : 1-4). I could not have put the essence of the mystery into more compact form myself. Those who had passed through the sea and the cloud were baptized *into Moses*; he was a personal revelation of this higher entity. Baptism *into Moses* exactly parallels Paul's idea of baptism *into Christ*. "They all ate the same 'pneumatic' food and all drank the same 'pneumatic' drink"—Philo says this very often about the manna in the wilderness and the water which issued from the great rock (Ex. ch. 16-7):[3]) the great rock with its stream of water was the Logos which came to relieve them. Paul's change is a simple one: "the rock was Christ."

Behind these verses in 1 Corinthians lies a hellenistic Jewish tradition which Paul has Christianized only by making the rock and its flow not Sophia or the Logos, but Christ. Paul certainly did not invent the idea that the passage of the Red Sea was a baptism *into Moses*. Here is indeed a survival from his earlier thoughtways. The cloud, the rock and the superhuman Moses are all depicted in the Dura Europos synagogue, in a fresco which might well be used among Christians to illustrate and explain Paul's text.[4]) Baptism "into" Christ and existence "in" him

---

[1]) [This is the theme of the first nine chapters of Light; it is summarized also in Introduction, 138-58.]

[2]) ["I do not see why recent translators make of the 'pneumatic' rock and food something 'supernatural'. That conception is quite foreign to the ancient mind," Symbols 12 : 171 note 44. Both RSV and NEB have "supernatural".]

[3]) [For a further discussion of "spiritual food and drink," see Symbols 6 : 198-216, where G. summarizes the Philonic material.]

[4]) [This paragraph is based on Symbols 10 : 135. Chapter 16 of Symbols 10 (105-39) is G.'s thorough discussion of the Moses-Exodus-Red Sea typology as it

would be instantly understandable to these familiar with this hellenistic Jewish "Moses" tradition.

Romans Ch. 8

The same theme continues: "There is now no condemnation for these who are *in* Christ Jesus, for the law of the spirit of life in Christ Jesus has set you free from the law of sin and death" (vs. 1f.).[1]) As they were baptized *into* Moses, we are now *in* Christ Jesus;[2]) the effect is very similar: we can rise from the lower law to the higher law which Christ embodies as Moses did. Christ has done away with the law of the flesh (vs. 3); the result is that we can fulfill the just requirement of the law by walking not according to the flesh but according to the spirit (vs. 4f.).[3]) This "just requirement" is surely *not* the Mosaic law; Paul has not gone through all of his experiences (his death with Christ in baptism, his emerging as a new creature in Christ) just so that he can more faithfully keep the Jewish law. Such an understanding he would have repudiated altogether. The Jewish law is something past and gone; instead there is a higher law which we obtain through Christ as did those Jews who were baptized into Moses before Sinai had issued a single commandment.

We are no longer in the flesh, but in the spirit, if the spirit of God really dwells in us—so says verse 9 in the peculiar, allusive speech of the mystic; we are in the spirit if the spirit is in us. One cannot press these mystic figures too closely; their purpose is to express union, without a concern for firm, logical terminology. The spirit is the spirit of Christ; if we lack this in us, we do not belong to him.[4])

---

applies to the Dura fresco mentioned here; he entitles it "Moses Leads the Migration from Egypt" and prints it as color-plate XIV in Symbols 11. For the relevant New Testament and early Christian material, with bibliography, see Symbols 10: 134ff.]

[1]) Cf. 2 Cor. 3: 6-18, which describes the giving of the spirit-law which *is* the Lord. [For an ingenious analysis of the source of this text, see Georgi's excursus, op. cit. 274-82.]

[2]) [In Psychology, 152ff., G. discusses some uses of "in Christ" imagery in the later Church.]

[3]) [G. points out that Paul's language here (e.g. living "according to the spirit" and "the mind of the spirit," 8 : 6) comes close to Philonic terminology, since "Philo often prefers to use the word Spirit when he speaks of the Logos in relation to man, how it comes in at inspiration, and abides in him as the higher mind," Introduction, 117 with note 5.]

[4]) [For an exhaustive study of the conception of "indwelling deity" in the ancient word, see J. Haussleiter, "Deus internus," Reallexikon fur Antike und Christentum 3 : 794-842 (1957), especially the sections on Philo and Paul, 815-20.]

The major part of this chapter is a peculiarly Pauline mixture of mysticism, eschatology and the doctrine of election, themes which appear again in chapters 9-11; Paul is working at the difficult task of describing Christian existence until the Parousia. Law-observance in the sense of pre-Christian legalism is an impossible solution, yet we are not live according to the flesh (vs. 12); we must set our minds upon the spirit. The spirit dwells within us (vs. 11, 13ff.) but our bodies are still mortal bodies (vs. 11); the final glorification (vs. 17) and the final gift of life (vs. 11) are still ahead of us, the whole creation sharing our "in-between" state (vs. 19-22).

We have the gift now only partially, only the first-fruits[1]) of the spirit (vs. 23); in our present struggle for obedience to the higher law, the law of the spirit, we will frequently fail, but the spirit helps us in our weakness, interceding for the saints according to the will of God (vs. 26).[2])

We have entered a new legal regime, a new order, a new way of life.

---

[1]) [In Symbols 5 : 86 G. suggests that this term "seems in itself to indicate Christ" at work within us. He further points out that Paul sometimes uses ἀπαρχή of Christ, and at other times, of certain Christians, e.g. the first converts in Asia (Rom. 16 : 5) and Achaia (1 Cor. 16 : 15). This "double implication" of the term occurs already in Philo, and, presumably, in the tradition upon which he draws. According to Philo "the Jews... had been set aside as the first fruits of the human race to the Creator and Father, a prerogative they attained... through the righteousness and virtues of the Patriarchs, 'which endure like immortal plants bearing an everblooming fruit that for their descendants is saving and profitable in every way' (*Spec.* iv, 180f.)... Just as the Christians become first fruits through the merits of Christ, the Jews had become first fruits through the merits of the Patriarchs. Christ as the saving first fruits has his prototype in Philo's Jewish saviors, the Patriarchs who are also first fruits," Symbols 5 : 89. For G.'s discussion of the other instances of *aparche* in the New Testament, see Symbols 5 : 84-91 and 12 : 104f.]

[2]) The distinctly hellenistic character of vs. 29 is usually obscured by translating it: "Those whom he fore-knew, he also predestined to be conformed to the image *of* his son," but what Paul is saying is rather: we are going to be "conformed to the image, i.e. his son," not to an image *of* Christ, but to Christ who *is* himself the image of God. "Image" (*eikon*) is frequently used by Philo in this fashion e.g. *Conf.* 97, *Fug.* 101, *Som.* i, 239 and ii, 45. In Col. 1: 15ff. the two chief functions of the *eikon* are "creating" and "ruling", exactly those of Philo's Logos [see the brief discussion in Introduction, 104ff. This topic is dealt with in two recent studies whose approach is indicated in their subtitles: J. Jervell, Image Dei: Gen. 1, 26f. im Spatjudentum, in der Gnosis und in den paulinischen Briefen, 1960, 271ff.; and E. Larssen, Christus als Vorbild: eine Untersuchung zu den paulinischen Tauf- und Eikontexten, 1962, 293ff. Larsson works chiefly with comparative material from the Old Testament, later Judaism and Qumran, while Jervell brings in gnostic texts, e.g. 122-70. For a brief summary of the Philonic and Pauline uses of *eikon* (*tou theou*), see the article by G. Kittel in Theological Dictionary of the New Testament 2 : 394ff. (1964).]

It is not yet perfect; *dikaiosune* in its fullest form is an attribute of God himself, and we shall not come into it in full perfection until we are rid of our bodies, or until our bodies have been transformed into spiritual entities. But through Christ we come into an entirely different order: in their blundering the gentiles have missed this and gone over to idols; the Jews thought they could win it by trying to obey with ever-increasing nicety the commandments of the Mosaic code. Neither of these will work. We have to die to our whole selves, die to our material nature, die to the flesh and come to live in the law of the spirit which is in Christ Jesus (vs. 2);[1]) only in this way do we approach the final *dikaiosune*.

Romans Ch. 9-11

In these chapters Paul turns to the heart-breaking problem of Israel's rejection of Christ. He finds his consolation in the whole history of Israel, for all the people who are fleshly descendants of Abraham by no means belong to Israel (9 : 6-8). Over and over again the people have rejected God, while whoring after other gods; God has had to reject them, but he has always kept a remnant. He is keeping a remnant now. There seems to be no way to distinguish between those who obey and follow, and so become a part of the remnant, and those who do not. Even in a family so exalted as that of Isaac, Jacob is accepted and Esau rejected (9 : 9-13). Why? That is a question we must not ask. Salvation is to come as an act of God, an act of mercy, and not by men's efforts. But why should some have this grace and others lack it? Again, this question we must not ask. Who are we to talk back to God (9 : 14ff.)? God does as he pleases with his own; he is a potter who may make vessels of honor and vessels of dishonor at his will. It is not for the clay to question the potter (9 : 20-23). The gift of grace and with it the gift of faith and with that the gift of righteousness—all these God has finally bestowed upon Jews and gentiles alike (9 : 24ff.).

Philo's idea of Israel is quite similar. The true Israelites are those who live not by the laws of the commands, but by the Logos and the powers in the higher law. But unlike Paul he does not say that those who are doing the best they can (the ordinary Jews with the Mosaic code) are rejected people. He would have been utterly impatient with

---

[1]) ["By simply omitting the reference to Jesus Christ in Paul's Romans viii, we have all been familiar from childhood with a description of the higher spiritual Law which can set one free from the law of the flesh and of sin, a description with which Philo would heartily have agreed," Light, 398.]

Paul's taking this position. For Philo there was the true Israel, and there was the mass of Israelites—what could you expect? The mass of people is not spiritually minded, not capable of the higher experiences, the higher ideas; consequently, they are mercifully given the law of Moses by which they live. Philo saw no cleavage or warfare between these two kinds of Jews. He himself wanted to live the life of the higher, inwritten law of the Logos and the powers, but he was a close fellow-worker with the Jews and would have nothing to do with those who rejected observing the law of Moses.[1] But Christ had made the higher law so vivid, so accessible, so real for Paul that he took the step which Philo would never have taken; he rejected those who tried by their own efforts to be saved. For Paul, salvation must be a matter of abandoning our effort and being given the grace, the gift of faith and of *dikaiosune* (10 : 3). The Jews who were ignorant of the righteousness that comes from God as his gift[2] sought to establish their own righteousness; they attempted to make themselves righteous by their own effort, and this was their fatal mistake. They could not and did not submit to God's true righteousness, the righteousness by gift.

It is not difficult to receive this gift; "the word is near us, on our lips and our hearts, that is, the word of faith which we preach" (10 : 8). We must cease our own efforts and pray to God for the gift, "for everyone who calls on the name of the Lord will be saved" (10 : 13). For this reason we spread the gospel as rapidly as possible by preaching, because no one can confess and believe what he has not heard (10 : 14f.).

We will not attempt to reconcile chapter 9 with chapter 10. Paul believes in preaching, in telling people, and yet everything is the work of God, foreordained and predestined.[3] Fortunately, for our purpose, the analysis of Paul's thought for hellenistic elements, the settlement of this controversy is not required. I suspect that Paul was a predestinarian very like most predestinarians; in some moods he submitted to God and felt that God did everything, in other moods human effort (even if only the effort of giving up and praying for God's help) seemed of some avail and God did listen. If predestinarians were not of this sort, the Calvinist churches would not have gone on with their

---

[1] [Cf. note 2, p. 40 above.]

[2] [On righteousness as a gift of God, see the Käsemann article cited above, note 2, p. 37.]

[3] [The same tension is apparent in the Dead Sea Scrolls; H. Ringgren suggests that "it is probable that the Qumran community itself was not aware of the contradiction, or in any case did not try to express its belief in a form which was free of contradiction," op. cit. (note 1, p. 44 above) 111.]

preaching. They were carrying the gospel to the people but (by strict) logic) if God did this directly for the elect, preaching and churches were quite supernumerary. The problem seems to me not specifically Jewish or specifically Greek; it is rather a problem which has arisen out of Paul's own experience of Christ.[1]) He received the great gift *as* a gift, with a sense that his effort was absolutely nil, that only when his efforts ceased was the gift bestowed. But did his own election mean that God turned a deaf ear when others piously asked for salvation and *pistis*? Paul could not say that, and the resulting contradiction is one within his Christian thinking. I see nothing comparable in Philo or in rabbinic texts.

Chapter 11 continues this theme: God has by no means rejected the whole of his people (11 : 1). Paul himself is proof of that, he himself is a Jew; all Jews have not been rejected. God has hardened the hearts of most Israelites however, so that the gospel will be spread among the gentiles, a thing which would have been most difficult had the Jews all eagerly accepted it and made it a part of their Judaism. Jews have been broken off, branch by branch, from the great olive tree, and gentiles grafted in their places (11 : 17ff.). But someday the broken-off branches will be taken back and put into the great, true olive tree. If you who have been grafted in begin to feel superior for that fact, you too will be torn off (11: 21). The only superiority is in God himself; it is fatal for you to have any pride or sense of accomplishment in yourself.

Romans: the Final Section

Paul's great exposition of the essentials of the Christian faith has come to an end. Chapter twelve brings us into the letter's final section, a combination of instruction and exhortation directed to specific issues and problems within a Christian's everyday life.[2])

Particular ethical statements in the Pauline letters are often quite like those of Jesus, e.g. in the Sermon on the Mount. Jesus too wanted men to live with neighborly love, as did the rabbis; he too was ready to disregard Mosaic proscriptions for the principles that lay behind them,

---

[1]) [The doctrine of predestination "was a natural and logical conclusion from the experience that Paul himself had... but logical conclusions are as dangerous in religion as they are in most of life," Toward a Mature Faith, 1955, 147.]

[2]) I include in this section chapters 12-15, since chapter 16 is generally recognized as a piece from another letter altogether. [In the article summarized above, note 1, p. 34, T. W. Manson rather calls chapter 16 a "covering note" sent to Rome with the summary of Pauline theology now called Romans 1-15. G. probably would not have quarreled with Manson on this point.]

thus, e.g. he goes beyond "Thou shalt not kill" to forbid even anger and words of derision (Mt. 5 : 21f.). There is to be no adultery, even in a look (Mt. 5 : 27f.); no resistance, even under attack (5 : 38ff.).[1]) But Jesus was a Palestinian in that he came to the higher meaning by generalizing the laws of the code themselves; Paul, on the other hand, worked to establish a morality that rises above specific precepts altogether, one that is based instead on the higher perception of right and wrong, on the higher immaterial law.

This difference between the ethics of the Sermon on the Mount and that of Paul is the result of the fact that Paul thinks in hellenistic terms; this becomes clear when we compare him with Philo.[2]) In his *de Specialibus Legibus* Philo approaches the specific laws of the Mosaic code much as Jesus does, but his *de Virtute* has interesting similarities to these last chapters of Romans. The *de Virtute* is a summary of the second major section of Philo's writings, the very long "Exposition of the Law,"[3]) which details God's giving of the law in the Old Testament, beginning with Creation. Philo's object here is to clarify God's law, the law which could be called the law of nature, since for theists nature in God. In the creation the law of nature[4]) is manifest; this is nothing less than the first great revelation of God's law. The second comes in the giving of the law to the *nomoi empsuchoi*,[5]) and then (since these were not enough) the giving of the law in the Ten Commandments, and finally the elaborate regulations of the Torah which Philo explicates in the four books of the *de Specialibus Legibus*.[6]) Paul has done nothing comparably elaborate; the whole of Romans is smaller than the little *de Virtute*. Philo, however, never lost his reverence for the Mosaic code in its literal form, as commandments; consequently he is driven to a long exposition of these regulations.

---

[1]) [For a detailed comparison of Jesus' view of the commands of the Torah with the views of later Judaism, primarily Qumran, see H. Braun, Spatjudisch-haretischer und fruhchristlicher Radikalismus, 1-2, 1957.]

[2]) [There are several useful comparisons between Pauline and Philonic ethics in Introduction, 112-33. On Philo's ethics, see also E. Bréhier, Les Idées philosophiques et religieuses des Philon d'Alexandrie³, 1950, 250-310; G. once mentioned that it was the first edition of this book which caused him to begin his study of Philo.]

[3]) [G. characterizes the different groups of Philonic writings and lists those treatises which make up this "Exposition" in his article "Philo Judeus" in Interpreter's Dictionary of the Bible 3 : 796f. (1962). His book Jewish Courts in Egypt, 1929, is an exhaustive treatment of *de specialibus Legibus*.]

[4]) [See note 2, p. 41 above.]

[5]) [See page 41ff. above.]

[6]) [See note 3, p. 40 above on the four levels of "law" in Philo.]

But once the specifics of the law have been explained, Philo leaves detailed laws behind altogether; he is writing for gentiles, for Romans who have their own ideas of morality and so, in the *de Virtute*, he summarizes the special laws under the general topics Courage, Humanity, Repentance and Nobility.

Here the commands are elevated into reminders of the universal laws. In his discussion of the commands to kindness, he transforms specific laws into a general principle. Many laws are quoted to show how kindness and consideration are required within the tribe; kindness is due also to proselytes and even to animals and plants. But then Philo summarizes: "With such instructions he tamed and softened the minds of the citizens of this commonwealth, and set them out of the reach of pride and arrogance, evil qualities grievous and noxious in the highest degree" (*Virt.* 161)—that is, all these many laws of Moses were actually established to teach the dangers of the great Greek sin *hubris*; they are to keep us humble and make us realize our own limits.[1]) We must never lose the remembrance of God; that is the one thing which will help us keep from falling into sin and pride, "for as when the sun has risen, the darkness disappears and all things are filled with light, so when God the spiritual sun rises and shines upon the soul the gloomy night of passions and vices is scattered and virtue reveals the peerless brightness of her form, and all is purity and loveliness" (*Virt.* 164). As Philo reminds us frequently in this book, this higher estate of the soul is called *dikaiosune*, righteousness. It alone will keep us as we should be, and it comes to us as we turn to God and let the brilliant sun of his person rise and shine upon the soul. When this happens, "the gloomy night of passions and vices scatters."

Paul's view is recognizably similar; for him the only way to avoid the sins of the flesh is to let the light of God so shine into us that the body with its desires and passions fades out of existence. This is our only hope. This is the way we will come into virtue, virtue pure, virtue unified, the virtue of God.[2])

---

[1]) [For a detailed examination of the hellenistic conceptions present in Philo's approach to the Torah, see I. Heinemann, Philons griechische und judische Bildung: kulturvergleichende Untersuchungen zu Philons Darstellung der judischen Gesetze, 1932. G. evaluates this book in Introduction, 11-13.]

[2]) Paul and Philo might well describe this result in the same terms; compare the "catalog of virtues and vices" in *Virt.* 182 with those in Paul [e.g. in Rom. 1: 29-31, 13: 13. See O. J. F. Seitz, "Lists, Ethical" in Interpreter's Dictionary of the Bible 3: 137-39 (1962) and add to the bibliography there, S. Wibbing, Die Tungend- und Lasterkataloge im Neuen Testament, 1959).]

When Romans 12-15 is compared to the Philonic writings in this way, it becomes clear that Paul's approach to the problems of ethics is as much like the *de Virtute* as his teaching (at its best in Romans) is *un*like that of Jesus.[1]) Indeed the evidence from Philo and Paul strongly suggests that there was a general tendency (among gentiles as well as among hellenized Jews) to admire the Jewish law for its reflection of general principles of morality;[2]) both men often appear to me to be capitalizing on such a situation.

While Paul and Philo thus approach the problems of ethics in the same way,[3]) Paul's great difference is that he has been so engrossed,

---

[1]) [On the use of non-Christian elements in early Christian parenesis and the place of Romans 12 in early Christian ethics, see E. Kasemann, "Gottesdienst im Alltag der Welt," Exegetische Versuche und Besinnungen II: 198-204 (1964) and the literature cited there.]

[2]) [Jewish apologists in the Diaspora were compelled to (and often eager to) relate and recommend their law to the gentiles around them. G. here discusses Philo's approach; other frequently mentioned examples are Ep. Aristeas 128-71 and Josephus, c. Apionem 2: 151-235, cf. E. Schurer, A History of the Jewish People in the Time of Jesus Christ², 2: 311-27 (1891). D. Georgi argues "dass das Medium der judischen Propaganda vor allem der Synagogengottesdienst und die hier dargebotene Gesetzesauslegung war," op. cit. 87, cf. 83ff. and his discussion of Juvenal and Horace, 105ff. The evidence indicates two things: 1) Many Jews realized that their law had to be taken with them into the gentile world; it was important to make Judaism attractive and available to gentiles, but if this were done by rejecting the Torah, the result could no longer be called Judaism. 2) As G. here suggests, the law-ordered life of an observant Jew was often highly attractive to his gentile neighbors. For both of these reasons, the law was a major element (perhaps the chief one) in the contacts between gentile and "apologetic" Jew, with both parties interested in stressing its general principles and universal scope rather than its Jewish particularity.]

[3]) [The similarity which G. stresses here extends to the literary forms used by Philo and Paul; both employ a common form of hellenistic moral exhortation, the diatribe, which has been characterized as follows: "Eine philosophische Unterweisung volkstumlichen Charakters mit vorwiegend ethischem Inhalt... In ihrer Anlage ist die D(iatribe) ein fingierter Dialog mit einem anonymen Gesprachspartner... (Sie) bedient sich der einfachsten u(nd) ausdrucksvollsten Kunstmittel der klassischen Rhetorik... Die Verfasser von D. lieben es, ein bestimmtes Repertorium von Themen aus der philosophischen Elementarethik abzuhandeln," H. I. Marrou, "Diatribe" in Reallexikon fur Antike und Christentum 3: 998 (1957). Marrou, 999f., finds the following examples of particular elements of the diatribe style in Romans: ethical exhortation, chaps. 12-15; imaginary dialogue or *apostrophe*, 2: 1, 9: 19; interjected protests, 9: 19, 11: 19; question and answer, 6: 1-19; personification of abstractions, 10: 6-8; *parataxis*, 2: 21f., 13: 7; parallelism, 12: 4-15; catalogue of vices, 1: 29(-31); imperatives, 12: 14f. On the diatribe in Philo, P. Wendland, "Philo und die kynisch-stoische Diatribe," in Beitrage zur Geschichte der griechischen Philosophie und Religion, 1895, 1-75; Wendland indicates (cf. 66) that Philo's attacks on gluttony, sexual license and other contemporary evils owe much to the Diatribe, his *de Vita Contemplativa* being one of the clearest examples of this influence. H. Thyen relies heavily on Philonic examples to

encompassed, engulfed by the vision of Christ that he no longer needs to defend the specific commands; indeed he rises above them altogether and looks toward a state where the higher mind, the higher vision, the higher self illuminated by God, is governing us, so that the body has become dead.

Paul's vision of Christ leads to many differences between his statements and those of Philo, but it is clear that both of them are trying to lead man into a life in which the higher part, the part engulfed by God, takes over and the fleshly impulses are no longer in control.[1])

---

demonstrate the similarities between hellenistic-jewish preaching and the Diatribe, Der Stil der judisch-hellenistischen Homilie, 1955. On Paul, see R. Bultmann, Der Stil der paulinischen Predigt und die kynisch-stoische Diatribe, 1910; Bultmann argues that the Diatribe has a limited but definite influence on Paul, cf. his conclusions, 107-09.]

[1]) [Both for Philo and for Paul "the only possible solution is that the higher mind conquer the lower members... The permanent adjustment is not, during this life at least, disembodied existence, but complete regeneration, the goal which Paul called 'the redemption of the body' but which he more commonly, like Philo, called by the legal-ethical terms, *dikaiosune* or justice. This term with both men still has the meaning which Plato gave it in the Republic: namely, a perfect regimentation of the state, civic or subjective, by which the higher faculties are in command, and the lower members perform their functions freely and fully, but keep each to its own business according to the laws fixed by the proper governor... Nothing distinguishes both thinkers more sharply from Stoic ethics than the refusal to build up the inner ethical harmony from within ...Philo like Paul despaired of achieving the end without a new union with the Universal Spirit: the fragment or extension (of that Spirit) within him was helpless against the forces of his lower nature unless it was freshly united and augmented in the divine Spirit or Logos as a whole," Introduction, 118. "On no point is the thinking of the two so similar as on the ideal adjustment of the soul and body for one who found the higher reality," 116.]

II
BIBLICAL STUDIES

ON THE PRESENCE OF GOD IN BIBLICAL RELIGION

BY

BARUCH A. LEVINE
Brandeis University

The late Erwin R. Goodenough devoted his best energies to the quest for meaning in graphic and glyptic representation and in ancient literary sources. He possessed great insight into the realms of both experience and doctrine, and showed considerable interest in the proper study of early Israelite religion, although that was not his primary area of inquiry. I dedicate this study to his memory, knowing his awareness of the limits of theology and his insistence on adherence to evidence in the study of ancient religions. I thus recognize my indebtedness to his intellectual leadership and to the methodology which he developed.*

"Where is God?" is the question of young children, but it constitutes as well the confrontation of mature men. Many of us have become accustomed to thinking that God is everywhere. We probably mean to convey that wherever man may find himself, the protecting God is nearby. "The Lord is near to all who call upon him" are the words of the Psalmist (Psalm 145: 18). The notion of God's omnipresence would afford a great measure of assurance to man, if it were fully convincing in its emotional aspects. It has seldom sufficed however, either for the modern believer or for his ancient predecessors; witness man's feeling that the divine being should be approached in special locales consecrated to him. Despite the many functions, other than cultic, that have always pertained to temples, it must be admitted that if men did not sense the need to build residences for deities so as to have the advantages of their proximity to the human community, the grandiose efforts devoted to temple building, and to the maintenance of elaborate cults, would have been expended on other enterprises.[1])

---

*) The author is indebted to the following scholars with whom he had the privilege of discussing the theme of the presence of God in biblical literature: to Profs. Yohanan Muffs, Nahum Sarna & Morton Smith. Aspects of this paper were treated in an address before the Society of Biblical Literature & Exegesis, Vanderbilt University, December, 1965.

[1]) See the discussion on "The Significance of the Temple in the Ancient Near East," *The Biblical Archaeologist Reader*, I, Anchor Books, 1961, pp. 145-185, and

In reading the Hebrew Bible with the question of God's whereabouts in mind, we observe that concern with the presence of God and his nearness is a major theme. Rarely does the biblical spokesman, be he priest, prophet, or Psalmist, assume the omnipresence of God.[1]) On occasion, biblical man is compelled to accept the fact that God may lay hold of him wherever he is (Psalm 139: 7-9). When, however, we attempt to penetrate to the motivations underlying religious activity in ancient Israel, we perceive that prayer and lamentation express the yearning for God's nearness, and that pilgrimages are undertaken so as to be close to the deity resident in the temple. Generally speaking, the desire for God's presence in the human community seems to motivate most of the regular aspects of religious life, and we shall proceed to show to what extent this is true of biblical culture.

The desire on man's part for the nearness of divine powers reflects universal human attitudes and conceptions. We normally visualize a protector, whether father or leader, as being nearby rather than far away, and love is identified with closeness. The child often experiences anxiety when he is left alone, and the adult must also come to terms with remoteness as a factor in his relationships. Moreover, divine beings are viewed as the source of life and power. Power, in turn, is thought to be conducted from the source to that which is infused with it, and man invariably expresses concern with identifying the channels through which power is conducted. He reasons that the closer the source, the more certain and plentiful the power. It is, therefore, understandable that the presence of God becomes synonymous with the material blessings and protection afforded by his power, and the

---

especially the statements of G. Ernest Wright, p. 169f., where he notes the difficulties for ancient man in accepting the omnipresence of God. We note here that all translations of biblical passages are the work of the author, and, where necessary, explanatory notes will be provided in justification.

[1]) See Ps. 72:19, where the hope is expressed that God's *kābôd* "presence" will fill the whole earth. Isaiah 6:3 may also mean that the *kābôd* infuses everything in the world: "His presence is the fullness of the whole earth." That passage is a crux. It may also mean that the earth, itself, is God's *kābôd*. In any event, both passages relate to the notion of omnipresence. On the sense of *kābôd* as "body, person" see H. L. Ginsberg, *Mordecai Kaplan Jubilee Volume*, Jewish Theological Seminary of America, 1953, pp. 246-247. Ginsberg was concerned with other passages (*inter alia* Isaiah 10:3, 16, 17:4, 22:18, Ps. 7:6, 16:9, Gen. 49:6) bearing on the sense of the term as applied to human beings. His discussion provides a starting point for establishing the sense of the term when applied to the deity. It obviously can mean "glory, honor", but in more cases than not, we should eliminate the elements of greater abstraction, so understandably evoked by divine associations, and emphasize rather the element of real presence.

very willingness of the deity to draw near is taken as a sign of favor. This assertion is not mitigated by the prophetic critique of practical religion; a critique aimed at changing the more conventional attitudes of ancient believers by injecting certain variables into the dynamics of the divine-human encounter.

The nearness of divine power had its dangers. Wrath and punishment are also features of God's relationship to man, and he may draw near to the human community in order to strike out at it. There are times when man may fear the nearness of God, but he normally must risk the dangers attendant on the divine presence for the blessings he hopes to receive from the divinity. It is our purpose here to explore the positive side of the relationship.

I

Where in biblical literature may we find the most fundamental expression of the desire for God's presence and nearness? The earliest indications are to be sought in biblical epic.[1]) In bringing together various pre-Israelite traditions about the gods and their exploits, traditions known in Ugaritic literature and in Mesopotamian sources, biblical poets preserved for later generations the vivid memory that, on certain momentous occasions, God descended to earth and acted on behalf of Israel and its leaders. There is, of course, more than one conception embodied in biblical epic, and most often several strains have been blended into a composite description. In at least one portrayal God accomplished his act of rescue from heaven: "He sends forth (his hand) from on high and takes hold of me; he draws me up from deep waters" (Psalm 18 : 17//II Samuel 22 : 17.[2]) The motif which becomes predominant in biblical epic is the portrayal of God as he descends to earth and approaches his people. In an early passage, which recurs with variations, God is seen approaching from the Negev and Dead Sea regions, variously Sinai, Paran, Seir, Edom, perhaps Kadesh, "the

---

[1]) See U. Cassuto, "Epic Poetry in Israel," (Hebrew), *Kenesset in Honor of H. N. Bialik*, 8, 1943-44, pt. 3, pp. 121-142. By "epic" we mean poetic collections relating the feats of God and the exploits of heroes. By "heroic" we mean prose accounts on the same subject, with perhaps more stress on the human hero. The difference between the two genres is to some extent a matter of form.

[2]) In these parallel passages it is stated that "he (God) bent the heavens and descended" (II Sam. 22 : 10//Ps. 18 : 10), but it is clear from the ensuing verses that the descent did not bring God down to Earth. Also see Ps. 68 : 5, 34.

wilderness" (Hebrew *yešîmôn*) and Teman. These passages most probably refer to a particular tradition about Israel's origins and describe their first encounter with Yahweh. The approach is tremendous:

Art. 7: On the Presence of God in Bibliycal Religion: Gedichten
> Yahweh! When you went forth from Seir,
> When you marched from the field of Edom,
> The heavens dropped rain, even the clouds let water fall,
> Water ran down the mountainsides.
> At the approach of Yahweh!
> Yonder Sinai, at the approach of Yahweh, the God of Israel.
> (Judges 5 : 4-5)

> God! When you went forth before your people,
> When you marched in the wilderness, Selah;
> The earth quaked, even the heavens dropped rain.
> At the approach of God!
> Yonder Sinai, at the approach of God, the God of Israel.
> (Psalm 68 : 8-9)

A probable variant of the same description is to be found in Deuteronomy 33 : 2:

> And he said:
> Yahweh came forth from Sinai,
> He shone upon them from Seir,
> And appeared from the region of Mt. Paran.
> He came from Riboth Kadesh.
> To his right were waterfalls.[1])

Of similar import is the description of God as a man of war in Exodus 15, and as the swooping eagle who encircles his nest, closely guarding his young, in Deuteronomy 32. We also have the reference to the battle with the powers of the sea, which begins:

---

[1]) On our translation of Dt. 33 : 2: For *qôdeš* read *qādēš*, the place name. *Ribebôt* may be a variant of *merîbôt*, elsewhere a part of the name. See Koehler-Baumgartner, *Lexicon in Veteris Testamenti Libros*, Leiden, 1958, s.v. *qādēš*. For the problematic ʾešdāt (presumably: "fire of the law") read ʾašādôt (or: ʾašēdôt) "waterfalls". See Jos. 10: 40, 12: 7-8. Approaching from the East, from Seir, one would have on his right two areas, one to the East and the other to the Northwest of the Jordan, which were called ʾašēdôt. See Y. Aharoni, *Carta Atlas of the Bible*, Jerusalem, 1964, map no. 7. The new Jewish Publication Society Torah translation tentatively suggests "lightning flashing". See E. König, *Kommentar zum alten Testament, das Deuteronomium*, Leipzig, 1917, pp. 216-218. A later echo of this epic theme is to be found in Habakuk 3 : 1f.

Why do you draw back your hand?
Hold back your right hand inside your bosom?[1])
My God! My king from of old!
The worker of acts of deliverance in the midst of the earth.
(Psalm 74 : 11-12)

Interestingly, the prophet Micah, and his contemporary Amos, invert the coin, and employ ancient images of the earth-striding deity to portray the approach of God, descending from heaven to earth, in order to devastate the idolatrous cultic centers:

For, behold! Yahweh is going forth out of his place,
And he will descend, treading on the high ridges of the earth.
The mountains will melt underneath him,
And the valleys will be split—
As wax before fire,
As water flowing down an incline.
(Micah 1 : 3-4, abbreviated in Amos 4 : 13)

Micah and Amos achieved unusual poignancy by transposing motifs associated in the minds of the people with God's saving power into the context of the punishment of Israel. The same approach, the descent to earth, becomes for them an inevitably disastrous act, but their referent is the tradition that God's presence on earth was a situation much to be sought. In the epic selections describing God's approach to Israel, the verbs employed, especially "he came, he marched, he went forth, he will tread" serve to create a scene of earthly activity.[2]) It is not only God's might that is recounted here, but his nearness.

This is the most fundamental expression of the notion, later to be-

---

[1]) V. 11b is problematic. We follow, in principle, the rendering of H. Gunkel, *die Psalmen, Gottinger Handkommentar zum alten Testament*, Gottingen, 1926, s.v. Ps. 74: 11. Gunkel reads *beqereb ḥēqekā tıklā)* "you hold back inside your bosom", for Massoretic *miqqereb ḥēqekā kallēh* which would have to mean: "draw out from inside your bosom". We do not have such a connotation attested for the Piel *kallēh*, which means "destroy, put an end to —." The word *klh* could, however, be a variant of *kl)* "hold back" and represent the ınfinitive absolute, *kālôh*.

[2]) In Dt. 33: 2 the verb *hôpı̄ʿa* "he appeared, he shone" (see Job 10 : 3) is used, as in other passages, to indicate the pose of the deity when he reveals himself. Cf. Ps. 50 : 2, 80 : 2, 94 : 1. The meaning "to shine" is not always used to describe sunlight. See Job 37 : 15, where it is said of God's protecting cloud. The verbs "come, go, shine" are elsewhere used to describe the sun, originally the sungod. On the verb *ypʿ* in Ugaritic, and regarding personal theophoric names which incorporate this verb, see C. H. Gordon, *Ugarıtıc Textbook*, Rome, 1965, glossary, no. 1133. On the quaking of nature at the approach of God, see S. A. Lowenstam, *ʿOz Ledavid, (Hebrew)*, vol. 15, Jerusalem, 1964, pp. 508-520.

come basic in Israelite religion, that God's nearness is prerequisite to the blessings afforded by his great power. The exercize of that power is recounted in referring to singular occasions in the past, in projecting descriptions of the redemption to come, and in appealing to God for rescue in the present. What the cult sought to do, in a sense, was to render permanent the epic relationship of God to Israel, and thus to assure the regular availability of divine power. The cult was to routinize the singular. Whereas prophets warned the people not to rely on past indications of favor as an assurance of victory, the cultic spokesmen instituted epic recitation for the very purpose of promoting faith in God's continuously protecting power.

II

The heroic traditions of the Bible reveal still another aspect of the concern with God's nearness and presence. We are here introduced to an accepted notion (one hesitates to use the term doctrine) of early biblical religion, which we shall call "the potent presence". Simply stated, it means that God's presence in the midst of the people is the actual cause of their victory and the success of their ventures, the basis of their peace and wellbeing. Conversely, God's absence or withdrawal permits other forces to control the situation, resulting in the defeat of Israel and in its misfortune. This notion affects both the individual hero and the military band as a whole, and, as in epic, usually finds its expression in the atmosphere of battle. Much has been said about the "charismatic" character of the Israelite hero, stressing that the "spirit of Yahweh" alights upon him and clothes him with prowess.[1] In the context of our discussion, the concern expressed by the hero for the presence of God in the midst of the people is of primary interest. It is Gideon's encounter with the angel of God which is most revealing in this regard (Judges 6). Gideon gives direct expression to the notion of the potent presence: "Pray, oh my lord, if indeed Yahweh is with us, why has all of this overtaken us?... For he must have abandoned us, and given us over into the hands of the Midianites" (Judges 6:13). Gideon is unwilling to take chances, and three successive signs are required to assure him of the divine presence, an absolute prerequisite to the success of the venture. That is the force of the preposition *'im*,

---

[1] J. Pedersen, *Israel: Its Life and Culture*, Copenhagen, 1953, vol. 3, pp. 34-39. R. de Vaux, *Ancient Israel*, New York, 1961, pp. 261-262.

which occurs four times in this passage.[1]) The hero seems to understand that God may, for a time, abandon his people, but he is extremely suspicious on the question of whether God has actually returned.

Once we realize that the notion of the potent presence was an unquestioned assumption in certain biblical traditions, we can better interpret a number of accounts which are predicated upon it.[2]) The book of Numbers records that after God had decreed forty years of wandering in the desert, a band of warriors attempted to advance by the direct route to Canaan and were repulsed. In warning them, Moses had said: "Do not go up, lest you be routed by your enemies, for Yahweh is not in your midst" (Numbers 14 : 42).[3]) Significantly, the ark does not budge from its place in the camp (*Ibid.* verse 44). What is most important here is the reasoning Moses employs in pleading for Israel. Moses argues that other nations would attribute Israel's extinction in the desert to God's impotence. The reasoning is as follows: God cannot have abandoned his people, since his presence is attested by the pillars of fire and cloud that go before the Israelites on their journeys. The people, nonetheless, perishes in the desert. Ergo: God is present, but he has become impotent (Numbers 14 : 13-16).[4])

This argument fails to consider aspects of God's relationship to Israel which figure elsewhere. It does not include the possibility that God merely refused to exercize the power of his presence, and that the decision not to exercize potency does not presuppose the actual withdrawal of the deity.

This becomes significant when we examine the account of the battle between the Israelites and the Philistines at Aphek (I Samuel 4 : 3f.), and compare it with the account of the battle fought some twenty years later against the Philistines at Mizpah (I Samuel 7 : 3f.). During the earlier battle, the Israelites had brought the ark from Shiloh in the hope that it would afford them victory, but they were defeated, nevertheless. In the terms of that account, the potency of the ark simply failed, and no explanation is given as to why. It is only later that Samuel explains the cause of the earlier defeat. Israel had committed idolatry. They would be victorious only if they sincerely returned to the worship of God. Samuel accepts the pledge of the people and en-

---

[1]) Judges 6 : 12, 13, 16, 17.
[2]) See de Vaux, *op. cit.*, p. 299.
[3]) Cf. Exodus 32: 11-12.
[4]) Cf. Zeph. 1 : 12. The prophet attributes to the people the view that Yahweh does nothing at all, which might mean that he has no power to act.

treats God on their behalf, and they are victorious. The presence of the ark had failed, for twenty years, to relieve the Philistine oppression, but the return of the people to the worship of God was efficacious.[1])

We see the difference between the essentially heroic tradition, when unaffected by prophetic superimpositions, and the interpretation of Israelite history in terms of disobedience to God and its consequences. In the heroic tradition, the mere presence of divine power is sufficient. It is a mechanically operating pneuma, subject at times to failure.

We can thus isolate three aspects in the structure of the idea of potent presence:

1. The alternatives of presence and absence, as reflected in the Gideon account.

2. The alternatives of presence, absence, and impotence, as reflected in Numbers 14: 13-16 and I Samuel 4: 3f.

3. The alternatives of exercized and unexercized potency. In this conception, presence is generally assumed, and is not the crucial factor, and impotence is inconceivable. This conception is reflected in I Samuel 7: 3f.

III

It has been necessary to deal with the general theme of God's presence before considering matters peculiar to the cult. Cultic notions are usually the particularized expressions of more widespread concepts operative in the culture at large, rather than the original creations of the cult itself.[2]) The religious establishment tends to sanction that which the culture has accepted. The notion that God's presence is necessary for securing the blessings of life was, as we have shown, intrinsic to the early traditions of Israel. It is against this background that we must now explore its cultic applications.

We begin by inquiring into the motivations surrounding the private and local altar-building projects recorded in the Pentateuch and in the historical books of the Bible. Two complementary factors must be considered: 1) The evident presence of the deity as the determinant in establishing the sanctity of a particular site, and 2) The construction of

---

[1]) Cf. Jos. 7: 4f.

[2]) This has been clarified by our researches into biblical cultic terminology. It is possible to demonstrate that the large majority of technical terms used in cultic texts derive from other contexts. See B. Levine, "Comments on Some Technical Terms of the Biblical Cult," (Hebrew), *Leshonenu*, The Academy for the Hebrew Language, Jerusalem, vol. xxx, 1965, pp. 3-11.

an altar, and the offering of sacrifices, as an effort to attract the deity to the place of sacrifice; to invite him to pay a visit.

The former aspect of the sanctity of cultic locales has been duly noted and discussed. A classic example is Genesis 28, the account of Jacob's experience at Bethel. The cult is there conceived as a human response to the presence of the deity. Generally, when sanction is sought for already existing cultic centers, much is made of the fact that the deity manifested his presence at those sites in the distant past.[1])

The problem of sanctions is, however, considerably more complex. In Exodus 20 : 19-23 (22-26), a passage containing some early regulations on the building of altars, verse 21 (24) states: "In every place where I cause my name to be pronounced, I will come to you and bless you."[2]) The point here is that God "comes" to the worshipper; he draws near to him when he is about to grant him blessings. Though a particular locale is known as a sacred site (a site where "I cause my name to be pronounced") it is not to be assumed, in the terms of this passage, that God is always present there. He must be invoked, and we are told that the deity will accept a proper invitation, and will "come." The altar must be constructed according to certain specifications, and nakedness may not be exposed in proximity to it.

The established sacredness of a site is thus subject to still another factor: the correctness of the cultic activity undertaken there. We may infer that improper rites may persuade the deity not to frequent certain sites, and he may come to despise them. This becomes a fundamental concept in prophetic literature, where it is fused with the overall prophetic critique of ritual to produce the idea that God rejects cultic sites, even places where he was present in the past, when those offering the sacrifices violate his laws of justice and love. For our discussion, it suffices to say that the tradition of Exodus 20 : 19-23 (22-26) viewed the altar rite as an invitation, and that it is predicated on the assumption that there are acceptable and unacceptable rites, a factor crucial irrespective of locale.

In the problematic Balaam account we are brought to a consideration of those efforts aimed at attracting the deity, a more emphatic project than inviting him to an already designated site. Magic would

---

[1]) See de Vaux, *op. cit.*, pp. 276-277. Pederson, *op. cit.*, vol. 3, pp. 201-214. Cf. J. Lindblom, *Hebrew Union College Annual*, Cincinnati, 32, 1961, pp. 91-106, and especially his treatment of the Gideon account on p. 103.

[2]) For exegesis, see M. Noth, *The Old Testament Library: Exodus*, Philadelphia, 1962, pp. 176-177. U. Cassuto, *A Commentary on the Book of Exodus*, (Hebrew), Jerusalem, 1959, pp. 176-178.

normally be involved in ritual activities having this objective, as was the case in the Balaam episode (Numbers 22 : 7, 24 : 1). For that reason, perhaps, biblical sources would shy away from openly stating that the worshippers were attempting to attract the deity to the place of sacrifice. The writer of Numbers is aware, however, that such motives enter into ritual, and he conveys that awareness in a setting at once removed from the normal context, and yet directly related to the God of Israel. Balaam orders that altars be built and sacrifices prepared as a means of inducing an encounter with God (Numbers 23 : 1-3). He had already explained that he could speak only what God put into his mouth (Numbers 22 : 38). The only matter to be determined was whether God would say something harmful to Israel.

The crucial term in these passages is the verb *qrh* (Numbers 23 : 3-4, 15-16). This root, in the Qal and Niphal, bears the connotation of establishing contact, of meeting up, and seems usually to include the nuance of a chance meeting.[1]) Although the writer of this account undoubtedly shared the belief that the deity selects certain sites where he manifests his presence, he thinks of this selection in more fluid terms. The deity may be attracted to a spot, by sacrifice and magic, where he had not been present previously, and without indication that he would visit the spot again. In such cases, certain fairly obvious factors would figure in the effort to attract. Mountaintops have definite advantages. If one is to direct his words at a specific area, a spot in full view of that area is where God might logically communicate (Numbers 23 : 13). But, withal, methods are employed to attract the deity to a place human beings consider to be well suited for their purposes, and this is something quite different from inviting God to visit a place which he has selected. Balaam walks away a distance from the altars to encounter God, but it is clear that they provide the basic attraction in this account (Numbers 23 : 3-4).[2])

---

[1]) See Koehler-Baumgartner, *op. cit.*, s.v. *qrh*, and cf. Exodus 3 : 18, Numbers 11 : 23.

[2]) Elijah's encounter with the priests of Baal (I Kings 18) may also reflect the same objective of attracting the deity. Elijah uses magical techniques. He digs a ditch and fills it with water (18 : 32-35). The response to Elijah's invocation comes in the form of fire which licks up the water and consumes the sacrifice (vs. 38-39). A. Goetze has presented a Hittite ritual of attraction which he calls Evocatio (J. Pritchard, *Ancient Near Eastern Texts Relating to the Old Testament*, Princeton, 1951, pp. 351-353). Materials such as oil, wine, etc. were placed in baskets along the way to make a trail for the gods to follow on their way back to Hattiland.

IV

We turn now to the royally sponsored cult at Jerusalem to determine in what manner the notion of the potent presence, and the effort to benefit from the nearness of God operated once a central cult was established.

I Kings 8:12-13 is a passage quoted from an ancient collection. Verse 13 states the purpose for which the temple was built: "I have surely built a princely house for you, a dais for you to sit upon forever." Less literally, we would render: "a set place for your residence." The temple is a residence for the deity.[1]) Once established, the Jerusalem temple and its attending cult produce certain reflexes in the religious attitudes of the people. One such reflex is the notion that God's presence in the Jerusalem temple guarantees the security of the city and its residents, an idea extended to include the whole people of Israel and its land.

This notion is attacked by the prophet Micah, who says of the leaders of the people in Jerusalem:

> Her leaders render judgment on the basis of bribes.
> Her priests practise divination for a fee.
> And they lean on Yahweh, saying:
> Is not Yahweh in our midst?
> No evil shall come upon us!
>
> (Micah 3:11)

Jeremiah also warns the people not to trust the words of the false prophets who say:

> The temple of Yahweh! The temple of Yahweh!
>
> (Jeremiah 7:3)

Jerusalem will fall just as did Shiloh, where God also resided. Psalm 46 presents the notion which Micah and Jeremiah are criticizing:

---

[1]) For exegesis, see J. A. Montgomery, H. S. Gehman, *Kings, The International Critical Commentary*, 1951, pp. 189f. V. 12 conveys the idea that the temple was meant as a place of concealment for the deity, thus reproducing his situation in the heavenly temple: "Yahweh intends to dwell in the dense cloud." See K. Baltzer, *Harvard Theological Review*, 59, 1965, p. 263f. The notion that the deity has "a set place" for residence met with some opposition. II Sam. 7:1f. preserves a tradition according to which God seemed to prefer the mobility afforded by the tent (v. 6). This passage may be simply an *ad hoc* explanation of why no temple was built until the time of Solomon, or it may indeed reflect a legitimate dissent from the growing nationalization of the cult which resulted from the establishment of the monarchy. See G. Ernest Wright, *op. cit.*, p. 172f.

God is for us protection and strength.
A most valuable source of help in trouble.
Thus, we have no fear when the earth is overturned,
And when mountains totter into the depths of the sea...
A river—its tributaries bring joy to the city of God,
The holy place of Elyon's residence.
God is in her midst, she shall not fall!
God will bestow help upon her before morning.

(verses 2-3; 5-6)

In this we have applied the notion of the potent presence to the Jerusalem temple, which became God's principal headquarters, and in time the only headquarters, for the Israelite. To put it in technological terms: God's power is produced in heaven, but it is distributed from the temple. This is conveyed by the author of Psalm 68:

Recount the might of God!
His majesty is over Israel,
And his might is in the heavens.
God is awesome from your temple buildings.
The God of Israel—he gives might and power to the people.
Blessed is God!

(verses 35-36)

It is from heaven that God's power originates, but it is from the temple that the deity appears and gives strength to the people.[1]

Although God never ceases to answer prayers from his heavenly abode,[2] the literature of supplications seems to indicate that it was primarily the temple from whence came the divine assistance requested in prayer and sacrifice.[3] This conclusion is supported by an analysis of the anxieties and passions of the religious man with respect to the temple, as expressed in the book of Psalms.

It was felt, first of all, that to be in the sanctuary is to be under God's protection, and the temple is actually equated with the shelter of God's wings.[4] In the same way, one senses great anxiety when he is distant

---

[1] Ps. 63 : 3.

[2] Thr. 3 : 44, Ps. 20: 7, 123 : 1, I Kings 8 : 30, 32, Neh. 9 : 27.

[3] In Ps. 20 we find the polarity of heaven and temple. The response comes from heaven (v. 7), but the help comes from the temple in Zion (v. 3). See J. A. Montgomery, *op. cit.*, p. 194. Cf. Ps. 14: 7, 53:7, 110 : 2, 138 : 1-3. In Ps. 28 it is clear, especially from v. 2, that the supplicant expects the requested help to come from the temple. Also cf. Jonah 2 : 8.

[4] Ps. 27 : 4f., 36 : 8-10, 61 : 5, 63 : 7, 65 : 2-3. The right of asylum in the sanctuary is clearly based on the concept that once in the temple a person is under God's protection, and dare not be harmed.

from the temple. The distressed supplicant, in the North or in Transjordan, recalls his joy in the cultic celebration, when he entered into the presence of God. He argues, albeit reverently, that since he remembers God from afar, God, in turn, should have him in mind when he is far from the temple (Psalm 42). The phrase *yešû ʾôt panâu* "his countenance is deliverance" (or: "deliverance is effected by his countenance") in Psalm 42 : 6 amplifies the thought that nearness to the temple meant actual nearness to God and his protection.[1] It is in the temple that one beholds God's countenance.[2]

Just as distance from the temple can produce anxiety, so may concern over being denied entry into the temple because of unfitness. The rites of entry referred to in Psalms 15 and 24 were a means of determining fitness, and although these Psalms are a stylized formulation of religious duties, they undoubtedly go back to an actual anxiety.

Looking at the other side of things, we find passionate expressions of the desire to be in the temple, and we sense the joy experienced there by the worshipper (Psalm 63 : 3, 7-8).[3] It is the pilgrim who experiences the peak of elation in the temple. After a long journey, during which God protected him from the dangers of the road and provided for his needs, he finally stands in God's presence:

> How endearing are your habitations, Yahweh of hosts!
> My soul yearns, even becomes faint for the courtyards of Yahweh.
> My heart and my flesh—they sing forth to the living God!
> Even as the bird finds a dwelling,
> And the swallow a nest for herself,
> Where she places her young—
> So are your altars, my king and God!
> Fortunate are they who dwell in your house!
> They shall continue to praise you, Selah.
> Fortunate is the man whose strength is from you!
> As they walk on the highways,[4]
> They who pass through the valley of Bākāʾ,
> They drink from a spring.

---

[1] The phrase *yešû ʾôt panai wēʾlôhai* in v. 12 is difficult. See H. Gunkel, *op. cit.*, s.v. 42 : 6. Perhaps: *yešû ʾôt panaû, ʾelôhai!* "My God- his countenance is deliverance!"

[2] Ps. 42: 3, 63 : 3, 84: 8, Jonah 2 : 5. Where the Massoretic text is vocalized *ʾērā*ʾ *eh* "I will be seen", in the Niphal stem, it is likely that the original was *ʾerʾ eh* "I will behold", as is the view of Gunkel. The change was tendentious.

[3] Ps. 26, 73 : 27-28, 118 : 19-20.

[4] In the phrase *mesillôt bilebābām* "roads in their hearts", the second word is perhaps to be read *belektām* "as they walk".

He (God) envelopes pools of water with rain.[1]
They proceed from wall to wall.[2]
He (finally) beholds God in Zion.
Yahweh, God of hosts, hear my prayer!
Give ear, oh God of Jacob! Selah.
Our shield, see!
God! Look at the face of your annointed!
For one day in your courts is better than a thousand (outside your courts)!
I prefer (merely) to cross the threshold[3] of the house of my God,
Than to dwell in the tents of wickedness!
For Yahweh, God, is a sun and shield.
Yahweh bestows kindness and honor.
He does not withold goodness from those who walk in uprightness.
Yahweh of hosts!
Fortunate is the man who puts his trust in you!
(Psalm 84 : 2-13)

In effect, this concern over the nearness of God produces the nexus of two factors: divine presence in the temple, and divine help. The worshipper needs the temple because he needs God's help. Note the following expressions of this nexus:

God is in her midst she shall not fall—
God will bestow help upon her before morning.
(Psalm 46 : 6)

Verily, I behold you in the sanctuary, seeing your might and glory—
For you have been a source of help to me.
(Psam 63 : 3,7)

God is awesome from your temple buildings—
The God of Israel—he gives might and power to the people.
(Psalm 68 : 36)

To you silence is praise, oh God in Zion!...
Oh hearer of prayer!
All flesh approaches you—
You have visited the land and given it water.
You enrich it profusely...
You have surrounded the year with your goodness.
(Psalm 65 : 1-2, 10, 12)

---

[1] For *ma ʿayān yešîtûhû* "they place for him a spring" read, perhaps: *yištûhû* "they drink it", or simply: *yištû* "they drink". See Gunkel, *op. cit.*, s.v. 84 : 7f. *Berākôt* "blessings" is to be vocalized *berēkôt* "pools".

[2] Hebrew *ḥayil* is to be vocalized *ḥêl* "wall". Cf. Ps. 48: 14. We see here a description of the approaching pilgrim. He proceeds inward, into the temple, until he stands before God. An alternative is to retain the vocalization *ḥayil* in the sense of "wealth" (cf. Ps. 49 : 11, 73 : 12, etc.). It would here refer to the fact that God provided for the needs of the pilgrim during his journey.

[3] *Hıstôpēp* is taken as a denominative from *sap* "threshold".

Fortunate are they who dwell in your house—
Fortunate is the man whose strength is from you.

(Psalm 84 : 5-6)

V

Another reaction to the Jerusalem temple, which testifies to its role as the locus of God's power on earth, is the anxiety over God's possible departure from the temple.[1]) This anxiety, like those others we have discussed, was not born in the experience of the cult. It was far more pervasive.

The Israelites challenged the authority of Moses at a moment when they thirsted for water: "Is Yahweh present among us or not?" (Exodus 17 : 7). This was a legitimate concern, coming from a group of people who found themselves in the Sinai desert without water. It is significant that when God arrives on the scene (verse 6), he does not rebuke the people or strike out at them. To the contrary, he acts to save them. In the mind of the biblical writer it was a lack of faith in God's reliability which prompted the taunt, but that should not make us unmindful of the genuineness of the anxiety itself.

At other moments in his career, Moses faced similar demonstrations of Israel's tendency to lose confidence in God and in the leadership of his appointed apostle. The people required periodic reassurance: "And he (Moses) said: If I have found favor in your eyes, oh my Lord, let my Lord go in our midst; for it is a stiffnecked people" (Exodus 34 : 9). Here, too, God's response is not wrathful. He promises Moses that he will perform wondrous acts in full view of the people, so that they may be convinced of his presence among them. No doubt the same fear that God had abandoned his people figured in the demand put to Aaron to produce a deity "who will walk before us" (Exodus 32 : 1).[2])

This fear over the departure of God was understandably intensified in the near-exilic and exilic periods, and it was the task of the prophets of that time to explain the destruction of temple and land in terms other than God's withdrawal from the midst of the people. The discussion of these developments is beyond our present scope, but a brief statement, focusing on the matrix of the problem, can be attempted here.[3])

---

[1]) Ps. 6 : 5, 10 : 1, Ps. 22, 34 : 19, 35 : 22, 38 : 22, 60 : 12//108 : 12, 90 : 13, 94 : 14.
[2]) Cf. the lament that God no longer "goes forth at the head of our hosts" in Ps. 60 : 12//108 : 12.
[3]) The prophets of the exile and the return further develop the notion of the

Ezekiel, pictured as residing in Babylonia, is transported to Jerusalem in a vision, and is there shown the idolatrous practices indulged by the leaders of the people within the temple itself (Ezekiel, chapter 8).[1]) In the text of the vision, a view is ascribed to the sinful elders of Israel and, for that matter, to most of the people: "Yahweh does not see us; Yahweh has departed from the land" (Ezekiel 8 : 12).[2]) In contrast, the prophetic view is presented through the words of God to Ezekiel. The idolatry of Israel and the pollution of the temple have angered God, and he issues an order for the destruction of the temple. At that point, the *kābôd*, or "presence" of God, withdraws from its position atop the cherub on the threshold of the temple, and moves into the courtyard (Ezekiel 10 : 4-5), a clear indication that God is departing and has consigned the temple to ruin.

May we not be a bit more objective than the prophet and suggest that there was real cause for anxiety in the years immediately preceding the final destruction and exile, and that an understandable, though not pardonable response would have been to turn to idolatrous cults in the hope that they would avail? It would be normal to conclude from the declining situation in Judea that the divine presence had actually departed. The prophet was juxtaposing cause and effect. In reality, idolatry was invoked because the situation appeared hopeless. This juxtaposition served two purposes for the prophet. If accepted, it might restrain further idolatry, and, what is perhaps more important, it would establish the sinfulness of the people as the cause for the national misfortune, thus refuting the pernicious notion that God had forsaken his people. In this light we can well understand Ezekiel's statement further on: "I will be for them a small sanctuary(?) in the lands to which they have come" (Ezekiel 11 : 16). God had, indeed, left Jerusalem, but only so as to be close to his exiled people in Babylonia.

---

potent presence (especially Ezekiel 20, 40f.), and in the post-exilic books, principally Chronicles, there is much material for consideration. Similarly, the priestly writings of the Pentateuch and the book of Deuteronomy present distinctive views on the subject of God's presence and nearness. Although it is *possible* (though we doubt it) that certain Psalms may reflect the influence of the priestly writings of the Pentateuch and the book of Deuteronomy, or of exilic and post-exilic views, we see no evidence, in the Psalms we have discussed here, of notions that clearly show such influence. It should be noted, in this connection, that God's selection of Jerusalem as the site of the temple is not, in itself, a Deuteronomic doctrine, but relates more clearly to the dynastic covenant with the House of David.

[1]) As presented, the vision is set in Jerusalem in the years immediately preceding the destruction. For the purposes of our discussion is it not necessary to determine whether this was a vision or an actual experience in Jerusalem.

[2]) Cf. Ezekiel 9: 9.

Ezekiel is still operating on the notion of the potent presence at this juncture, and does not really dispute the conclusion that a Jerusalem in ruins is a Jerusalem without its resident deity. In his vision, the deity departs before the destruction occurs. What the prophet does is to lend a new interpretation to the notion of the potent presence according to which the application of this notion exclusively to the Jerusalem temple is abrogated.

VI

Despite its weaknesses, the notion of the potent presence survived in biblical religion and continued to influence post-biblical Judaism as well. Prophets criticized and attacked it, and altered its force in the light of new situations. At times of crisis, even prophets betrayed their own belief, or hope, perhaps, that God's presence must surely bring deliverance. Jeremiah was audacious in his insistence that Jerusalem would fall despite the fact that the temple was God's residence, but he could not control his urge to appeal to the very belief he had attacked:

> Oh hope of Israel!
> His deliverer in time of trouble!
> Why are you like a sojourner in the land,
> Like a traveler who has turned aside (only) to spend the night?
> Why do you act like a stunned man,
> Like a warrior incapable of delivering?
> For you are in our midst, Yahweh,
> And we are called by your name!
> Do not forsake us!
>
> (Jeremiah 14 : 8-9)[1]

In an earlier period the Jerusalemite, Isaiah, never averse to attacking conventional reliance on the efficacy of the cult, was capable, nevertheless, of expressing great joy in the presence of the resident deity:

> Rejoice and sing, oh dweller in Zion!
> For the holy one of Israel is great in your midst.
>
> (Isaiah 12 : 6)

---

[1] Cf. Hosea 11 : 9 for similar thoughts.

THE CELEBRATION OF THE FEAST OF BOOTHS ACCORDING TO ZECH xiv 16-21

BY

WALTER HARRELSON

Vanderbilt University

I

Benedikt Otzen's recent study of Zech ix-xiv[1]) has done much to clarify and provide a plausible historical setting for the several sections of these troublesome chapters. This paper is intended to amplify Otzen's treatment of Chapter xiv. Otzen found it to be the latest of the materials in the collection. I agree with that judgment. No precise date can be fixed, although I find no reason to date the chapter to a period later than about 400 B.C.

We are interested especially in the last six verses: the nations' celebration of the feast of booths at Jerusalem. It is necessary first to look briefly at the contents of the entire chapter. Several recent scholars, including Otzen, consider the chapter to come from a single author, although a few glosses have been identified. Elliger thinks that the original was reworked rather considerably by a later hand.[2]) Using several motifs developed by earlier writers and perhaps deriving from the Israelite cultus, the author produced a fairly well unified picture of the Last Day. The chapter is in prose, although in verses 8-9 and 12 a rhythmic prose approaching poetry seems to me to be discernible.

I

The contents of the chapter may be summarized as follows:

Verse 1. The Lord's Day against Jerusalem. A summary word forecasting Jerusalem's invasion and despoiling.

II. Verses 2-5. An oracle of doom, in prose. At the Lord's initiative,

---

[1]) Benedikt Otzen, *Studien uber Deuterosacharja*. Copenhagen: Prostant apud Munksgaard, 1964. See especially pp. 199-212; 267-272.

[2]) Friedrich Horst (*Die zwolf Kleinen Propheten*; HAT, I, 14, 1938, 250) characteristically finds small independent units in the chapter. Paul Lamarche, *Zacharie, structure litteraire et messianisme* (1964) holds to the unity of the entire six chapters. Elliger (*Das Alte Testament Deutsch*, 25, 167-170) considers 4b-5, 10, 12, 15, 18, 20-21 to be later expansions. Gerhard von Rad allows for the possibility of some expansion (*Theologie des Alten Testaments*, II, 1960, p, 307). Otzen finds in vss. 13-14 the only major additions to the chapter.

the foreign nations attack Jerusalem. The Lord will bring the nations against Jerusalem; they will enter the city, plunder it, and take captive one-half of its inhabitants. Then the Lord will engage the nations in battle. He will divide the Mount of Olives and prepare a way of escape through the divided mountain for the survivors. (Textual emendation: in vs. 5 read *gē' hārîm*, "the valley of the mountains," translating "You will flee through the valley between the mountains").

III. Verses 6-11. A sketch of the Lord's inthronization in Jerusalem. Judah and Jerusalem will be transformed. The alternation of the seasons will cease. (Textual emendation: read *ḥom* for *)ôr* and translate "...there will be no heat, cold, or ice.") Perpetual day will prevail. Waters of life will go forth from Jerusalem to the west and the east. The Lord will rule as King over the entire earth. Jerusalem will tower above the land of Judah, for Judah will be transformed into a plain from its northern to its southern borders. Jerusalem's fortifications will be secured; its inhabitants will dwell in safety.

IV. Verses 12, 15. Oracle of judgment. The Lord's plague upon the nations. The nations will be afflicted with a loathsome disease. Their animals in the encampments will also be stricken.

(Verses 13-14 are probably a later addition.)

V. Verses 16-21. Admonitory summons to worship. Survivors among the nations celebrate the feast of booths. The nations will be required to come up to Jerusalem to celebrate the feast of booths. Those that refuse to come will be deprived of rain. Egypt in particular must come. If Egypt refuses, the Lord will smite the Egyptions with a plague (textual emendation: omit the second *welô)*). As the nations gather, they will be able to join in the festivities without restraints. Former distinctions between sacred and profane will be abolished. No traders will be in the Lord's house, apparently because no one will need to buy animals or other sacrificial objects.

This summary of the contents of the chapter reveals, I believe, that the last section—the nations' celebration of the feast of booths—is the culmination of the author's thought. This section should not be separated from the preceding ones, but it may be legitimate in a brief paper to concentrate attention upon it.

Formally, the chapter reveals a mixture of forms. The most characteristic formal element is the pilgrimage of the nations to Zion. We shall speak about the special features of this formal element later on. We also have a brief oracle of doom in prose (vss. 2-5), a prose sketch of the Lord's enthronement, apparently borrowed from the enthronement texts of the cultus (vss. 6-11), a brief oracle of judgment (vss. 12, 15), and a prose call to worship in admonitory tone (vss. 16-21). We observe a characteristic breakdown of literary forms in this eschatological-apocalyptic text.

II

The unknown author presents a distinctive picture of God's consummation of his purpose for the foreign nations. His literary sources are to some extent recognizable: Isaiah ii 2-4 (and Micah iv 1-4); Ezekiel xxxviii-xxxix; Isaiah lx, plus other materials from the Book of Isaiah.[1]) The author's bold image of the nations' worship at Jerusalem, however, goes beyond that found in any other OT texts. His identification of the occasion for the nations' worship is unique in the OT, so far as I have been able to determine.

The cultic sources of the author's imagery are much disputed. Is the gathering of the nations at Zion a part of the pre-Davidic Jerusalem's mythology, later celebrated in the City of David in connection with a royal Zion festival (von Rad, Kraus)?[2]) Or is this gathering to be connected with ancient ceremonies of covenant renewal?[3]) Or is it a motif in the celebration of the festival of the New Year?[4]) Judgments differ on this point as a result of differences in the understanding of the history of Israelite worship. I am convinced that Artur Weiser and those who follow him have gone too far in claiming the virtual ubiquity of the ceremony of covenant renewal. I am also convinced that the royal Zion festival of Hans-Joachim Kraus never existed.[5]) The imagery of this chapter seems to me clearly to derive from ancient celebrations of the New Year. The assembling of the nations against the holy city, the center of the earth, the source of the waters of life, is one such motif from New Year's Day celebrations. Another is the divine judgment upon the nations following upon their defeat. Creation imagery is unmistakable in the chapter: the picture of Zion as the city on the mountain from which the waters of life flow; the abolition of the alternation of the seasons and the establishment of perpetual day; the division of the mountain into two parts; the leveling of Judah into a plain dominated by the sacred mountain Zion. The motif chaos-cosmos is clear throughout the chapter; the Lord is transforming the

---

[1]) Otzen has a careful treatment of the author's sources; *op. cit.*, pp. 201-212. See also Von Rad, *op. cit.*, pp. 305-309, 312.
[2]) See most recently Hans-Joachim Kraus, *Gottesdienst in Israel*, 2nd ed. (1962), 239-253; Von Rad, *op. cit.*, pp. 305-306.
[3]) Artur Weiser, *The Old Testament: Its Formation and Development* (1961), pp. 33 and 275.
[4]) Otzen, *op. cit.*, passim, and many other scholars cited by him.
[5]) Elaborated by Kraus most fully in his *Die Konigsherrschaft Gottes im Alten Testament* (1950).

present world order by means of a convulsion of that order and the establishment of cosmos through and beyond the chaos.¹)

The structure of the chapter is reminiscent of the ritual of divine inthronization. The Lord brings the nations against Jerusalem. He then appears to rout the enemy. The chaos wrought by the nations is matched by the convulsions of nature brought by the Lord, as he clears the way for the Israelites to escape. The Lord then establishes his new order for the world. He takes his place as the one God of the nations (vs. 9), Zion appears as the center of the world, and the nations gather there for worship of the Lord their king.²)

Another element is present in the chapter, however. The occasion is the feast of booths. Despite the disclaimers of some scholars,³) it seems to me certain that in ancient Israel the fall festival was the occasion for annual renewal of the covenant between the Lord and his people. Under the kingship this festival became a New Year's Day festival in which the covenant between the Lord and the house of David was reaffirmed in Jerusalem. In Josiah's celebration of the Passover we may have a shifting of the festival to the spring; Josiah clearly engaged in an act of covenant renewal in connection with his reform (2 Kings xxii-xxiii).⁴) In post-Exilic times, however, we hear little of a national celebration regularly observed in Jerusalem which has the character either of a covenant renewal festival or one that continues the New Year's Day celebrations. On only one other post-Exilic occasion known to us does the feast of booths appear as a momentous festival: the occasion of Ezra's reform. In Neh vii 73-ix 38 (Heb vii 73-x 1) we have the record of that event. The celebration had not been observed, or had not been observed properly, since the days of Joshua. The date of the festival is remarkable in the Ezra story: public reading of Torah began on the first day of the seventh month. On the second day the seven-day celebration of the feast began. In the detailed priestly legislation for the

---

¹) See Otzen's fine treatment and the references cited there.
²) The author is thus influenced by actual cultic proceedings connected with the festival of divine inthronization. His use of this imagery is however, eschatological. The post-Exilic cult in Jerusalem no longer employed such themes in its actual celebration.
³) Alt argues for a 7-year ceremony; he has been followed by others, notably Kraus and Gerhard von Rad. My arguments for the annual celebration appear in *Interpreting the Old Testament* (N.Y. 1964), pp. 122-126.
⁴) Apparently, Josiah's shift of the festival to the spring was a part of a calendar reform, under Assyrian influence. Or the reforming king may have been altering the character of the spring festival already existent in Jerusalem as an Assyrian-influenced celebration.

feast, however, the celebration was preceded by a New Year's Day observance on the first of the month and on the tenth day the observance of the Day of Atonement (Lev xxiii). Since the Ezra celebration was a very special event, it is unwise to view it as decisive for the history of post-Exilic developments in Israelite worship. The priestly legislation may have been in existence prior to Ezra's day but not in operation. Even less decisive for the history of the festival is the account of an eschatological apocalyptic celebration like that in Zech xiv. The picture found here may have no connection with the regular cultic acts of the author's community.

The two references—that from Ezra's time and the Zech xiv passage—are significant witnesses to the import assigned to this festival by groups within the post-Exilic community. Ezra's celebration underscored the importance of Torah for the community. The ceremony of covenant renewal from ancient times was in effect reduced to a pledge of allegiance to Torah,[1] although the remarkable prayer attributed to Ezra reveals that the saving history continued to be an indispensable part of Torah (Neh ix). Emphasis fell on God's claim upon his people Israel. The foreign nations appear only as those from whom God's people must remain apart (Neh x).

III

In Zech xiv, the situation is decidedly different. Some scholars have maintained that the author's perspective is narrowly cultic and legalistic; that he carries to absurd extremes his interest in the cultic purity of the foreign nations; that only those persons who have scrupulously observed the ritual requirements will be acceptable guests at the ceremony.[2] Such a reading of the passage seems to me entirely wrong. The nations' observance of the feast of booths is perhaps a motif parallel to the nations' learning Torah from the Lord at Jerusalem

---

[1] Von Rad (*op. cit.*, p. 310) overstates this point. His insistence that the Torah became an absolute entity loosed from its saving-historical moorings is not defensible. Martin Noth's study (*Die Gesetze im Pentatuech*, 1940), on which he builds, also fails to make the case. Yet it is correct to distinguish between a priestly-theocratic picture of Torah and a prophetic-apocalyptic portrayal.

[2] Horst (*op. cit.*, p. 252) speaks of ritual holiness as the characterizing feature of the New Jerusalem and its environs. Mitchell (I.C.C., 1912) spoke of the author's "stress upon externals" (p. 242). Elliger points to contradictory impressions made upon the reader of the chapter. One discerns a true faith here, but one also sees an all too human concern for God, without understanding, which deepens the gulf between the narrow and the wider circle of God's saving works (*op. cit.*, p. 176).

(Isa ii 2-4). If so, the nations' observance of Torah may be implied in Zech xiv. Even that is doubtful.

When the whole of the passage is kept in mind, including its connection with verse 1-15, its import for the question of Israel's relation to the nations is striking. The author tells of a coming day on which the worship of the Lord in Jerusalem will be open to all the survivors among the foreign nations. They will be compelled to worship the one true God; but such worship will mean much more than their merely joining the Israelites in their ritual observances. Isiah lvi speaks of eunuchs and aliens who will have access to worship in the temple if they keep the Sabbath and hold fast to the covenant, doing those things that please the Lord.[1]) Zech xiv has nothing to say about observances other than the worship of the Lord at Zion on the great feast day, year by year. No conditions are imposed upon the foreign worshipers.

The fall festival was in ancient times the occasion for covenant renewal. Is it not in this text to be understood as the consummation of God's covenant with the foreign nations? We know from the Book of Jubilees (vi 17-18) that for at least one Jewish group the feast of Weeks or Pentecost was the occasion of God's renewal of the covenant with Noah. The sect at Qumran also had an annual celebration of covenant renewal, falling on the Day of Pentecost, according to several interpreters.[2]) The author of Zech xiv may very well have looked upon this coming festival as a time for the consummation of God's covenant with the nations.[3])

This possibility is made more probable when we turn to the picture of the abolition of distinctions between sacred and secular with which the passage ends. "Holy to the Lord" will be written on the bells or metal trinkets worn by the horses.[4]) Horses were viewed with suspicion by the Israelites; they were symbols of alien power. No longer will this be the case. Ordinary cooking pots in the temple will be just as sacred as will the bowls that receive the offerings to the Lord. Indeed, every pot in Jerusalem and in Judah will be acceptable for the offering of

---

[1]) Otzen points out the importance of Isa. lvi for an understanding of the chapter, but he does not call sufficient attention to the contract between the two passages (*op. cit.*, p. 211).

[2]) See Cross, *Ancient Library of Qumran* (1961), p. 219n, for references.

[3]) Otzen notes (*op. cit.*, p. 205) that the abolition of the alternation of the seasons also connects with the Noah covenant.

[4]) Horst (*op. cit.*, p. 252) sees this as a way of incorporating the power associated with the horse into the sphere of the Lord's holiness.

gifts to the Lord.[1]) Canaanites—i.e., traders who provided animals or other materials for sacrifice—will no longer be found in the vicinity of the temple (they were not allowed in the temple's inner courts at any time, in all probability). Those who come to worship may offer what they wish to offer, it would appear. The specifications for sacrifice on the occasion of the feast of booths found in Num. xxviii-xxix are not necessarily nullified, but the foreign worshipers, at least, seem to have free access to the temple.

The term "Canaanite" in verse 21 must refer to traders, not to the remnant of the foreign population in the land and not to the Samaritans.[2]) Traders who served the needs of worshipers were not being singled out for attack. This passage has no connection, I judge, with the NT stories of Jesus' cleansing of the temple.[3]) The best explanation is that mentioned above: in the Last Day the situation will have changed to such an extent that distinctions between sacred and secular will have vanished, just as the alternation of the seasons will have ceased. Worshipers may make such gifts to God at the temple as they have to make, no longer being required to exchange them for more appropriate ones. Or alternatively, the reference may mean that those who come up for worship will be blessed sufficiently to insure their having goods to sacrifice.

IV

The nations' worship of the Lord at Zion, then, seems to be the consummation of God's purpose for them. This passage may be considered the equivalent of Jeremiah's New Covenant (Jer. xxxi 31-34) and Ezekiel's picture of the giving of a new heart and a new spirit to Israel (Ezek. xxxvi 22-32). The latter two passages, however, do not include the foreign nations in the blessings to be bestowed on the Last Day.

Only the feast of booths is mentioned. Are the nations also to ob-

---

[1]) The two references to pots have caused great difficulty to interpreters. Horst and Elliger agree that the distinction between sacred and secular is to be transcended. Both of them hold, however, that the author is arguing for the ritual purity of the entire land and all its objects. (Horst, *op. cit.*, p. 252; Elliger, *op. cit.*, pp. 174-175.)

[2]) Elliger identifies the Canaanites with the Samaritan community and with the mixed population of the Philistine plain (*op. cit.*, p. 175).

[3]) So also Horst (p. 252). He maintains that sellers of consecrated pots to the worshipers will no longer be necessary because all the pots will be consecrated.

serve the other festivals of Israel? Apparently not. We need not conclude that Israel's festivals are to be reduced to this single event, although that possibility can hardly be excluded. In any case, the celebration of the one festival by the foreign nations in Jerusalem stands in remarkable contrast to the covenant renewal festival at Qumran on the Day of Pentecost, open only to the faithful members of the sect.

Zech xiv 16-21, then, reveals a feature of apocalyptic thinking in post-Exilic times all too frequently overlooked. It is unwarranted to speak of a Jewish community dominated by adherence to Torah as an independent entity, loosed from its *heilsgeschichtliche* moorings. It is wrong to focus attention upon the divine judgment of the heathen on the Last Day and overlook the promise of universal peace and blessing for mankind, for the nations as well as for Israel.

Some may find the notion of continuing sacrificial activity at Zion to be a mark of the author's spiritual limitations. Some may be less than happy with the idea that Zion still stands at the center of the nations' worship. But who will fail to see the boldness of this unknown Jewish author's thought? All who survive the divine judgment participate equally in God's blessing. Although the nations must come to Zion for worship, they gain life and participate in God's fulfillment of his promise for them as a result.

Our author was an apocalyptist. He shared the limited perspective of apocalyptists. He was also a man who knew that God's reign was to be universal. His picture of the nations' worship of the Lord at Zion qualifies, if it does not annul, the distinction between secular and sacral, between Israel and the nations. On that coming day, he said "the Lord will become king over all the earth"; "the Lord will be one, and his name one" (Zech xiv 9).

Our conclusion is evident: The author of this apocalyptic picture of the consummation of God's work was convinced that the foreign nations would participate with Israel in that consummation. The nations would not be "converted" to Israelite faith. They would not be required to observe Torah. They would be compelled, for their own good, to gather regularly for acknowledgment of the Lord as king of the universe. As they did so, however, they would participate in the goods and blessings of a renewed earth. God's covenant with Israel would have become a covenant with the foreign nations as well. Instead of the fixed world order characteristic of the Noah covenant, a new world order would prevail. The entire secular world order would be drawn into the realm of holiness. But if everything is holy, nothing is holy. Here we have one biblical witness to just that secularity which is so highly praised in recent theological essays on the Bible. And we have it in a post-Exilic, apocalyptic text.

PSALM 118: THE SONG OF THE CITADEL

BY
HARRY S. MAY
University of Tennessee, Nashville

A study of modern commentaries to Psalm 118 reveals several factors: a) that no two commentators agree on the dating of the Psalm; b) there is hardly any agreement as to the historical circumstances which served as the background for its recitation; and c) that the exegetes have used their linguistic tools to add new nuances and interpretations which seem unwarranted.

I

This study, dedicated to the memory of Prof. R. Goodenough, will present a new analysis of Psalm 118 based on an examination of the Masoretic Text plus the interpretation of facts emerging from recent archaeological and topographical findings in Israel. This analysis leads to the following conclusions about the Psalm which I have renamed The Song of the Citadel: 1) it is divided into three parts, with the first serving as an Invocation to God, the second, an Ode of Thanksgiving, a personal prayer of one poet-priest who found himself in a captive situation, and the third consisting of four separate fragmentary verses; 2) that it may have had its origin in the sanctuary of one of the royal border-fortressss along the Judaean frontier which were designed to ward off the physical and spiritual incursions of non-Israelite peoples; and 3) that it may well date back to the period of Hezekiah and Jerobam, but that it was not necessarily composed in connection with a specific political or historic event.

Part I

Verses 1-4 have been recognized as a preface and Invocation to the Deity. It is ancient in style, a repetitious formula reminiscent of an early Temple liturgy preceding either a procession or sacrifice. It sounds like a call to Divine Service with a caller, the Priest perhaps, making the tribal roll-call of all those present: the Aaronites, the Household of Israel and the Yirei Adonai. And the congregation answers with the refrain: His kindness is forevermore. W. Oesterley agrees with this formulation[1])

---

[1]) "vv. 1-4 clearly from an introduction. The first half of each verse here would

Who are these yirei Adonai?

Literally translated, we have the Fearers of the Lord (phoboūmenoi tōn teōn)[1] about whom J. Hastings states: "...they were drawn from heathenism by the higher ideals of Judaism... they found there an intellectual home... but they refused the final step that carried them into Judaism."[2]

What is perplexing is that the term "yirei Adonai" is almost exclusively identified by OT writers with proselytes and consequently used to create the impression that the Psalm's original date falls during the time of the Restoration or of Alexander the Great. But while it is true that the terms proselytes and yirei Adonai are used synonymously in post-biblical literature, we must keep in mind that it also connotes: the sojourner, the Cannanite, and even the backslider.[3] What is important is this: Yirei Adonai could be anybody who is called upon to serve God. And if these backsliders were even Hebrew "Returnees" (in the post-biblical sense) then there is no reason to designate them as proselytes. This opinion is supported by Arthur Weiser,[4] and also by Mowinckel, who states flatly that to regard the Yirei Adonai as post-exilic is wrong.[5] According to him, this Psalm should be dated as pre-Deutero-Isaiah. I propose, therefore, that we translate yirei Adonai as "Fearers of God" who have, in the words of H. S. W. Gesenius, "reverence for God."

Part II

Now we come to the body of the Psalm beginning with Verse 5, the most pivotal verse on which this interpretation rests. We have here

---

seem to have been sung as a solo, presumably by one of the priests, while the second half was taken up by the whole Levitical choir." W. Oesterley, *A Fresh Approach to the Psalms*, New York, 1937, p. 479.

[1] Hastings refers to the B'rit Milāh, or circumcision, as the final step.

[2] Hasting, *Dictionary of the Bible*, New York, 1909.

[3] *Ps.* 15:4: "Who may dwell on Thy Holy Hill?" (v. 1) Answer: "...but who honor those who fear the Lord!"

Ps. 25 vv. 12-14: "Who is the man that fears the Lord? Him will He instruct in the way that he should choose. He himself shall abide in prosperity and his children shall possess the Land.

The friendship of the Lord is for those who fear Him and He makes known to them His covenant!"

[4] Arthur Weiser: *Die Psalmen*, London, 1962, pp. 722-730.

[5] S. Mowinckel: *Psalmen Studien*, Amsterdam, 1961, p. 192. „Das halt aber kaum Stich. Die Reihenfolge: Israel-Ahron-die Gottesfurchtigen spricht dagegen: die nachstliegende Annahme ist, dass der Vers die beiden vorhergehenden Kategorien zusammenfasst: das ganze heilige, gottesfürchtige Volk" (ib. p. 192).

PSALM 118: THE SONG OF THE CITADEL

from Verse 5 through Verse 21 a prayer hymn, so unique in style, content, and intensity of feeling that it has become the personal favorite of the learned and the pious. So personal is this prayer that some critics hold that it was recited by the poet himself, not necessarily within the framework of the public Temple liturgy.

Traditionally, Verse 5 has been translated with slight variations as follows:

"From the Depth I call unto Thee, Oh Lord.
The Lord answered me and set me free."

The Septuagint, finds as an equivalent to "metsar", 'ek tlipseos ἐκ θλίψεως - מֵצַר, to mean "out of anguish." Plato and Strabo use the phrase syntlibo or tlipsis (συνθλίβω-θλίψις) as pressing together.[1]) This explains why Luther and later German commentators interpret *metsar* as *Angst, Bedrückung* or *Drangsal*.[2]) A further poetic version then suggests "innere Tiefe," the depth of man's heart or agony.[3]) Because of this chain of subtle changes from one language to the next and the implied psychological inferences that pressure and pain, *Angst* and *Bedrückung*, are identical with *metsar*, some remarkable interpretations of the message of the Psalm have been presented, by such scholars as Leslie, Weiser, H. J. Kraus, Dummelow, Buttenwieser and H. Gunkel.[4])

---

[1]) Strabo 1, 3, 6; Galen 27, 28B and 8, 142B.

[2]) Another difficulty in the case of Luther is, of course, our lack of knowledge about whether he chose his German phrase from either the Greek or Latin version of the Psalm. However, it is generally believed that he preferred reading either from the Greek or Latin rather than from the Hebrew text.

[3]) In Lam. 1 : 3 the term *metsar* assumes the meaning of "dire straits" and lastly in Psalm 116 : 3 it suggests "deep pain".

[4]) *Leslie* (*The Psalms*, New York, 1949, p. 113) translates v. 5:

"Out of Distress I cried to the Lord,
The Lord answered me with freedom."

And the author continues: "the experience of Israel across the centuries is here concentrated into a single sentence: 'Distress Cry to the Lord and the Lord answers'."

Arthur Weiser (*The Psalms*, London, 1962) translates it this way:

"Out of my distress I called on the Lord.
He answered me and set me free!"

Hans-Joachim Kraus: (*Die Psalmen*, Neukirchen, 1960):

„Aus der Drangsal rief ich zu Ja(hwe),
Ja(hwe) erhörte mich und schuf mir Raum!"

He comments himself: „...es antwortete mir in die Weite, Ja, es handelt sich hier

However, the Hebraic OT material reveals that *metsar* comes from the language of actual warfare, suggesting a siege, a fortification, a citadel. Etymologically, the old Semitic root *tsar* takes on the meaning of narrow or hard, like a stone flint. It is also used as foe and enemy. The verb "tsarar" takes on the meaning of restricted, cramped. As a noun it is used for rivalry.[1]) From this physical expression of matter to a higher psychological plain may be only one step, as we see in the various translations of the exegetes. But originally the term *tsar* is bound to a strictly physical description of a situation, and I maintain that the psychological translation and transformations are not justified. The word *tsar* can only be understood in the context of this Psalm in a setting of an ever-present hostility.[2])

---

um eine Breviloquenz die im Sinne der obengegebenen Übersetzung aufgelost werden kann."

J. R. Dummelow (in *A Commentary of the Holy Bible*, New York, 1935, p. 372) says "in distress" means literally "in a straight place". He "mistakes" *Metsar* with *merhav* in the same verse!

M. Buttenwieser (in *The Psalms*, Chicago, 1938, p. 661) translates v. 5:
"In my distress I cried to the Lord.
He heard my prayer: He has given me free soil."

Herman Gunkel (in *Ausgewahlte Psalmen*, Gottingen, 1917, offers this free translation:
„Aus der Bedrangnis rief ich zu Jah,
Jah fuhrte mich in die Weite!"

[1]) The Arab and Syrian root-equivalents imply a sharp-edged stone or flint.

[2]) In Dt. 20 vv. 19-20 we find this sentence: "...and when you *besiege a city*" (כִּי־תָצוּר אֶל־הָעִיר). And further down in Dt. 28 : 53 we read: "and you shall eat ...in the *siege and distress* with which your enemies shall distress you" בַּמָּצוֹר וּבַמָּצוֹק אֲשֶׁר יָצִיק לְךָ אֹיִבְךָ). What is interesting here is the use of two juxtaposed phrases, *matsor* and *matsok* (מָצוֹר – מָצוֹק). Both of them are combined to form a „Wortspiel", indicating the narrowness and tightness of a situation, and only then transposed into "siege and distress", clearly revealing that we are dealing here with a warlike happenstance. Furthermore, both ancient word pictures *Matsor* and *Matsok* came to mean a "narrow" and "tight" situation, both in Arabic and Ethiopian. (See also preceding v. 52.)

Dt. 28 : 57 continues: "...she will eat them (her children) secretly in the *siege and distress* with which your enemy shall distress your gates" (בְּמָצוֹר וּבְמָצוֹק אֲשֶׁר יָצִיק לְךָ אֹיִבְךָ בִּשְׁעָרֶיךָ). Again, this double application of *matsor* and *matsok* is definitely speaking of an emergency setting whicc is related to war, siege and the loss of life.

In Ps. 60 : 11 by adding the term "iȳr" (עִיר-city) to the term "matsor" (מָצוֹר), the psalmist speaks only in physical terms when he querries "And who will accompany me to the *city-fortress (citadel)*?" There is no inference of a "*depth or deep*" here, just the term "*iyr-matsor*" (עִיר־מָצוֹר).

The prophet Nahum (3 : 14) asks his listeners: "*Draw water for the siege*". And Habbakuk (2 : 1) makes it quite clear that he has a military situation to face when he states: "And I'll take my stand on the fortification (i.e., citadel)."

For additional examples, please see Zecharia 9 : 3 and 12 : 2 and Ezekiel 4 : 2, 3.

This conviction to retain the physical, literal meaning of the text is born out by the subsequent use of the word "B'merhavyah" in the very same verse. Here again, the original connotation of the term clearly indicates a broad, roomy place, a physical dimension. *Merhavyah* is then truly a spacious place of YHWH.[1]) In the Septuagint the term for merhav comes very close to its Hebraic antecedent. Platysmos (πλατυσμός) is used for broad space, extent, just as it is in Habbakuk 1 : 16.[2]) Despite this clear-cut translation, most exegetes have felt compelled to also interpret *Merhav* figuratively to mean freedom, simply because they have already interpreted metsar figuratively. On the other hand, if we try to combine these two important word-pictures by maintaining their physical meaning, we arrive at quite a different translation which this author proposes as follows:

"Out of this Citadel I cry unto Thee, Oh Lord.
Oh, answer me amid these wide open spaces, Oh God."

Part III

Beginning with verse 22 to the end there are several seemingly non-connected verses which I maintain are simply a series of fragments: A. The Two-stanza "Corner Stone Proverb" is seemingly a later interpolation, for it offers an entirely new idea after the passionate word-flow which had marked the personal prayer.[3]) B. Then suddenly, in verse 24, one encounters a change of mood as we hear the 'I' of the recitator change to the 'We'. This second fragment consists of vv.24-27 which seems to be the priestly intonations during a processional and sacrificial ceremony on the occasion of the Succoth Festival.[4]) C. The next fragment is verse 28 which has neither a tie with the Corner Stone Proverb nor the Processional. The language reverts back to the 'I' and continues in the same mood as Part II. This indicates that we have here the concluding sentence of the poet's prayer-solo. Perhaps this verse got lost somehow and was mistakenly put in the wrong place by an

---

In all these cases one can find the prophet's message in a descriptive use of physical words of hostility, based on *tsar* or its derivations.

[1]) One concordance states: Merhav is "extra-ordinarily spacious".
[2]) Hab. 1 : 16: מִרְחֲבֵי־אָרֶץ (pl. constr.) clearly means "expanses of the earth".
[3]) Christian scholars have noticed this and have given it a strictly theological interpretation. They suggest that the rejected stone (Jesus) has become the corner-stone upon which the new Church was built.
[4]) *Ana Adonai Hoshiah na*; *Ana Adonai hatzlihah-na*. "Save us, oh Lord, please! Give us success, oh Lord, we pray!" We can visualize a sacrificial processional led by the Aaronites and Levites and enjoined by the throng of worshippers, carrying palm branches to the altar.

editor. D. Finally we are left with verse 29 which concludes with the exact words as in the refrain used in Part I. This verse was obviously misplaced also.[1])

II

Next let us investigate the "time and place" element and the historic background of Psalm 118.

To begin with, let us review the contrasting opinions of the leading interpreters. Leslie and Mowinckel place the occasion on the Hebrew New Year's Festival.[2]) Ewald, Kirkpatrick and Baethgen hold the Psalm was recited on the Feast of Tabernacles.[3]) Wellhausen and Haupt think it was sung during the occasion of the Restoration of the Temple under the Maccabees.[4]) Delitzsch says that Ezra prayed thus as he rededicated the Temple.[5]) Cheyne gives it an eschatological interpretation,[6]) while Robinson identifies it with a Circumcision celebration.[7]) Duhm suggests it was recited on Nikanor-Day.[8]) And according to Buttenwieser the Psalm was inspired by the appearence of Alexander

---

[1]) Two possible interpretations offer themselves: 1) v. 29 was indeed a part of Part I (vv. 1-4), the opening Invocation to God, and somehow got tacked on at the end of the psalm; or 2) if v. 29 indeed belongs at the end of the psalm (where it is now), then perhaps vv. 1-4 might have been recited again after the ceremonial procession, but the duplication was omitted for unknown reasons either by the editor of the Psalm or inadvertently lost in the process of transmission.

[2]) Elmer. A. Leslie (*The Psalms*, ibid., pp. 112-116), "We can discern the worshipping throngs on New Year's Day moving through the Temple Gates and, as a climax to the worship, surrounding the altar... The leader of the procession summons the choir to praise: 'Oh give thanks unto the Lord.' The whole choir joins in the beloved response 'For His mercy endureth forever'."

S. Mowinkel (ibid.) tries to combine several ceremonial rites to determine the age of the Psalm: 1) he thinks that the presentation of „grune Zweige" (green branches) brings the Psalm closer („eher") to the Autumn-New Year's Festival („Herbst-Neujahrsfest"), p. 160, and then links this event 2) to a Coronation Ceremony, cultic in nature and filled with Thanksgiving, Part I, p. 92.

[3]) G. H. H. Ewald: *Commentary on the Psalms*, London 1880.
F. W. Baethgen: *Handcommentar zum A.T.*, Leipzig, 1898.

[4]) Wellhausen places the time element 300 years later, since he thinks Psalm 118 was sung „bei der Templeweihe der Maccabaeer." (In *The Psalms*, New York, 1898).

P. Haupt says that the occasion, which prompted its recitation, was the Hasmonean Simon's festive entry into Akra (I *Macc.* 13 : 51).

[5]) Franz Delitzsch: *Bibl. Kommentar Über die Psalmen*, Leipzig, 1873.

[6]) T. K. Cheyne: *The Origin and Religious Contents of the Psalter*, New York, 1892.

[7]) W. Robinson: *Psalms and Hymns*, New York, 1898.

[8]) B. Duhm: *Die Psalmen*, Tubingen, 1922.

the Great.¹) Hans Schmidt and W. O. Oesterley seem to come closer to the actual text when they stipulate that Psalm 118 is the product of a poet who finds himself imprisoned and soon to be liberated.²) Hans Jochaim Kraus puts it into the category of Temple-Gate liturgies.³) H. Gunkel is the only critic who rejects all attempts to give the Psalm a historic or political interpretation and warns us not to subject it to undue speculations⁴) and concludes that it was recited by one person because of „ein rein persönlichen Anlass". These then are some of the divergent views, exploring the origin of this Psalm in time and place. In my opinion the positions of Kraus, Schmidt, Oesterley and Gunkel are all well taken, though they do not go far enough. I should like to offer additional data to uphold my Citadel Theory, utilizing the most recent archaeological findings at Tel Arad which may put Psalm 118 into a new historical and psychological perspective.

For the past four years extensive excavations have taken place at Tel Arad, a few kilometers due East of Beersheva, under the leadership of Prof. Yohanan Aharoni of the Hebrew University. I had the opportunity to join this expedition during the summer of 1964. Located on the ancient Edom Highway, near the old biblical towns(s) of Arad, Tel Arad is a border fortress which harbored many secrets now coming to light, and which may prove important to the Bible historian and OT literary critic.⁵) Although most of the findings have not yet been published, some important factual data can already be presented.

---

¹) Moses Buttenwieser (*ibid.*, pp. 659ff.). To him Psalm 118 is a Victory Song, praising God for deliverance. He says: "Although 'I' runs through verses 5-27, the interpreters are agreed, with but one exception (Herman Gunkel), that 'I' is not the author speaking of himself, but the voice of the people speaking through him. He utters what moves and stirs the hearts of all of them." He summarily dismisses all the other commentators who have set the date for the composition prior to the advent of the Hellenic Conqueror.

²) Hans Schmidt (*Die Psalmen*, in *Handbuch Zum Alten Testament* (I No. 15) (Tubingen, 1934), identifies the poet with an actual worshipper.
W. O. Oesterley (*Psalms* II, pp. 479ff.) says that the Psalm clearly indicates that the poet, after a long imprisonment, finds himself liberated.

³) Hans-Joachim Kraus (*Psalmen* II, pp. 800ff.), while describing this poem as a Thanksgiving Prayer, classifies it with Psalm 15 and Psalm 24 as Temple-gate Liturgy.

⁴) Herman Gunkel, (ibid., pp. 506ff.) makes this definitive judgment: „Alle Versuche, den Psalm auf eine bestimmte politische Gelegenheit zu beziehen, sind gescheitert (p. 509)!" And he continues: „Solchen Krieg des Psalmisten gegen seine Feinde aber ist nicht ein wirklicher, sonder nur ein bildlicher!"

⁵) This specific Tel Arad is known to us (there are several "Arads" in the same general area) from early biblical times when the Canaanites ruled the country and held this military key-post against the invading Israelite tribes. In Nu. 21 : 1 we

First, the excavations brought to light the first Israelite Sanctuary located in the Negev plus a massive fortress gate. The dating of this discovery is also confirmed by many seals and ostraca which reveal the names of Priests and Levites mentioned in the Bible back to the 9th to 8th Centuries B.C.E. Second, the measurements of this Sanctuary correspond exactly with the dimensions of the Desert-Heḥal or Tabernacle which had been incorporated in the construction of the Holy of Holies of King Solomon's Temple in Jerusalem, as described in Exodus.) This Sanctum Sanctorum in the Royal Citadel of Arad was built deep into the rock, with three easily discernable stone-slab steps leading down into it. Two *matsevot*, or stelae, flank the entrance; a main-altar stands in the middle of it, with remnants of black ashes of burnt sacrifices still visible after almost 3000 years, and three smaller altars stand in back of the main altar. Third, under the Sanctuary a hidden cave about 15 meters deep, 9 meters long and 4 meters wide, with a secret passage leading into it, was uncovered.[1])

We know that "regular provisions were made (by the Kings of the pre-Josiah period) for the administration of Religion at other times and places."[2]) As I surveyed the excavations, it became quite clear to me that Tel Arad may have been such a place, which could very well have provided the setting for Psalm 118 during the turbulent period between the reigns of Jerobeam and Hezekiah. It is interesting to note that the Holy of Holies of the Tel was sunk down below the Citadel street level and that the central altar was built even still lower. We would normally expect a Fortress Sanctuary to be located on a high plateau for all people to see. The reason for this structural plan seems

---

read: "The King of Arad, the Canaanite, who dwelled in the South (Negev) heard that Israel came up via Atharım and he fought Israel." Though the invading-Hebrew tribes were initially beaten back between Horma and Se-ir by the combined forces of the Kings of Arad and the Amalekites (Nu. 14 : 45), Joshua eventually conquered the area, and with it some thirty-one city-kings, thus securing the Israelites entry into the northern part of Canaan. And the descendants of Jethro, Moses' Semitic father-in-law, became the rulers of Arad, and "they dwelled with the people," i.e., the Israelites (Ju. 1 : 16). After that account the Bible is silent regarding Arad. However, excavations in recent times have shown that the Judaean and Israelıte Kings built on top of those former Canaanite strongholds even stronger fortresses, all on mountain tops, i.e., above the hill-towns of the Negev. This was done for two reasons: a) to protect the caravan routes travelling from the North to the South (the Edom Highway), and b) to guard against the repeated invasions from the east, Moab and Edom.

[1]) Surprised, Prof. Aharoni exclaimed: "...considering the hardness of the rock and the primitive tools then available, the construction of this cave was a great engineering achıevement!"

[2]) Travers Herford, *The Pharisees* IV, p. 89. See also the recent excavations at Lahish!

to lie in the fact that this border sanctuary with its *bāmāh* incorporated into a military fort had to be protected against the effects of hostile attacks. Thus we can establish the thesis that a royally-sanctioned priesthood conducted YHWH worship at this Sanctuary's main altar, that the Holy of Holies served as a kind of "auxiliary Temple" which brought YHWH closer to enemy territory, to help assure victory for Israelite troups over their adversaries. Beyond that, the existence of side-altars leads one to assume that the non-Israelite, the sojourner and stranger also had opportunities to offer sacrifices there.[1]

What does all this mean within the context of our Psalm analysis?

The procession approaches the Citadel with the words: "This is the Gate of the Lord; may the righteous enter into it." At the open *bamāh* for all to see the Aaronites, the Israelites and the *yir'ē Adonai* (the non-Israelites), may now worship and offer their sacrifices. "Min ha-métsar karāti Yah; anáni b'mérhav-jah," now reveals a new meaning altogether. The poet, an educated, sensitive priest, serving a military and civilian congregation, calls upon YHWH from the deep of the Citadel's Holy of Holies, out of this beleaguered fortification somewhere in the Negev, in the wide-open spaces. And in this Citadel-Temple, he calls upon God to free him from the enemies all around—the Amonites, the Moabites and Edomites—who besiege him like bees. YHWH will assure victory, the poet prays, because He is omnipresent, even in this border fortress, so far away from Jerusalem.

To this writer it is hard to believe that a prayer of this kind would have been appropriate in the topographical setting of the Jerusalemite Temple. For the poet would hardly have spoken of a *merḥav* (i.e., wide-open spaces or extent) by looking from the top of the Temple Mount over the heavily populated hillsides of Jerusalem. *Merḥav* fits much better into the scenery of the empty Negev wilderness. And when the poet invokes God to help scatter the enemies, then the situation of potential warfare becomes even more plausible. A Festival occasion such as Succoth then assumes in such a setting the role of a morale-building prayer of thanks and entreaty. Yahweh is within the orbit of Israelite victory, and the potential religious threat to the Israelite community near the border of foreign lands *and* gods is averted. Monotheism is served and heathenism barred. What strikes me most poig-

---

[3] See Ju. 19 : 12; I King 8 : 41; Ex. 12: 43; Lev. 22 : 25 and Sam. 22 : 45.

The word נֵכָר foreigner, i.e., non-Israelite, often synonymous with the *yir'e Adonai*, comes from an old Semitic root. In Arabic 'nakarū' implies 'evil, bad,' to indicate that the foreigner is potentially also your enemy.

nantly is this: We seem to have here a synthesis of purely physical and psychological interpretations, where deep and depth of feeling actually merge.

One final observation: The Incarceration Theory of Hans Schmidt seems to have even greater merit than he himself fathomed, for it is quite possible that our Poet may have had the feeling of *Einkerkerung*, living and worshipping within the walled-in confines of a Citadel, surrounded by the seemingly endless spaces of the Judaean Desert. Such a person would long for freedom and the escape from ever-present hostile forces. There is even the possibility that the composer of this beautiful Ode to YHWH had been literally a captive or hidden in the cave under the Holy of Holies as a rebel or non-conformist, who longed to be free.

In conclusion, this writer is convinced that Psalm 118 is much older-than any of the critics acknowledge. Moreover, if we remain true to the Masoretic Hebrew Text, certain new vistas of plausible critique open up to us, giving this Psalm an even greater import than hitherto imagined. Psalm 118 may indeed be one of several "Citadel Hymns" which belong into a new non-Jerusalemite collection, which could have been composed at Tel Arad or other similarly constructed fortress-citadels (at Laḥish perhaps) and which deserve careful research and reclassification.

PSYCHOLOGICAL STUDY OF THE BIBLE

BY

FREDERICK C. GRANT

Union Theological Seminary, New York

The debates on Scripture and Tradition at the Second Vatican Council have raised once more the question of the sources of revelation —a question which has been debated since the Reformation. It has been one bone of bitter contention between Protestants and Catholics ever since the former, with their slogan *sola scriptura*, challenged the Roman Catholic Church, with its heavy burden of ecclesiastical tradition, much of it post-scriptural and to be harmonized with Scripture only by considerable straining of exegesis. But in principle and in origin Scripture and Tradition are inseparable, though "traditions" which arise *later* than Scripture may often be proved incompatible with the data contained in the sacred books; often they are the result of pious inferences or elaborations for which there was no real evidence save the on-going religious experience of Christians, or the "lively oracles" of the Church itself.

I

Scripture was cradled in Tradition, from beginning to end. The legends of Genesis, the myths of creation and the origin of the human race, the tales of the patriarchs, the story of Israel's election and enslavement in Egypt, the great drama of the redemption from bondage, the wilderness wandering, the entry into Canaan, the early history of the Hebrew people—the whole Hexateuch is a body of tradition. It is a traditonal cosmology, a traditional anthropology, a traditional law, a traditional account of national origins. Like all primitive writing of this nature it was not only traditional but also more or less casual, accidental, preserved for posterity by a principle of selection whose working can be seen only long *ex eventu* and by reading the story backwards from the present to the period of origins. The early Hebrew history with its tales of battle and bloodshed, courage, loyalty, and treason, heroic defense against the overwhelming odds held by the surrounding nations, especially by Assyria and Babylon—this record was also casual, like all ancient histories, and only happened to be written down and preserved, then revised and edited from a more highly developed religious point of view. What never got recorded was vastly more in quantity than what was set down in writing; and what failed to survive—e.g. "the chronicles of the kings of Judah and Israel"—was more than the brief extracts found in the "Former Prophets" (Joshua, Judges, Samuel, Kings) and in revised form in Chronicles, together with the memoirs of Nehemiah and Ezra. Clearly the stories of the early kings were traditional, as were the tales of the early prophets, from Samuel the seer to the first of the "writing" prophets, Amos of Tekoa. The "Latter Prophets" (from Isaiah to Malachi), whose written words survive, clearly wrought in a tradition, the "prophetic tradition", which embodied the principles of their teaching, their powerfully affirmed and absolutely intransigent monotheism, their abhorrence of idolatry, their unwavering loyalty to the principle of justice, their sharp criticism of compromise with paganism and the common substitution of cultic rites for moral behavior or righteousness. This growing prophetic tradition was something even greater than the prophets themselves. But it was only by looking backward that men could see "the hand of God in history" from Moses to the prophets, and again from the earlier prophets to the last of the great line.

Without question the Wisdom books enshrined a tradition much older than the collections found in Proverbs, in Sirach, or elsewhere. Hebrew poetry, like much of ancient poetry everywhere, was traditional—not in origin but in transmission. Traditions do not create poems; poets do. But poets often use traditional material, and their poems often get handed down orally, sometimes for generations, and occasionally they appear in divergent recensions, as do a few of the Psalms. As in the literature of Greece and India, as in fact in almost all ancient literatures, the place and the importance of tradition is undeniable, a conditioning factor at work everywhere from the earliest days.

The casual or accidental factor was equally important. These writings have survived. But if it was by divine choice, selection, preservation that they survived, then it must have been by divine purpose that they originated. This is the way the logic runs, not in the opposite direction. The prophets' conviction that they uttered the word of the Lord, the word divinely authorized and committed to them to deliver as God's message to His people, was carried over to the other Old Testament writings. Eventually the Hellenistic concept of divine inspiration was made to cover them as *littera scripta*, not just their subject matter which once had been committed to human voices for delivery. The theory went even farther. The history of the divine dealings with Israel was periodized, as in the Book of Jubilees or, far later, in the scheme of successive "covenants", fully elaborated by various Bible readers who reckoned seven covenants in all, from Adam to Christ or to the Holy Spirit or to the future Reign of Christ upon earth. But history is not like that, not even sacred history. History also is casual, as is man's whole existence, and that of the universe in general. Some better explanation of the origin—and the originality—of the teaching contained in Holy Scripture must be found than the rigid scheme of successive periods of revelation and of books explicitly setting forth the conditions and requirements for salvation in these successive epochs. The wonder of the canonization of Holy Scripture is the way in which these religious writings came to be made central, official, and authoritative. As I tried to show in my book *Translating the Bible*, the process was effected, as a rule, liturgically, i.e. by and in liturgical use. These books were found to be "profitable for teaching, for reproof, for correction, and for training in righteousness" and hence were believed to be "inspired by God" (2 Tim. 3.16). It was religious use and wont that chose these books; the canons of Old and New Testament were later and confirmatory.

The new religions in the New Testament period were found on the lower levels of society—as they still are in the twentieth century. The old, established national or nationalistic religions, i.e. cults, were part of the political and social "Establishment", then as now, and commanded wealth, prestige, and position, silvery bearded kings with golden crowns and mitred high priests with angelic attendants in raiment of white. Erwin Goodenough's great work on *Jewish Symbols in the Greco-Roman Period* studies both Jewish and Gentile religious art, an art which reflects the general intellectual level of the Hellenistic age. One inference we may draw from this art is that religious writers in the Hellenistic-Roman period cannot be credited with any great amount of philosophy: the Ritschlians and their successors were clearly wrong in wishing to get rid of "Greek metaphysics" in ancient Judaism (in the Diaspora) and in early Christianity. Philo was a lone star. So was Justin Martyr (supposing he was a philosopher). Popular religion under the early empire, Jewish, Christian, and pagan, was simply—popular religion! It was not theological, or philosophical, nor very artistic; at least its art was not on the classical level. And its sacred books did not rival the Greek classics—nor did they ever undertake to do so. Their greatness lay in another realm.

The New Testament also was cradled in tradition, like the Old. Behind the Gospels lay the "gospel tradition", forty years of it before Mark wrote, more years until the later evangelists wrote. The author of Luke-Acts explicitly appeals to the church's tradition, handed down from the "eyewitnesses and ministers of the word" (Luke 1.1-4), and in Acts 20.18-35 Paul's summary of his life work as exemplified in Ephesus is in thoroughly traditional terms. The Pauline letters stress the traditions Paul received and handed on: see 2 Thess. 2.15, 3.6; 1 Cor. 11.2. The tone and temper of the Pastoral letters is also traditional (e.g. 1 Tim. 1.3); so is that of Hebrews (e.g. 6.1-2) and the Catholic epistles (e.g. Jude 3 and 17). In fact the general tone of the New Testament as a whole is one of appeal to apostolic tradition for the facts, the teachings, the prophecies and predictions associated with Christ and the Church.

And again, as in the Old Testament, the narrative in casual. Not all the records were preserved, as the author of John insists (20.23f., 21.25), speaking either of his own work or, as some think, of all the gospels (i.e. if the final statement is a codicil to the whole "fourfold gospel canon" in the middle of the second century). And these were preserved, not for purposes of historical reconstruction or defense, but for evangelism, edification, apologetics and propaganda. These were the living traditions, as Papias later described them, which enable us to get inside and understand the Christian way of life and its inspiring dynamic, the power of the Holy Spirit active in the Church and still as realizable as in the days of the first apostles. This fact explains the difficulty of writing a life of Christ, or even a history of the early church. The material is fragmentary, and not wholly consistent. Divergent emphases and interpretations have been at work in the transmission of the tradition as well as in the actual writing of the New Testament books. If there had been only one evangelist, and only one Apostle to the Gentiles, and only one church historian, our problem might have been simpler—though three men could have set insoluble problems for later harmonists to solve. But if there had been only one, or two, or three, in solid agreement and consistency, the whole world would have passed the tale by as a bit of fiction, too consistent to be true. For history is never like that. The documents of religion or of political states or of wars and migrations, conquests and settlements, reigns and revolutions are never like that. They are always casual, sometimes circumstantial, sometimes not, always incomplete and fragmentary, always requiring comparison and interpretation, always tendentious, always written from a particular point of view—sometimes from more than one.

Now it is this casualness and fragmentariness of the records that have provided the insurmountable obstacle to a purely literary-critical interpretation of the Bible. For generations it was held that, the Bible being infallible, the records *must* harmonize. The theologians and the historians need only sharpen their wits and construct a narrative or an exposition that would be completely consistent and self-authenticating. It must fit the Scriptures, hand in glove, and it must support the current doctrinal system of the expert's own denomination. For the Catholic this meant the system of dogma set forth by the Schoolmen, especially St Thomas Aquinas, and by the Council of Trent. For the Protestant it must tally with either Reformed or Evangelical dogmatics. For the Jew, studying his sacred Scriptures, it must favor Orthodoxy or Conservatism or the Reformed synagogue. For liberals it had to come out with "the liberal Jesus" or "the liberal Paul", or "the rise of Christianity" based on "the letters and records of the Apostolic Age."—Not that all the historical research and the careful exegesis of the past two hundred years has been wasted! Only, something more is needed, not only in results but first of all in method. The creative mind of our late friend, Erwin Goodenough, saw into this problem and provided one way of advance in his great study of the Religious Symbols found in ancient Judaism and early Christianity.

First of all Goodenough's work makes clear the background of Diaspora Judaism and the early Church: it was the background of a decadent religious culture—as T. S. Eliot called it—a culture whose art was in decline, crude, barbarous, often tasteless. In the next place the scattered Jews throughout the empire and beyond were not all saints and scholars but very ordinary people, engaged in making a living but, like all Jews, everywhere and always, strikingly loyal to their religion and supporting it even at great sacrifice. The Christians, by contrast with the idealized pictures drawn in Sunday School literature, included, as Paul said, "not many... wise according to wordly standards, not many... powerful, not many... of noble birth" (1 Cor. 1.26). The "social triumph" of the early Church no doubt began in Rome, but under difficulties. And as Shirley Jackson Case held, it really did not come about until late in the second century. Hence the literary compositions of both the Jewish Diaspora and the early Gentile churches were not of classical quality and standard. They too were casual and fragmentary and often pedestrian. And the writers, no doubt endeavoring to do their best with the material at hand, were wholly untrained in the art of writing history or in oratory (now the Hellenistic standard of learning) or in poetry or philosophy. The one exception was the author of Hebrews, whose Greek was excellent and whose rhetorical arrangement of his homily disguises the thin stratum of historical acquaintance with both the Old Testament and the early Christian tradition, especially the gospel tradition: his *forte* was allegorical exegesis. In view of their actual accomplishment in the New Testament writings, the literary handicaps of the early Christian writers were not so important as we might expect. They wrote "out of faith and unto faith". What mattered was the present meaning, the present bearing of the episode or teaching or exhortation, not its purely historical *Einmaligkeit*, its uniqueness and its divine inspiration, once upon a time long ago.

In a precious *confessio fidei*, his autobiographical *Toward a Mature Faith* (1955), Dr. Goodenough pointed out the value and importance, even the necessity, of the psychological interpretation of the Bible. This is a new kind of biblical criticism. The earlier disciplines, Textual Criticism, Historical Criticism, Source Criticism, and Form Criticism, are all parts of or stages in Literary Criticism, necessary and important and not to be ignored. But Psychological Criticism opens up a wholly new and vast, far-reaching scene where the creative function of tradition and writing is fully recognized but where the real incentive comes from a far deeper spring, viz. the immediate testimony of the religious consciousness, its direct awareness of spiritual and moral truth, its "realization" of what is inevitably so because it has behind it the irrefutable *testimonium Spiritus sancti internum*. This testimony creates narrative by the dramatic skill of the devout imagination, narrative that often rivals successfully the more pedestrian testimony of "the eyewitnesses and ministers of the word." But the "history" thus produced is often—as in the Gospel of John—purely symbolic and really "super-historical", centered in some deep religious meaning rather than in a concrete historical event. Such were the accounts of Israel's deliverance from Egypt and the restoration after the Exile and the resistance to Antiochus and the divergent accounts of the Nativity of Christ and the equally divergent accounts of his Resurrection and the post-resurrection events, the story of Pentecost, the miracles of the saints. This factor in biblical narrative is as true in the New Testament as in the Old, and must henceforth be recognized by all interpreters of the Bible, whether concerned with the Old Testament or the New.

What Erwin Goodenough stressed was the importance of the symbolism at levels below the historical, factual, verbal statement or narrative. In a word, beyond the historical and exegetical interpretation of the Bible lies the whole new field of depth psychology and psychoanalysis. Quite apart from the question of Christ's resurrection on the third day, for example, the really important consideration is his glorification and his presence with the disciples, i.e. his appearances to them, then and now. Quite apart from the Virgin Birth, the meaning of Mary's virginity as a symbol of dedication, uniqueness, sacredness, holiness, mediation, as the instrument of the Incarnation—this lies in a wholly different dimension—not area but dimension—from the actual, factual narrative in Matthew 1.18-25 and its elaboration in the present text of Luke 1.26-38. (The text of vs. 34 probably contains a gloss, "since I know not a man;" for the Virgin's reply was an affirmation of faith and acceptance, not of doubt as in the case of Zechariah, Luke 1.18. Mary's question concerned only the mode, "How *shall* this be?", not "How *can* this be?" as in the RSV. See the Greek.)

This principle opens new doors to the fresh interpretation of Holy Scripture. For example, the promise to Peter in Matthew 16.17-19 is already interpreted by some scholars, even by some Roman Catholic scholars, as a post-resurrection saying, a view which would considerably ease the strain of historical interpretation. The Gospel of John locates the commission of Peter after the Resurrection, and its purely supernatural setting also seems presupposed by the language of Matthew. Peter is blessed because he has received the affirmation of Jesus' divinity as a direct revelation from God: he is one of the chosen who know who Christ is (Matt. 11.27), and the esoteric character of both the later revelation and Christ's promise fits better the whole of the rest of the New Testament and of early church history than an open avowal near Caesarea Philippi. But as a symbol of Peter's headship, as a psychological datum or guarantee, the scene is surely "supra-historical" (Martin Dibelius's term), and cannot be fitted into the Galilean ministry of Jesus. What needs to be studied is the world-historical significance of this saying, not its vanishing antecedents or its improbable location on the way to Jerusalem *via* Caesarea Philippi. No one has succeeded in locating the saying there, or in fitting it into Jesus' earthly life. How could it have thus been uttered, and then totally ignored in the subsequent history, or by the apostolic church, or in the rest of the

New Testament writings? John skirts the story in 6.66-71, but veers away from anything like an apostolic commission of Peter during Jesus' pre-resurrection life.

Or take the account of the Last Supper, whose details are almost indecipherable, and whose connection with the Passover seems extremely questionable—there is no roast lamb, no unleavened bread, no *seder*. It is only the "last supper" of Jesus with his disciples. The Passover element has been superimposed, but without success. Moreover the oldest form of the words spoken by Jesus are eschatological and concern the coming Kingdom, not his own death and resurrection. The fullest account of the latter references is the earliest, in 1 Cor. 11.23-26, which may have been "received from the Lord" in one or more of Paul's "visions and revelations" (2 Cor. 12.1-10), as some scholars hold, and not a part of the oldest tradition. Frankly, it is unthinkable that a Jew would command the eating of his own flesh and the drinking of his own blood, or of any human flesh or of any blood whatsoever. That this difficulty is no recherché scholar's fancy is clear from the psychological problems it presents today, even reflected in the church papers. One communicant wrote a letter to his diocesan *Bulletin*: "Sometimes at Holy Communion I've felt like a cannibal when I thought about eating, even symbolically, someone's body and blood." In another recent journal a small child is reported as crying out as his mother was about to receive the chalice, "Don't drink that blood! If you drink blood it will kill you!" In describing the concelebration at the closing service of the final session of the Vatican Council, one reporter pictured the twenty-four bishops "sipping the blood of Christ from spoons." True, the clergy do not often feel the force of this problem—they hear confessions, talk with (or to) the faithful who never protest, but rarely get into deep dialogue with those who share the horror of the act implied by the words of the Eucharist. The Roman Catholic Church has wisely withheld the chalice for many generations, and so escapes the words of administration of the Sacred Blood; moreover, the whole central action of the Mass is said secretly: *secrete, distincte et attente... attente, continuate, et secrete*. This wise and beautiful custom is now threatened by the demand for the whole service in the vernacular, clearly and openly pronounced. But the Eucharist, *above all* the Eucharist, needs to be studied psychologically and its real impact upon all the church's worshippers, not just the clergy and the faithful, made out exactly and reliably. The very drift away from language which stresses the crass realism of the ancient world and even of Protestantism up to three generations ago, a drift one can trace in the successive editions of church hymnals since 1900, ought to show the need for such a psychological study. Scholars have not created these problems: they only analyze them, and try for some kind of solution which will be loyal to the church's tradition and standards and will also speak to the new generation growing up around us, which is nursed on science—even weakly diluted—rather than the Bible and the Catechism. The efforts to stem this drift are unfortunate and foredoomed. For example, a young clergyman recently celebrated the Communion service with a peculiar emphasis on the verb in the words, "This *is* my Body... This *is* my Blood." But if the institution of the Eucharist took place in Aramaic there was no verb at all! Such an attempt to enforce an out-and-out Transubstantiationist view is completely misguided, and for one person who might be impressed there are a dozen who resent this crude maneuvre.

II

The Protestant-Catholic controversy over Scripture and Tradition during the past four centuries has warped the conception and the methods of biblical interpretation. If the Bible is infallible and is to be interpreted independently of the Church and its tradition, the main questions will relate to the origin and history of the individual books and the data behind them. The "truth' of the Bible will then consist in the accuracy of its records of the past, the firm connection with authoritative names in the past—Moses, David, Isaiah, Daniel, the Apostles, especially Matthew and John and Paul. If sources were used, they must be shown to be early, reliable, and consistent with one another. If interpolations occur, they must be old and reliable, and "reflect something" of value in the interpretation of the books concerned. Now all this study of origins, of sources, even the form-critical study of the tradition behind the sources, is valuable and by no means to be rejected. But it is merely preparatory to the main task of examining the scriptures. Their "truth" lies above and beyond the historical reliability of their data. Such data may be illusory, imaginary, fictitious, and yet profoundly true and valuable.

The "truth" of the Hexateuch is not the long preamble of primitive history contained in the Book of Genesis. It lies in the system of social and religious legislation which grew up during successive centuries when its various sources were produced and finally coalesced into the

Code. This Code is known as the *Torah* or Teaching. It is God's self-revelation set forth in a scheme of laws and promises. The "truth" of the Torah is its record or expression of this body of law, centered in the great revelation at Mt. Sinai and summed up in the daily *Shema*, "Hear, O Israel! The Lord is our God, the Lord alone. And you must love the Lord your God with all your heart and with all your soul and with all your might..." (Deut. 6.4-9). The symbol is the two scrolls kept in the ark at the front of every synagogue, where the Christian churches place the altar. These are the Law and the Prophets, Torah and Nebiim, the latter the books that interpret and apply the rules laid down in the former, sometimes commending, sometimes revising, sometimes expanding the legal Code. Many of the prophetic writings were older than the final form of the Code. But to the end, or rather to this present time, the principle is one and the same: "See, I have set before you this day life and good, death and evil. If you obey the commandments of the Lord your God... then you shall live" (Deut. 30.15f.).

This religion of the ancient Hebrews was out-and-out historical, and like all the higher Semitic religions it was expressed in a sacred law, given by God to safeguard his people's welfare. And so it did, though there were areas where further legislation—and not merely inference from laws already given—would have helped, as for example the duties of the Covenant people when incorporated within an alien society and government. The prophets looked in this direction, as Jeremiah bade the exiles seek the good of the city to which they were transported. Long later the rabbinic rule was stated, "The law of the land *is* law." But there was no explicit commandment enjoining or forbidding revolution. Revolutions were left to God and the slow-moving mills of history, i.e. to supernatural deliverance, as from Egypt, or the providential rise of Cyrus. But this situation created the crucial problem of the Zealots and the Qumran sectaries and the early Christians. On the whole the Old Testament, centered in the growing Torah, enabled Israel to live in a world of pagan violence and corruption, and to keep itself uncontaminated by the abominations of the surrounding heathen — though often at fearful cost. This was its function: to keep Israel loyal and faithful to Yahweh, and unspotted by the world. This is the point of view that must be maintained in our study of the Torah. How was this end achieved? What did it mean in later centuries, as Israel was forced into ever closer contact with paganism? (See the Mishnah *Abodah Zarah*.) How did it function in the de-nationalized era that followed the destruction of Jerusalem, and when its application was confined to private and community observance without the sacrifices and the free communal practice of judgment, administration of justice, commerce, festivals, and the whole round of social life in an independent nation? *There* lies the "truth" of the Torah, as a revelation of the divine purpose and requirement, *vis à vis* one people, Israel.

The "truth" of the Psalms is not their Davidic or non-Davidic authorship (David composed some of them), but their expression of the depths of Israel's soul, of individuals and of the whole people in relation to God. The "truth" of the Psalms is not ascertained or guaranteed by dating them, as ancient scholars tried to do (in the prefaces) or as Paul Haupt and others have undertaken to do, but is to be found in their psychological fidelity. These writers probed the depths of the human soul in its fullest experience of tragedy, sin and forgiveness, release and joy in the Lord. Such poems of utter trust in God, despite lowering skies in every possible direction, were unique; there are none quite like them anywhere else in the history of the world's religions.

The "truth" of Job is not that a man by that name once lived somewhere in the East, and suffered the vicissitudes described in the prologue and epilogue to this epical dialogue, nor in any vindication of its unity or justification of its interpolations. These questions are interesting and important; but the real "truth" is, once more, its psychology. The verse translated "Though He slay me, yet will I trust in Him" (13.15) may not be adequately rendered in the King James Version, but it is true to the attitude of utter loyalty commended by the author. In spite of total defeat and disillusion, frustration and despair, the Great Sufferer still has his God—even if he is compelled to admit that the ways of God are obscure and incomprehensible. This was the teaching of tragic experience, as *lived* by ancient Israel and by ancient individual Israelites, and by multitudes of Jews ever since then. The prophets had maintained that God can save "by many or by few" (1 Sam. 14.6); but later Israel went farther down into the dark depths of trial, and the writer of Judith propounded the revolutionary principle that God may decide *not* to save us at all! It may suit the divine purposes that we shall stand and die in our tracks, to the last man; if so, we have no alternative but to obey. We are "expendables", like a cut-off regiment, like a commando company assigned to carry out a hopeless raid. Our death, our suffering, our agony may serve the divine cause and fit the divine purposes more richly than would our rescue and deliverance (Judith 8.11-27). True, the Book of Daniel, almost contemporary, found an answer: the martyrs will live again (Dan. 12.1-3). But this highly apocalyptic solution has never reassured all men, not even all Jews, certainly not in the age which produced Ecclesiastes and other rationalistic writings. But the "truth" of Job—the book we are now concerned with—lies in the description of the "last stand" faith of multitudes in Israel who had been compelled to abandon hope and yet clung instinctively to the righteousness and wisdom of God, though they simply could not make it out or understand His present purposes. Again, this was something new and unique in religion, and it echoed the Psalmist's "If I make my bed in Sheol, thou art there!" (Ps. 139.8).

The "truth" of the Gospels is not the ease or the difficulty of disengaging the data for the life of Jesus or his teaching; or the probabilities of authorship, sources, dates, provenance, or early use of these four little books. Rather it lies in the proclamation of the meaning of Jesus' life, teaching, ministry, death and resurrection for the current generation and its church, in Rome, Antioch, Achaia, Alexandria, or wherever the gospels were written. The questions of introduction are important and not to be minimized; but they are only preliminary. The greater task of the interpreter is to find out how the gospels fit their own age, what they meant to it, i.e. to the Christians themselves at that time and also to outsiders, and what their "psychological" bearing and importance consisted in. Mark, the first, was a martyr-proclamation, an encouragement to those still facing possible death: "What does it profit a man to gain the whole world and forfeit his life?... What can a man give in return for his life?" "Whoever would save his life will lose it; and whoever loses his life for my sake and the gospel's will save it" (Mk. 8. 36f., 35). "Life" and "soul" are the same word in Mark. The "psychological" outlook of Mark suffuses the whole volume, and much of the gospels as a whole.

Matthew is a revision of Mark with a settled church in view, a teaching program, problems of relations with non-Christian Jews, eschatology, incipient Gnosticism, and the authority of the "law of Christ" as a substitute for (as Paul said) or a supplement to (as Matthew held) the ancient Jewish Torah. Luke is a thoroughly Gentile writing, though with much use of older Jewish and Jewish-Christian material, reflecting the poverty and discouragement of the period after the fall of Jerusalem in A.D. 70 and also the continued spread of the gospel in the Gentile world, recounted fragmentarily in Luke's second volume, the

Acts of the Apostles. Such a problem as the original form of the Beatitudes (Matt. 5.3-12, Luke 6.21-23), a problem that well illustrates the differences between Matthew and Luke, is important but not final: both versions have been influenced in the transmission of the gospel tradition by motives which are traceable elsewhere in Matthew and Luke. But the "psychological" interpretation of both is imperative.

John is wholly different, and its "truth" lies in the demonstration of the possibility of rewriting and reinterpreting the life of Christ to meet the demands of the quasi-philosophical Gnostic conception of God and the world, and yet fend off the full Gnostic view. If Christ was a divine being, as the church now held, he must have been related to the divine nature, the primal being of God, from all eternity. His coming to earth must have been a cosmic event. His death and resurrection must have had universal significance: "Because I live, you will live also" (John 14.19). The gospel now flowers into a fully developed religion of redemption, like others in the Hellenistic world under the early Roman empire, and yet wholly unlike any of them—achieving what others only attempted, some would say. It was now far removed from the original apocalyptic-eschatological message proclaimed at Jerusalem a few days or weeks after the crucifixion, when the risen Lord had appeared in glory and convinced his disciples of his coming triumph.

The "truth" of each of the gospels is not primarily historical or chronological or documentary but psychological: they set forth aspects of the new phenomenon, the Christian faith, *vis à vis* the new world which had now arisen, for Jews and Gentiles alike, in the days of the early Caesars. Every one of the gospels is more Gentile than Jewish in its content, aim, and outlook. The "historical" truth of the gospels is important for our understanding of them in their "psychological" orientation, their place in the full-orbed scene of religion in the first two centuries, the great turning-point in Western and Mediterranean religious history. It was then that our Western world began to move in the modern direction, and religion ceased to be nationalistic, indigenous, inherited, rooted in primitive rites and customs, and started to swing over toward what Ernst Troeltsch called the "conventicle" type, with emphasis on individual conversion and profession. Erwin Goodenough's *Symbols* belong to this era, and one can trace, in both Judaism and Christianity, their significance for this vast world of religious transition which they reflect: syncretism, spiritualization, individualism, deracination, personal loyalty. From now on, religion was directed more and more to the problems of the new world emerging in the West and to the problems set the individual living within this new, uprooted, still vastly unsettled world. Here is where the interpreter of the Bible must concentrate, if he would see the whole significance of the Holy Scriptures to the Church and to the world, and in relation to the on-going tradition of the Church. In grappling with the problems of the Mediterranean world and especially the West during these early centuries of the Christian era, the church tended to neglect the ethical teaching of the Bible in favor of theological interpretation. This heritage is with us still. The Mediaeval Church and the Reformation and its consequences have left the study of the Bible still off balance. Moral theology has not kept pace with metaphysical speculation. And Moral Theology has not shown signs of much vitality, adaptability, or creative progress in the modern world.

In this ultra-conservative post-war period of conformity—that is how the *Zeitgeist* has affected the churches—we may hesitate to set aside or mark for disuse any passage in Holy Scripture. "Take the Bible as is!"—this is the motto of many of our religious leaders, who reject Bultmann and Dibelius and Conzelmann and even Streeter! But there have been ages when bold spirits spoke out without hesitation, and were heard. St. Augustine forbade the public reading of the story of the Woman Taken in Adultery, who was forgiven and released without any sign of repentance, lest women in his diocese (Hippo, in North Africa) should follow her example, counting upon a similar lenity if discovered. Luther did not hesitate to brand the Epistle of James "an epistle of straw," since it apparently contradicted Paul's doctrine of Grace, "Justification by faith alone apart from works of the Law" as set forth in the Epistle to Romans 1.17, "The righteous shall live by faith." In fact Luther's view of the latter books of the New Testament was somewhat dismal. In his *Neue Testament Deutsch* (1522) the order of the books was rearranged and the last four were Hebrews, James, Jude, and Revelation, printed without *Sperrdrucke*, as stepchildren of the sacred collection (see the *Weimar-Ausgabe* of Luther's works, The Bible, Vol. 7 (1931) p. xliii). Not only Luther but even eminent Anglican scholars have deplored the inclusion of the Revelation to John in the New Testament—a book full of hatred and disloyalty, with not even a whisper of recognition of Rome's great services to public tranquillity, peace and order throughout the known world of the West in the first and second centuries, but only "blood up to the horses' bridles" (14.20)—the passage which so deeply offended Professor T. V. Smith.

There are passages in the Bible that ought never to be used in public worship, or even in private meditation. The last three chapters of Judges—and perhaps more of that book—might well be put in escrow. Isaiah 63 is another: "Who is this that comes from Edom, his garments spotted with blood?" This passage is read in the Anglican Prayer Book as the Epistle for Monday in Holy Week; in the Roman Missal it is appointed for Wednesday; and in both, presumably, a firm stroke of allegorical interpretation shifts it from the original and literal meaning (Yahweh's return from a foray of vengeance upon his traditional enemies and Israel's) to Christ upon the Cross, and so gives the passage meaning for the sacred season commemorating the Savior's death. But it is still bloody and awful, like the "blood up to the horses' bridles" in Revelation, or the allusion in the *Battle Hymn of the Republic*, still sung with gusto on patriotic occasions in the North—the words are straight from the passage in Revelation, as those of Revelation echo III Isaiah. But Christ was no butcher, his garments dripping blood, but a naked victim on a cruel cross in the blazing heat of a Near Eastern April day. One wonders why we Westerners tolerate such scenes in our devotional and liturgical anthologies. Are we still closely related to those cannibals who feasted in the Danube Valley about 2000 B.C., or the Druids who lived in the forests of Gaul in the days of Julius Caesar? In 1960 a crazed maniac broke into a Girls' Hostel in Birmingham, England, and chopped a young woman to bits. Then, his hands still dripping with her blood, he took a bus and rode for some distance to his domicile. He was seen in transit by a whole busfull of passengers, none of whom later volunteered to testify that they had seen him. Such scenes paralyze and even hypnotize people who fear to "get involved", persons who have nothing to gain but everything to lose by going to law for any purpose. The world is full of them. It is a real question if the *psychological* effects of such devotions as the Stations of the Cross, such imagery as the Crucifix, such hymns and scripture readings as magnify the details of death by torture ought to be encouraged. Their effect on non-historically minded persons is something that should be carefully studied. There is a story of a wayward boy who was sent to a Catholic school and immediately changed his ways. On being asked why (not a very good question), he replied, "There's a big picture at the end of the hall—a man nailed up on boards and left to die. That shows they mean business here, if you don't do what you're told." The story sounds apocryphal, but I am assured it is true. But even this *motif* is lacking in the devotional use of such symbols.

The portrayal of innocent suffering, with all its excruciating details, as in the Latin realism of much Passion art, cannot be shown to do any real good. It satisfies a sadistic demand for scenes of pain and horror—the kind the worst moving pictures supply. The psychological connection of this worship of Suffering—or of Sorrow, as Carlyle called it—with the fact that Christianity has been the bloodiest religion in history still remains to be made out. As for the fact, such a book as Professor Roland Bainton's *Horizon History of Christianity* with its full series of illistrations leaves this without doubt.

Another example of a questionable passage, from another and a different angle but still demanding psychological study, is the restoration of Peter in the appended chapter 21 of the Gospel of John. It calls for psychological analysis far more than for literary. Its flabby, saccharine "momism" is obvious to anyone who deplores that attitude and practice in the rearing of children, an attitude which makes the child absolutely dependent upon the mother, and encourages him to profess and claim a personal intimacy and devotion to the mother, and from her, superior to that of every other member of the family, especially every other child. This practice has led to endless tragedy, as any pastor must know who has really been close to his people and lived among them for a number of years—unless they have all been saints. The reiterated but pathetic question, "Lovest thou me *more* than these?" is unworthy of the majestic figure painted in this gospel, from chapter 1 to chapter 20, and it completely contravenes and contradicts the attitude of Jesus to his disciples as reflected in the pre-resurrection narratives of the Synoptics, especially his repeated reply to their ambitious query, "Who is the greatest among us?" That pathetic inquiry is now on Jesus' lips, not theirs! And the purpose of the episode in John is obviously aetiological, viz. to account for Peter's prominence in the early church, Peter's rather than James's or John's. Of course it fits the Roman claims, hand in glove. But the New Testament evidence for those claims, elsewhere already deeply suspect as false exegesis (see my *Rome and Reunion*), is here so obvious that it might almost be suspected of having been created to serve that very end—at the conclusion of the Four-fold Gospel Canon, which B. W. Bacon believed was compiled at Rome in the middle of the second century.

There was much more than the Donation of Constantine and the False Decretals and the myth of St Sylvester that needed to be pruned away from the mediaeval propaganda for the papacy. The tangled vines of legend root back all the way to the New Testament, and must be recognized and removed. Otherwise, the whole Christian Church stands to lose out in the current struggle for survival in an age which, since the 17th century, is less and less inclined to accept fiction for fact or pious fancy for demonstrated event. At least this is the way things are going among the educated. The extraordinary asseveration of veracity in John 21.24, instead of reassuring the modern reader, at once arouses his suspicion of the whole chapter—even of the whole book. There is no use in condemning the modern reader. Do we want him to read the New Testament or not? And are we willing to admit that the psychological insights of today must, on our view, be set aside when we come to the New Testament? How futile! The New Testament will continue to be read, and the modern reader will continue to apply the same tests to it that he would—and does—apply to any other ancient Hellenistic religious writing, Christian, Jewish, or pagan.

III

By "symbolism" and the "psychological" interpretation of the Bible we mean to suggest that the detailed incidents are sometimes supplied by imagination, by fiction—repeatedly in the Old Testament and often in the New. If the "truth" of the scene in John 21, Peter's restoration, is a fact of history—as it must have been—the story of the three-fold question and the three-fold commission must be fictitious: someone, the author of John or one of those who handed on the early Christian tradition, did his best to make the story vivid and realistic. But his gifts were limited and he was, like many of us, insufficiently critical of the result, and of his own powers. The psychological presuppositions of the story are maudlin and weak. A divine being risen from the grave would not talk like this. The appearance of the divine hero Heracles at the end of the *Philoctetes* is much more in character. The dialogue in John does not sound like either the historical Jesus or the Risen Lord. But the great "truth" which lies behind the story is not only Peter's restoration but, beyond that, the unquestioned sovereignty of the Risen Lord over his Church. Christ decides and chooses and appoints the leadership of his church, not at Caesarea Philippi but in Galilee, after the Resurrection. As in the Old Testament, so in the New, the tradition is frequently sound though the narrative telling of it is fanciful and imaginary. And the tradition comes first, not the dramatic retelling.

Dr. Goodenough also pointed out to us the universal symbolism of the Cup, chiefly as a token of fellowship and unity. This was undoubtedly its primary significance in the earliest church as reflected in the New Testament and in the church's oldest liturgy, in the *Didache*, where *both* the Cup and the Bread emphasize the unity of the believing congregation. Those churches of the present day which strongly emphasize the sacramental interpretation of the Eucharist but tend to ignore the implication of fellowship, do so to their own great loss and with resulting damage to the total Christian tradition. These symbols, the Cup and the Bread, described by the old theologians as self-effecting, i.e. symbols which both were and conveyed what they symbolized, are honored and observed not as a mechanism for private identification with Christ, as in too much of modern devotion, but in the common worship of and fellowship with the Risen Lord, who is present where two or three are gathered together (Matt. 18.20). Disloyalty to this sacramental presence is not the consequence of doubt as to its origin but of disregard for its meaning as the expression of fellowship, brotherhood, union with Christ and his Church. Alas, such disloyalty and treason was not limited to ancient Corinth! The Christian who partakes of this supernatural fellowship with Christ and his brethren, and then continues to lie, cheat, and steal—*he* has "profaned" the Lord's "body", which is not his "flesh" but his church. This is where the church's self-reformation has failed and must be revived, not in stronger emphasis on the "sacramental" interpretation of Christian rites but on their ethical implications. And this I take to be one of the most important practical inferences we should draw from the whole tremendous series on *Jewish Symbols in the Greco-Roman Period*, the *magnum opus* of our late friend Erwin Goodenough. May he rest in peace!

ROME IN THE EAST

BY

MORTON S. ENSLIN
Bryn Mawr College

At the time of the ministry of Jesus—"in the fifteenth year of Tiberius"—Palestine was firmly held by the possessive hand of Rome. The little land, "like all Gaul," was divided into three distinct parts: 1) Samaria, Judea, and Idumea constituted the province of Judea, governed by a Roman official resident in the land with his headquarters at Caesarea, a city which had been built by Herod fifty years before to provide his inhospitable coast with a harbor; 2) Galilee and a strip of land east of the Jordan known as the Perea constituted the tetrarchy of Antipas, a son of Herod the Great, who, a generation before, had held the whole territory, nominally a kingdom, but actually a frontier district of the expanding Roman empire; 3) the districts to the north and east of the Sea of Galilee, which had been added piece by piece a generation before to the growing domain of Herod in consequence of his demonstratedly able and effective administration of territories unable to control themselves, were now in the hands of another of his sons, Philip the tetrarch. The form of Roman control thus differed in these three sections of the little land, with considerable latitude and with marked deference to local customs and folkways. Nonetheless, be it in Jerusalem or in the nominally independent tetrarchies of Antipas or Philip, Rome was the mistress. The days of Jewish independence were long since past.

These facts are well known and frequently have been recited as an example of the bondage enforced by a greedy Rome upon peoples whom she had ruthlessly reduced to slavery. This emphasis is common today in view of the collapse of modern empires, in the course of which, in the name of freedom, the freed have been left to mismanage themselves and to violate the rights of their weaker neigbors. The question rises: Was the advent of Rome in the East the evil consequence of greed for domain and power of the city on the Tiber? It is a popular sport to appraise distant chapters in history and to return easy verdicts of "good" and "bad." The responsible historian is always on his guard here; before he renders his value judgment, "good" or "bad," he wants to know what the situation actually was and how it had arisen.

Although this subservience to a foreign lord who held possesion of a land popularly believed to be theirs by divine fiat was a source of constant irritation to the Jews and was destined to end, less than a half century after the crucifixion—a century and a quarter after it had begun—in the dreadful carnival of blood of the years A.D. 66-73, a good case for the contention can be made that in many ways the Palestinians were definitely better off than they had been before Rome's advent in the East. And the same may be said for other districts, notably Asia Minor, which, unlike Palestine, gratefully recognized it in the voluntary and unforced institution of emperor worship, in direct consequence of the freedom and protection from inroads from greedy boundary jumpers, which security the *pax Romana* had now made real.

The less-known story of Rome's advent in the East is a fascinating one and well worth the telling. This step eastward, which eventually led to the view that the Euphrates was her necessary eastern boundary, had been very reluctantly taken.

In 133 B.C. Attalus III of Pergamum, a rich and compact state in western Asia Minor, died and willed his territory to Rome. The reason for this act has been frequently debated. It would seem to me to have been largely due to Attalus' fear that his once powerful kingdom would fall prey to incursion. Relations with Rome had long been friendly. Pergamum and Rhodes had fought with Rome's assistance against the attacks of Philip V of Macedon and Antiochus the Great. At Magnesia in 190, it had been Rome who had ended the dreams of Antiochus for control over all Asia Minor and even Greece. Rome had aided Pergamum in subduing the lawless and vigorous Gauls (Galatians).

Rome was far from happy at this gift of a territory which might easily prove hard to control and protect. But Tiberius Gracchus, now at the peak of his "reforming," needed money to administer his land laws; thus he got a bill through the tribal assembly to take over this bequest from Attalus. This act was a distinct interference with senatorial rights, for it was the duty of the Senate to administer provinces. Tiberius was soon slain, and the Senate reassumed its right to administer foreign affairs. It more or less reluctantly accepted the bequest and turned it into the province of Asia, the first Roman province beyond the Aegean, as it had formed the provinces of Africa and Macedon a decade earlier after the III Punic War. But Rome had by no means adopted her later policy of "to the Euphrates" and, with a characteristic dislike of attempting to rule troublous districts, did some extensive pruning. She gave eastern Phrygia to Mithradates of Pontus; Lycaonia to Cappadocia; the Pamphylian and Pisidian tribes were set free to misrule themselves. Only Mysia, Lydia, and Caria were retained in the newly constituted third province.

Two years later (123 B.C.) Gaius Gracchus, the younger of the two crusadings brothers, needed money for his grain laws and got the assembly to interfere again in Asia and to take back Phrygia from Pontus. In addition, it put heavy tribute on several of the Greek cities which had been declared free a decade before, farming out the taxes to meet the extortionate demands. This action was to bear bitter fruit. It led to a growing restiveness and unrest in Asia and it aroused the anger of Pontus.

The second territory in Asia Minor to come into Roman hands was Cilicia. This was not by bequest but in consequence of the problem which all governments which have found themselves responsible for extraterratorial lands have had to face; you must protect what you have. Cilicia had long been a haunt of pirates whose depredations were both daring and costly. Pergamum and Rhodes had earlier policed the seas very efficiently to preserve their own commerce. But when in 133 Pergamum had been ceded to Rome, Rhodes got sick of spending her money in policing what was fast becoming a Roman lake. Rome hated to spend money on a navy, but the menace grew, aided by the lack of wisdom of having given independence to the southern and eastern parts of Pergamum, for these latter were clearly not ready for it. Both Cilicia and Pamphylia were now busily and uninterruptedly engaged in this lucrative piracy, even raiding the interior. Rome was forced to act, and finally sent a praetor, Antonius, with a fleet—requisitioned in large part from her Greek naval allies. Antonius effectively cleaned up the mess, and turned Cilicia into a province (102 B.C.). Lack of a standing army in Cilicia, however, left the work to be done over again years later by Pompey.

During the "Social War" which had ravaged Rome (90-88) Mithradates of Pontus found his chance for the invasion of the Roman province of Asia. He had come to the throne in 120, a mere boy of twelve. Soon he had expanded his kingdom to Armenia in the east, around the Sea of Azov to the north, and had then invaded southern Russia. As early as 93 he tried without success to gain Cappadocia, his southern neighbor, but had been repulsed by Rome who had driven out his young son Ariarathes whom he had placed on the Cappadocian throne. Three years later (90 B.C.) his attempt on Bithynia to the west had been thwarted by Rome, who restored the young Nicomedes III of Bithynia, whom Mithradates had driven out. In addition, the earlier indignity of having had Phrygia taken back by Rome, as already mentioned, still rankled. Now he saw his chance in this time of confusion in Rome and in the aggression against Pontus by Nicomedes of Bithynia at the instigation of Rome. He acted without delay. Retaking Bithynia, he raced south across Galatia into Asia. Here he was welcomed as a liberator by the inhabitants gouged by the rapacious tax collectors from Rome. Some 80,000 Romans and Italians are said to have been massacred in one day. Years later, in his famous speech in favor of Pompey, Cicero referred to the terrible financial panic in Rome caused by this massacre:

> We ought surely to keep in mind the lesson which this same Asia and this same Mithradates taught us at the beginning of the Asiatic war. For we know how payments of debts were stopped at Rome and credit shaken when so many had lost their property in Asia (*Manilian Law* 7).

Athens, in alarm at the fall of the island of Delos before Mithradates' ravages, was ready to make terms. Mithradates sent a force under Archelaus into Greece to make, if possible, a Pontic protectorate as far west as the Adriatic.

At this crisis Sulla appeared. He, a staunch aristocrat, had emerged from the disastrous social war as consul, since now once again the Senate was in the saddle. To him fortunately fell the lot to go against Mithradates. Before he could leave Rome fresh troubles blazed out in the so-called Sulpician riots, over the question of franchise for new citizens and freedmen. Marius, many times a consul and the hero of the wars against the Teutons and Jugurtha, long at odds with the Senate and a deadly enemy of Sulla, took a hand. Marius joined Sulpicius the tribune who had sparked the franchise agitation, in return for the promise that he be given the leadership, in place of Sulla, of the war against Mithradates. Though the resulting bill was entirely revolutionary—to depose a consul without charges!—it was raced through the assembly. At once Sulla marched on Rome and took the government by force. Sulpicius and Marius were driven out and later outlawed. To prevent a similar occurrence Sulla proposed a law forbidding the tribune to introduce bills before the assembly unless previously approved by the Senate. And this death warrant was carried out by the overawed Romans.

Although Sulla saw that his departure from Rome must result in the fall of his party, yet, good old believer in Roman tradition that he was, he could no longer delay his eastern campaign, and at once set forth for Greece. Athens was besieged and taken in 86. Sulla saved the city, despite some looting, and preserved its independence. Then at Chaeronea, where 250 years before Philip of Macedon had waged the battle which made him master of all the Greek states save Sparta, Sulla defeated Archelaus despite odds of five to one. Another force from Mithradates was equally unsuccessful. Now Mithradates really had his hands full. Not only checked in Greece but in Asia he had been attacked by another Roman army sent by the supporters of Marius, who, true to Sulla's fears, had promptly reentered Rome and had had Sulla proclaimed a public enemy.

Pushed on all sides, Mithradates offered terms of peace to Sulla, but the latter, taking no chances with the tricky Pontian, pushed into Asia to see the terms carried out. On his arrival, he forced Mithradates to surrender his Asian holdings, to return to Pontus, and to pay a 3,000 talent indemnity. Next he laid a fearful indemnity upon the Asian cities for their alleged aid to Mithradates and forced the generals of the Marian army to desert to him. Then he returned to Rome to reestablish the Senate in control after the bloody purge that Marius had staged upon his return to the city following Sulla's departure. This, the so-called I Mithradatic War, had lasted four years (88-84).

But Mithradates was still a menace. In 83 fresh troubles broke out, in the course of which the Roman commander. Murena, was worsted. It was during this inconsequential II Mithradatic War that Tigranes of Armenia overran the utterly demoralized Seleucid kingdom of Syria (83 B.C.) and held it until ejected by Pompey in 69.

In 75 more troubles were brewing in Asia Minor. Sulla, whom Mithradates had learned the hard way to respect and fear, was dead. Furthermore, Nicomedes Eupator, the king of Bithynia, who had recently died, had followed the earlier example of Attalus of Pergamum and had left his territory to Rome. Apparently this was for the purpose of preventing Bithynia from falling into the hands of Mithradates, for Rome alone was strong enough to oppose successfully this energetic encroacher and boundary jumper. Mithradates invaded Bithynia at once, to try to prevent the terms of the will from being carried out. This was the start of the III ("Great") Mithradatic War (74-63).

At once Rome sent both consuls, Lucullus and Cotta, against him. For two years the able Lucullus steadily and relentlessly pursued him, until finally Mithradates fled into Armenia. This flight had important consequences for Palestine which at that time was ruled by Alexandra, widow of Alexander Janneus. Tigranes, who, as was mentioned above, had gained control of Syria, was now moving south along the shore road, obviously intent on wresting Alexandra's kingdom from her, after his conquest of such seaport cities as Ptolemais. When he heard, however, the news of Mithradates' retreat into his own Armenia, although he had been quite ready to support Mithradates in the latter's ventures into Asia Minor, he had no desire to have this energetic ally in his own territory. At once giving up his plans for Jerusalem, he hastily returned to Armenia.

Temporarily freed from the menace of Mithradates, Lucullus in the interim had gone to Asia to attempt to remedy the bankruptcy of that province which had been caused by Sulla's crushing indemnity and the resulting usury of Syrian and Greek bankers. Believing, as all good Romans did, in the sacred rights of property, he had drastically reformed the financial arrangements, had disallowed two-thirds of the debts, dropped interest rates, and allowed the residue to be paid without interest in four annual installments, with the result that in four years Asia is said to have paid itself out of debt.

In 69, however, war was once again on. Tigranes had ralled to Mithradates' support, and the latter had raised a new army. This support, however, cost Tigranes Syria, for Lucullus proceeded against it at once. Instead of annexing it directly to Rome, he was content to expel Tigranes and to appoint the last of the Seleucids, Antiochus the grandson of Cyzicenos, as nominal king under the title Antiochus Asiaticus (Antiochus XIII). This latter puppet reigned for the ensuing four years (69-65). Other than this, Lucullus does not seem to have made any real further advances against either Mithradates or Tigranes, and in 67 he was recalled to Rome. He had become unpopular both with his own soldiers and in Rome—with the former because he was both a strict disciplinarian and had consistently prevented plundering; in Rome because of his drastic acts to protect the provincials from the greed of tax collectors and usurers.

In that same year 67, while he had been in Mesopotamia, his two generals who were holding Pontus had been defeated. Thus the definite gains of 72 had been lost. His victories during the first two years had apparently turned his head. He wanted a triumph. Instead he was recalled, and the consul Glabrio was sent to the East in his stead.

By 66 the latter had shown himself entirely incompetent, and his command was unceremoniously transferred to Pompey. Pompey was already high in public esteem. When Sulla had returned to Rome in 83,

Pompey had been his loyal supporter. Later, when Sertorius, the leader of the democrats, had fled to Spain, Pompey had been in charge of the war against him and had carried on a brilliant and successful campaign against this able opponent (76-72). Some years later (67) the Cilician pirates, earlier checked but not destroyed, had allied themselves with Mithradates and had become not only a nuisance but a definite menace. They had ventured to strike as far west as Delos and to loot its revered temples; even worse, they were robbing, burning, and kidnaping Italian and Sicilians for their slave markets. They had even ventured to seize Roman officials a few miles from Rome. In this crisis the tribune Aulus Gabinius had introduced the bill bearing his name making Pompey commander-in-chief against the pirates. Pompey met the most sanguine hopes. In a brilliant three-month campaign he cleaned the Mediterranean, sweeping the pirates into his net at the eastern end.

In consequence, now that Glabrio had shown so clearly his incompetence, Pompey was put in charge of the Mithradatic war by a bill presented to the Senate by Manilius and sponsored effectively by Cicero. This commission gave him full command over the East for an indefinite period. Once again expectations were not misplaced. At once he blocked all the harbors of Pontus and proceeded against Mithradates, completely crushing his power in little more than a year (66-65). Hoping to be able to make another attempt, Mithradates fled north, but finding his hope vain committed suicide after his own son had turned against him.

Now that this longtime menace was finally over, Pompey proceeded methodically to extend Roman control to the Euphrates. It was now clear that to hold these territories which Rome had more or less reluctantly assumed—Pergamum in 133; Cilicia in 102; Bithynia in 75—all of Asia Minor must be gained, either by arms or by treaties. Syria too, because of its position, constituted a grave problem to the tranquility of the growing Roman East. Antiochus XIII, whom Lucullus had put in nominal control, was thrust aside, and the remains of the once proud Seleucid empire was organized as a Roman province—her fourth in the East.

Palestine, at the moment involved in the clash of the two sons of Alexandra, Aristobulus II and Hyrcanus II, was slated to become part of the new province of Syria, for in the eyes of Pompey it was a revolting part of this territory which had temporarily broken away from it. Later events led him to modify his plans in this respect and to make it at first a virtually autonomous semidepartment of the new province, but with the Jewish high priest, Hyrcanus II, its local governor (ethnarch), directly responsible to the Roman propraetor of Syria, or at least under his direct oversight. Thus with the conquest of Jerusalem in 63 B.C. the end of actual Jewish independence had come. A Jewish king might eventually sit on the throne, as did both Herod and his grandson Agrippa; but they sat there because Rome had seated them, and well did they know it. All extra-Judean territory, save Idumea, was stripped off. The Greek cities of the seacoast and Transjordan were freed from what was to them a hated Jewish tyranny. Samaria and Galilee were appended to Syria. Many usurpers who had got control of cities or sections of the decaying Seleucid empire were summarily ejected. Others, like Tigranes, who could show claim to their territory and had learned to respect boundaries, were permitted to remain, with the clear recognition that it was definitely to their advantage to keep the peace and to prize Roman goodwill. Hyrcanus II, completely dominated by his mentor, Antipater, was one of these latter.

The next year Pompey spent in a complete reorganization of what had now become the Roman East. The province of Asia remained unchanged. Cilicia was substantially enlarged, extending along the Mediterranean to Syria and reaching inland to include such cities as Pisidian Antioch, Derbe, and Lystra. Lycia was not included in either Cilicia or Asia, but remained a confederacy of autonomous cities until, a century after Pompey, Claudius (A.D. 43) dissolved the confederacy "because of deadly intestine feuds" (Suetonius, *Claudius* 25,3). Bithynia and Pontus were turned into one combined province. Thus the East now saw four provinces: Asia, Bithynia-Pontus, Cilicia, and Syria. The remaining districts of Asia Minor, like Cappadocia and Galatia, with other small temple-states, were made into client kingdoms. Mithradates' son, Pharnaces was permitted to rule in the Crimaea. As has been noted, Armenia remained in the hands of its chastened king Tigranes.

In the provinces many new cities were established as centers of local government for the surrounding countryside. Many of the stabler features of Sulla's reforms were continued; the financial system was thoroughly overhauled. The powers of the governors were substantially increased, and the looting of provincials by greedy publicans, which had been the order of the day at the time when Gracchus had been eager to have the territory to finance his reform legislation and which had alienated the provincials, was drastically checked, or at least distinctly lessened. In no sense did Pompey seek to Romanize these newly organized lands. Rather, the earlier policy of Alexander the Great and of his successors, notably Seleucus, was continued. Greek culture and institutions, not Roman, were the order of the day. Greek, not Latin, was the language employed. Even the provincial governors were careful to translate their decrees into Greek. The towns and cities, of which there were over five hundred in Asia alone, continued democratic in government, with the town meeting the lawmaking body, precisely as the Sanhedrin in Judea continued to be. The towns continued to manage their own affairs with local courts having full power. Roman governors were content to see that law and order prevailed, that taxes due Rome were paid, that frontiers were respected, and that Roman citizens who chanced to be in their territories had the benefit of their presence to guarantee them their privileges and rights. Similarly in the case of religion, Roman governors never interfered unless practices were proving definitely detrimental. Even then, they sought to restrain, not to extirpate.

Early in 61 Pompey returned to Rome to celebrate a triumph and to have these various arrangements which he had made in Asia Minor and Syria ratified by the Senate. Difficulties at once broke out. Many, including Lucullus, were jealous of him, and he found many obstacles. Caesar, however, returned the next summer from the West. Thus Pompey was in a mood to throw in his lot with him. The breach of ten years standing with Crassus was superficially healed, and all three of them entered into the famous agreement known as the First Triumvirate (60-53) of which Suetonius later wrote: "Ne quid ageretur in re publica quod displicuisset ulli e tribus" (Suetonius, *Julius* 19,2). This power combine was destined to rule Rome until the death of Crassus in the East (53) dissolved it and brought Caesar and Pompey into open rivalry, with Caesar gaining more and more power from his brilliant campaigns in Gaul, while Pompey, in name the "Great Man," saw his influence slipping from him. He had preferred to remain in Rome than to go to his province in Spain which had fallen to him as proconsul after his first consulship with Crassus in 55.

The difficulties steadily worsened. Pompey and Caesar grew further and furhter apart. Julia, Caesar's daughter and Pompey's wife—a dynastic marriage which had tended to keep Pompey in line—died in 54. Finally after a year of confusion Pompey became sole consul, and Caesar saw the handwriting on the wall. Rome had become too small for them both. Caesar's commission, which had been renewed for five years, would shortly expire, and well did he know that once he became a private citizen he would be available to the courts and that Cato would have him indicted for treason. The Senate finally decreed that Caesar retire from office on July 1 or be declared a public enemy. Mark Antony, Caesar's friend, then tribune, vetoed the bill. Cicero sought a compromise. It was in vain. A week later the Senate passed its "last decree," throwing the government into the hands of the military, despite Antony's veto. Caesar no longer delayed, but crossed the the Rubicon onto Italian soil, with the never-to-be-forgotten word, "Alea iacta est," and proceeded at once against Rome.

The result was the dreadful period of civil war in Rome which lasted from Caesar's appearance in Rome until the death of Mark Antony at the hands of Octavian after Actium. All of this period of turmoil was reflected in the Roman East.

In Palestine Antipater, the real power behind the nominal ethnarch Hyrcanus II, naturally continued on the side of Pompey, as did all the East. When Pompey was treacherously murdered by the Egyptians, whither he had fled after his defeat at Pharsalia, Antipater made himself of such use to the pursuing Caesar that the latter not only confirmed both him and his nominal master Hyrcanus in their little territory, and restored it to the status of of an ethnarchy which it had shortly before lost because of a series of rebellions, but also exempted Jews from service in the Roman legions, thus safeguarding their religious prejudices. The death of Caesar on the fatal ides of March three years later was a sorry blow to Jewry. Antipater and his able son Herod were seen by Antony as valuable supporters and were warmly welcomed. As the years passed, Herod proved himself more and more able as an administrator and useful to Rome, and in 40 was appointed by the Senate king of the little Judean state at the insistence of Antony and Octavian who at the moment were acting hand in hand. As Antipater had nimbly changed from the side of Pompey to Caesar after Pharsalia, and as he and Herod had been welcomed by Antony after the assassination of Caesar and the resulting defeat of the conspirators at Philippi, so after Actium, where Antony and Cleopatra had been hopelessly defeated by Octavian, Herod, now longtime king in fact as well as in name, easily convinced Octavian that his retention as *rex socius* of the strategically important little frontier district of Judea was manifestly wise.

The battle of Actium rightly stands as one of the turning points in world history. It marked the end of the Roman republic, which, during those years of civil war, had become a republic only in name, and was the harbinger of the empire destined for many years to shape the history of the Mediterranean and the whole Near East. Octavian, despite his ingenious disclaimer, had imperial longings as had had his uncle Julius, but he was shrewd enough to guard himself against his uncle's fate. Since the end of the second triumvirate, which had eventually brought brought him into open rivalry with Antony whose mad ambition and antics in the East had finally become an open book, Octavian had had almost dictatorial power. This rested upon no constitutional basis but rather upon his own prestige, his annual consulship, and the subservience of the Senate. Now after a short time of quiet (27 B.C.), he made a great point of publicly declaring his desire for the restoration of the republic, wearied by war and eager for peace and quiet. He resigned all his extraordinary powers, including his command of the army and control of the provinces. The Senate, he declared, was and must be supreme. In return the Senate voted him 1) proconsular power over all frontier provinces, 2) the name *Augustus* and the title *princeps senatus*, and changed the month Sextilis to Augustus. He was thus in a completely secure position. He had voluntarily surrendered all claims to being a dictator, had disabused any nervous suspicion that he wanted to restore the hated kingdom, and had in regular and legal fashion regained command of the armies, for it was those provinces where legions were required—the frontier provinces—that had been tendered to him by a grateful Senate.

To prove that his was no idle gesture he left Rome for the West and did not return until 24 B.C. During his absence—had he expected it?—the Senate had shown itself utterly incompetent. Every request of his had been answered, "Your will is law." His fellow consul, Murenas, had plotted against him, but without success. His return to Rome saw marked and needed changes. He resigned his perennial consulship and in exchange received the *tribunicia potestas* for life. Thus he was doubly secure. By the vote of 27 he had been assured full control of the standing armies through his proconsular power over frontier provinces. Now this popular vote guaranteed him control of legislation and the veto. All was now in his hands without the onus of having stolen it from the Senate. The empire was born, and it had an able and astute master.

All this was highly acceptable to the provinces. Now instead of rival cliques in the Senate there was one strong hand in control, whose especial concern it was to make real the *pax Romana* and to end confusion and unrest; instead of irresponsible magistrates going out for a final year to the provinces with the firm determination to provide lushly for their years of retirement, these provinces received governors responsible directly and solely to Augustus. These officials remained in office so long as he determined, and this determination was based on their competence in keeping the peace without recourse to arms or violence. Military, judicial, and financial control were the responsibility of the governor, with the certainty that a lynx-eyed watch was kept on him in Rome. He received a fixed salary, not the right of taking as much as he could get as had been too often the case of the earlier incumbents. The abuses of taxation, so familar to all readers of Cicero's flaming arraignment, *Against Verres*, were no longer practised. Rome carefully audited the financial sheets of her provinces. A large proportion of the taxes was spent in improving the province itself—harbors, roads, water systems, public buildings. Most of the actual machinery of government—conspicuously was this the case in Judea, which was one of the lesser imperial provinces—was in the hands of native courts and officers. Religious prejudices were scrupulously safeguarded: Augustus' rule was that governors allow their provinces as much freedom from irksome control as possible. If they failed, their recall and dismissal was sure and swift, as in the case of Archelaus in A.D. 6, whose removal from office because of local discontent led to the transformation of the ethnarchy of Archelaus into a Roman province, with local resident governors, the fifth of whom was Pontius Pilate.

The *pax Romana* speedily became far more than a pleasant name. Boundary jumping—as by a Mithradates, Tigranes, or an Alexander Janneus—was over. Security was certain, travel was open and expedited; good roads made this possible, as a Paul was later to evidence. Actually the provincials were freer and more secure than they had been under their own kings. And this was gratefully recognized. Emperor worship, as earlier remarked, was the spontaneous reaction of many of the provincials in grateful recognition of the security and orderly government made possible by the new genius Roma and her embodiment in Augustus and—as the years went by—his successors.

As the historian reads these pages from the past he finds it hard not to feel that the coming of Rome into the East was far from being the unmitigated evil so often easily and lightly asserted.

GOD'S AGENT IN THE FOURTH GOSPEL

BY

PEDER BORGEN

University of Bergen, Norway

I. THE STATE OF RESEARCH

In his discussion of Christological ideas in the Fourth Gospel, C. H. Dodd finds that the status and function of the Son as God's delegated representative recalls the language of the Old Testament prophets. Certain peculiarities, such as the Son's complete and uninterrupted dependence on the Father, and the dualism between higher and lower spheres, suggest to him that this aspect of Jesus' human career is a projection of the eternal relation of the Son and the Father upon the field of time.[1]) This interpretation by Dodd does not take seriously the idea of the Son being commissioned and sent, but rather dissolves the idea of agency into an eternal and "Platonic" idea of relationship.

R. Bultmann, on the other hand, rightly places the commissioning and sending of the Son in the very center of the message of the Gospel. He also finds certain points of contact between the Johannine ideas and the prophets of the Old Testament. But John, according to Bultmann, goes beyond the thought of a prophet and interprets gnostic mythology about divine and pre-existent agents, commissioned by the Father and sent to the world. The Mandean literature is Bultmann's main source for his hypothesis.[2])

Close parallels found in the halakah encourage the investigation of the extent to which John's Christology and soteriology are moulded on Jewish rules for agency. K. H. Rengstorf had made a promising beginning at this point, although he does not think that the idea of agency plays any central role in the Johannine idea of Jesus as the Son of God.[3]) Also Théo Preiss and C. K. Barrett draw attention to the similarities between John and the halakah at certain places. Signifi-

---

[1]) C. H. Dodd, *The Interpretation of the Fourth Gospel*, Cambridge 1953, 254-262.
[2]) R. Bultmann, *Das Evangelium des Johannes*, Gottingen 1950, 187-188; and „Die Bedeutung der neuerschlossenen mandaischen und manichaischen Quellen fur das Verstandniss des Johannesevangeliums," *Zeitschrift fur die neutestamentliche Wissenschaft*, XXIV, 1925, 104-109.
[3]) K. H. Rengstorf, *Theologisches Worterbuch zum Neuen Testament*, ed. G. Kittel, I, Stuttgart 1933, 403-5; 421-22; 435-36.

cantly enough, Preiss discusses the idea of the Son as commissioned by the Father within the wider framework of the juridical aspects of Johannine thought. The importance of judicial ideas in John has been stressed by N. A. Dahl as well.[1]) In spite of the work of these scholars, the field is open to examine the degree in which halakhic principles of agent are reflected in the Fourth Gospel.

II. PRINCIPLES OF AGENCY

(a) The basic principle of the Jewish institution of agency is that "an agent is like the one who sent him."[2]) This relationship applied regardless of who was the sender. Thus, for example "the agent of the ruler is like the ruler himself."[3]) Consequently, to deal with the agent was the same as dealing with the sender himself:

> With what is the matter to be compared? With a king of flesh and blood who has a consul (agent) in the country. The inhabitants spoke before him. Then said the king to them, you have not spoken concerning my servant but concerning me.[4])

The saying in John 12 : 44 is a very close parallel to the saying by the king in the quotation from Siphre:

> John: he who believes in me, believes not in me but in him who sent me;
> Siphre: you have not spoken concerning my servant but concerning me.

Another saying which expresses the same idea, that dealing with the agent is the same as dealing with the sender himself, is found in all four gospels.[5]) The Johannine version occurs in 13 : 20:

> he who receives any one whom I send receive me;
> he who receives me receives him who sent me.

---

[1]) Theó Preiss, *Life in Christ*, *Studies in Biblical Theology*, XIII, London 1954, 9-31; C. K. Barrett, *The Gospel According to St. John*, London 1958, 216, 474; N. A. Dahl, "The Johannine Church and History," *Current Issues in New Testament Interpretation*, ed. W. Klassen and G. F. Snyder, New York, 1962, 137-142; See also P. Borgen, *Bread from Heaven*, Supplements to Novum Testamentum, X, Leiden 1965, 158-164.
[2]) Mek. Ex. 12: 3, 12: 6; Berakoth 5 : 5; Baba Metzia 96a; Hagigah 10b; Qiddushin 42b, 43a; Menahoth 93b; Nazir 12b, etc.
[3]) Baba Qamma 113b.
[4]) Siphre on Numbers 12 : 9, cited in K. H. Rengstorf, *Apostleship*, *Bible Key Words*, VI, translated from Kittel's *Theologisches Wörterbuch* by J. R. Coates, London 1952, 16.
[5]) See Matth. 10 : 40; cf. Matth. 18 : 5; Mark 9 : 37 and Luke 9 : 48. The paralells are discussed in C. H. Dodd, "Some Johannine 'Herrnworte' with parallels in the Synoptic Gospels," *New Testament Studies* II, 1955/56, 81-85.

There are also other similar sayings scattered throughout John:

5:23: he who does not honor the Son does not honor the Father who sent him;
12:45: he who sees me sees him who sent me;
14:9: he who has seen me has seen the Father;
15:23: he who hates me hates my Father also.

The halakhic principle that "an agent is like the one who sent him" usually meant that the agent was like his sender as far as the judicial function and effects were concerned. There were, however, rabbis who developed it into a judicial mysticism saying that the agent is a person identical with the sender.[1]) Thus not only his authority and his function are derived from the sender, but also his qualities. Qiddushin 43a formulates this mysticism in the following way: the agent ranks as his master's own person.[2])

In the Fourth Gospel the personal identity between the Son and the Father is stated in several different ways. One formula is "I and the Father are one" (10:30) and another formula is "the Father is in me and I am in the Father" (10:38; cf. 14:10-11 and 17:21-23). In 10:36-38 it is explicitly stated that it is the agent, the Son in the capacity of being sent into the world, who is one with the sender. Similarly, in 17:20-23, the unity between the Son and the Father shall make it possible for the world to recognize the Son as agent of the Father, "so that the world may believe that thou hast sent me". Moreover, in 10:37-38 and in 14:10-11 the oneness between the Son and the Father is made manifest in Jesus' words and works which also are said to be the works of the Father.

(b) Although John interprets the relationship between the Father and the Son in such legalistic terms, it is a legalism that is not seen in contrast to personal "mysticism." Thus Preiss' term "judicial mysticism" is a very apt one, and the personal element is further deepened by the fact that it was the *Son* who was the agent of the *Father*.[3]) It should

---

[1]) The phrase of judicial mysticism as clue to central ideas in John is suggested by Theó Preiss, *Life in Christ*, 25.
[2]) "He ranks as his own person" (הוה ליה כגופיה). Translation in *The Babylonian Talmud*, Nashim VIII, ed. by I. Epstein, London 1935, 216. Hebrew text in *Der Babylonian Talmud mit Einschluss der vollstandigen Mischnah*, by L. Goldschmidt, V, Leipzig 1906, 845.
[3]) See Theó Preiss, *Life in Christ*, 24-25: "the formulae suggestive of mystical immanence so typical of Johannine language are regularly intermixed with juridical formulae... Jesus reveals himself to be one with the Father as a result of the strict fidelity with which he waits upon him and utters his words and performs his task as ambassador and witness. (The bond between the Father and the Son) *coincides*

be added that the idea of the Son-Father relationship also implies that the Son is subordinate to the Father. This subordination fits very well to the principles of agency, since here the thoughts of unity and identity between agent and sender are modified by an emphasis on the superiority of the sender. The principle is stated in John 13 : 16 and Gen. R. 78:

> John: a servant is not greater than his master; nor is he who is sent greater than him who sent him.[1]
> Gen.R.: the sender is greater than the sent.

Matthew 10 : 24, cf. Luke 6 : 40, offers a parallel to the first part of John 13 : 16: "nor (is) a servant above his master." What in Matthew and Luke is said about pupil-teacher and servant-master relationship is in John specifically applied to agency.

(c) Another important area of agency centers around the specific mission of an agent. It was a legal presumption that an agent would carry out his mission in obedience to his sender.[2] as can be seen from Erubin 31b-32a, Qiddushin 2 : 4 and Terumoth 4 : 4:

> It is a legal presumption that an agent will carry out his mission (עושה שליחותו).[3]
> I appointed you for my advantage, and not for my disadvantage.[4]
> If a householder said to his agent (לשלוחו), "Go and give heave-offering," the agent should give heave-offering according to the householder's mind (כרעתו של בעל הבית).[5]

In accordance with this principle, Christ was an obedient agent who did as the Father had commanded. He said, "I have come down from heaven, not to do my own will but the will of him who sent me" (John 6 : 38). Likewise, the Christ always did what was pleasing to the one who sent him (8 : 29).

(d) The Johannine idea of the mission of Christ as God's agent is

---

with the bond formed by the obedience of a witness... Jesus is in the Father and the Father in him because he does the work of the Father (10 : 30, 37, 38). Inasmuch as he is the Son of Man sent as a witness from the height of heaven,... Jesus is according to rabbinical law "as he who sends him."

[1] See also John 15 : 20.
[2] Cf. K. H. Rengstorf, *Theologisches Wörterbuch* I, 415.
[3] Erubin 31b-32a; cf. Ketuboth 99b; Nazir 12a.
[4] Qiddushin 42b; cf. Baba Bathra 169b; Ketuboth 85a; Bekoroth 61b.
[5] Terumoth 4 : 4. Cf. the Mediaeval collection, Shulhan Aruq, Hoshen Mishpat, 188 : 5: „Stets wenn der Vertreter (שהשליח) von dem Willen des Vertretenen (מדעת המשלח) abweicht, is das Vertretungsverhaltnis ganzlich aufgelost." See M. Cohn, „Die Stellvertretung im judischen Recht," *Zeitschrift für vergleichende Rechtswissenschaft*, 36, 1920, 206.

seen within the context of a lawsuit. The statement in Baba Qamma 70a is of special interest for this question:

> Go forth and take legal action so that you may acquire title to it and secure the claim for yourself.

The principles reflected in this rule are also found in the Fourth Gospel. Although there is no scene of commissioning as pictured in the halakhic statement ("go forth," etc.), the commissioning itself is referred to in these words: "I came not of my own accord, but he sent me" (John 8:42); "For I have not spoken of my own authority; the Father who sent me has himself given me commandment what to say and what to speak" (John 12:49); "For he whom God has sent utters the words of God" (3:34); "My teaching is not mine, but his who sent me" (7:16); "...he who sent me is true, and I declare to the world what I have heard from him" (8:26); "...I do nothing on my own authority but speak thus as the Father taught me. And he who sent me is with me..." (8:28-29); "...the word which you hear is not mine but the Father's who sent me" (14:24).

According to the halakah the sender transferred his own rights and the property concerned to the agent.[1]) On this basis the agent might acquire the title in court and secure the claim for himself. The will of the sender, the Father, in John 6:39 makes just this transfer clear: "This is the will of him who sent me, that all that he has given me (πᾶν ὃ δέδωκέν μοι)..." The transfer is even more pointedly stated in 17:6: "thine they were, and thou gavest them to me" (σοὶ ἦσαν κἀμοὶ αὐτοὺς ἔδωκας).[2])

The next step is the actual acquiring of the title in court and the agent's securing of the claim for himself. John 12:31-32 pictures such a court scene:

> Now is the judgment of this world,
> now shall the ruler of this world be cast out;
> and I, when I am lifted up from the earth,
> will draw (ἑλκύσω) all men unto myself (πρὸς ἐμαυτόν).

There is close resemblance between the two phrases "I will draw all men to myself" (John) and "secure the claim for yourself" (halakah). In both cases the agent himself is to take possession of the property since the ownership has been transferred to him. John uses a different

---

[1]) See M. Cohn, *Zeitschrift fur vergleichende Rechtswissenschaft*, 36, 1920, 165-167; L. Auerbach, *Das judische Obligationsrecht*, I, Berlin 1870, 567-569.
[2]) Variants of the phrase occur in John 17:2, 6, 7; cf. 13:3.

verb, "draw" (ἑλκύσω) and not "secure" (ואפיק), but the Johannine term comes from judicial context. The verb renders with all probability the Hebrew משך, to draw, pull, seize.¹) Thus the Septuagint frequently translates משך by ἑλκύειν.²) And in the halakah of Judaism משך has received the technical meaning of "to take possession of" (by drawing or seizing an object).³) Thus the meaning of the phrase in John 12 : 32 and Baba Qaṁma 70a is the same.

Moreover, the legal acquiring of the title can be seen in John 12 : 31-32, although pictured in a negative way. The world and the ruler of this world are judged and cast out from the heavenly court.⁴) The ruler of this world is judged not to have any just title to or claim upon God's people.⁵) Thus it is implied that God's agent has the title and therefore can secure the claim for himself.

Although the ownership, for sake of the lawsuit, is transferred from the sender to his agent, the agent is, of course, still an agent of the sender. Thus as a matter of fact, the sender takes possession of the property when the agent does. The meaning of John 6 : 44 is to be understood along this line: "No one can come to me (i.e. the agent) unless the Father who sent me (ὁ πέμψας με, i.e. the sender) draws (ἑλκύσῃ) him." In other words, the coming to the agent, Christ, is the same as being in the possession of the Father, and only those who are included in the Father's claim come to His agent. Against this background it is logical that the rabbis discussed if an agent in such cases is to be characterized as partner to his sender.⁶)

(e) As Jesus has completed his mission (John 4 : 34; 5 : 36; 17 : 4; 19 : 30) he is to report to his sender. John 13ff. is dominated by this theme of Jesus' return to his Father: "Jesus, knowing that the Father had given all things into his hand, and that he had come from God and

---

[1]) So also A. Schlatter, *Der Evangelist Johannes*, Stuttgart 1930, 176, and R. Bultmann, *Evangelium*, 171, n. 7. These scholars have not, however, focused the attention upon משך as a judicial term.

[2]) Deut. 21 : 3; Neh. 9 : 30; Ps. 9 : 30 (10: 9); Eccl. 2 : 3; Cant. 1 : 4, etc.

[3]) Baba Metzia 4 : 2; Baba Metzia 47a; 48a; 49a. Cf. Ph. Blackmann, (ed. and trans.), *Mishnayoth*, IV, London 1951, 579.

[4]) See N. A. Dahl, *Current Issues in New Testament Interpretation*, (ed. W. Klassen and G. F. Snyder), 139; C. K. Barrett, *The Gospel According to St. John*, 355-6 ("The devil will be put out of office, out of authority. He will no longer be ἄρχων; men will be freed from his power").

[5]) Cf. that the children of Abraham have as Father God and not the devil, John 8 : 39-47.

[6]) Baba Qamma 70a, from which the above quotation was taken, discusses this very question: "He was surely appointed but a shaliach. Some, however, say that he is made a partner..."

was going to God..., etc." (13 : 3). And just as the judgment scene in John 12 : 31-32 was pictured in a proleptic way before its completion on the cross (19 : 30), so also is the Son's report given ahead of time in the form of the prayer found in John 17: "I glorified thee on earth, having accomplished the work which thou gavest me to do" (17 : 4).

It is in accordance with the halakah that an agent who is sent on a mission is to return and report to the sender. The return is mentioned in P. Hagigah 76d: "Behold we send to you a great man as our shaliach, and he is equivalent to us until such time as he returns to us." Although a constrast between human and divine agency is drawn in Mek. Ex. 12 : 1, the passage illustrates the point of return and report by an agent to his sender: "Thy messengers, O God, are not like the messengers of human beings; for the messengers of human beings must needs return to those who send them before they can report. With thy messengers, however, it is not so,... withersoever they go they are in thy presence and can report: we have executed thy commission." John does not draw this contrast between human and divine agents but applies rather the human principle of return and report also to God's agent, Jesus Christ.

(f) One question remains, namely, the actual effectuation of Jesus' mission after his return to his Father and beyond the limitation of his work in Israel. John found the solution of this problem in the halakhic rule that "an agent can appoint an agent" (Qiddushin 41a).[1]) Consequently at the completion of his own mission, Jesus said: "As thou didst send me into the world, so I have sent them into the world" (John 17 : 16).

At the last evening before his departure, Jesus therefore first made clear to the disciples the principles of agency, John 13 : 16.20, and then in his prayer reported to the Father about the sending (Ch. 17), and then after his resurrection the actual commissioning of the disciples took place: "Peace be with you. As the Father has sent me, even so I send you" (John 20: 21). Accordingly, the unity between the Father and His agent, the Son, is extended to these agents of the agent: "...as thou, Father, art in me, and I in thee, that they also may be in us, so that the world may believe that thou hast sent me" (John 17 : 21).

Thus there are striking similarities between the halakhic principles

---

[1]) There was discussion among the rabbis on this question, and some offered specific qualifications as to circumstances under which an agent could appoint an agent. See Gittin 3 : 5-6; Gittin 29b.

of agency and ideas in the Fourth Gospel, as (a) the unity between the agent and his sender—(b) although the agent is subordinate, (c) the obedience of the agent to the will of the sender, (d) the task of the agent in the lawsuit, (e) his return and reporting back to the sender, and (f) his appointing of other agents as an extension of his own mission in time and space.

III. HEAVENLY AGENT

On the basis of the analysis of agency in John one might be tempted to draw the conclusion that the Fourth Gospel represents the socalled normative and rabbinic Judaism,[1]) and not mystical Judaism which E. R. Goodenough so forcefully championed.[2]) Such a conclusion would be premature. The study so far has not explained the fact that Jesus according to John is not just a human and earthly agent but a divine and heavenly agent who has come down among men. Bultmann's hypothesis of gnostic mythology would offer an explanation of this point, since the gnostic agents were divine figures who were sent down to earth.[3])

The close similarities between agency in John and halakhic principles point in another direction. The question can be formulated in this way: Where do we find halakah applied to the heavenly world and man's relation to it? It is the merit of G. D. Scholem to have brought to the foreground the Merkabah mysticism and to have made manifest its halakhic character. Here we find a combination of halakah, heavenly figures and the heavenly world as is the case with the idea of agency in the Fourth Gospel.[4]) H. Odeberg, G. Quispel, N. A. Dahl and P. Borgen have suggested that the Fourth Gospel reflects early stages of Merkabah mysticism.[5])

Since Philo also is influenced by early Merkabah mysticism, his

---

[1]) The champion of "normative" Judaism is G. F. Moore, *Judaism*, I-III, Cambridge, Mass., 1927-1930.

[2]) See especially E. R. Goodenough, *Jewish Symbols in the Greco-Roman Period*, I, New York 1953, 3-58.

[3]) See reference in n. 2.

[4]) G. D. Scholem, *Major Trends in Jewish Mysticism*, 3rd rev. ed., New York 1961; *Gnosticism, Merkabah Mysticism and Talmudic Tradition*, New York 1960, 9-19.

[5]) H. Odeberg, *The Fourth Gospel*, Uppsala 1929; G. Quispel, ,,L'Evangile de Jean et la Gnose," in *L'Evangile de Jean, Recherches Bibliques* III, Lyon 1958, 197-208; and N. A. Dahl, *Current Issues* (ed. W. Klassen and G. F. Snyder), 124-142; P. Borgen, *Bread from Heaven*, have especially emphasized Jewish mysticism as background for John.

writings can throw ligth upon ideas in John.¹) In connection with the concept of agency, the Johannine idea of the vision of God can serve as a good point of departure for a comparison with Philo. According to John 12:45 God's agent mediates the vision of God: "he who sees me sees him who sent me." Moreover, in John the agent from God is a heavenly figure and the only one who has seen God:

> Not that any one has seen the Father
> except him who is from God:
> he has seen the Father (John 6:46).

John 6:46 as well as 1:18 ("No one has ever seen God; the only God (Son), who is in the bosom of the Father, he has made him known") are an interpretation of the theophany at Sinai. According to Ex. 33:20 there was a significant modification made to this theophany. Moses was not allowed to see the face of God; for no man can see God and live. John adds that one heavenly figure has had this full vision of God, namely the divine Son, the one who is from God.²)

The closest parallel to this heavenly figure is the idea of the heavenly Israel, "he who sees God." The idea is found in Philo, Conf. 146 and Leg. all. I 43:

> But if there be any as yet unfit to be called a Son of God, let him press to take his place under God's First-born, the Word, who holds the eldership among the angels, their ruler as it were.
> And many names are his, for he is called, "the Beginning," and the Name of God, and His Word, and the Man after His image, and "he that sees," that is Israel.
> ... the sublime and heavenly wisdom is of many names; for he calls it "beginning" and "image" and "vision of God."

Two observations support the theory that there is a connection between the Christ of the Fourth Gospel and the angel Israel. First, although there is no explicit etymological interpretation of the word Israel ("he who sees God") in John, the idea of Israel is tied together with the idea of vision in the interpretation of Jacob's vision, John

---

¹) Concerning elements of Merkabah traditions in Philo, see K. Kohler, "Merkabah," *The Jewish Encyclopedia*, Ed. I. Singer, VIII, New York 1947, 500.

²) Further discussion of ideas from the theophany at Sinai in the contexts of John 1:18 and 6:46 in M. E. Boismard, *St. John's Prologue*, Westminster, Md., 1957, 136-140; S. Schulz, *Komposition und Herkunft der Johanneischen Reden, Beitrage zur Wissenschaft vom Alten und Neuen Testament*, Funfte Folge I, (Der ganze Sammlung LXXXI), Stuttgart 1960, 40f.; N. A. Dahl, *Current Issues* (ed. W. Klassen and G. F. Snyder), 132; P. Borgen, *Bread from Heaven*, 150f.

1 : 47-51. Nathanael, the true Israelite is to see what his ancestor, Jacob/Israel saw. And the reference to the Son of Man (John 1 : 51) probably presupposes the idea of the heavenly model of Jacob/Israel.[1])

Secondly, important parallels can be seen between John and Philo as to the many other names of the heavenly figure. Both John and Philo identify him who sees with Logos (John 1 : 1,14 and Conf. 146, cf. the heavenly wisdom in Leg. all. I 43). He is furthermore called the Son, in John the only Son (μονογενής John 1 : 14; 3 : 16.18) and in Philo the firstborn Son (πρωτόγονος Conf. 146). It should be added that both John and Philo at times characterize the Logos and the Son as God.[2])

Two other parallel terms for the heavenly figure are Philo's "the Man after God's image" (see Conf. 146 and Leg. all. I 43) and John's "the Son of Man." The kinship between these two terms can be seen from the fact that both John and Philo associate this heavenly man with vision, with ascent into heaven, and with the second birth in contrast to the first birth.

At this point the ideas found in Quae. Ex. II 46 are of particular interest. Philo here says that when Moses, at the theophany at Sinai, was called above on the seventh day (Ex. 24 : 16), he was changed from earthly man into the heavenly man, and the change was a second birth in contrast to the first. John's ideas in 3 : 3-13 seem to be a polemic against the very idea expressed by Philo. John says that the vision of God's kingdom[3]) and the second birth from above are not brought about by ascent into heaven to the Son of Man. It is rather the heavenly man's descent which brings about the second birth.[4])

The conclusion is that John and Philo have in common the idea of a heavenly figure as the one who sees God, associate this figure with

---

[1]) See especially N. A. Dahl, *Current Issues*, (ed. W. Klassen and G. F. Snyder), 136-137 and foot notes with numerous references. It is even possible that the etymology of Israel meaning "he who sees God," is implied in John 1: 47-51. It would be more of pure speculation to try to find allusions to the etymology also in John 1: 18, that "No one has seen God" should render Hebrew לא איש ראה אל Concerning other places in which the idea of Israel and the vision of God are associated in John, see P. Borgen, *Bread from Heaven*, 175-177.

[2]) John 1 : 1.18; Somn. I 228-230 and Quae. Gen. II 62.

[3]) For the idea of seeing God's kingdom, see Wisd. 10 : 10.

[4]) This analysis of John 3 : 3-13 gives support to the interpretation suggested by H. Odeberg, *The Fourth Gospel*, ad loc., that v. 13 is a polemic against the idea of visionary ascent among Merkabah mystics. So also N. A. Dahl, *Current Issues*, (ed. W. Klassen and G. F. Snyder), 141; see also E. M. Sidebottom, *The Christ of the Fourth Gospel*, London 1961, 120-121.

Commentators have overlooked the importance of Quae. Ex. II 46 for the interpretation of John 3 : 3ff.

Israel, and also have in common several of the other terms and concepts which are crystalized around the same heavenly figure.

Although Philo in Conf. 146 says that Israel, "he that sees," mediates the vision of God, he does no apply the halakhic principles of agency to the concept. At this point John differs and says that the heavenly figure, the only one who has seen God, is sent as God's agent to mediate the vision. It is of interest to note that John in 8: 16-18 applies also another judicial principle to Christ and his mission. Here the Old Testament and halakhic rule of two witnesses has been applied to the idea of Jesus as the Son of the (heavenly) Father: the Father and the Son both witness.[1])

IV. CONCLUSION AND PERSPECTIVE

Thus the ideas of the heavenly figure who sees God (Israel) and ascent/descent are found in both Philo and John. Similarities have also been found between John and the rabbinic halakah about agency. The Fourth Gospel, therefore, shows that no sharp distinction can be drawn between rabbinic and Hellenistic Judaism.[2])

It has been suggested above that the Jewish background reflected in John should be characterized as early stages of Merkabah mysticism, in which we find such a combination of halakah, heavenly figures and the heavenly world. A strong support for this conclusion is found in text from Nag Hammadi, as reported by Doresse:[3])

> It [the Ogdoad] comprises a glorious palace, a throne erected upon a chariot surrounded by cherubim with faces like those of a lion, a bull, a man and an eagle. The chariot, we are told, has been taken for a model by the seventy-two gods who govern the seventy-two languages of the peoples. There are also seraphim in the forms of dragons, who perpetually glorify their lord. Near to Sabaôth stands a first-born who is named Israel, "the man who sees God".

This text shows close parallels to the ideas discussed from Philo and John, such as the heavenly Son, the firstborn who is the same as the

---

[1]) See C. H. Dodd, *The Interpretation*, 77 and H. L. Strack and P. Billerbeck, *Kommentar zum Neuen Testament aus Talmud und Midrasch*, II, Munchen 1924, ad loc.

[2]) Also E. R. Goodenough, "John a Primitive Gospel," *Journal of Biblical Literature*, LXIV, 1945, 145-182 rightly stresses the Jewish background of John. He draws, however, too sharp a distinction between legalistic rabbinism and Hellenistic (mystical) Judaism.

[3]) J. Doresse, *The Secret Books of the Egyptian Gnostics*, New York 1960, 167. (See also p. 176f.).

heavenly Israel, the man who sees God.[1]) It is significant that this heavenly figure has its place in the heavenly palace near the throne erected upon a chariot. This the influence of Merkabah traditions is unmistakable, a fact which shows that the same is the case with regard to the ideas discussed in John and Philo.[2])

Furthermore, the text from Nag Hammadi gives clear evidence for the fact that Jewish Merkabah traditions have influenced the gnostic movement. It is therefore quite probable that the ideas of heavenly agents in gnostic/Mandean literature similarly have been influenced by Jewish principles of agency and Jewish ideas of heavenly figures. In that case the gnostic agents do not explain the background of God's agent in the Fourth Gospel, as Bultmann thinks.[3]) The Fourth Gospel rather gives a clue to the Jewish background of the gnostic/Mandean mythology.

Not very long before the death of Dr. E. R. Goodenough, the eminent scholar to whose memory this volume is dedicated, I had the privilege of conversing with him about Philo of Alexandria. In the course of the conversation he said that it was the task of the younger generation of scholars to explore what light the Merkabah mysticism could throw upon Philo's work and upon Philo's relationship to rabbinic Judaism and the New Testament. The present study is meant to be a contribution towards the fulfillment of this charge given by Dr. Goodenough.[4])

---

[1]) See N. A. Dahl, *Current Issues* (ed. W. Klassen and C. F. Snyder), 136, nn. 21, 22; H. Jonas, "The Secret Books of the Egyptian Gnostics," *The Journal of Religion* XLII, 1962, 264.

[2]) See references to the works by J. Doresse and N. A. Dahl, p. 146, n. 4 and p. 147, n. 3

[3]) See references in footnote 2.

[4]) See also E. R. Goodenough, *Jewish Symbols*, I, 8 and n. 6.

THE SAMARITAN ORIGIN OF THE GOSPEL OF JOHN

BY

GEORGE WESLEY BUCHANAN
Wesley Theological Seminary

I. Views of scholars

Since the discovery of the Dead Sea Scrolls there have been several scholars who have either questioned the late date usually given to the Gospel of John or have claimed that it was the earliest of the Gospels. As early as 1945, however, Prof. E. R. Goodenough challenged the usual arguments given for a late dating of the Fourth Gospel, pointing out the problems that arise from presuming that John used Mark and Luke, and concluded that "the least likely solution of all is the one generally accepted, that the author of John took the stories from Mark."[1] Goodenough denied that the association of the Fourth Gospel with the Johannine epistles or the sacramentarianism of John required a late date. The absence of the virgin birth narrative and the different account of the eucharist, according to Goodenough, pointed to an early date for John. Hellenistic thought forms such as Light, Life, and Logos were all pre-Christian. "John," said Goodenough, "represents a primitive attempt to explain Jesus' person and work by seeing him in fulfillment of pre-Christian dreams of the Logos-Light of God made available to men."[2]

In Goodenough's judgment, that was the most important conclusion of his research. The place of origin seemed to him "relatively unimportant," but suggested "he (the author of the Fourth Gospel) might early have come in one of the Hellenistic synagogues of Jerusalem itself, or in Samaria, after the Hellenistic Christians had been dispersed in the persecution first led by Paul, or in Antioch, or in Ephesus (if you will), or in Alexandria. The strongly Semitic tone of the work, which even those admit who deny an Aramaic original, and the special feeling for Palestinian topography, make me incline to put the origin

---

[1] E. R. Goodenough, "John a Primitive Gospel," *JBL*, 64 (1945), 158.
[2] *Ibid.*, 182.

in Palestine, or to make the author a Palestinian Jew in exile."[1]

Pre-1945 scholarship

Goodenough was not the first to consider a Palestinian setting for the Gospel of John. As early as 1902, Schlatter showed that there were numerous idioms in rabbinic literature strikingly similar to expressions in the Fourth Gospel.[2] More than twenty years elapsed after Schlatter's work before Burney[3] and Raney[4] made further attempts to show the Semitic style of the author. Both believed that the gospel not only could be traced to a Semitic language, but they attempted to show that large sections of John were originally composed in Semitic poetry. Burney concluded that his evidence "should establish beyond question tha fact that the Gospel is a product of Palestinian thought."[5] Semitic style together with "the author's intimate knowledge of Palestinian topography, of Jewish festivals and customs, and of the current Messianic expectations at the time of the Lord" convinced Burney that "If the Gospel was written in Aramaic, it must surely have been written in Palestine or Syria; it could hardly have been written at Ephesus."[6] Cullmann, in 1930, supported Burney's conclusions from a comparison with *The Clementine Homilies*.[7] Shortly thereafter Torrey also published similar views. He said, "The material of our Four Gospels is all Palestinian, and the language in which it was originally written is Aramaic, then the principal language of the land; with the exception of the first two chapters of Lk, which were composed in Hebrew."[8] Torrey's conclusions were further supported by scholars like De Zwaan,[9] but most scholars held to Ephesus as the place from

---

[1] *Ibid.*, 182.

[2] A. Schlatter, *Die Sprache und Heimat des vierten Evangelisten* (Gütersloh, 1902). Revised, somewhat expanded, and more extensively interpreted in *Der Evangelist Johannes* (Stuttgart, c1960).

[3] C. F. Burney, *The Aramaic Origin of the Fourth Gospel* (Oxford, 1922) and *The Poetry of our Lord* (Oxford, 1925).

[4] W. H. Raney, *The Relation of the Fourth Gospel to the Christian Culture* (Giessen, 1933).

[5] Burney, *The Aramaic Origin of the Fourth Gospel*, 126. G. Dalman, *Jesus-Jeshua*, tr. P. Levertoff (New York, 1929), 26, said, "It is not surprising that Burney... should have considered the Gospel of John as a translation from the Aramaic original although he was not able to prove it..."

[6] Burney, *Ibid.*, 127.

[7] O. Cullmann, *Le Problème Littéraire et Historique du Romain Pseudo-Clementine* (Paris, 1930), 256.

[8] C. C. Torrey, *Our Translated Gospels* (New York, 1936), ix. See also *Documents of the Primitive Church* (New York, c1941).

[9] J. DeZwaan, "John Wrote in Aramaic," *JBL*, 57 (1938), 155-171.

which the Gospel of John originated. The reason for this conclusion is obvious. The earliest patristic report given for the Gospel relates its origin to Ephesus. Meyer, in 1884, insisted on that location, not just because of the early church witness, but "because the Gospel itself bears upon its very face proofs of its author's remoteness from Palestine, and from the circle of Jewish life..."[1] Even though scholars accepted the testimony of Irenaeus, most of them differed from Meyer and continued to relate the gospel to Palestine. Some, like Sanday[2] in 1921, following Von Dobschütz's earlier views,[3] did this by assuming that the Gospel was written by the Apostle John in his old age. This conjecture imagined that the author was only a teenager during Jesus' ministry, but wrote his Gospel during the reign of Trajan. Therefore the author who wrote in Ephesus, knew Palestine.[4] Bernard soon varied this hypothesis by suggesting that John the apostle was only one of a group of elders who actually composed the gospel in Ephesus and that the style was quite likely someone else's.[5] MacGregor thought there were three personalities involved in the composition of the Gospel. One was a young disciple of Jerusalem, not a member of the twelve, whose memoirs form a basis for the gospel. The second was the evangelist, a younger contemporary of the Jerusalem disciple. He was a Palestinian Jew who later moved to Asia Minor, residing for awhile in Antioch (a concession MacGregor made in deference to Burney) before finally settling in Asia Minor. The Evangelist wrote most of the Gospel, which was later edited by a final redactor, probably at Ephesus after the death of John of Ephesus.[6] This is only a slight variation of a theory proposed in 1902 by Wendt,[7] and explained in

---

[1] H. A. Meyer, *Critical and Exegetical Hand-Book to the Gospel of St. John*, tr. from German by W. Urwick; rev. and ed. by F. Crombie; preface by A. C. Kendrick (New York, 1884), 37.

[2] W. Sandey, *The Criticism of the Fourth Gospel* (New York, 1921), 98-99, 107-108, 121, 128-129.

[3] E. Von Dobschütz, *Probleme des Apostolischen Zeitalters* (Leipzig, 1904), 93.

[4] Sanday, *Op. cit.*, 98-99.

[5] J. H. Bernard, *A Critical and Exegetical Commentary on the Gospel According to St. John* (Edinburgh, 1928), I. lxviii-lxx. R. H. Strachan, *The Fourth Gospel* (London, c1917), 88, earlier suggested that the Elders of Ephesus were the persons who wrote John 21: 1-23 and were the ones designated "we" in John 21:24.

[6] G. H. C. MacGregor, *The Gospel of John* (New York, n.d.), lxiii-lxviii.

[7] H. H. Wendt, *The Gospel According to St. John* (Edinburgh, 1902), 211-213, said the "beloved disciple was probably John the son of Zebedee. The evangelist was a member of a Christian circle that stood in special relationship to John. It was this circle for which the Gospel was first written. The later editor, who was also the author of chapter 21, thought the author was John himself rather than just a member of his group.

greater detail by Bacon in 1933.[1] Bacon also supported Kundsin in observing that the evangelist was not interested in the geography of the Apostle John's time, but rather his own, and that the locations given were the places where Johannine communities were in greatest conflict with the Baptists and the followers of Simon Magus.[2]

Post-1945 scholarship

Some scholars since Goodenough's article have continued to be concerned about apostolic authorship. Braun,[3] Nunn,[4] Green-Armytage,[5] Edwards,[6] *et. al.* continued to uphold the traditional position in one way or another and received the criticism of Parker who showed the vast differences between the Son of Zebedee and the author of the Fourth Gospel.[7] Nearly ten years after Goodenough's article Barrett[8] and Dodd,[9] both with reservations, still accepted Ephesus as the probable place of authorship for the Gospel of John, but they also noted the author's familiarity with Palestinian geography, Jewish customs, and Semitic thought and idiom.[10] Dodd[11] and Barrett[12] both believed that John made use of a source or tradition from Palestine, which explained this familiarity. Much earlier Faure[13] followed in 1957 by Bultmann[14] and immediately afterwards by Wilkens[15] con-

---

[1]) B. W. Bacon, *The Gospel of the Hellenists* (New York, c1933), 423-429, concurred with Wendt in tracing the gospel back to the Apostle John.

[2]) Bacon, *Ibid.*, 71-72.

[3]) F.-M. Braun, *Jean le Théologien et son Évangile dans l'Église Ancienne* (Paris, 1959), I, 396-97, and "L'Arrière-Fond Judaique du Quatrième Évangile et la Communaute de L'Alliance," *RB*, 62 (1955), 5-44.

[4]) A. P. V. Nunn, *The Authorship of the Fourth Gospel* (Naperville, 1952).

[5]) A. H. N. Green-Armytage, *John Who Saw* (London, c1951).

[6]) R. A. Edwards, *The Gospel According to St. John* (London, c1954).

[7]) P. Parker, "John the Son of Zebedee and the Fourth Gospel," *JBL*, 81 (1962), 35-43.

[8]) C. K. Barrett, *The Gospel According to St. John* (London, 1955), 111, 113.

[9]) C. H. Dodd, *The Interpretation of the Fourth Gospel* (Cambridge, 1954), 424, 431, 452; *Historical Tradition in the Fourth Gospel* (Cambridge, 1963), 7.

[10]) Barrett, *Op. Cit.*, 138, 101-104, 107, 183, 193, 340, etc. Dodd, *Interpretation*, 453; *Historical Tradition*, 108, 206, 214, 240, 244-45, 309, 424. See also R. H. Lightfoot, *St. John's Gospel*, ed. C. F. Evans (Oxford, c1957), 3, 45, 47-48, 50. O. Merlier, *Le Qautrième Évangile* (Paris, 1961), 429-430, conjectured three sources plus one harmonising work and three revisions by different redactors.

[11]) Dodd, *Interpretation*, 453; *Historical Tradition*, 429.

[12]) Barrett, *Op. cit.*, 17.

[13]) Faure, "Die Alttestamentlichen Zitate im 4 Evangelium und die Quellenscheidungshypothese," *ZNTW*, 21 (1922), 107-112.

[14]) R. Bultmann, *Das Evangelium des. Johannes* (Göttingen, 1957), 78-79.

[15]) W. Wilkens, *Die Entstehungsgeschichte des vierten Evangeliums* (Zollokno, c1958), 5,30ff. Wilkens, like Faure and Bultmann, also conjectured other sources.

jectured a "Signs Source," but did not suggest that it was of Palestinian origin, even though Wilkens noted that four of the signs were performed in Galilee and three in Jerusalem.[1] Bultmann thought the "Speech Source" was of Semitic origin.[2] Cullman[3] in 1955 and Robinson[4] in 1959 wrote convincing articles to support a Palestinian origin for the Gospel of John. Robinson said that Jesus was not presented as a revelation to the Gentiles in the Gospel of John.[5] Nor does the Gospel show Jews in conflict with Gentiles. There is no instruction for admitting aliens into the fold at all. The Greeks in John were really Jews of the Diaspora in contrast to Palestinian Jews.[6] The material of the Gospel, according to Robinson, took shape in Judah, but later was reedited and prepared for Greek-speaking Diaspora Judaism as an appeal to those outside the church.[7] Cullmann, who had conjectured Palestinian setting for the Gospel of John in 1930, found more support for this position with the discovery of the Dead Sea Scrolls. The so-called Greek dualism of John is now apparent in the pre-Christian Dead Sea Scrolls, so that the Essenes, the Hellenists, and the Johannine Christians seem closely related.[8] He further said, "The Gospel of John is particularly interested in these Hellenists and their pioneer missionary work in Samaria. In fact this Gospel even undertakes a rehabili-

---

[1]) Wilkens, *Ibid.*, 30. B. Noack, *Zur Johanneischen Tradition* (København, 1954), noted many Semitisms in John but doubted that there was any "Sign Source," 113-114.

[2]) Bultmann, *Op. cit.*, 5, 29, etc.

[3]) O. Cullmann, "The Significance of the Qumran Texts for Research into the Beginnings of Christianity," *JBL*, 74(1955), 213-226, has basically the same argument as "L'Opposition contre le Temple de Jerusalem, Motif Commun de la Theologie Johannique et du Monde Ambiant," *NTS*, 5(1958-59), 157-173. The emphasis is slightly stronger on the opposition to the temple in the second article, but the major points are in both. Cullmann's conclusions about John and sectarian Christianity are supported by S. Schulz, *Komposition und Herkunft der Johanneischen Reden* (Stuttgart, c1960), 184-187. B. Reiche, "Traces of Gnosticism in the Dead Sea Scrolls?," *NTS* (1954-55), 137-141, also noted similar relationships between gnosticism and the Dead Sea Scrolls.

[4]) J. A. T. Robinson, "The Destination and Purpose of St. John's Gospel," *NTS*, 6 (1959-60), 117-131.

[5]) Robinson, *Op. cit.*, 120.

[6]) *Ibid.*, 124. Note the difference between Robinson's view and an earlier view of Strachan, *Op. cit.*, 50: "We feel instinctively that 'the Jews,' so frequently spoken of, mean for the Evangelist not merely the Jews of Palestine, but stand for that great body of organized opposition to the claims of Christ, which was represented in the Hellenistic Judaism of the Dispersion, when it came in contact with the Christian preaching."

[7]) *Ibid.*, p. 130-131.

[8]) Cullmann, *Op. cit.*

tation of the Hellenists."[1] John, he said, concurred with the Samaritans and Qumran sectarians in rejecting the temple at Jerusalem. Numerous other studies have recently been made that call attention to Semitisms,[2] the significance of the Temple cult,[3] or the interpretation of OT scripture in John, or the use of OT ideas;[4] but this evidence did not lead all scholars to accept a Palestinian origin for the Gospel of John. Smith thought it indicated that the author was trained in Alexandria.[5] Accepting Brandon's conclusion that Matthew was composed in Alexandria, Snape, in 1954, proposed the theory that John was written at about the same time in Ephesus. Palestinian Christianity came to Ephesus via Alexandria, and the pre-Pauline Johannine community at Ephesus was a daughter church of the church at Alexandria.[6] Three years later, Carroll[7] assumed that the author of the Gospel was a Gentile rather than a Jew and that he wrote of conditions in the second century rather than the first. In 1960 Teeple reacted against the claims of scholars like Albright, Cross, and Schubert who had held that as a result of the discovery of the Dead Sea Scrolls the Gospel of John must have come from Jewish Christianity. Teeple showed differences between the scrolls and John and concluded that the author was an anti-Jewish Gentile. He explained the Jewish traits of the Gospel by suggesting that the author might have been a "God-fearer" who had attended synagogues before becoming a Christian. Or he might have been a Gentile who acquired a knowledge of Judaism after he became a Christian. A third possibility is that he grew up in a pagan community

---

[1]) Cullmann, "The Significance of the Qumran Texts for Research into the Beginnings of Christianity," 122.

[2]) M.-E. Boismard, "A Propos de Jean V, 39. Essai de Critique Texetulle," *RB*, 55 (1948), 5-34; "Les Citations Targumiques dans le Quatrième Évangile," *RB*, 66 (1959), 374-378; P. Grelot, "A Propos de Jean 7:38," *RB*, 67 (1960), 224-225; "Jean VII, 38: Eau du Rocher ou Source du Temple?," *RB*, 70 (1963), 43-51.

[3]) A. Corell, *Consummatum Est* (London, 1958), 44-45; S. J. Louvain, "L'Arrière du theme johannique de vérité," *Studia Evangelica*, ed. K. Aland and others (Berlin, 1959), 311.

[4]) M.-E. Boismard, "Dans le Sein du Père," *RB*, 59 (1952), 23-29; P. Borgen, *Bread from Heaven* (Leiden, 1965); S. Schultz, "Die Komposition des Johannesprologs und die Zusammensetzung des 4 Evangeliums," *Studia Evangelica*, 355-56 and the same title in a book (Stuttgart, c1960; C. W. F. Smith, "Tabernacles in the Fourth Gospel and Mark," *NTS*, 9 (1962-63), 130-146; K. Stendahl, "A Study of the Relation of Isaiah to the Fourth Gospel," *ZNTW*, 46 (1955), 215-233.

[5]) C. W. F. Smith, *Op. cit.*, 130-146.

[6]) H. C. Snape, "The Fourth Gospel, Ephesus, and Alexandria," *HTR*, 47 (1954), 1-14.

[7]) K. L. Carroll, "The Fourth Gospel and the Exclusion of Christians from the Synagogue," *Bulletin of John Rylands Library*, 40 (1957), 31.

prior to his conversion to Christianity that had absorbed Jewish ideas and diction.[1] As early as 1950 R. Grant[2] denied the correctness of the testimony of Irenaeus on the Gospel of John,[3] and upheld the witness of Clement of Alexandria. Clement had referred to John as a "Spiritual Gospel," which Grant said meant a gnostic Gospel.[4] The "gnostic" Hellenists were in conflict with the "Ebonite" Judaisers, so in this sense the Gospel of John is a gnostic Gospel against Judaisers.[5] The author, said Grant, "lives between two worlds, the one that of the Palestinian Judaism out of which Christianity arose, the other that of Diaspora Judaism through which it reached the gentile world."[6] In preparing to teach the Greeks, the author "is compelled to reinterpret the gospel from beginning to end."[7] In a thought-provoking article that is basically sound, Van Unnik[8] said that the Christ, according to John, means the Messiah, and it holds the usual Jewish messianic expectations, such as the gathering in of the diaspora Jews. Van Unnik, commenting on Jesus' refusal to be made king, said, "It does not say that Jesus did not want, according to John, to be the king of the Jews but that he refused this manner of becoming king."[9] After he had made a strong case for believing that the concepts in the Gospel of John would have made no sense to Greeks, Van Unnik, possibly misled by Grant's article, strangely concluded "that the old tradition of Irenaeus, saying that the Fourth Gospel originated in Ephesus may be completely right."[10] Of course, Van Unnik held that it was for a *synagogue* in Ephesus, where Greeks could understand Jewish concepts, and his reasons for selecting a site in the diaspora was John 7:35: "'Where does this man intend to go that we shall not find him? Does he intend to go to the Dispersion among the Greeks and teach the

---

[1] H. M. Teeple, "Qumran and the Origin of the Fourth Gospel," *Novum Testamentum*, 4 (1960), 6-25.
[2] R. M. Grant, "The Origin of the Fourth Gospel," *JBL*, 69 (1950), 305-322.
[3] *Ibid.*, 316.
[4] *Ibid.*, 305-306.
[5] *Ibid.*, 316.
[6] *Ibid.*, 322.
[7] *Ibid.*, 322.
[8] W. C. Van Unnik, "The Purpose of St. John's Gospel," *Studia Evangelica*, 382-411.
[9] *Ibid.*, 394.
[10] *Ibid.*, 409. In his conclusion, Grant, *Op. cit.*, 322, said: "He lives between two worlds, the one that of the Palestinian Judaism out of which Christianity arose, the other that of Diaspora Judaism through which it reached the gentile world. 'Is he going to go to the diaspora of the Greeks and teach the Greeks?' (7:38). It is the Greeks who come to the Galilean disciple and ask to see Jesus (12:20-21)."

Greeks?'" Van Unnik asked, "Why this combination: dispersion among the Greeks? The Jewish Diaspora was spread all over the world: it would have been possible to speak about the dispersion in general: why is not Babylon, Egypt or Rome mentioned? There is only one explanation possible: because the writer was specially interested in this part of the world, and it is highly probable that we have here a typically Johannine piece of irony: what these Jews thought impossible, has happened, when the Christian missionaries came to that part of the world that was specifically Hellenic."[1] Van Unnik answered his own rhetorical question too easily,[2] but he has illustrated the tension that has gone into the Johannine problem of reconciling the Palestinian origins of Christianity to the patristic testimony of an Ephesian authorship of the Fourth Gospel. For many years scholars have sought satisfactory theories for reconciling all of the data. Although apostolic authorship has been a main factor for a Palestinian *Sitz im Leben* and patristic tradition, for an Ephesian origin, other reasons have been given in support of both localities. This conflict of scholarly opinion prompts a reexamination of the sources on which their conclusions were made. The first source will be the testimony of Eusebius and the second, the internal evidence provided by the Gospel of John itself.

II. Patristic testimony

Eusebius (H. E. V.viii.4) quoted Irenaeus (III.i.1) as follows: "Then John, the Lord's disciple who also reclined at his breast, himself also gave forth the gospel, while he was in Ephesus of Asia." Immediately following, Eusebius dealt with the Apocalypse of John and quoted Irenaeus concerning that author taken from a different context (H.E. V.viii.5-6; Irenaeus V.xxx. 1-3). In that context Irenaeus held that the author of Revelation lived toward the end of the reign of Domitian. In another instance, Eusebius quoted a later Dionysius' admission that the Book of Revelation was written by a certain John, but Dionysius did not believe that he was the son of Zebedee, who wrote the gospel and the catholic epistles, for the evangelist nowhere ascribed his own

---

[1] *Ibid.*, 408.
[2] There are other explanations possible, such as the proximity of the Greek Diaspora, a greater familiarity with Greeks than Babylonians, a reaction against the anti-Hellenistic feelings of the author's opponents, etc., but even if it were not possible for twentieth century scholars to think of alternate explanations, this would not mean that the one Dr. Van Unnik suggested was necessarily correct.

name, either to the gospel or to the epistles. In the gospel and the first
epistle no name was given at all, whereas in the second and third
epistles the title, elder, was given without a name. The author of
Revelation, on the other hand, referred to himself as John, but he did
not say that he was the beloved disciple, nor the brother of James, nor
the eye-witness and hearer of the Lord. If any of these qualifications
had been valid he would have used them. Dionysius commented
further that there have been many men named John, just as there had
been many named Paul and Peter, one of whom was John Mark, but
Dionysius did not believe John Mark wrote the Apocalypse because
he did not get to Asia, but returned to Jerusalem (Acts. 13:13).
Dionysius, however, believed the author of Revelation was one of the
occupants of the two tombs then at Ephesus, each of which was said
to be John's. Dionysius further compared the style and vocabulary of
the Book of Revelation with the Gospel and the Epistles and concluded that the same author could not have written both the Apocalypse on one hand and also the Gospel and epistles on the other (H.E.
VII.xxiv. 6-VII.xxv.27). Dionysius made such a point of insisting that
John was at Ephesus that scholars still locate the origin of the Gospel
at that place, but Dionysius clearly was not talking about the Evangelist and was careful to distinguish between the two Johns. His source
of information was evidently the Book of Revelation which included
letters to the seven churches, one of which was Ephesus, and probably
a tradition about the author of the Apocalypse related to Ephesus.
With this background information, he then looked for other evidence
in Ephesus related to the author of the Apocalypse, such as the two
tombs. He did not suggest that just because one of the tombs might
have been occupied by John the author of Revelation, that therefore
the other must have held the son of Zebedee. He may have meant that,
however, and later scholars have assumed that he took it for granted
that everyone knew the Apostle occupied the other tomb. Apparently
the Fourth Gospel was identified quite early with the Apostle John,
and the author of the Book of Revelation was confused with him,
because Justin Martyr[1] and Irenaeus both thought that John the son
of Zebedee wrote his gospel at Ephesus and Origen identified the
author of Revelation with the other Johannine books.[2] It is possible
that the Fourth Gospel really was composed in Ephesus, but the

---

[1]) Eusebius, *The Ecclesiastical History* IV. xviii.8.
[2]) *Ibid.*, III.xviii; V.xx,xxiv.

report of the Apostle's early death[1] and the possibility of confusing at least two of the Johns is so great that this conclusion should not be accepted unless internal evidence confirms it.[2] This will be the next step.

III. SAMARITAN BACKGROUND

Since the evidence for an Ephesian origin for the Gospel of John is quite weak, it will be necessary to consider carefully the reasons for thinking that the gospel may have come from a Palestinian *Sitz im Leben*. The evidence found in this enquiry suggests not only a Palestinian but a Samaritan Christian origin for the Gospel of John. This thesis will be defended in an examination of the Gospel of John.

Israelites and Samaritans

Nicodemus was described in John as a ruler of the Jews (3:1-2) and also a teacher of Israel (3:10). Israel here seems to be an inclusive term referring to the twelve tribes of Israel or the whole land of Palestine. In a somewhat similar use of terms in NT times, a certain Suzanna was referred to as a daughter of Judah (LXX text of Suzanna 22), the wife of an Israelite in Babylon (1-2,7) and also a daughter of Israel (LXX and Th. 48). It seems quite proper, then, to refer to a Jew also as an Israelite, but in this same document the daughters of Israel, who consented to masculine advances, were contrasted with a daughter of Judah, like Suzanna (56-57), who would not yield to them (56-57).[3] This means that in NT times the name Israel still held a distinctive connotation, meaning the Northern Kingdom as over against the

---

[1] See R. H. Charles, *A Critical and Exegetical Commentary on the Revelation of St. John* (New York, 1929), xlvii-l.

[2] Grant, *Op. cit.*, 316, said, "Our conclusion in regard to Irenaeus' statement concerning the purpose of the Fourth Gospel must surely be the denial of its correctness." Irenaeus's information about the place of authorship may also have been faulty. Parker, "John the Son of Zebedee and the Fourth Gospel," 36, said, "The fathers were by no means sure and unequivocal in ascribing this book to the son of Zebedee. While most of them thought it was by *somebody* named John, it was a very long time before any patristic writer declared, clearly and without reservation, that it was John the member of the Twelve and son of Zebedee." See also R. H. Charles, *Op. cit.*, I, xlv-l; R. A. Edwards, *Op. cit.*, 3-7; and B. P. W. Stather Hunt, *Some Johannine Problems* (London, c1958), 118-123.

[3] Th.: "And he said to him, 'You seed of Canaan and not Judah, beauty has deceived you—lust has turned away your heart. 57). Thus you used to do to daughters of Israel, and they, being afraid, used to 'associate' with you, but a daughter of Judah did not tolerate your lawlessness" (Suzanna 56-57).

Southern Kingdom, Benjamin and Judah. The Northern Kingdom was also known as Jacob, Ephraim, Joseph, and Samaria. Since this is true, it will be important to learn the meaning of Israel in the Gospel of John. Nicodemus, then, from the inclusive standpoint, was a teacher of all Israel (3:10), but he was also a Jew (3:1-2) as distinct from the Samaritans. Although he represented the highest in Judaism, Jesus told him he would have to be rebaptized and born again before he could enter the Kingdom of God (3:3-5).

When Jesus first met Nathaniel, he described Nathaniel—not as a Jew—but as a true Israelite in whom there was no guile (1:47). In response, Nathaniel said:

"Rabbi, you are the Son of God;
You are the King of Israel."

(1:49)

In the Gospel of John, Jesus was regularly referred to as the Son of God, which in this couplet had the same meaning as the King of Israel.[1] Jesus was also called the King of the Jews.[2] At his trial before Pilate, when Pilate asked if he were the King of the Jews, Jesus answered, "From yourself do you say this, or have others told you [thus] concerning me?" (18:33-34). But when Pilate asked simply, "Then, you are a king, aren't you?" Jesus responded, "You say that I am a king. I have been born for this and for this I have come into the world" (18:37). The author did not deny the tradition that Jesus had been crucified as King of the Jews (19:19), but he did not believe Jesus accepted this title nor that the rulers of the Jews approved of it (19:20-22). At the same time, Jesus acknowledged that he was a king, the King of Israel.

In the entry into Jerusalem, according to John, the crowd shouted:

"Hosanna!

---

[1]) For a consideration of the use of the title, "son of God," to mean "king," see H. Gressmann, *Der Messias* (Göttingen, 1929), 34-39, and S. Mowinckel, *He That Cometh*, tr. G. W. Anderson (New York, c1954), 123-131, 157, 360, 404.

[2]) Van Unnik, *Op. cit.*, 392, confused Israel with Judah in a very common way: "It has often been remarked that John is the only writer in the N.T. who used the original word 'Messiah' and that he speaks in the same connection of Jesus as 'the king of the Jews' (1:49)." E. A. Allen, "The Jewish Christian Church in the Fourth Gospel," *JBL*, 74 (1955), 89, said, "Nathaniel becomes the type of Jew who is studeous as well as sincere and devout." F.-M. Braun, *Jean le Théologien* (Paris, 1964), II. 56-57, identified the King of Israel of John 1:49 with the son of David in psalms of Solomon 17-18.

Blessed be he who comes in the name of the Lord,
Even the King of Israel!"

(12:13)

Parallels to this entry are as follows:
In Matthew:

"Hosanna to the son of David!
Blessed be he who comes in the name of the lord!
Hosanna in the highest!"

(Matthew 21:9)

In Mark:

"Hosanna!
Blessed be he who comes in the name of the Lord!
Blessed be the coming kingdom of our father David!
Hosanna in the highest!"

(Mark 11:9-10)

In the very place where Matthew and Mark called Jesus the son of David in his messianic entry, John, instead, called him "King of Israel." Whereas the synoptics and Paul (Rom. 1:3) confessed Jesus to be the son of David, John not only did not mention this Judaic designation, but he represented some of Jesus' opponents as taking for granted Jesus' Galilean origin and therefore held that he was not of the seed of David (7:41-42). Instead of the son of David, Jesus, in John, was called the son of Joseph (1:45; 6:42). The son of Joseph was a designation for the Messiah from Samaria just as the son of David was the Messiah from Judah.[1] In medieval Samaritan literature, Joseph was praised as a king *(Memar Marqah* I § 10), and righteous (V § 4) in contrast to Judah who sinned (IV § 6, 9). If it had not been for Joseph, in Samaritan opinion, God would not have accepted the repentence of Reuben, Simeon, and Judah (IV § 6,9).[2] While cursing Ezra and the things he had shamefully written, Samaritans anticipated the resto-

---

[1]) See further Sukkah 52a; Y. Ibn-Shmuel, *Midreshe Ge'ulah* (Jerusalem, 1953-54), 320; introduction to R. H. Charles, *Eschatology* (New York, c1963), xxii, and C. C. Torrey, "The Messiah Son of Ephraim," *JBL*, 66 (1947), 253-277.

[2]) J. Macdonald (ed. and tr.), *Memar Marqah the Teaching of Marqah* (Berlin, 1963, I, xx, has noted the familiarity of this Samaritan document with the Gospel of John. He said further, "It is possible that the traditions underlying Marqah's teaching reflect genuine Northern Israelite traditions" (p. xli). See John Macdonald, *The Theology of the Samaritans* (Philadelphia, c1964), *passim*, for the relationships between John and the Samaritans. Macdonald has assumed that Samaritans were influenced by the Fourth Gospel and not vice versa—not a necessary assumption *a priori*.

ration of the temple on Mt. Gerezim alone, with Jews asking to be admitted.[1] Medieval Jewish rabbis expected two messiahs: the one, the son of Joseph or Ephraim, was to come from Galilee. He was expected to lead the tribes of Ephraim, Manasseh, Benjamin, and part of Gad in battle against Armilos (Rome) and be killed in behalf of his people.[2] The son of Joseph was considered by medieval Jews to be the forerunner for the son of David who would destroy Armilos, claim his throne at Jerusalem, punish all the surrounding nations, and rule the people of Israel in peace.[3] The medieval Jewish expectation regarding the son of Joseph was probably not invented in the middle ages by Jews, but was recognized and put in subordinate position to the son of David expectation in the same way that the Gospel of John subordinated John the Baptist to Jesus (1:7-8, 15, 19-37).[4] John denied that Jesus was a sinner as the Jews claimed (9:16, 22-26, 31). It is not strange for a Samaritan to object to this designation from Jews, because the Samaritans were among those whom the Jews classed as sinners (see *Kuthim*), into whose cities the disciples were forbidden to enter according to Matthew (10:5-6). But the Samaritans were not treated unfavorably by John. The Jews called Jesus a Samaritan and said he had a demon. Jesus denied that he had a demon, but he did not deny that he was a Samaritan (8:48-49). Furthermore, he was willing to drink from the vessel of a Samaritan woman (4:7-28). The scene took place at the well that Jacob gave to *his son Joseph* (4:5) and recalled the scene of Rachel at the well (Gen. 24). In the same way, Nathaniel, the true Israelite, after confessing Jesus to be the King of Israel, was promised that he would see "the heaven opened and the angels of God going up and coming down upon the son of Man" (1:47-51)—a scene reminiscent of Jacob's vision at Bethel, in Samaria (Gen. 28:12).[5]

Although Israel, in the Gospel of John, may refer to all Israel, the term seems to be used from a North Israelite point of view. If this were

---

[1]) See A. Merx, *Der Messiah oder Ta'eb der Samaritaner* (Giessen, 1909), 29.
[2]) Ibn-Shmuel, *Op. cit.*, 320-323.
[3]) *Ibid*.
[4]) Scholars might consider the possibility that literature, such as the *Rule of the Community*, the *Two Column Scroll*, and the *Zadokite Document* which disclosed an expectation of a Messiah of Israel might be of North Israelite origin, whereas a document, like the *Twelve Patriarchs* which told of an expected Messiah of Judah, would be of Jewish origin.
[5]) Later Samaritans referred to Mt. Gerezim as "Beth-El," the house of God. See J. Macdonald, *The Theology of the Samaritans*, 328-330.

really so, then the Jews in John would be people of Judah who worshipped at Jerusalem in contrast to the people of Samaria who worshipped at Mt. Gerizim rather than people of the Jewish race in contrast to Gentiles. An examination will be necessary to learn whether or not this is true.

Jews and Judah

The attitude of hostility toward the Jews in the Gospel of John has been a problem to many scholars. But who were those Jews? Colwell said, "The Jews are a racial group outside the church."[1] Lightfoot[2] and Teeple[3] understood them in the same way, but noted that nonetheless there was a strong Jewish coloring in the gospel. Allen said that the author was hostile only to non-Christian Jews, but accepted "the type of Jew"[4] that Nathaniel represented. He thought the sheep in John 10 represented Jewish Christians, so that "salvation is indeed from the Jews."[5] Bultmann[6] was followed by Grässer[7] in holding that the Jews were not to be understood basically as a racial group in John, but rather theologically as a representation of the unbelieving world. Barrett said John reflected a rift between the synagogue and the church,[8] but since the author "speaks indescriminately of 'the Jew' and 'the Pharisees,'" he probably had "no clear knowledge of conditions in Palestine before A.D. 70."[9] Dodd said, "This writer uses the term οἱ ʼΙουδαῖοι imprecisely. Usually it means either (i) the general body of the Jewish people so far as they are hostile to or unfriendly to Christ, or (ii) the Jewish authorities in Jerusalem. Sometimes the two meanings are scarcely distinguished. Occasionally the term appears to be used in a geographical sense, meaning inhabitants of the province of Judaea. ('Judaeans' rather than 'Jews.')."[10] Dodd did not consider the possibility that all Jews in the Gospel of John might mean Judaeans, and he did not think the geography was a main point when it was the

---

[1] E. C. Colwell, *John Defends the Gospel* (Chicago, 1936), 44.
[2] Lightfoot, *Op. cit.*, 47-48.
[3] Teeple, *Op. cit.*, 24-25.
[4] Allen, *Op. cit.*, 89.
[5] *Ibid.*, 91.
[6] Bultmann, *Op. cit.*, 59, 213.
[7] E. Grasser, "Die antiJudische Polemik im Johannesevangelium," *NTS*, 10 (1964), 75-76, 85, 88-90.
[8] Barrett, *Op. cit.*, 280.
[9] *Ibid.*, 299; see also 145.
[10] Dodd, *Historical Tradition*, 242.

case. He said, "In any case οἱ 'Ιουδαῖοι seem always to be the enemies (or potential enemies) of Christ, and even if the geographical meaning of the term is present, the other meaning hovers about it."[1] As early as 1949 Cuming, in refutation of Lightfoot, said the Jews were Judaeans in contrast to Galileans rather than members of a different race.[2] Robinson said the conflict in John was between the true Israel and Judaism. John was not really anti-Jewish. "A true Jew and becoming a Christian are one and the same thing."[3] Schultz also objected to the accusation that John was anti-Jewish but said the evangelist only fought against lax illegitimate Judaism. John represented a sectarian Judaism in conflict with Pharisaic Judaism.[4] Cullmann was of the same opinion, but went one step further and suggested that John was very much interested in the Hellenists and their missionary work in Samaria[5] and that these Hellenists came from "a kind of Judaism close to this group."[6] This is very close to the hypothesis offered here, that the Jews were Judaeans or Palestinians who worshipped at Jerusalem and that the author came from another *Semitic* group, namely the anti-Judaean, Samaritan Christian Church.

The opponents of Jesus in the Fourth Gospel were the chief priests or high priest, the Pharisees, and the Jews. Most important for this discussion is that all three groups were from Judah. The important members of the priesthood, of course, were centered around the temple in Jerusalem, but the concentration of priests in Judah has an ancient origin. When Rehoboam fled to Jerusalem after the rebellion of Jeroboam, "the priests and Levites that were in all Israel resorted to him [Rehoboam] from all places where they lived" (II Chron. 11 : 13).[7] This left Israel with no priests considered legitimate by Judah. So Hosea could threaten that "the children of Israel shall dwell many days without king or prince [from the line of David, that is], without

---

[1] *Ibid.*, 242.

[2] G. J. Cuming, "The Jews in the Fourth Gospel," *Expository Times*, 60 (1949, 290-292.)

[3] Robinson, *Op. cit.*, 120.

[4] Schultz, *Op. cit.*, 184, 186-187.

[5] Cullmann, "The Significance of the Qumran Texts for Research into the Beginning of Christianity," 221.

[6] *Ibid.*, 224. Schlatter, *Die Sprache und Heimat des vierten Evangelisten*. 44, noted the following: "Ebenso sagt Jesus bei Johanan in Gespräch mit Nathaniel und Nikodemus 'Ισραήλ im Gespräch mit der Samaritarin und Pilatus dagegen 'Ιουδαῖος. Der messianische Name im Mund des Juden heisse: ὁ βασιλεὺς τοῦ 'Ισραήλ (1 : 50; 12 :18), im Mund des Römers ὁ βασιλεὺς τῶν 'Ιουδαίων (19 :19)."

[7] The report represents a Judaic point of view. For a Samaritan interpretation, see Macdonald, *The Theology of the Samaritans*, 20-24.

sacrifice or pillar, without ephod or terraphim" (Hosea 3:4). According to Hosea, the Israelites' only hope was to "return and seek the Lord their God, and David their king" (3:5).[1] Therefore a hostile feeling from Samaritans against the Jewish priesthood is not surprising. The Pharisees could trace their heritage of being separatists back at least to the Maccabean Revolt when Samaritans were more willing than Jews to compromise with the Hellenists,[2] or, perhaps even to the anti-Samaritan puritan movement led by Ezra and Nehemiah. Neither association would have ingratiated them with their Samaritan contemporaries or their NT descendants. The Jews, of course, were David's supporters in weakening Saul's kingdom and annihilating or rendering helpless his posterity, while taking over the Northern Kingdom. The Jabesh-gileadites who risked their lives to give Saul and Jonathan a proper burial (I Sam. 31:11-13; II Sam. 2:4-7) were not the only members of the Northern Kingdom who would not show David the same loyal support they had shown Saul.[3] Samaritans had not forgotten that it was a Jewish king, Ahaz (II Kings 16) who paid Tiglathpileser to sack Syria and weaken Israel so that it could later be taken into captivity (II Kings 17). The Samaritans also still remembered that the Jewish king, John Hyrcanus I, sent his sons to attack Samaria, force such conditions of famine upon them that the Samaritans were required to eat food not permitted by dietary laws, and afterwards the Jews razed the city to the ground and reduced its inhabitants to slavery (Josephus, *B.J.* I. 7 [64-66]). Medieval Samaritan literature said the Lord called Israel, "first born son," "special people," "holy," and "king." "Whoever does not preserve his Kingdom (ממלכתה), Judah is better than he *"(Memar Marqah* IV § 10). There is no hostility from outside the country that could compare with this

---

[1] The text is: 35 אחר ישבו בני ישראל
ובקשו את יהוה אלהיהם ואת דוד מלכם
ופחדו יהוה ואת טובו באחרית הימים

W. R. Harper, *A Critical and Exegetical Commentary on Amos and Hosea* (New York, 1905), 223, believed ואת דוד מלכם to be a gloss. This may be correct, but if so, באחרית הימים should also be considered a gloss to maintain the passage in poetry. Perhaps Harper was led to this judgment because he had already concluded that Hosea was a product of North Israel—a theory that is far from being proved.

[2] II Maccabees 6:2; Josephus, *Ant.* XII (257-64). Again, these are Judaic interpretations.

[3] David had gained support from the very Philistines Saul fought. When David fled from Absalom, Ittai and six hundred soldiers from Gath were among David's ranks (II Sam. 15:18-22). As late as the Maccabean period a fortress above Jericho bore the name, "Dagon" (Josephus, *B.J.* I [56]).

inner-family quarrel that had gone on for hundreds of years, mostly under terms that oppressed Samaria.[1] This hostility is reflected in the Gospel of John, but it is not anti-Semitism. This was an inner-Semitic quarrel in which the author was anti-Judaic.

Although the Jews were pictured as oppressors in John,[2] Jesus was recognized by the Samaritan woman as a Jew who believed salvation was from the Jews (4:9,22). He also had some disciples from the Jews but he did not trust them (8:31-41). Jesus was crucified as King of the Jews, but did not accept the title (18:33-19:22). His disciples (13:35) were called children (τεκνία) in distinction from the Jews (13:33). Jesus resisted his "brothers'," urging that he go to Jerusalem for the Feast of the Tabernacles (7:1-9). When he later went up (7:14ff.), he found himself in constant conflict with the Jews and Pharisees there who accused him of being a Samaritan (and therefore not a Jew in the sense that they were Jews (8:48). The Jews from Jerusalem (10:22-24) took up stones to stone him (10:31) at which time Jesus left Judah and went into Transjordan (10:40). Later he went again up to Judah (11:7) against the judgment of his disciples, because they remembered that the Jews there were seeking to stone him (11:8). After the raising of Lazarus at Bethany in Judah, Jesus finally left, no longer to walk about openly in Judaea. He went instead to a city called Ephraem, apparently a city in the tribe of Ephraem or Samaria (11:54).[3] The statement that a prophet is without honor in his own country (4:44), in Matt. 13:57 and Mark 6:4 was said just after Jesus came into his home country (Matt. 13:54; Mark 6:1) which was not named. Luke's expansion filled in the uncertainty by calling it Nazareth (Luke 4:16), but in John this was said before Jesus went to Galilee and his "own country" was classed together with Judah which he had just left (4:54). In Samaria Jesus was received with honor. When he went to his

---

[1]) See also Avi-Yonah *Geschichte der Juden im Zeitalter des Talmuds* (Berlin, 1962) 242.

[2]) See Colwell, *Op. cit.*, 45-46.

[3]) J. W. Jack, *Samaria in Ahab's Time* (Edinburgh, 1929), 1, fn. 1, said, "Ephraim (?'fertile region') was in reality a city (II Ch. 13:19; II S. 13:23), generally identified with modern *eṭ' Ṭaiyibeh*, south of Shechem, though the name was also applied to the tribe and afterwards to the northern kingdom. Mount Ephraim (הר אפראים) Jos 17:15; 19:50, etc.) was the designation of the western range of the hills (a single compact *massif*) from Esdrailon as far south at least as Bethel, just as Mount Judah (הר יהודה) was given to the whole tableland of Judah (Jos. 21:11, where the expression is translated 'hill country of Judah')." See also Jack's map between pages 70 and 71, and Josephus, *B.J.* IV (550-551), where Ephraim is listed with three other Samaritan locations.

own regions, his own people (the Jews) did not receive him (1:11). But in Samaria the fields were white with harvest (4:35), and many Samaritans came to believe in him (4:39).

In NT times the "house of Israel" from a Jewish point of view included Galilee but excluded Samaria (Matt. 10:5-6). This was because Galileans worshipped at Jerusalem and were therefore called Jews. On this basis Jesus, who was from Galilee (7:41) was called a Jew in the Gospel of John (4:9). This widens the geographical area of Judaism in John but does not distract from Palestinian limitations for the Jews in the Gospel of John.[1] In some cases the context requires that the Jews be understood locally because they were those who either lived in Judah or who had come to Jerusalem for the feasts held there. In the Fourth Gospel, the term, Jew, always makes good sense meaning a non-Samaritan Palestinian. In the Gospel of John, which has been recognized by scholars for many years as being the Gospel that gives the most accurate details about topography and geography, it is more than likely that the Jews mentioned also refer to citizens of a certain geographical area.[2] Furthermore the familiarity of the author with Near Eastern customs, idioms, and thought forms shows that he was very familiar with Palestinian Judaism. In fact, he thought in concepts very much like those of the Jews he maligned, except that they were his enemies. The person best qualified for this role would have been a Samaritan, a "true Israelite" (1:47).

Samaria and the prophets

The Gospel of John shows more interest in prophets than any of the Synoptic Gospels, but not those like Amos and Hosea, who criticized North Israel. Instead, his greatest interest was in the North Israelite prophets, Elijah and Elisha.[3] This is made apparent by comparing the signs Jesus performed with the miracles of Elijah and Elisha:

---

[1]) Contra Cumings, *Op. cit.*

[2]) For recent confirmations of this judgment in the light of modern archaeology, see S. Temple, "Geography and Climate in the Fourth Gospel," *The Joy of Study*, ed. S. E. Johnson (New York, 1951), 65-72; R. D. Potter, "Topography and Archaeology in the Fourth Gospel," *Studia Evangelica*, 329-337; Barrett, *Op. cit.* 102; Dodd, *Historical Tradition*, 139-140, 180, 236-38, 244-45, 309-310.

[3]) Judah did not assess the North Israel prophets favorably at first. Saul's association among the prophets was told to his discredit (I Sam. 10:9-13; 19:23-24). Amos would not accept the title "prophet" or "prophet's son." The Judaean revision of I and II Kings (I and II Chronicles) omitted the narratives about Elijah and Elisha.

Elisha Parallels	Miracles of Elijah	Miracles of Elisha
2	I. Stopped rain (I Kgs. 17:1-6)	1. Divided waters of Jordan (II Kgs. 2:14)
5,8,9	II. Provided widow's meal and oil (I Kgs. 17:8-16)	2. Purified water at Jericho (II Kgs. 2:19-23)
6,7,10,14	III. Revived widow's son (I Kgs. 17:17-24)	3. Called bears to destroy 42 boys (II Kgs. 2:23-24)
4	IV. Called down fire from heaven (I Kgs. 18:1-40)	4. Filled stream bed with water (II Kgs. 3:13-20)
3,11,13	V. Fire consumed Ahaziah's soldiers (II Kgs. 1:9-10)	5. Filled sons of prophet's wife's oil jars (II Kgs. 4:1-7)
	VI. Fire consumed Ahaziah's soldiers (II Kgs. 1:11-12)	6. Provided son for Shunamite woman (II Kgs. 4:8-17)
1,12	VII. Elijah parted waters of Jordan (II Kgs. 2:8)	7. Revived Shunamite's son (II Kgs. 4:18-37)
		8. Purified stew (II Kgs. 4:38-41)
		9. Multiplied loaves (II Kgs. 4:42-44)
		10. Cured commander's leprosy (II Kgs. 5:1-14)
		11. Afflicted Gehazi with leprosy (II Kgs. 5:19-27)
		12. Made ax head float (II Kgs. 6:1-7)
		13. Struck Syrians with blindness (II Kgs. 6:15-19)
		14. Man revived who touched Elisha's bones (II Kgs. 13:21)

When Elisha was granted a double portion of Elisha's spirit (II Kgs. 2:9-12), he evidently was given power to perform twice as many miracles as Elijah, but they were of the same nature. Elijah performed seven miracles, Elisha, fourteen, and Jesus, according to the Fourth Gospel, performed seven signs, which were very similar to those of the Israelite prophets, except that Jesus was credited with more healing miracles and none of the destructive miracles:

Elijah Parallel	Elisha Parallel	Signs of Jesus
II	2,4,5,8	1. Changed water into wine (2:1-11)

Elijah Parallel	Elisha Parallel	Signs of Jesus
	10	2. Healed centurion's son (4:46-54)
		3. Healed lame man at pool (5:2-9)
II	9	4. Multiplied loaves (6:4-14)
VII	1,12	5. Walked on water (6:16-21)
	13	6. Healed blind beggar at pool of Siloam (9:1-7)
III	7,14	7. Raised Lazarus (11:1-44)

"Wedding at Cana"

Jesus (John 2:1-11)	Elijah (I Kgs. 17:1-6)	Elisha (II Kgs. 4:1-7)
1. Woman recognized need; host unable to fulfill hospitality obligation.	Woman in need; embarrassed by hospitality obligation.	Woman in need; unable to meet obligation of creditor.
2. Asked Jesus for help.		Asked Elisha for help.
3. Response seemed unreasonable: "What have you to do with me?"	Request seemed unreasonable.	Response: "What shall I do for you?"
4. Mary: "Do whatever he tells you."	Elijah: "Do as you have said."	
5. Jesus ordered jars filled with water and taken to the steward.		Elisha ordered jars brought and filled.
6. Order fulfilled.	Order fulfilled.	Order fulfilled.
7. Abundance of wine.	Abundance of meal and oil.	Abundance of oil.
8. Hospitality obligation paid.	Hospitality obligation paid.	Financial obligation paid.

The miracles of Elisha are similar enough to each other in instances where he provided for people, that the Johannine sign has parallels with all of them (II Kgs. 2:19-20; 3:13-20; 4:38-41). But the parallels involving women, both with Elijah and Elisha, are closer types from which the Johannine story was probably formed.

"Centurion's Son"

Jesus (John 4:46-54)
1. Official's son ill.
2. Came to Jesus for help.
3. Jesus questioned his faith.
4. Jesus told him to leave; his son was well (distance healing).

5. Officer believed and left.

6. Son (a child) was well.

Elisha (II Kgs. 5:1-14)
Army officer had leprosy.
Came to Elisha, the Samaritan prophet (5:3), for help.

Elisha sent messenger to give directions (distance healing).
(3) [John out of sequence] Officer questioned that this would work.
Officer decided to follow instructions.
Officer's flesh restored like that of a child.

Two other healing miracles Jesus performed took place at pools. The first man healed (5:2-9) expected to have to be dipped in the pool as Naaman was directed by Elisha to go and wash, but Jesus told him to get up, take his cot, and walk. The blind man at the Pool of Siloam (9:1-7), however, was instructed to wash in the pool as Naaman had been told to bathe in the Jordan. Like Naaman, after he had done so, he was healed; he had received his sight.

"Multiplication of Loaves"

Jesus (John 6:4-14)
1. Great crowd arrived at Passover time.
2. Andrew brought boy with barley loaves[1]) and fishes.

3. Andrew, Jesus' disciple, said it was not enough.
4. Jesus blessed the food and had it distributed.

5. All ate and were filled and twelve baskets full of food were left over.

Elisha (II Kgs. 4:42-44)
Sons of prophets gathered.

Man from Beal-shalishah came with loaves of barley and fresh grain.
Elisha's servant said there was not enough.
Elisha commanded that the men be fed and promised some would be left.
All ate and they had some left as Elisha promised.

There is some resemblance between these miracles and the occasion when Elijah multiplied the meal and the oil for the widow (I Kgs. 17:1-6). In all instances, hospitality was required of people who apparently

---

[1]) John is the only gospel that agrees with II Kings in specifying that *barley* loaves were multiplied.

had not enough to provide it. In all instances the prophet involved performed a miracle which made the small amount of food there was become more than enough.

"Nature Miracles"

The power Jesus had over the forces of nature were shown in his ability to walk on the water (6:16-21). The same power was shown by Elijah and Elisha when they divided the waters of the Jordan and walked across on dry land (II Kgs. 2:8,14). Elisha showed that he had a double portion of his master's spirit by also making an ax head float (6:1-7). Details of these miracles are not very close.

"Raising the Dead"

Jesus (John 11:1-44)	*Elijah (I Kgs. 17:17-24)*	*Elisha (II Kgs. 4:18-37)*
1. Jesus had special relationship with family at Bethany.	Elijah had received hospitality from widow of Zerephath.	Elisha had received special hospitality from Shunamite woman.
2. Lazarus became ill and died.	Widow's son became ill and died.	Shunamite woman's son became ill and died.
3. Mary and Martha blamed Jesus: "If you had been here, my brother would not have died."	Widow blamed Elijah for son's death.	Shunamite blamed Elisha for deceiving her by giving a son and taking him away.

Some other details suggest that these similarities are more than coincidental. The picture of the Shunamite woman weeping at Elisha's feet after the death of her son (II Kgs. 4:27) resembles Mary who fell at Jesus' feet after the death of her brother (John 11:32). The resurrection miracle was the seventh miracle that Elisha performed and also the seventh that Jesus performed. Since Elisha had a double portion of Elijah's spirit, he also performed a second resurrection miracle, even after his death, when a corpse that touched his bones revived (II Kgs. 13:21). This was Elisha's fourteenth miracle. The miracles of Elisha follow a type that is similar to the miracles of Elijah. This does not mean that every miracle Elijah performed had exactly two counterparts in the Elisha stories. One has no parallel and another has four, but some are closer than others, and the total is exactly twice as many as Elijah had performed. The miracles of Jesus in the Gospel of John follow the typologies of Elijah and Elisha to about the same degree, being closer to the miracles of Elisha than Elijah.[1]

After Jesus fed the multitude with barley loaves as Elisha had done, the people referred to him as "the prophet" (John 6:14). In I and II Kings, "the prophet" always refers to Elisha, never Elijah unaccompanied by his name (such as I Kgs. 18:36; for Elisha, see II Kgs. 20:22; 5:13; 6:12; 9:4). Furthermore, Elisha was called „the prophet" in Samaria (II Kgs. 5:3), and Jesus, in Samaria, was recognized as a prophet (John 4:19). The Pharisees asked John the baptist if he were the Messiah, Elijah, or "the prophet" (1:25). "The prophet" following the new Elijah would have been the new Elisha, although according to John, the baptist qualified for none of these. But after the ascension of Elijah, his disciples followed Elisha (II Kgs. 2:15-18) just as the disciples of John followed Jesus (John 1:37). It was at the Jordan that John baptized so that Jesus might be revealed to "Israel." It was also there that John said he had seen the spirit descending upon Jesus (1:29-34). It was also at the Jordan where Elijah gave up his mantel and Elisha received a double portion of Elijah's spirit (II Kgs. 2:6-15). After the ascension of Elijah fifty men "sought him but they did not find him" (II Kgs. 2:17). Jesus likewise told the Pharisees, "You will seek me and you will not find me; where I am you cannot come" (John 7:34). Just as Elijah surrendered his leadership and disciples to Elisha, so John decreased while Jesus increased (John 3:30).

The obvious question at this point is: if Jesus was interpreted as the new Elisha in the Gospel of John, why did he not perform fourteen

---

[1]) Several efforts have been made to compare the Gospel of John with the Exodus typology, comparing the signs in John with the plagues of Egypt, considering Jesus as a prophet to be a second Moses, etc. H. Sallin, *Zur Typologie des Johannesevangeliums* (Uppsala, 1950); J. J. Enz, "The Book of Exodus as a Literary Type for the Gospel of John," *JBL*, 76 (1957), 208-215; R. H. Smith, "Exodus Typology in the Fourth Gospel," *JBL*, 81 (1962), 329-342; *et al.* Some of these suggestions are thought-provoking and may be correct. It is possible *a priori* for an author to have had John and Jesus parallel Aaron and Moses at the same time they paralleled Elijah and Elisha and even Eli and Samuel, for that matter. But parallels such as the Book of the Covenant (Ex. 20-23) with the "new commandment" of John 13:34 and Moses's finishing his work (Ex. 40:33b) with "It is finished" of John 19:30 (Enz, 210-211) or comparing the water turned into blood with the water turned into wine (Ex. 7:14-24; John 2:1-11) (Smith, 338) are not such striking parallels as the miracles of Elijah and Elisha. The healing of the official's son (John 4:46-54), for instance, is a closer parallel to the healing of the official by proxy at a distance by Elisha (II Kgs. 5:1-14) than to the plague on animals (Ex. 9:1-7) as Smith suggests (338). C. Goodwin, "How did John Treat his Sources," *JBL*, 73 (1954), 62, noted, "Five times he refers to the Prophet that was to come, but he never quotes Deut. 18:15ff."

miracles as Elisha had done. The answer is that originally the "signs" section in the Gospel of John probably existed as a separate document which included fourteen miracle stories attributed to Jesus. This then was later abridged; the number of miracles reduced in half; the prologue, the passion narrative, and the synoptic pericope (John 7: 53-8:11) added to make a Gospel out of a document patterned originally after I and II Kings, or at least the section of those books containing the Elijah-Elisha narratives. This conjecture will require more support than is briefly offered here, but this sort of a hypothesis would help explain the unevennesses in style and discontinuity of narrative now found in John. Many scholars have sought to reorganize the text to make the narrative continuous or explain its present lack of continuity.[1] It seems strange, for instance, for Jesus to have been in Jerusalem (5:1) and then to have crossed the Sea of Galilee (6:1) without traveling from Jerusalem to the Sea of Galilee. If the document had once been twice as large and composed of miracle stories, the editor who abridged the text probably had before him a text whose narrative was as unified geographically as the individual pericopes of John now are. But in choosing the seven best miracle stories, he necessarily broke the continuity. That the text as it is has been abridged and has omitted some of the signs is suggested by the summary in 20:30 which Faure, Bultmann, *et al.* accept as a part of the sign source: "Now Jesus did many other signs in the presence of the disciples which are not written in this book." Also the efforts made to show that John the Baptist was not Elijah even though in many ways he and John appear in the Gospel comparable to Elijah and Elisha, may indicate that the editor was intentionally omitting the Elijah sections of a book about John and Jesus as typologies of Elijah and Elisha. The original document may have shown both John and Jesus in the same critical relationship to Jerusalem leaders that Elijah and Elisha held toward the national leaders at Samaria.

This attempt to imagine non-existing documents, of course, is conjecture and not fact. But the major thrust of these arguments point to a Samaritan origin for the Gospel of John whether or not all of the details are correct. The Israelites in John appear to have been Samaritans and were viewed appreciatively; the Jews appear to have been

---

[1] Bultmann, *passim*; Barrett, *Op. cit.*, 18-21; Wilkens, *Op. cit.*, 4-5, 30; O. Merlier, *Op. cit.*, 426-27, 429-430; Faure, *Op. cit.*, 99-122; P. Parker, "Two Editions of John," *JBL*, 75 (1956), 303-314. Noack, *Op. cit.*, *passim*. S. Temple, "A Key to the Composition of the Fourth Gospel," *JBL* (1961), 221-232.

citizens of Judah and/or Galilee who worshipped at Jerusalem. They, together with the special classes of Judaeans, priests, and Pharisees, were always shown in conflict with Jesus. The author knew well the geography, topography, and customs of Palestinian Jews and Samaritans and their relationships together. He spoke and thought in Semitic idiom. He showed far greater knowledge of the country of Samaria than any other Gospel and devoted more space to Samaria and Samaritans than the Synoptic Gospels. His attitude toward the OT prophets and history was sympathetic with Israel's position more than Judah's.

The author may not have resided in Samaria, though that is the most likely conjecture. He may have been a member of the Diaspora and lived in Antioch, Ephesus, Alexandria, or any other possible location Goodenough would have approved. But if he belonged to a congregation in the Diaspora, then it was a congregation of the North Israelite Diaspora that had become Christian and maintained contacs with Samaria,[1] because the author was familiar with the geography at well as the feelings of first century Samaritans.

IV. THE AUTHOR AND THE APOSTLE JOHN

The problem that has claimed scholars' attention for many years is the relationship of the apostle, John, and the Fourth Gospel. A Samaritan *Sitz im Leben* for the Gospel might add some further data for consideration on this point.

When Paul returned to Jerusalem from Asia Minor for a conference with the Judaizing apostles, members of the council all agreed that Paul should go to the "nations" and James, Cephas, and John, would minister to the "circumcised" (Gal. 2:7-9). Paul's ministry to the nations, however, was not really limited to the physically uncircumcised (I Cor. 7:18-19; Gal. 5:6; 6:15; Col. 3:11). Instead he served both the circumcised and the uncircumcised among the "nations"—i.e. Asia Minor, and he planned to move farther west. The contrasting term, "circumcised," under the jurisdiction of other apostles, was evidently used in a general way to describe those within the territory promised to Abraham's seed rather than people physically circumcised.[2] When the apostles divided their duties, they seem to have done

---

[1]) For Samaritans in the Diaspora see Josephus, *Ant.* XII (10).

[2]) Ned. 3:11 seems to support a general use of the term, "uncircumcised" to mean those outside the Land of Palestine, circumcised or not and "circumcised" was taken to mean those inside the Land, circumcised or not, such as Goliath (I

it territorially, and Paul's division was to the "nations"—apparently meaning the inhabited world outside Palestine. Antioch was somewhere near the Northern boundary of the apostolic division of territory, because it was there that Paul and Cephas had contacts in their ministry. At first Cephas was willing to abide by the rules used in Pauline territory, but under the correction of "certain ones from James" (2:12), Cephas observed exclusive dietary rules. According to Eusebius, James was the first bishop in Jerusalem after the ascension of Jesus.[1] This seems reasonable, since those from James evidently were not always on hand. They had come from a distance, when they observed Cephas at Antioch. Cephas, on the other hand, was close by. He seemed to be ministering to the Christians in the North, perhaps Galilee and Syria. The concentration of geographical locations mentioned in the Gospel of Matthew, the gospel which heralded Peter as the rock of Christ's church (16:18), is in Galilee and Syria.[2] The territory between Jerusalem and North Palestine is Samaria, where the Gospel of John has disclosed the greatest familiarity with the geography. Without identifying authors, it is possible to put together these loose pieces to make a reasonable conjecture concerning the division of the church from which some of the canonical documents originated and the apostles to which they were attached: with James in Jerusalem and Cephas/Peter around Galilee and Syria, then John would have been allocated Samaria, the only territory left among the "circumcised" where his ministry took place (Gal. 2:7-9). With Paul in charge of "the nations" the whole Roman world was divided among the three great apostles and Paul. There is no reference to the apostles in the Gospel of John. The reason for this is probably that their headquarters were in the Judaic city at Jerusalem. A popular church leader in the Gospel was Philip (John 1:43-48; 6:5-7; 12:21-22; 14:8-9). According to Acts (6:5; 8:5-40), it was Philip who began the missionary work in

---

Sam. 17:36), in reality an uncircumcised Gentile and idolator, but one who lived within the territory considered the heritage of Israel. In which case, the "uncircumcised of Israel" would mean Gentiles in Palestine. If, instead, "Israel" were here understood to mean "Israelite," then the "uncircumcised of Israel" could only be Jewish males under eight days of age (and not yet really Jews), males exempted from circumcision for health reasons, etc.

[1]) H. E. II.xxiii, 1; II v.2; See also Acts 21:17-18 and Clementine Homilies XI.xxv.

[2]) So W. R. Farmer, "The Provenance of Matthew," *The Teacher's Yoke: Studies in Memory of Henry Tratham*, ed. E. J. Vardaman and others (Waco, 1964), 109-116. *Recognitions of Clement* I.xii also indicated that Peter's headquarters were at Caesarea Stratoni.

Samaria. After it had begun, the apostles, Peter and John, investigated the work and approved it (Acts 8:14-17). John may then have been the apostle in charge of Samaria, even though he did not do all of the work there. He may have had the same supervisory responsibility over Samaria that Paul had over Colossae, Hierapolis, and Leodicia, where Epaphras was the local pastor (Col. 1:2; 2:1; 4:12-17). To Samaritan Christians John could have been the one accepted as the "beloved disciple," just as to North Palestinian Christians, Cephas was the rock on which Christ would build his church. To the Church in Jerusalem, James was considered "the just." Paul was the great apostle in Asia Minor who ministered to the "uncircumcised." Documents composed from the churches founded by these particular leaders might have been ascribed to them, even though they were not the authors themselves. For instance, the pastoral epistles came from Asia Minor, Paul's churches, even though he did not write them. The essay attributed to James may have come from the Jerusalem church. Whether or not John is accepted as the founder of the Samaritan Church, it is clear that the Gospel attributed to John came from the Samaritan Christian Church.

---

[1] Read at the Society of Biblical Literature meeting, Nashville, Tennessee, December, 1965.

THE EARLIEST HELLENISTIC CHRISTIANITY

BY

ROBIN SCROGGS
Dartmouth College

Increased sensitivity to the pervasiveness of Hellenistic culture in Palestine is of crucial importance not only to better understanding of early Judaism, so greatly enriched by Professor Goodenough's researches, but necessary as well in any attempt to reassess the earliest beginnings of Christianity. For too long the old scheme has seemed in convenient to give up, that the earliest Christianity was uninfluenced by Hellenistic thought and culture, so that materials suggesting this influence reflect a non-Palestinian milieu and a later date than the 'Jewish' materials. Of course not many scholars have in recent years used this scheme in a rigid way; yet it stubbornly persists as a basic pattern. The fact is, however, that one need look no further than Jerusalem, not to speak of Galilee or Syria, to find all the presuppositions necessary for Hellenistic influence on the gospel.[1] In similar fashion, many scholars have for long been questioning the reliability of Acts as an historical document, particularly with regard to the basic historiographical and theological patterns stressed by its author. Yet how often does the view, that Christianity was from the first led by the former disciples in Jerusalem, from there gradually radiating out towards Greece and Rome, through Antioch, and always under the authority or pressure of the Jerusalem apostles, keep coming back to haunt us.

Acts does present us, of course, with an apparent exception in the figure of the Hellenistic Stephen. But while few have doubted that there was such a person or that there were such Hellenistic Jews in the Jerusalem church as Acts 6f explicitly asserts, scholarship has in general not known what to make of this evidence. Partly the perplexity is due to uncertainty about how to assess these chapters; partly it is due to the seeming disappearance of Stephen's followers due to

---

[1] As is pointed out by Goodenough, *Jewish Symbols in the Greco-Roman Period*, XII (New York, 1965), 55f.

the persecution and dispersion. As a result Stephen appears to many scholars as an isolated instance, a typical case of a man too radical to survive in his culture. In his very suggestive book on Stephen, Simon well sums up this viewpoint. "That Stephen stands as an almost solitary figure among the leaders of the first Christian generation seems pretty sure. His theological thought, with its strong anti-ritualistic trend, culminating in a deliberate hostility towards the Temple, is very personal and, if compared with other forms of primitive Christian thought, almost completely aberrant."[1] The point of this paper will be to argue the reverse: that in the Hellenistic Christians of Jerusalem is to be found the beginning of that Christian mission which in an apparently unbroken line advanced through Samaria and Antioch to the western world.[2] It is the beginning of that church which lay behind Paul and his fellow missionaries, in short the beginning of that church which was to survive to become the mother of western Christianity.

Purely apart from the evidence of Acts, a Christianity in contact with Gentiles can with some assurance be claimed for the earliest days of the church in Palestine.[3] Ernst Käsemann has demonstrated that in the material embedded in Matthew's gospel can be found evidence of a struggle between two early Christian viewpoints or churches.[4] One church, which is violently opposed by the Matthean material, has begun a mission to Gentiles and Samaritans (Matt. 10:5). Concomitantly it has rejected the law or at least reduced its requirements (Matt. 5:19). This church has as well emphasized the powers of the spirit as a criterion for the authentication of the believer (Matt. 7:21-23). I have argued elsewhere that material emanating from this group can be found in certain strata of the gospel of Mark, with the exception that the Markan material is favorable to the views of this church, not opposed

---

[1]) Marcel Simon, *St. Stephen and the Hellenists in the Primitive Church* (London, 1958), p. 98.

[2]) Cf. the discussion in B. W. Bacon, *The Gospel of the Hellenists* (New York, 1933), pp. 65-90.

[3]) Oscar Cullmann has been arguing this point in several recent articles, e.g., *The Early Church* (Philadelphia, 1956), pp. 185-92; *The Scrolls and the New Testament*, ed. K. Stendahl (New York, 1957), pp. 18-32; "L'Opposition contre le Temple de Jérusalem, Motif commun de la Théologie Johannique et du Monde Ambiant," *NTS*, V (1958-59), 157-73.

[4]) Cf. "Satze heiligen Rechtes im Neuen Testament," *NTS*, 1 (1954-55), 248-60; "Die Anfange christlicher Theologie," *ZTK*, 57 (1960), 162-85; "Zur Thema der urchristlichen Apokalyptik," *ZTK*, 59 (1962), 257-84. An earlier suggestion in the same direction was made by F. Jackson and K. Lake, *The Beginnings of Christianity* (London, 1920), I, 314-17.

as is the Matthean.[1] It might be added here that Mark 7:1-23 is further evidence of the views of this church. The traditions-history of the section is complex. What may be the original logion of Jesus in verse 15 has been gradually expanded until it has become a definite pronouncement against the food laws of the Torah, and the editorial comment of Mark (19*b*) makes certain no one will mistake the point.[2] Jesus himself, as far as our evidence goes, never made a programmatic denial of the validity of the Torah, and the law-free church gradually felt increasing need to have the authority of Jesus for its position. The material in Matthew cited above is also Käsemann's evidence for the existence of a church with opposing views. The law is maintained, and the criterion of the true believer is his obedience to the right interpretation of the law. The mission is limited to Jews, and even Samaritans are excluded. Certainly it is no accident that Matthew has so changed Mark 7 that Jesus is made to attack not the food laws found in the Torah but the purification laws of rabbinic tradition.[3]

As Käsemann has demonstrated,[4] the material in Matthew is very early, apparently going back to the beginning days of the church in Judea and perhaps in Galilee. The hostility to the Gentiles in the Matthean material certainly does not fit Matthew's own viewpoint (cf. Matt. 28:19f). Nor does the material in Mark always seem equatable with the final author's standpoint, insofar as this can be determined. Since Matthew probably was composed somewhere in Palestine or Syria, it is almost beyond doubt that the church which has turned to the Gentiles (and obviously to the Samaritans as well) existed in Palestine and/or Syria many years prior to the final redaction of the gospel. Furthermore, in the view of this writer, the arguments of Lohmeyer and Marxsen, that Mark was composed in or near Galilee, are convincing. Should this be the case, the Gentile coloring of this gospel need not be attributed to influence from churches in Greco-Roman areas but rather to Galilean or Syrian Christianity.

These two churches then existed side by side in the same geographical areas. With the church that limited itself to Jews I am not con-

---

[1] "The Exaltation of the Spirit by Some Early Christians," *JBL*, 84 (1965), 363-65, 373.

[2] Cf. V. Taylor, *The Gospel According to St. Mark* (London, 1957), p. 343.

[3] Matt. 15:1-20. Vss. 12-14 distinguish between the laws of God and those of men; the Markan explanation that Jesus by these words declared all foods clean (Mark 7:19*b*) is omitted and replaced by vs. 20 which interprets the words rather as opposed to the purification traditions.

[4] Cf. especially *NTS*, 1 (1954/55), 248-60.

cerned here. Unfortunately, at the present state of research, not too much can be said about the other community. For convenience it may be called the Gentile-centered church, since both Jews and Gentiles must have belonged to the same groups.[1] Aside from relaxation of the law and emphasis upon gifts of the spirit, however, not much can be conjectured. On the crucial issue of christology, for example, despite attempts that have been made, it is still unclear what distinctive elements, if any, are to be attributed to this church. Nor can it be said whether or not these Gentile-centered communities were led to any radical Hellenistic statement of the gospel. The evidence we possess from the Synoptics seems to me to suggest that in the main the issues confronting them were couched in biblical and apocalyptic categories. Certainly, however, we can imagine that the Hellenistic milieu which increasingly would be apparent in these groups must have been an important factor in the responses to the categories given them by the tradition.

The question then arises: Is it possible to trace this Gentile-centered viewpoint back to its origins? To suggest Paul as the creator of this church is impossible. The synoptic materials show no evidence of specific Pauline emphases and almost certainly stem from geographical areas untouched by Paul. It is much more likely that Paul can be explained by the prior existence of such a Gentile-centered community. Stephen and his followers is a much more obvious source, but to make such a claim in the face of the difficulties presented by the material in Acts requires a careful reassessment of the evidence.

I. Stephen and the Hellenistic Church

According to Acts, the earliest church in Jerusalem was composed of both Palestinian and Hellenistic Jews (Acts 6:1).[2] When a dispute arose concerning food distribution between these two groups, a party of seven men, all with Greek names, was elected to oversee this distribution so that the twelve apostles could give single-minded attention to proclaiming and teaching the gospel. Stephen, however,

---

[1] By 'church' I do not, of course, mean an organized group of churches, but independent units which shared similar basic points of view.

[2] Debate still goes on over the meaning of Ἑλληνιστής in Acts, cf. the commentaries *ad loc*. It at least means Greek speaking, and it may mean living according to the manner of the Greeks. Whatever 'Luke' meant by the word, the historical reconstruction of the Hellenists will give us the safest clue as to how much they were influenced by Greek culture.

suddenly appears (Acts 6 : 8ff) in the role not of a table servant but of an apostle with a provocative teaching and is soon haled before the Sanhedrin. His speech provokes the fury of the Jewish listeners and he is summarily killed. This event touches off a persecution of the entire Jerusalem church such that all the members are forced to flee with the exception of the apostles (8 :1). In the next scene we find another of the Seven, Philip, proclaiming the gospel to the Samaritans (8 :4ff).

Many scholars, seeing the impossibility of this narration, have raised two main objections.[1] 1. Stephen and Philip act as if they were proclaimers of the gospel, not distributors of food. 2. To imagine a persecution of the church such that the leaders remain but the members forced to flee is next to impossible. The remaining traditions in Acts assume that, while the church may have been sporadically harrassed, its membership as a whole was unmolested. As a result of these difficulties a reconstruction has often been suggested which, although no direct evidence exists to support it, must be taken with the utmost seriousness.[2] The group around Stephen demonstrates that a Hellenistic-Jewish church existed in Jerusalem along side of the church led by the former disciples. The Seven were probably the official leaders of this church, indicating that already some formal separation existed between the two groups, if not an outright split. When the Hellenistic Christians provoke the wrath of the Jewish populace in Jerusalem, Stephen is killed. What happens then is a persecution not of the entire church, but of Stephen's group alone. Only in this way is it credible how the apostles could have remained unharmed. The Jerusalem Jewish authorities must have distinguished between the two groups of Christians, found one acceptable, the other intolerable. Obviously simply the fact that some Christians were Hellenistic Jews cannot explain the persecution, since Hellenistic Jews themselves lived in Jerusalem and had their own synagogue or synagogues.[3] The reason then must have been some difference in theology between the two churches. Unfortunately only two pieces of evidence exist which can

---

[1] E.g., Jackson and Lake, I, 307f.; E. Haenchen, *Die Apostelgeschichte* (Göttingen, 1961), pp. 218-22; H. Conzelmann, *Die Apostelgeschichte* (Tubingen, 1963), pp. 43-52.

[2] Especially Haenchen and Conzelmann, *ad loc.*

[3] Acts mentions the Hellenistic synagogue at 6 :9, but the language is too uncertain to know whether he is thinking of one or more such synagogues. Cf. also the Greek inscription which must have come from a Jerusalem synagogue. Text and discussion are found in Jackson and Lake, IV, 67f.

tell us anything about the Hellenistic gospel. One is the narration of the arrest, trial, and martyrdom of Stephen (Acts 6:8-15; 7:54-60); the other is the speech of Stephen (Acts 7:2-53).

The narrative materials do not provide much certain information. Of chief importance are the accusations brought against Stephen, but here the problem is that there are two different charges. In verse 11 he is said to have spoken blasphemous words against Moses and God. In 13f the charge is that he speaks against the temple and the law: "For we have heard him say that this Jesus of Nazareth will destroy this place, and will change the customs which Moses delivered to us." Does this double charge indicate that two separate sources were used by the author of Acts? The following view has been suggested.[1] One source, containing the first accusation, pictures the death of Stephen as due to mob violence (6:9-11; 7:54-58a); the other indicates a judicial process was responsible for the execution (6:12-14; 7:58b-60). Conzelmann objects to the two source theory but does see that a division of some sort is necessary. He prefers to view the mob scene as the source, with the trial materials as Lukan additions.[2] In either view, the first charge, found in verse 11, seems to have more claim to belong to a pre-Lukan stratum. But here the difficulty is that the accusation is too vague to be helpful. It reads too much like a Christian 'interpretation' of Jewish hostility to put trust in its accuracy. To speak blasphemous words against God could mean anything, or nothing, while blasphemy against Moses is not by any means necessarily an expression for rejection of the law.

Commentators have frequently pointed out that the trial and death of Stephen were modeled by the author of Acts on the trial and death of Jesus. This similarity casts grave doubt on the historicity of the trial scene of Stephen. The author has, among other things, omitted the charge against Jesus about the temple (Mark 14:58) and made it the second accusation against Stephen. This is true for half of the charge—that Stephen is against the temple—but it does not explain the accusation that Stephen and Jesus are against the law. Why should the author of Acts have added this to the temple charge? It certainly fits ill with his own view, which is that Jewish Christians obey the law (cf. Acts 21:20ff). Nor does he get it from the speech which he has Stephen utter, for the speech affirms the law. Nor does he get it from any of the gospel material he uses about Jesus (he omits Mark 7:1-23

---

[1]) Jackson and Lake, II, 147-52.
[2]) P. 45. Cf. also Jackson and Lake, II, 151.

entirely). What is equally strange is the future tense of the charge on the law.[1] At face value this must refer to an eschatological alteration or abolition of the Torah. Nowhere, however, in the gospel is there hint of such a view. Jesus either upholds the law or he repudiates it. He does not say: In the future the law will be changed. As far as I can see, nowhere else in Acts is such an idea repeated. In short, the predicament with regard to the second accusation is that while the context demands that it be viewed as a creation of the author of Acts, the charge about the law makes this judgment a bit uncertain. Unfortunately in both accusations all we can be sure of—and all that may really be present—is that the author of Acts wants to say the charges against Stephen were completely false and due to Jewish envy and hostility. If any information about the content of the Hellenistic viewpoint is to be gleaned from Acts, one can search for it only in the very problematic speech of Stephen.

II. The speech of Stephen

While this long discourse is rich in material, it has presented scholars with difficult problems. What strikes most forcibly is its uniqueness among the speeches in Acts. In the case of every other speech, its content is relevant to the situation and replete either with explicit Christian theology and/or biographical accounts relating to the speaker's Christian experience. But in Stephen's speech, only the last three of the 53 verses are at all related to the occasion of the trial. The major part is a retelling of biblical history from Abraham to Solomon. No references to Jesus or anything Christian are to be found. Such summaries were for centuries popular among the Jews, examples of which can be found in the OT, Ben Sirach, and the Wisdom of Solomon.[2] Some scholars have inferred that the author of Acts has simply taken over such a Jewish summary, to which he may or may not have added some materials of his own.[3] This inference, however,

---

[1]) Unless it is determined by the future of the charge about the destruction of the temple, which 'Luke' may have taken from the accusation against Jesus in Mark.

[2]) Psalm 105, Sirach 44-49, Wisdom of Solomon 10f. Cf. Simon, pp. 40f.

[3]) Haenchen, for example, thinks the polemic sections were added by the author of Acts to a Jewish "Geschichtspredigt" which forms the nucleus of the speech, p. 240. The polemics seem too essential a part of the speech, however, to be eliminated, although I do agree with Haenchen in his emphatic statement that vss. 51-53 could not have been a part of the original speech.

founders on the puzzle, why 'Luke' would have remained content with a non-Christian source, when it is not his policy elsewhere—even Paul on the Areopagus ends his address with an explicit Christian reference. Furthermore, Hebrews 11 shows that the same form could, in fact, be used by Christians without significant reference in the account itself to specific Christian motifs.[1]

The following conclusions appear most likely. The author of Acts did not himself create the speech of Stephen (in distinction from the other speeches[2]) but followed what was probably a written document, although he reworked the language to conform to his own style. While there is no reason to think the speech in any way goes back to Stephen, the author must have obtained the document from some Christian group and thus can use it for the final speech of the first Christian martyr. Verses 51-53 however abruptly and radically change in mood and direction. This suggests they were composed by 'Luke' to make the transition from the speech proper to the event of the stoning.[3] Indeed, these verses are necessary to create the conditions for the stoning, since nothing in verses 2-50 could possibly be understood by the readers of Acts as provocative enough to merit such murderous rage. A final point is relevant here. The difficulty of determining the meaning of the speech is notorious and scholars have devoted much energy to an inconclusive search for the key.[4] The speech simply does not have an *explicit* point as it now stands. The reason must be that the end of the speech, where the issues would have become clear, was not used. 'Luke' has thus replaced the original conclusion with his own. Why he would have done this is, of course, impossible to know, but a suggestion close at hand is that the original conclusion was disturbing and theologically unacceptable to him.[5] Thus what we may have in 7:1-50 is a long fragment of a Christian

---

[1] Only 11:26 and 39f. are 'Christian'.

[2] Cf. on the other speeches the careful analysis of U. Wilckens, *Die Missionsreden der Apostelgeschichte* (Neukirchen, 1961).

[3] Up to verse 51 the speech makes no direct assault, nor does it really address the situation. Vss. 51-53, however, are a bitter attack upon the Jewish audience. Here also for the first time specific Christian phrases appear. The motifs of the holy spirit and 'The Righteous One' (Acts 3:14 and 22:14) are 'Lukan'. So also Haenchen: "Denn dass V. 51-53 nicht aus der benutzten 'Geschichtspredigt' stammen, sondern von der Hand des rhetorisch wirklich nicht unerfahrenen Lukas, ist deutlich," p. 240.

[4] Cf. the discussion below.

[5] As will be seen, the thought implicit or explicit in the speech disagrees with Luke's own theology.

retelling of Israelite history. Is it possible, despite the paucity of evidence, to go further and to determine the provenance and point of the sermon?

While Abraham and Joseph receive noticeable attention, it is the figure of Moses that dominates the speech in commanding fashion.[1] He was "beautiful before God" ἀστεῖος τῷ θεῷ (vs. 20), was instructed in the wisdom of the Egyptians and was mighty in words and deeds δυνατὸς ἐν λόγοις καὶ ἔργοις (vs. 22). Moses is the deliverer of Israel, a theme emphasized in three places. In verse 25 he knows that God is giving salvation (σωτηρία) to Israel through him. God is coming down to deliver (ἐξελέσθαι) Israel through Moses (vs. 34). God sent Moses as ruler (ἄρχων) and deliverer (λυτρωτής) (vs. 35). Special mention should be made of the particular style of verses 35-38.[2] Each sentence begins with the emphatic τοῦτον or οὗτος which, according to Norden, is one form of the encomium to the gods in Greek literature.[3] The effect thus achieved of piling up phrases in which Moses is exalted is an impressive and poetic climax to the entire section.

> This is the Moses whom they denied, saying:
> "Who appointed you ruler and judge?"
>
> This is he whom God sent as ruler and redeemer
> by the hand of the angel who appeared to him
> in the bush.
>
> This is he who led them out,
> doing wonders and signs in the land of Egypt
> and in the Red Sea and in the wilderness for
> forty years.
>
> This is the Moses who said to the sons of Israel:
> "A prophet for you God will raise up from
> your brethren who will be like me."
>
> This is he who was in the congregation in the wilderness
> with the angel who spoke to him at Mount Sinai,
> and with our fathers, who received living oracles
> to give to us.

---

[1] Here an instructive contrast can be made between Acts 7 and similar "Geschichtspredigten" in Sirach, Wisdom, and Hebrews. While Moses is mentioned in all of these, he assumes no ruling position as in Acts 7. Sirach seems, for example, more interested in Aaron than in Moses. In Acts 7, on the contrary, 20 of the 50 verses concern Moses.

[2] As Haenchen, pp. 233f., and Conzelmann, pp. 47f., have pointed out.

[3] E. Norden, *Agnostos Theos* (Stuttgart, 1956), pp. 164f., 223f.

Moses has a clear foil in the people of Israel. Deviating from the biblical account, the speech claims that the killing of the Egyptian should have indicated to the Israelites that Moses was to be their deliverer. They do not, however, understand this (vs. 25). The Israelite's retort, "Who made you a ruler and a judge over us?," is raised in importance out of all proportion and becomes a symbol for the entire people's rejection of their deliverer. The incident of the golden calf is also used to signal the complete rejection of Moses by Israel. "Our fathers refused to obey him, but thrust him aside, and in their hearts they turned to Egypt" (vs. 39). Here, then, we have a theology of the exalted Moses who is rejected by his own people.

Much less certain is the attitude toward the Mosaic law expressed in the speech. B. W. Bacon argues that the law is attacked by Stephen.[1] He contends that the ideas found here are closely related to radical Alexandrian Jewish views on the typological, spiritual understanding of the law as opposed to the literal.[2] Acts 7:51 shows that the circumcision mentioned in verse 8 is really a spiritual circumcision. Joseph and Moses have become types, an exegesis common to Hellenistic Judaism. Verse 42 indicates that the Mosaic ceremonial law is ordained as a punishment, and thus the 'living oracles' received by Moses are distinct from the actual Mosaic law. Bacon's position, while possible, is not probable. If, as suggested above, verses 51-53 did not belong to the original speech, the circumcision of heart mentioned there cannot be used to interpret the covenant of circumcision given Abraham in verse 8. Even should verse 51 have originally been a part, it does not prove what Bacon maintains. A notion of spiritual circumcision does not necessarily exclude acceptance of the physical rite. Nor does verse 42, "But God turned and gave them over to worship the host of heaven," prove that the Mosaic law is a punishment. The golden calf and the worship of other gods is precisely what the Mosaic covenant prohibits. Stephen is not saying the law is wrong but that the people are wrong for not being obedient to it. It hardly seems necessary to add that a typological use of the Old Testament heroes indicates nothing about an attitude toward the literal law, as Philo demonstrates again and again. In sum, none of Bacon's arguments militate against what is the simplest and obvious meaning of the "living oracles" given

---

[1] "Stephen's Speech: Its Argument and Doctrinal Relationship," in *Biblical and Semitic Studies* (New York, 1901), pp. 257f.

[2] Cf. Philo, *De Migratione Abrahami*, 89ff., where he attacks the view that the literal meaning of the laws can be neglected in favor of the spiritual.

to Moses. Just as Moses is exalted as prophet and lawgiver, so his words of Torah are the words of life. The speech is not primarily designed to put forward a position on the law, but I see no reason to doubt that the Torah accepted by Judaism was part of the author's religion. The speech assumes throughout that the law is valid.

Simon, on the other hand, argues that while Stephen's speech does not imply an abrogation of the Pentateuch, it does suggest that there is a difference between the true oracles given by God and a falsification of them begun with Aaron.[1] What we have in Stephen's church, believes Simon, is a group that uses a "revised and expurgated Pentateuch and Bible," following a method somewhat similar to the Pseudo-Clementines' distinction between true and false Scripture.[2] Simon's position, however, depends on his analysis of the attacks on sacrifice and temple. Since, as I will try to show, neither section is an attack on the Pentateuch itself, Simon's distinction is in the final analysis unnecessary.

What the speech actually says about sacrifice and temple must be very carefully examined. Moses, the exalted deliverer, has received the living oracles of the law. The Israelites, however, reject him, "Thrust him aside" and turn to idol worship, symbolized by the golden calf (vss. 39-41). At this point a startling innovation in the retelling of the events occurs, for the writer wants to say that the worship of the golden calf was not a once for all event, beaten down immediately by Moses (cf. Exod. 32), but rather one which resulted in a permanent apostasy of Israel. Because of the golden calf, "God turned and gave them over to worship the host of heaven."[3] Amos 5:25-27 is the proof for this apostasy.

> Did you offer to me slain beasts and sacrifices
>   forty years in the wilderness, O house of
>   Israel?
>
> And you took up the tent of Moloch,
>   and the star of the god Rephan,
>   the figures which you made to worship;
>   and I will remove you beyond Babylon.
>
> (Acts 7:42f)

---

[1] Pp. 81, 93.
[2] P. 93. He is dependent in part on H. J. Schoeps, *Theologie und Geschichte des Judenchristentums* (Tubingen, 1949).
[3] Acts 7:42. Notice the similarity with Rom. 1:24, 26, and 28.

A sharp distinction is made by Stephen between what God has commanded Israel through the law and what Israel actually did. Only if the worship of the host of heaven took place under the forms of sacrifices to Yahweh would Simon's distinction between a true and false Torah be possible. But nothing in the speech suggests such an interpretation, and I think the implications speak clearly against it. The references to the golden calf, the tent of Moloch, and the star of Rephan can only mean that outright idolatrous worship is charged against Israel.[1] The Torah commanded man how and whom to worship, but Israel forsook God's command, just as she forsook Moses. If this analysis is correct, the speech in no way rejects the Pentateuch or attacks the sacrificial cult ordained in it. What is attacked here, as always in the speech, is Israel's rejection of God.

The next section of the speech (vss. 44-50) contains a clear rejection of the temple, but again what this rejection does and does not imply must be carefully judged. "Our fathers had the tent of witness in the wilderness, even as he who spoke to Moses directed him to make it, according to the pattern that he had seen" (vs. 44). Here the tent of witness is accepted by the author as a valid part of the true worship of Israel, given by God through Moses. This can only mean that the sacrifices offered before the tabernacle were considered also as valid worship. What the speech rejects is the substitution of the temple for the tent of witness.[2] Solomon built the temple (vs. 47), but "The Most

---

[1] Cf. the discussion in Simon, p. 49. The difficulties in interpreting what Amos himself intended to say are well illustrated by W. R. Harper, *Amos and Hosea* (Edinburgh, 1905), pp. 136f.

[2] Vs. 46 presents certain problems of interpretation. David "found favor in the sight of God and asked leave to find a habitation for the God of Jacob," (RSV), εὗρεν χάριν ἐνώπιον τοῦ Θεοῦ καὶ ᾐτήσατο εὑρεῖν σκήνωμα τῷ θεῷ 'Ιακώβ. Here the author is drawing on the LXX of Ps. 132:5, where David says, ἕως οὗ εὕρω τόπον τῷ κυρίῳ, σκήνωμα τῷ θεῷ 'Ιακώβ. Simon argues that in the Psalm and in Acts the σκήνωμα is not the temple but the place in Jerusalem where the σκηνή, the tabernacle, rests, pp. 51f. Thus it is not said that David wanted to build the temple (as the Chronicler reports), but rather that David found a place for the tabernacle in contrast to Solomon who insisted on building a temple. This is an attractive suggestion, although it is not certain whether σκήνωμα can bear the interpretation Simon suggests. Certainly, however, the author of Acts does want to make a contrast between the σκήνωμα and the temple of Solomon; cf. also Michaelis in *TWNT*, VII, 386. A second problem is whether θεῷ or οἴκῳ is the correct reading in vs. 46. ACE and the received texts read θεῷ, as in the LXX. BA*DH read οἴκῳ. Despite the better witness for οἴκῳ, most commentators favor θεῷ, since otherwise αὐτῷ in the following verse is left hanging in air. A. F. J. Klijn, however, opts for οἴκῳ and argues that the verse wants to make a distinction between a house for Israel, which is what the temple really was intended to be, and Solomon's misunderstanding of it as a house for God, cf. "Stephen's Speech—Acts VII. 2-53",

High does not dwell in houses made with hands," Then follows another prophetic proof, from Isaiah 66:1f.

> Heaven is my throne,
> and earth my footstool.
> What house will you build for me, says the Lord,
> or what is the place of my rest?
> Did not my hand make all these things?

The form of the section on the temple is identical with that about sacrifices. First the legitimate and normative is described, Moses and the Torah in the one case, Moses and the tent of witness in the other. Next comes the false step of Israel, idolatry and temple. Finally, a prophetic text is quoted as proof for the argument. The structural similarity suggests that the temple is rejected as emphatically as idolatry. Simon demonstrates well that χειροποίητος is in Hellenistic Judaism a pejorative term, usually being reserved for attacks on pagan cults.[1] But here the term is used against the Jerusalem temple itself.

The question now becomes crucial: Why is the Jerusalem temple rejected if the previous section does not attack the sacrificial system of Israel as such? Confidence in any answer suggested here is lessened by the suspicion that the original speech was broken off at verse 50 by the author of Acts. Nevertheless, on the basis of what the text does say, the only reasonable answer is that what is rejected is the localization of worship to the particular center of the Jerusalem temple, or to any particular place. Not the worship itself is called into question, but the insistence that only at Jerusalem can it be carried on. God does not dwell in the Jerusalem temple; his throne is in heaven. And this means by implication that no center of worship has priority over others. Perhaps some idea of the issue involved can be gleaned from Psalm 132, which the author refers to in verse 46. In the Psalm the temple and Jerusalem are the dwelling place of God. "For the Lord has chosen Zion; he has desired it for his habitation: 'This is my resting place for ever; here I will dwell, for I have desired it'" (vss. 13f). In the Psalm the dwelling of God in Zion implies the exaltation and uniqueness of Zion. The temple *could* (though obviously not necessarily) signify the exclusiveness of the Israel according to the

---

NTS, 4 (1957-58), pp. 29f. This too is attractive, for it fits well with the motif of the speech. Yet the dangling αὐτῷ which would result from reading οἴκῳ is too jarring to overlook and τῷ οἴκῳ can be seen as a slip of a scribe whose eye was influenced by the αὐτῷ οἴκον of the following verse.

[1] Pp. 87-89.

flesh, and one can well understand how some early Christians, such as Hellenistic Jews with universalistic tendencies already ingrained in them, might have come to reject the temple precisely because it seemed to them to imply an idolatrous narrowing of God's favor to men. Through Christ the kingdom of God has burst the limitations of Zion's walls and is now offered to all men. The new Israel is inclusive in a way the old was not.[1]

In sum, the major points to be noted in the speech are 1) the exaltation of Moses and the correlative disobedience of Israel; 2) the implied acceptance of the law and sacrifice; 3) the rejection of the temple as the unique place where God dwells. It is important to note that the rejection of the temple in no way contradicts an acceptance of the Pentateuch, since neither the temple nor its location in Jerusalem is ever mentioned in the Five Books of the Law.

In addition several details of the sermon are of great interest and perhaps cumulatively of importance. According to Acts 7:16 Jacob and his sons after they died "were carried back to Shechem and laid in the tomb that Abraham had bought for a sum of silver from the sons of Hamor in Schechem." Here is a curious conflation of two

---

[1]) A somewhat related proposal sees one distinctive motif of the speech as being that God's revelation is not tied to the promised land. God appears to Abraham in Mesopotamia, guides Joseph in Egypt, appears to Moses in Midian and gives the law at Sinai. The true worship is not limited to one country or nation, thus implicitly opening the door for the Christian missionary activity. Such a view would be natural for Hellenistic Jews, who were accustomed to worship outside of the holy land. The observation that most of the theophanies do occur outside of Palestine is true, but that this fact is helpful towards determining the main motif of the speech is doubtful. In the first place, from the call of Abraham to the building of the temple, many of the important *heilsgeschichtliche* events narrated in the Bible *do* occur outside of the promised land. The preponderance of non-Palestinian theophanies is thus determined both by the necessity of selecting only key events and by the fact that the speech ceases where it does. In the second place, the holy land is mentioned a few times in a positive way. In 7:5 God promises the land to Abraham's descendants and in 7:7 the content of the promise is said to be worship in the holy land. It can hardly be fortuitous that in vs. 7, Exodus 3:12, which speaks of worship on Sinai, is reworked so that Palestine, not Mount Sinai becomes the place where God will be worshiped. Such a change would hardly have been made by someone hostile to the notion of the promised land. Reference to the promise is again made in vs. 17, while vs. 45 shows the Israelites entering into the promise by the power of God. The question which is really of interest here is *which* holy land is assumed to be promised.

While it is true that the speech does imply acceptance of the notion of a promised land, it must be emphasized on the other hand that this acceptance does not run counter to the strain of universalism we have seen implied in the section on the temple. Diaspora Jews did not necessarily feel that their union with the God of Israel was threatened by their abode outside of Palestine.

separate biblical traditions. According to Genesis 23, Abraham had bought a plot of ground for Sarah's burial from Ephron the Hittite. In Genesis this land is identified as Kiriath-arba, Mamre, Machpelah, and Hebron. The final redaction of the story clearly places this field at Hebron, that is, in southern Palestine, or Judea. In Genesis 25:9f, Abraham is reported to have been buried there, and in 49:29-32 and 50:13, Isaac, Rebekah, Leah, and Jacob are placed there as well. A separate tradition describes Jacob buying a plot of ground, for an unspecified purpose, at Shechem from the sons of Hamor. There Jacob builds an altar. But in Joshua 24:32 the bones of Joseph are taken from Egypt and buried at Shechem in the plot bought by Jacob. What the conflation in Acts 7:16 accomplishes is to remove the place of Jacob's burial from Hebron in Judea and place it at Shechem in Israel. Certainly the tradition followed by Acts cannot be simply derived from any particular text in the Bible, and it is hard to believe the conflation is to no purpose. Earlier, in verses 6f, God promises the land to Abraham and forecasts that after the enslavement Abraham's descendants will return and worship "in this place." Exodus 3:12 is quoted here but altered so that the prediction now concerns not the worship at Mount Sinai but the worship in the holy land. Is by implication "this place" the same as Shechem, which is by Mt. Gerizim? Or more broadly put, does the author assume that the holy land is really the old kingdom of Israel, now Samaria?

A second interesting alteration of the Bible is found in the quotation of Amos 5:25-27 in Acts 7:42f. The Hebrew of the MT presents certain difficulties and the LXX has apparently followed a slightly different version, perhaps one less corrupted than that the MT has preserved. But this does not concern us, since Acts follows the LXX almost word for word, with slightly different order. Yet the author of Acts makes one change justified neither by the MT, nor the LXX, nor by historical reality. Amos prophecies that Israel is to go into exile beyond Damascus, i.e., in the direction of Assyria which was, of course, the only threat to Israel at that time. According to Acts the people will go into exile beyond Babylon. This alteration is again hardly fortuitous. The author has deliberately changed a prophecy of doom against Israel into one against Judah. That is, the apostasy from the true worship in the wilderness is a or the cause of the end of the southern kingdom.

Many years ago, Paul Kahle reported a few variations of biblical quotations or allusions in Acts 7 which do not depend on either the

MT or LXX but are supported by the Samaritan Pentateuch.[1] In a recent work, Max Wilcox has supported and expanded upon the findings of Kahle.[2] These variations are as follows.

1. According to Acts 7:4 Abraham left Haran for Canaan after the death of his father, Terah.[3] Formally this involves a contradiction with the MT and LXX. Terah in Genesis 11:26 is said to have been 70 years old when Abraham was born. Abraham, in turn, was 75 years old when he left Haran (Gen. 12:4). This means Terah was 145 years of age when Abraham left. But since Terah lived to be 205 years old (Gen. 11:32), Abraham had to leave Haran many years before Terah died. While the LXX follows the MT in its dating, the Samaritan version, followed by the Samaritan Targum, gives the age of Terah at his death as 145. Thus, formally at least, Acts 7:4 agrees with the Samaritan as against the MT and LXX. The difficulty here is that the obvious sense of Genesis 11:32-12:1 is that Abraham in fact did go to Canaan after Terah's death, since the account of the death is immediately followed by the story of Abraham's departure. Unless one read the dates very carefully, he would never suspect otherwise. As Wilcox reports, Philo also reads the Genesis narrative in the same way.[4] Thus the author of Stephen's speech could be depending on the Samaritan Pentateuch, but one could just as easily account for the variation as a 'common-sense' reading of the biblical narrative.

2. In Acts 7:32 the text of Exodus 3:6 is given as follows: "I am the God of your fathers, the God of Abraham and of Isaac and of Jacob." The MT, however, reads very curiously, "I am the God of your father," as does the LXX. The Samaritan Pentateuch and Targum give the plural, Fathers, a reading clearly demanded by the sense of the sentence as well as by the appearance of the plural in other repetitions of the formula, such as found in Exodus 3:15. Thus Acts 7:32 is again in agreement with the Samaritan reading.[5] But does this mean Acts follows the Samaritan tradition? Again the answer is uncertain. Such a judgment is possible, but the similarity is also explicable on the basis of changes according to the sense of the passage.[6]

---

[1]) "Untersuchungen zur Geschichte des Pentateuchtextes," Abhandlung, *Theologische Studien und Kritiken*, 88 (1915), 399-439.
[2]) *The Semitisms of Acts* (Oxford, 1965), esp. pp. 26-30. He does not, however, refer to Kahle's investigation.
[3]) Kahle, p. 400; Wilcox, pp. 28f.
[4]) *De mig. Abr.* 177.
[5]) Kahle, p. 400; Wilcox, pp. 29f.
[6]) Wilcox argues that Acts 3:13 implies the same textual variation: "the God of

3. Kahle calls attention to the orderly course the speech takes through the events narrated in the Bible.¹ The section on Moses describes the events reported in Exodus: the theophany of the burning bush, the exodus itself, the giving of the law, the golden calf. In the midst of this account suddenly appears a verse from Deuteronomy 18:15, "God will raise up for you a prophet from your brethren as he raised me up." How is this abrupt insertion to be best explained? Kahle argues the answer is found in the Samaritan Pentateuch, which immediately following its version of the Decalogue in Exodus 20 inserts this very prediction of the future prophet, although the nearly identical verse, Deuteronomy 18:18, is used instead of 18:15.² The only significant difference between the two verses in Deuteronomy is the speaker, in the one case God, in the other, Moses. If the author of Stephen's speech had used the Samaritan Pentateuch, then he would have found the prediction embedded in the midst of the stories he is telling. In this instance Kahle's suggestion seems to me very illuminating.

4. Wilcox adds still a fourth 'Samaritanism'.³ In Acts 7:5 God is said to have given Abraham "no *inheritance* in it [the promised land], not even a foot's length, but promised to give it to him in possession and to his posterity after him." This seems to be a somewhat free adaptation of Deuteronomy 2:5 wrenched radically out of context. There God says to Moses with respect to territory belonging to the sons of Esau: "I will not give you any of their land, no, not so much as for the sole of the foot to tread on ..." Wilcox points out, however, that the greatest deviation from the Deuteronomic verse is the insertion in Acts 7:5a of the word "inheritance", κληρονομία, found neither in MT, LXX, nor the Jewish targum. Such a word is, however, found in the Samaritan Pentateuch, ירשה.

The evaluation of these 'Samaritanisms' is indeed difficult. Scholars who are expert in the area of textual studies seem to have reached the conclusion that textual traditions in the period under discussion were more fluid than the MT and LXX might seem to indicate. Kahle, for ex-

---

Abraham and Isaac and Jacob, the God of our fathers," cf. pp. 33f. While "fathers" does appear in the plural, the citation is freer than 7:32, and it would be even easier to interpret 3:13 as a quotation according to the sense rather than according to a textual tradition.

¹) Pp. 400f.
²) In vs. 15 the subject is in the third person; in vs. 18, in the first. Wilcox notes that the citation in Acts is in word order closer to vs. 18 than 15, p. 33.
³) P. 27.

ample, believes the Samaritan text represents a popular text tradition older than the Massoretic,[1] while Heller, on the contrary, sees the Samaritan version moving already in the direction of the midrashim and therefore later than the basic text represented by the MT.[2] Wilcox affirms that the deviations go back to non-MT or -LXX traditions exampled by Samaritan readings, but the fact that he finds parallels to these deviations in such varied places as Philo and the Jewish Targums apparently makes him cautious about locating the Samaritan-type readings in any one specific context.[3] Thus all the 'Samaritanisms' may indicate in Acts 7 is how widespread certain midrashic interpretations were.

Nevertheless, the cumulative impression these passages make is striking. No *text* outside the Samaritan Pentateuch and Targum supports any of the deviations we have discussed, and only Philo and possibly Justin are cited by Wilcox as showing any knowledge of these traditions. Also important is the fact that, as far as I can see, Wilcox makes no claim for any 'Samaritanisms' in Acts outside of chapter 7.[4] Thus we have only one chapter in Acts which shows any possibility of Samaritan relationship and this perhaps in four places.

What really makes one pay attention to this possibility, however, is that other features of the sermon mentioned above are extremely compatible with the suggestion that Stephen's speech has something to do with Samaria. The change of the prophecy of Amos, now directed towards the South rather than the North; the conflation of the burial places, so that the patriarchs are now all in Shechem, very close to the sacred Mt. Gerizim; the implication related to this that the holy land promised to Abraham is Israel, not Judea—all these motifs might well suggest a Samaritan point of view.

Even more important are the major motifs of the speech, the exaltation of Moses and the rejection of the Jerusalem temple. Both of these are key emphases of Samaritan theology. The centrality of Moses in Samaritan thought has recently been beautifully demonstrated by John MacDonald.[5] Although the extant documents apparently date at the earliest from the 3rd century A.D., the exaltation of Moses

---

[1]) P. 439.
[2]) C. Heller, *The Samaritan Pentateuch: An Adaptation of the Massoretic Text* (Berlin, 1923).
[3]) Pp. 51-55.
[4]) With the exception, the uncertainty of which has already been noted, of a citation in Acts 3:13 similar to that in 7:32.
[5]) *The Theology of the Samaritans* (Philadelphia, 1964), pp. 147-222.

appears to have been a constant factor throughout all periods of which we have knowledge, as the additions to the Decalogue in the Samaritan Pentateuch clearly imply.[1] The great *Memar*, the Teaching of Marqah, a theologian who lived probably in the third century A.D. according to MacDonald, is filled with hymns and benedictions of praise to Moses the Man of God, not unlike the encomium found in Acts 7:35-38. One example may suffice.

> Where is there anyone like Moses and who can compare
>   with Moses the prophet, the like of whom has
>   not arisen and never will arise?
> Where is there ayone like Moses and who can compare
>   with Moses, to whom his Lord revealed what He
>   had never before revealed to any man?
> Where is there anyone like Moses and who can compare
>   with Moses, who was strengthened with much
>   wisdom from the light of the Divine One?
> Where is there anyone like Moses and who can compare
>   with Moses, whom his Lord entrusted over
>   His possession?
> Where is there anyone like Moses and who can compare
>   with Moses, for whose sake manifold wonders were revealed?"[2])

Then immediately follows the sentence, "Great is the mighty prophet Moses and what he said in that address, which is wholly life (-giving)" חייה. Moses is exalted as the savior of Israel.[3] A striking parallel to Moses' awareness of his mission as early as his murder of the Egyptian (Acts 7:23-25) is given by MacDonald. "As far as the Samaritans are concerned, the appearance of Moses as a young man intervening in a dispute between an Egyptian and a Hebrew indicated his undying concern for his people, the Hebrews, and his later determination to deliver them from the hand of the oppressor."[4]

---

[1]) After the tenth commandment in Exodus 20, which concerns the Gerizim temple, various passages are added, some from Deut. 5, as well as Deut. 18:18: "I will raise them up a prophet from among their brethren, like unto thee, and will put my words in his mouth. And he shall speak unto them all that I shall command him." Cf. the text in A. von Gall, *Der hebräische Pentateuch der Samaritaner* (Giessen, 1918) and a translation in M. Gaster, *Samaritan Oral Law and Ancient Traditions* (London, 1932), pp. 189f.

[2]) *Memar*, IV, 1. Translation by J. MacDonald, *Memar Marqah* (Beihefte zur *ZAW*, no. 84), II, 135. It should be noted that MacDonald thinks Christian influence can be seen in the development of Samaritan concepts of Moses, *Theology*, pp. 150-52.

[3]) *Theology*, p. 195.

[4]) *Ibid.*, MacDonald does not give any source documentation for this idea.

Samaritan opposition to the temple at Jerusalem is common knowledge. It was rooted very early in Israelite history, although the Samaritan version of the story is in many ways different from that found in the biblical writings, or at least deduced by scholars on the basis of the Bible.¹ For our purposes it is sufficient to note that in the Samaritan judgment Solomon's building of the temple was outright apostasy, clearly violating the tenth commandment.²

In sum, the speech of Stephen contains many features which are compatible with Samaritan biblical tradition and theology. At the same time it cannot be said that the speech is entirely consonant with Samaritan ideas, for in at least three instances differences emerge.

1. In Samaritan thought God directly gives the Pentateuch to Moses, without the mediatorship of angels (contra Acts 7:38).³

2. As we have seen, at two crucial places concerning worship and temple, Jewish prophets are quoted. The Samaritans acknowledged only one prophet, Moses, and the messianic prophet, the Taheb, who would either be just like Moses or a Moses *redivivus*. Whether the Samaritans were actively hostile to the prophetic writings is not, however, as clear. MacDonald notes only one clear instance in the *Memar* of an anti-prophetic statement.⁴ "The book we possess is a book of truth, but all the writings of the prophets are foul things." Thus while the prophetic books of Israel would not have been used by Samaritans, it is conceivable that such writings would not have created extreme hostility if used in addresses *to* Samaritans. We have already seen how the quotation from Amos is altered to make it refer to Judah, not Israel.

3. The reason given in Acts for the rejection of the Solomonic

---

¹) *Ibid.*, pp. 15-21.

²) The tenth commandment reads as follows in Gaster's translation, p. 189. "And it shall come to pass when the Lord thy God will bring thee into the land of the Canaanites whither thou goest to take possession of it, thou shalt erect unto thee large stones, and thou shalt cover them with lime, and thou shalt write upon the stones all the words of this Law, and it shall come to pass when ye cross the Jordan, ye shall erect these stones which I command thee upon Mount Garizim, and thou shalt build there an altar unto the Lord thy God, an altar of stones, and thou shalt not lift up upon them iron, of perfect stones shalt thou build thine altar, and thou shall bring up upon it burnt offerings to the Lord thy God, and thou shalt sacrifice peace offerings, and thou shalt eat there and rejoice before the Lord thy God."

³) MacDonald, *Theology*, p. 287, although the angels were present at the law-giving. The mention of the angel at the burning bush in Acts 7:30 is, however, consonant with Samaritan teaching, cf. *Memar* I, 1.

⁴) *Memar*, VI, 2. Cf. note in translation at p. 218.

temple is obviously different from that which would be accepted by the Samaritans. In Acts the reason is that God does not dwell in any temple. According to Samaritan thought, God ordained only one temple and that at Gerizim. It should not be forgotten, however, that the rebuilt Samaritan temple had been destroyed by John Hyrcanus in the late second Century B.C. Thus the Samaritans, while they continued to worship on Mount Gerizim did not worship in a temple. By implication at least the argument in Acts 7 is strikingly close to the passage in John 4 where Jesus addresses the Samaritan woman. "Woman, believe me, the hour is coming when neither on this mountain nor in Jerusalem will you worship the Father.... But the hour is coming, and now is, when the true worshipers will worship the Father in spirit and truth, for such the Father seeks to worship him" (vss. 21,23). Here too worship at any particular place—Jewish or Samaritan—is rejected in favor of the true worship in spirit, which for John is through Christ. Jesus' word acknowledges the inadequacy of the Jewish claim; yet at the same time it cuts through the Samaritan as well with the argument that the true worship is of another order, freed from place and nation and universalized by the potential omnipresence of God's spirit. In the post-war period in Judaism the rabbinic leaders with apparent success guided their people away from an unhealthy attachment to a destroyed temple,[1] and it is not at all impossible that a Christian mission with such universal emphases might have had success with the Samaritans who long before had lost their temple. John 4 has often, and I believe rightly, been considered as a reflection of the Christian mission to Samaria.[2] Is it possible that the *locus* of Stephen's speech is the same?

The cumulative weight of the evidence suggests that such a *locus* is not only possible but also probable. The author seems to know the Samaritan Pentateuch. He harmonizes at several points the biblical narrative with Samaritan interests. He accepts the high exaltation of Moses they insist upon, at the same time acknowledging the eschatological overtones of this exaltation (Acts 7:37). He sympathizes with Samaritan feeling about the Jerusalem temple. He says nothing to antagonize the high esteem with which the Torah was regarded. It is not the Torah which is defective, but the people's response to God's

---

[1]) Cf. J. Neusner, *A Life of Rabban Yohanan ben Zakkai* (Leiden, 1962), pp. 138-46.

[2]) E.g., Cullmann, *The Early Church*, pp. 185-92; recently W. Meeks, "Galilee and Judea in the Fourth Gospel," *JBL*, 85 (1966), 163-69.

will found in the Torah. At the same time an inplicit christology can be seen, as has often been noticed, in the exaltation of Moses and the hint of the eschatological prophet who is to be like him. One can imagine the end of the speech, assuming it to have been replaced by the present ending, proclaiming Christ as that prophet, the Taheb who had come to reveal the truth, but who, instead of reconstituting worship on Mt. Gerizim as the Samaritans thought would happen,[1] has shown that no temple can be the *locus* of worship. Whether it would be possible to imagine a motif even closer to the theology of the gospel of John, that Christ has taken the place of the temple, is too problematical to suggest. However, it can be pointed out that in John 4 Jesus is clearly invested with traits of the Taheb. The Samaritan woman perceives him to be a prophet (John 4:19). In verses 25 and 29 the Messiah is said to be the revealer of the truth, just as Samaritan thought affirmed.[2] Jesus himself claims in verse 26 that he is such a Messiah, and in verse 29 the woman raises the question whether Jesus is this Messiah on the basis that he has revealed to her truths about herself. Of course the woman's reason for her confession betrays the usual Johannine separation between the superficial and the true levels. At the end of the pericope, however, the other Samaritans independently confess that Jesus is the savior of the world. As we have already seen, savior is a title ascribed to Moses (and therefore the eschatological prophet) by Samaritan thought as well as by Acts 7. Thus while not all the characteristics of Acts 7 are compatible with Samaritan thought, they are at least all comprehensible within the framework of a Hellenistic Christian mission to Samaria.

III. The mission of Stephen's church

Before drawing final conclusions about Acts 7, the historical situation, insofar as it can be reconstructed, of the Hellenistic mission must be considered.[3] According to Acts 8, the persecution drove Philip to Samaria where he conducted a successful mission. Even a superficial glance at this chapter shows that 'Luke' has put together a number of disparate traditions about contacts between Christians and

---

[1] MacDonald, *Theology*, p. 365.
[2] *Ibid.*, p. 364.
[3] Cf. Bacon, *Gospel of the Hellenists*, pp. 65-90, and Jackson and Lake, I, pp. 300-20 for interesting statements which move in the same direction as the following. For a divergent view cf. W. Schmithals, *Paul and James* (Naperville, 1965), pp. 16-37.

Samaritans, harmonized them as best he could and molded them to his own theological viewpoint.[1] Aside from the legends linked with Simon Magus, the author does not appear to have much specific tradition, not even being able to say in which Samaritan city Philip evangelized (cf. Acts 8:5). Nevertheless, there seems hardly any reason why 'Luke' would have wished to ascribe the origins of this mission to the Hellenists without basis in tradition, particularly since he so clearly wishes to give Peter (i.e. the apostles) the real credit wherever possible. In fact, the encounter between Peter and Simon inserted into the narrative about Philip (Acts 8:14-25) shows precisely this tendency. Furthermore, the region of Samaria would have been the nearest safe refuge from the Jewish persecution. Josephus suggests that Jewish discontents often, in fact, fled to Samaria to escape various punishments.[2] There seems to me no reason to doubt the tradition that the Hellenists evangelized Samaria.

The persecution, dispersion, and Samaritan mission must have happened very early in the life of the church. The Hellenistic Christians never again appear in Acts as residents of Jerusalem, so that these events belong to the earliest reports 'Luke' has collected. Furthermore, just as the church of the apostles was not persecuted, so Paul's persecution of the Christians can only mean a persecution of the Hellenistic church which, in some way, had deviated from norms acceptable to the Jewish authorities in Jerusalem. Since Paul's conversion can not have occurred many years after the death of Jesus, the dispersion of the Hellenists is shown independently of Acts to be a very early phenomenon. Paul had reached Damascus in his activities before he was converted, indicating that the Hellenistic mission must already by that time have pushed through Judea and Samaria to Syria.[3]

The question of the admission of Gentiles into the church probably arose for the first time in critical fashion in Galilean and Syrian regions.[4]

---

[1]) Cf. Haenchen, *Apostelgeschichte*, ad loc., and "Gab es eine vorchristliche Gnosis?", *ZTK*, 49 (1952), 344-48.

[2]) *Ant.* XI. 346f. "And, whenever anyone was accused by the people of Jerusalem of eating unclean food or violating the Sabbath or committing any other such sin, he would flee to the Shechemites [i.e. the Samaritans], saying that he had been unjustly expelled." Trans. by R. Marcus, Loeb Library edition. The passage is referring to the late 3rd century B.C., but it is doubtful Josephus is thinking only of past history at this point.

[3]) As Gal. 1:17 implies; cf. also Acts 9.

[4]) The Samaritans were probably considered renegade Jews, rather than Gentiles. This is the attitude of some, at least, of the rabbis and is what Acts implies by putting the mission to the Samaritans before Peter's first Gentile conversion.

Philip travels to Caesarea at the northern edge of Samaria (Acts 8 : 40), and we find him in residence there later (Acts 21 : 8). Embedded in Acts 11 is a tradition which says explicitly that the group radiating out from Stephen reached Phoenicia, Cyprus, and Antioch and at Antioch proclaimed the gospel to the Gentiles. "Now those who were scattered because of the persecution that arose over Stephen traveled as far as Phoenicia and Cyprus and Antioch, speaking the word to none except Jews. But there were some of them, men of Cyprus and Cyrene, who on coming to Antioch, spoke to the Greeks also, preaching the Lord Jesus" (vss. 19f).[1] These verses cannot have been created by the author of Acts, for they do not fit his own *tendenz*, which is to give precedence to the Jerusalem apostles. This *tendenz* is, in fact, evident in verses 22f, where 'Luke' tries as hard as possible to make Jerusalem responsible for the real establishment of the Antiochean community. Verses 19f almost certainly belong to the traditions of the Hellenistic church, other remnants of which are found in Acts 6-8. I see no real reason to doubt, further, that the Gentile mission at Antioch happened much earlier than Acts reports and, in fact, probably not long after the Samaritan mission and before the conversion of Paul. The author of Acts could not have reported the founding of the Antiochean church by the Hellenists any sooner than he did. For according to his view, the mission to the Gentiles is originated by Peter at God's command (Acts 10 : 1-11 : 18). Thus he cannot say prior to this that any Christians evangelized Gentiles. But once Peter has made the move and it is sanctioned by the church at Jerusalem (11 : 1-18), then the author is free to narrate other traditions he has of the beginnings of the Gentile mission. This he does immediately, joining together the tradition of 19f with the beginning of Paul's mission (vss 25f). His structure is obviously artificial. In all probability the Gentile mission by the Hellenists antedated that of Paul and Peter.[2]

The evidence thus suggests, I believe, that the church of Stephen, so far from being an isolated and too-radical phenomenon in the early church is really that church which quickly and successfully sprung Christianity loose from the notion that it was a sect within Judaism, a Christianity which moved through Samaria and then Syria, preaching

---

[1]) The reading Ἕλληνας is to be preferred to Ἑλληνιστάς on the grounds of sense as well as textual witnesses.

[2]) Haenchen suggests that the original version of Philip's conversion of the Ethiopian was the Hellenistic church's story of the first Gentile conversion, parallel to the apostolic church's version of Peter and Cornelius, *Apostelgeschichte*, p. 265. An intriguing and perhaps correct conjecture.

eventually a law-free gospel to the Gentiles. It is this church which Paul persecuted and into this church he was converted. While Paul is its most famous representative, he is far from being its founder. The activity and theology of Paul is in fact inexplicable apart from the Hellenistic church which originally stemmed from the days of Stephen in Jerusalem.

IV. Conclusions

We have, on the one hand, evidence that the Hellenistic church did conduct a mission to Samaria. On the other we have a speech placed in the mouth of the hero of this church by the author of Acts, a speech which it seems clear he did not himself create. This speech can coherently be interpreted as a fragment of a Christian proclamation to the Samaritans. Is it likely that the Samaritan background of Stephen's speech is entirely fortuitous? Is it not more likely that 'Luke' possessed a document which he knew had been created in the missionary activity of this Hellenistic church and which, for this reason, he felt appropriate to insert into his tradition of the martyrdom of the church's hero? Obviously an affirmative answer rests upon a number of arguments which are in the final analysis unprovable. Yet the suggestion does make sense both of the speech of Stephen, and of its insertion into its present context, despite the fact that superficially at least it is so irrelevant to the occasion, contrary to the custom and ability demonstrated elsewhere by the author of Acts. Should this conclusion be correct, Stephen's speech becomes an immensely important document for historians attempting to learn about the earliest church. It reveals to us something of the thinking which lay at the roots of that church which is, in the final analysis, the mother of the church that survived. As already suggested, some of the material in Mark reveals further evidence of this church as it existed in Galilee or Syria. Thus Mark and Acts 7 may open windows into the earliest wrestling on Palestinian soil of that Christianity which was to prove of such decisive importance for later eras and different lands.

This essay opens a great many problems which cannot be solved here. I want to conclude, however, with a brief mention of four of them.

1. Although Acts 7 must be dated post-Stephen, can it shed any light on the cause for the actual persecution of the Stephanic group in

Jerusalem? Haenchen's reconstruction of the events leads him correctly to believe that only some major deviation of the Hellenistic group from Jewish beliefs could account for the persecution.[1] He acknowledges two possible causes, belief in Jesus as the Messiah and rejection of the law. Only the latter, he concludes, can be the real explanation, since the apostles were not persecuted for their belief in Jesus. But Haenchen overlooks one possibility, and this is just what the speech of Stephen emphasizes: the rejection of the temple. Josephus narrates a story which makes it clear how sensitive and excitable Jerusalem Jews were about the sanctity of the temple. The slightest suggestion of deprecation could create riot conditions.[2] The incident of Paul's arrest (Acts 21) is another case in point, and it is not at all impossible that Jesus' word about the destruction of the temple was an important factor in his arrest and execution.[3] An explicit rejection of the temple would be ample explanation for the killing of Stephen and the persecution of his group.

Moreover should our suggestion about the Samaritan *locus* of Stephen's speech be correct, the implication is that the Hellenistic church had at the time of the Samaritan mission not yet reached a negative judgment about the law. Of course, with the Samaritan emphasis upon the Torah, a mission which did not attack it would obviously be more immediately successful. But Acts 7 is not simply silent about the law; here it is positively accepted as living oracles from God. Furthermore a church willing to face persecution from the Jews for the sake of its belief would hardly adopt a more pragmatic attitude towards the Samaritans. If then the law was still accepted at the time of the Samaritan mission, how much more likely would the group while still in Jerusalem have accepted it. I would thus suggest that rejection of the temple rather than the law was the cause of Stephen's death.

2. At what point, then, did the Gentile-centered church reject the law? It must first be said that the church could missionize Gentiles without explicitly breaking with the law. The Gentiles could become Jewish converts, i.e., be circumcised, or they could be given the status of god-fearers. That there was a Gentile mission prior to and apart

---

[1] *Apostelgeschichte*, p. 221.

[2] *War*, II, 223-27, where an indecent gesture by a Roman soldier in the temple during Passover started a riot in the temple itself (between 48-52 A.D.).

[3] Cf. M. Goguel, *Jesus and the Origins of Christianity* (New York, 1960), II, 508, and a fuller treatment in his "A propos du procès de Jésus," *ZNW*, 31 (1932), 289-301.

from Paul seems to me proven by Acts 11:19f and the materials in Matthew and Mark already mentioned. That this mission from the beginning proclaimed a law-free gospel is not as certain. The teaching of Jesus is not unambiguous on the question of the law, and in fact nowhere does there seem to be preserved a word authentically Jesus' which makes a general pronouncement about it.[1] The Hellenistic church would have had to proceed by implication and the involved process which seems to be evident in the structure of Mark 7 may suggest it was not an easy progression. On the other hand, certain statements which Paul makes about his call and mission are easiest to explain if he was converted into a church which had already relaxed its views toward the law.[2] There is so little evidence one way or the other that any suggestion is extremely tenuous, but the possibility has to be considered that the break with the law took place after the Samaritan mission had begun but not later than the time the missionaries had reached places like Antioch and Damascus.[3]

3. The existence of a *Hellenistic* Christian mission to Samaria presents no more problems than the existence of such a Christianity in Jewish Palestine. If anything, Samaria may have been more Hellenized. Certainly the national elements that existed within the borders had been for centuries less homogenized than in Judea.[4] According to Josephus, the Samaritans were quite happy to accede to the program of Hellenization by Antiochus Epiphanes and there seem to have been no Samaritan Maccabeans to turn the tide.[5] There was a Samaritan diaspora just as there was a Jewish.[6] According to Kahle, a Greek translation of the Samaritan Pentateuch existed[7], and Eusebius pre-

---

[1]) The extreme statements in Matt. 5:17ff. are clearly church formulations, and if Taylor is correct, the authentic kernal in Mark 7 is too general to be taken as a specific pronouncement on the law, cf. Taylor, *Mark*, p. 343. In his or his disciples' actions, evidence may be seen for the breaking of some *traditions* over the meaning of the biblical ordinances, but it cannot be inferred from this that Jesus felt he was breaking the biblical ordinances themselves.

[2]) He interprets his encounter with the risen Lord as a prophetic commission to the Gentiles, cf. Gal. 1:15f. If this reflects what he in fact did think shortly after he became a missionary with a law-free gospel, it is easiest to assume he knew that other Christians had already begun such preaching to the Gentiles.

[3]) As Acts 11:19f. in fact says.

[4]) E. Wright, for example, argues that the tradition that Alexander populated the city of Samaria with Macedonians is true, cf. "The Samaritans at Shechem," *HTR*, 55 (1962), 357-66.

[5]) *Ant*. XII. 257-64.

[6]) Cf. J. Bowman, "Samaritan Studies," *JRLB*, 40 (1957-58), 298.

[7]) P. 403.

serves a fragment under the name of Eupolemos, which must have been written by a Hellenistic-Samaritan apologist.[1] Whatever hostility showed to Hellenistic Jews by Samaritans thus would presumably be due more to their Jewishness than to their Hellenism.

What is difficult, however, is to know from just what sort of Hellenistic Judaism the Stephanic Christians originated. Were they, as Bacon argues, radical Hellenists who had already before becoming Christians renounced the literal meaning of temple, sacrifice, and law?[2] As is well known, Philo polemicizes against such people, while he himself upholds the necessity to honor temple and cult.[3] The Alexandrian, however, himself sits rather loose to the literal meaning despite his protests. What this may suggest is that many Hellenistic Jews, regardless of their intent to remain loyal to the temple, had at best divided feelings.[4] This same kind of uncertainty may be supposed to have insinuated itself into Stephen and his followers. Otherwise the division over the temple in the earliest church between the apostles and the *Hellenistic* church is not comprehensible.[5]

---

[1] *Praep. Evang.* IX, 17.

[2] "Stephen's Speech," pp. 237-75.

[3] *De mig. Abr.*, 87-93.

[4] Cf. the discussion in H. Wenschkewitz, *Die Spiritualisierung der Kultusbegriffe* (Leipzig, 1932), pp. 67-87.

[5] Cullmann believes that it *is* explicable on other grounds, namely, that the Hellenists are really an outgrowth of Qumran, cf. esp. "The Significance of the Qumran Texts for Research into the Beginnings of Christianity," now in *The Scrolls and the New Testament*, ed. Stendahl, pp. 18-32. His argument, however, seems to rest primarily on the rejection of the temple both by the Hellenists and Qumran and by the insertion of the author of Acts into the stories about the Hellenists the information that many priests became Christians (Acts 6:7). Yet the evidence seems to be that Qumran did not reject the temple itself but the priests who conducted the sacrifices there. If this is so, there is really no relationship at all between the views of Acts 7 and Qumran on the temple. Haenchen's judgment appears to me entirely correct. "Sie [Stephen's rejection of the temple] hat nicht das geringste zu tun mit dem Nein, das man in Qumran zum Jerusalemer Tempeldienst sprach," *Apostelgeschichte*, p. 241. Haenchen also comments that the number of Jewish priests must so far have outnumbered those at Qumran that it is stretching the imagination to prefer to take Acts 6:7 as a reference to Qumran priests rather than to Jewish priests. Cullmann is not able either to extract himself from the difficulty that the Stephanic people are called 'Hellenist'. His answer is that "there was no other way to describe those who did not belong to official Judaism" (p. 29). The name was chosen to label representatives of "Hellenistic syncretism." While it is true that some Greek documents have been found at Qumran, which is hardly a real surprise, to call the thought of this group as it is revealed by documents like IQS and IQH as Hellenistic syncretism is going entirely in the wrong direction. Cullmann has, however, found supporters, e.g., A. Klijn, *NTS*, 4 (1957/58), 25-31, and P. Geoltrain, "Esséniens et Hellénistes," *ThZ*, 15 (1959), 241-54. E. Blair in *Jesus in the Gospel of Matthew* (New York, 1960),

That these Hellenistic people in Jerusalem had, prior to becoming Christians, rejected the temple, as Bacon thinks, is quite another matter. What has to be explained in this hypothesis is why they were not persecuted before becoming Christians rather than afterwards. As we have seen, Jewish feelings about the temple were so sensitive that a programmatic rejection of it by any Jews in Jerusalem would have caused strong reaction. Of course, there may have been persecutions of Hellenistic Jews with these radical views before the persecution of the Stephanic Christians, but then one has to wonder how there could have been such Jews left in Jerusalem to become Christian. For whatever the account may contain of historical information, in Acts 6 it is said to be the Hellenistic Jews in Jerusalem who cause Stephen to be brought before the authorities in the first place, perhaps further indication that Stephen's followers had come to hold different views from their fellow Hellenistic Jews.

While Hellenistic Jewish *uncertainty* about the temple is to be seen as a necessary presupposition for the Stephanic attitude, the arguments of the previous paragraph lead to the conclusion that something in the *Christian* understanding of the Hellenistic church must have been the catylist in the move toward rejection of the temple. What this could have been is also a most difficult question, for the church of the apostles apparently found no difficulty in their loyalty to the temple. In fact this raises the basic question, which becomes the more urgent the earlier we push back the Hellenistic church, how a split within the church over basic beliefs could have happened so soon after the death of Jesus when, presumably, his ideas were still fresh in the minds of the disciples.

4. We are thus led, in the final consideration, to the question: What

---

accepts Cullmann's views and then tries to derive a relationship between the Hellenists and Matthew, pp. 143-61. While relationship might be possible between Matthew and Qumran, his attempt to relate Matthew and Acts 7 seems completely unconvincing to me.

Nevertheless, the new finds at Qumran have created some surprises. The discovery there of a text of Exodus which seems to follow the Samaritan version has opened up the possibility that some relation might exist between the Samaritans and Qumran, cf. Geoltrain, *ThZ*, 15 (1959), 251f.; M. Black, "The Patristic Accounts of Jewish Sectarianism," *JRLB*, 41 (1958/59), 296f.; and J. Bowman, "Contact between Samaritan Sects and Qumran," *VT*, 7 (1957), 184-89. The last-named scholar sums up his findings: "Direct points of contact between Samaritan sects and Qumran probably never existed, but both grew out of a similar background," p. 189. In view of this, dogmatically to deny any possible relationship between Acts 7 and Qumran is rather precarious. To be convincing, however, the arguments proposed will have to be more cogent than the ones Cullmann mounts.

is the relation, if any, between the view of this Hellenistic church and those of Jesus? Here there are at least four possibilities.

a. Jesus upheld the temple and the Stephanic group is wrong.
b. Jesus rejected the temple and the apostles are wrong.
c. Jesus made no unambiguous proclamation, and each group drew what it felt were the correct implications.
d. Regardless of what Jesus said, the death, resurrection, and the resulting kerygma about Jesus led the Stephanic group to its view.

Any argumentation here is of necessity too subtle and complex to mount in this essay. It can at least be said, however, that had Jesus made a programmatic statement for or against the temple, how either group could have consciously turned against him is hard to see. Thus possibilities (a) and (b) are probably to be excluded. What may be the most likely is a combination of (c) and (d). The number of references to Jesus' supposed prediction of the destruction of the temple are so numerous that many scholars believe some authentic saying lies behind the various traditions.[1] Goguel draws the intriguing, if radical, conclusion from these sayings that Jesus had in fact made a complete rejection of the temple.[2] This judgment in my opinion founders among other reasons on the extreme difficulty of understanding how the original disciples could have so immediately rejected such a definite and central feature of his message, one which as Goguel conceives it, was at the very heart of Jesus' final proclamation. Nevertheless, Goguel may be more correct than those scholars who take as normative the view that Jesus 'cleansed' or 'purified' the temple. The statements about the destruction of the temple in the gospel traditions are all predictive. What this may mean is that the destruction of the temple was seen by Jesus as an eschatological event to be associated with the tumultuous happenings of the messianic woes, just as Mark implies in chapter 13. Should this be the case, Jesus, perhaps influenced by a pessimism over the real value of the present temple, rejected any notion of a glorified temple in the eschatological era, such as was

---

[1]) Cf. R. Bultmann, *Die Geschichte der Synoptischen Tradition* (Göttingen, 1957), pp. 126f., for a convenient discussion.
[2]) *Jesus*, II, 412-424, 507-509. He is followed by M. Simon, "Retour du Christ et reconstruction du Temple dans la pensée chrétienne primitive," *Aux Sources de la tradition chrétienne* (Neuchatel, 1950), 247-50.

hoped for by some Jewish traditions.[1] This is at least the implication of Mark 13:2 and Acts 6:14, and is not necessarily opposed to Mark 14:58 where Jesus is charged with prophesying a rebuilding of a temple not made by hands, ἀχειροποίητος, (cf. Acts 7:48). Such a temple might not at all be the glorified eschatological temple but a symbol, as it is in Hebrews, for an entirely different way of relating man to God.

At any rate, the prediction of the removal of the temple in the eschatological era would be just the kind of statement that *could* explain the deviation in early Christian belief.[2] If the death and resurrection of Jesus proclaimed in the kerygma were taken as the inbreaking of the eschatological eon, then the Stephanic group could argue, with some relief, that the days of the temple are over (again, just as Hebrews does). On the other hand, if the eschatological day begins only with the return of Jesus as the exalted Messiah, then the temple could be seen as still a valid part of Jewish-Christian piety. The evidence of the divergent churches in Matthew and Mark comes to our aid here, for the emphasis by the Gentile-centered church upon the gifts of the spirit would seem to suggest that this church thought the spirit-filled eschatological days had begun. The contrary seems to have been the case with the Jewish-centered church (cf. Matt. 7:22). Paul and the enthusiasts he fights are further instances of a belief in the presence of the kingdom held by the Gentile-centered churches. If these conjectures contain any truth, it cannot be said that the Hellenistic Christians proclaimed *the* message of Jesus. Yet one wonders whether they were not more open than the church of the apostles to the radical implications of his proclamation.

---

[1] Cf. Tob. 14:4f.: I Enoch 90:28f. and 91:13. Cited by Strack-Billerbeck, *Kommentar zum Neuen Testament aus Talmud und Midrasch* (Munich, 1956), I, 1003.

[2] A similar approach is taken also by W. Foerster, "Stephanus und die Urgemeinde," in *Dienst unter dem Wort* (Gütersloh, 1953), pp. 9-30.

THE PURPOSE OF THE HELLENISTIC PATTERNS IN THE EPISTLE TO THE HEBREWS

BY

ROBERT S. ECCLES

De Pauw University

Influence of Hellenistic thought upon the Epistle to the Hebrews has long been recognized. Comparisons have frequently been made between Hebrews and Philo Judaeus.[1] Usually such comparisons have been of sporadic nature, and have served primarily to raise questions concerning the background of Hebrews, or even occasionally to support some theory concerning the authorship of the epistle.[2] Recently it has been argued that the typology of Hebrews need not be attributed to a supposed influence by Philonic-Alexandrian thought, since Old Testament influence is sufficient to explain it.[3] The deficiency of most theories concerning possible Hellenistic or Philonic influence upon Hebrews lies in the fact that they fail to consider the total pattern and purpose of the epistle. It is in the intention of the present study to consider the Hellenistic elements within Hebrews in the light of its central purpose.

The central feature of Hebrews is its interpretation of the saving work of Christ as the work of a heavenly high priest. Representation of Christ as priest is in the New Testament unique to Hebrews. How does this serve the author's purpose? Viewing the epistle as a whole, what can we discern concerning its intention and purpose? It is strongly hortatory in its warning against rebelliousness (3:12ff.), and against faltering in faith (2:1ff.; 10:23ff.). Hebrews warns its readers against falling back into Judaism, but with its great preoccupation with matters of the sanctuary and priestly sacrifice, it hardly seems possible that it intends to warn against reversion to the Judaism that

---

[1] See James Moffatt, *Hebrews*, International Critical Commentary, New York, 2nd ed., 1924, lxi.

[2] As for example, Apollos. See Luther, *Sämmtliche Werke*, Erlangen Ausg., Bd. VII, 2e Aufl., 1866, S. 190.

[3] Charlest T. Fritsch, "TO ANTITUPON," to be published in a forthcoming Festschrift for Vriezen.

Paul has in mind in Galatians and Romans. The clue to the major purpose of Hebrews is to be found in 3:1-6. In these verses the author argues that Christ in his high priesthood is superior to Moses as builder to house, and as servant to son. This raises two questions. First, why in the peculiar role of *priesthood* should Christ be declared superior to Moses? Secondly, to whom could the idea have occurred that Christ was *not* superior to Moses? Nowhere else in the New Testament is the question even raised.

It is at this point that the studies of Philo by E. R. Goodenough have rendered great service in making possible a more comprehensive interpretation of the Hellenistic patterns in Hebrews, especially making possible a better explanation of the author's purpose in representing Christ as heavenly high priest.[1] Students of Philo tend to divide into two camps. Some find Philo's philosophy to be of primary importance, and his Judaism simply a framework around which he erected his philosophical structure.[2] Others find Philo's religion to be primary, and his philosophy simply the support for what to him was all important, his Jewish religion.[3] Goodenough belongs to the second group.

In the Hellenistic world before the beginning of the Christian era the mystery religions commanded the devotion of countless individuals.[4] Likewise philosophy exhibited a clear strain of mysticism. Whereas many persons of all classes of society in the Hellenistic world found satisfaction for their spiritual needs in the mystery religions with their solemn rituals, many intellectuals sought satisfaction rather in philosophy. Edward Caird declares that with the decay of the state religions "philosophy had to step into the vacant place and to supply, at least for the educated classes, the kind of spiritual nutriment which

---

[1] *By Light, Light, the Gospel of Mystic Judaism*, New Haven, 1935. Henceforth referred to as *BLL*.

[2] James Drummond, *Philo Judaeus, or the Jewish-Alexandrian Philosophy*, London, 1888, 2 vols. gives an earlier treatment, whereas the most important modern treatment of Philo as philosopher is in Harry Wolfson, *Philo*, Cambridge, Mass., 1948, 2 vols.

[3] Edward Caird, *The Evolution of Theology in the Greek Philosophers*, Glasgow, 1904, 2 vols., esp. vol. ii, pp. 184-209; Hans Windisch, *Die Frommigkeit Philos und ihre Bedeutung fur das Christentum*, Leipzig, 1909; Heinemann, *Philons griechische und judische Bildung*, Breslau, 1932; Pascher, 'Η ΒΑΣΙΛΙΚΗ 'ΟΔΟΣ: *Der Konigsweg zu Wiedergeburt und Vergottung bei Philon von Alexandreia*, Paderborn, 1931 (Studien zur Geschichte und Kultur des Altertums XVII, Parts 2 and 4).

[4] Angus, *The Religious Quests of the Graeco-Roman World*, London, 1929; Willoughby, *Pagan Regeneration*, Chicago, 1929.

they required."[1] It is in this situation that Philo made his contribution.

Goodenough shows that Philo was always loyal to the tradition of Judaism as he understood it, unwavering in his loyalty to the Torah. Yet in his allegorical interpretation of scripture Philo shows how deeply he was influenced by Hellenistic philosophy and mysticism.[2] Goodenough concludes that although Philo was repelled by the paganism of the mystery cults, the patterns of philosophical mysticism were congenial to him, and in his interpretation of the Torah he represents the religion of Judaism as a mystery, indeed as two mysteries, the Lower Mystery of Aaron, and the Higher Mystery of Moses.

The Lower Mystery of Aaron provides for the worship of God from the point of view of the material world through the symbolism of the Jerusalem cultus of temple and priesthood. Only Jews are invited to participate in the Mystery of Aaron.[3] Gentiles, however, are invited by Philo to share in the Higher Mystery of Moses.[4] In Philo's description of the Higher Mystery, as Goodenough shows,[5] he was influenced by the Hellenistic idea of kingship. Sharing in cosmic rulership was characteristic of the Hellenistic concept of the ideal king. One of the important functions of Moses' kingly office according to Philo was that of priest. While on Mount Sinai Moses was instructed in the "mysteries of his priestly duties".[6] However much Philo might think of Moses as king, however, ultimately for him God alone is supreme heavenly king.[7] It is the identification of Moses by Philo as high priest which makes comparison between Philo and Hebrews imperative for fuller clarification of the basic purpose of Hebrews.

It is possible that other elements in the thought-pattern of Hebrews

---

[1] *Op. cit.*, ii, p. 49.

[2] Heinemann (*op. cit.*, pp. 78ff.) asserts that there is nothing in Philo's conception of the sacrificial law and the temple cultus which he could not have derived from Greek sources.

[3] *BLL*, ch. 4, *passim*.

[4] *Ibid.*, ch. 5, *passim*.

[5] *Ibid.*, pp. 38ff.

[6] *Moses*, ii, 74f. (Citations and quotations from Philo are from *Philo, with an English Translation*, by F. N. Colson and G. H. Whitaker, London and New York: Loeb Classical Library, vols. I-X, 1949-1962; and *Philo, Supplement*, by Ralph Marcus, London and New York: Loeb Classical Library, vols. I, II, 1953. Abbreviations of the titles of Philo's works are those of Colson-Whitaker, vol. I, p. xxiiif.)

[7] On this point see Goodenough, *BLL*, 38ff., and Goodenough, *The Politics of Philo Judaeus*, with a general bibliography of Philo by Howard L. Goodhart and E. R. Goodenough, New Haven, 1938, p. 90f.

may have been colored by the concept of Hellenistic kingship. For instance, the very Hellenistic description of Christ that: "He is the effulegence of the glory of God and bears the very stamp of his image" (1:3) may be compared with a statement from Ecphantus quoted by Stobaeus: "Accordingly the king, as a copy of the higher king, is a single and unique creation, for he is on the one hand always intimate with the one who made him, while to his subjects he appears as though he were in a light, the light of royalty."[1] To this may be added Philo's description of Moses' appearance after his descent from Sinai so that the eye-witnesses could not "continue to stand the dazzling brightness that flashed from him like the rays of the sun."[2] Significantly this passage stands within Philo's discussion of Moses as high priest. Even though the claim of Hebrews that Christ was God-begotten rests upon the Old Testament (1:5, cf. Ps. 2:7), the possibility of Hellenistic influence cannot be ruled out. Ecphantus' statement supports the idea of the divine sonship of the king. Philo describes Moses' ascent of Sinai as essentially a second birth "better than the first. For the latter is mixed with a body and had corruptible parents, while the former is an unmixed and simple soul of the sovereign, being changed from a productive to an unproductive form, which has no mother but only a father, who is (the Father) of all."[3] In this study, however, we must confine ourselves to consideration of the concept of the high-priestly mediator as found in Hebrews, and compared with Philo and other representatives of Hellenistic Judaism.

In Philo there is a significant convergence of concepts. At one time Philo represents Moses as high priest, but at another time it is the Logos which is high priest. Finally Moses is also identified with the Logos. A comparable convergence of concepts in Hebrews would suggest the sharing of elements of a common thought-pattern by both Philo and the author of Hebrews. Philo says that Moses was qualified for priesthood by his natural piety and natural gifts in which "philosophy found good soil."[4] Before Moses could exercise his function as high priest he had to be clean in soul and body. He followed a preparatory discipline which resulted in his remarkable growth in grace

---

[1] Stob., IV, vii, 64, 65, 66 (IV, 271ff.) quoted in Goodenough, "The Political Philosophy of Hellenistic Kingship," *Yale Classical Studies*, I (1928) 53-102, Yale University Press, p. 75.
[2] *Mos.*, ii, 70.
[3] *Q.E.*, ii, 46.
[4] *Mos.*, ii, 66.

which gave him access to the sacred mountain, Sinai, where during a period of forty days he enjoyed the heavenly vision. While on the mountain Moses was instructed in the mysteries of his priestly duties, the first of which was the building and furnishing of the tabernacle[1]. Of this Philo comments:

> It was fitting that the construction of the sanctuary should be committed to him who was truly high priest, in order that his performance of the rites belonging to his sacred office might be in more than full accordance with the fabric.[2]

Elsewhere Philo discusses the high priesthood of Moses in such terms as to represent his nature as on the boundary between the mortal and the immortal.[3]

> The good man indeed is on the border-line, so that we may say, quite properly, that he is neither God nor man, but bounded at either end by the two, by mortality because of his manhood, by incorruption because of his virtue. Similar to this is the oracle given about the high priest: "When he enters," it says, "into the Holy of Holies, he will not be a man until he comes out."
>
> (Lev. 16:17)

Philo makes much of Moses' preparation for his role of supreme religious mediator and high priest.[4] Unlike the other patriarchs who undergo great struggles of discipline in order to achieve the mystic vision, Moses is a special type of superior incarnation ruling over the whole mortal realm of his existence, not even like a king, but like a god.[5]

Goodenough in interpreting Philo's discussion of the meaning of Moses' sitting "outside the camp" declares: "Moses sitting outside the camp is really then a type of the perfect mystic who, having gone beyond the experience of the Logos in the Cosmos, comes to the higher doctrines of the Mystery, and can live simply and continuously on that level. *Indeed he is that Logos itself.*"[6]

Just as there appears to be a convergence of the conceptions of high-priesthood and of the Logos in Philo's representations of Moses, so in Hebrews there seems to be a similar convergence of these conceptions

---

[1] *Ibid.*, 67-73.
[2] *Ibid.*, 74f.
[3] *Som.*, ii, 231f., cf. 189.
[4] *Gig.*, 54f.
[5] *Sac.*, 9.
[6] *BLL.*, p. 211. See *Gig.*, 51f. Italics are those of the author of the present study.

applied to Christ. The classic representation of Christ as Logos in Hebrews appears at the very beginning of the epistle, suggesting the importance which this idea held in the theology of the author. "In these last days he has spoken to us by a Son, whom he appointed the heir of all things, through whom also he created the world. He reflects the glory of God and bears the very stamp of his nature, upholding the universe by his word of power." (1:2f.). The view has been widely held by scholars that this passage intends to identify Christ with the Logos.[1] Windisch finds in Philo close parallels to the ideas in the passage in Hebrews 1:2f., and regards the terms *apaugasma* and *charaktēr* within the passage as "Termini und Anschauungen einer jüdisch-Hellenistischen Spekulation."[2]

Hebrews argues that Christ is of the order of Melchizedek. This stems from the author's application to Christ of Psalm 110. The crucial verse is: "He is without father or mother or genealogy, and has neither beginning of days nor end of life, but resembling the Son of God he continues a priest forever" (7:3). Rabbinic tradition includes little reference to such speculation,[3] consequently it is necessary to look elsewhere for possible influences upon the thought of Hebrews giving rise to such speculation on the part of its author. The Christ of Hebrews, of the order of Melchizedek, is superior to Levi and Aaron. As perfect Son of God he is priest forever, and he ministers in the true heavenly sanctuary. He also mediates the new covenant of Jeremiah's prophecy, hence the old ordinances and sacrifices of the Levitical priesthood are futile, for Christ by his death and the shedding of his own blood accomplished the perfect sacrifice. Finally, the Levitical sacrifices are only symbolic, and are not efficacious in themselves.[4]

In Philo we find relatively few references to Melchizedek. He is the ideal king,[5] and he is the Logos, heir of Being who grows the wine

---

[1]) Moffat, *op. cit.*, p. 5; Windisch, *Der Hebraerbrief*, Tubingen, 1931 (*Handbuch zum Neuen Testament*, Nr. 14), p. 10; Clemen, *Primitive Christianity and its Non-Jewish Sources*, Edinburgh, 1912, p. 73f.

[2]) *Op. cit.*, p. 10f., Philo, *Mig.*, 6, *Sac.*, 8.

[3]) Strack-Billerbeck, *Kommentar zum Neuen Testament aus Talmud und Midrasch*, iv, p. 464 cites the only two known rabbinic references to Melchizedek as messianic high priest: Aboth de Rabbi Nathan, 34, and Pesiqtha (de Rab Kahana) 51. The lateness of these references and the complete absence of any apparent orientation of Hebrews to the rabbinic tradition makes rabbinic influence seem improbable. Windisch (*Hebräerbrief*, p. 61f.) finds Hebrews much closer to Philo than to rabbinic tradition.

[4]) For the full development of this argument see Heb. 7:26-10:18.

[5]) *LA*, iii, 79ff.

that produces in men the Sober Intoxication of divine ecstasy.[1] Melchizedek, just as he is without antecedents, is priest "whose tradition he had learned from none other but himself."[2] Goodenough regrets the loss of the section in Philo's treatise *Quaestiones in Genesin* that would have treated Genesis 14:17ff. where Melchizedek is mentioned. He surmises that it might have told us more of the significance of Melchizedek and so have thrown more light on the Epistle to the Hebrews.[3] Goodenough remarks that Hebrews suggests that the Philonic interpretation of Melchizedek was a current one.[4]

In the 19th century M. Friedländer suggested that a mystery cult was very early formed about the figure of Melchizedek, and that both the Melchizedekian and Ophite heresies of early Christianity were actually pre-Christian in their origin.[5] Friedländer believed that Melchizedekianism was the form of early Christian Gnosticism by which Alexandrian philosophical mysticism passed rapidly into Christianity. He called attention to significant similarities between the views of the Melchizedekian sectaries and views of Philo concerning Melchizedek.[6] More recently A. R. Johnson has sought the source of Melchizedek speculation in the development of the role of the king in the Jerusalem cultus.[7] He thinks that the Davidic kingship may have been based on an earlier form of the Jerusalem cultus originally centered in a pre-Israelite deity known in Jerusalem as El Elyon, the "Most High God."[8] This god was also the personification of SEDEK, the focus of loyalty or right relation of the social unit, and so the source of its wellbeing. After the capture of Jerusalem Saul's successors found in the Jebusite cultus of the High-god Elyon and its royal-priestly order of Malkisedek a valuable means of emphasizing the ideal unity of the kings. The least to be said for these theories is that they suggest how widespread speculation about Melchizedek may have been in the Hellenistic-Jewish tradition, and how important it is to seek the environment of the thought-pattern of Hebrews.

---

[1]) *Ibid.*, 82.
[2]) *Cong.*, 99.
[3]) *BLL*, p. 145, n.
[4]) *Ibid.*, p. 151, n.
[5]) "Melchizedek et l'épitre aux Hebreux," *Revue des Etudes Juives*, v, vi (1882) 1-26; 188-98.
[6]) *Ibid.*, p. 22.
[7]) "The Roles of the King in the Jerusalem Cultus," in *The Labyrinth*, ed. Hooke, London, 1935, ch. 5.
[8]) Hooke, *Myth and Ritual*, London, 1933, ch. 5.

Of major significance to the present study is a collection of fragments of a Jewish liturgy derived by W. Bousset from a study of the *Apostolic Constitutions*.[1] Bousset concluded that fragments preserved in the Christian document were drawn from a Hellenistic Jewish background. The Jewish material was taken over by Christians and adapted to Christian use by slight interpolations. Goodenough's fresh study of this material renders the additional service of indicating the milieu in which such a Jewish liturgy might have originated, namely in Hellenistic-Jewish mysticism closely akin to that of Philo.[2] Two passages within this Jewish liturgical material refer to Melchizedek. The first is in the context of baptismal instruction which includes the injunction, "Let him be taught how God... did glorify the saints in every generation—I mean Seth, and Enos, and Enoch, and Noah, and Abraham, and his posterity, and Melchizedek, and Job, and Moses, and Joshua, and Caleb, and Phineas the priest, and those that were holy in every generation."[3] Of this passage Goodenough remarks, "The Patriarchs selected as 'glorified' are, except Job, precisely those of Philo... What is here is unmistakably the Judaism of the Mystery."[4] Another of the liturgical passages concludes the names of almost exactly the same list of patriarchs, including Melchizedek, and in the same order, except that Abel, Isaac, Jacob, Joseph, and Aaron are mentioned, and Caleb and Phineas are not.[5] Most interesting of all is the inclusion of Melchizedek in a patriarch list comprising nearly all of the same names mentioned in the two preceding passages, in which all are described as *priests*.[6] Goodenough declares that such a list could come only from the Mystery, by whose Judaism alone these patriarchs were accounted as priests.[7]

In the light of these data it is not unreasonable to suppose that while the author of Hebrews is undoubtedly influenced by the messianic interpretation of Melchizedek found in Psalm 110, he is at the same time influenced by an exegetical tradition of mystic Judaism. Although

---

[1] "Eine jüdische Gebetssammlung im siebenten Buch der apostolischen Konstitutionen," in *Nachrichten von der k. Gesellschaft der Wissenschaften zu* Göttingen, Philologische-Historische Klasse, 1915 (1916), pp. 435-485.
[2] *BLL*, pp. 306-358.
[3] *Const.* VII, xxxix, 2-4, in Goodenough, *BLL*, p. 326.
[4] *BLL*, p. 327.
[5] *Const.*, VIII, xii, 6-27, in Goodenough, *BLL*, p. 330.
[6] *Const.*, VIII, v, 1-4, in Goodenough, *BLL*, p. 330.
[7] *BLL*, p. 331.

Philo most fully exemplifies this tradition, he is not its only spokesman as the liturgical fragments suggest.

The distinctiveness of Hebrews lies in its interpretation of Christ's saving work as a high-priestly act performed in the heavenly sanctuary. Christ is "minister in the sanctuary and the true tent which is set up not by man but by the Lord" (8:2). This is in contrast to the work of the earthly priests who "serve a copy and shadow of the heavenly sanctuary; for when Moses was about to erect the tent, he was instructed by God, saying, 'See that you make everything according to the pattern which was shown you on the mountain'" (8:5). In Hebrews 9 the contrast between the earthly and heavenly tabernacles is continued with a somewhat detailed description of the sacred furnishings, the daily sacrifices offered by the ordinary priests, and the entry into the Holy of Holies by the high priest on the Day of Atonement. The author remarks, "By this the Holy Spirit indicates that the way into the sanctuary is not yet opened as long as the outer tent is still standing (which is symbolic for the present age)" (9:8f.).

According to Hebrews under the system of sacrifices practiced in the earthly temple the ritual regulations cannot perfect the conscience of the worshipper, and are imposed only until the time of reformation. "But when Christ appeared as a high priest of the good things that have come, then through the greater and more perfect tent (not made with hands, that is, not of this creation) he entered once for all into the Holy Place, taking not the blood of goats and calves but his own blood, thus securing an eternal redemption" (9:11f.). The more perfect sanctuary is heaven itself (9:24). In the contrast between the earthly and heavenly tabernacles and references to the earthly as but a shadow of the heavenly realm students of Hebrews see the clearest evidence of the influence of Hellenistic thought-patterns.[1]

Philo refers to the world as God's house in the realm of sense-perception. "It is a 'sanctuary', an outshining of sanctity, so to speak, a copy of the original."[2] "There are," says Philo, "two temples of God: one of them this universe, in which there is also as High Priest His First-born, the divine Logos (Cf. Christ as Logos in Hebrews 1:2-3!), the divine Logos, and the other the rational soul, whose Priest is the

---

[1]) See Eager, "The Hellenistic Elements in the Epistle to the Hebrews," *Hermathena*, XI (1901) 263-87; Moffatt, *An Introduction to the Literature of the New Testament*, Edinburgh, 3rd ed., 1918, p. 427f.; and Kennedy, *St. Paul and the Mystery Religions*, London, 1913, ch. 2.
[2]) *Plant.*, 50.

real Man."[1] Of the latter the Levitical priest is the outward, visible image. He in wearing the priestly tunic, "which is a copy and replica of the whole heaven" symbolizes the fact "that the universe may join with man in the holy rites and man with the universe."[2] Philo's ultimate conviction would appear to be that the worshipper's concern ought to center upon the higher spiritual reality which the earthly sanctuary only reflects.[3] Ultimately no earthly tabernacle is adequate for God. "It is not possible genuninely to express our gratitude to God by means of buildings and oblations and sacrifices, as is the custom of most people, for even the whole world were not a temple adequate to yield the honor due to Him."[4]

In three separate descriptions of the Lower Mystery of Aaron, each varying in detail from the others, Philo gives extended descriptions of the tabernacle.[5] The table, the candlestick, the tabernacle and its curtains, and altar of sacrifice, and the veil separating the Holy of Holies for Philo all serve as symbols of the progress of the worshipper through the stages of the Mystery toward the ultimate goal of contemplation of and communion with God.[6] Clement of Alexandria reproduces a description of the tabernacle remarkably similar to that of Philo, but gives an allegorical interpretation which differs from Philo's. It appears that Clement drew from a different account of the Hellenistic Mystery of Aaron than that reproduced by Philo. Josephus likewise records a symbolic interpretation of the temple fundamentally the same as that of Philo, yet so different in detail that Josephus can hardly have drawn his material from Philo. We may conclude then that Jews of the Hellenistic period in a variety of ways made the Temple and its furnishings represent the mystic rise from material confusion, through the cosmos mystically and philosophically interpreted, to the *kosmos noētos* and to God. The very variety of detail is important because of the unity of purpose underlying the variety. This suggests a single and widely familiar tradition of philosophic mysticism characterized by broad divergences. However, all persons who were familiar with this tradition saw in the sanctuary of tabernacle or temple the symbol of the worship of immaterial reality by way of the material elements.[7]

---
[1] *Som.*, i, 215.
[2] *Ibid.*, 216. Philo expresses similar ideas in *Ebr.*, 132 and *Spec.*, i, 66f.
[3] *Heres.*, 112.
[4] *Plant.*, 126, cf. *Heres.*, 123.
[5] *Mos.*, ii, 66-108; 136-140; *Spec.*, i, 71-97; *QE*, ii, 69-123.
[6] *Mos.*, ii, 71-135; cf. Goodenough, *BLL*, p. 97.
[7] *BLL*, p. 99.

If we consider the discussion of the tabernacle in Hebrews against this background the purpose of the epistle is seen in new perspective. The author seems to presuppose on the part of his readers a knowledge of the symbolism present in Philo and other sources. Hebrews declares that the earthly tabernacle is a copy of the divine pattern, and that the earthly tabernacle has a heavenly counterpart. The order of details in the description of the tabernacle in Hebrews is remarkably similar to that of Philo's description.[1] However, the author of Hebrews simply catalogs the sacred furnishings, and makes no effort to explain their symbolism. He concludes with the tantalizing comment, "Of these things we cannot now speak in detail" (9:5). Surely the author was prepared to say more on the subject, and there is no reason to suppose that he considered these details irrelevant. It is more reasonable to suppose that he is addressing a group of Christians already familiar with the philosophic and mystical interpretation of the sanctuary widespread in Hellenistic Judaism. This would lend force to his reproof of them in another connection in which he chides them for having become "dull of hearing", and at a time when they themselves "ought to be teachers" they need someone once again to teach them the "first principles of God's word" (5:11f.).

In addition to his symbolic treatment of the heavenly sanctuary, the author of Hebrews speaks symbolically of the heavenly city. Abraham "looked forward to the city which has foundations, whose builder and maker is God" (11:10). Of Abraham a multitude of descendents were born, all of whom lived as "strangers and exiles in the earth, ... seeking a homeland", for they desire a better, heavenly country. "Therefore God is not ashamed to be called their God, for he has prepared for them a city" (11:13-16). To the terror of the Israelites before Sinai Hebrews contrasts the triumphant joy of those who "have come to Mount Zion and to the city of the living God, the heavenly Jerusalem" (12:22f.). The author of Hebrews characterizes his readers in precisely the same terms in which he represented Abraham and his descendents, "For here we have no lasting city, but we seek the city which is to come" (13:14). From what source did the author of Hebrews derive this symbolism?

In a recent monograph Charles T. Fritsch has proposed an answer to this question.[2] Fritsch's special interest is in the use of the term *to antitupon* in two places in the New Testament because of the new

---

[1]) To *Mos.*, ii, 66-108 compare Heb. 9:1-5.
[2]) *Op. cit.*

dimension of thought which it adds to the Biblical concept of typology. The first is in 1 Peter 3:21, "Baptism, an antitype *(antitupon)* of this (i.e., the flood waters), now saves you ..." This demonstrates the prophetic, or horizontal, typology in which the Old Testament type, or *Vorbild*, is fulfilled in the New Testament antitype. The other instance is in Hebrews 9:24, "For Christ has not entered into a sanctuary made with hands, the antitype of the true one *(antitupa tōn alēthinōn)*, but into heaven itself. ..." This demonstrates what Fritsch calls a "vertical" typology in which the heavenly type, or *Urbild*, is disclosed in the earthly antitype.

Fritsch concludes that since the reference to the earthly tabernacle as the antitype of the heavenly model is based on Exod. 25:9 and 25:40, it is unnecessary to go outside the Old Testament to find the sources of the typology of Hebrews. Although Fritsch admits that in the ancient world every temple had its celestial archetype, as did every important city, and though he cites one Assyrian example, he nevertheless declares that the celestial-terrestrial Jerusalem motif as developed in Jewish writings and in the New Testament went far beyond the astrological myths of the Babylonians and Assyrians.

Of greatest significance to our present study is Fritsch's conclusion that the view that the typology of Hebrews has been shaped by a combination of Platonic, Philonic, and Alexandrian ideas is an unnecessary assumption, for the Old Testament is adequate to account for this. As he says, "The author of Hebrews regarded the earthly adumbration of the heavenly order as ordained by God for the purpose of redemption, and not as a philosophical explanation of the nature of the universe in terms of two contrasting orders, the world of matter and the world of ideas, the ephemeral and the eternal, the phenomenal and the noumenal, as Platonism had done. In other words, redemption, not cosmology, is the main interest of the author of Hebrews."[1]

Fritsch's conclusions are open to criticism on at least two points. First, in selecting only one element of the symbolism of Hebrews, he is in danger of misconstruing its sources through failure to consider the main purpose its author had in employing the imagery. Secondly, in dismissing the aim of Philo and the Alexandrian school as simply that of finding a philosophical explanation of the nature of the universe, he fails to recognize the importance of the religious quests of the Hellenistic world. Goodenough has shown that Philo's aim was a

---

[1] *Ibid.*, p. 5.

religious one, consequently his aim and that of the author of Hebrews cannot at the outset be declared to be totally divergent from each other.

Gunkel in his study of New Testament backgrounds concluded that the tradition of the heavenly Jerusalem is not to be explained entirely by the apostolic tradition.[1] It is an independent tradition of a mythology which stems from the idea that heaven is a city of the gods. That this myth was borrowed by the Jews, and the heavenly city was name by them Jerusalem, is shown by the attributes assigned to the heavenly city: adornment with precious stones, light, and splendor. Earlier Judaism stressed the glorification of the earthly Jerusalem, and only certain details were borrowed from the heavenly-city myth. Later Judaism took over completely the concept of the heavenly city. These conclusions should caution us against seeing in the heavenly city of Hebrews simply its author's own typological interpretation of the Old Testament, as Fritsch proposes, or simply the reflection of Jewish apocalypticism, as Windisch has concluded.[2] We must suppose, rather, that although the author of Hebrews may indeed reflect a tradition of biblical and theological interpretation which is both Palestinian and rabbinic, at the same time he is under the influence of an extremely rich religious tradition in which Jewish and Hellenistic elements are closely intermingled.

Philo also speaks of the heavenly Jerusalem.[3] But to him the Great City is the present universe in both its visible and invisible aspects, whereas in Hebrews the Heavenly City is a realm apart from the present universe, the messianic realm which stands beyond the earthly realm. For Philo the ideal city, the universe, is only the reflection of the Divine Absolute, whereas in Hebrews the Heavenly City is the ultimate abode of the Divine. Also Hebrews presents the image of the Heavenly City in terms of a contrast between the terrors of the revelation to Moses and the Israelites at Sinai, and the gracious welcome extended to those who "have come to Mount Zion and to the city of the living God, the heavenly. Jerusalem" (12:22).

This brings into relief a primary purpose of Hebrews, to show the Christian way of salvation in sharp contrast to a different system of salvation centered in Moses as its chief religious mediator. To Moses,

---

[1]) *Zum religionsgeschichtlichen Verständnis des Neuen Testaments*, Göttingen, 1903, pp. 48ff.
[2]) *Hebräerbrief*, p. 113.
[3]) *Som.*, ii, 50.

the mystagogue and mediator of the sacred mysteries of God, as Philo sees him, Hebrews contrast Christ, the one who upon entering the heavenly sanctuary within the heavenly city became the supreme Mediator and High Priest who eternally supplants and outshines the lesser mediator and inferior rites of the earthly cult.

In pointing out the superiority of the way of salvation through faith in Christ over the supposed way of salvation through Moses and the earthly rites, the author of Hebrews does not distinguish, as Philo does, between a Lower and a Higher Mystery. With respect to the heavenly sanctuary Hebrews contrasts the mortality of earthly priests and the ineffectualness of their sacrifices with the heavenly exaltation of Christ the eternal High Priest, and the ultimacy of his sacrifice. Here the contrast would seem to be to the Mystery of Aaron as conceived by Philo. On the other hand, Hebrews by its claim of the superiority of Christ to Moses would seem to be effecting a contrast between the Christian way and the Mystery of Moses. Thus Hebrews dismisses as inferior to the Christian way all mystic Judaism of whatever kind.[1]

The cryptic words, "the way into the sanctuary is not yet opened as long as the outer tent is still standing" (9:8f.) would seem to make sense only if the Jewish temple were still standing when the author of Hebrews wrote. The eschatology of the passage, foreign to Philo's thought, gives Hebrews its characteristic note of urgency which is especially evident in chapter 10. This appears in such passages as, "Since we have a great priest over the house of God, let us draw near with a true heart in full assurance of faith" (10:21f.); and "Recall the former days when, after you were enlightened, you endured hard struggle with sufferings... Therefore do not throw away your confidence, which has a great reward" (10:32, 35). All this would suggest that the author is exhorting his readers, in the light of the imminent eschaton, to devote themselves to the true worship of Christ, and not revert to the practice of any form of Judaism however it might be related to the temple and its rites. This might give a clue to the *terminus ad quem* as well as to the purpose of Hebrews.

One of the most notable chapters of Hebrews is the eleventh in which the author seeks to stir up the faith of his readers by a great

---

[1]) Goodenough (*BLL*, p. 120) reminds us of the fact that Josephus presents a Mystery of Aaron, but not a Mystery of Moses, suggesting that a cosmic interpretation of the temple cultus may have been familiar to Palestinian Judaism as a Higher Mystery was not. This may account for the lack of distinction between two types of Jewish Mystery in Hebrews.

roll-call of the past heroes of Israel's faith. These heroes extend from Abel to the Maccabean martyrs. The Jewish liturgical fragments, already referred to above in connection with Melchizedek, furnish the most important clues to the significance of the hero-list in Hebrews 11. One fragment must be quoted.[1]

> In the first place Thou didst respect the sacrifice of Abel, and accept it as Thou didst accept of the sacrifice of Noah, when he went out of the ark; of Abraham, when he went out of the land of the Chaldeans; of Isaac at the Well of the Oath; of Jacob in Bethel; of Moses in the desert; of Aaron between the dead and the living; of Joshua the son of Nun in Gilgal; of Gideon at the rock, and the fleeces, before his sin; of Manoah and his wife in the field; of Samson in his thirst before the transgression; of Jephtha in the war before his rash vow; of Barak and Deborah in the days of Sisera; of Samuel in Mizpah; of David on the threshingfloor of Ornan the Jebusite; of Solomon in Gibeon and in Jerusalem; of Elijah on Mount Carmel; of Elisha at the barren fountain; of Jehoshaphat in war; of Hezekiah in his sickness, and concerning Sennacherib; of Manasseh in the land of the Chaldeans, after his transgression; of Josiah in Phassa, of Ezra at the return of Daniel in the den of lions; of Jonah in the whale's belly; of the three children in the fiery furnace; of Hannah in the tabernacle before the ark; of Nehemiah at the rebuilding of the walls; of Zerubbabel; of Mattathias and his sons in their zeal; of Jael in blessing. Now also do thou receive the prayers of Thy people which are offered to Thee with gnosis, *through Christ in the Spirit*.

Bousset finds it incredible that a Christian of the time of the *Apostolic Constitutions* in which this fragment is embedded could have based all his precedents for prayer or sacrifice upon this list of patriarchs down to the Maccabean period, and not have gone on to mention the prayer or sacrifice of Christ or the achievements of the apostles.[2] It is similarly remarkable that the hero-list of Hebrews 11 mentions Samuel as the last hero to be mentioned by name in v. 32, and thereafter refers only to anonymous heroes and martyrs. Of further importance to our present study is the fact that in the list just quoted from the liturgical fragments, all the names listed in Hebrews 11 appear. Moreover, it includes the names of Gideon, Barak, and Jephtha which are not included in any of the other fragments identified by Bousset. This suggests an answer to a question which puzzled Moffat: why, since Jephtha is one of the four "judges" with the poorest reputation of all

---

[1] *Const.*, VII, xxxvii, 1-3, in Goodenough, *BLL*, p. 312f.
[2] Bousset, *op. cit.*, p. 446, cf. Goodenough, *BLL*, p. 313.

those named by Hebrews, was Jephtha included at all?[1] The evidence leads to the following conclusion. The author of Hebrews adapted a patriarch and hero-list from a Jewish liturgical source, applying it to a Christian purpose much in the same way that the Christian redactor incorporated the material into the *Apostolic Constitutions*. In this liturgical tradition upon which the author of Hebrews drew, patriarchs could sometimes be represented as priests, and comparatively unimportant individuals such as Gideon, Barak, and Jephtha achieved a special significance which made their inclusion in a list of spiritual heroes appropriate in the mystical Jewish tradition, although the reason is not apparent to us.

Persuasive as the evidence is that Hebrews has been influenced by the thought-patterns of the Hellenistic-Jewish Mystery, it is equally clear that Hebrews is dominated by another theme and pattern which are alien to Philo and the liturgical fragments. The theme is eschatology, and the pattern is that of the Christian kerygma. For Hebrews the goal is not the mystical ascent of the enlightened spirit, but rather the goal is the ultimate achievement by the believer of a place within the community of the redeemed in the Heavenly City. The author expresses his urgent concern that his readers "once having been enlightened" not through lethargy, fear of persecution, or decay of faith throw away their one and only opportunity for salvation so graciously proffered by Christ, and very presently to be fulfilled to those who do not fall away in faithlesness. The employment of Hellenistic patterns for the expression of the Christian faith in Hebrews serves only to enhance in the mind of the author his sense of eschatological urgency.

It is now necessary to show another thought-pattern at work in Hebrews, that of the kerygma. We follow the summary of the kerygma as analyzed by C. H. Dodd.[2] Dodd notes that the first point of the apostolic kerygma is that the age of fulfillment announced by the Old Testament prophets has now dawned in the advent of Jesus Christ. Hebrews announces this at the very outset: "In these last days he has spoken to us by a Son, whom he appointed the heir of all things" (1 : 2*a*.). Secondly, the fulfillment has occurred through the ministry death, and resurrection of Jesus. Hebrews is notable in that for all its concern to represent the resurrected Christ in the most exalted terms, it makes pointed reference to the earthly ministry of Jesus, the "pioneer of our salvation", made "perfect through suffering" (2:10), the one who

---

[1]) *Hebrews*, p. 185; cf. Heb. 11 :32.
[2]) *The Apostolic Preaching and Its Developments*, New York, 1949, pp. 21ff.

partook of the same nature of those who "share in flesh and blood", that "through death he might destroy him who has the power of death" (2:14). Christ, the Heavenly High Priest in Hebrews is identified with "one who in every respect has been tempted as we are" (4: 15), Jesus, who in the days of his flesh "offered up prayers and supplications, with loud cries and tears, to him who was able to save him from death" (5:7). The whole imagery in Hebrews of Christ's self-sacrificial act and his entry through death into the heavenly sanctuary is a celebration of his death and resurrection.

The third point of the kerygma concerns Christ's resurrection, by virtue of which he has been elevated by God as the Messianic head of the new Israel. Of this Hebrews leaves no doubt. "When he had made purification for sins, he sat down at the right hand of the Majesty on high" (1:3). The author reiterates this point throughout chapter 1 through quotations from messianic psalms. The fourth point of the kerygma is that the Holy Spirit in the Church is the sign of Christ's present power and glory. Hebrews does not dwell on this point, but rather presses on to emphasize the final point of the kerygma, that the Messianic Age will shortly reach its consummation.

Dodd has pertinent observations to make concerning the presence of the pattern of the kerygma in Hebrews. He notes instances in which the Pauline kerygma differs in detail from the Jerusalem kerygma of Acts. One such point which Hebrews shares with Paul is the assertion that the exalted Christ intercedes for us. Hebrews says that the exalted Christ "always lives to make intercession" for those who "draw near to God through him" (7:25, cf. Rom. 8:34).

It is well known that Rudolf Bultmann analyzes the New Testament kerygma in ways sharply different from those of Dodd. While Bultmann looks to formula-like expressions as evidence in the New Testament of a general Christian kerygma,[1] he is less willing than Dodd to identify a set of propositions such as Dodd finds in speeches in Acts with the kerygma. Bultmann finds most examples of the kerygma in the New Testament already to be colored by theological interpretation. Allowing for these differences in approach to the kerygma in Dodd and Bultmann, it is instructive for our purpose to note examples of Bultmann's recognition of the presence of the kerygma in Hebrews. He confines his notice of these to his chapter on "The Kerygma of the Hellenistic Church Aside from Paul".[2]

---
[1] *Theology of the New Testament*, New York, 1951, i, p. 64.
[2] *Ibid.*, pp. 63-183.

Bultmann notes that the call to believe in the one true God is at the same time a call to repentance, and he notes in Heb. 6:1 "repentance from dead works" in relation to "belief in God" stands at the threshold of Christianity."[1] In the primitive church the preaching of the resurrection from the dead is not to be separated from the preaching of God's judgment, and this idea appears among the "elementary doctrines" mentioned in Hebrews 6:2.[2] An inner causal connection between Jesus' resurrection and the general resurrection is subject for reflection in the kerygma, and appears in Hebrews 2:14f.[3] Bultmann notes that "according to the oldest view, Christ's resurrection coincides with his *exaltation* to heavenly glory." Hebrews speaks of this repeatedly (1:3, 13; 8:1; 10:12; 12:2).[3] Christ's death as a sacrifice is prominent in the kerygma of the Hellenistic church, and to this Hebrews makes abundant references (7:27; 9:26; 28; 10:10, 12).[5]

In a passage important for our purpose Dodd gives recognition to the distinctive way in which the pattern of Hellenistic thought has in Hebrews been interwoven with eschatological and kerygmatic patterns. He says, "The 'Age to Come' is identified with that order of eternal reality whose shadows or reflections form the world of phenomena. The death of Christ, therefore, which in the primitive preaching was the crisis of the eschatological process, is here His passage into the eternal order (9:12, 24) ... The death of Christ, therefore, is the point at which history becomes fully real, exhibiting no longer mere shadows, but 'the very image of realities' (10:1). The eschatological valuation of the death of Christ thus receives a new interpretation, which gives the clue to this writer's doctrine of His eternal priesthood."[6]

What conclusions may be drawn from the evidence that has been considered? No matter how far the author of Hebrews may go in representing Christ as the Mediator of a Christian Mystery, it is the Christian kerygma that he intends to proclaim, and not a Christian gnosticism. *Heilsgeschichte* dominates the argument of Hebrews. Christ is not the Mystagogue who, like the Moses of Philo, leads the individual illumined soul to the mystic vision of the Absolute. In Hebrews Christ is the incarnation of God within history, the one in whom the

---

[1] *Ibid.*, p. 73.
[2] *Ibid.*, p. 77.
[3] *Ibid.*, p. 81.
[4] *Ibid.*, p. 82.
[5] *Ibid.*, p. 85.
[6] *Op. cit.*, p. 45.

eschatological fulfillment of the *Heilsgeschichte* occurs. Salvation comes to those who accept the kerygma in faith, and are thereby granted the gift of eternal life and membership in the eschatological community.

To whom was the epistle originally addressed? It is well accepted that Hebrews was not addressed to Christians at large, but to a special community.[1] We must suppose that it was a community well acquainted with Hellenistic thought-patterns. Since there was no locality within the ancient Mediterranean world in which Hellenistic influences were not felt, the Hellenistic elements in Hebrews hardly serve to indicate its destination. The only clue to the point of origin of Hebrews is the reference to "those of Italy" in 13:24. It is perfectly reasonable that Hebrews originated in Hellenistic circles in Italy. If 9:8f. indicates that Hebrews was written while the Jerusalem temple was still standing, it is not impossible that the original recipients were themselves located in Palestine and were acquainted with a mystical form of Judaism comparable to that of Philo's Mystery of Aaron with its allegorization of the temple cultus. Yet the earliest references to Hebrews are found in writings issuing from the Roman church.[2] With the destruction of the temple in A.D. 70, and the resulting dispersion not only of Jews but of Jewish Christians from Jerusalem and Palestine, it is reasonable to suppose that members of the group to whom Hebrews was originally addressed migrated to Italy, perhaps to join with Christians from the church from which the epistle originated. Thus it would be possible for the original epistle, or a copy, to be returned to its point of origin.

The situation of Hebrews may be reconstructed somewhat as follows: The author, a convinced Christian, at the same time versed in Hellenistic thought, is writing from Italy to a Christian group somewhere in the provinces about whom he has received some communication. What he has learned of them arouses his concern for their advancement from elementary to mature Christian doctrine. His promise to visit his readers shortly (13:23) may indicate that he has been with them before, and perhaps was their very founder and teacher. Their failure to mature in their Christian faith to the degree that their teacher had a right to expect lies in their inability to see for themselves that Christ's way of salvation entirely supersedes the religion to which they previously adhered. We may suppose that this was a form of mystical Judaism in which, as in the thought of Philo,

---

[1]) Moffat, *Hebrews*, p. xv.
[2]) *Ibid.*, p. xiiif., citing 1 Clem. 36:2ff.; 2 Clem. 11:6; Shep. Herm. 3:2f.

Moses was revered as the supreme spiritual mediator. Perhaps the readers were still under the influences of their former mode of religious thought.

Their situation is an alarming one. They are being tempted to revert to their original Judaism for several reasons. First of all they face persecution, perhaps at the hands of Jews to whom they now appear by their adoption of Christianity to be apostates and renegades. In the face of opposition the readers have experienced a cooling-off of their faith. A further reason for their falling away from Christian faith lies in their disillusionment with the barrenness of Christian theology as they have known it. To them the Christian kerygma may have seemed indeed barren in contrast to the rich elaboration of allegory in the interpretation of scripture and cult in their former mystical Judaism.

The author of Hebrews meets these problems head-on. He shows how firmly anchored in the Jewish scriptures Christ and his saving work actually have been. Whatever claims for the mediatorship of Moses might be made in mystic Judaism, these pale in their inadequacy before the ultimate claims which Christians may make for the supreme saviorhood of Christ, their Heavenly High Priest. The very persecutions which the readers face may be a stimulus to their faith, since these are the advance notices of the last times now dawning, in which those whose faith is perfected may be joined to their heavenly Mediator. As a climax to his whole argument and exhortation the author rehearses the great acts of faith of the spiritual heroes of Israel's past in whose procession the readers may take their place if they do not abandon their own faith.

Throughout the epistle the author of Hebrews has affirmed the kerygma in the strongest possible terms. But he has succeeded in giving it an amazingly rich theological elaboration in terms of Hellenistic thought-patterns for the edification of those very Christians to whom such a way of thinking would seem most convincing. Yet all of this elaboration has but one goal, the stirring up of fundamental Christian faith. This is made plain in the climax of the epistle: "Therefore, since we are surrounded by so great a cloud of witnesses, let us also lay aside every weight, and sin which clings so closely, and let us run with perseverence the race that is set before us, looking to Jesus the pioneer and perfecter of our faith" (12:1f.).

NEW TESTAMENT AND GNOSTIC CHRISTOLOGY

BY

CARSTEN COLPÉ
Göttingen University

In the academic year 1963/64, when I was vicariously holding the chair of the History of Religions at Yale, which previously had been made world-famous by Erwin R. Goodenough, I had several impressive discussions with him about the intentions and aspects of his life-work. He told me that he originally had started what became later the monumental 12-volumes monograph on "Jewish Symbols" merely in order to know enough about Hellenistic Judaism for a solid N.T. exegesis. But now he had come, apart from the immense extension of his subject, also to postbiblical non-Christian times and would have to place N.T. concepts into a historical development whose end would be neither the N.T. itself nor the history of the early church. Here I mentioned, as an analogon, the problems which I was dealing with at that time for a paper.[1] This interested Erwin Goodenough greatly, and his contributions were in some respect clarifying to me. So it seems to me right to dedicate the substance of this paper to his memory.

The word "Theology" strongly suggests the implication that the early Christians should have been primarily oriented toward a doctrine of God. In these terms Christology would be a special case among the statements which could be made about God. Indeed, many manuals of Christian doctrine and even older books on New Testament Theology are oriented precisely this way. Still more, the succession of elements in the later creeds, i.e. the succession from God to Christ, makes it appear as if the early Church were concerned with Christ only secondarily (after its concern with God).

However, the fact that this is not the case is already indicated by the respective lengths of the two elements in these affirmations of faith. And apart from this, the history of the early church shows repeatedly that one was easily on the verge of heresy whenever one sought to

---

[1]) I read it on March 3, 1964 at Drew University, on May 4, 1964 at Harvard Divinity School, and on July 1, 1964 at Claremont School of Theology. For the help with the translation I have to thank Mssrs. R. Ezzell and W. Mount.

understand the first and third elements in themselves, instead of in their relation to the second element, namely, Christ. Systematic considerations about why this was so find their exegetical support and adequacy in the evidence which has recently been brought forth in various ways. According to this evidence, the oldest creedal formulas are without exception christologically oriented. I Corinthians 8:6 contains one of the few N.T. confessions which mention both Christ and God the Father at the same time. And it is precisely characteristic for this confession that the separation between God as Creator and Christ as Redeemer is unknown. In fact, the confession mentions creation with regard to both God and Christ: "... (yet for us) there is one God, the Father, from whom are all things and from whom we exist, and one Lord, Jesus Christ, through whom are all things and through whom we exist" (RSV). Both elements (God and Christ) deal with creation. The difference lies only in the prepositions: with God they are ἐξ and εἰς; with Christ it is διά ("... *through* whom are all things..."). And it is not only in this old formula that we encounter the notion of Christ as Mediator of the creation. On the contrary, we can trace this notion further through the entire N.T., e.g. John 1:3; Colossians 1:16. But the strongest expression of this notion is found in Hebrews 1:1o, where precisely the "founding of the earth" is ascribed to Christ, and the heaven is designated as "the work of his hands".

In other earliest confessions which deal with God, God appears, not as Creator, but on the contrary as the "Father of Jesus Christ". He is brought in as the One Who raised Christ from the dead (Polycarp 2:1ff.). Finally Oscar Cullmann[1] demonstrated that all the functions which are in the later creedal formulas associated with the Holy Spirit, the third element, are named as direct functions of Christ in the early christological formulas, for example, the forgiveness of sins and the resurrection.

This content increases the significance of contemporary research directed toward Christology. Of course, this significance originally lay in the interest in the, as-it-were, "classical" works of Christ. Here these works can be summarized only inadequately by the word "Redemption". In addition, the intensity of the question concerning the historical Jesus may certainly be viewed in light of this interest, even if those concerned with the historical Jesus are not primarily

---

[1]) O. Cullmann, *Die ersten christlichen Glaubensbekenntnisse*, 2nd ed., Zurich 1949.

concerned with Christology; that is, if they are less concerned with what is preached about Christ and more concerned with what he said himself. For until today in N.T. research, there is still no consense about where the beginning of Christology is to be placed: with Jesus or with the early Christians only after the Easter event. This alternative is the result of differing historical judgments. However, as a presupposition for both possible alternatives, one can appropriate the insight developed by that historical theory which makes begin Christology in the early Church. This insight is that Jesus' whole attitude implies a Christology and that the explication of this Christology is only later achieved by transfering certain titles to Jesus. The modification of this insight would be that the denotation of certain activities of Jesus by means of certain titles need not necessarily be achieved only within the early Church. Instead, in individual instances even Jesus himself could have taken up these denotations. And this is true though certainly Jesus' divine consciousness and his corresponding speech and behavior were present prior to any objectification of that divinity by means of titles.

The titles in question are various. Either they point to the origins of those groups in the early Church which transfered these titles to Jesus, or they express which aspects of Jesus' activity should be especially emphasized and pointed up. And so it is that, for what ever the particular characterization of the work of Christ, his person takes on and bears the most divers titles: Prophet, High Priest, Mediator, Servant of God, Lamb of God, Messiah, Son of David, Son of Man, Judge, the Holy One of God, Lord (Kyrios), Saviour, King, Logos, Son of God, God[3].

All these titles come from pre-Christian traditions. In those traditions these titles expressed quite different ideas of Majesty, Divinity, Lordship, and Redemption, and were bound up with the corresponding hopes and expectations. Whether Jesus himself transfered these titles to himself or whether they were transfered to him by the early Church is a matter which involves separating out each title and then examining every instance. But in general, to the extent that these titles were transfered to Jesus, he himself and the early Church (or: he himself or the early Church) wanted to present him as the fulfillment and completion of those hopes which were bound up with those titles. These titles have their sources in the Old Covenant, or in

---

[3]) Following the impressive survey in the table of contents in O. Cullmann, *Die Christologie des Neuen Testaments*, 2nd ed., Tubingen 1958.

ancient Judaism, or in pre-Christian Hellenism. Viewed in light of these sources, the contents of faith and the hope which find expression in these titles are all the result of a long history full of sorely-tested religious devotion and of disappointed hopes. In a most diverse way men found in the figure of Jesus of Nazareth an answer to the decisive questions for their lives, questions which arose from that long history. Depending on their own spiritual or religious origins, men believed in Jesus as Israel's Messiah or the Saviour of the world; they believed in him as the Atoning Servant or the obedient Son of God, as the last of the prophets or the highest of all priests, as the judge, Lord and King of all men, as the Mediator of God or as God Himself.

Of course, in each case the content and meaning of these titles changed as they were transfered to Jesus. In part, this change is due to the new stamp which a given title took on by virtue of the new things Jesus had said and done and by virtue of the new kind of relation in faith in which the early Church stood to Jesus, both after Easter and already even before Easter. And in part, this change is due to the fact that these titles, originally quite heterogeneous, now influenced each other reciprocally as they were all transfered to one individual person. This is most clearly seen in the connection of Servant of God and Son of Man. In view of this interaction of titles, how does one find the specific meaning of the christian Redeemer-doctrine, in contrast to other doctrines of a Redeemer? Precisely because of this interaction, the legitimate and always productive way is first to ascertain the christian meaning of the title, and then to compare the title in its new content with the title in its old content. In order to do this—I am repeating self-evident matters—one must be acquainted with the Soteriology of those circles which believed in those other redeemers, whose names and deeds these circles then used in light of their new faith to designate Jesus of Nazareth.

The origin of these believers is to be found in various areas, and often only in various currents, of the many-sided world of that time. In part, we can already define the areas rather precisely, as, for example, the apocalyptics, the priestly circles, the withdrawn martyr theologians, the rabbinic scribes, and groups centered around emperor cults. But in other cases the sought-for areas evade a more exact specification. I want to limit the discussion to the relation of early-church Christology to one particular current. For some scholars this current can be described very precisely. For others this current is very difficult to grasp and is of a problematic size. This current is Gnosis. Two of the titles mentioned above have drawn attention to the relation between Gnosis and the N.T. These two titles are Son of Man and Logos.

Not only in the investigations arising out of R. Bultmann's school, but also in books taking a different direction, for example O. Cullmann's "Christologie des N.T.", these titles are taken as valid indices for Gnostic redeemer doctrines. These doctrines are taken to be background for Christology. And a difference of opinion actually exists just as to whether these doctrines are to be taken directly or indirectly as fruitful for interpretation. We must decide what kind of confrontation can best serve exegesis and whether any kind of confrontation is appropriate at all to the Gnostic Redeemer doctrine. But before we can decide this, we must delineate a context in which both of these notions have a fixed place. Thus, again we are forced to make a selection from a great body of material. Let us select the speculations in the material from Philo of Alexandria.[1] We take Philo, because, on the one hand, it has been maintained that these speculations contain traces of the Gnostic myth of Urmensch-Redeemer. On the other hand we take Philo because also in our opinion his speculations deal with the problem, though, to be sure, in a sense which can only later be demonstrated. With regard to the notion "Son of Man", we don't have to look precisely for this, but just to "Man". For this is the meaning of the Aramaic equivalent of υἱὸς τοῦ ἀνθρώπου.[2]

In Philo's variously expressed and often directly contradictory thought, only God in the O.T. sense has a fixed place. Any investigation of Philo's system must be repeatedly oriented to this God. This God has a universal image (likeness, form), εἰκών. On the one hand, this image is to be thought of and imagined as a spiritual (rational, intellectual) or conceptual world, κόσμος νοητός. On the other hand, it is to be thought of and imagined as a heavenly man, ἄνθρωπος οὐράνιος. This is the universe. So far as in the Platonic sense the spiritual (intellectual) is taken as the true universe, so, in the main, the universe is carried over in contemplation, in the thought, and as a conception, into that power which ultimately animates the universe. But at the same time, this power also remains identical with the universe, and therefore, in the same way this power includes everything

---

[1]) I need not say what I have learned from E. R. Goodenough's books on Philo. The following is the result of my own approach, checked with *By Light, Light* (New Haven 1935).

[2]) This statement does not involve that the evangelists should better have translated with ἄνθρωπος.

which it also animates. This power is chiefly Logos, but also—though not always—identical with *nous, logismos, pneuma,* or *phronesis*. The Logos can be taken as the actual center of the world, although, as God's instrument of creation, it also existed before the world. Its image, that is, a second eikon or *eikon mimema*, is in the broader sense of the term the world of sense perception, κόσμος αἰσθητός. In the narrower sense it is the earthly man. The prototype of the earthly man is the heavenly man, who, just as is Logos, is the best part of earthly man. Or, the heavenly man is the inner man in the earthly or outer (ἔξω) man. Thus, Logos and heavenly man, or inner man, are interchangeable notions. They designate the same thing under different aspects.

Here I would like to introduce a modern word with which the two notions can be indicated: That is, the Self. With this word I intend the innermost essence, that which is real in the world and in man—or even the highest part of the human or world soul. The Logos/Self places man as part of the earthly world into the dynamic structure of the universe. Thereby, Logos/Self gives man share of God by means of the heavenly *eikon*. And thereby, man can himself become *eikon* or heavenly man. This is redemption, *Soteria*, in the Philonic sense. Here it is to be noted that God, not ἄνθρωπος stands as σωτήρ. Anthropos, or the Self, only mediates *Soteria*. Unfortunately, we cannot here spell out in detail the very interesting anthropology this view involves.

We will want to investigate whether and to what extent this presentation reflects Gnosis or a Gnostic Redeemer myth. But before we can do this, we must turn to the N.T. way of conceiving such conceptualization. For a third time I must make a choice from much too large a body of material. Many things could be considered: The Sophia- and Pneuma idea of the Corinthians letters; the Adam-Christ typology in Romans 5; and many others. But I limit myself to the Christology of the Fourth Gospel. I do this because this Christology is exemplary for the content under investigation and because here we find side by side both notions with which we are concerned. Certainly, here I do not need to quote the Logos-Prologue at length. Rather, I simply call attention to the twelve occurrences of Son of Man.[1] In contrast to the apocalyptic picture which dominates still in the Synoptics, the this-wordly work of the Son of Man is especially striking in the Fourth

---

[1]) This is a summary just with regard to the problem of the presence of the Gnostic redeemer, for which also cf. R. Schnackenburg, "Der Menschensohn im Johannesevangelium," in : *NTS* 11, 1965, pp. 123-137.

Gospel. It is precisely right here on earth that the man born blind believes in Jesus as the Son of Man (9:35-38). Precisely here on earth Jesus gives man food which endures to eternal life (6:27), the food which consists of his own flesh and blood (6:53). Precisely in the fact that he is on earth—that he "has been sent"—Jesus brings the fulfillment of Grace and Salvation which exists also in the judgment (5:27). Correspondingly, even on earth he remains in contact with heaven (1:51). And the dignity of the Son of Man as Redeemer is consistent with his origin from heaven (3:13), into which he will also be taken up again (3:14; 6:62; 8:28; 12:34, twice). This event, which coincides with his crucifixion, is synonymous with his glorification (12:23; 13:31).

Nowadays, it is often considered a well-established fact that the foregoing conception does not rest upon the Synoptic, and at last the Jewish-Apocalyptic, view of the Son of Man. Instead, the Gnostic doctrine of the Urmensch-Redeemer is supposed to lie primarily behind this conception,—the same Gnostic doctrine, which, by the way, sometimes is supposed to be the root also of the Jewish-apocalyptic Son of Man expectation. In this regard, the Gnostic doctrine is supposed to stand indirectly in the background, even when one views the Synoptic teaching about the Son of Man as the direct presupposition behind the Johannine view.

In either case, the interpretation takes something like the following course:[1] In speculative Gnosis, when the Redeemer comes into being as Man, this does not happen as a revelation in terms of an illuminating happening which adresses itself to men. Rather, it is a cosmic process. The Redemption is accomplished when the souls of men are collected and born upward by the Redeemer who has become Man. Human souls are held to be scattered bits of light from a figure of light which was captured by darkness in the primordial beginning. By bearing the souls upward, the Redeemer frees his second Ego, or himself, i.e. the primordial figure of light which fell in the primordial beginning. Through their *physis*, the preexistant souls are determined for salvation. And the entire process of redemption is the disentanglement of the unnatural mixing of the *physis* of the divine with the demonic dark. This process affects the individual man insofar as he is a cosmic being and stands in the context of a cosmic event. When one speaks

---

[1] I am summarizing mainly R. Bultmann' view, given e.g. in *Theologie des Neuen Testaments*, Tubingen 1953, § 45-50, and *Das Evangelium des Johannes*, 10. Aufl. Göttingen 1941, pp. 102-115.

of soul and body and redemption, one cannot strictly speak of *my* soul, *my* body, and *my* redemption. Rather, one must speak of *the* soul, *the* body, and *the* redemption, together and in general. The redemption is accomplished as a sublime, grand, natural act which, as it were, almost passes *me* by. The redemption is absolutely incomprehensible as a happening of my own temporal and historical life. And correspondingly, the redeemer is in fact not a concrete temporal and contingent man, but rather an *Urmensch*. The where and when of his becoming a man is basically a matter of indifference. By contrast, revelation and redemption in the Fourth Gospel would be understood, not as a mythical cosmic process, but as a temporal and historical concrete event. The Fourth Gospel has broken away the idea of the preexistent soul, an idea, which is constitutive of the Gnostic myth. And with this disappears the doctrine of the ascent of soul to heaven. In the Fourth Gospel the fate of the soul is determined through faith and unfaith, not on the basis of *physis*. This comes to decision in the encounter to the Son of Man on whom may still be expressed, in contrast to myth, that he came down from heaven and will again go up into it. Moreover he is no longer the means of revelation, but revelation itself. He is no longer the mystagoge who knows and shows the way to the truth, but rather, he is the way and the truth itself. The Johannine Redeemer does not become superfluous after he has brought the redeeming Gnosis. Rather, as the one who has become man, he poses to every man the decisive question of how each man relates himself to him, the Redeemer. Unlike the case in myth, the Redeemer does not give man merely an occasion for reflecting on his own situation. Instead, in the encounter he creates a new situation which is eschatological and which he must accept in a personal decision for his own salvation.

To the extent that there are sufficient reasons for supposing a fully developed, pre-Christian Gnostic Redeemer doctrine, then it is undeniable that the direct and immediate confrontation of Gnostic and Christian concepts can account for all the indications of evidence for explaining the actual sense of the Christology contained in these concepts. This results in an impressive over-all view. That is, Christology is taken to be temporalizing and historizing a mythical Redeemer concept. For man, this temporalizing exposes the fact that the possibilities for his own, self-redemption are illusory. Further, this temporalizing reveals the legitimation and perhaps even the historical basis for modern understanding of existence. Here, then, would be an absolutely ideal case of how the realization of man as man can and must take place in the personal encounter with the One who is sent to man and who himself has become man. And this ideal case is mutually corroborated, both by historical-exegetical findings and by the uncontested modern analysis of existence.

However, the matter is, unfortunately, more complicated. First, I must make two historical corrections whose bases, unfortunately, I cannot explicate here. The first correction is: It cannot yet be assumed that the Gnostic Redeemer doctrine is as explicit in pre-Christian times as it is claimed to be. Even Philo's speculations do not constitute evidence for such a claim. Of course, to the extent that the Logos, or heavenly man, or the Self, binds the earthly and heavenly world and man together, then man is not only a unity, but also a dual being. But he is not divided. In spite of Philo's distinction between the immortal soul and the mortal body, nevertheless man's lower part is not to be taken as exiled in a demonized world into which this part is supposed to have fallen in its pre-existence and from which this lower part must be freed by its upper part which comes down to the lower as an alien being. Herein lies a basic distinction to Redemption in Gnosis. In Gnosis it is not the Philonic, basically Stoic-harmonistic values which are pre-supposed. Rather, here Gnosis presupposes only the important concepts of the Philonic world picture.

The second historical correction is: The Johannine Son of Man is primarily rooted in the Jewish apocalyptic tradition, which also remains recognizable in the Synoptics.[1] And the Fourth Gospel's identification of Jesus with the Son of Man does not have its basis in the fact that the Evangelist wanted Jesus to suppress or temporalize a Gnostic redeemer-figure. Instead, the identification is based on the fact that the early Christian community took Jesus to be the Son of Man, and apparently this is precisely because of Jesus' own words prior to Easter. Here we recall the insight into the explication of Jesus' acts by means of certain titles. As Willi Marxen has recently shown[2] the futuristic-apocalyptic relation of the Son of Man to humanity is used in the Synoptics as an eschatological qualification of the relation of Jesus to man. For example, when Jesus says: "I tell you, everyone who acknowledges me before men, the Son of Man will also acknowledge before the angels of God" (Luke 12:8 RSV), then all the weight is laid on the this-wordly relation between Jesus and man, on the

---

[1] Cf. Siegfried Schulz, *Untersuchungen zur Menschensohn-Christologie im Johannesevangelium*, Göttingen 1957.

[2] W. Marxen, *Anfangsprobleme der Christologie*, Gutersloh 1960, esp. p. 24ff.

eschatological qualification of earthly man's decision for or against Jesus. When Jesus himself is designated as Son of Man, then simultaneously as the one who is coming as well as the one who has already come. Going beyond Marxsen at this point, I would like to assume that Jesus himself gave the explication of his earthly functions, symbolizing his surety to become consummated by means of the title *Son of Man*. And he does so in the following eight passages[1]; Mt 24:37/Lc 17:26; Lc 17:30; Mt 24:27/Lc 17:24; Mt 24:30*a*; 10:23; Lc 18:8; 22:69; 21:36. And the author of the Fourth Gospel completes what has been inaugurated, both with regard to the identification of Jesus with the formerly apocalyptic Son of Man, as well as with regard to the transference of his works into the presence.

But at the same time, there are indications that John also wanted to suggest to his readers the idea of a non-apocalyptic man. Of course, he did not want to suggest the *Urmensch* of the Gnostic myth, but rather, a heavenly man of the sort we find in Philo, for example. This is all the more clear as, in the Prologue, John even identifies Jesus Christ with the equivalent idea of the heavenly man, the Logos. Clearly, the enormity of what is being said here is concealed when one deals with the merely formally correct statement that Gnosis also witnesses to the Redeemer's becoming man. In Gnosis the Redeemer of course is sometimes called "man", along with *Logos* and other terms. This is all the more to be expected because of the marked variety of terminology for Self-speculation which the Gnostic myth presupposes. But the Johannine Prologue does not speak at all about the Logos' becoming man, but rather of the Logos' becoming flesh. Only this expression is a synthetic one in which something new is said and to which there is no parallel. By contrast, "the Logos became man" would have been an analytical expression to illustrate an alleged content which is already known.

And this suggests a reason why John has this Prologue at all and why he puts it at the beginning of the Gospel. This reason is an internal one. Here it is unnecessary to employ any form-critical or literary-critical consideration about whether such Logos and man speculations were previously available to the evangelist or to the writers of an earlier stratum in the Fourth Gospel. There should be no debate over the fact that the Fourth Gospel presupposes such traditions. What may be regarded to be new is the nuance that the pre-

---

[1] The exegetical reasons will be given in my article ὁ υἱὸς τοῦ ἀνθρώπου c I 1 in *Kittelsches Worterbuch*, vol. 8.

Gnostic *Anthropos* terminology also belongs precisely within these traditions. Thus, when the Fourth Gospel says that the Logos became flesh, this means exactly the same as the statement that this *Anthropos* descended, or was sent. Both the Logos' becoming flesh and the early activity of the Son of Man express a new fact which is decisive for man's redemption or rejection. Thus, the contrast to the previous view must not be seen as it occurs in the afore-mentioned confrontation with the entire Gnostic myth. Rather, the contrast must be seen in something like the following way: The Logos is no longer the one who inspires, but is the concrete, real, incarnate one who encounters men. The heavenly man no longer encompasses the entire world with his corporeal counter-images, that is, earthly men. Nor does he thereby mediate *Soteria* to men. Instead, for every earthly man, he becomes one of their own kind and shares their sin and their death. This is more than and different from the mere temporalization and historization of a mythological happening. It is, first and foremost, something substantially and phenomenologically new, something totally inadequate to the old material of conceptions and imaginations.

But one cannot say that the Christology set out over against the Gnostic Soteriology gives a false viewpoint in the whole. After all, what we have called Self-speculations are pre-Christian, not yet exclusively Gnostic, but they do tend toward Gnosis. In fact, with regard to these traditions it must be said that something soteriologically new has been expressed by relating them to Jesus. And the content of this new expression no longer has anything to do with the soteriology to which these traditions originally belonged. In the face of this fact, a satisfactory N.T. hermeneutic is free to arise, and for the most part, it often does in fact arise.

But, the history is not yet completed. After all, the relations continue to exist, on the one hand, between Self-speculation and the Redeemer-myth and, on the other hand, between Johannine and Gnostic soteriology. And they now demand another explanation, different from the one which has just been rejected. From what has been said previously, it follows that one may no longer ask where and how the Redeemer became man. Instead, one must ask where and how *man became Redeemer*. Here I would like to assume that this *structural change* took place in a Gnosis which absorbed and assimilated the Christian Son of Man into its speculations over the heavenly man which was already known to Gnosis.[1] It cannot be assumed from the outset that the identification of heavenly Anthropos and redeeming Son of Man is clearly evident as such in the sources. For Gnosis the more important matter was the resultant Anthropos Soter. And for the sources which we have, it is simply unimportant how this Anthropos Soter was conceived. In this material either the origin could be no longer known or else it was simply not historically problematical. Even if this were the case, still we could do nothing better than to have recourse to our hypothesis concerning that identification. But as a matter of fact, there seems to be evidence which proves it. Naturally, we are concerned here only with those passages in which *man* occurs expressedly as *Son of Man*. Here the word "Son" must be understood sometimes in the Greek sense as an expression for parentage, sometimes in the Aramaic sense as an expression for individuality. Here, for the fourth time we must make a selection from a great quantity of material. In my opinion, our thesis can be verified by the Gnostic systems of the Sethians, of Markus, of the Peratians, and of Basilides. But because it provides the most easily and briefly demonstrable verification, let us here take the system of the Ophites. The Ophites held an absolutely revolutionary belief about the serpent which corrupted Adam and Eve. Instead of damning the serpent as the instrument of the devil, the Ophites dared to revere the serpent as the bringer of Knowledge which makes the knower like God.

According to Irenaeus' account of the Ophite system[2] the first man, who is the father of all, exists in Bythos as the primordial light. The *Ennoia* which has emanated from him is the second man, or Son of Man. In this account it is striking that a feminine spiritual power of the first man is hypostatized, not as his daughter, but as his son. Even when one takes into account the imprecision of Gnostic thought, such a change in meaning cannot be explained merely as varying reflections on a single word. This change in naming is understandable only if one assumes that "Son of Man" was a notion already well-established. The Greek understanding of the term itself placed the Son of Man into the same relation to the heavenly man in which Ennoia already stood as Emanation. From there it was only a short step to the identification

---

[1]) The Christian Gnosis is not the only tradition where this structural change took place. In pagan Gnosis we find a convergent development, even with regard to the Urmensch, cf. C. Colpe, Die Thomaspsalmen als chronologischer Fixpunkt in der Geschichte der orientalischen Gnosis, in: *Jahrbuch für Antike und Christentum* 7, 1964, pp. 77-93, esp. p. 91.

[2]) Adv. Haer. I, 30, 1-6.

of Ennoia with Son of Man. As a result of this, also the direct identification with the *first* man became possible for two reasons. First, just as in every Gnostic notion, *Ennoia* retained its original meaning of "to-be-in-the-father". And this meaning had been the term's characteristic before that of its character as Emanation. Second, behind the expression "Son of Man" the meaning of "man" is still recognizable. Indeed, this meaning is expressly there. And because it is, it presented the occasion for placing the second man besides of the first close to a complete identity. And this also explains how the first and second man, along with the feminine *Pneuma*, beget the third man, Christ. A man and his son were nearly felt to be one. For even the Gnostic sensitivity, which penetrated deeply into the mysteries of the sexes, could not carry out the idea of a double fatherhood.

In addition to Christ, *Dynamis* also emanated from *Pneuma*. *Dynamis* contained in itself the so-called *Prounikos* or *Sophia*. From Sophia the world and individual men are descended in different, parallel ranks. In particular, the first son of the *Prounikos* (Sophia), Jaldabaoth (the son of *Chaos*), creates the angels, *dynameis*, powers, *nous*, and the evil of this world. As the account reads: "Then Jaldabaoth rejoiced and boasted of that which took place at his feet. And he said: 'I am their father and God, and there is no one over me'. But when his mother heard this, she retorted: 'Do not lie, Jaldabaoth, for over you is the father of all, the first man, the Son of Man!'" In Prounikos' (Sophia's) reply the identification of the two "men" into one figure finds expression again. And according to the image of this figure, Jaldabaoth creates earthly men, and they are through the usual means, that is, "Emptying from light" or "Pouring out of light", bereaved of the possibility of redeeming themselves. Sophia takes pity on the first pair of men. She also speaks to men through the prophets and finally begets Jesus and John. She and Christ, both of whom are children of the *Pneuma* and the first-second man, descend upon Jesus, who then becomes the earthly Christ. It is he who brings the redeeming Gnosis. Then he is crucified and goes up to heaven, but only as Jesus (I 30, 13).

In my opinion, in this system two things come about through the entrance of the Christian Son of Man into Gnostic speculation. First, there is the hypostatic differentiation of concepts. Above all, this is especially true of the Anthropos concept which, exactly as Logos, designates the Self of the universe and, in so doing, there comes about an independent redeemer. Second, there is the transfer, and thereby the structural change, of the redemptive activity from the highest God to a descendent of Anthropos who can also be called Anthropos. It is no contradiction to the statement made before that the Christian redeeming Son of Man was in fact identified with the higher man. For, contrary to earlier views, such as those of W. Bousset[1] and H. Lietzmann[2], there was a yet no independent Redeemer with which the Son of Man could have been identified or whom the Son of Man could have displaced. The Gnostic descendant redeemer became existant just with this identification. In any case the upper Anthropos-Logos retained his place as the Self which stands behind all the hypostatized differentiations of the universe. But at the same time, this Anthropos-Logos became creator of the Redeemer. For this reason, and also because the Anthropos-Logos is identical with the Redeemer in another regard, the upper Anthropos also achieves indirectly a soteriological character. And this character is typologically different from that of the pre-mythological Soteria which, as in Philo for example, is constituted through the Self.

As an aid to understanding this mythological speculation, let us consider briefly Irenaeus' report concerning the so-called Ptolemeans and Colorbaseans (I 12,4). In this report two directions are cited which, in a rather typical way, designate Anthropos as creator of the twelve Aeons, as the pre-beginning or all-encompassing power, that is, as the Self of the universe. Into this Anthropos a figure was simply inserted, and the name "Son of Anthropos" was tradited for it. According to the witness of the Fourth Gospel, this was the Redeemer. In this way, the Anthropos gained for itself a further, independent emanation which, as such, was the Redeemer. But at the same time, this emanation could continue to bear the name of its father *Anthropos*. This rather simple speculation is probably a primordial form of the doctrine of Anthropos as Redeemer. And thereby, even anthropos qua Logos-Self attains indirectly the quality of Redeemer because of the constant tendency toward identification. In any case, redeeming hypostatizations, which were not themselves called Anthropos, could now also emanate from Anthropos. This could abundantly be verified in numerous systems, even in those of the Valentinians and Manicheans.

With the introduction of the Son of Man Christology into their speculation, the Gnostics thus gained for themselves two moments by means of which they could expand the Self. Whereas originally the

---

[1] *Hauptprobleme der Gnosis*, Göttingen 1907, p. 162 and 263f.
[2] *Der Menschensohn*, Freiburg-Leipzig 1896, p. 62ff.

Self existed as a timeless function of being, the Gnostics could now expand the Self into the substratum of a process with a temporal schema.

The one moment was the historicity and temporality of the notion "Son". If the Anthropos had a son, then the son had to be born or raised at some time. Thus, there must have been a time when the Anthropos was alone and afterwards a time in which he had a son. Once this initiative was carried to the development of a temporal line, then the development could easily be carried further. Here the typical Gnostic technique of dealing with notions was useful in two ways. First, there is the mythical-alogical approach which involves an inability to formulate general concepts and specific concepts, or to distinguish between a thing and its attributes. Instead, this approach permits the specific concept of attribute to be an hypostasis which follows in a natural way from the general concept or thing. Second, there is an unclarity of concepts which itself never permits identifications to achieve a sharp, precise unity. But precisely this unclarity could range over great, internal, substantially wide divergence and split it into a hypostatic reduplication. In any case, once the development of a temporal schema was given, such reduplication tended toward the order of a temporal continuum. Thus, with the help of these ways of thinking, speculation could at will continue the genealogy of the original father-son relation in any desired direction. And by means of secondary genealogies, this speculation could expand the genealogy into a complete pleromatic fullness. In the process of carrying out such speculation the Gnostic, of his own accord, referred to a temporal schema which arose simultaneously with and in the speculative enterprise.

The other moment by which the Gnostics could expand the Self was the historicity of the Christian revelation. As the Fourth Gospel attested for the Gnostics the Son of Man had preached the redeeming Gnosis on earth at a time which could be specified historically. Prior to this preaching, the Son of Man had already had a history as the one descended from the heavenly man, or even as the Logos. And the Son of Man would resume this history after he again ascended. Of course, the pre- and postexistence of the Redeemer had to be related to the pre- and postexistence of the world and of man. In antiquity this pre- and postexistence, as such, was not problematical for beliefs concerning creation and immortality. Since this world is evil and the human soul suffers in this world, it was to be assumed that the Redeemer, already in his preexistence, had attempted to prevent creation, or in other words, he had attempted to save the soul. And similarly, after man's death the Redeemer had to provide for the salvation, both of the soul which already knows its place of origin by means of Gnosis, and also even of the soul which is still totally ignorant. Thus, in Gnostic speculation, the Christian process of redemption was transformed into a preexistent, earthly-historical, and postexistent process. This is a remarkable temporal reversal of the Christian eschatology. In some instances conceptual difficulties arose when one and the same Redeemer was always permitted to act. In those instances one took as supplement the analogous and likewise temporally structured speculation which led to Aeon-genealogies and reduplication of concepts. Thus, a multiplicity of redeeming hypostatizations were arrived at in which the dominant place could also be allotted to the Logos. Each of these hypostatizations is a repetition of the preceding ones, adapted to the development of the cosmogonous-soteriological process. With regard to preexistence, the Valentinian system offers the richest pleromatic display. With regard to contemporary existence, it is the Mandean system, while with regard to postexistence, it is the Manichean system.

The Christian Gnostic Redeemer myth is drafted in this way.[1] Only in this form does the myth have in itself the dramatic moment which is constitutive for it, and without which one cannot speak of a myth-"tale". But for the Gnostic, whose Logos contained the myth in itself, redemption proceeded that way, that for him the present redemption, effected by revealed Gnosis and experienced mainly in contemplation, was a repetition and renovation of an archetypal and prefiguration of a posthumous process. This is why, for example, psychology of character created by C. G. Jung is interested in this phenomenon.

Thus, it cannot be simply said that Gnosis appropriated a Redeemer-figure for the first time only under Christian influence. The docetic Christ-figure appears in many systems. But besides of this, we have the phenomenon that Logos and the heavenly Anthropos become a Redeemer. We have demonstrated that this phenomenon does not merely presuppose Christian Christology, but in fact also develops pre-Christian traditions.

And from this fact perhaps an awareness is achieved which is rele-

---

[1]) Of course, this is not the only way in which the myth was conceived. There are other ways in post-Christian pagan Gnosis (Mandaeans and Manichaeans), in pre-Christian pagan Gnosis (Simonians), and in Valentinianism.

vant today. That is, aided by actually inadequate notions from the philosophical-soteriological language of its time, Christology achieved with difficulty its own original, individual assertion. And after this achievement, Christology itself went on to develop and make pregnant in a new sense these old, inadequate notions. But precisely through these notions Christology, then, comes to be threatened by the danger of being metaphysicized, mythologized, and psychologized. This danger is one more of the many humanely fascinating topics which are the subject matter of history of religion. History of religion can investigate *how* this danger came to be. But it is the work of N.T. exegesis to guard against the actual occurance of this danger.

JEWISH INFLUENCES ON THE "HELIAND"

BY

GILLES QUISPEL

Utrecht University

When I last saw my good friend Erwin Goodenough, some weeks before his death, he told me with impressive courage about the nature of his illness and mentioned his intention to write now the book about St. Paul, which he ever had in mind when he was working at the *Jewish Symbols*. Few of us do not have such a last perspective for their work, a last and decisive word that is never spoken and inspires us during our whole life.

So the present writer would like to write, but probably never will do so, a "History of the Churches". Not of the Church, but of the Latin, Greek and Syrian Churches. In such a book conventional labels would be avoided. Calvin would be just an extreme representative of African, Augustinian theology, Nestorianism nothing more than a reform, due to Barsauma, of the indigenous Syro-Palestinian Semitic type of Christianity, Messalianism nothing but an interesting and perfectly legitimate revival of a very old and very Syrian spirituality. Then a phenomenological description of these three varieties of religious experience would be possible.

Latin Christianity was so practical and unspeculative as the Romans always were, only interested in the great realities of existence, guilt and grace, sober and efficient in its cult as the Old-Roman pagan Prayerbooks once were, stressing order, obedience, stability, all good, old, conservative Roman virtues, aiming at a theocratic order of society, the rule of God's commandment over the whole world. *Tu regere imperio populos, Romane, memento.*

How different from the very beginning the Greek Christians were: their cult a mystery, an initiation, their life a new being, their christology a synthesis of Being and time (Christ is "ho Ōn"), their mysticism an oceanic experience. No doubt that the ontological aspirations of the Greek found their fulfilment in their type of the Christian religion.

The Syrian Christian, on the contrary, was not interested in the ontological speculations of the Greeks. Aphraates, though catholic and orthodox, does not contain the slightest echo of the dogmatic controversies which shook the Greek world during his lifetime, the fourth century. Syrian Christianity is not a holy Empire, or a logos about Being, but a Way towards an eschatological horizon. The Syrian was primarily a wanderer, critical about bourgeois institutes like marriage and property, always on the move in the steps of that great Foreigner from Galilee. And this is understandable. It becomes more and more clear, that Christianity has been brought to Syria by Jewish missionaries from Palestine; and even when it spread over Asia, towards India and China, it preserved its Syrian liturgy and its Semitic character. Syrian Christianity has integrated the eschatological restlessness of the Jewish mind.

It is my aim to show in this paper that this Syrian Christianity of Jewish origin has remained an important factor in Western developments. As an example I choose the Old Saxon *Heliand*, written about 830 A.D. under the reign of Lewis the Pious. Curiously enough the English speaking peoples are not very interested in the *Heliand* though this beautiful poem belongs without any doubt to world literature, was inspired by English epical poets like Caedmon and both by its language and by its subject matter, an epical presentation of a Biblical subject, seems to be closely connected to English literature.[1]

During a certain period the *Heliand* was considered by German scholars to be typically German: combining certain data of the language of the poem with the results of the study of modern dialects, they concluded that the *Heliand* had been written in the Eastern part of the Saxon realm, in Magdeburg or some other German city. But it has been established that the language of the *Heliand* is artificial or rather artistic, like the idiom of Homer, with strong English and Frisian elements; therefore dialect-study is of no avail for the localisation of the *"Heliand"*.[2]

Other scholars thought that the poem originated from Fulda, the monastery of St. Boniface, because it is based upon a Gospel Harmony, a version of the *Diatessaron* of the Syrian Tatian, like the *Codex Fuldensis*, once used by St. Boniface. Its author was supposed to have used as a source this latter very vulgatised recension of the *Diatessaron* and was therefore localised at Fulda. But the discovery of the *Gospel of Thomas* and the light it threw on the various recensions of the *Diates-*

---

[1]) Text: O. Behaghel, *Heliand und Genesis*, 6 ed., Halle 1948. Translation: Wilhelm Stapel, *Der Heliand*, Munchen, 1953.

[2]) T. A. Rompelman, *Heliandprobleme*, Wilhelmshaven, no year.

saron, English, Dutch, Italian, German, Latin, Arabic, Persian, Armenian, Syriac, has ruined this hypothesis.[1] It is an established fact that the Latin *Diatessaron* upon which the *Heliand* is based was much wilder and had preserved many more authentic Tatianic elements than the *Codex Fuldensis*.[2] Therefore the *Heliand* was certainly not written at Fulda, but possibly at the monastery of Werden, near Essen, which was founded by the Frisian missionary Liudger, who had come there from Holland in order to tame the pagan and agressive Saxons by means of the Gospel. The *Diatessaron* of the *Heliand* has many elements in common with the Dutch *Diatessaron*. This hints in the direction of Holland. The latest theory is that the *Heliand* was composed at Werden by Bernlef, a Frisian poet converted to Christianity by Liudger, and who worked under the guidance of Liudger. To this end Liudger is supposed to have made a copy of the Latin *Diatessaron* which was kept at Utrecht at the famous international school of Gregory, a Frankish missionary among the Frisians, where Liudger had studied.[3] This would explain the curious parallels between the Dutch *Diatessaron* and the Gospelsource of the *Heliand*: they go back to the same archetype supposedly existant in the Low Countries even before 830, the date of the *Heliand*.

So we are beginning to discern the hidden ways of history, the eradiation of a Syrian text, the *Diatessaron* of Tatian, brought in a Latin version probably from Italy to Holland and from there to Germany, where it became the source of the famous poem. But then we must not forget that the *Diatessaron* of Tatian contained Jewish Christian Gospel tradition. The same is the case with the *Gospel of Thomas*: if the two writings have so many variants in common, it is because they used the same source, an independent Aramaic Gospel tradition, brought by Jewish missionaries to Mesopotamia, where both Tatian and the author of the *Gospel of Thomas* lived. And so the *Heliand*, based as it is upon a Tatianic Gospel harmony has preserved distinct echoes of this Palestinian tradition. I quote one example which has not yet been published in detail. I underline the elements which the *Heliand* has in common with the *Gospel of Thomas* as against the *Vulgate* and the established Greek New Testament. The passage is 1. 2538-

---

[1] *L'Evangile selon Thomas et le Diatessaron*, Vigiliae Christianae, 13 (1959), pp. 87-117.
[2] *Der Heliand und das Thomasevangelium*, Vigiliae Christianae, 16 (1962), pp. 121-153.
[3] J. J. van Weringh, *Heliand and Diatessaron*, Assen, 1965.

2574 of the *Heliand*. The corresponding passage is *Matthew* 13, 24-31. My own version, made from the Old Saxon, aims to be literal and cannot possibly be adequate or idiomatic.

> "So he showed forth with words. Many people stood around the child of God, heard him with many images tell with words about the end of this world. Quoth he that once a man of nobility sowed upon his field pure corn with his hands. He wanted there to acquire lovely harvest, beautiful crop. Then went there his enemy after him with evil mind and oversowed it all with weeds, with the worst weeds of all. Then grew up both the corn and the herb. So his servants came to his house, said to their master, the squires to their lord with confident words: "What, you have sown pure corn, good lord, unmixed, upon your field. Now nobody sees anything but weeds growing. How could that happen so?" Then the noble man spoke to his people, the lord to his squires, quoth that he might well suppose a hostile man, an enemy, to have sown there after him the evil herb. 'He did grudge me the fruit, spoiled the growth.' Then his friends answered, his followers, they said that they wanted to go there, to come in force and *take* away the weeds, to get them with their hands. Then the *lord* answered *them*: 'I do not *want you* to *weed* it, for you can not avoid, prevent on your way, though you prefer not to do it, that you destroy much corn germinating, tread it under your feet. Let them both grow forth and before harvest cometh and when in the field the fruits are ripe, ready on the acre, then let us go there all, to fetch it with our hands and gather the pure corn, cleanly together, and put it in my barn, keep it there so that it be not spoiled, and *take* the weeds, bind them into sheafs and throw them into the bitter fire, let them be caught by the hot blaze, the unsatiable flame.'"

At first sight the variants might appear slight and unsignificant. But to the trained eye they reveal a very important historical process. One must keep in mind that the *Heliand* has a host of variant readings in common with the various *Diatessarons* and with the *Vetus Latina* and the Old Syrian *Sinaiticus* and *Curetonianus*. On the other hand, the *Heliand*, as all other recensions of the *Diatessaron*, has many variants in common with the *Gospel of Thomas*. We give here only a sample of a much richer material. But that also this passage contains very old and very important deviations from the canonical text is shown by the following comparison between our version and the Vulgate:

2559: lôsian (take) ∼ Mt. 13, 28: colligimus: Dutch Diat.: *trekken ut;* Venetian Diat.: *chavaimo;* Persian Diat.: *strappiamo;* Ar. Diat.: *séparer.*
2560: herro (the lord) ∼ Mt. 13, 29: ait: Ven. Diat.: lo *segnore* disse; Dutch Diat.: die *here* antwerdde hen; Cf. Aphraates: *dominus.*

2560: sprac im angegin (answered them) ∼ Mt. 13, 29: et ait: Dutch
Diat.: *antwerdde hen;* Ar. Diat.: *il leur dit.*
2561: ne uuelleo ik (I do not want) ∼ Mt. 13, 29: non. Ven. Diat.:
non voio; Aphraates: non sinit.
2571: uuiod niman (take the weed) ∼ Mt. 13, 30: colligite zizania:
Ven. Diat.: *toi.* Persian Diat.: *strappino* et separino.

The remarkable fact is that all these variants, as so many more in other *Diatessarons*, are to be found in the *Gospel of Thomas*, logion 57:

> Jesus said: The Kingdom of the Father is like a man who had good seed. His enemy came by night, he sowed a weed among the good seed. *The man* did not *permit* them (the workers) to *pull* up the weed. He said *to them:* Lest perhaps you go to *pull up* the weed and pull up the wheat with it. For on the day of harvest the weeds will appear, they will *pull* them up and burn them.

Authoritative scholars do agree that this is an independent tradition of a parable of Jesus. And indeed it is so different from the canonical version (*Mt.* 13, 24-30) that it hardly can have been taken from the *Gospel of Matthew*. Note that here only the point of the parable becomes clear: the weed is so similar to the wheat, that only at the latest stage of growth the weed becomes manifest and can be removed. Recently Helmut Koester has accepted this thesis, in an important article.[1] He agrees that the *Gospel of Thomas*, written in Syrian Edessa before 140 A.D., contains an independent tradition of the Sayings of Jesus, brought to Mesopotamia by Jewish Christians and also witnessed by the *Diatessaron* of Tatian. But then must not we rather suppose that Tatian, when writing his *Diatessaron* about 170 A.D. somewhere in Mesopotamia, used the *Gospel of Thomas*, written about 140 A.D. in Edessa? ,

I think the *Gospel of Thomas* clearly shows this parable to have been taken from a written source, because its wording is so clumsy:

It says that the man *had* a good seed; the source must have said that he *sowed it in his field*; it does not mention the workers; but its source must of need have referred to them.

This source, I should guess, must have been an Aramaic Gospel, the *Gospel of the Hebrews* or the *Gospel of the Nazorees*: logion 2 of the *Gospel of Thomas* gives an amplified quotation from the *Gospel of the Hebrews*.

---

[1] Helmut Koester, *The origin and nature of diversification in the history of Early Christianity*, Harvard Theological Review, 58, 3, 1965, pp. 279-318.

So the latter was a source of the *Gospel of Thomas*. Why not also in the case of logion 57?

I am confirmed in this conviction when I observe that Aphraates *does* mention the workers, in a passage which is very near to the *Gospel of Thomas* and very far from *Matthew*:

> *Dominus* sementis *servos* non sinit triticum
> a zizaniis ante messem purgare.
> Aphraates, *Demonstratio* VII, 25, Parisot p. 355.

The Jewish Christians in Beroea, but also the author of the Syriac *Liber Graduum*, and Aphraates, and Tatian all knew a Jewish Chrisitan Gospel.[1]

Is not it wise then to assume that Tatian and the author of the *Gospel of Thomas* used a common source, the Aramaic *Gospel of the Hebrews* or the *Gospel of the Nazorees*, if there is any difference between these two?

This has its consequences for the *Heliand* which now turns out to have been influenced not only by the Syrian Tatian but even by an Aramaic Palestinian Gospel. Our findings give a completely new and rather surprising perspective to the beautiful poem.

The *Heliand* is not a German, but an anti-Germanic writing. It was possibly composed by a Frisian poet from the Low Countries, Bernlef, and probably written down in Werden, a spearhead of European civilisation and occupation in Saxony. It formed part of that blessed endeavour of Charlemagne and his son Lewis the Pious to subdue an aggressive enemy. It was based on the Gospel harmony of a Syrian, which contained Jewish Gospel tradition.[2]

Whether one likes it or not, this seems to be true. It explains a whole set of remarkable, but undeniable facts. For there is no doubt that the *Heliand*, the various *Diatessarons* and the *Gospel of Thomas* have many variants in common. These facts can be interpreted as witnesses of a historical process, the mission of Jewish Christians in Mesopotamia and the use of the *Diatessaron of Tatian* as a tool in the christianisation of Germany. All this becomes clear if we only keep in mind that Jewish Christianity, especially in Mesopotamia, remained an important factor in the history of the Church.

We have now an admirable history of the Jews in Mesopotamia,

---

[1] *The Gospel of Thomas and the Gospel of the Hebrews*, New Testament Studies, July, 1966.

[2] Compare the contrary view of W. Krogmann, *Heliand, Tatian und Thomasevengelium*, Z.N.W., 41, 1960, pp. 255-268.

owing to the exertions of Jacob Neusner. These Mesopotamian Jews, who in part were Christians, now turn out to have played an important part even in the history of the West. If the historian is ready to focus his attention on them, he can uncover some hidden ways of history.

Let us therefore follow the example of Erwin Goodenough, who discovered many things, because he was inspired by the paintings in the synagogue of Dura-Europos. He found that the West had influenced the Jews. But in some cases the reverse is also true.

III

APOCRYPHA
AND PSEUDEPIGRAPHA

THE PRAYER OF JOSEPH

BY

JONATHAN Z. SMITH

University of California, Santa Barbara

In a period of renewed interest in non-canonical literature sparked by the discoveries in the Dead Sea area and at Nag-hammadi and in the remains of hellenistic Judaism so ably researched by E. R. Goodenough, it is imperative that there be a re-examination of the apocryphal literature of Judaism and Jewish-Christianity comparable in scope to Hennecke-Schneemelcher's *Neutestamentliche Apokryphen*.[1]) Much of this literature has suffered from scholarly neglect, certainly none more so than the fragments of a Jewish apocryphon quoted by Origen under the title, *The Prayer of Joseph* (Προσευχὴ 'Ιωσήφ).[2])

---

[1]) While the recent unrevised reprinting of R. H. Charles, *Apocrypha and Pseudepigrapha of the Old Testament* by the Oxford University Press was long overdue, an edition of texts on a scale comparable to Hennecke-Schneemelcher still remains a *desideratum*. The often artificial source-criticism of Charles', his emendations and faulty texts must be corrected by newer techniques of analysis. Likewise many of Charles' historical judgements are suspect in the light of our increased understanding of the diverse phenomena of post-Biblical Judaism. The many omissions (e.g. *Joseph and Asenath*, the *Testament* and *Apocalypse of Abraham*) as well as the failure to include representative Hebrew and Aramaic works of a similar character (such as those published by Jellinek in his *Bet ha-Midrash*) and the discovery of new material such as the so-called *Genesis Apocryphon* from Qumran render Charles inadequate for present use. The recently reprinted collection of P. Riessler, *Altjudische Schrifttum ausserhalb der Bibel* 1ed. (Augsburg, 1928) has a wider selection of texts in translation but no critical commentary. See especially the programmatic essay of A.-M. Denis, "Les pseudépigraphes grecs d'Ancien Testament," *Novum Testamentum* 6(1963), pp. 310-19 and two recently inaugurated series *Pseudepigrapha Veteris Testamenti Graece* and *Studia in Veteris Testamenti Pseudepigrapha*, eds. A. M. Denis and M. de Jonge.

[2]) Henceforth cited as *PJ*. The major treatments of which I am aware are: R. Simon, *Histoire critique des principaux commentateurs du Nouveau Testament* (Rotterdam, 1693), Vol. II, pp. 238-42; J. Fabricius, *Codex Pseudepigraphus Veteris Testamenti* (Hamburg, 1722), Vol. I, pp. 761-71; Abbé Migne, *Dictionnaire des Apocryphes* (Paris, 1858), Vol. II, p. 419 n. 475; A. Dillmann, "Pseudepigraphen des Alten Testaments", in Herzog *et al.*, *Real-Encyklopadie fur protestantische Theologie und Kirche* 2ed. (Leipzig, 1883), Vol. XII, p. 362; J. T. Marshall, "Joseph, Prayer of," in J. R. Hastings ed., *Dictionary of the Bible* (New York, 1899), Vol. II, col. 778b; P. Batiffol, *Studia Patristica* (Paris, 1889), Vol. I, pp. 16-18; A. Resch, *Agrapha* (Leipzig, 1906), pp. 295-8; E. Schurer, *Geschichte des judischen Volkes* 4ed. (Leipzig,

In the standard editions of Origen, the major fragment (A), preserved in the *Comm. in Ioann.* II,31, occupies some fifteen lines of Greek encompassing eight periods. An additional fragment (B) is given in the *Philocalia* XXII,15, but this adds only a single line. That this only constitutes a fraction of the whole work may be seen from the *Stichometry* of Nicephorus who reports that the *PJ* contained 1100 *stichoi*.

The fact that only so small a remnant remains, that testimonies to the work are sparse and quotations from it even rarer should not be allowed to obscure the interest or importance of the text.[1]) The legend

---

1909), Vol. III, pp. 359f.; E. Norden, *Agnostos Theos* (Leipzig-Berlin, 1913), p. 300; A. von Harnack, *Der kirchengeschichtliche Ertag der exegetischen Arbeiten des Origines* (Leipzig, 1919), Vol. II, p. 48 cf. Harnack, *History of Dogma* (New York, 1958 rp.), Vol. I, pp. 102f. n.2 and Harnack, *Geschichte der altchristlichen Literatur bis Eusebius* (Leipzig, 1958 rp.), Vol. I:2, p. 853; L. Ginzberg, *Eine unbekannte judische Sekte* (New York, 1922), pp. 36f.; Ginzberg, *Legends of the Jews* (Philadelphia, 1925), Vol. V, pp. 275 and 310f.; H. Strack-P. Billerbeck, *Kommentar zum Neuen Testament aus Talmud und Midrasch* (Munich, 1924), Vol. II, pp. 340f.; R. Cadiou, *La jeunesse d'Origène* (Paris, 1935), p. 79; W. L. Knox, *St. Paul and the Church of the Gentiles* (Cambridge, 1939), p. 49 and notes 5, 6; N. A. Dahl, *Das Volk Gottes* (Oslo, 1941), pp. 114f. J. Ruwet, "Les 'Antilegomena' dans les oeuvres d'Origène", *Biblica* 24 (1943), pp. 50f.; Ruwet, "Les apocryphes dans les oeuvres d'Origène," *Biblica* 25 1944), p. 144 and pp. 368f.; P. Winter, "ΜΟΝΟΓΕΝΗΣ ΠΑΡΑ ΠΑΤΡΟΣ", *Zeitschrift f. Religions- und Geistesgeschichte* 5 (1953), pp. 351-2, 358, 361; R. P. C. Hanson, *Origen's Doctrine of Tradition* (London, 1954), pp. 135f.; P. Winter, "Zum Verstandnis des Johannes-Evangeliums", *Theologische Literaturzeitung* 80 (1955), cols. 147 f. J. Daniélou, *Théologie du Judéo-Christianisme* (Tournai, 1958), pp. 182-5 (abridged and revised in the English translation, *Theology of Jewish Christianity* Chicago, 1964, pp. 132-4); R. M. Grant, *Gnosticism and Early Christianity* (New York, 1959), pp. 18f.; E. Schweizer, "Die Kirche als Leib Christi," *Theologische Literaturzeitung* 86 (1961), cols. 167f. D. S. Russell, *The Message and Meaning of Jewish Apocalyptic* (Philadelphia, 1964), p. 67; M. Smith, "The Account of Simon Magus in Acts 8", *Harry Austryn Wolfson Jubilee Volume* (Jerusalem, 1965), pp. 748f. The only relatively full studies of the *PJ* are those of M. R. James, *The Lost Apocrypha of the Old Testament* (London, 1920), pp. 21-31 and E. Stein, "Zur apokryphen Schrift 'Gebet Josephs'", *Monatschrift f.d. Geschichte und Wissenschaft d. Judenthums* 81 (1937), pp. 280-86. For general treatments of Origen's use of Jewish apocrypha see Harnack, *op. cit.*, Vol. I, pp. 34-50; Ruwet, *op. cit.*, *Biblica* 24 (1943), pp. 18-58 and *Biblica* 25 (1944), pp. 143-66, 311-34; G. Bardy, "Les traditions juives dans l'oeuvre d'Origène", *Revue Biblique* 34 (1925), pp. 217-52 esp. pp. 226f.; and A. C. Sundberg, Jr., *The Old Testament of the Early Church* (Cambridge USA, 1964), pp. 134-8.

[1]) Testimonies, besides the *Stichometry* of Nicephorus (in Th. Zahn, *Geschichte d. neutestamentlichen Kanons* [Erlangen-Leipzig, 1890] Vol. II:1, p. 300) are: the list of "Sixty Canonical Books" (in Zahn, *op. cit.*, p. 292); the *Synopsis* of pseudo-Athanasius (in Zahn, *op. cit.*, p. 317); a list by the Armenian, Mechithar of Arivank (in Zahn, *Forschungen d. neutestamentlichen Kanons* [Leipzig, 1893], Vol. V, p. 109); Michael Glycas, *Annales* II.171 (ed. Bekker, *Corpus Scriptorum Historiae Byzantinae* xxvii [Berlin, 1836], p. 321) refers to a contest between Jacob and the angel

it narrates is unique. This, and the problem of determining the date and provenance of the apocryphon render its interpretation extremely difficult.¹) Within the scope of this paper, I can only discuss briefly the various motifs; at a later date I hope to publish a detailed commentary.

The text, as it has survived, appears to be a midrash on the Jacob narrative in Genesis (most particularly Gen 32.24ff.). As such, it takes its place within an established literary tradition represented by works such as Jubilees, the pseudo-Philonic *Biblicarum antiquitatum*, the complex Testament-literature and the recently discovered "Genesis Apocryphon". The text bears definite verbal affinities to Genesis 48-49, especially in the Septuagint. Thus M. R. James concludes: "the book contained a dying speech of Jacob, of which we have a portion. I am tempted to think that it was addressed to Joseph and his sons Ephraim and Manasseh. The grounds are naturally slight: (a) We already have, in Genesis xlix, the full address of Jacob to the twelve; (b) there are coincidences of language with the episodes of Joseph's sons in Gen. xlviii."²) However this would not explain the title Προσευχή 'Ιωσήφ (although Joseph is mentioned in a context of prayer in Gen 48.18;

Raphael (sic!) being found in an apocryphal volume entitled προσευχή 'Ιωσήφ; Procopius of Gaza paraphrases fragment B of the *PJ* as being the *testimonium ab Jacobo dictum ex oratione Josephi* (*Comm. in I Gen.* 29, *MPG* LXXXVII :1, cols. 95f.); the reference in the *Ascension of Isaiah* 4.22 to "the words of Joseph the just" have been taken by some critics to refer to the *PJ* (cf. A. Dillmann, *Ascensio Isaiae Aethiopice et Latine* [Leipzig, 1877], p. 69; R. H. Charles, *The Ascension of Isaiah* [London, 1900], p. 39; E. Tisserant, *Ascension d'Isaie* [Paris, 1909], p. 127n.; and G. H. Box-R. H. Charles, *The Ascension of Isaiah* [London, 1919], p. 41 n.2); the question in Priscillian, *Liber de Fide et de Apocryphis* (ed. Schepss [Vienna, 1889], pp. 45f.) "Who ever heard of a prophecy of Jacob *(profetiam Jacob)* being included in the canon?" may well refer to the *PJ* where Jacob appears to be the chief speaker and possesses prophetic powers (so M. R. James, *The Testament of Abraham* [Cambridge, 1892], p. 13). Fabricius (*op. cit.*, Vol. I, p. 438) along with several other authorities, has misread the Gelasian list: *Liber qui appellatur Testamentum Job, apocryphus* as *Liber qui appellatur Testamentum Jacob, apocryphus* which has been interpreted as referring to the *PJ*; but this is manifestly an error.

Fragment A is quoted only in Origen, *loc. cit.*; paraphrased in Origen's *Philocalia* XXIII.19; and alluded to in Glycas, *loc. cit*. Fragment B occurs in Origen, *Philocalia* XXIII.15,19; Eusebius, *Praep. evang.* VI.11.64 (ed. E. H. Gifford [Oxford, 1903] Vol. I, p. 373); and Procopius, *loc. cit.*

¹) The dating of Origen's *Commentary* prior to 231 provides the *terminus ad quem*. The parallelism of terminology and motifs between the *PJ*, Philo and other hellenistic Jewish material would suggest a possible first century dating and an Alexandrian provenance. M. Smith, *op. cit.*, p. 748 appears to suggest a Palestinian provenance and dates the *PJ* as being probably from the first century. P. Winter, "ΜΟΝΟΓΕΝΗΣ," p. 352 dates the *PJ* from "post-Valentinian times."

²) James, *op. cit.*, p. 26.

50.5 and 50.25). From what has survived, one might well have anticipated the title being Προσευχὴ 'Ιακώβ. This may, of course, simply be a problem of what has survived being unrepresentative of the whole, and James may be quite correct in assuming "that the book must have contained a prayer or prayers of considerable bulk uttered by Joseph (as *Asenath* contains a long prayer by Asenath). On what occasion it was offered, whether in the pit or in prison, or on his deathbed, there is no certainty."[1]) I would suggest, as an alternative, the possibility that the *PJ* follows the format of the Testament-literature where, quite consistently, it is the previous patriarch who appears and speaks to the patriarch in the title, most usually at the point of the latter's death (e.g. Abraham to Isaac; Isaac to Jacob).[2]) One might well expect heavy influence from Genesis 48-50 as well as Jacob's role as a heavenly figure within such a setting. However, it must be emphasized that the text does not permit final certainty on these questions.

Fragment A (Origen, *Comm. in Ioann.* II,31)

If one accepts from the apocrypha presently in use among the Hebrews the one entitled "The Prayer of Joseph," he will derive from it exactly this teaching... (namely) that those who have something distinctive from the beginning when compared to men, being much better than other beings, have descended from the angelic to human nature. Jacob, at any rate, says: "*I, Jacob, who am speaking to you, am also Israel, an angel of God and a ruling spirit. Abraham and Isaac were created before any work. But I, Jacob, whom men call Jacob but whose name is Israel, am he who God*
(5) *called Israel, i.e. a man seeing God, because I am the firstborn of every living thing to whom God gives life.*" And he continues:
"*And when I was coming up from Syrian Mesopotamia, Uriel, the angel of God, came out and said that I had descended to earth and I had tabernacled among*
(10) *men and that I had been called by the name of Jacob. He envied me and fought with me and wrestled with me saying that his name and the name of him that is before every angel was to be above mine. I told him his name and what rank he held among the sons of God: 'Are you not Uriel, the eighth after me and I Israel,*
(15) *the archangel of the power of the Lord and the chief captain among the sons of God? Am I not Israel, the first minister before the face of God?' And I called upon my God by the inextinguishable name...* But we have made a lengthy digression in considering the matter of Jacob and using as evidence a writing not lightly to be despised to render more credible the belief concerning John the Baptist which maintains that he... being an angel, took a body in order to bear witness to the light.[3])

---

[1]) *Ibid.*
[2]) e.g., W. E. Barnes, "The Testaments of Abraham, Isaac and Jacob" in M. R. James, *The Testament of Abraham* (Cambridge, 1892), pp. 133-161.
[3]) In the editions of A. E. Brooke, (Cambridge, 1896), Vol. I, pp. 97f. and E. Preuschen, (Leipzig, 1903, *GCS*), pp. 88f. The standard English translation, un-

fortunately, remains that of A. Menzies in the *Ante-Nicene Fathers* (Grand Rapids, n.d.), Vol. X, pp. 340f. But see the English renderings in James, Ginzberg, Daniélou and Grant in their works cited above (253 n.2).

There are several translation difficulties to be noted: (1) A, 7-10 ἐξῆλθεν Οὐριήλ... καὶ εἶπεν ὅτι κατέβην ἐπὶ τὴν γήν... καὶ ὅτι ἐκλήθην ὀνόματι 'Ιακώβ. I have treated the whole as indirect discourse with the first ὅτι as introducing the reporting of Uriel's speech and the second ὅτι as a continuation of the quotation. (G. W. Lawell of the Yale Dept. of Classical Languages has made the suggestion that the second ὅτι be read as ὅτε. This is possible; but is not required). In both clauses, Uriel is the speaker and the behavior of Jacob-Israel is the subject of the discourse —the whole being reported by Jacob-Israel. Thus Jacob-Israel narrates that Uriel claims that Jacob-Israel has descended to earth, tabernacled among men and taken the name of Jacob. Daniélou (*Theology*, p. 133f.) treats the second ὅτι as the beginning of a new quotation and holds that both clauses refer to Uriel: "Uriel said: 'I have come down...' and: 'I am called by the name Jacob.'" This forces him to the conclusion that "each of the characters present claims the name of Jacob..." Father Daniélou informs me (in a letter of February 17, 1965) that he now believes "the terms κατέβην, κατεσκήνωσα and ἐκλήθη refer to the angel Israel and not to the angel Uriel" and withdraws his previous interpretation.

(2) A, 11-12 λέγων προτερήσειν ἐπάνω τοῦ ὀνόματός μου τὸ ὄνομα αὐτοῦ καὶ τοῦ πρὸ παντὸς ἀγγέλου. James (*op. cit.*, p. 22) suggests translating this as either "saying that his name (i.e. Uriel) should have precedence over my name and that of the angel that is before all" or "that his name and the name of the angel that is before all should have precedence over my name." This would introduce a third angelic actor (presumably a figure such as Michael or Metatron) who is the superior angel. This, however, would run contrary to the persistent emphasis in the *PJ* on the superiority of Jacob-Israel (A, 5,14-18). Schurer (*loc. cit.*) emends the text to read πρὸ τοῦ παντὸς ἀγγέλου but this is not required. Ginzberg (*Legends*, Vol. V, p. 310) believes the reference here is to the suffix -*el* which is frequently attached to the names of angels, referring to YHWH, and proposes to emend: "and the name of him who is after every angel." There is no justification for such a flagrant disregard of the given text. Daniélou (*Theology*, p. 133) suggests: "saying that his name which is the name of him that is before all the angels would prevail over mine." Either this has Uriel claiming YHWH's name, which is no where suggested in the text; or, this translation is required by Daniélou's thesis that both Jacob and Uriel are claiming the name Israel which "is not the true name of either" (*op. cit.*, p. 134).

(3) A,13 καὶ πόσος ἐστιν ἐν υἱοῖς θεοῦ James (*op. cit.*, p. 22 n.1) suggests emending πόσος to πόστος which is possible; but not required. Fabricius (*op. cit.*, Vol. I, p. 766) erroneously reads: καὶ πρωτός ἐστιν ἐν υἱοῖς θεοῦ!

(4) A,18-19 καὶ ἐπεκαλεσάμην ἐν ὀνόματι ἀσβέστω τὸν θεόν μου. The problem is the relation of this clause to the preceding. All editors from Fabricius to Preuschen place the question mark after μου. This might suggest that a part of Israel's λειτουργία before YHWH was the utterance of the name and that Israel is here enumerating one more instance of his superiority (so James, *op. cit.*, p. 29). One would, however, have expected an imperfect of habitual action rather than the aorist ἐπεκαλεσάμην. The tense would seem to suggest that this should be treated as a new sentence, following Israel's address, in which the angel invokes the name of God. The question mark should then be placed after ὁ ἐν προσώπῳ θεοῦ λειτουργὸς πρῶτος (as Grant, *loc. cit* has translated). In A,18 the adjective ἄσβεστος has called forth some comment. I have treated it as a synonym for αἰώνιος. James (*op. cit.*, p. 29) remarks "the expression 'inextinguishable name' I have not found elsewhere, though I believe it to exist." For an occurrence of this term, see Esaias, *Oration* 4.9 (ed. Augustinos [Jerusalem, 1911], p. 26. Previously known only in Latin trans-

Fragment B (Origen, *Philocalia* XXIII,15)

...like a book of God, in a manner of speaking, the whole heaven may contain the future. The saying of Jacob in the "Prayer of Joseph" should be understood in this manner: *For I have read in the tablets of heaven all that shall befall you and your sons.*[1])

Because of its importance for section III of this paper, I add also the paraphrase of Fragment A and quotation of Fragment B given in Origen's *Philocalia* XXIII, 19:

And moreover, Jacob was greater than man, he who supplanted his brother and who declared in the same book from which we quoted *I read in the tablets of heaven* that he was a chief captain of the power of the Lord and had, from of old, the name of Israel; something which

---

lation, cf. *MPG* XL, col. 1118B). However the context (a homily on Gen. 28) is quite different than the *PJ*, the name clearly referring to God's promise to Jacob, that his name would not be forgotten (vss. 13-15). Ginzberg (*Legends*, Vol. V, p. 310) suggests that a Hebrew idiom may be behind the expression and compares it to שמות שאינן נמחקין citing BT, *Shab.* 35a. This is scarcely a parallel. The reference in BT, *Shab.* 35a (cf. PT, *Rosh hash.* 1.56d etc.) "there are divine names that may be erased and such as may not be erased" refers to the ruling that, on a piece of paper, one may erase the attributes of YHWH but not His names (see further: M. *Sanh.* 7.8; Jastrow, *Dictionary*, Vol. II, pp. 763f. s.v. מחק; Levy, *Worterbuch*, Vol. III, pp. 80f. s.v. idem; J. Z. Lauterbach, "Substitutes for the Tetragrammaton," *Proceedings of the American Academy for Jewish Research*, 1930-1931, pp. 43f.). For a contrary opinion, see BT, *Shab.* 116a (on a writ of divorce "the Name, written in holiness, may be blotted out").

I should like to express my gratitude to Prof. Hiram J. Lester for his valuable criticism of my translation and this note.

[1]) In the edition of J. A. Robinson, Cambridge, 1893, pp. 203f. The Greek text in Eusebius, *Praep. evang.* VI.11.64 is identical. The Latin version preserved in Procopius of Gaza, *Comm. in I Gen.* 29 reads: *Praetera, ut magis suam opinionem stabilant, adducunt illud testimonium ab Jacobo dictum ex oratione Josephi: Legi in tabulis coeli quanta contigent vobis et filius vestris* (*MPG* LXXXVII :1, cols. 95f.). The reference in Origen's *Comm. ad Ioann* I.31 to the γράμματα θεοῦ which the ἅγιοι may read and declare that they have read the future ἐνταῖς πλαξὶ τοῦ οὐρανοῦ is too general to allow one to assume, as does Brooke (*op. cit.*, Vol. I, p. 41 margin) that this is a reference to Fragment B of the *PJ*. The image of the "tablets of heaven" is widespread in apocalyptic literature (e.g. it occurs some 20 times in *Jubilees* in a variety of contexts). Cf. H. Bietenhard, *Die himmlische Welt im Urchristentum und Spätjudentum* (Tubingen, 1951), ch. xi. and G. Widengren, *The Ascension of the Apostle and the Heavenly Book* (Uppsala-Leipzig, 1950), passim, and F. Notscher, "Himmlische Bucher und Schicksalsglaube in Qumran," *Revue de Qumrân* 1 (1958-9), 405-411. The reference in the *PJ* is most likely to Genesis 49.1-2. Note that an almost exact parallel occurs in *Jubilees* 32.21 "And behold an angel descended from heaven with seven tablets in his hands, and he gave them to Jacob, and he read them and knew all that was written thereon which would befall him and his sons throughout all the ages." (Charles, Vol. II, p. 62).

he recognizes while doing service in the body, being reminded of it by the archangel Uriel.[1])

The "Prayer of Joseph", as it has survived, is dominated by (I), the lofty role of Israel who is called (1) Ἰακώβ, (2) an ἄγγελος θεοῦ, (3) a πνεῦμα ἀρχικόν, (4) an ἀνὴρ ὁρῶν θεόν, (5) as being the πρωτόγονος παντὸς ζώου, (6) the ἀρχάγγελος δυνάμεως κυρίου, (7) the heavenly ἀρχιχιλίαρχος (8) and the λειτουργὸς πρῶτος ἐν προσώπω θεοῦ; (II) the conflict between Jacob-Israel and Uriel, each claiming ascendency over the other and (III) the curious myth relating the descent to earth of Jacob-Israel. It is on these three elements that this paper will focus.

I. THE TITLES

There is a remarkable consistency to the titles given Jacob-Israel in the *PJ*. Indeed, it is striking that many of Jacob-Israel's titles are applied by Philo to the *Logos*, by rabbinic literature to Michael, by Jewish mystical literature to Metatron and by Jewish Christianity to Jesus. This suggests, without arguing direct literary dependence, a community and continuity of tradition. It would appear that the center of this continuity must be located within hellenistic mystical Judaism as described by Erwin Goodenough in *By Light, Light* and in his magisterial *Jewish Symbols in the Greco-Roman Period*.[2]) More specifically, I

---

[1]) In Robinson, *op. cit.*, p. 208. Some scholars identify the unnamed *libellus* in Origen's *Hom. ad Num* XVII.4 (ed. W. A. Baehrens [Leipzig, 1921], p. 162 *GCS*) as the *PJ*: *sicut et in libello quodam legitur quia Iacob domus sit Istrahel, hoc est corpus eius Iacob dicatur et anima Istrahel*. There is nothing in the surviving lines explicitly quoted from the *PJ* to suggest that Jacob is considered the body and Israel, the soul. But this may represent an interpretation of the earthly Jacob and angelic Israel as given in the text. For the identification of this *libellus* with the *PJ*, see: Harnack, *op. cit.*, Vol. I, pp. 18f.; Baehrens, *op. cit.*, p. 162 note ad line 1; A. Méhat, *Origène: Homélies sur les Nombres* (Paris, 1951), p. 351 n.1 and Daniélou, *Théologie*, p. 183 n.1.

[2]) This does not imply an acceptance of Goodenough's tendency to postulate radical discontinuity between hellenistic Judaism and rabbinic circles of the time; nor his portrait of "Pharisaic domination" of Palestinian Judaism which is the basis for his dichotomy. For a corrective to Goodenough at this point see M. Smith, "The Image of God: Notes on the hellenization of Judaism with especial reference to Goodenough's work on Jewish Symbols," *Bull. John Rylands Library* 40 (1958), pp. 473-512, esp. pp. 488f.; J. Neusner, "Notes on Goodenough's *Jewish Symbols*," *Conservative Judaism* 17 (1963), esp. pp. 79-82; Neusner, "Judaism at Dura-Europos," *History of Religions* 4 (1964), esp. pp. 95-101 and E. J. Bickerman, "Symbolism in the Dura Synagogue," *Harvard Theological Review* 58 (1965), esp. pp. 129-135. Goodenough has only partially corrected his position in *Jewish Symbols*, Vol. XII, pp. 65-7 et passim.

would suggest that in the *PJ* we are given a precious fragment of a mythology concerning the Mystery of Israel, a mythology which continues in the later Merkabah and Metatron speculation and which is presented in a 'de-mythologized' form in the writings of Philo.[1])

1. *Jacob*

In the *PJ*, the titles that are given apply exclusively to Jacob-Israel's heavenly nature. Indeed, it would appear that Jacob is his only earthly title, that by which he is known to men (A, 3: ὁ κληθεὶς ὑπὸ ἀνθρώπων 'Ιακώβ).[2]) Although in Manichaean and hellenistic sources there is an angel Jacob, in the *PJ* Israel is the name borne by the angel; Jacob, by the man.[3])

---

[1]) Goodenough's remarks on the angelology of Philo in comparison with that of the Sadduccees and Pharisees in *By Light, Light* (New Haven, 1935), pp. 79f. are to the point here.

[2]) This is a standard feature of hellenistic revelation-literature. The heavenly revealer possesses a (secret) celestial name while being known on earth by another name. See already Homer, *Iliad* I, 403-4 "Ὂν Βριάρεων καλέουσι θεοί, ἄνδρες δέ τε πάντες Αἰγαίων and XX, 74 "Ὂν Ξάνθον καλέοοσι θεοί, ἄνδρες δὲ Σκάμανδρον. And compare Mandaean texts where Ptahil-Utra is named Gabriel: "He summoned Ptahil-Utra. He put names on him which are hidden and preserved on their place. He called him Gabriel, the apostle..." (*Right Ginza* III in M. Lidzbarski, *Ginza* [Göttingen-Leipzig, 1925], p. 98:7ff. I have followed the English translation of G. Widengren, *The Ascension of the Apostle*, p. 59. Cf. the parallels cited in K. Rudolph, *Theogonie, Kosmogonie und Anthropogonie in den mandaischen Schriften* [Gottingen, 1965], p. 198); and the catalogue of both the heavenly names and the names by which men call the five archons in *Pistis Sophia* 137 (C. Schmidt-W. Till, *Koptische-gnostische Schriften* [Berlin, 1962], Vol. I, p. 235 cf. A. D. Nock, "Greek Magical Papyri," *Journal of Egyptian Archaeology* 15 [1929], p. 227 n.5). Cf. the material collected in E. Norden, *Agnostos Theos* (Leipzig-Berlin, 1913), pp. 177-239 and, more recently, H. Becker, *Die Reden des Johannes-evangeliums und der Stil der gnostische Offenbarungsrede* (Gottingen, 1956), esp. pp. 14-41.

[3]) *Yākōb prēstag* (i.e. *ferestak*, see A. Ghilain, *Essai sur la langue Parthe .. d'après les textes manichéens du Turkestan oriental* [Louvain, 1939], p. 98) "the angel Jacob" occurs in the Manichaean Turfan fragments M. 4 and M. 20 as edited and translated by F. W. K. Müller, "Handschriftenreste im Estrangelo-schrift aus Turfan. Teil II," *Abhandlungen d. kon. Akad. d. Wissenschaften* Berlin, 1904 (Anhang, phil-hist, Kl. Abh. II). M. 4 (fol. 6) reads, in Muller's translation, "Ich verehre Gott, Jakob den Engel mit den 'Glorien', den 'Kraften', den guten Geistern, welche uns selbst beschutzen mogen mit Kraft starkei. ...Ich *bekenne in Freude die Kraft, die starke, Jakobs, des Engels, des Anfuhrers der Engel... Neue Kraft komme von Jakob, dem Engel, neue (?) von allen Engeln..." (*op. cit.*, pp. 56f.) M. 20 contains a brief catalogue of angelic names: "der Damon, Jakob der Engel, der Herr Bar Simus, Qaftinus, der machtige. Raphael, Gabriel, Michael, Sarael, Narsus, Nastikus." (*op. cit.*, p. 45). For a detailed description of these two manuscripts and a guide to their secondary literature, see M. Boyce, *A Catalogue of the Iranian Manuscripts in Manichaean Script in the German Turfan Collection* (Berlin, 1960), pp. 2f. The occurrence of Jacob as an angelic name in these manuscripts was

briefly noted by A. von Harnack and F. C. Conybeare, "Manichaeism," *Encyclopaedia Britannica* 11e. (1911), Vol. XVII, p. 575; F. C. Burkitt, *The Religion of the Manichees* (Cambridge, 1925), p. 91 and H. Gressmann, *Die orientalischen Religionen im hellenistischen und romischen Zeitalter* (Berlin, 1930), p. 168. Its connection with the *PJ* was first suggested by T. Schneider, "Der Engel Jakob bei Mani," *Zeitschrift f.d. neutestamentliche Wissenschaft* 33 (1934), pp. 218f. and, more strongly, in Daniélou (*Theology*, p. 134 n. 146). It should be noted that *prēstag* carries the same force as the Hebrew מלאך and the Greek ἄγγελος i.e. it has the root sense of "messenger, one who has been sent" (see G. Widengren, *The Ascension of the Apostle and the Heavenly Book* [Uppsala, 1950], p. 37 cf. Widengren, *The Great Vohu Mana and the Apostle of God* [Uppsala-Leipzig, 1945], p. 30 and n. 4 and *Mesopotamian Elements in Manichaeism* [Uppsala-Leipzig, 1946], pp. 167-75; H. Corbin, *Avicenna and the Visionary Recital* [New York, 1960], p. 358 n.1 cont'd.) Thus, *Yākōb prēstag* could, conceivably, be translated "the apostle James" (see: E. Waldschmidt-W. Lentz, "Der Stellung Jesu im Manichaismus," *Abhandlungen d. preuss. Akad. d. Wissenschaften* [Berlin, 1926], phil-hist. Kl. no. 4, pp. 8f. and H. H Schader, "Iranica 2:Fūlin", *Abhandlungen d. Gesellschaft d. Wissenschaften z. Gottingen* 1934, phil.-hist. Kl. F. 3, no. 10, p. 32 n. 3). However, the context of both citations would clearly suggest the angel Jacob rather than the apostle James. Ginzberg, (*Legends*, Vol. V, p. 275 n. 35 cont'd) suggests that in the *PJ* "the patriarch Jacob is confounded with the Semitic god Jacobel mentioned in an Egyptian inscription. Many an angel is nothing more than a degraded god." I know of no such Semitic god. As is well known, Ya' qob-el occurs as a place name in the fifteenth century list of Thutmose III (in Pritchard, *ANET*, p. 242 cf. S. Yeiven, "Ya'qob'-el", *Journal of Egyptian Archaeology* 45 [1959], pp. 16-18) which may be what Ginzberg is referring to. It is now suggested that *Ya'qob-el* is to be translated "May El protect" (so J. Bright, *A History of Israel* [London, 1960], p. 83) but the previous generation of scholars translated "Jacob is God" (e.g. Oesterley-Robinson, *History of Israel* [Oxford, 1932], Vol. I, pp. 52f. and 91).

'Ιακωβ occurs as the name of a supernatural being in the *Sword of Dardanus* (a charm which forms part of the Great Paris Magical Papyrus). To fashion the amulet, the user must take a magnetic stone, engrave on it a figure of Aphrodite and, under her, the figure of Eros. Under Eros must be engraved certain names including Adonai, Jacob and Iao. On the reverse of the amulet is to be carved the figures of Eros and Psyche embracing. Cf. the editions of C. Wessely, "Griechische Zauberpapyrus von Paris und London," *Denkschriften d. Akad. d. Wissenschaften* 36:2 (Vienna, 1888), p. 88, lines 1735-7 and K. Preisendanz, *Papyri Graecae Magicae* (Berlin, 1928) Vol. I, p. 126 (Papyrus IV, lines 1735-7). For a discussion of the significance of this amulet, see esp. A. D. Nock, "Magical Notes," *Journal of Egyptian Archaeology* 11 (1925), pp. 154-8; M. Smith, "The Account of Simon Magus", p. 749 has related this text to the *PJ*. R. Mouterde, "Le Glaive de Dardanos: Objets et inscriptions magiques de Syrie," *Mélanges de l'Université Saint-Joseph* 15:3 (1930), esp. pp. 56f. has discovered such an amulet with the fragmentary inscription [... ΧΛΑΔW NAIEBACMAXA ... WIA KWBICAKW] which is to be restored, on the basis of the papyrus (line 1735): [(Αχαπα) χ (α)(?) 'Αδωναῖε Βασμ-(α)/χα/ (ρακ) ω 'Ιακωβ 'Ισκκω (?)]. Another striking instance is an amulet (Newhall Collection No. 35) bearing on its obverse the inscription: ΙΑΚΩΒ/ΑΚΟΥΒΤΑ/ ΙΑΩ/ΒΕΡΩ/ published by H. C. Youtie, "A Gnostic Amulet with an Aramaic Inscription," *Journal of the American Oriental Society* 50 (1930), pp. 214-20 (cf. C. Bonner, *Studies in Magical Amulets* [Ann Arbor, 1950], fig. 275 and pp. 171, 299) Youtie suggests that the text be read: Jacob/the likeness (עקובתא) /YHWH/ his son (ברו) and that there may be an attempt to derive an etymology of the name Jacob as the "image of God" IA (Ω) AKOΥB(TA). In his article (*op. cit.*, pp. 218f.),

2. Israel, an angel of God

The angel Israel appears in several Jewish mystical documents such as the *Sefer Raziel*, but he possesses such a diffuse character in these works that generalization is impossible.[1]) In hellenistic sources, the name *Istraēl* is found in a wide variety of texts and may well represent

---

Youtie compares the notion of Jacob as the son of God with the description of Jacob in the *PJ*. The chief difficulty in Youtie's interpretation, of which he is well aware, is that עקובתא is a *hapax legomenon* in BT, *Sanh*. 96a (end) and is usually translated "buttocks" (e.g. Jastrow, *Dictionary*, Vol. II, p. 1105 and all translations that I am familiar with). Youtie, following Levy's *Wörterbuch* (Vol. III, p. 682) argues from an Arabic cognate that the word means "image". However, this must remain conjectural. Bonner (*op. cit.*, p. 171) suggests that ακουβτα and βερω may simply be *voces magicae*. Ganschinietz, in his article "Jacob" (Pauly-Wissowa, *Realencyclopadie*, Vol. IX :1, cols. 623f.) notes the tendency to combine the name 'Ιακωβ with the divine name 'Ιαω (which might suggest a heavenly Jacob). He cites P. Paris 1736 'Ιακωβιαωη, P. Paris 1803 'Ιακωβ' ιαω, P. Paris 224 'Ιακουβιαι, P. Mimaut 'Ιωκουβια and P. Lugd. J. 384 'Ιαια 'Ιακουβια to which may be added the close association of these names in the material just discussed. Other possible occcurrences of the name Jacob in a supernatural context are 'Ιακουβ as one of the *nomina sacra* in a love-charm (Preisendanz, *PGM* Vol. II, p. 29, line 649); 'Ιακουβια in P. London 121 (ed. Leemans [Leipzig, 1888], p. 51 line 715) which M. Schwab, *Vocabulaire de l'angelologie* (Paris, 1897), p. 291 translates as Jacob; 'Ιακωπ which is one of the παρέδρους τοῦ μεγάλου θεοῦ in the Great Paris Magical Papyrus (P. Paris 574 in Preisendanz, *PGM*, Vol. I, p. 118, line 1377); and Ιακου βαι on an engraved gem described in H. Carnegie, *Catalogue of Antique Gems formed by James, Ninth Earl of Southesk, K.T.* (London, 1908), p. 195 N84 (cf. Goodenough, *Jewish Symbols* Vol. II, p. 274 "It is hard to think which basis this word could have other than the name Jacob."). ιακ which occurs as an angelic name in various Coptic magical papyri bears no relationship to the figure of Jacob and should not be confused with him. e.g. P. London 6795 (in M. Kropp, *Ausgewahlte koptische Zaubertexte* [Brussels, 1931], Vol. II, p. 99, line 36 also C. D. G. Muller, *Die Engellehre der koptischen Kirche* [Wiesbaden, 1959], p. 297) and London Ms. Or. 6794 (in Kropp, *op. cit.*, Vol. II, p. 107, line 46 cf. Goodenough, *Jewish Symbols*, Vol. II, pp. 166-8 who treats this as a purely Jewish charm). Cf. Kropp, *op. cit.*, Vol. III, pp. 29f. and 45-7 for a discussion of this angel.

[1]) ישראל appears as a conquering angel, lord of the seventh day of the week with dominion over the month of Shebat in *Sefer Raziel* (Amsterdam, 1701), f. 41b and is related to the sign of the Bull in *Sefer Raziel*, f. 4b (see M. Schwab, *op. cit.*, pp. 151f.). שריאל is invoked, along with other angels, in the Hebrew *Sword of Moses* (M. Gaster, ed. *Studies and Texts in Folklore, Magic, Medieval Romance, Hebrew Apocrypha and Samaritan Archaeology* [London, 1928], Vol. III, p. 71, line 2. Cf. Gaster's translation, *op. cit.*, Vol. I, p. 314). The angel יוראל in *Sefer Raziel* f. 6b, who possesses dominion over fire and flame, may be a corruption of Israel (so Schwab, *op. cit.*, p. 146). Possibly an angelic Israel is implied in *Zohar* II. 4b (translation: J. de Pauly [Paris, 1908], Vol. III, p. 16): "the 'children of Israel' refers to the angels who are the children of the heavenly Israel." I regret that it has proved impossible to determine whether the angel Jacob (or Israel) appears in M. Margoliot's new reconstruction of the *Sefer Ha Razim*.

a corruption of Israel.¹) In Justin's *Baruch* (Hippolytus, *Ref.* V, 26,2), one of the three *archai* is a female who is called Israel, a tradition which Resch suggests may be reflected in the *PJ*'s description of Israel as a πνεῦμα ἀρχικόν (an inference which is speculative at best and should be rejected).²)

In Jewish mystical literature, the community of Israel chanting the *Kedusha* has become personified into a heavenly figure named Israel who leads (as does Michael or Metatron in parallel traditions) the celestial worship before the Throne. Thus, I would suggest, from the two-level action depicted in an anonymous *baraitha* in BT, *Hullin* 91b:

> Israel is beloved before the Holy One, blessed be He, even more than the ministering angels. For Israel repeats the song every hour while the ministering angels repeat it only once a day... Furthermore the ministering angels do not begin the song above until Israel has started it below...

---

¹) 'Ἰστραήλ appears as an angelic name in the Greek manuscript of 1 *Enoch* 10.1 (R. H. Charles, *Apocrypha and Pseudepigrapha*, Vol. II, p. 193n.). He figures prominently in the Great Magical Paris Papyrus as part of the "Sword of Dardanus." The "sword" must be inscribed on a gold leaf along with the acclamation Εἷς Θουριὴλ Μιχαὴλ Γαβριὴλ Οὐριὴλ Μισαὴλ Ἱρραὴλ Ἰστραήλ. The gold leaf is to be swallowed by a partridge, the partridge is to be killed and the leaf recovered, a sprig of παιδέρως is to be inserted in the leaf and the whole hung around ones neck (Preisendanz, *PGM*, Vol. I, p. 128 esp. lines 1815f. cf. Nock, *op. cit.*, p. 157). Ἰστραήλ also occurs in BM 46 (Wessely, *op. cit.*, p. 130, line 118); P. Oslo 36 (Preisendanz, *PGM*, Vol. II, p. 173, line 310 cf. Goodenough, *Jewish Symbols*, Vol. II, p. 199); in an inscription from Kodja-Geuzlar published by W. Ramsey, *The Cities and Bishophrics of Phrygia* (Oxford, 1897), Vol. I:2, p. 541 no. 404 and in an engraved gem (Palestine Archaeological Museum no. 36-1856) described in Goodenough, *Jewish Symbols*, Vol. II, pp. 275f. and Vol. III, fig. 1078. E. Peterson, "Engel- und Damonennamen. Nomina barbara," *Rheinisches Museum* 75 (1926), pp. 403f. declares that *"Istrael* appears *in der Namensform Israel* in the Prayer of Joseph," an opinion most recently put forth by J. Michl, "Engel, V", *Reallexikon f. Antike und Christentum*, Vol. V, cols. 217f. G. Scholem, *Jewish Gnosticism, Merkabah Mysticism and Talmudic Tradition* 2ed. (New York, 1965), pp. 95f. has suggested a possible connection between 'Ἰστραήλ, 'Ἀστραήλ, and אסטר (*Aster*, in both Aramaic and Latin sources. See the literature cited by Scholem, *op. cit.*, pp. 89, 95n. 8 and 96n. 9). Ganschinietz, "Israel", Pauly-Wissowa, *Realencyklopadie*, Vol. IX:2, col. 2234 cites as further possible corruptions of the angelic name Israel 'Οσραήλ and Εσράηλ in P. Paris 3034, to which may be added 'Ἰστρήλ which occurs in close proximity to 'Ἰστραήλ in BM P. 46 (ed. Wessely, *op. cit.*, p. 129, line 112 and p. 130, line 118). Burkitt, *op. cit.*, p. 91 suggests that Sarael in Manichaean literature "appears to be a miswriting of Israel"—a suggestion with which I cannot concur. Whether there is a possible relationship between the Arabic archangel Izra'il or the angel of death Israfil and the angel Israel, I cannot determine. A. J. Wensinck's derivation of the former from אסריאל and the latter from Serafim appears unconvincing to me (*The Encyclopaedia* of *Islam* [London, Leiden, 1927], Vol. II, pp. 570-1 and 554).

²) καλεῖται δὲ Ἐδὲμ αὕτη ἡ κόρη καὶ Ἰσραήλ. Cf. Resch, *op. cit.*, p. 298.

there developed a vision, in the *Pirke Hekhaloth*, of "the angel who bears the name of Israel standing in the center of heaven and leading the heavenly choir."[1]) The antiquity and distribution of this tradition has recently been unexpectedly confirmed by the Coptic Codex II from Nag-hammadi which presents a description of the heavenly Throne. In this Merkabah text there stands, amidst Cherubim and Seraphim, near to Sabaoth, "a firstborn (ⲟⲩϣⲡⲛ̄'ⲙⲙⲓⲥⲉ) whose name is Israel, the man who sees God (ⲡⲣⲱⲙⲉ ⲉⲧⲛⲁⲩ ⲉⲡⲛⲟⲩⲧⲉ)."[2]) Here, in just one line, we find two of the major titles given Israel in the *PJ* (the firstborn and a see-er of God), set within the context of a celestial liturgy before the heavenly Throne.

Biblical and midrashic traditions concerning the Patriarch Jacob-Israel have likewise contributed to the *PJ*. Titles appropriate to the earthly Jacob have been attracted to the angel, Israel. The phrase in the *PJ* (A, 3-4) "I, Jacob, whom men call Jacob, but whose name is Israel, am he who God called Israel" appears to be based on Genesis 32.29 where Jacob receives the name, Israel. The notion of Israel as an angel in the *PJ* may be based on an exegetical tradition which connects שרית עם אלהים, "you have striven with God" (Gen 32.29) with שר "prince", and interprets the verse to mean "you are as a prince with God" i.e. as one of the angels.[3])

---

[1]) G. Scholem, *Major Trends in Jewish Mysticism* (New York, 1954), p. 62 paraphrasing Jellinek, *BHM*, Vol. III, pp. 161-3. Cf. Ginzberg, *Legends*, Vol. V, p. 307n. 253; Goodenough, *Jewish Symbols*, Vol. X, pp. 71-72. The pattern, in BT, *Hullin* 91b, of the angels not beginning their song above until Israel has begun it below is also found in the *Hekhaloth* material. See M. Smith, "Observations on Hekhalot Rabbati," in A. Altmann, ed., *Biblical and other Studies* (Cambridge USA, 1963), p. 143.

[2]) A. Bohlig-P. Labib, *Die koptisch-gnostische Schrift ohne Titel aus Codex II von Nag Hammadi* (Berlin, 1962), plate 153, lines 23-5, pp. 52-5. Cf. J. Doresse, *The Secret Books of the Egyptian Gnostics* (New York, 1960), p. 167; P. Borgen, *Bread from Heaven* (Leiden, 1965), p. 177. Daniélou (*Theology*, p. 133n. 43) was the first to relate this text to the *PJ*. Codex II has proved difficult to date with any security (see the review of Bohlig-Labib by G. Quispel, *Vigiliae Christianae* 17 [1963], pp. 50-4). Bohlig-Labib (*op. cit.*, p. 54n.) compare to this passage the *Apocryphon of John* 30.7 (W. C. Till, ed., *Die gnostischen Schriften des koptischen Papyrus Berolensis 8502* [Berlin, 1955], pp. 100f.) which narrates the birth of *Monogenes*, the divine Self-born (ⲁⲩⲧⲟⲅⲉⲛⲏⲧⲟⲥ) and First Born (ϣⲣⲡ̄ ⲙⲙⲓⲥⲉ) Son of All—which is not as relevant a parallel as the *PJ* which they fail to cite.

[3]) In Jerome, *Liber Hebraicarum Quaestionum in Genesim* (*MPL* XXIII:1038): *Sarith* (שרית) *enim, quod ab Israel vocabulo derivatur, principium sonat. Sensus itaque est: Non vocabitur nomen tuum supplantator, hoc est, Jacob; sed vocabitur nomen tuum princeps cum Deo, hoc est, Israel.* Cf. the notes on this passage in L'Abbé Bareille, *Oeuvres complètes de Saint Jérôme* (Paris, 1878), Vol. III, p. 549 and the discussion of Jer-

Finally, we may relate the conflict motif in the *PJ* to a tradition that the mysterious figure with whom Jacob wrestled in Genesis 32 was an angel called Israel (or, in Jewish-Christian sources, was the *Logos* or the Christ who is named Israel). Thus, in the *Pirke de Rabbi Eliezer* 37: "And the angel called his name Israel like his own name, for his name is called Israel."[1])

3. *a ruling spirit*

I am unable to account for the title πνεῦμα ἀρχικόν (A,2). It may well be related to astrological angelology in which the various angels are assigned planetary spheres of influence, days of the week, months, signs of the Zodiac, etc. (analogous to the hellenistic and Gnostic *archai*), but I have not been able to locate this particular phrase in any astrological text.[2]) More probably, this title is to be related to the concept of a national angel. While it is usually Michael who is the angel of Israel, it may well be that in the *PJ*, Israel's ruling angel is himself named Israel.[3])

4. *a man seeing God*

This title has its biblical origin in Genesis 32.31 where Jacob after wrestling with the angel and receiving the name Israel, exclaims "I have seen God!" (ראיתי אלהים). However the interpretation of the name Israel to mean "a man seeing God" (ἀνὴρ ὁρῶν θεόν = ראה אל איש) received its most massive development in Philo. This phrase occurs twenty-three times in the Philonic corpus and is expressed or

---

ome's exegesis in Roger Bacon, *Opus Majus* III : 6 (R. B. Burke, translation [Philadelphia, 1938], Vol. I, pp. 93-6). Cf. the medieval Jewish commentaries of Ibn Ezra, Gersonides and Hezekiah b. Manoa ad Genesis 32.29.

[1]) G. Friedlander, *Pirke de Rabbi Eliezer* (London, 1916), p. 282 in an anonymous tradition. Cf. the Slavonic *Ladder of Jacob* (translated in M. R. James, *op. cit.*, p. 98) in which the archangel Sarakl says to Jacob after the vision at Bethel. "What is your name?' and I said, 'Jacob'. Then he said, 'Your name shall no longer be called Jacob, but your name shall be like my name, Israel.'" James, *loc. cit.* suggests that the *Ladder of Jacob* may contain "a dim reflection" of the *PJ*. For Christian interpretation of the wrestling narrative, where Christ who is called Israel gives his name to Jacob see esp. Justin Martyr, *Dial. c. Trypho* 125.5 and, more generally, Origen, *Comm. in. Ioann.* I.35 (40).

[2]) It is not possible to maintain, as Resch (*op. cit.*, pp. 295-8) suggests, that this relates the *PJ* to the gnostic Archontic sect. Resch's thesis is rightly rejected by R. M. Grant, *op. cit.*, p. 190 n.36. Nor is it possible to accept Stein's attempt (*op. cit.*, p. 283 n.6) to derive the chronological force of ἀρχή from ἀρχικόν, and thus relate it to the *Logos* as ἀρχή in Philo.

[3]) cf. *Jubilees* 35.17 "the guardian of Jacob is great and powerful and honored and praised more than the guardian of Esau." See below, pp. 274-276.

implied in some twenty-six additional texts.¹) As the derivation rests on a Hebrew *jeu de mots* and as it is never argued but rather assumed by Philo, there is good reason to suggest that he is drawing upon an earlier tradition.²) However, except for the *PJ*, Christian sources possibly dependent upon Philo, two Jewish(?) prayers and a late(?) Hebrew midrash—it occurs nowhere else.³) The Philonic parallels to the *PJ* are far more extensive than this one point of contact. Indeed, as already suggested, the majority of the titles applied to Jacob-Israel

¹) It should be noted that Philo nowhere employs the phrase ἀνὴρ ὁρῶν θεόν. For the phrase Ἰσραὴλ (ὁ) ὁρῶν (τὸν θεόν) in Philo see: *L.A.* II, 34; III, 186, 212; *Sac.* 134; *Post.* 62,92; *Conf.* 56, 72, 146, 148; *Mig.* 113, 125, 201; *Haer.* 78; *Cong.* 51; *Fug.* 208; *Somn.* I, 173; II, 44, 173; *Abr.* 57; *Leg.* 4; *QG* III, 49 and IV, 233. Cf. *L.A.* III, 15, 172; *Plant.* 58, 60 and *QE* II, 22 which mention vision in a context which suggests Israel. τὸ ὁρατικὸν γένος as a synonym for Israel occurs in *Immut.* 144; *Conf.* 91; *Mig.* 18, 54; *Mut.* 109, 189, 258; *Somn.* II, 279 cf. *Somn.* II, 44 where Judah is the king of the nation that sees. The substantivised forms ὁ ὁρῶν *Conf.* 159 and *QE* II, 47 (in *Sobr.* 13 this may apply to either Moses or Israel. The former seems probable from *Agr.* 81) and οἱ ὁρατικοί *Plant.* 46f. and *QE* II, 38 are also employed. Synonymous expressions applying other verbs of seeing and contemplation to Israel are θεορεῖν *Sac.* 120; *Haer.* 279; σκέπτομαι *Haer.* 279; βλέπω *Somn.* I, 114. Note further ὁρατικός plus some organ with reference to Israel: ψυχή *Ebr.* 111; διάνοια *Mig.* 14; νοῦς *Mut.* 209 (cf. *Somn.* II, 173) and ὀφθαλμός *Conf.* 92; *Mut.* 203. For a discussion of this etymology in Philo see esp. W. Michaelis, *TWNT* Vol. V, pp. 337-338 n.113 and, further, the penetrating treatment of the ideology contained in this etymology in P. Borgen, *op. cit.*, pp. 115-118, 175-179 esp. p. 177 where the "affinities" of this concept with Merkabah mysticism are suggested.

²) So E. Stein, *op. cit.*, pp. 282f. Cf. Stein, *Die allegorische Exegese des Philo aus Alexandria* (Giessen, 1929), pp. 20f. There is no evidence for or against S. Baron, *A Social and Religious History of the Jews* 2ed. (New York, 1952), Vol. I, pp. 182f. who assumes that the etymology in the *PJ* "antedates" Philo. While the Philonic derivation is to be rejected as having no linguistic claim, note that E. Sachsse, "Die Etymologie und älteste Aussprache des Names Israel," *Zeitschrift f. d. alttestamentliche Wissenschaft* 32 (1914), p. 3 has suggested that Israel could be derived from a root שׁוּר "to behold." For a review of the present state of the discussion concerning the etymology of Israel, see G. A. Danell, *Studies in the Name Israel in the Old Testament* (Uppsala, 1946), pp. 22-8.

³) Christian sources which may be presumed to be dependent upon Philo include the following forms: 1) ὁ ὁρῶν τὸν θεόν in Clement Alex., *Paed.* I, 9 (*MPG* VIII, 341); Origen, *Princ.* IV, 3 (*MPG* XI, 395); Eusebius, *Praep. evang.* XI, 6 (ed. Gifford, 519b) etc. Cf. *Israhel est videre deum* in Jerome, *Heb. Quaest. in Lib. Gen.* ad Gen. 32,28-9 (*Corpus Christianorum* LXXII, 40f.) and Jerome (?), *Liber Interpr. Heb. Nom.*, Ex. (idem., 75); 2) νοῦς ὁρῶν τὸν θεόν in Macarius, *Hom.* XLVII, 5 (*MPG* XXXIV, 800); 3) ὁ τῷ ὄντι διορατικός in Clement Alex., *Strom.* I, 5 (*MPG* VIII, 725). The alternative form ἀνὴρ ὁρῶν θεόν or ἄνθρωπος ὁρῶν τὸν θεόν in Hippolytus, *Contra Noetum* 5 (*MPG* X, 809); Eusebius, *Praep. evang.* VII, 8 (ed. Gifford, 525b) cf. Nag-hammadi Codex II quoted above (p. 264)—a form *never* found in Philo, appears to represent a quite different strain of tradition, one perhaps closer to Hebraic sources depending upon the significant role of the heavenly אִישׁ in Genesis 32. Prof. Nils A. Dahl of Yale University has suggested, in a private communi-

in the *PJ* are applied to the *Logos* by Philo.¹) The most dramatic instance, as has been noted by several scholars, occurs in *De confusione linguarum* 146:

---

cation, that this distinction may "support the view that the etymology in the *PJ* antedates Philo" as Stein (*loc. cit.*) held. Note that in Origen, *Hom. XI*, 4 *in Num.* (*MPG* XII, 648), the name Israel is applied to the angels who see God: *Nomen enim Istrahel pervenit usque ad angelicos ordines, nisi quia multo verius illi appellabuntur Istrahel, quanto verius illi sunt mens videns Deum; hoc enim Istrahel interpretatur*. On this theme in Origen, see M. Simonetti, "Due note sull'angelologia origeniana," *Rivista di cultura classica e medioevale* 4 (1962), esp. pp. 165-79. Cf. Clement Alex., *Stromata* V, 35,1-2 and *Excerpta ex Theodoto* 10-12 where the seven angelic πρωτόκτιστοι are those who see the face of God (on the relationship of this scheme to Origen, see Simonetti, *op. cit.*, p. 166; for its possible dependence upon Philonic tradition see W. Bousset, *Jüdisch-christlicher Schulbetrieb im Alexandria und Rom* [Gottingen, 1915], pp. 231f. and R. P. Casey, *The Excerpta ex Theodoto of Clement of Alexandria* [London, 1934], pp. 105f. Cf. F. Andres, "Die Engel-und Damonenlehre des Klemens von Alexandrien," *Römische Quartalschrift* 34 [1926], p. 137). The phrase, in its Philonic form, appears twice in the *Constitutiones Apostolorum* VII, 36,2 τὸν ἀληθινὸν ᾿Ισραήλ... τὸν ὁρῶντα θεόν, and VIII, 15,7 ὁ θεὸς ᾿Ισραὴλ τοῦ ἀληθινῶς ὁρῶντος which Goodenough (*By Light, Light*, pp. 306-58 esp. 312, 330, 340), following W. Bousset, "Eine judische Gebetssamlung im siebenten Buch der apostolischen Konstitutionen," *Nachrichten von d.K. Gesellschaft d. Wissenschaften zu Göttingen* phil.-hist. Kl. 1915 (1916), pp. 435-85 esp. 444, quite rightly treats as prayers derived from hellenistic Judaism. The only occurrence of the etymology of Israel as a man seeing God in rabbinic sources appears to be a late midrash on Hosea 9.10 in *Seder Eliyyahu Rabbah* 27 (ed. Friedmann [Venice, 1900], pp. 138f.) אל תיקרי ישראל אלא איש ראה אל on which see Ginzberg, *Legends* Vol. V, p. 307 n.253. I should like to express my debt of gratitude to Prof. N. A. Dahl who criticized this note in a previous draft and made several valuable suggestions which I have incorporated.

¹) (a) Jacob is not a title for the Logos in Philo (see E. R. Goodenough, *The Theology of Justin Martyr* [Jena, 1923], pp. 171-172); (b) Israel as a title for the Logos occurs, as cited above, in *Conf.* 146; (c) Logos as angel or archangel occurs in *L.A.* III, 177; *Immut.* 182; *Haer.* 205; *Mut.* 87; *Conf.* 146; *Somn.* I,240 etc.; (d) πνεῦμα ἀρχικόν occurs nowhere in Philo, but one might compare the notion of the Ruling Power, especially in texts such as *Abr.* 125 τὴν ἀρχικήν, ἣ καλεῖται κύριος in the context of interpreting Abraham's vision of the Three (cf. Goodenough, *By Light, Light*, pp. 23-47 and *Jewish Symbols* Vol. X, pp. 87-96). See further *QE* II,64,66, 68; (e) Logos as "the one seeing God" in *Conf.* 146; (f) to Israel as the "firstborn of all living things" compare the Logos as πρωτόγονος *Agr.* 51; *Conf.* 63 or as the πρεσβύτατος θεοῦ υἱός *L.A.* III,175; *Det.* 118; *Mig.* 6; *Conf.* 146; *Haer.* 205; *Somn.* I,230 and perhaps ἀρχή in *Conf.* 146 and *L.A.* I,43; (g) ἀρχιχιλιάρχος does not occur in Philo, but one may compare the Logos as ἡγεμών *Conf.* 174 (Goodenough, *By Light, Light*, p. 302 calls attention to the Logos being "recognizable as the χεὶρ καὶ δύναμις of God that fights with us as our ally" in *Somn.* II,265-7 and notes that "in comparison to God, the Logos is only ὕπαρχος, lieutenant" citing *Somn.* I,241); (h) To Israel as the λειτουργός might well be compared Philo's Logos as ἱερεύς or ἀρχιερεύς *L.A.* III,82-88; *Spec.* I,230; *Gig.* 52; *Mig.* 102; *Fug.* 108-110 (see E. Kasemann, *Das wandernde Gottesvolk* [Gottingen, 1939], pp. 125-140) and perhaps ὑπηρέτης *Mut.* 87; *Immut.* 57.

God's first-born, the *Logos*, who holds the eldership among the angels, an archangel as it were. And many names are his for he is called: the Beginning and the Name of God and His Word and the Man after His Image and He that Sees i.e. Israel.

Jacob-Israel is likewise called in the *PJ* "firstborn" (A,5), an "archangel" (A,15) and Israel "a man seeing God" (A,4f.).[1]

5. *the first-born of every living thing to whom God gives life*

The claim ἐγὼ πρωτόγονος παντὸς ζώου ζωοπαουμένου ὑπὸ θεοῦ which bears such a striking resemblance to Colossians 1.15,17 πρωτότοκος πάσης κτίσεως... καὶ αὐτός ἐστιν πρὸ πάντων[2]) has its biblical origin in Exodus 4.22 where God declares that "Israel is my firstborn son" (Υἱὸς πρωτοτόκος μου 'Ισραήλ cf. Ps 89.27). While God is here clearly speaking of the Nation (cf. 4 *Ezra* 6.58), some rabbis interpreted the passage to refer to the Patriarch (e.g. R. Nathan in *Exodus R* 19.7). This concept was developed into the doctrine that the Patriarchs were formed before the Creation (a tradition alluded to in the *PJ* A,2f 'Αβραὰμ καὶ 'Ισαὰκ προεκτίσθησαν πρὸ παντὸς ἔργου[3]) or that Israel (clearly the Nation, but capable of being interpreted as the Patriarch) was so formed.[4])

---

[1]) The correspondence has been noted by E. Stein, *op. cit.*, p. 283 and Daniélou, *Theology*, p. 133. Cf. the remarks on this passage in H. Wolfson, *Philo* (Cambridge USA, 1947), Vol. I, pp. 377-9.

[2]) Especially in the Syriac Peshitta which reads "the first born of all creatures" rather than "of all creation" (see G. Widengren, *Mesopotamian Elements*, p. 23). M. R. James has failed to translate this passage but remarks (*op. cit.*, p. 26), "If Jacob is the first begotten of every living thing, is he the senior to Abraham and Isaac? One must doubt whether the author had thought this out." This is an all too typical example of the failure of scholars to appreciate the thought-forms of the material they are treating. One does not need to go beyond John 8.58 to see that the problem James poses was both raised and answered by first-century thought.

[3]) προκτίζω is applied to Christ in a similar context in Christian literature. See Didymus Alex., *De Trinitate* III,4 (*MPG* XXXIX :832) and Gelasius Cyz., *Historia concilii nicaeni* II,16 (*MPG* LXXXV :1257). Cf. the πρωτόκτιστοι in Jewish-Christian literature. See P. E. Testa, *Il Simbolismo dei Giudeo-Cristiani* (Jerusalem, 1962), pp. 61 et passim. and 267 n. 3 above.

[4]) In *Tanhuma* (ed. Buber) *Numbers, Naso* 19, the fathers of the world and Israel are among those created before the world; in *Midrash Tehillim* and Psalm 93.3, Israel is pre-existent. Cf. Romans 11,2 οὐκ ἀπώσατο ὁ θεὸς τὸν λαὸν αὐτοῦ ὃν προέγνω. See the discussion by L. Blau, "Preexistence", *Jewish Encyclopedia*, Vol. X, pp. 182-4 esp. p. 182 and the convenient collection of texts in Strack-Billerbeck, *Kommentar*, Vol. III, pp. 256-8. See further: J. Jervell, *Imago Dei* (Göttingen, 1960), pp. 78-84 and further the discussion of the title "Firstborn" in P. Winter, "ΜΟΝΟΓΕΝΗΣ", pp. 335-365, and S. Buber, *Midrash Tehillim* (Wilna, 1892), p. 414 n.11.

6. *the archangel of the power of the Lord*

This is one of the earlier occurrences of the term ἀρχάγγελος in hellenistic literature and appears here, especially with the qualifier δυνάμεως κυρίου to be a reflection of the traditional vocabulary associated with Michael as the שר הגדול (Dan 12.1; Resh Lakish in BT *Hag.* 12b etc.)[1])

7. *chief captain among the sons of God*

The title ἀρχιχιλίαρχος appears to be *hapax legomenon* in this document;[2]) but it would seem to be parallel to Michael who is the ἀρχιστράτηγος τῆς δυνάμεως κυρίου in hellenistic Jewish literature (Dan 8.11 in the LXX and Theod.; 2 Enoch 22.6f. and 33.10f; 3 Baruch 11.1ff. etc.).[3])

W. L. Knox, *op. cit.*, p. 49 n.6 raises the possibility that the notion of the pre-existent patriarchs implies that the *PJ* also considers Abraham and Isaac to be angels. There is considerable debate as to the day on which the angels were created. The rabbinic view may be summarized in the dictum of R. Luliabi b. Tabri in the name of R. Isaac that "all agree that none were created on the first day" (*Gen. R.* 1.3 but see *Jubilees* 2.2 and the material collected in Ginzberg, *Legends*, Vol. V, pp. 20f. which represent "reminiscences of the old view according to which angels were created on the first day.") For the Christian discussion, see the material collected in G. W. H. Lampe, *Patristic Greek Lexicon* (Oxford, 1961), fasc. 1, p. 10 s.v. ἄγγελος sect. IIB,3-5. Note that Clement Alex. terms God's covenants with Adam, Noah, Abraham and Moses ἄγγελοι πρωτόκτιστοι *Ecl. proph.* 51 (*MPG* IX:722).

[2]) See, on the occurrence of this term in the *PJ*, G. Kittell, "ἀρχαγγέλος", *TWNT* (English translation), Vol. I, p. 87.

[3]) Sophocles, *Lexicon* s.v. ἀρχιχιλίαρχος cites only the passage in Origen which quotes the *PJ* as does Stephanus, *Thesaurus graecae linguae* Vol. I:2, col. 2128; D. Demetrakos, *Mega Lexikon tēs hellēnikēs Glōssēs* (Athens, 1936), Vol. II, p. 1023 and Lampe, *op. cit.*, fasc. 1, p. 241. Professor C. Bradford Welles of the Yale Department of Classical Languages informs me that he knows of no occurrence of this term in hellenistic papyri. I should like to acknowledge the assistance of Professor Hardin Craig, Jr. of the Fondren Library, Rice University and Mr. Douglas Gunn of Yale University in attempting to further trace this word.

[1]) esp. in texts such as the *Assumptio Moysis* 10.2 *qui est in summo constitutus* (O. F. Fritzsche, ed., *Libri Apocryphi Veteris Testamenti* [Leipzig, 1871], p. 719). Cf. the *Prayer of Joseph and Asenath* 14 where Michael appears to Asenath declaring: 'Εγώ εἰμι ὁ ἀρχιστράτηγος κυρίου τοῦ θεοῦ, καὶ στρατιάρχης πάσης στρατειᾶς τοῦ ὑψίστου ... In this version, Michael assumes the form of Joseph! (καὶ ἰδοὺ ἀνὴρ ὅμοιος κατὰ πάντα τῷ 'Ιωσήφ) P. Batiffol, ed., *Studia Patristica* (Paris, 1889) Vol. I, p. 59, lines 11-16 cf. the Latin text, p. 101, line 31-p. 102, line 4 and Batiffol's discussion, pp. 32-4; M. R. James, *Joseph and Asenath* (London, 1918), p. 45. For Michael as warrior in Jewish tradition see the material collected in W. Luecken, *Der Erzengel Michael in der Überlieferung des Judentums* (Marburg, 1898), pp. 13-30. For Christ or the *Logos* as warrior see J. Barbel, *Christos Angelos* (Bonn, 1941), pp. 234f. (this tradition may reflect the LXX of Joshua 5.13 as well as assimilation to Michael).

8. *the first minister before the face of God*

It is possible that the angel Israel's service before the "face of God" (as well as the motif of his "seeing") may be based on the title *Peniel* conferred by Jacob upon the place of wrestling in Genesis 32.30. More particularly, in light of the tendency of the *PJ* to utilize for Israel titles frequently associated with Michael, Gabriel and Metatron (e.g. titles 1, 2, 6 and 7), ὁ ἐν προσώπῳ θεοῦ λειτουργὸς πρῶτος, is almost an exact translation of שר הפנים applied quite consistently to these figures in Jewish mystical literature.[1])

An examination of the various titles applied to Israel in the *PJ* has revealed that they all may be placed within a Jewish context. While some are derived from the Old Testament and its haggadic exegesis, some more frequent within circles of hellenistic and Merkabah mysticism as well as related Wisdom-theology, others more closely akin to Philo—no title requires that an extra-Jewish influence be postulated (e.g. from Christian, hellenistic or Gnostic tradition). This will be of crucial importance in investigating the second and third motifs: the combat of Jacob-Israel and Uriel and the myth of the descent of Jacob-Israel, for here scholars have suggested the presence of such influences.[2])

In this section, I have resisted a univocal interpretation of any given title, preferring instead to suggest a variety of possible backgrounds within Jewish tradition. Nevertheless certain generalizations are possible. The majority of the titles seem to be drawn from material associated with the Patriarch Jacob, especially the narrative of Genesis 32 (i.e. titles: 1, 2, 4, 5, 8) or from material associated with Michael, Gabriel or Metatron (i.e. titles: 1, 2, 3?, 6, 7, 8). Secondly, some of the titles appear to be drawn from traditions concerning the celestial

---

For Michael as warrior in Christian material see e.g. M. Bonnet, *Narratio de miraculo a Michaele archangelo* (Paris, 1890), p. 3.

[1]) Note, however, that the occurrence of ἄγγελοι λειτουργοί in Philo (*Virt.* 73), οἱ λειτουργοῦντες... πρὸς κύριον (*T. Levi* 3.5) or λειτουργικὰ πνεύματα (Hebs. 1.14) as synonyms for angels suggests that this is an element in the general technical angelic vocabulary of hellenistic Judaism. On this possibility see C. Spicq, "L'Epître aux Hébreux, Apollos, Jean-Baptiste, les hellénistes et Qumran," *Revue de Qumran* 1 (1959), esp. pp. 377f.

[2]) Let me stress that I do not mean by this to imply an isolation of Judaism from its environment. Judaism, like Christianity, is to be treated within the context of the history of Mediterranean religions in the hellenistic period. I mean only to suggest that the *PJ* is representative of a type of Judaism, drawing upon specifically Jewish traditions as well as reflecting common hellenistic patterns such as the descent-ascent of a heavenly figure (see below pp. 287-291). It is only a reductionistic view of the complexity and diversity of Judaism within this period that requires "borrowings" to be postulated in order to explain a text such as the *PJ*.

liturgy (i.e. titles: 2, 6, 7, 8 and Israel's calling upon the "inextinguishable name of God" in A,17f). As will be noted below, the legend of Jacob wrestling with the angel, the figures of Michael, Gabriel and Metatron and the performance of the heavenly liturgy are combined in both hellenistic Jewish and rabbinic sources, thus strengthening the possibility of their mutual influence on the *PJ*.

II. THE CONFLICT

(1) The conflict between Jacob-Israel and Uriel is, without doubt, the most debated portion of the *PJ*. There have been five major approaches to its interpretation. The first may be represented by R. H. Charles who declares that "the work was obviously anti-Christian" and J. T. Marshall who detects "an anti-christian *animus*".[1]) Or, more circumspectly, the opinion of M. R. James that the text was Jewish and that the author "knew something of Christian theology and indulged in some side hits at it. Whether this was the main object of the book we cannot tell..."[2]) The second interpretation takes the other extreme, as in the article of V. Burch who states that the text has an "anti-Jewish character".[3]) A third position is held by J. Daniélou who suggests that the text is Jewish-Christian.[4]) A fourth viewpoint, exemplified by R. M. Grant, maintains that the text, while Jewish, "is certainly protognostic because of the rivalry between Jacob-Israel and Uriel".[5]) The fifth, with which I would concur, accepts Origen's statement that the *PJ* is a Jewish text.[6])

For those who see an anti-Christian polemic in the work, Uriel

---

[1]) R. H. Charles, "Apocalyptic Literature," *Encyclopaedia Britannica* 11ed., Vol. II, p. 173; Charles, *The Ascension of Isaiah* (London, 1900), p. 39; J. T. Marshall, *loc. cit.* and, most recently, D. S. Russell, *The Method and Message of Jewish Apocalyptic* (Philadelphia, 1964), p. 67 who finds in the *PJ* "hints here and there of an anti-christian bias."

[2]) James, *op. cit.*, p. 31.

[3]) V. Burch, "The Literary Unity of the *Ascensio Isaiae*", *Journal of Theological Studies* 20 (1918-19), esp. p. 21.

[4]) Daniélou, *Théologie*, pp. 28,184; *Theology*, pp. 16f. In his contribution to J. Daniélou-H. Marrou, *The Christian Centuries* (New York, 1964), Vol. I, p. 76, Daniélou lists the *PJ* among "Jewish works, in particular some of Aramaic origin" which were re-written by the Jewish-Christians.

[5]) Grant, *op. cit.*, p. 19. Cf. P. Batiffol, *op. cit.*, p. 17 who declares the *PJ* to be "*de la pure gnose juive.*"

[6]) e.g. Fabricius, *op. cit.*; Dillmann, *op. cit.*; Schurer, *op. cit.*; and Schweizer, *op. cit.*, esp. col. 167 who terms the *PJ* a "*reinjudischen Apokryphon.*" (I am indebted to Prof. N. A. Dahl for this latter reference).

must be equated with Christ and Jacob-Israel with a Jewish attempt "to claim for the three patriarchs the same sublime and supernatural characteristics as the Christians claimed for the Lord Jesus".[1]) The identification of Uriel with Christ is not impossible as it occurs within at least two Ethiopian Christian documents.[2]) And furthermore, within early Christian literature, the one who wrestled with Jacob is declared to be the *Logos*, the pre-existent Christ (e.g. Justin Martyr, Origen etc. see above p. 265 n. 1). Thus by demoting Uriel, the status of Christ is attacked. This interpretation as advanced by Charles and Marshall is clearly secondary to their notion that the titles assigned to Jacob-Israel are conscious imitations of Christian titles already assigned to Jesus. It is this assumption which determines the identification of the two angelic actors. However, the *religionsgeschichtliche* inquiries of the past fifty years, the material quoted above from Philo etc. would make it at least possible to reverse this chronology. Rather than the Jews imitating Christological titles, it would appear that the Christians borrowed already existing Jewish terminology. Thus this line of interpretation must be called into question.

The same objection may be brought against the view advanced by James. He cites as examples of familiarity with Christian theological terminology the pre-existence of the patriarchs, the notion of a heavenly figure "tabernacling among men", the "first born of every living thing" and the phrase "his name shall have precedence over mine"— each of which may be documented from Jewish sources (especially from Wisdom literature and Philo).[3]) Furthermore, it is impossible to comprehend how Origen could declare of a presumed anti-Christian work that it is "a writing not lightly to be despised" (οὐκ εὐκαταφρόνητον γραφήν), unless one assumes that he had completely misunderstood the character of the text.

Burch's anti-Jewish theory is based on an alleged relation between

---

[1]) Marshall, *loc. cit*.

[2]) *Narrative of St. Clement*, translated by E. A. W. Budge, *The Contendings of the Apostles* (London, 1899), pp. 479f. and Urâ'el as a name of Christ in the Ethiopian *Lefâfa Sedek*, translated by E. A. W. Budge, *The Bandlet of Righteousness* (London, 1929), fol. 5a, p. 64. Only the former text has been cited by advocates of this identification.

[3]) For the pre-existence of the Patriarchs, see the material cited in p. 268 n.4 above; for "tabernacling among men" see, *Ecclus*. 24.8; *Baruch* 3.36-7; for the "first-born of every living thing" see Philo *Conf*. 146; *Agr*. 51; *Mig*. 6 and *L.A*. III,175 (cf. Goodenough, *By Light, Light*, p. 341 "the phrase πρωτοτόκος πάσης κτίσεως seems only a variant of Philo's πρωτόγονος."); "his name shall have precedence over mine," see Philo *Conf*. 146.

the *PJ* and the *Testimonia adversus Iudaeos*. He declares the "chief theme" of the *PJ* to be "the surpassing of one angel appearance of the Christ by another—Uriel by Israel"; that, as in Cyprian's *Testimonia* so in the *PJ* "Jacob and Israel are as prototype and type of the Christ".[1]) His argument hinges on the Ethiopian *Narrative of St. Clement* which contains the unique passage:

> And I (i.e. Peter) gave them commandments concerning circumcision according to the Law of Moses and God (i.e. Christ) appeared to me in the form of the angel Uriel and commanded me to do away the Old Law and to bring in the New.[2])

But this text precisely reverses the direction Burch has assumed. Rather than Israel supplanting Uriel as would be required by Burch's thesis, the Ethiopian text portrays Uriel abolishing Israel's Law. Furthermore, it would be difficult to reconcile Origen's statement that the *PJ* was "in use among the Hebrews" (τῶν παρ' Ἑβραίοις φερομένων ἀποκρύφων τὴν ἐπιγραφομένην Ἰωσὴφ προσευχήν) with an alleged anti-Jewish bias.[3])

Daniélou's suggestion of a Jewish-Christian origin is based on two questionable premises. The first is an appeal to the researches of Resch as decisively demonstrating the *PJ*'s link with Jewish Christianity. However, Resch only maintained (on extremely slight evidence) that the origins of the *PJ* were to be sought among the *Archontikoi*, a group that does not fit Daniélou's usual definition of Jewish Christianity and, to my knowledge, is never so labeled by him.[4]) The second is Daniélou's contention that Origen's location of the text παρ' Ἑβραίος is not an argument against its Jewish Christian character, that Origen consistently calls Jewish Christians Ἑβραῖοι when he relates their traditions. However the texts Daniélou cites do not bear out this interpretation.[5]) Daniélou's printed interpretation of the conflict is that Uriel (i.e. Jacob) tabernacles among men until he is contested by the true Israel (i.e. the *Logos*, Christ). However, Father Daniélou now

---

[1]) Burch, *op. cit.*, p. 20. Burch cites Cyprian's *Testimonia* I.20 as containing the view that "Jacob and Israel are as prototype and type of the Christ." I find no such typology in the text he cites.

[2]) See p. 272 n. 2 above.

[3]) Burch, *op. cit.*, p. 21 n.5 cites this text and declares, without offering any supporting argument, that it is not against the view that the *PJ* was anti-Jewish.

[4]) Resch, *op. cit.*, pp. 295-8; Daniélou, *Théologie*, p. 184 n.2. See p. 265 n.3 above.

[5]) In two of the texts Daniélou cites (*Théologie*, p. 185 n.1) *Hom. in Num.* 13.5 (ed. Baehrens, p. 114) and *Hom. in Jer.* 20.2 (*MPG* XIII : 501) the reference is not

informs me that he considers the verbs κατέβην, κατεσκήνωσα and ἐκλήθη to refer to Jacob-Israel and not Uriel, thus invalidating his exegesis.¹)

Grant's thesis as to the "proto-gnostic" character of the text appears to rest simply on the fact that there is rivalry between Jacob-Israel and Uriel. However, the mere presence of conflict or, for that matter, dualism is not in itself sufficient to term a text "gnostic."²)

(2) On the basis of Jewish sources, I find that there are at least three possibilities of interpretation. The first approach would be to suggest that the *PJ*'s narration represents a projection of the conflict between Jacob and Esau. As presented in the biblical account, this struggle begins within Rebekah's womb (Gen 25.22-6), continues through Jacob's acquisition of Esau's birthright (Gen 25.29-34) and of the

---

to the general group of Ἑβραῖοι but to a specific individual (a Ἑβραῖος) who has converted from Judaism to Christianity. The third instance, *in Ezech.* 9.2 (*MPG* XIII : 800), the context is not sufficiently clear to allow final security. On the use of the term Ἑβραῖος in these three passages cf. Bardy, *op. cit.*, pp. 221-3 and W. L. Knox, *op. cit.*, p. 49 n.5 who declares "There is no hint of Christianity in the fragments preserved by Origen who regards it as an orthdox Jewish work of an almost canonical character. But Origen's standard of orthodoxy is not high." Both the argument from Resch and the argument concerning the use of the term Ἑβραῖοι have been omitted from the English translation of Daniélou's work; but Father Daniélou informs me that he should have allowed them to remain.

¹) *Théologie*, p. 184. Father Daniélou writes, in a letter of February 17, 1965: "... in fact the terms κατέβην, κατεσκήνωσα, and ἐκλήθη refer to the angel Israel and not to the angel Uriel. The arguments that are developed in the paragraphs in question lose their foundation."

²) It must be admitted that the harshness of the rivalry between Jacob-Israel and Uriel is striking. If the *PJ* is employing a traditional scheme of either four, six or seven archangels—Jacob-Israel's taunt "Are you not Uriel the eighth after me?" (A,14) would appear to remove Uriel from the ranks of the chief hierarchs before the Throne. He has been excommunicated! (so Daniélou, *Théology*, p. 134. The English translation is in error at this point and should read: "then the *former* does not fall..."). However if, as I believe, a scheme of eight heavens and principal angels is being employed, Uriel would remain within the hierarchy as the lowest of the seven archangels and Jacob-Israel would assume the role of the *Dynamis* of the eighth, highest and secret heaven (cf. Scholem, *Jewish Gnosticism*, pp. 65-71). N.B. the similarity in angelological structure between the *PJ* and Clement of Alexandria's *Excerpta ex Theodoto* 10-12 (cf. *Stromata* V, 35,1-2 and p. 267 n.3 cont'd above) where there are three orders of angelic beings: (1) the Son who is the Face of God; (2)the seven πρωτόκτιστοι who behold the Face of God which is the Son and (3) the archangels. Jacob-Israel would appear to play a role in the *PJ* similar to the Son in Clement's scheme. See further the remarks of H. Corbin, *op. cit.*, pp. 65 and 287-88 n.14 comparing the Son and the seven πρωτόκτιστοι in Clement's *Excerpta* with the angelology of 3 *Enoch*. W. L. Knox (*op. cit.*, p. 49) suggests a seven-fold order of angels led by Jacob-Israel with a "rebellious hierarchy" of angels below, led by Uriel. See further, sect. III below.

blessing (Gen 27). Basing itself on texts such as Genesis 25.23, haggadic literature extended this conflict to the descendents of Esau and Jacob and to a final eschatological conflict between their sons and their guardian angels.[1])

The oldest strata of material which reveals this conflict may well be that which, basing itself on passages such as Genesis 36. 1, 8, 9, 43 identifies Rome as Esau, Edom, Seir etc.[2]) and depicts conflicts between the guardian angel of Israel (i.e. Jacob) who is most usually Michael and the guardian angel of Rome (i.e. Esau) who is most usually Sammael.[3]) Scholars agree that such identification is to be dated about the time of Herod the Idumean. The equation Esau-Rome was, at a later date than the *PJ*, transferred to the Christian (i.e. Roman) Church and produced polemic material which resembles in broad outline the conflict between Uriel and Jacob-Israel.[4])

As one may expect, the various elements of the biblical narrative which tells of twin brothers struggling in the womb and throughout their lives (including the haggadic extension which has Esau finally slain by Jacob)[5]); the distinctions of one being smooth, the other hairy; the one light, the other "ruddy" etc. lent themselves to dualistic symbolism. But this material is all late and does not appear to have influenced the *PJ*.[6])

There is one biblical-midrashic tradition that does appear to be reflected in the *PJ*. The name Jacob is derived in Genesis 25.26 from עקב (the heel, one who takes by the heel i.e. the supplanter cf. Gen 27.36; Hos 12.3; עקוב in Jer 17.9). This is continued in Philo who regularly assigns the title πτερνιστής to Jacob before he received the

---

[1]) For the conflict between the descendants of Jacob and Esau, see esp. *Midrash Wa-Yissa'u* in *Yalkut* I, 132 (ed. Jellinek, *BHM*, Vol. II, pp. 1-5 cf. Ginzberg, *Legends*, Vol. V, pp. 321f. n.317). Earlier fragments of this legend are preserved in *T. Judah* 9.4 and *Jubilees* 37-38.

[2]) e.g. strikingly in PT, *Ab. Z.* I.2 (2b) cited in H. Odeberg, *The Aramaic Portions of Bereshit Rabba* (Lund-Leipzig, 1939), Vol. II, p. 147.

[3]) e.g. BT, *Yoma*, 38b; *Gittin* 57b etc.

[4]) See the collection of late texts illustrating the application of Esau, Edom, etc. to Christians in L. Zunz, *Die synagogale Poesie des Mittelalters* (Frankfurt a.M., 1920), pp. 437-52. For an earlier example of an anti-Christian polemic which contains the theme of illegitimate assumption and forcible expulsion see PT, *Nedarim* 38a where R. Aha declares in the name of R. Huna: "Esau the wicked will put on his *tallith* and will sit with the righteous in the Garden of Eden in the time to come. But the Holy One, Blessed be He, will drag him out and cast him forth from there."

[5]) *T. Judah* 9.3; *Jubilees* 38.1-4 cf. *Yalkut* I.132; *Midrash Tehillim* ad Ps. 18.159-60 and Ginzberg, *Legends*, Vol. V, pp. 321f.

[6]) See especially the collection in *Yalkut Reubeni* ad Genesis 32.25-33.

name, Israel.[1]) This is one element in Uriel's charge against Jacob-Israel, that he has taken advantage of Uriel in descending to earth and unlawfully claiming precedence over him. I would suggest that this may be a reflection of Jacob's deception of blind Isaac, gaining Esau's blessing by putting on the goatskins. In light of the widespread metaphor which speaks of the incarnation of a heavenly soul as a putting on of garments (at times specifically garments of goatskins),[2]) the legend in Genesis 27 would lend itself to such an interpretation. Note that in a late mythological fragment preserved in *Yalkut Reubeni* (ad Gen 32.29), the angel Gabriel disguised as Esau appears before Jacob and accuses him of being an imposter in claiming to be Isaac's firstborn.[3]) It is possible that in the *PJ*, Uriel represents Esau and Israel, Jacob. However this identification of Uriel as the guardian angel of Esau would then be, to my knowledge, a unique instance in Jewish or Christian literature.

(3) While details of the conflict between Jacob and Esau might have influenced the tradition represented in the *PJ*, the most likely source of the setting of the conflict between Jacob-Israel and Uriel within our text is the wrestling of Jacob with the mysterious figure in Genesis 32.24ff. Indeed, several points of verbal contact between this text and the *PJ* may be noted. The dispute between Uriel and Jacob-Israel occurs when the latter is coming up from Μεσοποταμία τῆς Συρίας the standard Septuagint rendering of *Padan-aram*. The encounter by the Jabbok occurred as Jacob was journeying up from *Padan-aram* to rejoin his father in Canaan having fled from there to Laban's house to avoid Esau. Of the three-fold description of the conflict in the *PJ*, "he envied me and fought with me and wrestled with me" (A, 10f), only the latter verb is to be found in the biblical account. The notion of envy supplies the motivation so strikingly lacking in the Genesis narrative.[4])

---

[1]) *L.A.* I,161; II,89; III,15,93; *Sac.* 42,135; *Mig.* 200; *Somn.* I,171; *Mut.* 81; *Heres.* 252.

[2]) See my article, "The Garments of Shame," *History of Religions* 5 (Winter, 1965), pp. 217-238, esp. pp. 231f. and notes.

[3]) Paraphrased in Ginzberg, *Legends* Vol. V, p. 310. *Yalkut Reubeni* cites as its source the *Pirke de R. Eliezer*, however it is not found in the present text of this midrash.

[4]) Compare, however, P. Winter's interpretation of the verb in "ΜΟΝΟΓΕΝΗΣ," p. 352. "Israel's rank in the order of existence is so high that Uriel, the angel of God, tries to impersonate him (ἐζήλωσε = he was jealous, he vied with, he emulated, he imitated) to maintain his superiority. But Israel tells him exactly where he stands...".

Rabbinic literature tends to provide brief and fragmentary interpretations of the conflict. Usually it is held that the angel wrestled with Jacob in order to strengthen him for his struggle with Esau or to punish him for fearing Esau. Another view is that the angel fought with Jacob in order to remind him of his promise to tithe his possessions.[1]) The identity of the mysterious heavenly combattant is likewise controversial. I know of only one instance in a Jewish or Christian source where it is Uriel, and that is most probably dependent on the *PJ*.[2]) Most usually he is identified as either Michael, Gabriel or Metatron. The view of R. Hama b. R. Hanina in *Genesis Rabbah* 77.3

---

[1]) For a convenient summary see Ginzberg, *Legends* Vol. I, pp. 384-388 and the literature cited.

[2]) L. Réau, *Iconographie de l'art chrétien* (Paris, 1956), Vol. II:1, p. 151 lists three traditional Christian identifications of Jacob's angelic combatant, concluding: "D'après une troisième tradition, ce serait l'Archange Uriel." As Réau gives no reference, I can only presume he is referring to the *PJ*. The reference in a homily attributed to John of Jerusalem in Ms. Reims 427 (fol. 62): *Et pugnavit cum angelo Oriel* should, most likely, be assumed to refer to the conflict in the *PJ*. See G. Morin, "Le catalogue des manuscrits de l'abbaye de Gorze au XIe siècle. Appendix: Homélies inedites attribuées à Jean de Jerusalem," *Revue Bénédictine* 22 (1905), p. 14 cf. James, *op. cit.*, pp. 24f. Several suggestions might be tendered as to the origin of this identification. Within the Ethiopian *Enoch* literature, Phanuel stands, at times, in Uriel's place in lists of the four arch-angels (1 *Enoch* 40.9; 54.6; 71.8, 9,13). If this name can be related to the Peniel-Penuel of Gen. 32.30—as has been suggested by J. E. H. Thomson, *The Samaritans* (Edinburgh, 1919), p. 189 cf. A. Z. Aescoli, "Les noms magiques dans les apocryphes chrétiens des Éthiopiens," *Journal asiatique* 220 (1932), p. 109—then this might be one link in the chain of identification. *Midrash Aggada* ad Exodus 4.5 (ed. Buber, p. 132) names Uriel as the one who attempted to slay Moses in the desert. Ginzberg suggests that this may be a parallel to the negative role of Uriel in the *PJ*. See *Eine unbekannte judische Sekte* (New York, 1922), p. 37 and *Legends*, Vol. V, p. 310 n.273. In the Falasha *Mota Muse* it is Suriel, the angel of death, who slays Moses (see the English translation by W. Leslau, *Falasha Anthology* [New Haven, 1951], pp. 107-111 esp. p. 109). As Ginzberg (loc. cit.) has noted, his suggestion is supported by this text in light of the widespread tendency to equate Suriel and Uriel. On this identification, see especially H. Malter, "Der Tod Moses in der aethiopischen Ueberlieferung," *Monatschrift f.d. Geschichte und Wissenschaft d. Judenthums* 51 (1907), p. 711 n.3; J. H. Polotsky, "Suriel der Trompeter," *Muséon* 49 (1936), pp. 231-43 esp. pp. 232-5 and cf. Peterson, *op. cit.*, pp. 418f. Note that in BT, *Ber.* 51a, Suriel is both a revealing angel and the prince of the Divine Face (see Scholem, *Major Trends*, p. 356 n.3). A further suggestion of a negative role for Uriel is found in the tradition that he is the chief angel of the realm of the dead, especially within the Enoch-literature (see 1 *Enoch* 20.2; 33.3; 72.1; 74.2 etc.) and possibly in the *Testament of Solomon* 10 where the demon Ornias is an "offspring of Uriel, the power of God" (F. C. Conybeare, translation. *Jewish Quarterly Review* o.s. 11 [1899], p. 17). For general treatments of Uriel, see especially P. Perdrizet, "L'archange Ouriel," *Seminarium Kondakorianum* 2 (1928), pp. 241-276 and J. Michl, "Engel, IX", *Reallexicon f. Antike u. Christentum* Vol. V, cols. 254-256.

and 78.3 that Jacob wrestled with Esau's guardian angel may be assumed to be a projection of the fraternal conflict. Nonetheless, incidental details in these *midrashim* reveal remnants of what must have been a rich combat tradition which may well have influenced the *PJ*. Thus a hint of a possible angelic contest between Uriel and Jacob might be seen in the narrative of R. Huna, a third century tradent:

> Eventually he (the angel) said to himself: Shall I not inform him with whom he is engaged? What did he do? He put his finger on the earth, whereupon the earth began spouting fire. Jacob said to him: Don't think you can terrify me with that! Why I am altogether of that substance! Thus it is written: AND THE HOUSE OF JACOB SHALL BE A HOUSE OF FIRE (Obad 1.18).[1]

Uriel, according to at least one tradition, is derived from אור אל "the fire of God"—and the action of the angel in Huna's account would be thoroughly consistent with that role.[2] Jacob claims an equally exalted, if not superior, role. He is made wholly of fire and, hence, should probably likewise be understood to be claiming an angelic nature.[3]

(4) The content of Uriel's envy is the rank of Jacob-Israel among the heavenly host (A, 11f.). The notion, in apocalyptic literature, of a conflict between the angels of God and the "fallen" angels is familiar; but is not suggested in the *PJ*. Nor do we here have an example analogous to Satan's envy of the newly created Adam and his refusal to worship him. For though Israel has descended among men, both Israel and Uriel are clearly heavenly figures and their conflict is concerned with their relative position within the celestial hierarchy. The theme of one angel gaining domination over another is not unknown in Jewish sources, most particularly in political allegories which narrate the ascendency of one national angel over another.[4]

---

[1]) *Gen. R.* 77.2, cf. *Midrash R. ad Cant.* 3.6.3. See further W. Bacher, *Die Agada der palastinensischen Amoraer* (Strassburg, 1899), Vol. III, p. 286.

[2]) Isidore Seville, *Etym.* VII,5 (*MPL* LXXXVII, 273) and L. Blau, "Uriel", *Jewish Encyclopaedia* Vol. XII, p. 383. The text quoted from Obadiah 1.18 בית יעקב אש (ὁ οἶκος Ιακωβ πῦρ) would be sufficient to suggest a conflict between Jacob and the angel of fire (i.e. Uriel). The alternative etymology derives Uriel from אור אל "light of God."

[3]) Cf. *Ex. R.* 15.6 "God compared Israel to the angels ... The angels are called fire because it is written THE FLAMING FIRE, YOUR MINISTERS (Ps. 104.4) and Israel is also so called, as it is written AND THE HOUSE OF JACOB SHALL BE A FIRE (Obad 1.18)."

[4]) See especially the narrative of Gabriel and Dubbiel in BT, *Yoma* 77a (omitted in most mss.) On this passage see E. Langton, *The Ministeries of the Angelic Powers* (London, n.d.), pp. 178f. and Ginzberg, *Legends*, Vol. VI, p. 434.

The theme of angelic rivalry before the Throne may be found in both hellenistic and Hebrew Merkabah literature.[1]) Thus, in the early apocryphon, the *Apocalypse of Abraham*, which Scholem notes "more closely resembles a Merkabah text than any other in Jewish apocalyptic literature"[2]) Jaoel (who plays the role assigned in Hebrew texts to Metatron) is the one "who hath been given to restrain, according to His commandment, the threatening attack of the living creatures of the Cherubim (i.e. the *hayyoth*) against one another" (ch. X), while in the vision of the Throne in chapter XVIII, Abraham sees that when the *hayyoth* have finished their singing:

> ...they looked at one another and threatened one another. And it came to pass when the angel who was with me saw that they were threatening each other, he left me and went running to them and turned the countenance of each living creature from the countenance immediately confronting him, in order that they might not see their countenances threatening each other. And he taught them the song of peace which hath its origin (in the Eternal One).[3]

---

[1]) Central to this tradition is Job 25.2, "Dominion and fear are with him; he makes peace in his heights." See R. Meir(?) *Num. R.* 11.7 "Great is peace, for the name of the Omnipotent is called Peace as it says 'The Lord is peace' (Judges 6.24). Great is peace for the angels on high need peace as it says (Job 25.2)." cf. bar Kappara in *Lev. R.* 9.9 and, for *Shalom* as the name of God, see A. Mamorstein, *The Old Rabbinic Doctrine of God* (Oxford, 1927), Vol. I, pp. 104f. Cf. the angel סמוסלם in Scholem, *Jewish Gnosticism*, pp. 76 and 134. Frequently combined with Job 25.2 is a conflict between Michael as snow and Gabriel as fire (see esp. R. Simeon b. Lakish in *Deut. R.* 5.15; R. Simeon b. Yohai in *Midrash R. ad Cant.* 3.11.1; R. Abib in *Num. R.* 12.8, *Midrash R. ad Cant.* 3.11.1. cf. Leucken, *op. cit.*, p. 55). Dependent on, or giving rise to this tradition is the notion of angels being composed half of snow and half of fire (cf. *Gedulath Moshe* 15 in Gaster, *Texts and Studies*, Vol. I, p. 129; *Midrash 'Asereth ha-dibberoth* in Jellinek, *BHM*, Vol. I, p. 66, translated in A. Wunsche, *Aus Israels Lehrhallen* [Leipzig, 1909], Vol. IV, p. 74). The whole complex may ultimately depend on cosmogonic imagery of creation as a mixture of fire and snow or water (see R. Yohanan BT, *Rosh hash.* 23b, *Gen. R.* 10.3, *Deut. R.* 5.12; R. Jacob of Kephar-chanin in *Peskita* 3a, PT, *Rosh.hash.* 58a. Cf. 2 *Enoch* 29.2; 3 *Enoch* 42.7 translation H. Odeberg [Cambridge, 1928], pp. 131f.) See, on aspects of this material, G. H. Box, *The Apocalypse of Abraham* (London, 1919), pp. 62f. n.13 and p. 87 additional note ii. Of direct relevance to the *PJ* is the anonymous midrash on Canticles 3.11 in *Num. R.* 12.8 and *Midrash R. ad Cant.* 3.11.1. "Another explanation is that UPON KING SOLOMON means Upon the king who brought about peace between his handiwork and those who love him. He made peace between the fire and Abraham, between the knife and Isaac and *between the angel and Jacob*. Another explanation is that UPON KING SOLOMON means Upon the king who makes peace between his creatures. The hayyoth were of fire and the firmament of snow... Yet neither did the latter extinguish the former nor did the former consume the latter." [emphasis mine, J.Z.S.]

[2]) Scholem, *Jewish Gnosticism*, p.23 cf. Box, *op. cit.*, pp. xxix-xxx.

[3]) I have followed the translation of G. H. Box, *op. cit.*, pp. 47 and 63.

As G. H. Box has pointed out, this picture is paralleled by a text in *Tanḥuma, Bereshit* (ed. Buber, Vol. I, p. 10 with correction) which contains a midrash on Job 25.2 "Dominion and fear are with him, he makes peace in his high places". The text in *Tanḥuma* interprets "dominion" as Michael and "fear" as Gabriel and the latter part of the verse as God's action in keeping peace among the angels

> ...for even the heavenly ones need peace. The constellations rise, Taurus says 'I am first and I see what is before him;' the Gemini say 'I am first and I see what is before him' and so each one in his turn says 'I am first.'

It is perhaps significant that in the *Pirke Hekalot* the angel Israel has the function, as one of the *ḥayyoth*, of keeping order among the heavenly choir[1]—a role in close agreement with that of Jaoel in the *Apocalypse of Abraham*. The rivalry in the *PJ*, however, more closely resembles that depicted in *Tanḥuma*.

(5) What is most crucial to our understanding of the *PJ* is that in documents representing both hellenistic and rabbinic Judaism the motifs of Jacob's wrestling by the Jabbok and the theme of angelic rivalry before the Throne are combined. In a variety of midrashim, the angel with whom Jacob wrestled had to return at dawn (Gen. 32. 26a) in order to chant before the Throne. This Jacob prevented until he secured the angel's blessing or until he learned the angel's name (Gen. 32.26b-27).[2]) This, coupled with a traditional etymology found in scattered texts of the name Israel as "trying to sing in the place of the angels"[3]) suggests the possibility that there was a tradition of angelic rivalry between Jacob-Israel and the archangels similar to that reflected in the *PJ*. This supposition is strengthened, moreover, by the fact that in several sources YHWH not only keeps peace between the angels before His Throne but also between Jacob and the wrestling angel.[4])

---

[1]) Jellinek, *BHM* Vol. III, pp 161-3.

[2]) Pseudo-Philo *Biblical Antiquities* 18.5 (G. Kisch, *Pseudo-Philo's Liber Antiquitatum Biblicarum* [Notre Dame, 1959], p. 159); *Gen. R.* 78.2; *Midrash R. ad Cant.* 3.6.3; *Pirke de R. Eliezer* 37 and implied in BT, *Ḥullin* 91b. In *Pirke d. R. Eliezer* 37, Jacob appears to have successfully prevented the angel from returning above to sing at dawn.

[3]) *Tanḥuma* (ed. Buber I,127). Ginzberg further cites *Haserot* in Wertheimer's *Batte Midrashot* Vol. III, p. 4 (*non vidi*. See Ginzberg, *Legends*, Vol. V, p. 307 n. 253). I can see no sense in which *Gen. R.* 78.2 may be interpreted as implying that Jacob attempts to sing instead of the angels as Ginzberg (*loc. cit.*) maintains.

[4]) *Num. R.* 12.8; *Midrash R. ad Cant.* 3.11.1 See above p. 279 n.1.

Thus, while the conflict between Jacob-Israel and Uriel in the *PJ* gains its setting from the contest between Jacob and the angel by the Jabbok in Genesis 32 (sect. II,3) and draws upon the narratives of Esau and Jacob for the content of the conflict (sect. II,2)—the text is more likely to be explained on the basis of the mystical theme of angelic rivalry before the Merkabah (sect. II,4,5). As in our study of the titles, so here in considering the conflict, we have found nothing that requires the postulation of non-Jewish influence (sect. II,1) and have once more located the *PJ* within circles of mystical Judaism.

III. THE DESCENT MYTH

(1) As M. R. James has noted:

> The leading idea of the principal fragment is that angels can become incarnate in human bodies, live on earth in the likeness of men, and be unconscious of their original state. Israel does so apparently in order that he may become the father of the chosen people. It is, I believe, a doctrine which is unique in Jewish teaching.[1]

Indeed it is remarkable! though not unique.[2] The paradigm that is employed here appears to be the Gnostic one of the descent of the heavenly soul, its incarnation in ignorant flesh and its recollection of its supra-mundane origin on encountering a heavenly revealer i.e., the familiar movement from λήθη and ἄγνοια to γνῶσις by means of ἀνάμνησις. The language of Origin's paraphrase of the *PJ* in *Philocalia* XXIII,19 quite strikingly employs the vocabulary of this Gnostic paradigm: καὶ ὄνομα κεκτημένος 'Ισραήλ. ὅπερ ἐν σώματι λειτουργῶν ἀναγνωρίζει, ὑπομιμνήσκοντος αὐτόν τοῦ ἀρχαγγέλου Οὐριήλ. The simplest solution to the problem posed by this text would be to declare that the descent myth that is quoted from the *PJ* in Origin's *Commentary on John* (A, 8-10) contains no suggestion of Jacob-Israel's forgetfulness nor of Uriel's positive role in reminding him of his former state. One might assume that, as the passage in the *Philocalia* is manifestly a paraphrase, Origen simply employs the Platonic language

---

[1] M. R. James, *op. cit.*, p. 30.
[2] M. Smith, in his recent contribution to the *Wolfson Festschrift* (*op. cit.*) has endeavored to demonstrate that "the belief that a particular individual might be a supernatural Power come down to earth and appearing as a man, was reasonably common in first century Palestine" (*op. cit.*, p. 749). He cites the examples of Dositheus, John the Baptist, Jesus, Simon Magus and Menander (p. 743) and included Jacob-Israel in the *PJ* within this category (pp. 748f.).

which was natural for him.¹) Or, as a variant to this approach, one might suggest that the sending of angels as revealers into the material world where they become incarnate as the Patriarchs of Israel is a theological motif within Origen's thought. Therefore it might be the case that Origen is here betraying his own interests rather than faithfully reporting the text.²) So little of the *PJ* has actually survived that it is difficult to have confidence as to a judgement on the accuracy of Origen's report. But the fact that an analogous use of Platonic language and a mystical interpretation of the Patriarchs occurs in Philo leads me to assume that Origen had reason for employing the terms he did. It will be necessary to inquire whether extant Jewish sources contain material that would clarify this mythologoumenon.

(2) The language of the descent myth in the quotation from the *PJ* in Origen's *Commentary on John* clearly derives from the Jewish Wisdom-Shekinah theology that has been the preoccupation of many students of the Prologue to the Fourth Gospel since the pioneering researches of J. Rendel Harris: ὅτι κατέβην ἐπὶ τὴν γῆν καὶ κατεσκήνωσα ἐν ἀνθρώιποις, καὶ ὅτι ἐκλήθην ὀνόματι 'Ιακώβ (A, 8-10). The two terms for descent καταβαίνω and κατασκηνόω are both witnessed to in pre-Christian Wisdom literature as well as in their New Testament adaptations. The clearest parallel to the *PJ* is *The Wisdom of Ben-Sira* 24.8 where Sophia, after wandering all over creation, is told by God who ὁ κτίσας με κατέπαυσεν τὴν σκήνην μου to 'Εν 'Ιακὼβ

---

¹) The standard treatment of this remains H. Koch, *Pronoia und Paideusis: Studien uber Origines und sein Verhaltnis zum Platonismus* (Berlin-Leipzig, 1932). M. Joel, *Blicke im die Religionsgeschichte zu Anfang des zweiten christlichen Jahrhunderts* (Breslau, 1880), Vol. I, pp. 118f. attempted to find a Jewish counterpart to the Platonic doctrine of *anamnesis* in the notion that the soul (or embryo) knows everything before it is born, forgets during life and is reminded of what it has known by an angel at death (R. Simlai in BT, *Niddah* 30b cf. the treatise *Seder Yezirat ha-Walad* in Jellinek, *BHM*, Vol. I, pp. 153-5 and the brilliant short story on this theme by I. B. Singer, "Jachid and Jechidah" in *Short Friday* [New York, 1964], pp. 81-90). The parallel is scarcely striking. The Platonic experience of recollection occurs during life; in the Jewish material it occurs at the point of, or after, death. It would appear that the Jewish tradition is secondary to the discussion of the purity of the soul before birth and debates concerning the point at which the *Yetzer ha-ra* is able to exercise influence on an individual.

²) *De princ.* IV,3,12 etc. This theme employs the allegory of the descent into Egypt being a descent into the material world (cf. the interpretation of Genesis 46.3 in *Hom. ad Gen.* 15.5 etc.) an interpretation which is Philonic. See on this theme, J. Daniélou, *Origen* (New York, 1955), pp. 247-9; Daniélou, "Les sources juives de la doctrine des anges des nations chez Origène," *Recherches de Science Religieuse* 38 (1951), p. 134; H. Crouzel, *Origène et la "connaissance mystique"* (*Museum Lessianum*, 1961), pp. 98-101, 305-12.

κατασκήωσονκαὶ ἐν 'Ισράηλ κατακληρονμήθητι. Here Sophia is identified with the Torah accepted by Israel after the other nations have refused it (cf. vs. 23 and *Apoc. Baruch* 3.37f.). Likewise Israel's title in the *PJ*, πρωτογόνος as well as the notion that Abraham and Isaac προεκτίσθησαν πρὸ παντὸς ἔργου would appear to derive from speculation as to the role of Wisdom-Torah in the Creation.[1]) But, as was noted above (see p. 268), if theories as to the pre-existence of the Law and the nation Israel might be personified; so here, in the text from *Ben-Sira*, a mystical interpretation would read that Sophia became incarnate in the Patriarch, Jacob-Israel. This sort of mystical reading is represented by the Philonic model of a *hieros gamos* between the Patriarchs and Sophia, as elucidated by Goodenough.[2])

(3) The uniqueness of the decensus myth in the paraphrase of the

---

[1]) Thus W. L. Knox (*op. cit.*, p. 112) explains the tradition in the *Assumptio Moysis* 1.14 *itaque excogitavit et invenit me, qui ab initio orbis terrarum praeparatus sum* (ed. Fritzsche, p. 703 cf. the Greek citation in Gelasius Cyz., *Comm. Act. Synodi. Nic.* II.18). "Firstborn" appears to be used as a title for Jacob by R. Nathan in *Ex. R.* 19.7.

Possibly there is some relation to the doctrine within heterodox Judaism of the world being created by an angel e.g. in the teachings of Simon Magus, Menander, Saturninus (cf. Grant, *op. cit.*, pp. 15-18); the doctrine of the Magharians (see L. Nemoy, "Al-Qirqisāni's Account of the Jewish Sects and Christianity," *Hebrew Union College Annual* 7 [1930], pp. 363-4, H. A. Wolfson, "The Preexistent Angel of the Magharians and Al-Nahāwandi," *Jewish Quarterly Review* 51 [1960], pp. 89-106.). Daniélou (*Theology*, p. 134) compares a Novatianist inscription first published by A. M. Calder, "Epigraphy of Anatolian Heresies," *Anatolian Studies presented to Sir William Mitchell Ramsay* London, 1923, pp. 76f. no. 4: πρῶτον μὲν ὑμνήσω Θεὸν τὸν πάντει ὁρόωντα δεύτερον ὑμνήσω πρῶτον ἄγγελον OCTI CAITPCIN (cf. H. Grégoire, "Epigraphie chrétienne," *Byzantion* 1 [1924], pp. 699f. and idem., "Un nom mystique du Christ," *Byzantion* 2 [1925], pp. 449-53). Possibly, one might also relate the tradition which renders בראשית in Gen. 1.1 as ראשית and reads either "In the beginning God created a Son" or "In the Son, God created" which is found in several Jewish-Christian texts e.g. Jerome, *Quaest. Heb. in Gen.* 1.1: *in Altercatione Jasonis et Papisci scriptum est ... in Hebraeo haberi, in Filio fecit Deus caelum et terram.* (*MPG* V:1279 and notes 39, 40) Cf. Irenaeus, *Dem.* 43 (following J. P. Smith, "Hebrew Christian Midrash in Irenaeus," *Biblica*, 38 [1957], pp. 24-34); Tertullian, *Adv. Prax.* 5; Hilary of Poitiers, *Tract. Psalm.* II,2 and several polemic documents (see A. L. Williams, *Adversus Judaeos* [Cambridge, 1935], p. 29 n.3) See further Harnack, *Evagrius' Altercatio Simonis et Judaei et Theophili Christiani* (Berlin, 1883), p. 130f. and Daniélou, *Theology*, pp. 167f. For a general survey on the relationship of Wisdom-Creation-Son traditions see J. R. Harris, *The Origin of the Prologue to St. John's Gospel* (Cambridge, 1917); Knox, *op. cit.*, ch. v; C. F. Burney, "Christ as the 'Αρχή of Creation," *Journal of Theological Studies* 27 (1926), pp. 160-77; W. D. Davies, *Paul and Rabbinic Judaism* 2ed. (London, 1958), ch. vii and Daniélou, *Theology*, pp. 166-72.

[2]) Goodenough, *By Light, Light*, pp. 157-60, 164 *et passim*. I would agree with Goodenough that "the passages are not altogether satisfactory" in depicting a marriage between Jacob and Sophia but that it may be clearly inferred.

PJ in Origen's *Philocalia* is that it is not the heavenly Sophia who incarnates herself or marries Jacob, but the heavenly Israel who becomes incarnate in his earthly counterpart, the Patriarch Jacob. Any speculation that is relevant to the *PJ* concerning descent-ascent must be related to the figures of the heavenly and earthly Jacob-Israel. The obvious point of focus about which such speculations would cluster is "Jacob's Ladder" in the vision at Bethel (Genesis 28.10-27). For here is a moment of contact, of entry and re-entry between the celestial and terrestrial realms as well as an explicit reference to angels "ascending and descending".

The biblical narrative presents the familiar picture of Jacob sleeping on the ground, the heavenly ladder with angels ascending and descending on it and, at its summit, the figure of YHWH. The *Targumim* provide a motivation for the angel's movement and, incidently, attempt to explain why angels should first ascend, then descend:

> ...the angels who had accompanied him from the house of his father ascended to make known to the angels on high saying, Come, see Jacob the pious whose image is on the Throne of Glory and whom you have desired to see. And behold, the holy angels of the Presence of the Lord descended to look upon him.[1])

The tradition of the face of Jacob engraved on the Merkabah in early rabbinic sources most likely indicates a tendency to merge the Patriarchs with the *hayyoth*; but may also be a reflection of, or possibly the source of the tradition of the heavenly Israel.[2]) Thus in a remarkable

---

[1]) *Jerusalem Targum* ad Genesis 28.12, M. Ginsburger, ed., *Das Fragmententhargum* (Berlin, 1899), p. 16. I have adapted the translation of J. W. Etheridge, *The Targums of Onkelos and Jonathan* (London, 1862), Vol. I, pp. 252f.

[2]) Cf. the anonymous Tannaitic *baraitha* in BT, *Hullin* 91b "They ascended to look at the image above and descended to look at the image below": *Gen. R.* 68 : 12; 78 : 3 etc. Joel, *op. cit.*, Vol. I, p. 117 unconvincingly attempts to provide a hellenistic parallel.

For the tradition that "the Patriarchs are the Merkabah" see R. Simeon b. Lakish in *Gen R.* 47 : 6; 69 : 3; 82 : 6 (on this dictum see Scholem, *Major Trends*, p. 79; M. Smith, *op. cit.*, p. 507 and n. 3). Cf. *Zohar* I. 173b (Sperling-Simon translation, Vol. II, p. 164) "AND GOD WENT UP FROM HIM IN THE PLACE WHERE HE SPOKE WITH HIM. R. Simeon said, From here we learn that Jacob formed the Holy Chariot together with the other patriarchs, further that Jacob constitutes the supernal Holy Chariot which will restore the full light of the moon and that he forms a Chariot by himself..." A reflection of the Jacob as the Merkabah tradition is to be seen in the interpretation of a saying of R. Simon b. Lakish (that God showed Jacob a three legged throne) by R. Levi, "Thou (i.e. Jacob) are the third leg" (*Gen. R.* 68 : 12). Abraham and Isaac are clearly the other two legs (cf. Goodenough, *Jewish Symbols*, Vol. IV, p. 183 n. 124). Cf. the mystical interpretation of YHWH standing "over" Jacob in the Bethel vision in the *Zohar* I. 150a (Sperling-Simon, Vol. II, p. 81) "the

passage in *Hekhaloth Rabbati* 9, God embraces, kisses and caresses the image of Jacob engraved on the Merkabah when Israel chants the Kedusha.[1])

The extended elaboration of this theme may be seen from a discussion between two first century Palestinian Amoraim, R. Ḥiyya and R. Yannai:

> R. Ḥiyya and R. Yannai differed (as to the meaning of בו in Gen. 28.12b), the one said: The angels ascended and descended on the ladder (בסולם); the other said: They ascended and descended on Jacob (ביעקב), they praised him and slandered him,[2]) they ran about him, on him, sneered at him—for it is written, YOU, O ISRAEL, IN WHOM I WILL BE GLORIFIED (Is. 49.3),[3]) that is said in the sense of: You are he whose image is engraved on high. They ascended on high and saw his image, they decended on earth and saw him sleeping. This is like a king who sits and judges; they ascend to his throne room and find him seated in judgement, they descend to his chamber and find him sleeping... They (i.e. the angels) would have tried to harm him, but THE LORD STOOD BESIDE HIM. R. Simeon b. Laḳish said: If it were not thus written, it would have been impossible for us to say it. The Lord was like a father fanning his sleeping child to keep the flies away...[4]) R. Ḥiyya and R. Yannai differed (as to the meaning of עליו in Gen. 28.13a), the one said: The Lord stood beside the ladder; the other said: He stood beside Jacob...R. Simeon b. Laḳish said: It shows that the Patriarchs form the Merkabah (i.e. taking על in the sense of "upon" and the masculine suffix to refer to Jacob).[5])

In the debate between Ḥiyya and Yannai and the interpolated comments of Simeon b. Laḳish, many of the motifs we have been considering are gathered together: the heavenly image of Jacob on the Throne, the contrast between the heavenly image of Jacob and the figure of the Patriarch sleeping below, the Patriarchs as constituting the Merkabah, the hostility of the angels toward Jacob-Israel and the

---

Lord was standing over him (i.e. Jacob) so as to form the Divine Chariot, with the community of Israel, embodied in Jacob, as the uniting link in their midst..."

[1]) Jellinek, *BHM* III, 90. Translated by P. Bloch in J. Winter - A. Wunsche, *Die jüdische Literatur seit Abschluss des Kanons* (Berlin, 1897) Vol. III, p. 238. I am indebted to Prof. N. A. Dahl for calling my attention to this important text.

[2]) מעלים ומורידים בו might this be interpreted more literally "they raised him up and put him down"?

[3]) This link between the hostility of the angels towards Jacob and the glorification of Israel may be paralleled in the midrashic elaboration of the refusal of the angels to glorify Adam, the "image" of God. See the sources in Ginzberg, *Legends*, Vol. V, pp 69f. and M. Smith, "The Image of God", pp. 478-80 and 480 n.l.

[4]) R. Simeon b. Laḳish's dictum is attributed to R. Abbahu in BT, *Ḥullin* 91a and *Gen. R.* 63. 12.

[5]) *Gen. R.* 68. 13-69. 3.

ascent-descent of the angels. In addition, R. Yannai's interpretation of בו as יעקב implies a mystical growth of Jacob to cosmic size, a theme present in the Fourth Gospel's allusion to the Ladder vision (ὄψεσθε τὸν οὐρανὸν ἀνεῳγότα καὶ τοὺς ἀγγέλους τοῦ θεοῦ ἀναβαίνοντας καὶ καταβαίνοντας ἐπὶ τὸν Υἱὸν τοῦ ἀνθρώπου Jn. 1.51)[1]) and, perhaps, in the figure of Metatron as the personified Ladder of Jacob in late mystical literature.[2])

More crucially for the *PJ* and the question of the apparent Gnostic terminology in Origen's paraphrase in the *Philocalia* is the distinction between the image of Jacob on the Merkabah above and the sleeping figure below. Regardless of how the rabbis quoted may have understood the contrast, in view of the widespread metaphor of sleep as ignorance of God or of one's true self,[3]) such a distinction may well have given rise to the picture in the paraphrase of the *PJ* of Israel's forgetfulness of his heavenly origin.[4])

---

[1]) See C. F. Burney, *The Aramaic Origin of the Fourth Gospel* (Oxford, 1922), pp. 115f. and H. Odeberg, *The Fourth Gospel* (Uppsala-Stockholm, 1929), pp. 33-42. Some suggestion of this tradition may also be reflected in Philo's allegory of the Ladder in *Somn.* I, 146f. My attention was first called to the notion of the soul growing to cosmic size as a motif distinct from the *Himmelreise der Seele* by Professor Carsten Colpe in his discussion of *Corpus Hermeticum* IV, 4f. and X. 25 (see the privately printed minutes of his seminar on the *Hermetica* at Yale University, 1963-1964, p. 18).

[2]) See the texts cited in H. Odeberg, 3 *Enoch* (Cambridge, 1928), "Introduction", p. 123.

[3]) See the excellent collection of texts in H. Jonas, *The Gnostic Religion* 2ed. (Boston, 1963), pp. 69f., 80-6, 92 *et passim*. (*idem.*, *Gnosis und spatantiker Geist* 3e. [Gottingen, 1964], Vol. I, pp. 113-15, 126-34 *et passim*.). Here the stress is upon the sleep of Adam. In addition see the striking text in *Corpus Hermeticum* I. 27 which most likely reflects Jewish background (see C. H. Dodd, *The Bible and the Greeks* [London, 1954], pp. 159f., 178f., 187f.). In Jewish literature, sleep is most usually the state in which the soul "wanders" from the body and may receive revelation by either vision or mystic ascent. These two notions of sleep as ignorance and precondition for revelation are not necessarily antithetical. See *Corpus Hermeticum* I. 1 where they are combined.

[4]) H. Odeberg, *The Fourth Gospel*, pp. 37f. (accepted by R. Bultmann, *Das Evangelium des Johannes* [Gottingen, 1962], p. 74 n.4cf. his *Erganzungsheft* [Gottingen, 1957] p. 19 *ad loc.* See further C. H. Dodd, *The Interpretation of the Fourth Gospel* [Cambridge, 1958], pp. 245f.) who argues from the passage in Gen. R. 68. 18 : "The Divine utterance 'I will be glorified in thee' does not refer to Israel as he is in his earthly appearance (i.e. as Jacob) but to his ideal counterpart in heaven, his celestial appearance (i.e. as Israel properly). The *contrast* obtaining between man's celestial and terrestrial appearance is thus emphasized by the dictum. In view of the simile used as illustration (the King in judgement contrasted with the King in sleep) there is not a doubt but that the celestial appearance is meant to be conveyed as the real man. Further, the 'sleep' is also, in all probability, taken in a mystical sense: the earthly man is, in regard to his real life, as one who sleeps." In a private

The one element not to be found in any Jewish source that I am familiar with is the notion that the celestial Israel descended or the terrestrial Jacob ascended,[1]) but the ascent-descent of the angels on "Jacob's Ladder" would be, in itself, sufficient to provide the origin of this motif.

In this section, as in the preceding ones, I have sought to demonstrate that there is nothing in the *PJ* which is not explicable in terms of Jewish tradition. Specifically, with respect to the descent myth, I have attempted to defend the reliability of Origen's paraphrase in light of traditions surrounding Jacob's vision at Bethel.

(4) The *PJ* may be termed a myth of the mystery of Israel. As such it is a narrative of the descent of the chief angel Israel and his incarnation within the body of Jacob and of his recollection and ascent to his former heavenly state. This myth bears striking resemblance to a variety of traditions within the hellenistic Mediterranean world. The descent of a celestial being to earth, his forgetfulness of his previous state, his recollection upon meeting an angelic figure and his return (at times with combat) above fits well into what might be termed the common Gnostic pattern.[2]) Whether we are to interpret the earthly Jacob-Israel as a thoroughly docetic figure (similar to the pattern of Cerinthus' Christ); as an appearance and incarnation of a heavenly power (analogous to Morton Smith's discussion of Dositheus, John, Jesus, Simon and Menander) or as a heavenly messenger (as elucidated in the works of G. Widengren) remains, for me, a moot question.[3])

---

communication (April 26, 1965) Professor Morton Smith has persuasively argued against Odeberg's interpretation of the simile. "Odeberg should have asked himself How can a King who sits and judges be in two places at once? The answer is, because in the judgement hall there is a statue representing him judging which can be seen even while the real King is at home asleep. So the image of Israel, as it should be, is on the throne while the real Israel is asleep below—and thus, the angels both praise and denigrate him."

[1]) Indeed Jacob's ascent is specifically denied in the wide spread allegory of the guardians of the other nations partially ascending the Ladder while Jacob is afraid to do so—thus condemning his descendants to serve other nations. See *Sifre*, Numbers 119; *Midrash Tehillim* 78. 6; *Leviticus R.* 29. 2 Cf. *Gen. R.* 68. 14; *Pirke d. R. Eliezer* 35 and the late adaptation of this legend in the Slavonic *Ladder of Jacob* 4-5. However, compare R. Jacob in *Shir Ha-shirim Zuta* 1. 4 on the phrase in Gen. 35.1 "Arise, go up to Bethel. This teaches that the Holy One, blessed be He, showed him (i.e. Jacob) one level above another and showed him also the celestial realms"—clearly a fragment of an ascent-legend in connection with the Ladder vision.

[2]) See above, p. 281.

[3]) See especially G. Bardy, "Cérinthe", *Revue Biblique* 30 (1921), 344-373; M. Smith, "The Account of Simon Magus", *Wolfson Festschrift* and G. Widengren,

However it is characteristic of all of these patterns that the myth may be ritually appropriated by its believers, that the 'objective' narrative has a 'subjective' correlative. That which is accomplished by the paradigmatic figure of the Patriarch Jacob-Israel may, presumably, also be achieved by the "sons of Jacob". The pattern of this 'subjective' experience would be the ascent of the mystic to the Merkabah, an ascent fraught with peril from angelic adversaries, an ascent which results in a vision of the form of God on the celestial Throne.[1]) The way of ascent for a son of Jacob, as I suspect it was for Jacob-Israel, is the *scala Iacobi* (significantly, such an interpretation is at least hinted at in Origen, *Contra Celsum* VI,21).[2]) Thus the *PJ* takes its place among a host of texts witnessing to what I have come to believe is *the* fundamental pattern of hellenistic Mediterranean religions—an astrological

---

The Great Vohu Manah and the Apostle of God; Mesopotamian Elements in Manichaeism; The Ascension of the Apostle and the Heavenly Book and *Muhammed, the Apostle of God and his Ascension* (Uppsala-Wiesbaden, 1955). To the last two patterns might be compared the much discussed issue of angel-Christology. See, especially, A. Bakker, "Christ an Angel?", *Zeitschrift f. d. neutestamentliche Wissenschaft* 32 (1933), 255-265; J. Barbel, *Christos Angelos* (Bonn, 1941); M. Werner, *Die Entstehung des christlichen Dogmas* (Leipzig, 1941), pp. 302-389 and cf. W. Michaelis, *Zur Engelchristologie im Urchristentum* (Basel, 1942). For a brief review of recent literature see M. Werner, *The Formation of Christian Doctrine* (London, 1957), p. 130 n. 1; J. Barbel, "Zur Engelchristologie im Urchristentum," *Theologische Rundschau* 54 (1958), cols. 49-58, 103-112.

[1]) See, in general, M. Smith, "Observations on Hekhalot Rabbati", in A. Altmann, ed., *Biblical and Other Studies* (Cambridge USA., 1963), pp. 142-160 which effectively points to parallels between hellenistic and rabbinic ascent materials, a point already suggested in a preliminary way by W. Bousset, "Die Himmelreise der Seele", *Archiv fur Religionswissenschaft* 4 (1901), p. 153. See further, G. Scholem, *Jewish Gnosticism*, pp. 75-83. One might also profitably compare the mythologem of heavenly enthronement especially as elucidated by Scandinavian history of religions research. See G. Widengren, "Den himmelska intronisation och dopet", *Religion och Bibel* 5 (1946), 28-61 especially p. 29; Widengren, "Baptism and Enthronement in some Jewish-Christian Gnostic Documents" in S. G. F. Brandon, ed., *The Saviour God: Comparative Studies in the Concept of Salvation presented to Edwin Oliver James* (New York, 1963), pp. 205-217; H. Reisenfeld, *Jesu transfiguré* (Copenhagen, 1947) and P. Beskow, *Rex Gloriae* (Uppsala, 1962), pp. 127-131 cf. pp. 103-106, 147-156.

[2]) H. Chadwick, *Origen: Contra Celsum* (Cambridge, 1953), pp. 333f. This observation as well as others made in this paper renders imperative that a careful study be made of the use of Gen. 25 : 10-17 in Jewish and Christian tradition. The only recent treatment that I am familiar with is C. A. Patrides, "Renaissance Interpretations of Jacob's Ladder", *Theologische Zeitschrift* 18 (1962), pp. 411-418. While I think his interpretation excessive, note Goodenough's discussion of Exodus 19. 4; Deut 32. 11 and *Assumption of Moses* (Charles, Vol. II, p. 422) as capable of being understood as referring to the astral ascent of Israel. Once again, what might be said of the Nation could be read as referring to the Patriarch.

mystery involving the descent-ascent of a heavenly figure, the *Himmelreise der Seele* of the believer through the astral-angelic spheres and magical-theurgic practices.¹) What distinguishes the *PJ* from other ascent-literature is the paradigmatic figure of Jacob-Israel, for, within Hebrew and Aramaic Merkabah texts, the Patriarch's play no normative role (save in Simeon b. Laḳish's dictum that the "Patriarchs are the Merkabah" quoted above).²)

However, as Goodenough has demonstrated in *By Light, Light*, within hellenistic Judaism, the Patriarchs play just such a role.³) Thus, without attempting a detailed demonstration, it should be noted that elements I find within the theology of the *PJ* appear reflected in Goodenough's discussion of the symbolism of the great "reredos" in the Dura Synagogue.⁴) The reredos is dominated by the great Vine which is, in part, a ladder.⁵) To one side, at the foot of the Vine, is the reclining figure of the Patriarch Jacob; in the branches is the figure of

---

¹) For general treatments of these motifs see W. Bousset, "Die Himmelreise der Seele", *Archiv für Religionswissenschaft* 4 (1901), 136-169, 229-273 (reprinted Darmstadt, 1960); A. Dieterich, *Eine Mithrasliturgie* 1e (Leipzig, 1903), pp. 179-212 (I regret that the two subsequent editions are not available to me at this writing); F. Cumont, "Le mysticisme astral dans l'antiquité", *Bulletin de l' Academie Royale de Belgique* 1909 (Classes des lettres), pp. 256-286; A-J. Festugière, *La révélation d'Hermès Trismégiste* Vol. I *L'astrologie et les sciences occultes* 3e (Paris, 1950); M. Nilsson, "Die astrale Unsterblichkeit und der kosmische Mystik", *Numen* 1 (1954), pp. 106-119; J. Lewy, *Chaldean Oracles and Theurgy* (Cairo, 1956) and the works cited above, p. 288 n. 1. Goodenough's treatment of this theme in *Jewish Symbols* Vol. VIII, pp. 167-218 seems to me to be one of his weaker sections.

²) See p. 284 n. 2, above. Also the traditions collected by M. Smith, "The Image of God", pp. 478-81 on the deification of the righteous through worship by being given the name of God. To the extent that this tradition is based on Genesis 33. 20 where Jacob erects an altar at Shechem and called it אל אלהי ישראל it is relevant to our text. Cf. BT, *Meg.* 18a "R. Aḥa said in the name of R. Eleazer: Where do we learn that the Holy One, blessed be He, called Jacob by the name of *El*? It is said (quoting Gen. 33.20). . this means AND JACOB WAS CALLED EL. Who called him thus? the God of Israel." Cf. R. Simeon b. Lakish in *Gen. R.* 79. 8 "Jacob meant: Thou art the Lord of all heavenly things and I am the lord of all earthly things"; and *Zohar* I. 138a. Note that in *Gen. R.* 79.8, R. Huna rejects R. Simeon b. Lakish's exegesis (cf. Sifre, *Deut.* 355; *Midrash ha-Gadol* I, 552f. etc.). A similar tradition is connected with the name *Jeshuran* e.g. R. Berekiah in the name of R. Simon, "There is none like unto God. Yet who is like God? Jeshuran which means Israel the Patriarch. Just as it is written of God AND THE LORD ALONE SHALL BE EXALTED (Is 2.11) so also of Jacob AND JACOB WAS LEFT ALONE (Gen 32.25)." in *Gen. R.* 77.1.

³) Goodenough, *By Light, Light*, esp. chs. v and vi.
⁴) Goodenough, *Jewish Symbols*, Vol. IX, pp. 78-123.
⁵) *ibid.*, pp. 80 and n. 86. Cf. Vol. VIII, pp. 148-57 and M. Eliade, *Patterns in Comparative Religion* (New York, 1958), pp. 102-11.

Orpheus, the heavenly singer; and, at the summit, is the Throne and the Powers. While the emphasis in the *PJ* is on the descent of Israel and, in Goodenough's exposition of the Dura fresco, on the ascent, the "value" remains similar:

> ...blessed at the bottom by the Patriarch wearing the white robe of a man of God on earth, Israel can go up to stand permanently beside the Throne with the Powers.[1])

A further parallel is found in a hellenistic Jewish papyri entitled Προσευχὴ 'Ιακώβ![2]) Here the petitioner, after invoking God and his saving acts, prays:

> Fill me with wisdom, empower me, Master. Fill my heart with good things, Master, because I am an angel on earth, because I have become immortal, because I have received the gift from thee.

Here, in the name of Jacob (most likely, though not demonstrably, the Patriarch) we gain a picture of the 'subjective' experience of one who, receiving the "gift" of *sophia*, realizes that he is "an angel on earth" (ὡς ἄγγελον ἐπίγειον),[3]) and has thereby "become immortal".

It is within such a circle of hellenistic Judaism which speaks of the ascent of the Patriarchs to the full reality of their heavenly (angelic) nature that the *PJ* is to be located. The Προσευχὴ 'Ιωσήφ is the narrative of the "objective" mythology of the heavenly figure; the Προσευχὴ 'Ιακώβ is the expression of the 'subjective' experience of this salvation within the individual believer.

The complete pattern might be illustrated by the figure of Enoch, especially as he appears in the Slavonic *Enoch* which contains much old tradition. Here Enoch was originally a man (I, preamble); ascends

---

[1]) *ibid.*, p. 107.
[2]) Berlin, P. gr. 13895 in Preisendanz, *PGM*, Vol. II, pp. 148f. It would be difficult to improve on the superb English rendering of this text in Goodenough, *Jewish Symbols*, Vol. II, p. 203 or to disagree with his conclusion that the *Prayer* is "quite unimpeachable as a product of hellenized Judaism...the prayer seems to me to be one which Philo himself could have repeated from beginning to end, or could himself have written, since it is a prayer for transfiguration" (pp. 203f.).
[3]) Cf. the material collected in H. Corbin, "Cyclical Time in Mazdaism and Ismailism" in J. Campbell, ed., *Man and Time: Papers from the Eranos Yearbooks III* (New York, 1957), pp. 114-172 esp. pp. 164,167 on "angelomorphosis" and in his *Avicenna* pp. 46, 71, 83, 90, 111, 114, 182 on the concept of *fereshtagi* i.e. "angelicity" See further the important summary statement on p. 21 on the "connection, little analyzed hitherto, between angelology and mysticism".

to heaven *and becomes an angel* (XXII, 4-10 cf. 3 *Enoch* 10.3-4 and 48C); returns to earth as a man (XXXIII,5-10) and finally returns above to resume his angelic station (LXVII,2).[1])

I have attempted to demonstrate that the *PJ* must be placed within the environment of first or second century Jewish mysticism by examining the most striking elements in the text: the titles of the angel Jacob-Israel, the conflict between Jacob-Israel and Uriel and the decent of the heavenly Israel. In each instance I have sought to point to parallel traditions in available hellenistic Jewish and rabbinic documents.

The existence of an angel Israel is implied in both hellenistic (Jewish) magical papyri and in late Jewish mystical literature, in rabbinic material concerning the name of the angel with whom Jacob wrestled and in Hekhaloth literature which speaks of a heavenly Israel who leads the angelic liturgy before the Throne (sect. I,2). While the various titles given to Israel in the *PJ* are paralleled by those borne by Michael in rabbinic and apocalyptic texts, Metatron in Jewish mystical documents and Christ in Jewish-Christian authors (sect. I, 2,3,6,7,8) as well as titles applied to Jacob-Israel within the Old Testament and its midrashim (sect. I,1,2,4,5,8)—the most striking parallels are to be found in those assigned to the *Logos* by Philo (esp. sect. I,4).

In considering the contest between Jacob-Israel and Uriel, I dismissed the arguments of previous scholars that this represents either anti-Christian or anti-Jewish polemic or that the conflict stems from Jewish gnosticism, maintaining that the *PJ* is a positive Jewish document (sect. II,1). Certain features appear to be drawn from the legends of conflict between Jacob and Esau (sect. II,2); but the setting is clearly to be traced to Jacob wrestling with the angel in Genesis 32 (sect. II,3). I sought to place the conflict within the context of angelic rivalry before the Throne of God as witnessed to in both hellenistic and rabbinic mystical literature (sect. II,4,5).

The problem of the gnostic language of the descent myth, especially as presented in Origen's paraphrase of the *PJ* in the *Philocalia*, was likewise to be interpreted on the basis of Jewish material (sect. III,1,2). I suggested that the mythologies of Israel's incarnation in Jacob and

---

[1]) The classic study of Enoch remains, in my opinion, H. L. Jansen, *Die Henochgestalt: Eine vergleichende religionsgeschichtliche Untersuchung* (Oslo, 1939). See further H. Odeberg, "Forestallningarna om Metatron i äldre judisk mystik", *Kyrkohistorisk Årsskrift* 27 (1927), 1-20 especially p. 6.

ignorance of his heavenly origin might be drawn from first century discussions of Jacob's Ladder with the angels ascending and descending between the image of Jacob on the Merkabah and the sleeping figure of the Patriarch below (sect. III,3). Finally, I pointed to two witnesses from hellenistic Judaism which appeared to give the 'subjective' correlative of the ascent-experience 'objectified' in the descent myth and suggested that the emphasis on the archetypal role of the Patriarch (an emphasis lacking in rabbinic Merkabah texts) most probably locates the *PJ* within the sphere of hellenistic mystical Judaism (sect. III,4).[1])

ADDENDA

p. 256 n. 2. A possible connection between Joseph and a prayer of Jacob might be suggested by *T. Benj.* X,1 (ed. M. de Jonge, *Testamenta XII Patriarcharum* [Leiden, 1964], p. 84) which records that when Joseph was in Egypt, Benjamin longed to see him. Through the prayers of Jacob (δι' εὐχῶν 'Ιακώβ), Benjamin has a vision of Joseph. (The suggestion of R. H. Charles, *The Testaments of the Twelve Patriarchs* [London, 1908], p. 212; *Apocrypha and Pseudepigrapha*, Vol. II, pp. 355 and 359 that this verse be emended and transferred to *T. Benj.* II,1 should be rejected). See further Jacob's role as the 'narrator' of Joseph's 'secret' in *T. Benj.* III,2-5 as reconstructed from the Armenian by R. H. Charles (*op. cit.* Vol. II, p. 355). The Armenian version, however, is probably not to be relied on (see M. de Jonge, *The Testaments of the Twelve Patriarchs* [Assen, 1953], pp. 23-34). This passage is lacking in the better Cambridge Univ. Library Ms. Ff 1,24 as edited by de Jonge (*op. cit.*, p. 80).

Further research needs to be done on the pattern of these patriarchal traditions within the *Testament* literature. With respect to my suggestion above "that the *PJ* follows the format of the Testament-literature where, quite consistently, it is the previous patriarch who appears and speaks to the patriarch in the title", see the valuable Appendix VI, "Valedictions and Farewell Speeches", in E. Stauffer, *New Testament Theology* (London, 1963), pp. 344-347.

p. 260 n. 3. For *angelos* as prophet-angel in hellenistic Jewish sources, see W. D. Davies, "A Note on Josephus, *Antiquities* 15.136", *Harvard Theological Review*, 47 (1954), pp. 135-140 nd F. R. Walton, "The Messenger of God in

---

[1]) I am deeply indebted to Prof. Nils A. Dahl, who first aroused my interest in the *PJ*, for his careful critical reading of the final draft of this paper and for graciously sharing with me his own unpublished lecture on the subject; though we disagree in our interpretation of the PJ, his comments, criticisms and suggestions have been a precious source of aid; to Professors H. Lester, W. Meeks, J. Neusner, M. Smith and K. Stendahl for reading this paper in various drafts and for their incisive criticisms and suggestions; to Père J. Daniélou for his courteous response to my questions; to Professors H. Craig, Jr., G. Lawell, G. Quispel, C. Bradford Wells and Mr. D. Gunn for suggestions and assistance on specific problems.

Hecateus of Abdera", *ibid.* (1955), pp. 255-257. Cf. *sukkalmah* in Elam as the "exalted messenger" who can be either as prophet or an angel according to G. C. Cameron, *History of Early Iran* (Chicago, 1936), p. 71.

In addition to *Ya'qob-el*, see the name *Ia-ah-qu-ub-él* in an eighteenth century text cited by C. J. Gadd, "Tablets from Chagar Bazar and Tall Brak, 1937-38", *Iraq*, 7 (1940), p. 38.

ιΑΚΟΥ ιΒ appears as one of the Powers of Ialdabaoth, creating the right shoulder of man in *Apocryphon Johannis* 65.11 (ed. S. Giversen [Copenhagen], 1963, p. 79).

p. 262 n. 1. See further the discussion of Israel as an angel in *Sefer Raziel* 41b in T. Schrire, *Hebrew Amulets* (London, 1966), pp. 106f.

Another probable occurrence of Israel as an angel occurs in London Ms. Or. 6796(4), line 21: "I am Israelel, the Dynamis of Iao Sabaoth, the great Dynamis of Barbaraoth", (in Kropp, *op. cit.* Vol. I, p. 48; Vol. II, p. 58).

p. 263 n. 1. *Istraël* occurs as an angelic name in London Ms. Or. 5987, line 93 (in Kropp, *op. cit.* I, p. 25; II, p. 152). On Istrahel and the angel of death, see further, W. Bousset, *Des Religions d. Judentums* 3e (Tubingen, 1926), pp. 328f.

p. 267 n. 1. To item (*g*), compare the Logos as *stratēgos* in the pseudo-Justin, *Oratio ad Graecos* 5. For the relationship of this text and title to Philo and hellenistic Judaism, see E. R. Goodenough, "The Pseudo-Justinian 'Oratio ad Graecos'," *Harvard Theological Review*, 18 (1925), pp. 194-195 and, further, P. Beskow, *Rex Gloriae* (Uppsala, 1962), pp. 209-210.

p. 268 n. 2. For a comparison between the *PJ* and Col 1.15, see H. Windisch, *Die gottliche Weisheit der Juden und die paulinische Christologie* (Leipzig, 1914), p. 225n. and, most recently, C. F. D. Moule, *The Epistles of Paul the Apostle to the Colossians and to Philemon* (Cambridge, 1962), p. 63.

p. 268 n. 4. In Christian material, see especially οἱ ἅγιοι ἄγγελοι τοῦ Θεοῦ οἱ πρῶτοι κτισθέντες in *Hermas*, Vis. III, iv, 1.

p. 270 n.1. N. Turner, "Joseph, Prayer of", *The Interpreter's Dictionary of the Bible* (New York-Nashville, 1962), Vol. II, p. 979 states, "The riddle of the book is not yet solved, but it must have been anti-Christian to some extent at least".

p. 271 n. 4. J. Daniélou, *Message évangélique et culture hellénistique au IIe et IIIe siècles* (Tournai, 1961), pp. 451f. speculates that the text of the *PJ* may well reveal Christian influence. Though he has nowhere spelled this out in detail, this remark coupled with his note in Daniélou-Marrou, *op. cit.*, Vol. I, p. 76 appears to suggest that Daniélou is developing a complex redaction-history of the *PJ* involving a Jewish (Aramaic?) *Grundschrift* and one or more Christian redactions.

p. 274 n. 2. On the motif of seven angels, see the classic paper of G. H. Dix, "The Seven Archangels and the Seven Spirits", *Journal of Theological Studies* 28 (1927), pp. 233-250 and, further, G. Furlani, "I sette angeli del Yezidi", *Rendiconti della reale academia dei Lincei*, Ser. VIII, Vol. 2 (1947), pp. 141-161, esp. pp. 146-154.

p. 277 n. 2. T. Schrire, *op. cit.*, p. 108 describes Uriel as "he who wrestled with Jacob". Schrire cites no source for this identification.

On the figure of Suriel, see further, G. Furlani, *op. cit.*, pp. 157f.

p. 288 n. 2. On *Contra Celsum* VI,21 see further, F. Cumont, *Afterlife in Roman Paganism* (New York, 1959), pp. 153f. and, especially, W. L. Knox, *Some Hellenistic Elements in Primitive Christianity* (London, 1944), p. 59 n. 1 who compares it with Aristides, *Hieroi Logoi* iii.48.

A further instance of Gen 28 understood as a ladder of mystical-initiatory ascent occurs in the Naassene exegesis of the Attis Hymn in Hippolytus, *Ref.* V. 8.18-21 in which Psalm 24.7,9; Gen 28.17 and John 10.9 are correlated with the ascent of Anthropos.

p. 289 n. 1. From the perspective of History of Religions, the larger question must ultimately be raised as to the structural parallels between these Hellenistic and

Jewish ascent and theurgic practices and other ecstatic initiatory procedures. See, in a preliminary way, the specialized study of J. W. Hauer, *Die Dhāraṇī im nordlichen Buddhismus und ihre Parallelen in der sogennanten Mithrasliturgie* (Stuttgart, 1927), esp. pp. 20-25 which is not, however, very satisfactory. More generally, see M. Eliade, *Shamanism* (New York, 1964), esp. pp. 375-403, 487-494.

pp. 290-91. The passages from Slavonic *Enoch* have been cited according to W. R. Morfill-R. H. Charles, *The Book of the Secrets of Enoch* (Oxford, 1896). In the new text and translation by A. Vaillant, *Le Livre des Secrets d'Hénoch* (Paris, 1952) XXII-IX (pp. 25-27); XXXIII-XI (p. 33); LXVII-XVIII (p. 65).

THE CONCEPT OF THE MESSIAH IN IV EZRA

BY

MICHAEL STONE

Hebrew University, Jerusalem

In IV Ezra the Messiah is mentioned or referred to only in certain sections of the book. While this raises problems about the literary unity of the work, it also facilitates an examination of its views bearing on the Messianic idea. These we here explore along three lines of question. These concern first, the nature and functions attributed to the Messiah; second, the consistency with which these are found in the passages dealing with him; and third, his function in the total eschatological scheme of the book. Such questions receive some sharpness because of the title "Man" given the Messiah in chapter 13 and the possible connection of this title with the title Son of Man in I Enoch and in the New Testament. The question of the Messiah as the son or servant of God, arising from expressions occurring in 7:28, 7:29, 13:32, 13:37, 13:52 and 14:9, must remain the subject of a separate study which the writer hopes to complete in the future.

I

Definite reference is made to the Messiah in the following passages: 7:28ff., 11:37-12:1, 12:31-34, 13:3-13,25-52, 14:9. It has been suggested that the son in the fourth vision is the Messiah but this seems unlikely.[1]

In 7:28ff. he is titled "my Messiah" and "my servant the Messiah." He is said to be revealed together with his company which suggests pre-existence. He makes those who survive the Messianic woes rejoice for four hundred years and at the end of this period he dies together with all men. The only tradition similar to that of the death of the Messiah here is Ap. Bar. 30:1.[2] Most sources, such as the Rabbinic

---
[1] See Erik Sjoberg, *Der Menschensohn im ÄthiopischenHenochbuch* (Lund: Gleerup, 1946), 134-139 for both a bibliography and an excellent critique of this view.

[2] This is similar to the idea of the snatching away of the Messiah remarked upon by W. Zimmerli and J. Jeremias, *The Servant of God* (London: SCM Press, 1957), 99n. One of their references. I En 70 : 1, seems to refer to Enoch's own elevation. Yet at least I En 71 : 14 strongly suggests that Enoch can be identified

materials, do not deal with the specific fate of the Messiah. This is also true of IV Ezra elsewhere. In this passage there is no suggestion that he plays any part in the events preceding the end of this world.

II

The Messiah plays a significant role in the fifth vision, that of the eagle symbolizing the Roman Empire. In chapter 11 the lion, speaking in a human voice (37) indicts and sentences the eagle (38-45). As he speaks the eagle's last head and last two little wings disappear, its body is burnt and the earth greatly rejoices (12:1-3). In the angelic interpretation the lion is identified with the Davidic Messiah, preserved by the Most High for the end (12:32). He will come and rebuke the last of the four world empires, "he will first set them up in judgment (Syriac, Arabic, Armenian: his judgment) while they are alive, and it shall be when he will have rebuked them he will destroy them" (12:33). He will then deliver the rest of the people in the land of Israel and rejoice with them until the time of the end and the day of judgment (12:34).

The most important function here attributed to the Messiah is indictment and punishment, referred to in the interpretation as judgment. The Messiah is pre-existent, he will rule over the people in the land for a time and then the end will come. In contrast to 7:28ff. where the Messiah plays no part in the events preceding the end, his role here is central. On the other hand, his rule over the temporary Messianic kingdom is explicit in both passages and the language of rejoicing and the term survivors are common to both. Additional features presented by this vision are the Davidic geneology, the Palestinian locale of the kingdom and the forensic aspects of the description of his activity. Pre-existence, which was hinted at in 7:28ff., is made explicit.

G. H. Box, author of the most recent, major, English edition of IV Ezra, suggests that chapters 11-12 were drawn from an independent source document. His arguments directly supporting this have been largely refuted by the work of J. Keulers and, although further considerations can be urged in support of Keuler's views, they are sufficiently strong in themselves.[1]) More important for the student of the

---

with the Son of Man (if our present text is to be trusted). Thus perhaps Zimmerli[i] and Jeremias' reference to I En 70 : 1 can be justified. IV Ezra's reference to the death of the Messiah remains unparalleled.

[1]) G. H. Box, *The Ezra-Apocalypse* (London: Pitman, 1912), xxiii-xxiv. Keulers'

author's Messianic thought is Box's contention, associated with this first proposition, that editorial adjustments have been made within the vision.[1]) This is significant because these supposed adjustments were made to verses dealing with the Messiah. Thus, Box suggests that the phrase "whom the Most High hath kept unto the end of days" in 12: 32 is secondary because it implies transcendence which contradicts the Davidic descent. Further, all of 12:34 referring to the deliverance of the survivors and their joy in the Messianic kingdom until the day of judgment is an addition, for it is "out of harmony" with the purely political expectation of the vision.

Against this view Keulers points out that, alongside 12:1-3 the admittedly genuine verses 12:32f. must speak of the leaders of the Roman empire, for the empire itself had already disappeared. Thus, at this point, there is a combination of the Messiah as king and the Messiah as judge, which latter function points beyond a merely political hope. He further observes that the Davidic geneology is traditional so it is introduced in spite of the apparent anomaly.[2]) It is illuminating to compare this Messianic figure, with its supposedly incompatible heavenly origin and Davidic descent, with the figure of Melkizedek presented by the materials associated with II Enoch. There Melkizedek is born before the flood and assumed to heaven in order to appear later at the appointed time.[3]) To the author of this document the supposed incompatibility did not seem important. This highlights the sort of inappropriate assumptions which Box makes.

---

views may be found in his "Die eschatologische Lehre des vierten Esrabuches," *Biblische Studien*, 20, Nos. 2-3 (1922), 47ff. Additional considerations arise, for example, from a careful exegesis of 4:26ff. which does not support the transcendent and dualist eschatology of the S source as Box maintains. The general weight of Keulers' argument is that the contrasts between the documents are not as great as Box would have them and therefore the Eagle vision cannot be proved to be an independent source on this basis. Keulers admits the general possibility that Vision V-VII are based on written traditions reworked by the author. Nonetheless he adduces further detailed considerations in favour of the substantial common authorship of the supposedly different documents, including terminological consistencies, *ibid.*, 53-55.

[1]) Only those "adjustments" relevant to the Messianic thought are discussed in detail here.

[2]) Keulers, *Biblische Studien*, 1922, 115.

[3]) W. R. Morfill and R. H. Charles, *The Book of the Secrets of Enoch* (Oxford: Oxford University Press, 1896), 91f., ch. 4 of text. [This observation is confirmed by the Melkizedek text from Qumran, published after the above was written, cf. A. S. van der Woude, "Melchisedek als himmlische Erlosergestalt in den neugefundenen eschatologischen Midraschim aus Qumran Hohle XI," *Oudtestamentische Studien* 14 (1965), 354-373. See also D. Flusser's article "Malchizedek and the Son of Man," *Christian News from Israel* (April, 1966), 23-29.]

Over and above these particular points, however, it is necessary to come to grips with Box's basic contention about the eschatology of the eagle vision which, in fact, determines these other matters. Box characterizes the eschatology of the vision as an obsession with the might of Rome and purely political hopes centered on this world whose consummation will be the overthrow of the Roman empire. 11:46, which he recognises as genuine, is thus a crucial verse for him. If it refers to the final judgment, it extends the nature of the author's hope beyond the purely political realm. To the contrary, Box argues, the end has come with the annihilation of the eagle (see 11:45) and therefore, in v.46 "the judgment and mercy of Him who made it (the earth)" must refer, not to final judgment, but to the character of the rule of God which is to follow the overthrow of the Roman empire.[1]

This argument is based on the unstated premise that if the end is the destruction of the Roman empire, then no further eschatological events can possibly ensue. It appears, however, that (for IV Ezra) which particular event is called the end in any given passage is determined by the immediate context. It is clear that "end" was a technical term in eschatological contexts, for it is used alone and without any referrent in such contexts.[2] Yet it is equally clear that it does not always refer to the same event (cf. 7:113, 12:34, 11:39-46, 6:25). "End" evidently signified for the author something like "the decisive point in the eschatological sequence." If so, then variation is to be expected as to its precise location in that sequence, conditioned by the context and purpose of the passage in which it occurs.[3] Now, as Box himself rightly notes, the main prepossession of this vision is with the Roman Empire and of necessity, its climax is the destruction of that empire. This event is thus called "the end" but it does not follow that this is perforce the final event of the eschatological sequence. It may just be the climax of the particular aspect of that sequence on which the author's attention has been concentrated.

Were there further support in the vision or in its interpretation for the view that 11:46 refers to the theocratic rule of the Messianic kingdom, Box's view might be still acceptable. The only other reference to what succeeds the destruction of the eagle is to be found in 12:34. If this is secondary, as Box would have us believe, then in the interpre-

---
[1] Box, *Ezra-Apocalypse*, 247ff.
[2] Thus, for example, 5:41, 6:15 *et al.*
[3] 7:113 and 12:34 both clearly state that the end is the day of judgment, 11:36-39, 6:25, 6:7-10, 5:41 and 14:9 all are best interpreted as placing the end immediately before the Messianic kingdom.

tation of the vision there is no reference at all to the nature of the Messianic rule and in chapters 11-12 only 11:46 would provide information about it. Box's interpretation of 11:46 can only stand, as has been seen, if there is other evidence to support it. In his "original" text of the vision there is none and therefore his interpretation must be rejected.

Further, 12:34 has been rejected on the basis of its lack of harmony with the views of the vision. Such views are to be found, however, only in 11:46. Since Box's interpretation of this verse cannot be supported on grounds independent of the text of the vision, and receives no support within the vision, 12:34 cannot be rejected as being in conflict with it. Moreover, if 12:34 is genuine, then there is no doubt whatsoever that 11:46 refers to final judgment, after the end of the Messianic kingdom. Further, the awkwardness of Box's interpretation of 11:46 is highlighted by his own confusion. On the one hand he says that "judgment" in 11:46 "means the judicial process by which the Roman Empire is condemned and destroyed,"[1] while on the other, he claims that it suggests "the mild rule of the theocratic king, *i.e.*, God himself."[2]

To this argument one further consideration should be added. In Daniel 7, for example, where the eternity and universality of the Messianic kingdom of Israel are proclaimed, they are made explicit both in the vision and in its interpretation.[3] To this the situation here stands in strong contrast. If 11:46 is proclaiming the eternal kingdom of the Messiah then it is obscure and misleading. 12:34 excludes this concept and if it is secondary then that kingdom is ignored altogether in the interpretation.

It appears therefore that 12:34 is original and that "judgment" in 11:46 refers to final judgment to follow the Messianic kingdom. In light of the main interest and emphasis of the vision, the placing of the climax at the destruction of the empire is not anomalous, even though the author also believes in a temporary Messianic kingdom and day of judgment. The perfunctory nature of the description of the events following this destruction emphasizes the almost exclusive preoccupation with Rome in the vision. The eschatology of the vision extends, therefore, beyond the purely political and encompasses final judgment.

The judicial aspect of the function of the Messiah and yet the distinctness of his activity from the final judgment raise the problem of

---

[1]) Box, *Ezra-Apocalypse*, 260, n.i..
[2]) *Ibid.*, 247.
[3]) Dan. 7 : 14,27.

the relationship of that judgment to the other events which involve the separation of the righteous from the wicked. Here this is done for the last generation by the Messiah. In 7:27ff. it is effected by the woes, the troubles which precede the coming of the Messiah—the concept of the survivors presupposes this. Another case in which this problem arises is in the separation of the souls of the righteous and wicked after death in 7:75ff. The question of the relationship between the prefiguration of judgment in the form of the survivors concept and final judgment is one of the factors at work in 5:41ff. There the answer was, in effect, that the day of judgment has a decisiveness and permanency unlike any other event.[1]) These are precisely the most prominent features of the day of judgment in the description of it in IV Ezra. In light of this, the apparent anomaly of the judicial function of the Messiah need not be seen as an obstacle to the eschatology put forward by this vision.

Box's point about the different functions of the Messiah here and in 7:28ff. seems quite valid. There the Messiah appears after the end of the convulsions which precede his kingdom. Here, however, he appears when the wickedness of the last heathen empire reaches its peak, and he is directly responsible for its overthrow. Further, his activity is described in legal terms, reminiscent of the language of God's judicial activity, for example in 7:37. Baldensperger pointed out that in Daniel 7 the eschatological battle is given a forensic formulation and sees this as relevant to the language used here of the Messiah.[2]) The Son of Man as cosmic judge is one of the most remarkable features of the Similitudes of Enoch. The comparison with Daniel 7 on the one hand and the Similitudes of Enoch on the other will help us better to evaluate the significance of the legal formulation applied here to the activity of the Messiah.

In Daniel 7, of course, the theme of judgment is explicit. It is judgment by the Ancient of Days, that is God, and it is cosmic in nature. He sits on the Throne with his attendant hosts before him, the heavenly books are opened and judgment is given.[3]) The cosmic ex-

---

[1]) Thus, although the starting point of the discussion in 5 : 41 concerns the inequality of reward for the survivors and those to be resurrected, the solution to the problem is clearly found in the nature of the day of judgment (5 : 42). The primary interest in this passage is in reward, not inequality. R. Kabisch, *Das vierte Buch Esra auf seine Quellen untersucht* (Gottingen: Vandenhoeck und Ruprecht, 1889), 68 touches on the pre-figuring of judgment in the Messianic kingdom.

[2]) Wilhelm Baldensperger, *Das Selbstbewusstsein Jesu im licht der messianischen Hoffnungen seiner Zeit*; I. "Die messianisch-apokalyptischen Hoffnungen des Judentums" (3ed. rev.; Strassburg: Heitz und Muendel, 1903), 98f., cf. 161.

[3]) Dan. 7 : 9f., 26.

tent of this judgment is unmistakable. In the Similitudes judgment, although performed by the Son of Man, has the same cosmic, universal aspects. He sits on the Throne of Glory as judge over the sinners.[1] The universal and ultimate nature of his function is greatly stressed.[2]

In the vision here under examination the elements of judgment are also clearly present. 11 : 38-43 are the indictment, 45-46 the pronouncement of sentence, and 12 :1-3 its execution. In the interpretation, 12 : 33 is even more explicit. The Messiah will set up the leaders of the fourth kingdom in judgment while they are still alive and then he will destroy them.[3] Yet the elements of universality and resurrection generally associated by IV Ezra with final judgment do not appear, neither do those features which serve to highlight the cosmic nature of the judgment in Daniel 7 and I Enoch. There is, for example, no enthronement. This vision is greatly influenced by Daniel 7 as is evident not only from the explicit reference to that chapter in 12 :11 but from many other elements in the structure of the vision.[4] This renders the lack of these cosmic features the more striking.

The question thus arises of the origin of the Messiah's function of judgment in the form in which it is presented here. Is it to be seen as a modification of the concept of the Messiah as cosmic judge as it occurs, for example, in I Enoch or rather as one outcome of the legalizing of the eschatological, cosmic battle, another of which is the concept of the Messiah as cosmic judge? In this connection it is important to examine the vision in Ap. Bar. 39-40. Although the Syriac Baruch has many connections with IV Ezra, there is clearly no *literary* connection between this vision and IV Ezra 11-12. It is, like IV Ezra 11-12, a four empires vision. The anti-christ features which influenced the indictment in IV Ezra 11 : 38-43 are also evident in Ap. Bar. 39 :5, and both stem from the characterization of the little horn in Daniel 7. Here, strikingly, the legal form, in particular the judgment of the *leader* of the last empire (40 :1) and the temporary Messianic kingdom (40 :3) occur. The cosmic and universal elements are totally absent.

---

[1] I En. 62 : 2,3,5, 69 : 27 etc.

[2] See also Sjoberg, *Menschensohn*, Ch. 3, 61-82. The Similitudes, which do not occur at Qumran, have been lately dated variously between the middle of the first century B.C.E. and the first or second centuries C.E. See the discussion by J. Starcky, "Les quatre Etapes du Messianisme à Qumran," *Revue Biblique*, 70 (1963), 501f. Whatever the situation be, they are close enough to IV Ezra to serve as comparative material.

[3] Keulers, *Biblische Studien*, 1922, 115.

[4] See Keulers, *ibid.*, 109ff., Baldensperger, *Das Selbstbewusstein Jesu*, I, 160, Box *Ezra-Apocalypse*, 283f., etc.

This tends to indicate that the cosmic judgment of the Messiah is not the background of these visions. Had some hint of this appeared in either of these two visions, unrelated as they are in their literary form, the situation would have been different. In both, the features of judgment must be seen as a function of the legalizing of the eschatological battle leading to the description of the activities of the Messiah in legal terms. This is seen as the introduction to the Messianic kingdom. For Baruch and for Ezra final judgment is the realm of God. When the eschatological battle became separated from final judgment as is the case in Ezra and Baruch, the Messiah as warrior took over some aspects of the judgment language, but final judgment remained the prerogative of the Most High.[1])

The coincidence of a number of common elements in the visions of Ezra and Baruch tends to suggest a distinct associational complex. The two visions have in common first, the vision form and the use of nature symbolism, second, the four empires theory, third, the last most wicked empire and its overthrow by the Messiah, fourth, the formulation of the Messianic activity in forensic terms, fifth, the judgment upon and destruction of the leaders of that empire, and, finally, the concept of the temporary Messianic kingdom. Yet in spite of all this there is no literary interdependence.

The roots of most of these elements lie deep in apocalyptic tradition and especially in Daniel 7. It is quite possible that there developed in the two hundred and fifty years after the composition of Daniel, a traditional complex which might be called "the Four Empires Vision complex" and which was characterized at least by the basic elements of the symbolic vision form, the four empires and the military-legal function of the Messiah. IV Ezra 12:11 makes it evident that the author is dependent on a tradition of interpretation or rather re-interpretation of Daniel 7 and he may not have been the first so to be. In any case, the deeply traditional nature of the materials in this chapter may be the explanation of the introduction of the forensic features of the Messiah, whether or not a crystallized complex of elements such as that suggested here actually existed.

Thus it may be concluded that the legal language used here to describe the Messiah's activities is not to be taken to indicate that judgment is the prime characteristic of that figure. The foremost features are still military, the overthrowing of the great Roman Empire

---

[1]) It is precisely the Son of Man's assuming the functions of universal judgment that makes the Similitudes so problematic in the eyes of many scholars.

and the description of this activity in legal terms is one of the elements of the tradition here involved.

The traditional nature of this vision doubtless is the explanation of those differences from the first part of the book which have led many scholars to posit an independent source for it. Yet it is clear that the vision is not an adaptation of a written source. The overall congruence of vision and interpretation, in spite of minor problems, weighs against this. This becomes even clearer when the vision is compared with that of chapter 13. There the vision and interpretation are far from harmoniously related and it will be seen that there is reason to think that the vision is an independent piece while the author tried to write an interpretation to it.

Here both unevennesses and differences from other places in the book are best regarded as the result of the author's employing a highly traditional complex of ideas, a complex which probably imposed certain features, such as the function of the Messiah, upon him who employed it. It is easier to see in these terms the divergences in the concept of the Messiah between this vision and 7:28ff. than to explain in their similarities, as Box does, as the result of editorial adaptation of a divergent eschatology to that of the first part of the book. If the similarities are the result of editorial adaptation then it must be admitted that this adjustment is unbelievably clumsy. After all, the Messianic figure does not fit that of 7:28ff., the warlike and judicial functions remain and the new eschatology is most inadequately affirmed. It is best, therefore, to see the vision as the composition of the author, employing a literary form well known to him from tradition.

III

The second major vision in which the Messiah plays a large role is the Son of Man vision, chapter 13. Here the Messiah is called "as the form of a man" or "the man" in both the vision and its interpretation. It is clear that the former title is simply a result of the mysterious style that the apocalypticists liked to affect, for in the overwhelming majority of cases he is just called "the man" or "that man."[1] In the interpretation he is also called "my servant."[2] He is pre-existent and is revealed, according to the interpretation, together with his companions (cf. 7:28). He delivers the survivors and presumably rules

---
[1]) Thus vss. 3,4,12,25,51, "as the form of a man," v.3, cf. v.32.
[2]) Vss. 32,37,52

over them, but the element of rejoicing common to 7:28 and 12:34 is not mentioned. As in the Eagle vision, he plays a central role in the events preceding the end. He is not said to be of Davidic descent, but in the interpretation his kingdom is in Palestine and the forensic features also appear.

H. Gunkel in his treatment of Visions IV, V, VI pointed out the need to distinguish between materials composed by an apocalypticist as allegories and materials which existed previously, often in mythical form, and which are employed by the apocalyptic writer as allegories. The former, he maintains, have no independent meaning while the latter do. He is not certain into which category Vision VI falls.[1]) It seems possible that a third class of materials exists, original allegories used by a later writer with a new interpretation.

If either the second or the third situation obtains it is important to bear in mind that, even if the vision was originally an independent piece later employed by the apocalypticist for his own purposes, what is important to the student of the thought of the writer is the understanding of the vision offered in his interpretation. The independent meaning of the allegory, if such be present and can be determined, may well be important from other points of view. As far as the author is concerned, he is using this allegory to convey his own ideas and provides an interpretation to make these ideas explicit.

Box maintains that this is an independent source and that the redactor is responsible for 13b-24, the middle phrase of 26, all of 29-33, 36, 48 and the reference to the companions of the Messiah in 52.[2]) The arguments against it being an independent source are in general the same as those brought to bear in the case of the Eagle vision and as there, the crucial question is one of eschatology. Box points to the following distinctive features of this source: the fact that all the heathen powers and not just the Roman empire are involved, the transcendental Son of Man as opposed to the Davidic Messiah, and the ten tribes tradition which he claims implies a situation before 70 C.E.[3])

---

[1]) Hermann Gunkel, "Das vierte Buch Esra" in *Die Apokryphen und Pseudepigraphen des alten Testaments*, II, edited by E. Kautzsch (Tubingen: Mohr, 1900), 346f.

[2]) Box, *Ezra-Apocalypse*, 286.

[3]) Box, *ibid*. C. Clemen, "Die Zusammensetzung des Buch Henoch, Ap. Baruch und IV Ezra, "*Theologische Studien und Kritiken*, 71 (1898), 244 claims that the tradition behind this vision must have been formed before the time of Pompey, for Rome does not figure as a world power. See, however, the consideration urged in the text here.

The first and third of these features are not really convincing. In the Eagle vision the author is in the context of a four empires vision and thus must talk of the Roman empire, while here he is drawing on the tradition of the eschatological war. Besides, it may be questioned whether to an author of the first century C.E. there was a great distinction between the Roman empire and all the heathen world. The ten tribes tradition is here combined with the survivors in the land and is only isolated because Box excises v.48. The features of the Messianic figure will be discussed below and then an assessment of Box's second proposition will be made.[1]

There are, however, severe literary problems which have not been treated adequately by past scholars of the book. The chapter falls into three sections: the vision (1-13a), the seer's thoughts about the vision (13b-24), and the angelic interpretation (25-53). The structure of the vision itself is fairly clear. Some seemingly anomalous features have been noted by past scholars, but these are no more problematic than those found in other apocalypses.[2] Problems of far greater gravity arise, however, in the interpretation.

The interpretation of the man is given in v.25 while that of his rising from the sea is added only at the end of the interpretation in vss.51ff. Further, vss.27f. state that the weaponlessness of the man and his fiery breath are to be interpreted. The explanation of these elements should follow immediately. Instead, there intervene seven verses (vss.

---

[1]) The basic weakness of Box's arguments for redactoral adjustment is that the work of the redactor can be distinguished from the "genuine" material only by contrasting its ideas with the "original" eschatology of the vision. This in turn can only be determined from the "original" vision without the adjustments, which of course is circular.

[2]) Thus Box, *Ezra-Apocalypse*, 282, Keulers, *Biblische Studien*, 1922, 123 and many others. Keulers, for example, raises two problems. The man both rises from the sea and flies on the clouds, and if in v.4 everyone has melted, who makes up the innumerable host of v.5? The man rising from the sea is problematic. Generally, only evil forces rise from the sea, cf. Dan. 7 : 3. In Sib. III : 72ff. a flaming power arises from the sea and destroys Beliar and in Ap. Bar. 56 : 3 a white cloud, symbolizing the length of days of the world also comes up from the sea. Gunkel, quoted by Box, and Box himself think that this may come from a star-god myth, see Box, *Ezra-Apocalypse*, 282. Gressmann, against this, is inclined to regard it as a secondary feature borrowed from Daniel 7, see H. Gressmann, *Der Ursprung der israelitisch-judischen Eschatologie* (Gottingen: Vandenhoeck und Ruprecht, 1905), 354. The Gunkel-Box explanation needs more support than is adduced. If Gressman is not correct, and his explanation is likely, then it must be concluded that the origins and nature of the tradition of good forces rising from the sea are obscure. Keulers' second problem surely arises from an overly literalistic approach to what is clearly apocalyptic hyperbole.

29-35) containing a prophecy of the woes, the gathering of the host including a reference to the man's voice which was mentioned in v.4 and which is not interpreted elsewhere, and an explanation of the mountain. Only in v.36 does the interpretation mentioned in v.28 finally appear.

Moreover, the ten tribes material seems to be an originally independent pericope. From the point of view of the vision it is unnecessarily detailed. V.48 shows signs of its integration into the interpretation.[1]) It is, however, clearly original in the present form of the piece. Another difficulty is that the companions of the Messiah introduced in v.52 are mentioned nowhere else in either the vision or the interpretation.

These considerations lead to the conclusion that the author is here writing his own interpretation to a previously existent allegory. This seems more likely than the interpolation theory developed by Box, for his hypothesis does not solve the problems of the interpretation: his original displays much the same difficulties as the text as it now stands. One other possibility is a radical reworking of an original interpretation. This might be thought to be suggested by two features. The first is the separation of the two parts of the explanation of the man rising from the sea. The other is the seemingly double explanation of the mountain.[2]) If this is so, then in any case it must be admitted that the original interpretation is now submerged beyond recovery. Only the attempt to give a new interpretation to a previously existent vision

---

[1]) The verse has no main verb in Latin and Arabic¹. This also seems to be the case in Ethiopic and Arabic² which combine it syntactically in differing ways with the preceding. Ethiopic adds at the end of v.47 instead of "in peace," "were brought up and were found in my land"; Arabic² reads "(47) and the multitude which you saw...(48) are those who remain of my people on the holy mountain." One suspects that v.48 serves to relate the ten tribes pericope, which may preserve a block of old legendary material, to the peaceful multitude of v.12 in the vision, which in context must include the survivors. This, if it is the case, is no reason for the verse to be ungrammatical. Even if it were redactional (as Box maintains) the redactor was, presumably, capable of writing complete sentences. The state of the versions indicates that the verb was lost early in the history of transmission and Syriac retains the best reading. "Your people" alongside "my borders" worries Violet, see Bruno Violet, *Die Apokalypsen des Esra und des Baruch in deutscher Gestalt* (Leipzig: Hinrichs, 1924), *ad loc*. In context, however, "your" could well refer to Ezra and the remaining two and one-half tribes in contrast to the other nine and one-half, for he is in charge of "Israel" (5 : 16). For the reading "mountain" in the Arabic versions, cf. Arabic¹ of 9 : 8, perhaps a confusion of ὄρος and ὅριον (Hilgenfeld).

[2]) Since, however, Zion and Mt. Zion are to be regarded as virtually identical, this point is not very strong.

can explain on the one hand the contrast between the closely structured allegory and the confused interpretation and on the other the general contrast between this interpretation and the clearly formulated interpretation of the Eagle vision whose originality there is no reason to doubt.

It was observed above that the Messiah is called "man" in both vision and interpretation while the title "servant" occurs only in the interpretation. "Messiah" as a title is not found. The "man" is identified in the interpretation as "my servant" in v.32 and "my servant" continues to be the subject of action in v.37. "Man" is treated by the interpretation as a symbol employed in the vision for "my servant." It thus occurs in the expository formula which first mentions the symbol to be interpreted and then gives the interpretation[1]) while on the remaining occasion, in 13:32, an identification is also given. "The man" is never the subject of action in the interpretative sections. This is significant in assessing the role of this figure in the vision as a whole; "the man" is treated in the interpretation as a symbol, just as the lion was in chapter 12. It is the symbol of the Messiah who is called "my servant."

Thus, although the representation in the vision is of a man, for the author of the interpretation this figure has to be identified as "my servant." Box, as already has been noted, characterizes the Messiah in this vision as the transcendent Son of Man. Box, Volz and others have suggested, on the basis of the title, that this man is to be identified with the *Urmensch*.[2]) In his treatment of the much more clearly defined Son of Man in I Enoch, Sjöberg concluded that while the figure was influenced by the *Urmensch*, it was not identified with him. Adam, he pointed out, takes over some of the primary features of the *Urmensch*, but the Son of Man is identified neither with Adam nor with the *Urmensch*.[3])

The actual form "Son of Man" is not found in this vision and although originally this title probably meant simply "man", the consistent use of the expression "Son of Man" in the Similitudes and the New Testament clearly shows that it early became formulaic.

---

[1]) Thus vss. 25,51. For this type of formula compare 10 : 43, 45, 47, 48, 12 : 17, 19, 22, 26, 31 and many other places in apocalypses.

[2]) Box, *Ezra-Apocalypse*, 283, P. Volz, *Judische Eschatologie von Daniel bis Akiba* (1 ed; Tubingen und Leipzig: 1903) 214f., 216f.

[3]) Sjöberg, *Menschensohn*, 190-198. On the relationship of Adam to the *Urmensch* see A. Altmann, "The Gnostic Background of the Rabbinic Adam Legends," *Jewish Quarterly Review* 35 (1944-45), 371-391.

It seems of significance for the evaluation of the place of the concept Son of Man in thought of this general period that, even if the Man in the previously existent vision of Chapter 13 was the Son of Man, this figure was not understandable as such either to the author or to his readers. Indeed, in the interpretation, not only has the author of IV Ezra shorn this figure of all its special characteristics but he even treats it as just a symbol. This would be inconceivable if the Son of Man concept was readily recognizable to him and his readers.

The major feature of the figure in the vision is as warrior, and this is emphasized far more here than it is in chapters 11-12. Contrariwise the judicial function is completely absent from the vision and is introduced only in the interpretation. The symbolism used to describe this figure in the vision is ancient, cosmic language drawn largely from the terms of Yahweh's epiphanies, especially of his epiphanies as Divine Warrior. The winds regularly precede the epiphanies of Yahweh,[1]) the clouds come before him or are his chariot.[2]) These elements also feature in Daniel 7 and, of course, this may be their direct source. Fire is also typical of theophanies and is one of the main instruments of divine destruction of enemies.[3]) The "melting" of the enemies is also appropriate to the Divine Warrior.[4])

All of these elements had been freed from the complex of God's Holy War by the time of IV Ezra, but doubtless the cosmic aura still surrounded them. It is significant, therefore, that none of them except the fiery elements is mentioned in the interpretation and these are interpreted in judicial terms. The mountain may also be connected with cosmic war as Box points out, but the interpretation clearly thought of it as Mt. Zion.[5]) Further, the figure of the mountain is obviously derived from Dan. 2:45 as the element of its unknown origin (v.7) indicates.

The cosmic features of the Son of Man in I Enoch have been mentioned. Inasmuch as the Messiah acts as warrior in the eschatological war, it is natural that the symbolism connected with the Divine Warrior be transferred to him. Yet it may be observed that one significant feature of the interpretation is the exclusion or re-interpretation

---

[1]) Cf. I Ki. 19 : 11-12, Job 40 : 6, Zech. 9 : 14 etc.
[2]) Preceding epiphanies, Ezek. 1 : 4, I Ki. 8 : 10f., Ex. 19 : 9, 16, 13 : 21, Nu. 12 : 5, 14 : 4; as the chariot of the Deity, Ugaritic Baʿal as *rkb ʿrpt*, also Ps. 104 : 3, 68 : 5, Ex 19 : 19, Nah. 1 : 3, Isa. 14 : 14, 19 : 1 etc.
[3]) Ps. 97 : 2-3 cf. I Ki. 19 : 12, II Sam. 22 : 9f. 11, Ps.18 : 9f., Ezek. 10 : 2.
[4]) Thus Ps. 97 : 5, Mic. 1 : 4, cf. Judith 16 : 15, I En. 1 : 6.
[5]) See Box, *Ezra-Apocalypse*, n.y on p. 295 and references there.

of all the cosmic elements of the vision. The forensic aspect is less prominent here than in the Eagle vision, but the treatment of it in the interpretation is virtually identical with the description there, both rebuke and destruction are present. The element of sentencing seems to be absent although this may be the meaning of v.38.[1]) In any case, the righteous word as an instrument of destruction is well known.[2])

Therefore, in view of the title "man" and the cosmic imagery applied to this figure, it may be that in the vision the Son of Man is involved. The understanding of this man in the interpretation, however, is substantially that of the Messiah in chapters 11-12. The cosmic aspects are played down, the judicial element is introduced, and features connected with the Messianic kingdom such as the woes, the survivors in the land, and so forth appear. Thus, not only does the man, central to the vision, play little role in the interpretation, but there are features of the Messiah presented by the interpretation which are not hinted at in the vision. The legal features of vss.37f. already noted, are present only in the interpretation. In contrast with this, in chapters 11-12 legal features are found in both vision and interpretation and are more strongly emphasized than here (cf. 11 : 38ff., 12 : 32ff.). The showing of wonders (v.50) has no parallel in the vision nor do the companions (v.52). The cosmic features of the vision, as noted above, are suppressed in the interpretation.

Other additional eschatological elements are to be found in the interpretation. One such is the function of the Messiah after the destruction of the host (vss.26,49f.). There is no hint of this in the vision which ends with the approach of the joyous multitude in v.13. The woes in vss.29ff. are not mentioned in the vision while such elements as the heavenly Jerusalem in v.36 and the survivors in vss.26,48 are, at most, only implicit in it.

It is surely significant that it is those elements either not mentioned or only implicit in the vision but explicit in the interpretation which show greatest connection with the rest of the book. In the case of certain of these this may be simply because the interpretation is more detailed than the vision. In the case of others, however, this is not the explanation. Some, such as the heavenly Jerusalem, occur in Box's

---

[1]) This verse may also be a reference to future judgment for "torture" is a technical term for eschatological punishment, see 8 : 59, 9 : 9, 12 (ultimate fate of the wicked), 7 : 36, 38 (Gehenna as place of torment), 7 : 75, 76, 80, 84, 86, 99 (intermediate state of the wicked souls).

[2]) See I En. 62 : 2, Wisd. Sol. 12 : 9, 18 : 15f., Isa. 11 : 4, II Thess, 2 : 8 cf. Isa. 49 : 2. Compare destruction by rebuke in chapters 11-12.

"interpolations" but others, like the companions (v.52) and the showing of wonders (v.50) are in his "original" text. Further, the special traits of the vision, the cosmic features and the outright military formulation of the Messianic figure in particular, both of which are toned down in the interpretation, are not found anywhere else in the book. Thus it may be concluded that the notion of the Messiah as formulated in the interpretation is substantially in accord with that of the Eagle vision while that of the vision, as far as can be determined, is rather different. This supports the thesis that the vision represents an independent piece while the author of the book is responsible for the interpretation.

As in chapters 11-12 and opposed to 7:28ff., the activity of the Messiah commences before the beginning of his kingdom and he is active in the overthrow of the evil nations. This is a traditional feature of the Messianic figure, one especially connected with the Messiah as warrior. The absence of the great opponent of the Messiah, the leader of the enemy host who was referred to in the four empires visions in IV Ezra and in Ap. Bar. 39ff. and who is mentioned in 5:6 may be imposed by the originally independent vision. The same reason could be argued for the activity of the Messiah before the end, but it seems safer to say that this is typical of the concept of the Messiah as warrior. In short, the Messiah presented by the author of the interpretation of chapter 13 is largely in accord with the Messiah presented elsewhere in the book. The differences that are observed are explicable in terms of the variety of traditions which are available to the author.

The only incidental reference to the Messiah in the book is to be found in 14:9. Here, in connection with the promise of assumption made to Ezra, the Messiah is introduced. The Messiah, together with the assumed righteous, is preserved until the end of times. He is called "my servant" but no information about his function and nature other than pre-existence is presented.

IV

In general, while few features of the Messianic figure are found in all passages, most are found in a majority of them and only few are completely contradictory. The Messiah is pre-existent in all texts. Where information is provided, he is expected to take care of the righteous survivors.[1] Although his kingdom is only stated to have an

---

[1] All sources except 14:9 and the vision of chapter 13.

end in 7:28ff., 12:34 cf. 11:46, it is nowhere asserted to be eternal. He is said to come with his company in 7:29, 13:52 and 14:9. This is not mentioned in chapters 11-12 or in the vision of chapter 13. The term "survivors" is common to all sources where the subject is raised except the vision of chapter 13. He is called "Messiah" in 7:26 and 12:32 and "servant" in 7:29, 13:32,37,52 and 14:9. "Man" as a title is found only in the vision of chapter 13.

Although there is some variety of tradition, the common features of the concept of the Messiah stand out. This is emphasized by certain other aspects of the material. Kingship nowhere figures in the concept of the Messiah in the book and his rule is never described in these terms. He is said to make the survivors rejoice (7:28ff., 12:34) or deliver them (12:34 cf. 13:26), to defend them (13:49) or order them (13:26). He never reigns over them. Thus the reference to the Davidic descent of the Messiah in 12:32 should probably be regarded as a traditional element and not at all central to the concepts of the book.[1]) Again, although the temporary nature of the period of Messianic rule is made explicit only in 7:28ff., 12:34 cf. 11:46, that rule is never found associated with the characteristic features of the day of judgment. It is found in the interpretation of chapter 13, however, connected with the "survivors" and the "wonders", both belonging to the cycle of ideas associated with the Messianic kingdom, even though nothing is said in that chapter about its duration. This tends to indicate that in this instance too the Messianic rule belongs to the complex of ideas which may be dubbed the "Messianic kingdom" and generally this kingdom is temporary.

The paucity of information about the nature of the Messianic age given in the two visions of chapters 11-13 highlights their emphasis on the end of the present world order, to the exclusion of any real interest in the nature of the times of the Messiah. Conversely, in 7:28f. the Messianic kingdom is only important as a stage towards the final day of judgment which is the point of emphasis of 7:26-44. But it is this passage which raises the main contradiction in the views of the Messiah and the time of his appearance. This may be a function of these differing emphases. There are two distinct traditions, but they

---

[1]) M. J. Lagrange, "Notes sur le Messianisme au temps de Jesus," *Revue Biblique* N. S. 2 (1905), 499 regards this as interpolated, see also *Revue Biblique*, N. S. 4 (1907), 615 in his review of Vagany. Perhaps, however, the lion as a symbol for the Messiah in Ch. 11-12 was suggested by the Messianic interpretation of the "lion of Judah" in Gen. 49:9f., and is a hint in the direction of the royal Messiah. Compare the use of this idea in Rev. 5:5.

are not frequent enough in occurrence in the book for it to be established whether they stem from distinct associational patterns. The overall congruence of terminology and of the view of the Messiah is, however, adequate evidence for the substantial common authorship of these passages.[1])

The role of the Messiah in the total eschatological thought of IV Ezra is difficult to assess. He takes up the whole attention of chapter 13 and plays a significant role in chapters 11-12. It would seem, therefore, that he is of considerable importance. The Messiah, however, figures in few passages outside these two visions. He is mentioned only once in the first three visions with their detailed discussion of eschatological matters. This is the more significant when it is recalled that that single reference (7:28f.) is in the most comprehensive catalogue of eschatology. The reason for this may well be that the Messiah was not the answer to the questions that Ezra was asking. His absence from 6:25 adds further weight to this conclusion. Thus the place of the Messiah in the author's eschatological scheme cannot be doubted, yet it is misleading to see him as the exclusive center of his aspirations.

---

[1]) The view of the independent piece, the vision of chapter 13 is rather different. The title "man," the cosmic elements, the out and out military function, and the absence of any of the other common features except pre-existence distinguish this passage.

IV
HISTORY OF JUDAISM

ON THE SHAPE OF GOD AND THE HUMANITY OF GENTILES

BY

MORTON SMITH

Columbia University

In an article, "The Image of God: Notes on the Hellenization of Judaism, with especial reference to Goodenough's work on Jewish symbols," printed in 1958 in the *Bulletin of the John Rylands Library*,[1]) I presented evidence which seemed to me to show that, on the one hand, passages in rabbinic literature justified Goodenough's interpretation of a number of symbols, notably those of the menorah and the tree, as, at least occasionally, images of God, on the other hand, these and similar passages cast grave doubt on his account of "the rabbis" as out of touch with Hellenistic culture and hostile to the religion of the majority of Greco-Roman Jews, the religion expressed by the pictures on the archaeological material.

In 1960 appeared J. Jervell's *Imago Dei: Gen.* 1.26 *f. im Spätjudentum, in der Gnosis und in den paulinischen Briefen*,[2]) which included (pp. 71-121) an extended study of the rabbinic notions as to the image of God in man. Jervell had evidently not seen my paper (which must have come out shortly before or after his book went to the publisher). In any event, the results of his study not only differed from, but in some points contradicted, those which I had reached. The differences resulted in part from a difference of purpose: Jervell's concern was to survey the whole of rabbinic teaching on the subject; mine, to point out one important but neglected strand of it. These differences need not concern us further. The contradictions, however, deserve discussion, and I think it appropriate to discuss them here, not only because my former paper dealt with Goodenough's work, but also because the questions involved—the range of rabbinic opinions concerning the human body's likeness to God, and therefore concerning

---

[1]) Vol. 40, No. 2, pp. 473-512. Offprints are available from, The Librarian, The John Rylands Library, Deansgate, Manchester, 3, England.

[2]) Göttingen, Vandenhoeck and Ruprecht, 1960 (*Forschungen zur Religion und Literatur des Alten und Neuen Testaments*, N. F. 58).

gentiles—are fundamental for study of one of the great problems Goodenough's work has raised, that of the relationship between the material which he collected and the rabbinic literature. To have raised such problems was among Goodenough's most important accomplishments; the study of them henceforth should be seen as a continuing tribute to his memory.

Let me begin this study by summarizing the results of Jervell's survey. He distinguishes what he thinks the public, "official" teaching from the discussions of the rabbinic schools. The public teaching, he finds, was primarily concerned to maintain that God alone created man, that man was not created in the image of God, and that man was not created androgynous (p. 119). The school discussions, on the other hand, were concerned to explain the statement, that man was created in the image of God, so as to make it useful either for ethical teaching or for pseudo-historical glorification of Israel and the Law. For these purposes they started from common suppositions: The Law was the motive and means of creation. Israel was created to observe the Law. So was Adam. Adam before his fall was therefore the prime and perfect Israelite; the creation of man was the creation of Israel. Consequently the non-Israelite is not a man. Consequently, in rabbinic school-discussions, the term "man", when used without further specification, means "Israelite", and only Israelites have any likeness to God (pp. 78-84).

Starting from these presuppositions, two interpretations of Gen. 1.26 f. developed. One was "ethical-anthropological": It maintained that man was created in the likeness of the angels, whom the Old Testament sometimes calls "gods"; he was like the angels in possessing *da'ath*, standing erect and speaking Hebrew, but not in body.[1] *Da'ath*, his most important likeness to the angels, is essentially the power both to distinguish and to choose between good and evil; but only those who choose good retain it(?), at any rate, true likeness to "God", *sc.* to the angels, is possessed only by righteous Israelites. Other men are like animals except for upright stature and economic life. Consequently, all obligations towards "men" *qua* images of "God" are obligations only towards Isrealites (pp. 84-96). The other interpretation was "speculative-protological": It admitted that Adam was created in the image of God, declared him greater than the angels, but found his likeness to God essentially in his *kabod* which was above all "*eine mora-*

---

[1] How it is possible to be alike in upright stature without having some bodily likeness, Jervell does not explain. Cp. his statements on pp. 86 and 90.

lische Grösse", *i.e.* it consisted in his being a Law-abiding Israelite. This was lost at the fall, so all men are Adam's descendants, but only the Israelites are in his image, since they only can possess the *kabod* which, with the Law, was given Israel at Sinai (pp. 96-119).

It must be said at once that this summary is necessarily somewhat unfair, since one cannot summarize without suppressing the author's recognition and discussion of material which he thinks divergent from the main pattern. Jervell several times recognizes the danger of systematization, but, in the end, he produces a system, and one which is itself, like the above, a summary, and shares the same necessary weakness. At all events, we are concerned here with only two points in his summary, the propositions that man's likeness to God is not a matter of bodily form, and that in rabbinic usage *'adam* ("man") means "an Israelite." "Cattle and heathen are not אדם." (*sic*, p. 82.)

First as to bodily form: For his conclusion on this point—that man's bodily form is not thought an element of his likeness to God—Jervell argues (pp. 88 ff.) that Adam was thought to possess knowledge of good and evil before the fall when he was "as One," *i.e.* as God, Targum Jonathan on Gen. 3.22. (But here the likeness is said to be, not knowledge of good and evil, but uniqueness.) From Adam will arise a people able to distinguish between good and evil, *ib.* (But this is merely a forced exegesis of ממנו לדעת טוב ורע; its purpose is to avoid the plain sense of *mimmennu* and it has nothing to do with the question of the nature of Adam's likeness to God.) Further, when Adam ist justified at the end he will be as God, Gen. Rabba 21.2 (read 21.1. This likeness will result from justification, but what it will consist of is not stated.) That he "was as one of us" is explained by his having been created in God's image, Num. Rabba 16.24 (16.15 in my edition. But here the likeness is said to have been immortality.) "See also" Eccles. Rabbati on 7.29 (here the likeness is righteousness) and Cant. Rabba on 1.9. (This last is one of a set of texts collected by Theodore in his notes on Gen. Rabba 21.5. They include the Mekilta passage which Jervell cites as "Beschalla—*sic*—7,73 ff". meaning, ed. Lauterbach, p. 248, lines 73 ff., and further parallels which he does not cite. The tangle offers only one explanation of Adam's likeness to God—his uniqueness.) Further Jervell cites Abot 3.14, where Akiba says Adam (or, "man?") was created in the image of God, but gives no indication of what he thought this meant; knowledge of the Law can hardly be intended, since the same saying declares *that* a greater blessing given to Israel. (Against Jervell's attempt to limit the reference of the entire saying to Israelites, see Tosafot Yom Tob, *ad loc*, which argues at length for reference of the first half to all children of Noah.) Next comes Dt. Rabba 4.4 and, as parallels to it, Midrash Pss. 17.8 and 50.3 (a false reference.) Dt. Rabba 4.4 says that an angelic escort precedes the righteous man and proclaims, "Make way for the image of God," and Jervell takes this as proof that the image exists *only* in the righteous. *Non sequitur*. Finally he concludes, p. 90, that "The passages cited above indicate that the human body has no likeness to God." This is false. Some of the passages indicate some respects in which man is or may be like God, but none discusses at all the question of bodily likeness, and there is no justification for an argument from silence about a matter with which they are not concerned.

To strengthen this argument Jervell now cites Sifre Dt. 306, ed. Friedmann 132a, where it is said that man's soul is heavenly, but his body earthly; therefore if he obeys the Law he will be, like the heavenly creatures, immortal, "for it is written, 'I said, "You are gods, and all of you sons of the Most High;"'" if not, he will be like the earthly creatures, "for it is written, 'None the less, you shall die like men'". This concerns the substance of man and is irrelevant to the question of similarity of *form*, which is the normal relationship of an image to its original. The same is true of the cognate passages Jervell cites in this connection: Tanhuma, ed. Buber, *Bereshit* 15, and Pirqe R. Eliezer 11. Pesiqta Rabbati 21, ed. Friedmann "108b" (read a-b), which he also cites, does not say as he supposes that "only ... the soul has been created in God's image," but that the soul was created in God's likeness (דמות) and the body was joined to it and made like God's image (צלם); it thus expounds the two words as referring, one to the soul, the other to the body, and is explicit evidence that some rabbis thought man was *bodily* like the image of God.

Other evidence for the same opinion is plentiful. It was discussed at length by A. Marmorstein, *The Old Rabbinic Doctrine of God, II, Essays in Anthropomorphism*,[1]) who advanced the thesis that in Palestinian Judaism there were two schools of thought, one which took the anthropomorphisms of the Bible literally, another which allegorized them. Though many of the particular applications which he made of this theory remain dubious, he gave strong evidence for his main contention, "that there was a school in Judaism, and an important one, too, that believed in a God who accompanies man in human form and shape" (p. 52). To this Jervell, though citing the work in other connections,

---

[1]) Oxford, 1937 (*Jews' College Publications*, 14).

did not refer. Marmorstein also fully documented the anti-anthropomorphic side of Jewish tradition, which is, of course, familiar. His thesis has now been greatly strengthened by G. Scholem's demonstration, in *Jewish Gnosticism, Merkabah Mysticism, and Talmudic Tradition* (2 ed., N.Y., 1965, pp. 36 ff.) that the so called *Shi'ur Qomah* speculation, which concerns the dimensions of the various parts of God's anthropomorphic body, goes back, as an important secret doctrine within rabbinic circles, at least to the second century A.D. and probably beyond.

In this connection a number of the passages which I cited in *The Image of God* would, at first sight, seem conclusive. So, for instance, Lev. Rabba 34.3, which reports that once, when Hillel was about to leave his disciples, they said to him, "'Rabbi, where are you going?' He said to them, 'To perform a commandment.' They said to him, 'And what, then, is this commandment?' ... He said to them, 'To bathe in the (public) bath.' They said to him, 'And is this a commandment?' He said to them, 'Yes. If the man who is appointed to take care of the images of kings, which (the gentiles) set up in their theaters and circuses, scours them and rinses them, and they provide his livelihood, and not only that, but he occupies an important place among government officials; then we, who were created in the image and in the likeness (of God) ... *a fortiori*.'" Substantially the same story appears in Abot de R. Nathan, text B, ch. 30 (ed. Schechter, 33b), as a comment on the words, "And let all they acts be for the sake of Heaven," (*i.e.* of God). It should be noticed, by the way, that the failure to specify *whose* image and likeness, can hardly be thought significant as an avoidance of anthropomorphism (*contra* Jervell, p. 85). This is a standard form of reference to a text everybody knew by heart, the omission of "God's" is merely a scribal abbreviation. This is particularly clear from the fact that often, when the abbreviation is used, a proof text, commonly Gen. 9.6, with "God's" written out in full, immediately follows. So it does, for instance, in the passage just cited.

This passage, as remarked above, would at first sight seem conclusive. If Hillel expected reward for washing the image of God, and considered that man's likeness to God made bathing a religious obligation, one would suppose there would be little doubt as to where he thought the likeness lay. He was not going to wash his observance of the Law. But a theologian might argue that the body was reverenced only as the instrument for the observance. Jervell presumably had some similar argument in mind when he cited, p. 81, from Abot de Rabbi Nathan

"2" (read, text A, 2) the statement that Adam must have been born circumcised because it is said that God created Adam in his image. (Jervell's citation contains six mistakes in ten words of Hebrew.) The naïve reader might suppose this indicated belief in a circumcised deity, but Jervell glosses the statement, "Das heisst, dass er צדיק und תמים (sic) war." Circumcision is merely the symbol of legal observance; since the deity is the cause of the Law, the circumcised man resembles Him as effect resembles cause. But rabbinic texts contain very few philosophic arguments of this sort, and a great many anthropomorphisms. Therefore (though I should insist that many rabbis had some acquaintance with philosophy, cf. *Image of God*, pp. 474 f.) I think it more plausible to suppose that the anthropomorphisms indicate their usual way of thought, and that philosophical arguments are not to be read into rabbinic texts without good reason.

In this instance, moreover, there is good reason for supposing anthropomorphism: Midrash Tannaïm on Dt. 21.23 (ed. Hoffmann, p. 132) explains the commandment that the *dead* body of an executed criminal is not to be left hanging on a tree over night, "'because a hanged man is an insult to God.' Rabbi Me'ir said, ...' (It is like) two brothers who were identical twins and lived in the same city. One was made king, and the other became a bandit. The king commanded (that the bandit be hung up after execution) so they strung him up. Everyone who saw (the dead body) said, "The king has been hung up." So the king commanded and they took him down.'" It seems that the similarity supposed here was not the executed criminal's obedience to the Law, nor his dead body's capacity to obey it, but the sheer similarity of external, physical form. R. Me'ir's exegesis was taken over, with his name, into the legal collections, Tosefta San. 9.7 (Zuckermandel 429); San. 46b.

It seems, then, that the Biblical statements concerning man's likeness to God were interpreted in many different ways which were not thought to be mutually exclusive, and that among the interpretations was the opinion, held by some very important rabbis, that man's body was made as an image of God. From this opinion it follows that all men are images of God in one respect at least, since all possess essentially the same bodily form. This conclusion might be taken as a refutation of Jervell's claim that only Isrealites were thought to be images of God, and the term "man" referred only to them. On the other hand, Jervell would argue that this claim, which he had established with other evidence, refuted our conclusion. We must therefore examine his evidence.

First, however, it must be admitted that the normal usage of *'adam* ("man") in rabbinic material is determined by the contexts in which it occurs. These are mostly legal, and since the Law was accepted only by Israel most of its provisions concern Israelites alone. Thus when the Mishnah says that the sages ruled the *shema'* must be read before midnight "in order to keep a man far from transgression," (Berakot 1.1) or that the school of Shammai says, "in the evening all men should recline when they read it," (*ib*. 1.3) the reference is of course to Israelites only. But it would be absurd to take such passages as evidence that the rabbis always used "man" in this restricted sense or thought those who did not read the *shema'* were not human.

Such an interpretation would, moreover, be indefensible, because there are many passages in rabbinic literature where *'adam* and *bene 'adam* ("children of men," *i.e.* men) are used to refer to all human beings. For instance, Baba Qama 38a, in a dispute as to whether or not gentiles are rewarded for observance of the Noachite laws, reports, "Rabbi Me'ir says, 'Whence (do we know) that even a gentile who works at the Law is as a high priest? (Because) the Bible says that "if a man will practice (my laws and my judgements) he will live, as a result of them." (Lev. 18.5). It is not said, "If priests, Levites and Israelites (will practice them)," but "If a man." Hence you must conclude that even a gentile who works at the Law is as a high priest." This is repeated in Sanhedrin 59a with the added explanation that "a gentile who works at the Law" is one who observes perfectly the Noachite commandments, and also in 'Abodah Zarah 3a with the explanation that gentiles who perform these commandments are not rewarded as performing commandments (since God long ago withdrew the Noachite commandments because of the gentiles' general failure to perform) but as persons who do good deeds without being commanded. (So their performance is *not* observance of the Law; they are wholly outside the Law.) A third repetition in Sifra, *'ahare mot* 13, on Lev. 18.5, has been contaminated with a different saying which limited the benefits of the Law to the righteous, as opposed to all Israel. It is worth noting that this opinion of Rabbi Me'ir accords with his opinion cited above, that the human likeness to God is *inter alia* a matter of similarity of form, wherefore all men are images of God. For other passages which clearly recognize that *'adam* refers to "human beings", including gentiles, see the exegeses of Ex. 9.9 f.; Lev. 18.5; Num. 31.40; II Sam. 7.19; Jer. 32.20; Ezek. 28.2; Jonah 4.11; Pss. 115.16; 118.6. These suffice to determine the reference in many other usages, for instance the technical expression, *ma'akal 'adam*, "human food," as opposed to food fit only for the lower animals, *ma'akal behemah*. For the same sense of *bene 'adam* see Gittin 47a, where Ps. 115.16 ("As for the heavens, the heavens belong to Yahweh, but he gave the earth to *bene 'adam*.") is used to prove that gentiles may acquire land in Palestine in order to develop water supplies there. In Sanhedrin 104b one Israelite prisoner says to another, about their guard, "The camel walking in front of us is blind in one of its eyes, ... and of the two *bene 'adam* who are leading it, one is an Israelite and the other a gentile." In Nedarim 32a (end) Abraham is said to have been at fault because, after defeating the kings, he permitted the *bene 'adam* in the spoil to be taken away from him; he should have made them proselytes. In Tosefta Baba Mezi'a 9.33 (Zuckermandel 393) we have the ruling that if a lessee sublets a piece of property the owner may tell him, "I have no contract with any man (*'im kol 'adam*) except you." (*i.e.* you continue to be responsible for everything specified by your lease, regardless of what the subtenant does). Clearly, *'adam* here excludes gentiles as well as Israelites, and so it does in many similar negative passages. These, in turn, justify the supposition that the same sense is to be understood in many other passages, for instance Tosefta Baba Qama 2.12 (Z. p. 349), when it states that cattle customarily walk in the center of a road, and *bene 'adam*, on the sides; or in the common expression, דברה תורה כלשון בני אדם, "the Law expressed itself as men ordinarily do."

Thus the primary meaning of *'adam* ("human being") was well established in rabbinic usage, but in legal contexts the word was commonly used to mean "a man," *sc.* "any ordinary man to whom the law under discussion applies," *i.e.* any male, adult, free, sane Israelite. When the Mishnah lists the things "a man" must say on the eve of Sabbath (2.7), it of course does not bother to add that the obligation is not incumbent on women, children, slaves, fools and gentiles. But in other contexts the reference of the term, as the reference of the law, may be extended to include any or all of these classes. Consequently there are many discussions as to the exact extent of reference of one or another law.

One group of these discussions did much to mislead Jervell. It consists of a number of passages in which Ezekiel 34.31 ("And you, my flock, ... you are *'adam*.") is used to prove that in one or another Biblical law the word *'adam* refers only to Israelites. This application of Ezekiel 34.31 seems to have been first thought of by Rabbi Simon ben Yohai, who used the verse to prove that the laws on the impurity of a dead body, since they begin with the words, "Should an '*adam* die in a tent," (Num. 19.14) apply only to Israelites; gentiles, he argued, being excluded from the scope of this law, were (*in this respect*) like animals, which admittedly neither produced nor contracted this sort of uncleanness. Ben Yohai's exegesis and conclusions did not go unchallenged. It was objected that in Num. 31.40 and Jonah 4.11 the word '*adam* undoubtedly referred to gentiles. He agreed that this was so, but argued that in those passages the word for "human being" had to be used to refer to gentiles for the sake of the contrasts, required by the contexts, between them, *qua* humans, and animals; in Num. 19.14 there was no such contrast, therefore the narrower interpretation, indicated by Ezekiel's statement, might be used. He thus acknowledged the broader meaning of '*adam* and argued only for its more limited sense in this particular law. (Thus Yebamot 61a, Baba Mezi'a 114b.) In Keritot 6b we find ben Yohai(?) again using Ezekiel 34.31, to prove that Ex. 30.32, which prohibits the application of sacred ointment to the flesh of an '*adam*, prohibits its use only on Israelites, not on gentiles. Here, too, he has to meet the same objections, and meets them by the same admission. His arguments found some acceptance. For example, later Rabbi Levi, interpreting Gen. 9.5 ("From the hand of a the '*adam* ... I shall require the life of the '*adam*.") used Ezekiel 34.31 in the same way to limit the reference of (*only*) the second '*adam* to Israelites. The survival of both interpretations is shown by the exegesis of Gen. 9.6 ("He who sheds the blood of an '*adam*, by an '*adam* shall his blood be shed.") Here one string of passages takes the first '*adam* as referring only to Israelites (Tosefta Sanhedrin 11.4, Z. 431; Sifre Zutta on Num. 35.12; Sanhedrin 72b; etc.) while another takes the law as one of the commandments given to and therefore originally concerning all the children of Noah (Sanhedrin 57a; Gen. Rabba 34.14, etc.).

Of the above passages Jervell (82 f.) neglects those indicating the broader sense of '*adam* and misunderstands those which limit the sense to Israelites. He does not realize that they are concerned with the question of the scope of particular laws, but thinks them definitions of the term '*adam* regardless of its context. Thus he arrives at the amazing conclusions summarized above. These he bolsters by a great number of false arguments, of which the largest collection is on pp. 81 ff. These pages I shall now go through point by point:

Abot de Rabbi Nathan 2 (*sc.* of text A) says Adam was like God because circumcised; Jervell concludes that only the circumcised are like God. But it is possible to resemble God in other respects, see above. (Here Jervell cites, as if in support of his opinion, Goldin's translation, p. 180, n. 5. Read 45. But the note points out that circumcision is merely one condition of prefection. It is evidently supposed that there are others.)

Abot de Rabbi Nathan 37 (again text A): Man is like the angels because he speaks Hebrew. Jervell: Therefore only those who speak Hebrew are like the angels. Again one has to add, "in this respect"! Moreover, the parallel in Gen. Rabba 8.11 omits "Hebrew," which suggests that the similarity was originally the gift of speech. This suggestion is confirmed by the fact that the other similarities specified— erect stature, understanding, and the ability to see out of the corners of the eye—are also universal human characteristics, two of them, by the way, bodily, which settles the question of the shape of angels, who were also made "in the image and in the likeness" of Guess Who (cp. Jervell, pp. 84 f.).

Gen. Rabba 8.12 Jervell has evidently quoted from an inferior text. In Theodore's edition the passage in question reads, "Rabbi Hanina said, 'If (Adam) lives a virtuous life, (the commandment, Gen. 1.28), "Have dominion (over the animals), "(will be fulfilled), and if he does not live a virtuous life, (the prophecy), "And they shall be subject" (to the animals).'" (This "prophecy" is produced by a different vocalization of Gen. 1.26.) "Rabbi Jacob of Kefar Hanan said, 'To that which is in our image and our likeness (*i.e.* Adam before the fall), "Let them have dominion" (applies); to that which is not in our likeness (Adam after the fall), "And they shall be subject."'" This is the familiar notion that Adam lost the divine likeness as a result of the fall. As we have seen, it by no means prevented many rabbis from recognizing that men were still, at least in some respects, images of God. The notion and the recognition were by no means irreconcilable: Likeness to God seems often to have been thought of as a complex relationship, of which some elements could be lost and others retained.

"Mekilta, *Shir* 9" (ed. Lauterbach, pp. 75 f., lines) "120 ff. on Ex. 15.16 says that (*sic*), וארץ (*sic*) שמים (cp. Gen. 1.1) is Israel." (pp. 81-82). It does not. "See also Kohelet Rabbati I.4 § 4" (*i.e.* 1.9, on 1.4). This says that in the Bible the term *'erez* (*sometimes*) refers to Israel, as in the expression, "the captivity of the *'arez*" (Judges 18.30), which is literally "the captivity of the land," but of course means, "the captivity of Israel." Therefore the commentator concludes that in Eccles. 1.4 *'erez* may also refer to Israel. And Jervell takes this as evidence that the first man created was an Israelite! "And Sifre Deut. 37, 76a+b." This, too, is irrelevant (praise of Palestine).

To prove that "man" means "Israelite", Jervell uses Mishnah Sanhedrin 4.5, which he reads as saying, "the Biblical text indicates that anyone who destroys one Israelite life is as guilty as if he destroyed a whole world." In n. 46 (p. 82) he remarks that Beer-Holtzmann, in their edition of the Mishnah, said that some MSS omitted the word "Israelite" and preferred this reading. This preference, Jervell says, was a mistake, due to the fact that they did not understand that "man" means "Israelite". Thus the reading proves the principle and the principle determines the reading (and the circle is the most elegant form of argument).

Ex. Rabba 30.16: Anyone who strikes the image of a king must die, so must anyone who destroys a single Israelite life. Rabbi W. Braude tells me that A. Hallevi, in his edition of Ex. Rabba, omits "Israelite" (*beYisra'el*) and cites in support of his omission the Oxford and Jerusalem MSS and the parallel in Makiri, Here Jervell, n. 47, again refers to Goldin's ed. of Abot de Rabbi Nathan, this time to p. 204, n. 4. But Goldin there says that Schechter's addition of "Israelite" in a cognate passage (ARN, text A, 31; parallel San. 4.5, see above) is *not* justified by the sources. "Also in Num. Rabba 16.24 the original likeness to God is referred only to Israel." I can find nothing in or near Num. Rabba 16.24 which might justify this statement, but editions differ.

"See also Ex. Rabba 40.1." This is one of the instances discussed above, where Ezek. 34.31 is used to determine the extent of the reference of '*adam* in a Biblical verse, here Job 28.28, God said to '*adam*, "The fear of the Lord, that is wisdom." This is interpreted (perhaps correctly) as meaning, God said to Israel. Jervell seems to have taken this as justifying his statement that "The heathen first becomes human when he is converted to Judaism." To this he appends a note (48a) appealing, for further support, to the many statements: (1) That the newly baptized proselyte is as a newborn child. (This is a legal fiction meaning that he has lost all debts, including those of suffering due for sins, and also all property rights, including claims over children, claims to have fulfilled commandments, etc. These consequences are also misunderstood by Jervell in his n. 51. The legal fiction does *not* include making the convert a born Israelite. In prayers, for instance, when referring to the patriarchs, he must say "their"—Israel's—"ancestors", not "our ancestors", *cf*. Bikkurim 1.4 etc.) (2) That one who converts a heathen is, as it were, his creator, (3) That an Israelite who repents is, as it were, a new creature. (These are homiletic exaggerations from the simple fact that conversion and repentance are means of salvation *i.e.*, life; the same sort of thing is given legal consequence in the equally frequent statements that a man's obligation to his teacher takes precedence of that to his parents. This has obviously nothing to do with the question whether gentiles—or Israelite parents—are human.) Here belong the references to Cant. Rabba 1.3 § 3 (*i.e.* 1.22 on 1.3) and Bekorot 47a, misplaced in Jervell's text. And from here he goes on to argue from Baba Meziʻa 114b; Keritot 6b; and Yebamot 61a, all of them passages of which his misunderstanding has been discussed above.

The question as to whether or not Cain was an Israelite (pp. 82-3) is irrelevant to that of the humanity of gentiles after the flood, all of the latter being descendants of Noah.

Gen. Rabba (read, 39.14) 39.4 "is another example of the homiletic exaggeration" considered in the preceding paragraph, class (2).

Hullin 91b does not justify the statement that Israel is considered the "himmlisches Urbild des Menschen".

This concludes the main body of Jervell's arguments for his thesis that rabbinic thought on the question of man's likeness to God began from the assumption that only Israelites are human. It seems to me that the quality of the arguments, as revealed by this examination of the main body, makes it unnecessary to deal in detail with the minor, collateral ones scattered through the rest of the work. The origin of the error was presumably in a misunderstanding of the texts discussed above, pp. 323-325, but the extension of this misunderstanding to so many irrelevant passages and the neglect of almost all the evidence to the contrary seem to me the results of a gift for systematic theology which is a great handicap in the study of rabbinic literature.

THE FACADE OF HEROD'S TEMPLE, AN ATTEMPTED RECONSTRUCTION

BY

M. AVI-YONAH

The Hebrew University, Jerusalem

Jewish tradition knows of four ways of interpreting the Scriptures —all summed up in the mnemonic word *PaRDeS* (lit. "orchard"), which is formed of the first letters of the words *Peshat, Remez, Derush, Sod*, referring respectively to the plain, the typological, the homiletical and the symbolic method of interpretation. E. R. Goodenough was a master of both the *remez* and the *sod*; in the following pages an attempt will be made to apply the "plain" method of archaeological interpretation to two items in his monumental work.[1]) By combining them with other remains of Jewish and Classical antiquity we shall try to arrive at an idea how the facade of Herod's Temple might have looked.

We shall begin with the earlier of the two objects in evidence: the representation of a tetrastyle facade on the obverse of the tetradrachms of Simeon Bar Kosiba (Bar Kochba). (Pl. I). This representation has been the subject of a recent study;[2]) in the following paragraphs we have drawn on the rich material collected by Mrs. Alice Muehsam in her monograph. We shall take as our guiding principle that "architecture on coins always represents an actual building." The coin engraver might omit, abbreviate or simplify, but he did not invent.[3])

With this rule in mind there can be only one building represented on the coins of a Jewish ruler who took arms at the time when a foreign conqueror threatened to set up a pagan temple on the hallowed site of the ancient Sanctuary. The image on the coin could refer neither to an imaginary Temple "in heaven" not to the Torah shrine or "Ark of

---

[1]) *Jewish Symbols in the Greco-Roman Period*, New York, I, 1953, pp. 276-277, III, No. 692, and Vol. IX, 1964, pp. 68-71, Pl. III and Fig. 66.
[2]) Alice Muehsam: *Coin and Temple* (Near Eastern Researches, I) Leeds, 1966.
[3]) Ibid. p. 2, quoting Bluma L. Trell: *The Temple of Artemis at Ephesus* (NNM 107), New York, 1945, pp. 4-6, 12 and D. F. Brown: *Temples of Rome as Coin Types* (NNM, 90), New York, 1940, p. 13f.

Law."[1]) The latter, actually a cupboard in which the scrolls were kept in places of prayer, was in itself a highly venerated object, but one found in hundreds of synagogues in the Holy Land and the Diaspora. It might have been used by the Maccabees, who rose in the defence of the Law. Hadrian however, against whom the revolt of Bar Kosiba was directed did not (at this stage) endanger the survival of the Torah. The "Torah shrine" which was the visible symbol of the Law would hardly be a suitable symbol for the obverse of the largest denomination struck by a revolutionary government, dedicated to the defence of the Holy City and the Temple Mount against a proposed desecration, and marking its coins with the legend "Deliverance of Israel", "Freedom of Israel" and "Jerusalem". Notwithstanding the various difficulties with which we shall deal in the following, we shall take it *a priori* that the building represented is the Temple.

It might be argued that at the time the tetradrachms of Bar Kosiba were struck the Temple had been in ruins for sixty-two years; but even so its remains must still have been a landmark in liberated Jerusalem. The sanctuary erected by Herod was built of marble,[2]) wood gilt copper and gold. Assuming that the wood had burnt and the metals were melted down and looted, there would still remain an enormous mass of stone, enough for a building with a facade 164 feet high and wide as much. As far as we know there were no building activities on the Temple Mount between 70 and 132; for the preparations for the erection of the temple of Jupiter Capitolinus as planned by Hadrian could hardly have been far advanced when the revolt broke out. There could thus be no serious difficulty for the engravers commissioned by Bar Kosiba to depict the fallen sanctuary as still standing and thus express the hope of its speedy restoration. Moreover there were surely a few old men still alive in Jerusalem who remembered the Temple in all its glory. We learn from Haggai 2:3, that in 519 B.C. there were in Jerusalem people who had seen the First Temple, (i.e. after 67 years), as compared with the 62 years separating the revolt of Bar Kosiba from the fall of Jerusalem.

In fact we cannot even exclude the possibility that the facade shown on the coins became a reality in the course of time. Bar Kosiba and his men held Jerusalem for about three years, during most of which the

---

[1]) For the latter view see Goodenough, *op. cit.* (p. 327, note 1), I, p. 277; Muehsam, *op. cit.* (note 2 above), p. 13; A. Reifenberg: *Ancient Hebrew Art* New York, 1950, p. 122; B. Kanael: *Die Kunst der antiken Synagoge*, Munchen, 1961, p. 15.

[2]) *Bab. Sukkah* 51 b lists the three kinds of marble used in the Temple.

PLATE I

Tetradrachm of Bar Kosiba (obverse).

Plate II

Temple of Bel, Palmyra. (short side).

Dura-Europos synagogue. Fresco over Thorah shrine.

PLATE III

PLATE IV

1. Drawing of the ornament on dome, Double gate.

2. Tetradrachm of Bar Kosiba, showing wavy Crenellation.

fighting was fairly distant from the Holy City. During this time there was no rival authority in Jerusalem, and there were no fratricidal struggles such as marred the First Revolt. There was therefore nothing which would divert the energies of the priestly authorities, headed by "Eleazar the Priest" who sometimes appears on the coins of the Second Revolt, from restoring the Temple facade. There was certainly a scriptural precedent for the resumption of the sacrifices, as happened during the interval between the destruction of the First Temple and the dedication of the Second.[1]) There was no reason therefore why the architectural design on the coins of Bar Kosiba should not have been clothed in the course of a couple of years with a show of substance.

If we compare the details of the representation on the coin with the extant literary evidence, we find that neither of our principal sources, the Mishna or Josephus, have anything to say about how the facade of the Temple looked actually. We are only told of an enormously high open portal, leading into the "porch."[2]) This AV term (*'ulam* in Hebrew) has been wrongly understood to refer to a prostyle. The so-called "porch" was however—as we learn from the Mishna—a room enclosed by walls, which served as the antechamber of the Sanctuary proper. In any case the four columns represented on the coin could not have been freestanding for technical reasons, as we shall see.

At this point we may compare the Temple of Jerusalem with another contemporary edifice, which shows a similar mixture of Greek and Oriental elements, the temple of Bel at Palmyra, built between 44 B.C. and A.D. 32.[3]) The similarity between the political and social conditions and the artistic tendencies prevalent in Palmyra and Jerusalem is in evidence throughout the Herodian period.[4]) The temple in Palmyra differs from that in Jerusalem in its plan, for its is a peripteral broadhouse. If we compare, however, the *short* side of its cella (Pl. II) with the facade represented on the Bar Kosiba coin, the resemblance is

---

[1]) Ezra 3 : 3.
[2]) Mishna *Middot* 3 : 7; "40 cubits high, 20 cubits wide"; Josephus, *War* V, 208: "75 cubits high, 25 wide". Notwithstanding the contrary opinion of L. H. Vincent and Alice Muehsam (*op. cit.* p. 6) the Mishna seems on the whole the more trustworthy evidence. The Jewish sages who compiled it expected it that future generations would rebuild the Temple according to the specifications transmitted, and had therefore every inducement to be scrupulously exact, whereas Josephus, who wrote for Gentiles about a buulding in ruins at the time of writing, had no such motivation.
[3]) L. Crema: *L'architettura romana*, Torino 1959, p. 180, Figs. 173-174; for date see H. Seyrig, *Syria* 31 (1940), p. 326.
[4]) M. Avi-Yonah: *Oriental Art in Roman Palestine*, Roma, 1961, pp. 25-26.

striking. The whole wall at Palmyra is divided into three units by a pair of half pillars in the corners and a pair of half-columns in the centre.[1]) If we consider the height of the Temple facade the impossibility of freestanding columns 164 feet high is evident; but this objection does not apply to engaged columns such as were used in Palmyra.

If we assume that the tetrastyle on the Bar Kosiba coins is an image of Herod's temple, we have next to identify the arched entity shown between the two columns in the centre. The current identification of this image is with the Ark of the Covenant,[2]) mainly on the strength of the representations of this object in the Dura frescoes and the Capernaum synagogue. This interpretation is, however, only acceptable if we regard the structure shown on the coin as an imaginary reconstruction of the Temple of Solomon. For while it is true that—following a numismatic convention of the period—the engraver could space out the centre columns of a prostyle temple in order to show the cult-image within the cella (and thus identify the temple itself), this would by no means apply to the present case, since the Jews knew well enough that the Ark was one of the object of the First Temple which was missing from the Second[3]) and could by no means serve to identify the latter.

In order to arrive at a solution of this conundrum we have to call to our aid another representation of a tetrastyle connected with a Jewish source, the central object in the fresco above the Torah niche in the synagogue of Dura-Europos (Pl. III). This structure has from the very time of its discovery been compared with the tetrastyle on the Bar-Kosiba coin. The similarity between the two is indeed striking and has been noted by all commentators.[4]) With regard to the edifice as a whole there is indeed a discrepancy in the partial fluting of the columns as depicted in the fresco when compared with the full-length flutings on the coin. However in all other details, from the partitioned "crepidoma" to the semi-circular antefixes[5]) the parallel is most convincing.

Matters are different, however, as regards the centre of the representation. At Dura-Europos we have indeed again an arched struc-

---

[1]) A. Champdor: *Les ruines de Palmyre*, Paris, 1953, p. 104 and plate facing it.
[2]) Muehsam, *op cit*.. (p. 317, note 2), pp. 7-14 and the literature quoted there, to which add A. Kindler- *Thesaurus of Judaean Coins*, Jerusalem, 1958, No. 19a. Others saw in it the Ark of the Law, see note 4 above.
[3]) *Bab. Yoma* 21 b.
[4]) Du Mesnil de Buisson: *Les peintures de la synagogue de Doura-Europos*, Paris, 1939, p. 19f.; C. H. Kraeling: *The Synagogue* (Excavations at Dura Europos VIII, 1), New Haven, p. 60.
[5]) *ibid.*, p. 59 f.

ture, but this is clearly an arched portal with double doors, each door having a boss in its upper part. The portal is flanked by two fluted columns with knobs set at intervals between the flutings of the shafts. The lintel, which is surmounted by a conch, is shaded in a way suggesting moulding.

Scholarly opinion has been divided as regards the interpretation of this tetrastyle (as in the parallel case of the Bar-Kosiba coin) between those considering it an interpretation (real or imaginary) of the Temple and those recognizing in it a Torah shrine.[1])

On this point we subscribe entirely to the opinion of those who see in the Dura tetrastyle a representation of the Temple. The painter must have followed one of the traditional images of the Herodian sanctuary, another of which had already served the engraver of the Bar Kosiba coin, even if the fresco is over a century later than the coin and 164 years later than the ruin of the Temple. The arguments in support of the identification of the tetrastyle as a Torah shrine (apart from the metaphysic one derived from the importance of the Law in Judaism) are mainly based on the frequent and unmistakeable representations of this object in later synagogue reliefs and mosaics. It should be remarked, however, that with one or two exceptions, these representations show the Torah shrine as a closed cupboard, surmounted by a gable,[2]) sometimes horned. The arched roof appears only in a recently discovered pavement at Beth Shean (possibly of a *Samaritan* synagogue) and a very late one at Jericho. At Beth Shearim we have the representation of a Torah shrine flanked by columns, but it is surmounted by a Syrian gable and not a straight entablature.[3]) In later synagogues the *picture* of the shrine, flanked by seven-branched candlesticks and by (real or symbolic) images of lions, is to be found in the mosaic floors in a position facing directly the supposed real shrine with real candlesticks and possibly real statues of lions, set against the wall over it. The picture on the floor served thus as a kind of reflection of the reality cast on the pavement. But how can one compare such pavement images with an alleged representation of a shrine *over* its real counterpart, together with *one* candlestick instead of a pair, and the depiction of the Sacrifice of Isaac on the opposite side. The central position of the tetrastyle suggest forcibly that it is an image of the focus

---

[1]) *Ibid.*, p. 60; Goodenough, *op. cit.* (p. 327, note 1) IX, pp. 68-71; Muehsam, *op. cit.*, p. 13.
[2]) Goodenough, *ibid.*, III, No. 471 (Capernaum).
[3]) *Ibid.*, Nos. 58-62, cf. also Nos. 639, 649, 666.

of Jewish faith, which derived its standing from Divine light (the candlestick) and from the readiness for a supreme sacrifice by which Abraham sealed his Covenant with the Almighty; an act of sacrifice which was moreover located in later times at the very spot where the Temple stood.

We suggest therefore that the image on the coin and that on the fresco had a common prototype in reality. Some scholars have interpreted the differences between the coin and the fresco by assuming that the fresco painter had misunderstood his subject and had misrepresented the Ark of the Covenant as a portal.[1]) It is our contention that exactly the contrary is the case, and that in both representations the original object was a door, which was simplified on the coin but was represented in detail on the fresco. We are thus returning to an old view, voiced by Merzbacher already in 1877.[2])

The objections to this identification have been recently summed up by Mrs. Muehsam as follows:[3]) (1) the object has clearly recognizable feet; (2) the Mishna (*Middot* 2:3) states that all doors in the Temple (save one) had lintels and the coin image shows none; (3) a door would be expected to have two wings and show a vertical dividing line. Without wishing to minimize the weight of the first and third argument (for the second does not apply—the text of the Mishna in the passage quoted refers to the gates of the Inner and Outer Temple and not to the doors of the Sanctuary; and besides the object on the coin has a clearly drawn lintel below the arch), the differences between coin and fresco is not as great as has been suggested. In several details the two show considerable similarity: the image on the coin has the double outline of the arch, the moulded lintel (shaded in the fresco and indicated by five horizontal dots on the coin), the knobs on the column shafts flanking the door and the two bosses on the door (although the latter have been almost universally interpreted as the ends of the shafts for carrying the Ark of the Covenant). The lower line of the "Ark" can represent a door-cill; thus it is only the dividing line of the doors which is missing.

We suggest therefore that the balance of probability—together with the parallel image on the fresco—is in favour of regarding the arched construction on the coin as a door.

---

[1]) Du Mesnil, *op. cit.* p. 19 f.; cf. E. Wendel: *Der Thoraschrein im Altertum*, Halle, 1950, p. 20.
[2]) E. Merzbacher, *Zeitschrift fur Numismatik*, 4 (1877), p. 353, No. 95.
[3]) *Op. cit.*, p. 7.

Our next question must be: the door to what? It cannot be the huge portal of the "Porch" (*'ulam*), for this was a rectangular opening surmounted by a complicated arrangements of wood and stone,[1]) which stood open, with only a veil, the *parokhet* or *katapetasma* in it. However the back wall of the *'ulam* was the front wall of the Sanctuary proper, the door of which was visible through the portal when the veil was lifted. Now we learn from the Mishna (*Middot* 4:1): "The entrance to the Sanctuary ... had four doors, two within and two without"—i.e. from without it had the appearance of a double door. Over the door there was a lamp, the gift of Queen Helena of Adiabene, which in the

Fig. 1: Facade (reconstructed) of Hinnom tomb.

opinion of some scholars, quoted in the Jerusalem Talmud,[2]) had the shape of a conch (*qônkhitâ*).

We submit that the door shown in the fresco and the coin was the double door to the Sanctuary, the one object visible in the Temple facade between the columns, with the conch-shaped lamp above it. The open portal was disregarded because it did not impinge in the same measure on the visual consciousness of the beholder who viewed it from the low viewpoint of the Court of the Israelites.

We should like to draw attention in this connection to a tomb facade belonging to a rock-cut tomb in the Hinnom Valley outside Jerusalem.[3]) It has been dated by some to the period after the fall of Jerusalem, but

---

[1]) Mishna *Middot* 3 : 7.
[2]) *Jer. Yoma* 3 : 3-41 a.
[3]) R. A. S. Macalister, *Palestine Exploration Quarterly Statement*, 1901, pp. 216-218; K. O. Dalman, *Zeitschrift d. Deutschen Palastina-Vereins*, 62 (1939), pp. 190-208; Goodenough, *op. cit.*, I, p. 84.

for no satisfactory reasons.[1]) In fact apart from its decoration and some special features it fits in quite well with the general type of monumental rock-cut tombs around Jerusalem. This tomb is marked by two features which are of interest here. Firstly, its facade has in its centre a door arched over, with a conch over the lintel. (Fig. 1) The door itself is flanked by two pilasters. Its outline is thus identical with the suggested shape of the door of the Sanctuary and corresponds in general with the door in the Dura fresco. This central door of the Hinnom tomb is

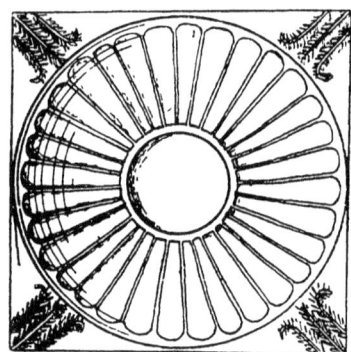

Fig. 2: Hinnom tomb; rock-cut ceiling in main hall.

flanked by two smaller ones, thus confirming its resemblance to the door of the Sanctuary, for we read in Mishna *Middot* (4:2): "The great gate had two wickets, one to the north and another to the south."

Secondly, the arrangement of this tomb facade is only one of the links connecting this sepulture with the Temple. For another we have to look at the rock-cut ceiling in the main hall of the tomb (Fig. 2). It is cut to resemble a flat dome, filled with a carved rosette, with four "acanthus cups" in the corners of the square room, suggesting filled-in pendentives.[2]) A similar design (Pl. IV, 1), with a rosette in the centre and acanthus plants in the corners appears—together with several other minor decorative elements—in one of the two domes over the Double Gate of the Temple, which is still standing.[3]) Such resemblance cannot be coincidental.

---

[1]) N. Avigad in *Sefer Yerushalayim* (ed. M. Avi-Yonah), Jerusalem, 1956, p. 346 (Hebrew).

[2]) Goodenough, *op. cit.* III, No. 37.

[3]) M. Cohen in *Jewish Art* (ed. C. Roth), Jerusalem, 1959, Fig. 52 a on p. 118 (Hebrew). The design is copied in this drawing from an unpublished photograph in the archives of the Departement of Antiquities. (The figure was not reprinted in the English edition of the same book, Jerusalem, 1961).

To sum up: The facade of the Herodian Temple was subdivided by four engaged columns or—more in accordance with classical architecture—by two engaged corner pilasters and two columns. The double portal showed the arched-over door of the Sanctuary, with a conch above it and two smaller doors flanking it. The facade was crowned by

Fig. 3: Reconstruction of the facade of Herod's temple.

antefixes, probably not the simplified round type of the Dura fresco and some of the Bar Kosiba coins (Pl. IV, 2) but by crenellations such as are common in Palmyra and Petra.[1]

The principles of the reconstruction outlined here have been applied by us in the model of ancient Jerusalem (1:50) now in the course of construction (Fig. 3).

---

[1] E. g. Champdor, *op. cit.* pp. 36, 37 and 93.

HELLENIZATIONS IN JOSEPHUS' PORTRAYAL OF MAN'S DECLINE

BY

LOUIS H. FELDMAN

Yeshiva College

The fact that Josephus presents us in the first eleven books of his *Antiquities* with a systematic and comprehensive paraphrase of the Bible, such as no Talmudic rabbi has left us, and anterior, often by several centuries, to the extant collections of homiletic expositions by the rabbis, gives a special significance to this part of his work. Josephus (*Antiquitates Judaicae* 1.17) tells us in his prooemium that he will set forth the "precise details" (τὰ ... ἀκριβῆ) of what is written in the Scriptures (ἀναγραφαῖς), "neither adding nor omitting anything" (οὐδὲν προσθεὶς οὐδ' αὖ παραλιπών).[1]) His work, he says (*AJ* 1. 5),

---

[1]) For similar professions that Josephus is following the Bible strictly see *AJ* 1. 26, 2. 347, 4. 36, 8. 159, 10. 218; and *Ap.* 1. 54. R. B. Sobel, *Josephus' Conception of History in Relationship to the Pentateuch as a Source of Historical Data* (unpubl. diss. M. A., Hebrew Union College, Cincinnati, 1962) has attempted to list all of Josephus' divergences from the first five books of the Bible, but he has relied upon Thackeray's translation in the Loeb Library to the exclusion of the Greek, has made little attempt to explain these differences, and has failed to analyse the Greek influences working upon Josephus. S. Rappaport, *Agada und Exegese bei Flavius Josephus* (Wien 1930), whose work is the only one that systematically attempts to note Josephus' divergences from the entire Bible, has missed many details and suffers from having assumed that Josephus' additions always parallel rabbinic tradition, even though he must admit (Introduction, xxx) that there are some additions not found in extant rabbinic or Apocryphal literature, and even though he must likewise concede (xxxiv) that there are places (e.g., *AJ* 10. 106-107) where Josephus definitely shows his independence of rabbinic exegesis. Rappaport fails to see that some of these additions, as is perhaps true of some of Philo's embellishments, may have been originated independently by Josephus insofar as the explanation emerges simply and naturally from the Biblical text. Finally, he fails to give due weight to the fact that Josephus is writing for a Greek audience and that many of his embellishments are attempts to impose a Greek flavor upon the Biblical narrative. In saying that he has changed nothing, perhaps Josephus is merely implying that, compared to the other Hellenistic historians, such as Eupolemus, he is really close to the Bible. H. St. J. Thackeray, *Josephus the Man and the Historian* (New York 1929) 34, cites our passage (1. 5) as evidence that Josephus used the word "translate" loosely and that therefore when he speaks of translating (μεταβαλών) his *Jewish War* from the Greek, this does not indicate that the translation was literal since, in fact, our version of the *Jewish War* shows no trace of Semitic parentage.

"will embrace our entire ancient history (ἀρχαιολογιάν) and political constitution (διάταξιν τοῦ πολιτεύματος) translated (μεθηρμηνευμένην) from the Hebrew records (ἐκ τῶν Ἑβραϊκῶν... γραμμάτων). The word μεθηρμηνευμένην may mean either "translated" verbatim or "interpreted" with some freedom.[1]) A century before Josephus, Cicero (*De Optimo Genere Oratorum*, 4. 14) contrasts a translation which proceeds word for word (*verbum pro verbo*) with his own translation as an orator, whereby he preserved only the general style and form of the original; and indeed in Cicero's own translations from Plato he does take considerable liberties. Horace (*Ars Poetica*, 1. 33) goes even further and says that the faithful translator (*fidus interpres*) will take care not to render word for word (*verbum verbo*, almost Cicero's phrase).

It is obvious to even the most casual reader that Josephus has made numerous changes of omission, for example, the cunning of Jacob in connection with Laban's flock (Gen. 30. 37-38), the Judah-Tamar episode (Gen. 38), Moses' slaying of the Egyptian (Ex. 2. 12), Miriam's leprosy (Num. 12), the story of Moses' striking the rock to bring forth water which speaks of Moses' disgrace (Num. 20. 10-12), the story of the brazen serpent (Num. 21. 4-9) whereby Moses cured those who had been bitten by the fiery serpents, and the building of the golden calf (Ex. 32),[2]) as well as of commission, for example, his portrayal of

---

Josephus clearly states in the *Antiquities* (1. 5) that he has altered *nothing*, and it is here suggested that the γραμμάτων (1. 5) and the ἀναγραφαῖς (1.17) which Josephus promises not to modify and which must, as the words themselves indicate, refer to written works, refer not to the Bible but to the Jewish tradition generally. This would imply that some of the Midrashic tradition had by Josephus' time been committed to writing; and while such a statement two decades ago would have been considered most unlikely, inasmuch as the earliest rabbinic midrashim date from a century after Josephus, we now have midrashim in the Dead Sea Scrolls (notably the Genesis Apocryphon, dated by its editors, N. Avigad and Y. Yadin, *A Genesis Apocryphon* [Jerusalem 1956] 38, on palaeographical grounds, as having been written between the end of the first century B.C.E. and the middle of the first century C.E. [so also E. Y. Kutscher, "The Language of the Genesis Apocryphon: A Preliminary Survey;" *Scripta Hierosolymitana*, 4 (1958) 22; G. Vermès, *Scripture and Tradition in Judaism: Haggadic Studies* (Leiden 1961) 96, n. 2, prefers an early second century date], which Josephus parallels at several points which antedate Josephus or are contemporary with him. Cf. also Vermès, 4-10, who cites the work of R. Bloch, who investigated the Biblical origins of the midrash in certain books of the Bible itself.

[1]) See *LSJ*, s.v. μεθερμηνεύω.
[2]) It is important to note that Josephus' omissions do not coincide with the omissions advocated by the rabbis (Mishnah, *Megillah* 25 a). According to the rabbis, the following passages are read in the synagogue but not translated: the incident of Reuben's intercourse with this father's concubine Bilhah, the second account of the Golden Calf (Ex. 32. 21-25), the blessing of the priests (Num. 6.

Abraham as a philosopher, scientist, and general, his romanticizing of the story of Josephus and Potiphar's wife in the vein of the Hippolytus-Phaedra story,[1]) his depiction of Moses as a general, employed by the Egyptians against the Ethiopians, who marries the daughter of the Ethiopian king, his heightening of erotic, heroic, and dramatic interest in his picture of Samson, his portrayal of Saul as a kind of Jewish Achilles, his presentation of Solomon as a kind of Jewish Oedipus, and his introduction into his Esther narrative of motifs found in Hellenistic novels.[2]) There is rabbinic precedent (*Megillah* 25 a-b) for omitting the translation of certain Biblical passages because of the embarrassment involved (though the list there given does not completely coincide with Josephus'); and when Josephus says that he has neither added to nor subtracted from what is written, he presumably means not merely what is written in the Bible but also that which was included in the Jewish tradition of interpretation and which was regarded as an integral part of that tradition. Whether we should stress that the word γραμμάτων and the later word ἀναγραφαῖς refer to written records used by Josephus and that the Midrashic traditions incorporated in the *Antiquities* had already been recorded by his time—which indeed would be an important finding—or whether he was relying upon the *written* Bible (and the Septuagint) and the *oral* traditions of Midrashic interpretation,

---

24-27), the incident of David and Bath-Sheba (2 Sam. 11. 2-17), and the beginning of the incident of Ammon son of David and Tamar (2 Sam. 13. 1). Of these Josephus omits the first three but not the last two. Moreover, the rabbis (*ibid.*) expressly declare that the incident of Judah and Tamar (Gen. 38) and the first account of the golden calf (Ex. 32. 1-20) are both read and translated, whereas Josephus omits both. In the Gemara on the above passages, the rabbis add to the list of passages that are to be read and translated (*Megillah* 25 a-b) the account of creation (Gen. 1), the story of Lot and his daughters (Gen. 19. 31-38), the curses and blessings promised to Israel (Lev. 26 and Deut. 27), the story of the concubine in Gibeah (Jud. 19-20), the passage from Ezekiel (16. 1) about Jerusalem's abominations, and the rest of the incident of Ammon and Tamar (2 Sam. 13. 2-22). Josephus has all of these but does not actually enumerate the blessings and curses and omits the passage from Ezekiel (as he does most prophetic passages).

[1]) On Josephus' reworking of the episode of Joseph and Potiphar's wife see M. Braun, *Griechischer Roman und Hellenistische Geschichtsschreibung* (*Frankfurter Studien zur Religion und Kultur der Antike*, no. 6; Frankfurt am Main 1934); and H. Sprodowsky, *Die Hellenisierung der Geschichte von Joseph in Aegypten bei Flavius Josephus* (Diss. Greifswald: *Greifswalder Beitr. z. Lit. u. Stil.* 18 [1937]). These remain the only studies of Hellenization in any given episode in Josephus (and both deal with the same episode). The whole area of Josephus' historiography has been much neglected, as a perusal of my critical bibliography, *Scholarship on Philo and Josephus* (1937-1962) (*Studies in Judaica*, no. 1) (New York 1963) 48-49, will show.

[2]) The author is presently engaged in writing a series of studies of these and of other episodes analyzing Josephus' technique in Hellenizing the Biblical narrative.

we should, I believe, take Josephus at his word that he has not added or subtracted, except insofar as he was a free translator writing as a kind of orator, defending the cause of the Jews before a Greek audience in terms intelligible to them. If ἀναγραφαῖς refers only to the Bible and if Josephus had taken excessive liberties with it, he could easily have been detected, since the Septuagint, at any rate, must have been accessible to his Jewish and to some of his non-Jewish readers, as the quotation from it in his earlier contemporary, pseudo-Longinus, shows; hence the phrase for Biblical tradition must be understood to include midrashic exposition as well. It is here proposed to discuss one brief passage in Josephus as an example of his "translation" or "interpretation," and, in particular, of his Hellenizing technique, namely, his account of the Golden Age and of the decline of civilization that followed the sin of Adam and Eve.

At the very beginning of his account, Josephus presents his narrative within a Greek framework. The notion of a stream, the Okeanos, flowing around the earth, is found among the Greeks from an early period; and while Herodotus (2. 23) disclaims any knowledge of a river called Okeanos, he does confirm the antiquity of the notion by conjecturing that Homer or some earlier poet invented the name and introduced it into his poetry. Even when the Greeks accepted the idea of the spherical shape of the earth, they continued to apply the name Okeanos to the great outer nature of the earth as against the inner seas. This conception of a stream encircling the entire earth is introduced by Josephus (1. 38) in his description of the river that went out of Eden to water the garden (Gen. 2. 10); he thus presents Biblical geography in terms intelligible to his Greek audience.[1] This feature of Josephus' geography is, as Rappaport[2]) admits, unknown to the Agada, and is plainly an attempt to present Biblical geography in Greek terms. The same tendency to identify Biblical places with those familiar to the Greeks is found in Josephus' identification (1. 38) of the river Pishon (Gen. 2. 11) with the Ganges River and of the land of Havilah "where there is gold" and which it encompasses as India.[3]) Josephus here follows the many classical writers—Herodotus, Diodorus, Strabo, and

---

[1]) Rappaport (above, p. 336 n. 1) 76, n. 10, refuses to equate this stream with the Okeanos, and notes that Josephus distinguished between the waters surrounding the planet earth and the river flowing around the earth. But it is precisely the latter, not the former, that the Greeks identified with the Okeanos.

[2]) Rappaport (above, p. 336 n. 1) 2, n. 8.

[3]) Most of the rabbis identify the Pishon with the Nile River: see Rappaport (above, p. 336 n. 1) 76-78, notes 11-12.

Pliny—who identify India as the land of gold. Similarly Havilah in Genesis 10. 29 is identified by Josephus with India. Just as Herodotus in his travels sought to identify strange and exotic foreign place-names with those familiar to the Greeks so that they would not appear so remote, so Josephus (1. 39) likewise adopts the old identification of the River Gihon (Gen. 2. 13) with the Nile.[1]) Similarly, in his listing (1. 122-129) of the lands settled by Japheth's sons, Josephus identifies them with various Greek countries.

Josephus (1. 41) adds to the Biblical narrative (Gen. 3. 1) that in the earliest period all the animals spoke a common language(ὁμοφωνούντων). Such a detail is, to be sure, found in the Book of Jubilees (3. 28) and in a few places in rabbinic literature.[2]) The more common rabbinic view, however, is that only the serpent produced speech.[3]) Ginzberg[4]) has noted that the older rabbinic literature does not know of the original common language spoken by man and the animals, and that, in any case, the serpent is said to have spoken Hebrew, while the other animals spoke their own language. It is interesting that Philo (*De Confus. Ling.* 6) ascribes the view of a common language of animals to mythologists (μυθυπλαστοί), perhaps, we may conjecture, the same mythologists who are the source for Plato's picture (*Statesman* 272 *C*)[5]) of primitive man, who had the power of holding intercourse not only with men but with brute creatures as well. Josephus may well have been influenced by the fact that in the earliest period animals, in the Greek as in the Jewish tradition, are said to have the possibility of speech, as we see in the case of Achilles' horse in the *Iliad* (19. 404-417) and in Aesop's fables.[6])

The typical picture of the early generations of man in Greek liter-

---

[1]) See Rappaport (above, p. 33n. 1) 3, no. 12, and 79. n. 16, who cites the Septuagint on Jer. 2. 18, Ecclesiasticus 24. 27, and a number of other texts that make this identification.

[2]) See Rappaport (above, p. 336 n. 1) 79-80, n. 18; and A. Schalit's translation of Josephus' *Antiquities* into Hebrew, 2 (Jerusalem 1944) 8, n. 15.

[3]) Josephus apparently knew this view, for he says (1. 50) that speech was taken from the serpent, the assumption being that only the serpent had previously possessed this faculty.

[4]) L. Ginzberg, *The Legends of the Jews*, 5 (Philadelphia 1925) 94, n. 58.

[5]) Cited by A. Lewinsky, *Beitrage zur Kenntnis der religionsphilosophischen Anschauungen des Flavius Josephus* (Breslau 1887) 54, n. 3.

[6]) Cf. W. Headlam, "Prometheus and the Garden of Eden," *CQ* 28 (1934) 65, who notes that such animal fables, prefaced by the phrase "in the days when all the beasts talked," are still current among the Arabs—for instance, the story of the lizard whose foot writes the name of Allah with its print. For parallels from Russian, Norse, and other folktales about speaking animals see F. Bender, *Die marchenhaften Bestandteile der Homerische Gedichte* (Darmstadt 1878) 15-17.

ature is of man in close contact and friendship with the gods. Thus Hesiod (*Op.* 120) speaks of men during the Golden Age as friendly with the immortal gods (φίλοι μακάρεσσι θεοῖσιν).[1]) Even in the later heroic age, Homer (*Od.* 1, 22-26) speaks of the god Poseidon as associating with the Ethiopians, enjoying himself by sitting at their banquets. Again, Nausicaa (*Od.* 6. 203) tells Odysseus that the Phaeacians are very dear to the gods. And Alcinous, the king of the Phaeacians (*Od.* 7. 201-206), notes that the gods appear in manifest form among them, feast among them, and sit together with them, since they are related to them (ἐπεί σφισιν ἐγγύθεν εἰμέν). Josephus, in an addition to the Bible, presents (1. 45) a similar picture of Adam as being wont to resort to God's company (εἰς ὁμιλίαν αὐτῷ) and as taking delight in associating with him (ἡδόμενος τῇ πρὸς αὐτὸν ὁμιλίᾳ). The approaching end of this Golden Age is signalled by the fact that Adam, who had previously been associating so freely with God, withdraws when God enters the garden after his sin.

In his developed picture of the original bliss of mankind (1. 46), which has no parallel in the Bible, Josephus follows a tradition found in many authors from Hesiod on. Smith[2]) finds almost a hundred references to the Golden Age in classical writers, and he quotes the author of the *Aetna* (16), who says that descriptions of the Golden Age are so common that "non cessuit cuiquam melius sua tempora nosse." Josephus describes this life of bliss (βίον εὐδαίμονα) as one in which men are unmolested by any evil (κακοῦ παντὸς ἀπαθῆ), with no care (φροντίδι) to fret (ξαινόμενοι, "mangle") their souls, where all things that contribute (συντελεῖ) to enjoyment (ἀπόλαυσιν) and pleasure (ἡδονήν) spring up, through God's providence (πρόνοιαν), spontaneously (αὐτομάτων), without toil (πόνου) or distress (ταλαιπωρίας) on the part of man, where men live long lives and where old age (γῆρας) does not soon overtake them. And in imposing his punishment upon Adam (Gen. 3. 17), God says, in Josephus' version (1. 49), that the earth will no longer produce anything of herself (αὐτομάτως) but only in return for toil (πονοῦσι) and grinding labor (τοῖς ἔργοις τριβομένοις).

The notion that early man lived free from evils and toil and that old age did not soon overtake him is found in Hesiod's description in the *Works and Days* (90-93), which employs several of the words found later

---

[1]) On Hesiod's account of the Five Ages and its sources T. G. Rosenmeyer, "Hesiod and Historiography," *Hermes* 85 (1957) 257-285.

[2]) K. F. Smith, "Ages of the World (Greek and Roman)," *Hastings Ency. of Rel. and Ethics* 1 (1908) 194.

in Josephus: "For ere this the tribes of men lived on earth remote and free from ills (κακῶν) and hard toil (πόνοιο) and heavy sicknesses which bring the Fates upon men; for in misery men grow old (καταγηράσκουσιν) quickly."[1]) In his description of the Golden Age, Hesiod (*Op.* 112-120) says that men lived like gods without sorrow of heart, remote and free from toil (πόνων) and grief, that they avoided old age (γῆρας),[2]) that the earth of its own accord (αὐτομάτη) gave them fruit abundantly. "They dwelt in ease and peace upon their lands with many good things," he concludes, "rich in flocks and loved by the blessed gods" (118-120).[3]) In contrast, in his description of the Iron Age, Hesiod (*Op.* 176-178) stresses that men never rest from labor and sorrow by day, nor from perishing by night, "and the gods shall lay troublesome cares upon them." Josephus elsewhere (*AJ* 1. 108) mentions Hesiod's report that the ancients lived for a thousand years and notes (*Ap.* 1. 16) that the historian Acusilaus often corrects Hesiod; and he may well have had Hesiod's passage in mind while writing his own description of the primitive age of bliss.

The notion of food springing up spontaneously, mentioned several times here in Josephus' description of the Golden Age (1. 46, 1. 49, 1. 54), is also found in Homer's description of the Cyclopes (*Od.* 9. 109), for whom grain sprang up without sowing or plowing. Josephus mentions Homer several times in his works (*AJ* 7. 67, *Ap.* 1. 12, 2. 14, 2. 155, 2. 256), and quotes a verse (*Il.* 14. 90-91) from him at one point (*AJ* 19. 92); and the fact that he is able to state (2. 155) that Homer *nowhere* employs the word "law" would indicate perhaps that he had studied his works thoroughly, though, of course, he may have derived this fact from a handbook. Likewise, in Plato (*Statesman*, 272 A), the Golden Age is described as a period when the fruits of the earth grew of themselves (αὐτομάτης). Again, Josephus shows considerable interest in his works, particularly the *Republic*, and mentions him a number of times (*Ap.* 2. 168, 223-224, 225, 256, 257-261).[4]) Philemon

---

[1]) Translated by H. G. Evelyn White (Loeb Classical Library, Cambridge, Mass. 1914). All other translations in this paper are from the Loeb Library.

[2]) Cf. Horace, *Odes* 1. 3. 27-33, who remarks that after Prometheus' theft of fire "death, that hitherto had kept withdrawn and came but slowly, quickened its pace. Headlam (above, note 14) 66, notes that in Genesis this part of the punishment does not appear until Noah (Gen. 6. 3).

[3]) Hesiod's description of the ages of the world may well come from the doctrine of Zarathustra that there will be four ages of the world, symbolized by a tree with four branches—gold, silver, steel, and iron. Cf. R. Reitzenstein, in *Warburg Bibliothek* 7 (1926) 38ff.

[4]) On Josephus' intimate knowledge of Plato and on actual Platonic terminology

(fr. inc. 4) contrasts the miserable lot of man who must always toil with the lot of the other animals for whom the earth gives bread of its own accord. The Peripatetic Dicaearchus of Messene (fl. c. 310) explains (fr. 49)[1]) that primitive man's ignorance of agriculture caused him to be dependent upon food that grew spontaneously (αὐτόματα). He states that in the Golden Age men lived long lives of leisure, without toil (πόνων) or care (μερίμνης) and without disease. Iambulus in his utopia (*ap.* Diodorus Siculus 2. 57. 1) remarks that foodstuffs were there produced of themselves (αὐτομάτους), and that the inhabitants lived extremely long lives, reaching the age of one hundred and fifty (2. 57. 4).

From the vehemence with which Josephus criticizes (10. 277-280) the Epicureans for excluding Providence from human affairs, a criticism which he later repeats (*Ap.* 2. 180), we can see that he was well acquainted with the doctrines of this group. Likewise his picture of the Golden Age is reminiscent of that in Lucretius, with whose Latin Josephus probably was not acquainted,[2]) though he might have been since he wrote his *Antiquities* after spending twenty years in Rome, and who remarks (2. 1158) that at first the earth of her own accord (*sponte sua*) created crops for men, who now must toil for a lesser result. Similarly Lucretius (5. 933-938) describes the primitive age of man as one when man did not use the plough, but depended merely upon the sun and rains to bring forth what the earth had earlier created of its own accord (*sponte sua*). Cicero (*N. D.* 2. 63) recalls the Golden Age, when, "as the poets say," no force was ever applied by man to produce crops from the soil. In his picture of the return of the Saturnian Age, Virgil[3]) (*Ecl.* 4. 18-20) declares that the earth, untilled, will pour forth ivy and foxglove; and in another picture of this Golden Age (*Geor.* 1. 125) he notes that no ploughman then tilled the soil.[4]) Ovid (*Met.* 1.

---

in Josephus see B. Brune, *Flavius Josephus und seine Schriften in ihrem Verhaltnis zum Judentum, zur griechischen-romischen Welt and zum Christentum* (Gutersloh 1913) 195-198.

[1]) *Ap.* Porphyry, *De Abstinentia* 4. 2, in F. Wehrli, *Die Schule des Aristoteles, Texte und Kommentar*, 1 (Basel 1944) 24.

[2]) So Thackeray (above, p. 336 n. 1) 118: "Josephus, we may be sure, had but slight acquaintance with Latin litierature, and these reminiscences doubtless came from an assistant."

[3]) On Virgil's picture of the Golden Age see M. E. Taylor, "Primitivism in Virgil," *AJP* 76 (1955) 261-278; and I. S. Ryberg, "Vergil's Golden Age," *TAPA* 89 (1958) 112-131.

[4]) For an excellent analysis of Virgil, *Georgics*, 1. 121-146, and its relation to Lucretius' theory of progress see Ryberg (above, note 3) 119-123, who notes the originality of Virgil's view of man's progress in the arts as evidence of God's wisdom and providence. Josephus, in contrast, has the more conventional view,

101-104), too, in his description of the Golden Age, says that the earth gave forth food of itself (*per se*) without compulsion (*nullo cogente*). "The earth, untilled," he continues (1. 109-110), "brought forth her stores of grain; and the fields, though unfallowed, grew white with the heavy, bearded wheat." Elsewhere (*Amores* 3. 8. 39-40) he repeats the theme that in that age the earth produced fruits without the use of the ploughshare.

Josephus' picture of primitive man as being unmolested (ἀπαθῆ) by any evil is reminiscent of the Stoic goal of ἀπάθεια. The Stoic Seneca quotes (*Ep*. 90. 37) the passage from Virgil's *Georgics* cited above, and then remarks (90. 40) that in those days "the very soil was more productive when untilled, and yielded more than enough for peoples who refrained from despoiling one another." Similarly, pseudo-Seneca (*Octavia* 404-405) remarks that in that age the glad earth of her own accord (*ultro*) laid bare her fruitful breast. The unknown author of the *Aetna* speaks (9-16) of the carefree Saturn in whose age "no man subdued fields to his will or sowed grain in them." It is true that in the rabbinic Agada[1]) we find the notion that it was unnecessary to till the soil in the Garden of Eden to produce fruit, and this is, in fact, implied in the Biblical text itself, but the correspondences both in ideas and in words between Josephus and the Greek authors, especially those whom Josephus cites elsewhere, are closer.[2]) And, in the last analysis, even if Josephus' version is sometimes paralleled by rabbinic midrashim, the fact that he chooses to select a given tradition, while omitting so many others, is an important indicator of his aim and method.

According to the Bible (Gen. 3. 16), one of the punishments meted out by God to Eve is that man shall rule thereafter over woman.

---

found in Hesiod and others, that toil is God's punishment inflicted on man for his sin.

[1]) See Rappaport (above, p. 336 n. 1) 5, no. 18, and 82, note 24.

[2]) On the original state of mankind in the Golden Age see J. W. Klingender, *De Aureae Aetatis Fabula Disputatio* (Cassel 1856); H. E. Graf, *Ad Aureae Aetatis Fabulam Symbola* (Leipzig 1884); J. B. Bury, *The Idea of Progress* (London 1920); R. H. Murray, "The Conception of Progress in Classical and Renaissance Writers," Appendix in his *Erasmus and Luther: Their Attitudes to Toleration* (London 1920) 401-446; L. Séchan, "Pandora, l' Ève grecque, "*Bull. de l'Assoc. G. Budé* (1929) 3-36; H. Turck, *Pandora und Eva: Menschwerdung und Schopfertum im griechischen und judischen Mythus* (Weimar 1931); W. Headlam (above, p. 340 n. 6) 63-71; A. O. Lovejoy and G. Boas, *Primitivism and Related Ideas in Antiquity* (Baltimore 1935); and F. J. Teggart, "The Argument of Hesiod's *Work and Days*," *JHI* 8 (1947) 45-77. Of these the fullest collection of sources is that by Lovejoy and Boas, but they are little concerned with the terminology used or with comparing the sources with one another.

During the Hellenistic period the status of women was greatly ameliorated;[1]) and presumably to avoid the accusation that Judaism places the woman in an inferior position, Josephus (1. 49) completely omits this statement. He does, however, repeat (1. 49) the common classical theme of the evil wrought by womanish counsel when he says that God imposed punishment on Adam for yielding (ἥττονα—being inferior to) to a woman's counsel (γυναικείας συμβουλίας). Though this is ostensibly similar to the Bible (Gen. 3. 17), which says that God punished Adam because he hearkened to the voice of his wife, Josephus generalizes about womanish counsel, and in this he is reminiscent of Homer's *Odyssey* (11. 436-439), where, after Agamemnon has described how he met his death through the contrivance of his wife Clytemnestra, Odysseus replies: "Ah, verily has Zeus, whose voice is borne afar, visited wondrous hatred on the race of Atreus from the first because of the counsels of women (γυναικείας βουλάς). For Helen's sake many of us perished, and against thee Clytemnestra spread a snare while thou wast afar." One is reminded of Josephus' attacks on women (5. 294) in connection with the betrayal of the riddle by Samson's wife, that nothing is "more deceitful than a woman who betrays our speech to you."

One of the difficulties in the Biblical text, pointed out by such non-believers as Julian the Apostate (*Gal.* 364 E-347 C) and Ḥiwi al-Balkhi[2]) is that God is apparently capricious in accepting the sacrifice of Abel while rejecting that of Cain (Gen. 4. 4-5). The Septuagint (Gen. 4. 7) explains God's rejection of Cain by stating that he failed to cut his sacrifice into pieces properly.[3]) Philo (*De Sacrificiis Abelis et Caini* 88-89), followed by Julian (*op. cit.*), goes to great pains to explain the difference between Cain's offering, which, he says, was lifeless, second in age and value, and weak, and that of Abel, which was living, first in age and value, and possessed of strength and superior fatness. Similarly the rabbis[4]) stress that Cain's gift was of the poorest quality. But, as

---

[1]) See W.W. Tarn and G. T. Griffith, *Hellenistic Civilisation*³ (London 1952) 98-100.

[2]) See J. Rosenthal, "Hiwi al-Balkhi," *JQR* 38 (1947-48) 323.

[3]) Genesis 4. 7 is so difficult to understand that the rabbis (*Yoma* 52 a-b) numbered this among the five verses in the Torah the grammatical construction of which is undecided. Josephus resolves the problem by completely omitting the verse.

[4]) *Genesis Rabbah* 22. 5 and other passages cited by V. Aptowitzer, *Kain und Abel in der Agada, den Apokryphen, der hellenistischen, christlichen, und muhammedanischen Literatur* (Wien 1922) 37-41, 142-144. E. Stein, *Philo und der Midrasch* (Giessen 1931) 10-11, states that since the Septuagint was not in favor in Palestine, the source of the rabbis' comment that Cain incurred God's displeasure through an improper division of the sacrifice is "Hellenistic midrash."

Cassuto[1]) well points out, the Bible itself does not contrast the gifts of Cain and Abel but merely conveys the impression that Abel brought the finest of his flock (Gen. 4. 4), while Cain was indifferent (Gen. 4. 3). To show that God was not capricious in preferring Abel, Josephus (1. 54) condemns Cain because his gift had been forced from the soil "by the ingenuity of grasping man" (τοῖς κατ' ἐπίνοιαν ἀνθρώπου πλενέκτου [καὶ] βίᾳ πεφυκόσιν). In addition, Josephus (1. 53) stresses Abel's respect for justice, his piety, and his virtue generally, in contrast to Cain's depravity and eagerness for gain.[2]) Josephus thus, like Philo (*De Sacrificiis Abelis et Caini* 2), connects Cain's name, which means "acquisition" (κτῆσις), with this quality in his character.

It was characteristic of the Stoics in antiquity to seek etymologies of proper names;[3]) and Josephus elsewhere (e.g., 1. 180, Melchisedek) adds etymologies that are not found in the Bible. The Bible, to be sure, often does give etymologies, but it omits (Gen. 4. 2) the etymology of the name of Abel, a fact that bothered some of the great medieval Jewish commentators, one of whom, Nachmanides, noted that the reason for this omission was that the Bible did not wish to make explicit the pessimism inherent in the meaning of the name "vanity" (*hebel*). The Hebrew reader, as Cassuto[4]) remarks, can immediately see how apt the name of Abel is in view of the fate in store for him; but this is of course not true for the Greek reader. Hence Josephus (1. 52) gives the meaning of Abel's name as "nothing" (οὐθέν).

Similarly Josephus' added detail (1. 59) about Cain's fear that in his wanderings he would fall a prey (ἀλώμενος περιπέσῃ) to wild beasts is a familiar theme from Greek and Roman literature. Thus Lucretius (5. 982-987), in his vivid description of the life of primitive man, notes that tribes of wild beasts often made rest dangerous for primitive man, who would flee in terror at night at the approach of a foaming boar or

---

[1]) U. Cassuto, *A Commentary on the Book of Genesis*, Part 1: *From Adam to Noah* (Jerusalem 1961) 205.

[2]) Similarly the Agada praises the righteousness of Abel (see Rappaport [above, p. 336 n. 1] 5, no. 22) and citations on 83, n. 28) and condemns Cain's acquisitiveness (see Rappaport, 5, no. 23, and citations on 83, n. 30). But the rabbinic parallels speak of Abel in terms that would appeal to a traditional Jewish audience: thus (*Tanch. Balak* 11) he is referred to as righteous (zaddik), whereas Josephus describes his virtues in terms comparable to the cardinal virtues spoken of by Plato and Aristotle.

[3]) See, e.g., Cic. *N. D.* 2. 7. 64-69. For further examples and bibliography see A. S. Pease, *M. Tulli Ciceronis De Natura Deorum*, 2 (Cambridge, Mass. 1958) 709.

[4]) Cassuto (above, note 1) 202.

a lion.[1]) Likewise Josephus' exaggeration (1. 60) of Cain's travels (πολλὴν δ' ἐπελθὼν γῆν), in contrast to the Bible's statement (Gen. 4. 16) that Cain "went out from the presence of the Lord," is reminiscent of Greek parallels, notably the wanderings of Oedipus.[2])

Josephus (1. 60-62) elaborates considerably on Cain's wickedness after the murder of Abel, and his language is highly reminiscent of Greek and Roman descriptions of the decline of man from the age of primitive simplicity.[3]) The ancients generally, starting with Hesiod, agreed that the chief cause of man's decline was his greed and selfishness. Hesiod describes the Iron Age, the age in which he himself lived, as one in which man used the right of might (χειροδίκαι: *Op.* 189, and δίκη δ' ἐν χερσί: 192) and in which man praised the evil-doer and his insolence (κακῶν ῥεκτῆρα καὶ ὕβριν: 191).[4]) Plato, in his description of primitive man (*Laws* 3. 679 B 3-C 2) notes that men in those days were neither rich nor poor, and hence they were free from insolence (ὕβρις), injustice (ἀδικία), jealousies (ζῆλοι), and envies (φθόνοι). These men were simple-minded (εὐήθεις), believed to be true what they heard about gods and men and lived according to truth. They did not know how to suspect their fellow men of falsehood. Similarly Aratus (*Phaenomena* 108-109) describes the Golden Age as a time when justice ruled and men had not knowledge of "hateful strife, or carping contention, or din of battle," while he depicts the Silver Age as one marked by wars and cruel bloodshed (*Phaen.* 125). Lucretius, who differs from Hesiod and Aratus in not seeing a continuous decline in man's history, condemns (5. 1105 ff.) the building of cities and the establishment of

---

[1]) The Agada (*Gen. Rabbah* 22.12 and other citations in Rappaport [above, p. 336, n. 1] 85-86, n. 37) is not as close to Josephus in remarking that the animals assembled to demand Abel's blood. Philo, *Quaest. in Gen.* 1.74, which Rappaport cites as a parallel, similarly says that Cain "feared the attacks of beasts and reptiles, for nature produced these for the punishment of unjust men."

[2]) Cf., e.g., Soph. *O. C.* 20: "For an old man thou hast traveled far." On Josephus' or his assistant's acquaintance with Sophocles see Thackeray (above, p. 336, n. 1) 100-120.

[3]) There was also in antiquity a theory that man had risen from his former estate (e.g. Aesch. *Pr.* 447-506), as well as a theory (cf., e.g., Lucretius, 5. 925-1457: see A. O. Lovejoy and G. Boas [above, p. 344, n. 2] 192-221) that man had in some respects improved while in other respects he had declined; but the prevailing theory, as Smith (above, p. 341, n. 2) 192, states, was that man had progressively degenerated. The typical presentation is that of Horace, *Odes* 3.6. 46-48: "Aetas parentum, peior avis, tulit / nos nequiores, mox daturos / progeniem vitiosiorem."

[4]) Cf. G. H. Macurdy, *The Quality of Mercy* (New Haven 1940) 51-55, for a parallel between Hesiod's descriptions of evils attending the wicked and of the happiness attending the righteous and those of Amos and Micah the Hebrew prophets.

citadels by kings to be a stronghold and refuge, and in particular attacks the introduction of the institution of property and gold, "which easily robbed the strong and beautiful of honor, since, for the most part, however strong men are born, however beautiful their body, they follow the lead of the richer man" (5. 1113-1116). During the Iron Age, according to Ovid (*Met.* 1. 127-131), modesty, truth, and faith fled the earth, to be replaced by tricks and plots and snares (*fraudesque dolusque insidiaeque*), violence (*vis*), and a cursed love of gain (*amor sceleratus habendi*). Whereas, he adds (1. 135-136), the ground, like the sunlight and the air, had previously been the common possession of all men, it was now carefully marked out by boundary-lines. During this age (1. 139-150) wealth was discovered, which led men on to crime and war and plunder and which vanquished piety. It was (15. 99-103) an age in which the trustfulness (*credulitas*) of the fish and the innocuousness and simplicity of the beasts did not result in their being caught, since all things were free from snares (*insidiis*), fear and deceit (*fraude*), and full of peace. The Stoics[1] similarly had a glowing picture of a Golden Age, during which men lived in harmony with nature and had no blind love of gold (Sen. *Phaedra* 486 and 527-528), and of a decline from that ideal, so that (Ps.-Sen. *Octavia* 427-428) "luxury arose, deadliest of ills, a luring pest."

Josephus' picture (1. 60-62) of the decline from a Golden Age is within this classical tradition. Cain, he says, in his supplement to the Biblical account, indulged in every bodily pleasure, increased his substance with wealth (παλήθει χρημάτων) amassed by rapine (ἁρπαγῆς) and violence (βίας), and incited to luxury (ἡδονήν) and pillage (ληστείαν) all whom he met.[2]

In particular, Josephus' non-Biblical additions of Cain's introduction of boundaries of land, his building and fortifying a city, and his ending

---

[1] See the passages collected by Lovejoy and Boas (above, p. 344, n. 2) 260-286. To be sure, however, many of the Stoics, as I. S. Ryberg (above, p. 343 n. 3) 121, and M. E. Taylor (above, p.343, n. 3) 264-266, remark, for example, Panaetius (*ap.* Cic. *De Off.* 2. 15-16), did acknowledge that there was some progress in the history of civilization.

[2] Cf. Ovid, *Am.* 3.8. 35-36, who refers to the Age of Saturn, when "the deep earth kept all lucre in darkness." Josephus (5. 179-180) similarly notes as marks of the degeneracy of the Israelites before their deliverance by the judges their drifting into living in accordance with their own pleasure (ἡδονήν) and caprice (βούλησιν) and luxury (τρυφήν). It is the increase in wealth (πλοῦτον) which leads to luxury (τρυφῆς) and voluptuousness (ἡδονῆς), and these lead to disregard of the laws (5. 132). Cf. Moses' extra-Biblical attack (4. 167) on the tribes of Gad, Reuben, and Manasseh for seeking to live in luxury and ease (τρυφᾶν ἀπόνως) and Josephus' attack on Samuel's sons for abandoning themselves to luxury (τρυφή) and rich food.

of the life of simplicity have close classical parallels which Josephus may well have had in mind. In his description of the Germans, Caesar (*B.G.* 6. 22), in apparent praise, notes that they do not have definite quantities of land or estates of their own. Virgil (*Geor.* 1. 126-127) remarks that in the Saturnian Age it was unlawful to mark out fields and to divide them with boundaries. Tibullus (1. 3. 43-44) notes that in that age there were no boundary-stones in the fields. Ovid (*Am.* 3. 8. 41) similarly remarks that in that period surveyors did not mark off the soil with boundaries. Seneca uses similar language (*Phaedra* 528-529) in noting that no sacred boundary-stones separated fields; in contrast, in the present age (Ps.-Sen. *Octavia* 420-422), the characteristics of decline are that men have marked out boundaries, have established kingdoms, have built cities, have guarded their own dwellings, or, bent on booty, have attacked other dwellings with weapons.

To Virgil (*Ecl.* 4. 32-33) the fact that man, even with the return of the Golden Age, will gird towns with walls is an indication that traces of his old sin remain. Similarly Seneca (*Phaedra* 531-532), in his picture of the primitive age of man, notes that cities were not then surrounded by massive walls, set with many towers. And Pseudo-Seneca (*Octavia* 401) similarly notes that they were not then accustomed to surround their cities with walls.

Josephus condemns Cain for putting an end to the guileless (ἀκέραιον) and generous (μεγαλόψυχον) simplicity (ἀπραγμοσύνην—a word which occurs only here in Josephus) and ignorance (ἀμαθίας) in which men had lived previously and converted them to a life of knavery (πανουργίαν). This, too, is in line with the classical portrayals of the primitive age of simplicity in Homer, Plato, Virgil, and Ovid, as noted above.

In a further addition to the Biblical narrative, Josephus (1. 66) notes in vivid detail the continued deterioration in Cain's descendants, each generation becoming worse than the previous one through inheriting and imitating its vices. "They rushed incontinently (ἀκρατῶς) into battle," he adds, "and plunged (ὡρμήκεσαν) into brigandage (λῃστείαν); or if anyone was too timid (ὀκνηρός) for slaughter, he would display other forms of mad recklessness (ἀπόνοιαν θράσους) by insolence (ὑβρίζων) and greed (πλεονεκτῶν).[1] Later, in describing (1. 72) the

---

[1] On the depravity of Cain's posterity see also Philo, *De Post. Caini* 42-43. Philo here speaks of "a life beset with passions and vices, with its treachery and unscrupulousness, its villainy and dissoluteness." While the picture is similar, Josephus uses none of Philo's terms in describing the depravity of Cain's descendants. Cf. also *Pirke de R. Eliezer* 22, which speaks of the descendants of Cain as those

deterioration of Seth's descendants, Josephus remarks that they no longer rendered to God his due honors nor showed justice in dealings with their fellow men but showed a zeal (ζήλωσιν) for vice (κακίας) twice as great as they had shown previously for virtue. All this is Josephus' embellishment of a single Biblical phrase (Gen. 4. 17): "And he [Cain] built a city."

Schalit[1]) has well remarked that the fact that Josephus speaks in immediate juxtaposition of the wickedness of Cain and of his building of a city indicates that he regarded the act of Cain as sinful.[2]) In this Josephus may well have had in mind the story of Romulus, who slew his brother Remus because of an argument over the city wall of Rome.[3]) The account may have been familiar to him from Dionysius of Halicarnassus, with whose work, as Thackeray and Shutt have shown,[4]) Josephus was probably acquainted.

Josephus (1. 64) adds to the Biblical account (Gen. 4. 22) of Tubal-Cain, whom he calls Jubel, by connecting the latter's invention of the forging of metal with the art of war, a connection similarly made in Ovid's account of the Iron Age (*Met.* 1. 142-143). Josephus' account is likewise reminiscent of the account of the Greek Telchines, semi-divine beings in Rhodes who were skilled in metal-work, found in Strabo (14. 2. 7, pp. 653-654) and Eustathius (*ad Iliad*, p. 771. 55ff.). The added statement that Jubel distinguished himself in the art of war, procuring thereby the means of satisfying the pleasures of the body, is reminiscent of Lucretius' attack on war (5. 1000-1001).[5])

---

who rebel and sin and defile themselves with all kinds of immorality; but the picture and the language are more Biblical than Josephus' Hellenized version. Cf. Rappaport [above, p. 336, n. 1] 7, no. 33, and 86-87, n. 41.

[1]) Schalit (above, p. 340, n. 2) 11, n. 28.

[2]) The Midrash (*Genesis Rabbah* 23.1) likewise regards this as sinful but does not give details such as Josephus gives. Pseudo-Philo (*Biblical Antiquities* 2.3) adds that Cain continued to build cities until he had founded seven of them.

[3]) Cf. Livy 1. 7.2 and 1.16; D. H. 1.87.4; and Plut. *Romulus* 10. On the comparison of Cain and Romulus, see P. Kretschmer, "Remus and Romulus," *Glotta* 1 (1909) 301, who cites Propertius, 3.9.50 ("caeso moenia firma Remo") and Tibullus, 2.5. 23-24, as indicating that the death of Remus was understood as a building-sacrifice. See also A. Ehrenzweig, "Kain und Lamach," *ZATW* 35 (1915) 1-9; A. Ehrenzweig, "Biblische und klassische Urgeschichte," *ZATW* 38 (1919-20) 65-86; and O. Gruppe, "Kain," *ZATW* 39 (1920-21) 67-76.

[4]) H. St. J. Thackeray, *Josephus*, 4 (Loeb Classical Library; Cambridge, Mass. 1930) ix-x; and R. J. H. Shutt, *Studies in Josephus* (London 1961) 92-101.

[5]) Cf. Philo, *De Post. Caini* 117: "All these people are war-makers, and that is why they are said to be workers in iron and bronze," Similarly, as Rappaport (above, p. 336, n. 1) 6, no. 31, and 86, n. 39, notes, the Agada (see *Gen. Rabbah* 23.3 and Rashi on Gen. 4.22) condemns Tubal-Cain for inventing the weapons by means of which men can kill each other.

The exalted picture of Seth's descendants (1. 69), completely missing from the Bible (Gen. 5. 6), as inhabiting the same country without dissension (ἀστασίαστοι) is reminiscent of Thucydides, who especially bewails (3. 80-83) civil strife, and of Plato (*Laws* 3. 678 E 9-679 A 2), who, in his description of the development of society after the great deluge, remarks that primitive men felt affection and good will towards one another and had no occasion for internecine quarrels about their subsistence. And the fact that they lived "in prosperity, meeting with no untoward incident to the day of their death" is reminiscent of Aristotle, who remarks (*Ethics* 1. 8. 1099 A 31-1099 B 8) that true happiness requires external goods (τῶν ἐκτὸς ἀγαθῶν), "for which reason some identify happiness with good fortune (εὐδαιμονίᾳ), though others identify it with virtue." Aristotle further stresses (1.9.1100 A 4-9) that not only is complete virtue required, but also a complete life, since many vicissitudes occur, as witness the case of Priam, who fell into misfortune in his old age; "and one who has experienced such chances and has ended wretchedly no one calls happy." Finally, Aristotle quotes Solon (1.10.1100 A 10-11) as saying that no one should be called happy until he has seen the end of his life.[1])

An interesting addition to the Biblical text made by Josephus (1.70) is Adam's prediction[2]) of "a destruction (ἀφανισμόν) of the universe, in one case by a violent fire (κατ' ἰσχὺν πυρός) and in another by a mighty deluge of water (κατὰ βίαν καὶ πλῆθος ὕδατος).[3]) While it is true that the rabbis (*Zebaḥim* 116a and other passages cited by Rappaport)[4]) speak in juxtaposition, describing the tumult that occurred when God gave the Torah at Sinai, of the possibility that the noise is

---

[1]) Josephus' knowledge of Aristotle is clear from his several mentions of Aristotle by name (see the index to my Loeb volume, s.v. "Aristotle") and from his acquaintance with Aristotelian terminology (see the numerous examples cited by Brune [above, p. 342, n. 4] 210-214).

[2]) Rappaport (above, p. 336, n. 1) 7, no. 37, and 88, n. 45, notes that the picture of Adam as predicting the future is very widespread in the Agada, but he notes that the rabbis do not picture him, as does Josephus, as predicting catastrophes to his contemporaries.

[3]) Rappaport (above, p. 336, n. 1) 88, n. 94a, concludes that from Josephus' language it is not possible to be sure whether Josephus means "the one time ...the other time," i.e., two catastrophes, or "partly... partly," i.e. one catastrophe, though he tends toward the view that Josephus is speaking of one catastrophe. But Schalit (above, p. 340, n. 2) 13, n. 45, contends that Josephus refers to two catastrophes, noting the close parallel with the *Vita Adae*, 49-50, which, like Josephus, speaks of two catastrophes and two tablets. It seems more likely, however, that one catastrophe is referred to: in the one case (fire), the brick pillar will survive, while in the other case (water), she stone pillar will survive.

[4]) Rappaport (above, p. 336, n. 1) 90, n. 52.

that of the destruction of the world by flood of water or by flood of fire, they do not present this as a prediction and in fact deny (the words are put into the mouth of Balaam) that this will take place, since God has sworn that He will not destroy mankind. It is just as likely, however, as Hölscher[1]) remarks (though without citing evidence), that Josephus' notion is Greek. In point of fact, Plato (*Timaeus* 22 C 1-3) remarks that there have been and will be many destructions of mankind, the greatest of them being caused by fire and water. And in interpreting the myth of Phaethon (*Timaeus* 22 C-D) Plato explains that it signifies one of the great conflagrations upon the earth occurring after long intervals. Heraclitus (*ap.* Diog. Laer. 9.8 = Heraclitus, fr. 66 D., 26 B.) likewise speculates about the conflagration (ἐκπύρωσις) which will consume the universe, and this doctrine of the ultimate absorption of the universe at the end of the *annus magnus* in a primal fire played a prominent role in the writings of the Stoics, so that Clearchus (*ap.* Stobaeus, *Ecl.* 1, p. 171) speaks of successive reintegrations of the universe from fire, and Marcus Aurelius (6.4) notes that in the conflagration all things that exist will either pass into vapor or else be dispersed into their constituent atoms. Ovid (*Met.* 1.253-261) similarly notes that it was fated that the universe, including the sea, land, and sky, would be destroyed by fire, and so Zeus, to punish man's wickedness, decided to send a flood.

There is obvious Hellenization in Josephus' treatment of the sons of the angels of God (Gen. 6.4), for he actually compares (1.73) their bold exploits with those ascribed by the Greeks to the giants.[2]) Josephus then discusses the punishment by God of these sons of angels in language reminiscent of Greek tragedy, for, whereas the Bible (Gen. 6.5) remarks merely on their wickedness and on their evil thoughts, Josephus notes (1.73) that they were overbearing (ὑβριστάς) and disdainful (ὑπερόπτας) of every virtue, being over-confident of their strength.

Hellenizations such as these that have been noted in Josephus' account of the Golden Age and of man's decline therefrom are to be seen throughout the part of the *Antiquities* which parallels the Bible, as the present author will attempt to show in a number of studies in which he is now engaged. While it is true that some of these Hellenizations

---

[1]) G. Hölscher, "Josephus," *RE* 9 (1916) 1959.
[2]) Rappaport(above, p. 336, n. 1) xxv, n. 2, rightly cites this as an example to refute M. Gaster's contention (*The Asatir* [London 1927] 63) that Josephus adhered strictly to the Biblical narrative and avoided syncretism with Greek mythology.

have parallels in rabbinic midrashim, the parallels with classical sources, particularly those whom Josephus cites by name elsewhere, are generally closer both in idea and in language; and it seems more likely that in attempting to defend Judaism before a Greek-speaking audience Josephus would clothe the Biblical narrative in a classical dress familiar to them. Finally, even where Josephus' embellishments have rabbinic parallels, one must stress the significance of Josephus' choice of those which would especially appeal to a Greek audience.

MOSES AS GOD AND KING

BY

WAYNE A. MEEKS

Indiana University

Erwin Goodenough, more than any other single scholar, has demonstrated the astonishing degree to which many Torah-true Jews were involved in the syncretism that pervaded the Mediterranean world in the Greco-Roman period. As a corollary to his achievement—a corollary he himself grasped only near the end of his work—the impervious barriers which were once commonly supposed to separate such circles as "normative" or "Palestinian" Judaism from "Hellenistic" Judaism and from Samaritanism are now exposed as a modern illusion.[1]) Consequently there is every reason to hope for a new era in the comparative and historical study of Jewish, Samaritan, early Christian, Gnostic, and Islamic traditions. What is offered here is a very small step in that direction: an analysis of some variations on the theme of Moses' heavenly enthronement in Philo, the midrash aggada, and Samaritan sources.

I. The Enthronement of Moses

Goodenough showed that Philo's *Life of Moses* depicted the "Lawgiver" and "Protoprophet" of the Jews as a perfect example of Hellenism's ideal king,[2]) with the necessary subsidiary functions of legislation, prophecy, and the high priesthood. Philo offers several explanations for Moses' selection for the highest office, of which this is the most interesting:

> Therefore, since he bade farewell to accumulation of goods and to the wealth that has such force among men, God honored him by giving him the greatest and most perfect wealth ... For, deeming him worthy to appear as partner of his own fortunes, (God) remitted to him all the

---

[1]) See, most recently, E. Bickermann, "Symbolism in the Dura Synagogue," *HTR* 58 (1965), 129-31; and J. Neusner, "Judaism in Late Antiquity, A Review Essay", *Judaism*, 15, 2, 1966, 230-240.

[2]) *By Light, Light*, pp. 181-87; *An Introduction to Philo Judaeus*, pp. 33f.

world as a possession suitable for (his) heir.... And perhaps that is not to be wondered at, for if, according to the proverb, "friends' things are common," and the prophet was declared the friend of God, then it follows that he would share also in his possessions, according to what was needful. For while God possesses everything but needs nothing, the good man possesses nothing properly speaking, not even himself, but partakes, so far as he is able, of God's treasures. ... What then? Did he not also enjoy an even greater partnership with the Father and Maker of the universe, being deemed worthy of the same title? For he was named god and king *(theos kai basileus)* of the whole nation. And he was said to have entered into the darkness where God was, that is, into the formless and invisible and incorporeal archetypal essence of existing things, perceiving things invisible to mortal nature. And, like a well-executed painting, openly presenting himself and his life, he set up an altogether beautiful and God-formed work as an example for those who are willing to imitate it.[1])

Here Moses' kingship is an intermediary status between God and the rest of men. Having perceived the invisible good, he so models his own life after it that he becomes a paradigm for his subjects. Goodenough has shown that this concept of double imitation is a common theme in Hellenistic writings on kingship.[2]) But there is one thing peculiar about the Philonic passage: here Moses' paradigmatic office is founded on a mystic vision, which in turn is identified, by a midrash on Exodus 20.21, with his ascent of Mt. Sinai. The implication is that Philo is uniting the Hellenistic ideology of kingship with an existing midrashic tradition that interpreted Moses' ascent of Sinai as an ascension to heaven.

The double title "god and king" is also puzzling. The first title, "god," Philo takes directly from Exodus 7.1,[3]) "See, I have made you a god to Pharaoh." But the scriptural context has no connection with the Sinai theophany, nor does it mention kingship. We are left with the question how Philo came to connect Moses' installation as ideal king with (1) a mystic ascent, read into the Sinai episode, and (2) the scriptural report that Moses was called "god."

At this point we receive unexpected clarification from a rabbinic midrash in the group of homilies collected under the name of R. Tanḥuma. The homily interprets Num. 10.1-2, "The Lord said to Moses, 'Make for yourself two trumpets of silver,'" by introducing

---

[1]) *Mos.* i. 155-58.
[2]) "The Political Philosophy of Hellenistic Kingship," *Yale Classical Studies*, I, 88-91; cf. p. 74; *By Light, Light*, p. 186.
[3]) See *Leg. all.* i. 40, *Sac.* 9, *Det.* 161f., *Mig.* 84, *Mut.* 19, *Som.* ii. 189.

Psalm 24.7, "Lift up your heads, O Gates ...," which, according to the midrash, was spoken by Solomon when he brought the Ark into the Temple. The connection between the two passages is not at once apparent, for the cardinal point, that the trumpets are a sign of royalty, does not emerge until the end of the homily. Once introduced, however, the Psalm text is expounded:

> What (does this mean): "The Lord of hosts, he is the King of glory"? (This means that) he apportions some of his glory to those who fear him according to his glory. How so? He is called "God," and he called Moses "god," as it is said, "See, I have made you a god to Pharaoh" (Ex. 7.1). He vivifies the dead, and he apportioned some of his glory to Elijah, for the latter vivified a dead person ... (1 Ki. 17.22). Thus the Holy One, blessed be He, apportions some of his glory to those that fear him. To the King Messiah he grants to be clothed in his robes ... (Ps. 21.6). Our rabbis teach us that no mortal king rides on God's steed or puts on his robes or uses his crown or sits on his throne, but the Holy One, blessed be He, apportions all these to those who fear him, and gives them to them. How do we know this? It is said, "In storm and whirlwind are his ways" (Nah. 1.3), and he gave this to Elijah, as it is said, "And he went up in a whirlwind to heaven" (2 Ki. 2.11). And none puts on his robes. What is written? "Thou art clothed in splendor and majesty" (Ps. 104.1). And of the King Messiah it is written, "Splendor and majesty thou dost put on him" (Ps. 21.6). And none makes use of his crown. What is written of Moses? "And Moses did not know that his face beamed with light" (Ex. 34.29). And none sits on his throne. It is written, "Solomon sat on the throne of the Lord as king" (1 Chr. 29.23). And none makes use of his sceptre, for it was given to Moses, as scripture says, "Take this rod in your hand," etc. (Ex. 4.17). What is written of the Holy One, blessed be He? "God has gone up with a shout, the Lord, with the sound of the horn; [Sing to God, sing; sing to the King, sing; for God is King over all the earth; sing a Maskil. God reigns over the nations; God sits on his holy throne"] (Ps. 47.6-9). The Holy One, blessed be He, said to Moses, "I have made you a king," as Scripture says, "He became king in Yeshurun" (Deut. 33.5). Just as they blow trumpets before the King when he goes forth, so in your case, when you go forth they will sound trumpets: "Make for yourself two trumpets of silver."[1]

The last sentence compares Moses not with earthly kings, but with God who is preceded by the sound of the Shofar when he "goes up" as king. The silver trumpets, which were not to be used, according to tradition, by any earthly king except perhaps David,[2] are therefore

---

[1] Tanh., ed. S. Buber (1885), IV, 51f., cf. 53; repeated in Bamidbar R. 15.13.

[2] Tanh., ed. Buber, IV, 53f. = Bamidbar R. 15.15; Midr. Kohelet R. 8.8 (end); cf. Sifre Num. 75 (on Num. 10.8).

understood as a sign that Moses shared *God's* kingship. This accords with the theme of the whole homily, that God "shares his glory with his worshippers." As God the supreme king made Moses "god," so also he made him "king."

It is immediately apparent that the core of the homily is the same as Philo's midrash. (1) The main theme of both is that "God shares his glory with those who fear him," or, in Philo's language, "The good man partakes, so far as he is able, of God's treasures." (2) Both hinge on the verse, "I have made you a god to Pharaoh." (3) This verse is interpreted to mean that God made Moses "king" as well, since "king" is one of the attributes of "God." This point is only implicit in Philo's statement, but absolutely necessary for his argument.

The other peculiarity of the Philo passage, the connection of Moses' naming as "god" with the Sinai ascent, is not quite clear in the Tanḥuma homily, although it is implied in the proof-text Deut. 33.5 and in the identification of Moses' corona of light with the "crown of God." Moreover rabbinic traditions did commonly connect Exodus 7.1 with Moses' ascent to heaven, as shown by the midrashim on the phrase "Moses, the man of God" (Deut. 33.1), which was interpreted "Moses, a man, god." One of several variants is this:

> "A man, god": "A man" when he ascended on high; "god" when he descended below. "And Aaron and all the sons of Israel saw Moses and behold! his face emitted beams of light."[1]

Thus it was in heaven, at the time of the Sinai assembly, that Moses was made "god" and, therefore, "king."

From the extant Samaritan sources, which unfortunately do not allow us to see very clearly before the fourth century C.E., it is evident that a very similar tradition existed in the Samaritan religion, for which Moses was the hero of heroes. The "vesting" of Moses with God's name and "crowning with light" are the major elements in a heavenly enthronement that was the foundation of Moses' whole mission:

> Exalted is the great prophet Moses whom his Lord vested with His name. He dwelt in the mysteries[2] and was crowned with the light. The True One was revealed to him and gave him His handwriting; He made him drink from ten glorious fountains, seven on high and three below.[3]

---

[1] Pesikta R. K. 32, f. 198b; cf. Debarim R. 11.4; Midr. Tehillim 90.1.

[2] I.e., "in heaven." The "unseen" realms, *ksi'ātā*, are contrasted in Sam. with the "visible," i.e. earthly, *gli'ātā*.

[3] *Memar Marqah* ii.12, trans. Macdonald, pp. 80f.

In other passages, Moses receives not only a "crown of light," as in the Tanḥuma homily, but a "robe of light" (which in Tanḥuma was reserved for the King Messiah!):

> They assembled on Mount Sinai on the day when the Scriptures came down.
> The Shofar began to proclaim,
> and the voice of the prophet was raised.
> And the Good said: "A prophet shall be exalted; the prophet shall be magnified; his prophecy shall be exalted."
> And he adorned and glorified and brought (him) to Arafel,
> when he was clothed with a garment in which no king is able to be clothed;
> when he was hidden in the cloud
> and his face clothed with a beam of light,
> that all peoples should know that Moses is the servant of God and faithful[1].)

Other passages speak directly of Moses' installation with royal status in heaven: "God gave him a rank which no king is able to possess, and God appointed him below and entrusted him with the unseen world,"[2] Like Enoch in some Jewish traditions Moses "sat on a great throne and wrote what his Lord had taught him.[3]) Similarly, the rod he received from God ("from the fire") is a sceptre of sovereignty: "This will be a wonder to you—in it is great and powerful rulership (*salṭanu*)."[4]

The crown, the robe, the throne, the sceptre received from God: all these are varying aspects of the imagery of Moses' enthronement in heaven at the time of the Sinai revelation. This Samaritan imagery is

---

[1] From the 6th hymn of the *Durran* cycle by Amram Darah; text in A. E. Cowley, *The Samaritan Liturgy* (1909), I, 40f.

[2] From the first hymn of the *Durran*, Cowley, I, 38, lines 24-26; cf. *M. Marq.* v.3, text p. 126, line 6.

[3] *M. Marq.* iv.6, trans. Macdonald, p. 156; cf. 1 Enoch 12.3, 4; 15.1; Jub. 4.23; Targ. Ps.-Jon. on Gen. 5.24; see G. Scholem, *Jewish Gnosticism, Merkabah Mysticism and Talmudic Tradition* (1960), p. 51, n. 24.

[4] *M. Marq.* i.2, trans Macdonald, p. 7. On the staff as an emblem of kingship received from a god, see G. Widengren, *The Ascension of the Prophet and the Heavenly Book* (1950), p. 9 and n. 1. The rod of Moses, which had been Adam's and, in one tradition at least, cut from the tree of life (ARNb, ed. Schechter, p. 157; Widengren regards this as a Babylonian motif), plays an important part in diverse Jewish as well as Sam. traditions. See Artapanus in Eusebius, *Praep. Ev.* ix.27; Ps.-Philo, *Bibl. Antt.* 19.11; *Asatır*, ed. Gaster, ix.22; cf. L. Ginzberg, *The Legends of the Jews*, II, 291-93 and n. 88; III, 19 and n. 31; III, 477; John Bowman, "Samaritan Studies," *BJRL* 40 (1958), 303f.; José Ramón Díaz, "Palestinian Targum and New Testament," *Nov. T.* 6 (1963), 78; B. Murmelstein, "Adam. Ein Beitrag zur Messiaslehre," *Wiener Zeitschr. f. d. Kunde d. Morgenlandes* 36 (1929), 55.

much more concrete than Philo's, but it is strikingly similar to that of the Tanḥuma homily quoted above and also to that of a Greek Jewish source much older than Philo. The latter, a verse drama of "The Exodus" written by a certain Ezekiel sometime before the first century B.C.E.,[1]) casts Moses' enthronement in the form of a dream. Moses sees a "noble man" (*phōs gennaios*) seated on a "great throne" at "the peak of Mt. Sinai." The figure gives to Moses his own "royal diadem," "mighty sceptre," and the throne itself.[2]) The interpretation of the dream predicts that Moses "will establish a great throne;" the dream itself has made clear that his reign is on behalf of God.

II. Moses and the Name of God

In all the variant traditions of Moses' enthronement we have examined, the central theme is that Moses, when he received the Torah at Sinai, was made God's vice-regent.[3]) Philo elaborated this theme in a peculiar way by drawing upon the popular Hellenistic philosophy of kingship; Ezekiel, the Tanḥuma homily, and the early Samaritan sources depict the vice-regency with graphic symbolism. Elsewhere the Samaritan sources speak explicitly of Moses' status, as when God is made to say to him, "You are my second [*tinyāni*] in the lower world,"[4]) Significantly this extraordinary designation of Moses is derived precisely from the verse that was central to the tradition we found represented in Philo and the Tanḥuma homily: Exodus 7.1.[5]) Thus the incomparable status of Moses is directly connected with the implications of the biblical report that he was called "god."

It is especially in the Samaritan literature that the naming of Moses with God's name is elaborated and emphasized.[6]) The name with which Moses was "crowned"[7]) or "clothed"[8]) is always Elohim, as

---

[1]) E. Schurer, *Die Geschichte des jüd. Volkes*, 4. Aufl., III, 469.

[2]) Text in Eusebius, *Praep. Ev.* ix.29; ET in E. H. Gifford, *Eusebii Pamphili Evang. Praep.*, III/1, pp. 469f. Goodenough discusses the passage, *By Light, Light*, pp. 289-91, and *Symbols*, IX, 101.

[3]) The transmission of the "heavenly book" as the major instrument of a divinely established kingship is the subject of Widengren's monograph cited above.

[4]) *M. Marq.* 1.2, trans. Macdonald, p. 12.

[5]) *Ibid.*, Marqah assimilates Ex. 7.1 and 4.16, substituting *tinyāni*, "my second," for *'elohîm*.

[6]) E.g., *M. Marq.* 1.2,9; ii.12; iv.1; v.3,4 (ET, pp. 5, 18, 31, 81, 137, 203, 207); Cowley, I, 32f., 54.

[7]) *M. Marq.* i.9.

[8]) *Ibid.*, ii.12; v.1; Cowley, I, 54, etc.

distinguished from YHWH, "the name which God revealed to him."[1]) Furthermore the tradition is univocal that it was "on the top of Mount Horeb" that Moses was thus named. For the Samaritans this is one of several motifs that serve to connect the Exodus and the Sinai theophany typologically with Creation:

> The first name, with which Genesis opens, was that which he was vested with and by which he was made strong. *See, I make you as God to Pharaoh* (Ex. vii.1; Targ.).
> As I began then, so now I begin. In the beginning I began a goodly world and now I begin a righteous world.[2])

In the new "righteous world" it is clear that Moses has pre-eminence, for the sharing of God's name with Moses means in addition the sharing of his functions and status:

> Then He said, I am the God of your fathers (Ex. iii.6).
> Take from me divinity ['*elāhû*] and with it make your prophethood strong.[3])

Indeed Moses' ascension on Sinai was often regarded as in some sense a deification. Thus the late "Book of Joshua" praises Moses as the one "who went out from the boundaries of humanity and human power into the Divine power."[4]) However, this interpretation was much older than this source, as comparison of a passage in Memar Marqah with one in Philo demonstrates:

> At the time God said to him, "*Come up to me on the mountain*" (Deut.x.1; Targ.), when he went up to Him and cloud covered him for six days,... He ascended from human status to that of the angels [*weslêq mîn metûbît barnašitā 'el metûbît mal'akiā*.][5])

And Philo, expounding the parallel verse, "Come up to me to the mountain and be there ..." (Ex. 24.12a, LXX), says:

---

[1]) *M. Marq.* ii.12, ET p. 81. See also v.1, where the statement, "The name with which he was vested on the top of Mount Horeb asks its Lord that death should not come near him," is followed by an acrostic on ELOHIM. Macdonald's suggestion that the identification of Moses' name with God's depends on the equation *mšh* = *šmh*, "the Name" (circumlocution for the Tetragrammaton) is mistaken.

[2]) *M. Marq.* ii.12, trans. Macdonald, p. 81. Cf. *ibid.*, i.9, "On the seventh day ... I established your name then also—my name and yours therein as one ..." On the Exodus and Covenant as a new creation, see J. Bowman, "The Exegesis of the Pentateuch among the Samaritans and among the Rabbis," *Oudt. Studiën*, 8 (1950), 248f.

[3]) *M. Marq.* i.2, trans. Macdonald, p. 5.

[4]) Trans. O.T. Crane, *The Samaritan Chronicle* ... (1890), p. 32.

[5]) *M. Marq.* v.3, trans. Macdonald, p. 206.

This signifies that a holy soul is divinized by ascending not to the air or to the ether or to heaven (which is) higher than all but to (a region) above the heavens. And beyond the world there is no place but God.[1]

When compared with these texts the traces of a similar notion in the rabbinic midrashim can no longer be ignored. The notion is clearest in the passages, already referred to, that interpret *mošeh 'iš hā'elohîm* (Deut. 33.1) against all rules of syntax as "Moses, man and god": "A man when he ascended on high, a god when he descended."[2] This peculiar exegesis can only be a relic of the tradition that Moses, during his heavenly ascension at Sinai, received from God both the name Elohim and a share of the status and functions which that name entailed.

This conclusion is strengthened and further illuminated by an observation made by Morton Smith, who has called attention to rabbinic exegesis of Isaiah 43.7, understood in this way:

> Everyone who is called by my name, him have I created, formed and made that he should also share my glory.[3]

From this a Talmudic tradition concludes that Adam before the fall and the righteous at the end of days are worshipped by angels.[4] Smith offers the very plausible suggestion that the naming with God's name here implies the restoration of God's image, which the first man had but lost at the fall. His suggestion is abundantly supported by analysis of a further recurrent element in the legend of Moses' ascension, the crown or robe of light, to which we now turn.

III. THE CROWN OF LIGHT AND THE IMAGE OF GOD

It was only natural that the *qeren 'orah* Moses received on Sinai (Ex. 34.29ff.) should come to be regarded as a "crown of light" as it is throughout the Samaritan literature and in the rabbinic traditions referred to above. The astral or solar crown was very common in the symbolism first of Eastern, then of Hellenistic kingship.[5] Always it

---

[1] *QE* ii.40 (trans. R. Marcus, Loeb ed., *Supplement* II, 82f.). On Moses as god and man in Philo, see Goodenough, *By Light, Light*, pp. 224-29.
[2] Pesiqta R.K. (ed. Buber, 1868), f. 198b. Cf. Debarim R. 11.4 and Midr. Tehillim on Ps. 90.1; contrast Sifre Deut. § 342.
[3] "The Image of God," *BJRL* 40 (1958), 478.
[4] Talm. B., Baba Bat. 75b. See Smith's discussion, pp. 478-81, and other references he cites.
[5] See Goodenough, *Yale Classical Studies*, I, 78-83; K. Keyssner, "Nimbus," Pauly-Wissowa, XVII/1, cols. 591-623, esp. 595f., 610-615.

seems to have signified that the wearer was or became in some sense divine.[1]) This is no less true in the Moses legends, in which the crown of light is God's own crown. Moses—but no other mortal—is now permitted to use it, that is, to exercise divine prerogatives.[2]) Hence Exodus 34.30 provided the secondary proof-text in the midrash on Deut. 33.1 that Moses became "god" during his ascent.[3]) A special twist is given to the Jewish and Samaritan traditions, however, by the identification of the light-crown with the *image* of God, Gen. 1.26f. This passage from the Memar is particularly revealing:

> Where is there any like Moses, apostle of the True One, faithful one of the House of God, and His servant? He drew near to the holy deep darkness where the Divine One was, and he saw the wonders of the unseen—a sight no one else could see. His image [*ṣalmēh*] dwelt on him. How terrifying to anyone who beholds and no one is able to stand before it! His mouth was like the Euphrates, rolling with living waters which quench the thirst of all who drink of them. His tongue was like a drawn sword victorious in wrath and turning back speedily. His heart was like a garden; all its fruit life from death. His thought was like the tree of Life; to eat of it keeps one from death. His mind was like an appetizing dish, the taste of it the taste of truth. His reason [*ḥašabēh*] was like a candlestick [*menôrāh*], its lamps trimmed by the King who created them. He who is guided by it will never stray; the light before him will lead him to salvation.[4])

The comparison of Moses' God-inspired intellect with the menorah, following so closely upon the statement that God's image "dwelt on" him during his heavenly ascension, cannot fail to remind a Goodenough pupil of the remarkable relief carving of a man bearing a menorah on his head in the Beth Shearim cemetery.[5]) In a brilliant discussion of this figure Morton Smith has called attention both to the comparison of the

---

[1]) See Philo's description of the mad Caligula masquerading as Apollo, *Leg.* 95.
[2]) Cf. Tanḥ., ed. Buber, IV, 51, quoted above. G. Scholem has shown that the term I have translated "make use of" *(hištammeš be-)* is often "a term for theurgic practice" and offers examples from Jewish mystical texts for the notion of magical "use" of God's crown. The crown and the *name* of God, moreover, are closely connected in his examples, as they are in the passages we have examined (*Jewish Gnosticism*, p. 54 and n. 36).
[3]) Above, p. 357; cf. the description of Enoch-Metatron's enthronement (3 Enoch 12.3f.): "And he made me a royal crown in which were fixed forty-nine costly stones like unto the light of the globe of the sun. For its splendour went forth in the four quarters of the '*Araboth Raqia*', and in (through) the seven heavens, and in the four quarters of the world. And he put it on my head" (trans. Odeberg). Enoch receives the throne name "Yahweh Qaton"!
[4]) *M. Marq.* vi. 3, trans. Macdonald, pp. 223f.
[5]) *Symbols*, III, illus. 56; discussed I, 92.

menorah to a wreath or crown (Sifre Zuta 8.2) and to Apion's story, answered by Josephus (*C.Ap.* ii.112ff.), of a fake epiphany in the Jerusalem temple, employing a headdress set with lamps. Thus, Smith argues, the menorah or a crown of light was nothing less than the visual symbol for the image of God.[1]) Jacob Jervell, moreover, has shown that in Jewish Adam-speculation the image of God was typically regarded as "gerade auf dem Antlitz eingeprägt."[2]) Jervell argues that this conception of the *imago* was especially connected with the notion that Adam had been God's vice-regent, the first "king of the world."[3]) When the *imago* is identified with Moses' divine crown of light, it is quite clear that the same kind of connection is implied. The similarity is not accidental, for further examination of the enthronement traditions about Moses shows that these stories link Moses very closely with Adam.

Again the Samaritan sources are most illuminating. In a midrash on Deut. 34.7 Marqah shows the identity between Moses' crown of light and Adam's lost *imago*:

> *Nor his natural force abated*, for he was vested with the Form [*salmā*] which Adam cast off in the Garden of Eden; and his face shone up to the day of his death.[4])

In another passage Marqah lists a point-by-point correspondence between the creation of Adam and the establishment of the Covenant by the hand of Moses. In both cases there was a theophany; for both

---

[1]) *BJRL* 40, pp. 500f.

[2]) *Imago Dei; Gen.* 1,26f. *im Spätjudentum, in der Gnosis, und in den paulinischen Briefen* (1960), p. 45. Correspondingly, God's *kabôd* was visualized as the gleam of his "face," as in the Targ. on Song of Songs 5.10: "... the effulgence of the glory of whose face is brilliant as fire ..." (quoted by R. Loewe, "The Divine Garment and Shi'ur Qomah," *HTR* 58 [1965], 156 and n. 23).

[3]) *Ibid.*; cf. p. 25. One of the clearest statements of the connection is in the Syriac Christian "Cave of Treasure," certainly incorporating an older Jewish tradition: see the ET by E. A. W. Budge, pp. 52f. That the *imago* meant kingship is also clear in this fragment from Philo: "In his material substance *(ousia)* the king is just the same as any man, but in the authority of his rank he is like the God of all. For there is nothing upon earth more exalted than he. Since he is a mortal, he must not vaunt himself; since he is a god he must not give way to anger. For if he is honoured as being *an image of God*, yet he is at the same time fashioned from the dust of the earth, from which he should learn simplicity to all" (text in Mangey, II, 673, quoted by Goodenough, *Introduction*, p. 71, italics added.). Cf. Ps.-Clem. *Hom.* ix.3, where Noah is said to have been "a king according to the image of the one God."

[4]) *M. Marq.* v.4, trans. Macdonald, p. 209. It should be noted that one MS (Kahle) reads, instead of "vested with the Form ... Eden," "vested with a beam of light and radiance."

the angels assembled as witnesses; Moses like Adam received the spirit from God; the one received "a perfect mind," other "a powerful illumination;" one was "glorified with speech," the other "with perfect knowledge." And, of first importance, "the two of them were clad in two crowns of great light."[1]

Also in Jewish sources the notion that Adam's lost glory was returned at Sinai is familiar, and the identification of the lost image with the light of Moses' face is not unknown. For example a midrash on Prov. 31.29 contains this dialogue:

> Adam said to Moses, "I am greater than you, for I was created in the image of the Holy One, blessed be He..." (Gen. 1.27) He replied, "I am superior to you. The glory which was given to you was taken from you... (Psalm 49.21), (but) I kept the radiance of my face which the Holy one, blessed be He, gave to me, forever..." (Deut. 34.7).[2]

Philo, moreover, repeats a tradition that identified the ascendant Moses with the "heavenly man" created in God's image on the seventh day:

> But the calling above of the prophet is a second birth better than the former. He was called above on the seventh day, by this differing from the first-formed man, because the latter was composed of earth and with a body, while the former is without a body. Therefore the appropriate number six was assigned to the earthborn, while to the other (was assigned) the most sacred nature of the hebdomad.[3]

It is impossible to say to what extent one common tradition may have underlain the various passages from such diverse provenience that we have examined. The evidence is sufficient, however, to demonstrate that related and very similar traditions about the ascension of Moses were cultivated not only in Samaritanism, but also in some circles within both Palestinian and diaspora Judaism. In this constellation of

---

[1] *Ibid.*, vi.3, trans. Macdonald, p. 221.

[2] Debarim R. 11.3; also in the collection *Yalkut ha-Makiri* on Prov. 31.29 (ed. E. Grunhut, rp. Jerusalem, 1964, p. 102b) and on Ps. 49.21 and 68.13 (ed. Buber, 1899, I, 270 and 330). See further Murmelstein, *WZKM* 35 (1928), 255 and n. 3; 36 (1929), 56, and Jervell, pp. 45, 88, 100-103, 114-19.

[3] *QE* ii.46; I translate the Greek fragment preserved in Procopius (printed in the Loeb ed., *Suppl.* II, p. 251), which is slightly shorter than the Armenian version trans. by Marcus (*ibid.*, p. 91). On the creation of the "heavenly man" on the seventh day, see *Leg. all.* i.5, 31, 88, etc. In *QG* ii.56 Philo follows a different, partially contradictory tradition, in which the incorporeal man was created on the sixth day, the "moulded man" on the seventh; cf. *Opif.* 66ff. and Jervell, p. 65. For Marqah also the number "seven" in Ex. 24.16b indicated Moses' superior status, but by comparison with God (Gen. 2.4) rather than Adam (*M. Marq.* i.9).

traditions Moses' elevation at Sinai was treated not only as a heavenly enthronement, but also as a restoration of the glory lost by Adam. Moses, crowned with both God's name and his image, became in some sense a "second Adam," the prototype of a new humanity. Primarily, it seems, his typological identification with Adam was conceived of in functional terms. Moses fulfilled the commission as "Apostle" and vice-regent to which Adam had also been called, but in which he had failed.[1])

IV. THE FUNCTION OF THE TRADITION

No description of the development of a religious tradition can be regarded as complete without some attempt to reconstruct the tradition's *Sitz im Leben*, to discern what function the tradition exercised in the communities that cultivated it. Such extrapolation from traditional motifs back to the social and cultic activities which produced or shaped them is the most difficult task of all, one which inevitably involves conjectural and circular arguments. The proportion of conjecture to solid inference will be inversely related to the degree of our primary and independent knowledge of the groups and their activities. Our knowledge of the diverse Jewish and Samaritan groups of the period dealt with here is so incomplete that I can offer only some working hypotheses. Let us then consider four functions which the traditions of Moses' heavenly enthronement might have served.

When folklore describes an extraordinary experience of a hero regarded as a founder of the community, one is naturally led to ask whether the legend may be an aetiology. Could the legends of Moses' enthronement as God's agent and vice-regent have served to authenticate an existing royal or prophetic institution?[2]) This possibility could be supported by the survival in several forms of a tradition about the successors of Moses.[3]) Nevertheless there is no positive evidence for

---

[1]) On Adam as "king of the whole world," see ARNa, ed. Schechter, p. 4 (ET, Goldin, p. 10); Pesikta rab., ed. Friedmann, 192a; Philo, *Opif.* 84, 148; *QG* i.20, 21; cf. *Opif.* 88; *QG* ii.56; 2 Enoch 31.3; 58.3; 4 Ezra 6.54; Syr. Bar. 14.18; Jervell, pp. 25, 38-40; Murmelstein, *WZKM* 35 (1928), 271.

[2]) Widengren has suggested that the OT stories of Moses' receiving the Torah may themselves have served as an aetiology for the oldest Israelite kingship, specifically for the "royal protocol" (*Ascension*, pp. 24-29; *Sakrales Konigtum im Alten Testament und im Judentum* [1955], pp. 29-33). For a searching criticism of Widengren's presuppositions see M. Noth, "Gott, Konig, Volk im Alten Testament, *ZThK* 47 (1950), 157-91.

[3]) Josephus, *Antt.* iv.165; *C.Ap.* i.40; Justin, *Dial.* 52.3; Eupolemus, *apud* Eusebius, *Praep. Ev.* ix.30; ps.-Philo, *Bib. Antt.* 49.7, cf. 57.4; *Peṭirat Mosheh* in

an aetiological function, and the formal characteristics of an aetiology are missing from the accounts of Moses' ascension. There is nothing to indicate any connection between these legends and the one group we should expect to have sought such legitimation, the Hasmonean kings—who were, to be sure, of Moses' tribe. Moreover the legends themselves in almost every instance emphasize the *uniqueness* of Moses' experience and mission. In the Samaritan liturgy for example, Deut. 34.10 is frequently paraphrased, "who can compare with Moses the prophet, the like of whom has not arisen and never will arise ?"[1])

If no "prophet like Moses" was expected in the present age, however, the hope for such a prophet at the end of days was certainly not excluded.[2]) Therefore our second hypothesis might well be that the stories of Moses' heavenly enthronement laid the foundation for an eschatological ideology. The pattern, "As was the first redeemer, so will be the last redeemer," is quite familiar from rabbinic midrash,[3]) and the Samaritan *Taheb*, despite Merx's argument to the contrary,[4]) cannot be understood except on the basis of Moses typology.[5]) A legend of

---

Jellinek, *Bet ha-Midrasch*, I, 122. Such a succession seems also implicit in some of the passages which designate Moses as "Father" or "Teacher" of all the prophets who followed him: ARNb, c.1, ed. Schechter, p. 3; Sifre Num. § 134 (ed. Friedmann, 50b); Seder Eliahu R. 5, 6, 13; Eliahu Zuta 12 (ed. Friedmann, pp. 21, 33, 68, 194), Midr. Mishle 25.97; Wayikra R. 1.3; Debarim R. 1.10; Midr. Tehillim on Ps. 5.11; Shemot R. 42.8; Sam. Joshua, chap. ii.

[1]) Cowley, I, *passim*; M. Marq. ii.9; iv.2, 9, 10; v.4; cf. J. A. Montgomery, *The Samaritans: The Earliest Jewish Sect* (1909), p. 229.

[2]) See especially F. Hahn, *Christologische Hoheitstitel* (1963), pp. 351-404; cf. 334-40; also H. Teeple, *The Mosaic Eschatological Prophet* (1957); A. S. van der Woude, *Die messianische Vorstellungen der Gemeinde von Qumran* (1957), pp. 76-89; J. Giblet, "Prophétisme et attente d'un Messie prophète dans l'ancien Judaïsme," *L'attente du Messie*, ed. L. Cerfaux *et al.* (1954), pp. 85-130; R. Schnackenburg, "Die Erwartung des 'Propheten' nach dem Neuen Testament und den Qumran Texten," *Studia Evangelica*, ed. K. Aland *et al.* (1959), pp. 622-39. The application of Moses typology to the Qumran "Teacher of Righteousness" (N. Wieder, "The 'Law-Interpreter' of the Sect of the Dead Sea Scrolls: the Second Moses," *Jour. Jewish Studies* 4 [1953], 158-75; van der Woude, pp. 84-87, 165; G. Vermes, "La figure de Moïse au tournant des deux testaments," *Moïse, l'homme de l'alliance*, ed. H. Cazelles *et. al.* [1955], pp. 79-84, *Scripture and Tradition in Judaism* [1961], pp. 59-66; for a contrary view see G. Jeremias, *Der Lehrer der Gerechtigkeit* [1963], pp. 297f.) also belongs here rather than to aetiology, since the Teacher—and the whole community—is understood in an eschatological context. In any case the *ascension* traditions play no part in published Qumran texts.

[3]) E.g. Kohelet R. on 1.28. See Renée Bloch, "Quelques aspects de la figure de Moïse dans la tradition rabbinique," *Moïse, l'homme de l'alliance*, ed. H. Cazelles *et al.* (1955), pp. 156-61; J. Jeremias, "Mousēs," *ThWbNT* IV, 860ff.

[4]) A. Merx, *Der Messias oder Ta'eb der Samaritaner* (1909), pp. 41-49.

[5]) See J. Bowman, "Early Samaritan Eschatology," *Jour. Jewish Studies* 6 (1955), 63-72; *Oudt. Studiën* 8 (1950), 226f.; J. Macdonald, *The Theology of the Samaritans*

Moses' installation in heaven as God's vice-regent could very well support a doctrine of a final reign on earth, when this vice-regency would come to its ultimate fruition.[1]) The Targumin on Deut. 33.5—the usual rabbinic proof-text for Moses' kingship—attest an eschatological interpretation of the Sinai assembly heads. As Moses, when "he gathered the elders together," "became king in Yeshurun,"[2]) so "a king will arise from the house of Jacob, when the head of the people are gathered together."[3]) What is not clear, however, is just what role the ascension as such would have played in such ideology.[4])

Perhaps the most common function of ascension stories in literature of the period and milieu we are considering is as a guarantee of esoteric tradition. In the apocalyptic genre the ascension of the "prophet" or of the ancient worthy in whose name the book is written is an almost invariable introduction to the description of the secrets which the ascendant one "saw." The secrets, therefore, whose content may vary from descriptions of the cosmic and political events anticipated at the end of days to cosmological details, are declared to be of heavenly origin, not mere earthly wisdom. This pattern is the clear sign of a community which regards its own esoteric lore as inaccessible to ordinary reason but belonging to a higher order of truth. It is clear beyond dispute that this is *one* function which the traditions of Moses' ascension served. In the Book of Jubilees, for example, the Secret revelation to Moses stands as the guarantee that the sectarian calendar and associated

---

(1964), pp. 362-71; M. Gaster, *The Samaritan Eschatology* (1932), pp. 185-90 *et passim;* W. Meeks, *The Prophet-King* (1967), pp. 229f., 249-54.

[1]) Some such typology is evident in the peculiar mixture of temporality in the 1 Enoch "similitudes," in which the Son of Man is "named before the Lord of Spirits" "before the stars of the heaven were made" but enthroned as God's vice-regent to judge the nations at the end of days (1 Enoch 46.1-3; 48.2-6; 62.7; 51. 1-3; 52.9; 69.26-29; chaps. 70-71). The Enoch and Moses traditions show many other similarities; cf. Philo, *QG* i.86, where just Enoch, Moses, and Elijah are said to have ascended to heaven. See also Heb. 1, where Jesus' enthronement (as High Priest) is both pre-temporal and eschatological. Cf. N. A. Dahl, "Christ, Creation, and the Church," *The Background of the New Testament and Its Eschatology*, ed. W. D. Davies and D. Daube (1956), p. 433.

[2]) So Targ. Ps.-Jon.; cf. Ibn Ezra in the rabbinic commentaries *ad loc.*

[3]) The fragmentary Pal. Targ., trans. J. W. Ethridge, *The Targums* ... (1862), II, 673. Cf. *Midrasch Tannaim*, ed. Hoffmann, II, 213.

[4]) It is easier to discern the eschatological use of the traditions that Moses did not die, but ascended at the end of his earthly mission. Though not essential to the belief that he would return at the end of days (both some rabbinic and some Sam. traditions speak of Moses' resurrection prior to the general resurrection), the ascension legends did facilitate such belief and doubtless stand behind the NT Transfiguration legend and Rev. 11.

cultic practice of the Qumran sectaries—in distinction from the "orthodox" practice at the Jerusalem temple—is divinely ordained. The notion of secret, especially apocalyptic, teachings delivered to Moses at Sinai is well-known from Hellenistic Jewish sources, such as 4 Ezra:

> I told him many wondrous things,
>   showed him the secrets of the times,
>   declared to him the end of the seasons:
> Then I commanded him saying:
> These words shalt thou publish openly, but these keep secret.[1])

But "normative" Judaism could appeal to Moses in exactly the same way for authentication of the "oral Torah," including "the Mishna, the Talmud, and the Aggada, even the questions that a perceptive student would someday ask his master."[2]) The case is even stronger in the Samaritan traditions, in which Moses is the man "to whom his Lord revealed what He had never before revealed to any man."[3]) To him were revealed "signs and wonders" and "mysteries new and old;"[4]) he learned "what had been and what was yet to be"—the characteristics of God's own knowledge.[5]) Specifically this meant that "his span includes the knowledge of the Beginning and it goes on to the Day of Vengeance,"[6]) that is, the Torah contained cosmological secrets concealed in Genesis as well as eschatological secrets which were thought to be particularly concentrated in the "song of Moses" (Deut. 32).[7]) The notion that Moses received cosmological secrets led to elaborate descriptions of his "heavenly journeys," very similar to those attributed elsewhere to Enoch. The fullest descriptions are in the medieval

---

[1]) 4 Ezra 14.5.
[2]) Talm. Yer. Peah 2.4 (13a), following Schwab's translation; same with slight variations in Kohelet R. on 1.9; see also Talm. B. Megilla 19b, Abot 1.1, and G. Vermes, *Moïse*, p. 77.
[3]) *M. Marq.* iv.1, trans. Macdonald, p. 135.
[4]) *Ibid.*, ii.9, p. 67; cf. i.1, p. 4; Cowley, I,77, lines 17-19.
[5]) *M. Marq.* ii.3, cf. i.1. The formula, "to know what was, (what is,) and what is to be," is used of Moses also in the poem by Ezekiel (Eusebius, *Praep. Ev.* ix.29: *ta t'onta, ta te pro tou, ta th'husteron*) and in Yalkut Shim. (Warsaw, 1925), I, 483 (on Num. 12.6-8). It is not necessarily a gnostic formula, as Scholem has suggested, referring to Ḥag. 2.1 and the rather different formula in *Excerpta ex Theodoto* § 78 (*Major Trends in Jewish Mysticism* [1961], p. 74), but characterizes the true *prophet*. Thus Marqah has God say, "Were it not for your prophethood, I would not have revealed myself ..." (*M. Marq.* i.9, p. 32), and the "Prophet of Truth" in the pseudo-Clementines is defined as "he who always knows all things—things past as they were, things present as they are, things future as they shall be..." (Hom. ii.6).
[6]) *M. Marq.* v.1, trans. Macdonald, p. 193.
[7]) *Ibid.*, iv.1; cf. iv.3 *passim*.

Jewish *Gedulat Mosheh*,¹) but the journeys are also mentioned in the Biblical Antiquities of pseudo-Philo (12.1) and in Syr. Baruch (4.2-7, cf. chap. 59), while they are already clearly implied by Marqah's statement that Moses saw "the forces of the unseen," i.e. "glory," "angels," "the light," "the darkness," "the wind," "the fire," "the water," "the foundations," "the two luminaries and the stars."²) Therefore the statement in Num. 12.6, that Moses was "entrusted with all (God's) house," is interpreted by both Samaritan and rabbinic midrash to mean that Moses was entrusted with both heaven and earth, "the hidden and the revealed things."³)

The foregoing examples, which could be multiplied, are sufficient to indicate that one, and perhaps the major, function of the ascension legends was to emphasize Moses' role as guarantor of the traditions, cosmological, halakic, or eschatological, of the particular group cultivating the stories. There are some aspects of the ascension traditions, however, which are scarcely related to this function. Especially Moses' *kingship*, which is so central to the forms of the tradition with which we began, seems to play no role here. We must reckon with the probability, therefore, that the legends are composites of the strands which at some earlier stage served disparate functions.

The final possible function we must consider is the one which Goodenough championed so vigorously: that the stories of Moses' ascension were intended to serve as paradigms of mystical experience, perhaps in the context of an organized "Jewish mystery." The true "disciple of Moses" would be the person who was fitted by intellectual and psychological endowment and continuous self-discipline to follow the "royal road" opened by Moses and thus attain the vision of God, or at least of his Logos.⁴) It is impossible here, of course, to enter into a discussion of all the evidence which Goodenough adduced or of the psychological theory which he employed in evaluating it. We can only ask whether there are elements in the legends we have described which would shed further light on his hypothesis. On the whole the answer is negative, for the notion of a mystical imitation of Moses' ascent to heaven is nowhere, outside of Philo, directly suggested in these legends.

---

¹) Jellinek, I, 58-64, cf. II, x, xivff., xixf.; two versions were translated by M. Gaster, "Hebrew Visions of Hell and Paradise," *Jour. Roy. Asiatic Soc.* (1893), 573-90; reprinted in *Studies and Texts*, I, 124-43.
²) M. Marq. iv.1.
³) *Ibid.*, iii.6, cf. vi.6 (of God!); Cowley, I, 77; Midr. Tehillim on Ps. 24.1.
⁴) See Philo, *Conf.* 95-97; cf. *QG* iii.8 and Goodenough, *By Light, Light*, chap. viii.

Nevertheless, we cannot fail to observe that the *descriptions* of Moses' ascent contain several motifs which are common coin in descriptions of mystical practice and experience. Thus Moses, like any practicing mystic, receives his heavenly vision only after ascetic preparation, including fasting and abstention from sexual relations.[1]) The ascent itself was accompanied by terrible threats, for the angels opposed his entrance into heaven,[2]) and he was in danger of being devoured by heavenly fire.[3]) To escape the latter danger, according to some sources, his flesh was transformed into fire or into light—a notion possibly related to the image of God motif.[4]) Possibly we should include in the same category the scattered suggestions that in heaven Moses shared the angels' food[5]) and participated in the heavenly liturgy.[6]) It may be, however, that all these motifs serve rather to emphasize the promethean quality of Moses' triumph in acquiring the heavenly Torah for his people[7]) than to provide a handbook for a would-be imitator.

V. Conclusions

We have seen that in very diverse sources there persist the remnants of an elaborate cluster of traditions of Moses' heavenly enthronement

---

[1]) Philo, *Mos.* ii.68; ARNa, chaps. 1, 2 (ed. Schechter, pp. 1, 10; ET, Goldin, pp. 3, 19; see also J. Goldin, "The First Chapter of Abot de Rabbi Nathan," *Mordecai M. Kaplan Jubilee Volume*, pp. 278-80); Tanḥ., ed. Buber, III, 46; cf. Scholem, *Major Trends*, p. 49; F. O. Francis, "Humility and Angelic Worship in Col. 2:18," *Studia Theol.* 16 (1963), 114-19.

[2]) Syr. Bar. 59.5-11; ARNa, chap. 2, p. 10 (ET, Goldin, p. 20); Midr. Tehillim on Ps. 8.2; Talm. B. Shab. 88b; Shir R. 8.11; Peṭirat Mosheh, Jellinek, I, 128; 3 Enoch 15B (Odeberg, pp. 40-43).

[3]) Philo, *QE* ii.28; 3 Enoch 15B; the Sam. sources especially praise Moses for having "trod the fire," which became "like dew beneath his feet": *M. Marq.* ii.12 (text p. 51), v.3 (p. 125), vi.2 (p. 135), vi.3 (p. 137), vi.11 (p. 147), and frequently in the liturgy. In the 14th century "Samaritan Poem about Moses" published by T. H. Gaster in *The Joshua Block Memorial Volume* (1960), this motif is transferred to Moses' birth (lines 8-10, pp. 119, 125).

[4]) 3 Enoch 15B; Midr. Tehillim 90.1; cf. Debarim R. 11.4; cf. Ps.-Clem. Hom. xvii.16, "For the excess of light dissolves the flesh of him who sees, unless by the secret power of God the flesh be changed into the nature of light ..."

[5]) *M. Marq.* iv.6 (ET, pp. 155f.); Philo, *Mos.* ii.69; cf. Josephus, *Antt.*, iii.99; Tanh., ed. Buber, II, 120; Shemot R. 47.5 (cf. 3.1); L. Bieler, *Theios Anēr* (1936), II, 33; G. Widengren, *Ascension*, p. 46, n. 2.

[6]) For the Samaritans Moses became "Priest of the unseen world," "priest of the angels": *M. Marq.* iv.6 (ET, p. 155); v.3 (ET, p. 202), *et passim*; "A Samaritan Poem" (Gaster), lines 20-22, pp. 139f., 150.

[7]) This is quite clearly indicated in the medieval *Peṭirat Mosheh*, where Moses states that he has "conquered the heavenly household" (Jellinek, I, 128).

at the time of the Sinai theophany. These traditions were closely connected with scripture and at the same time thoroughly syncretistic. Central to the midrashic themes is the notion that, when God gave to Moses his own name (*'elohim, theos*), he conveyed to him a divine status and a unique function among men. Here the usual Hellenistic conception of the "divine man" was modified by combination with the Semitic notion of the agent (*šalîaḥ, apostolos*), as well as by the concept of the image of God. Thus Moses' enthronement in heaven, accompanied by his receiving the name "god" and God's crown of light, meant that the lost glory of Adam, the image of God, was restored to him and that Moses henceforth was to serve on earth as God's representative, both as revealer (prophet) and as vice-regent (king).

The traditions we have traced here resist confinement within any of the conventional groupings of sources-"normative," "hellenistic," "Palestinian," "diaspora," even Jewish over against Samaritan. What is needed for a full understanding of these legends is not an attempt to force them into these categories, but the discovery of new categories more narrowly and specifically related to the traditions as such, what the German form-critics call the *Tradentenkreise*. As a step in that direction we have here been able only to suggest four possible functions the traditions may have served in the circles that preserved them. Further efforts in the same direction would be well repaid, if they follow the example set by Erwin Goodenough: first with rigorous care to describe "what one sees," then with boldness and imagination to propose what may have been happening in the ancient circle that produced what one now sees from afar.

STUDIES IN CYNICISM AND THE ANCIENT NEAR EAST: THE TRANSFORMATION OF A *CHRIA*

BY

HENRY A. FISCHEL

Indiana University

I

The late Professor Erwin Goodenough was among the first to whom I made known my working hypothesis that a number of cultures of the ancient Near East showed considerable inroads of Cynicism. He showed great interest in the preliminary results I had at that time—results which indicated that tannaitic literature, in particular, showed traces of Cynical literary and ethical modes.

Meanwhile, these investigations have crystalized in a complete work on a partial aspect[1]) of the over-all project.[2]) The present essay will concentrate on a single specimen of a specific cynicizing literary category in order to touch upon problems that could not be discussed in the larger work.

It seems that among the literary creations of the Greek world one form in particular, the cynicizing *chria*, χρεία, *sententia* or *exemplum*—although developed centuries earlier and based on a still older but less extreme form—experienced a great upsurge from the Roman Civil Wars on, both in Greece and Rome, which paralleled the goundswell of Graeco-Roman rhetoric and the strong political activities and effective propaganda of Neo-Cynics and Neo-Stoics under Early Imperial Rome.[3]) Even prior to this renaissance, the *chria* was popular

---

[1]) *Tannaitic and Amoraic Literature and the Cynicizing Chria*, to be published in the near future by the American Academy for Jewish Research. Henceforth called *Cynicism*.

[2]) *Studies in Cynicism and the Ancient Near East:* "Transmission, Reception and Transformation, Function and Structure of Cynic Ideas, Values and Literary Forms in the Mediterranean Area of Near Eastern Cultures." This project is partially supported by research grants from Indiana University.

[3]) The most important Cynics of this period are Demetrius and Dio of Prusa (Chrysostom) in the first ct., Demonax, Oenomaus of Gadara and Peregrinus Proteus in the second ct. Propagators of the ideal of the Noble Cynic are Seneca, Musonius Rufus, Epictetus, Lucian, Favorinus, and Maximus of Tyre. *Cf.*

with the grammarians and literary critics and it penetrated into the "handbooks" for orators and the grammatical exercises of the schools.)[1] The work of the *doxographoi* and biographers of the philosophers increased its distribution still further, and the Roman satire popularized its content in a new literary form.[2]) The final attenuation of poetic creation in the last phases of antiquity with its resultant stress on prose and the collection and codification of the work of earlier exemplary periods, in gnomologies and related works, gave it a prominent place in literature until the Byzantine Age.

The *chria*, in general,[3]) is a terse, realistic anecdote, originally and usually on a Sage-Philosopher, that culminates in meaningful action or a truth in form of a gnome, apophthegm or proverb. The Cynic (or cynicizing) *chria* distinguishes itself by the odd, extreme, and often even burlesque action (or basic situation or final statement) of the central Sage-Hero that becomes the basis for a demonstration of Cynic ideals and values. The climactic finale is usually witty, approximating a "punch-line." *Double entendre*, invective and altercation abound. It was thus an ideal vehicle for the teaching of the non-conformist ideas of the Cynics, for their task of παραχαράττειν τὸ νόμισμα,[4]) to "falsify" (i.e. remint) the coin (of convention). The ancient literary critics spoke of the forcefulness of the chriic style. Indeed, the *chria* was "useful"— this is the etymology of the Greek term—in a time of change, of an ever growing complexity of life and the ensuing political and social stress. It taught ataraxy, self-control and contentment, the happiness that

---

Chronological Table, below. *Cf.* D. R. Dudley, *A History of Cynicism*, London 1937 and M. I. Rostovtzeff, *The Social and Economic History of the Roman Empire*, 2nd ed., 2 vols., Oxford 1926.

[1]) J. Barns, "A New Gnomologium," *Classical Quarterly* 44 and 45, 1950 and 1951, 126-137, 1-19. E. Norden, *Die Antike Kunstprosa*, 5th ed., 2 vols, repr. Darmstadt 1958. E. Ziebarth, *Aus dem griechischen Schulwesen*, 2nd ed., Leipzig 1914. G. M. A. Grube, *A Greek Critic: Demetrius on Style*, Suppl. Phoenix IV, Toronto 1961 and *The Greek and Roman Critics*, Toronto 1965. *Cf. Cynicism* on Quintilian, Caesius Bassus, Hermogenes and Theon (Section 8.9).

[2]) *Cf.* G. C. Fiske, *Lucilius and Horace*, U. of Wisc. Studies in Lang. and Lit., Madison 1920. P. Lejay, *Oeuvres d'Horace, Satires*, Paris 1911. E. Haight, *The Roman Use of Anecdotes...*, New York 1940.

[3]) Apart from the standard histories of ancient literature and the encyclopedias, especially: G. Rudberg, "Zur Diogenes-Tradition" and "Zum Diogenes Typus," *Symbolae Osloenses*, Fasc. 14 and 15, Oslo 1935 and 1936, 1-18, 22-43. G. A. Gerhard, *Phoinix von Kolophon*, Leipzig 1909. R. Hirzel, *Der Dialog*, I, Leipzig 1895. G. V. Wartensleben, *Begriff der griechischen Chreia...*, Heidelberg 1901. W. Gemoll, *Das Apophthegma*, Vienna 1924.

[4]) Diogenes Laertius' *Vitae philosophorum* VI.20 and 71. (D.L.) This famous formula of the Delphian oracle is purposely ambiguous.

comes from the simple and even primitive life, the "short cut to virtue," the use of reason over the emotions. According to the present state of scholarship in the problems of ancient Cynicism it seems now assured that the *chria* was used to celebrate and "idolize" Founder Sages important to the later Cynic school regardless of historical facts or the appropriateness of the new portrait.[1]) Philosophers thus affected are Socrates, the father of all post-Socratic schools, Antisthenes, the founder of theoretical Cynicism, Diogenes, the founder of "practical" Cynicism, and Crates, the founder of its philanthropical variant. After subsequent rapprochements founders of related (but initially hostile) schools were equally affected, such as Zeno, founder of Stoicism, Cleanthes, the founder of its religious trend,[2]) and Aristippus, the founder of the hedonist Cyrenaic school.[3]) At a somewhat later stage the primeval Seven Sages, the *palaioi*, were affected, among whom were soon included Anacharsis, the Scythian critic of Greek civilization (in the *chria*) and Aesopus. In the last late phase of this development even Aristotle was affected.[4]) Diogenes, however, remained by far the most popular figure of chriic imagination—we have on him probably over one thousand items. New *chriae* were continuously created out of the smallest chriic thematic elements, which combined and recombined unendingly within the framework of the established narrative and plot patterns.

In the aforementioned work of the present writer, the attempt has been made to demonstrate that there is a Hebrew *chria* that has all the aspects of structure of the Greek cynicizing *chria* and appears in all its literary forms, i.e., terse, full, elaborate or composite, "direct" or "reported." It shows the same typical situations, actions, moods, and keywords, and often the same social values and, consequently, the same type of gnomic finale. It either reproduces complete Greek items

---

[1]) In this respect Dudley's work is somewhat lagging. *Cf.* Rudberg, *opp. cit.*, K. v. Fritz, *Quellenuntersuchungen zum Leben und Philosophie des Diogenes von Sinope*, Suppl. Philologus 18.2, 1926. Over-critical: F. Sayre, *Diogenes of Sinope*, Baltimore 1938 and *The Greek Cynics, ibid.*, 1948. But so already A. Packmohr, *De Diogenis Sinopensis apophthegmata quaestiones selectae*, Diss. Muenster 1913.

[2]) Together with his successor Chrysippus, the re-founder of the Stoa, the aforementioned form a *diadoche*, a chain of tradition, of seven in the doxographic-biographic works, such as *D.L.*

[3]) Aristippus the Elder, a companion of Socrates, is seen as the founder in the *chria*. The actual founder may have been his grandson of the same name.

[4]) O. A. Gigon, "Interpretationen zu den antiken Aristoteles-Viten," *Museum Helveticum* 15, 1958, 146-193. I. Duering, *Aristotle in the Ancient Biographical Tradition*, Göteborg 1957.

or recombines thematic elements in the same "atomistic" fashion.[1]) It has the same function: to celebrate and elevate the Founder-Sage, in this instance almost exclusively Hillel the Elder, *fl. c.* 30 B.C.E.—10 C.E., i.e., Hillel is described as an ideal Cynic-chriic Sage. In other words, a Hellenistic form of honoring a great sage figure has been adopted in the tannaitic Jewish culture. The knowledge of this Graeco-Roman practice must have come to Judaea through the acquaintance with ubiquitous Hellenistic rhetoric, either in its oral or its literary form.

In Hebrew culture, wisdom, and with it, the figure of the Sage, had always been central. The wisdom aspects of much of Graeco-Roman rhetoric may therefore have facilitated the process of transmission. Besides, the accounts of the radical actions of the Hebrew prophets which, on the surface, resembled those of the chriic sages (but are quite different in essence, as we shall see presently), favored the adoption of the *chria*. The well-known political and social crises that prevailed in post-Socratic Greece seemed to repeat themselves in Imperial Rome and tannaitic Judaea and became catalysts in the process of transmissions of chriic modes both in Rome and in Judaea.

All 20-25 stories told on Hillel the Elder originating in the tannaitic period proved to be *chriae* and use chriic material in practically every detail.[2]) For this reason, they cannot be used as a historical source for Hillel's life, activities or beliefs. They indicate, though, the existence of a Sagelike figure and innovator, be he a scholar, philosopher, bureaucrat-administrator, or lawgiver.[3]) That any historical figure should deliberately or subconsciously have played out the stories of the ideal Cynic Sage, is little probable, and would not account for stories in which the Sage does not act himself but is acted upon by others. In the contrastive study presented here, one such intercultural *chria* will be discussed in detail. It could be called "The Spoiled Meal." There are

---

[1]) In detail: my *Cynicism*, ch. IV.

[2]) *Cynicism*, ch. V. These do not include historical notes, abstract halakhah, or sayings, which are of a different literary type and origin.

[3]) Owing to the inclusion of the Seven Sages into the chriic cycle, statesmen (Pittacus) and lawgivers (Solon) finally emerge in the *chria*, although only marginally. The immediate companions of the original Cynic-chriic heroes are necessarily also drawn into the chriic narrative, if not for any other reasons so as partners of dialogues. We see thus finally also Alcibiades (more below) via Socrates, and Pericles, his guardian, through him, emerge in the *chria*. Xenocrates probably was affected through his succession to the leadership of the Peripatos. Thematic elements from the chriic material of all these appear also in the Hillel cycle, although its main material stems from Socrates-Antisthenes-Diogenes-Zeno-Cleanthes stances.

nine major Greek variants and one Hebrew equivalent. The challenge of this inquiry consists in the fact that in this case the Greek pattern of the Hebrew is much less obvious than in all other Hillel anecdotes, but certainty of dependence should emerge gradually in the progress of this investigation.

Chronological Table of Chriic Sources

(+: our texts)	Oxford Class. Dict. or other major opinions	Median or round figures or fl.
+ Xenophon	c. 430–c. 354	390 B.C.E.
* Theocritus of Chios		350
* Metrocles, Cynic		325
* Demetrius of Phalerum	c. 350–Ptolemy II	300
+ Bion-(Teles-Theodorus-Stobaeus)	c. 325–c. 255	290
* Cleanthes	331–232	280
* Ariston of Chios, Cynic		250
* Fr. Papyrus Hibeh 1.17	(Barns, *op. cit.*, p. 14f.)	250
Fr. Papyrus Reinach 85	c. 280–220	250
+ (Bion-) Teles (-Theod.-Stob.)	c. 235	235
+ *Vita Aesopi* (Samos Section)	c. 500 B.C.E.–200 C.E.[1])	150
* Hecato(n) of Rhodes	*fl.* 100 B.C.E.	100
** Cicero, especially his *Tusc. Disput.*	106–43 45	75 45
** Philo Alex. (Judaeus)	c. (22 or) 30 B.C.E.–c. 45 C.E.	13 C.E.
** Seneca, Luc. Ann.	c. 5 or 4 B.C.E.–65 C.E.	30
+ (Bion-Tel.-) Theod. (-Stob.)	1st ct. (Hense)	50
** Vienna Papyrus, ed. Croenert	50 B.C.E.–150 C.E.[2])	50
** Synoptic Gospels	55–85[3])	70
** Dio of Prusa (Chrysostom)	40–after 112	80
** Plutarch	c. 46–after 120	85
+ (Arrian-) Epictetus	c. 55–135	95
+ Tannaitic Hillel *chriae*	c. 30–190[4])	110
** Pseudo-Cynic Letters	c. 5 B.C.E.–250 C.E.	125
+ Arrian (-Epictetus)	second ct.	150
** Lucian (esp. *Demonax*)	c. 120–after 180	155
+ Athenaeus	*fl.* 200	200
+ Aelian	170–235	205
+ Diogenes Laertius	*fl.* first half 3rd ct.	225

(+: our texts)	Oxford Class. Dict. or other major opinions	Median or round figures or fl.
+ Derech Erets Rabbah central chapters	200–550[5])	375
+ (Bion-Tel.-Theod.-) Stobaeus	probably 5th ct.	450
+ Gnomologium Vindobonense	not datable	

*) supposed creators or editors of *chriae* (as distinguished from the appearance of some of them as heroes of *chriae*).
**) heavy users of cynicizing *chriae* (except papyri frr.).

[1]) *Cf.* H. Zeitz, "Der Aesoproman und seine Geschichte," *Aegyptus* 16, 1936, 225-257. *Der Kleine Pauly*, ed. K. Ziegler, W. Sontheimer, I, Stuttgart 1964, *s.v. Aisopos*.

[2]) W. Croenert, *Kolotes und Menedemos*, Studien zur Palaeographie und Papyruskunde VI, Leipzig 1906, and average major opinions.

[3]) Average major opinions.

[4]) 30 C.E.: to allow for formation of legend after Hillel's death; 190 C.E.: close to end of tannaitic activities.

[5]) 200 C.E.: material not included in Mishnah, becomes *baraita*. 550 C.E.: latest possible revision of central chapters (inclusion of quotations from Babylonian Talmud).

II. Sources. "The spoiled meal."
(Without guests).

1. Aelian(us), *Varia Historia*, ed. R. Hercher, Leipzig 1887; XI. 12, p. 116 (henceforth Ael.[1])

> Πλακοῦντα ὁ Ἀλκιβιάδης μέγαν καὶ ἐσκευασμένον κάλλιστα διέπεμψε Σωκράτει. ὡς οὖν ὑπὸ ἐρωμένου ἐραστῇ πεμφθὲν δῶρον ἐκκαυστικὸν τὸν πλακοῦντα διαγανακτήσασα κατὰ τὸν αὐτῆς τρόπον ἡ Ξανίππη ῥίψασα ἐκ τοῦ κανοῦ κατεπάτησε. γελάσας δὲ ὁ Σωκράτης 'οὐκοῦν' ἔφη 'οὐδὲ σὺ μεθέξεις αὐτοῦ.'

—Alcibiades sent to Socrates an extremely large and very pleasantly prepared cake. Like on the approach of an inflammatory present sent by the lover to the beloved, Xanthippe, greatly irritated according to her way, tore the cake out of the basket and trampled it under foot. Laughing(ly) Socrates said: "Now you will have no share of it either." (End of *chria*. Moral follows).—

[1]) From here on, a special way of quoting our sources has been used in order to assure maneuverability in the tables and yet eliminate ambiguity, especially in view of the fact that three different sources come from Plutarch's *Moralia*.—Text-critical annotation has been reduced to a minimum and is limited to questions essential to this study.

This is the traditional understanding of the finale. However, Socrates would thus be somewhat sullen and childish. On the grounds of the moral suggested by Aelian it is probable that he understood the finale somehow as follows: "Now, would you not have your share of it?" I.e., he is still willing to pick up the food and eat it (which is the case in the Stobaeus item, No. 7, below).

Moral:

> εἰ δέ τις οἴεται περὶ μικρῶν με λέγειν λέγοντα ταῦτα, οὐκ οἶδεν ὅτι καὶ ἐκ τούτων ὁ σπουδαῖος δοκιμάζεται ὑπερφρονῶν αὐτῶν, ἅπερ οὖν οἱ πολλοὶ λέγουσιν εἶναι κόσμον τραπέζης καὶ δαιτὸς ἀναθήματα.

—If someone thinks that I have told trifles, he does not now know that the Sage is recognized by the fact that he holds in contempt what the vulgar call the decorum of the table and the niceties of the banquet.—

2. Athenaeus, *Deipnosophistae* (643e f.), in H.F.A. v. Arnim, *Stoicorum Veterum Fragmenta*, vol. III, Leipzig 1923, under "Antipater of Tarsus," p. 257, #65 (henceforth Ath.)

> ἡμεῖς δὲ ἃ μετεγράψαμεν ὀνόματα πλακούντων, τούτων σοι καὶ μεταδώσομεν, οὐχ ὡς τοῦ ⟨ὑπ'⟩ Ἀλκιβιάδου πεμφθέντος Σωκράτει ὃν Ξανθίππης καταγελασάσης ὁ Σωκράτης ,,οὐκοῦν, ἔφη, οὐδὲ σὺ μεθέξεις τούτου." (τοῦτο δὲ ἱστόρησεν Ἀντίπατρος ἐν τῷ πρώτῳ περὶ Ὀργῆς) ἐγὼ δέ, φιλοπλάκουντος ὤν, οὐκ ἂν περιεῖδον τὸν θεῖον ἐκεῖνον ἐξυβριζόμενον πλακοῦντα.

—We, however, will indeed share with you the names of cakes which I have written out—unlike (the case of) the one sent by Alcibiades to Socrates regarding which, when Xanthippe had trampled it under foot, Socrates said laughing(ly): "Now, you will not have a share of it either." (Athenaeus postscript): 'As for me, being a lover of (flat-)cake, I would not have allowed'[1]) that divine cake to be (so arrogantly) disdained. (Reading καταπατησάσης, γελάσας).—

Stories with Guests

3. Plutarch, Moralia 471 B, *de tranquillitate animi*, ed. W. C. Helmbold, vol. VI, The Loeb Classical Library, London, Cambridge, Mass. 1939, p. 202 (henceforth P. P., i.e., Plutarch on Pittacus)

> ὁ γοῦν Πιττακὸς ἐκεῖνος, οὗ μέγα μὲν ἀνδρείας μέγα δὲ σοφίας καὶ δικαιοσύνης κλέος, εἱστία ξένους· ἐπελθοῦσα δ' ἡ γυνὴ μετ' ὀργῆς ἀνέτρεψε τὴν τράπεζαν· τῶν δὲ ξένων διατραπέντων, "ἑκάστῳ τι," ἔφη, "ἡμῶν κακὸν ἔστιν· ᾧ δὲ τοὐμόν, ἄριστα πράττει."

---

[1]) quoted from a comic poet.

—Now, when that well-known Pittacus—whose fame was great for bravery and great for wisdom and justice—was entertaining guests, his wife came in a rage and upset the table. While the guests were confounded, he said: "Everyone of us has some affliction; he who has mine only[1]) is doing admirably (very well)."—

4. Plutarch, Moralia 461 D, *de cohibenda ira*; item on Arcesilaus, *ibid.*, p. 142 (henceforth P. A., i.e., Plutarch on Arcesilaus)

Ἀρκεσιλάου δὲ μετὰ ξένων τινῶν ἑστιῶντος τοὺς φίλους παρετέθη τὸ δεῖπνον, ἄρτοι δ' οὐκ ἦσαν ἀμελησάντων πρίασθαι τῶν παίδων. ἐφ' ᾧ τίς οὐκ ἂν ἡμῶν διέστησε τοὺς τοίχους κεκραγώς; ὁ δὲ μειδιάσας, "οἷόν ἐστιν," ἔφη, "τὸ συμποτικὸν εἶναι τὸν σοφόν."

—Arcesilaus was once entertaining his friends together with some strangers, and when dinner was served, there was no bread, the slaves having neglected to buy any. In such a situation, which one of us would not have torn the walls apart with shrieks? But the former (merely) smiled and said: "How fortunate it is that the Sage is convivial."[2])—(This item is immediately followed by 5.)—

5. Plutarch, *ibid.*, item on Socrates and Euthydemus, *ibid.*, p. 142. henceforth P. E. (i.e., Plutarch on (Socrates and) Euthydemus)

Τοῦ δὲ Σωκράτους ἐκ παλαίστρας παραλαβόντος τὸν Εὐθύδημον, ἡ Ξανθίππη μετ' ὀργῆς ἐπιστᾶσα καὶ λοιδορηθεῖσα τέλος ἀνέτρεψε τὴν τράπεζαν, ὁ δ' Εὐθύδημος ἐξαναστὰς ἀπῄει περίλυπος γενόμενος· καὶ ὁ Σωκράτης, "παρὰ σοὶ δ'," εἶπεν, "οὐ πρῴην ὄρνις τις εἰσπτᾶσα ταὐτὸ τοῦτ' ἐποίησεν, ἡμεῖς δ' οὐκ ἠγανακτήσαμεν;"

—Once, when Socrates invited Euthydemus[3]) from the palaestra, Xanthippe, standing (threateningly) about and scolding, finally overturned the table. Euthydemus, greatly saddened, rose and got not a ready to depart when Socrates said: "At your house, the other day, did bird fly in and do this very same thing, yet we did not get angry?"[4])—

6. *Vita Aesopi*. B.E. Perry, *Aesopica*, Urbana 1952. Codex G, pp. 34-77. (Codes W, pp. 81-107, and *Vita Lolliniana*, pp. 110-130, for some variants only) (henceforth V. Ae.)

---

[1]) Τοῦτο μόνον, mss.
[2]) i.e., the Sage is ready to replace at a moment's notice bread with the symposium, i.e., wine, conversation, or both.
[3]) Sophist, of Chios. In Plato's *Euthydemus* he is a ridiculous figure, the butt of Plato's criticism of Antisthenes. *Cf. Oxford Classical Dictionary*, s.v. *Cf.* Xenophon, *Mem.* IV.ii.f. More below.
[4]) In the epilogue, Plutarch explains that at a meal one must show cheerfulness towards friends and not spread fear among the slaves. He continues with the *bon ton* of table manners, which includes the rejection of fussiness and anger.

39. Ὁ Ξάνθος εὑρὼν φίλους εἰς τὸ βαλανεῖον τοῖς τῶν φίλων παιδαρίοις δοῦναι <ἐκέλευσε> τὸν Αἴσωπον τὰ ἱμάτια, καὶ λέγει αὐτῷ "ὕπαγε, Αἴσωπε, εἰς τὴν οἰκίαν, καὶ ἐπειδὴ διὰ τὴν μανίαν τῆς γυναικός μου συνεπατήθη τὰ λάχανα, ἀπελθὼν φακὸν. ἔψησον ἡμῖν...
ὁ Ξάνθος σὺν τοῖς φίλοις αὐτοῦ λουσάμενος λέγει "ἄνδρες, δύνασθε πρὸς ἐμὲ εὐτελῶς ἀριστῆσαι; πρὸς φακὸν γὰρ ἡμῖν ἐστιν. οὐ δεῖ δὲ τῇ πολυτελείᾳ τῶν ἐδεσμάτων τοὺς φίλους κρίνειν, ἀλλὰ τῇ προθυμίᾳ δοκιμάζειν ·...

(39), p. 49: When Xanthus[1]) found some of his friends at the bath, he told Aesop to give the robes to the friends' servants and said to him: "On with you, Aesop, and home! And since because of the temper of my wife the vegetables are trampled upon, be off and prepare us lentil"[2]) ... When Xanthus together with his friends had had their bath, he said: "Men, will you share my simple fare? We have lentil. One should not judge friends by the costliness[3]) of their food but recognize them (approve of them) by their good intention"[4])...

For further reference: Codex G, #44, p. 50:

ἐξελθὼν οὖν λέγει καθ' ἑαυτόν· "νῦν καιρός ἐστιν τοῦ μετελθεῖν με τὴν μῆνιν τὴν πρὸς τὴν κυράν, ἀνθ' ὧν με ἀγορασθέντα ἔσκωψεν καὶ ἐκακολόγει, καὶ ὅτι τὰ δωρηθέντα μοι ὑπὸ τοῦ κηπουροῦ λάχανα σκορπίσασα συνεπάτησεν, καὶ οὐκ ἀφῆκέν μου τὴν δωρεὰν εὐχαρῆ τῷ δεσπότῃ μου γενέσθαι. ἐγὼ αὐτῇ δείξω ὅτι πρὸς εὔνουν οἰκέτην οὐδὲν ἰσχύει γυνή · ἐπὰν γὰρ ὁ δεσπότης εἶπέν μοι ὅτι 'δὸς τὰ μέρη τῇ εὐνοούσῃ', νῦν ὄψεται τίς αὐτῷ εὐνοεῖ."

7. *Ioannis Stobaei Anthologium* (i.e., *Eclog.* and *Flor.*) ed. C. Wachsmuth and O. Hense, repr. Berlin 1958 (1894), vol. III, ch. 1.98 (Meineke 5,67), p. 37ff. Also: O. Hense, *Teletis Reliquiae*, 2nd ed., Tuebingen 1909, ch. II, p. 5ff. From the Epitoma Theodori of Teles' *peri autarkeias*. (henceforth Sto.)

In the critical apparatus and introduction to the latter work, Hense

---

[1]) Xanthus is the Sage in V.Ae., Aesop his slave-Sage (very frequent in the *chria*, cf. for Diogenes D.L. VI. 29ff. from a satire by Menippus (or Hermippus). Philo was well acquainted with this material).

[2]) Intentionally singular. The (scribal?) addition ὄσπριον, "pulse," is rightly cancelled by Perry (missing in W and V.L.) since is spoils the second *chria* by which Ae. serves a single lentil (41) to teach his "master" precise language (who finally recognizes, in a third *chria*, that he has acquired a teacher, and not a slave—shades of Diogenes (40))! The serving of one lentil represents a second meal, spoiled by the slave (pigs' feet are finally served), similar to P. A.— On composite *chriae* more below.

[3]) Codex W reads ποικιλίᾳ,, diversity (p. 88, #39, line 9).

[4]) Codex W ends here. *Vita Lolliniana* has instead: Sed non est ad amicum saturare ventrum sed bona voluntas sufficit omnia (p. 119, #39). Our Codex G continues to elaborate (*cf.* the end of the Stobaeus item for the same style) that "on occasion the most humble dishes afford a more profound pleasure than more luxurious ones, if the host serves them with good intention" (Perry reads μετ' εὐνοίας instead of μετανοίας).).

has tried to reconstruct the Teles text and free it from the accretions of Theodorus, an otherwise unknown epitomator.[1] Hense's attempts have not been unanimously accepted, see Pauly's *Realencyclopaedie der classischen Altertumswissenschaft* (Wissowa-Kroll-Mittelhaus), vol. V (10), sec. ser., Stuttgart 1934, *s.v.* Theodorus #34, col. 1831f. Furthermore, Hense, p. LXV, believes that our item is inspired by Bion and refers to D.L. IV. 52 where mention is made of Bion's use of "vulgar names" (.. φορτικοῖς ὀνόμασι ..). Hense sees indications of the Bionic style in Xanthippe's being called a goose, D.L. II.37 and Sto. 98, in the prelude to our text, below, and in the use of ὀξυρεγμίᾳ σπαράσσειν (*cf.* Aristophanes fr. 473 K.) and of ὄρνιθος κορυζώσης and γυνὴ ὑώδης, below.

Item for further reference (Hence, p. 18):

... καὶ γυναικὸς χαλεπότητα πράως ἔφερε κἀκείνης βοώσης οὐκ ἐφρόντιζεν· ἀλλὰ Κριτοβούλου εἰπόντος 'πῶς ἀνέχῃ ταύτης συμβιούσης;' 'πῶς δὲ σὺ τῶν παρὰ σοὶ χηνῶν;' 'τί δέ μοι μέλει ἐκείνων;' φησίν 'οὕτως οὐδ' ἐμοὶ ταύτης, ἀλλ' ἀκούω ὥσπερ χηνός'.

Main item, Hense, p. 18 (p. 48, W.-H.):

καὶ πάλιν παρειληφότος αὐτοῦ 'Αλκιβιάδην ἐπ' ἄριστον, ὡς ἐκείνη παρελθοῦσα τὴν τράπεζαν ἀνέτρεψεν, οὐκ ἐβόα οὐδ' ὠδυνᾶτο δεινοπαθῶν 'ὦ τῆς παρανομίας, ὥστε ταύτῃ πάσχειν', ἀλλ' ἀναλέξας τὰ πεσόντα, παραθέσθαι πάλιν ἐκέλευσε τὸν 'Αλκιβιάδην· ὡς δὲ ἐκεῖνος οὐ προσεῖχεν ἀλλ' ἐγκαλυψάμενος ἐκάθητο [αἰσχυνόμενος], 'προάγωμεν δή' φησίν 'ἔξω· φαίνεται γὰρ ἡ Ξανθίππη ὀξυρεγμίᾳ σπαράσσειν ἡμᾶς.' εἶτα μετ' ὀλίγας ἡμέρας αὐτὸς ἀριστῶν παρὰ τῷ 'Αλκιβιάδῃ, ὡς ἡ ὄρνις ἡ γενναία ἐπιπτᾶσα κατέβαλε τὸν πίνακα, ἐγκαλυψάμενος ἐκάθητο καὶ οὐκ ᾑρίστα· ὡς δὲ ἐκεῖνος ἐγέλα καὶ ἐπυνθάνετο εἰ διὰ τοῦτο οὐκ ἀριστᾷ ὅτι ἡ ὄρνις ἐπιπτᾶσα κατάβαλοι, 'δῆλον ὅτι' φησί 'σὺ μὲν πρῴην Ξανθίππης ἀνατρεψάσης οὐκ ἐβούλου ἀριστᾶν, ἐμὲ δὲ οἴει νῦν <ἂν> ἀριστᾶν τῆς ὄρνιθος ἀνατρεψάσης; ἢ διαφέρειν τι ἐκείνην ὄρνιθος κορυζώσης ἡγῇ;' 'ἀλλ' εἰ μὲν ὗς' φησίν 'ἀνέτρεψεν, οὐκ ἂν ὠργίζου, [οὐκ ἂν διηνέχθης] εἰ δὲ γυνὴ ὑώδης;' ὅρα παιδιάν.

—And on another occasion, when he had received with him Alcibiades for breakfast, as she (Xanthippe) came in and overturned the table, he did not shout and did not feel distress, having suffered this terrible thing (such as exclaiming): "Oh, for this outrage, that I have to put up with this," but having picked up what had fallen down bade Alcibiades to serve up again.[2]) When the latter did not comply but covered up (his face) and sat there deeply ashamed, he said: "Let us proceed outside,

---

[1]) assigned by Hense to first century Neo-Cynicism (C.E.), *op. cit.*, p. XIII, n.
[2]) reading παραθέσθαι acc. to Hense or ἅπτεσθαι, "to touch it," with Bucheler in W.-H. Gnomological variants suggest ἐπιθέσθαι, "to apply himself (to the table)."

for Xanthippe seems to wish to make us convulse with heartburn."[1]) Then, after a few days, when he himself had breakfast at Alcibiades' house and this "noble" bird flew in and overturned the plate, he (S.) covered himself, sat still, and did not eat. When the former laughed and inquired if he was not eating because the flying bird had overturned (the plate, *Gnom. Par.*), he said: "It is obvious that the other day when Xanthippe upset (the table), you did not want to eat; do you think I then would want to eat now that the bird overturned (the table)? Or do you think that she is different from a dribbling bird?"—"Now, if a pig," he continued,[2]) "overturned it, you would not become angry [nor would you have thought it made a difference], but if a swinish woman (does so, you do)? Note the moral![3])—

(8) *Diogeni Laertii Vitae Philosophorum*, ed. H. S. Long, 2 vols., Oxford, 1964. D.L. II.34, p. 71:

Καλέσας ἐπὶ δεῖπνον πλουσίους, καὶ τῆς Ξανθίππης αἰδουμένης ἔφη, "Θάρρει· εἰ μὲν γὰρ εἶεν μέτριοι, συμπεριενεχθεῖεν ἄν· εἰ δὲ φαῦλοι, ἡμῖν αὐτῶν οὐδὲν μελήσει."

—When he had invited some rich men to a meal and Xanthippe felt ashamed (because of the simplicity of the dinner) he (S.) said: "Be confident, for if they are fair, they will accomodate themselves, and if they are mean, we shall not worry about them."—

For further reference: D.L. II.36-37:

πρὸς Ἀλκιβιάδην εἰπόντα ὡς οὐκ ἀνεκτὴ ἡ Ξανθίππη λοιδοροῦσα, "ἀλλ' ἔγωγ'," ἔφη, "συνείθισμαι, καθαπερεὶ καὶ τροχιλίας ἀκούων συνεχὲς καὶ σὺ μέν," εἶπε, "χηνῶν βοώντων ἀνέχῃ;" τοῦ δὲ εἰπόντος, "ἀλλά μοι ᾠὰ καὶ νεοττοὺς τίκτουσι," "κἀμοί," φησί, "Ξανθίππη παιδία γεννᾷ."

---

[1]) Understood as *dat. instrument.*, and σπαράσσ(ττ)ειν acc. to Liddell and Scott, item 4, "to wretch or convulse" in accordance with Bionic style and the many parallels in *chriae* (ill effects of eating odd things, cf. D.L. VI. 76, but also 64).

[2]) The opaqueness of Stobaeus is notorious, especially the lack of indication who the speakers are.

[3]) The last phrase and the square brackets are accretions acc. to C. B. Cobet, "Stobaei ad Florilegium," *Mnemosyne* 9, 1860, 86-148 (p. 102). However, the terse form of the *chria* and the spoudaiogeloiically or rhetorically enlarged forms exist side by side. *Cf.* D.L. II.21 (Socrates is kicked, does not retaliate): εἰ δέ με ὄνος ἐλάκτισε, δίκην ἂν αὐτῷ ἐλάγχανον; "If an ass had kicked me, should I have adopted his law?" and Syriac Pseudo-Plutarchus (P. Lagarde, *Analecta Syriaca*, 1858) and J. Gildemeister and F. Buecheler, "*Pseudo-Plutarchos* περὶ ἀσκήσεως," *Rhein. Mus. f. Philologie*, n.s. 27, 1872, 520-538 (p. 528): "It seems to me as if you would get angry, if an ass kicked me on the road, and would kick it because it kicked me; you do not refrain from anger, although you know that there are many people whose manners are not different from those of a beast of burden and the rest of the animals."

9. *Gnomologium Vindobonense*, or *Wiener Apophthegmensammlung*, ed. C. Wachsmuth, in *Festschrift zur Begruessung der 36. Philologenversammlung*, Karlsruhe 1882, 3-36. Parallels in printed editions: Maximus Confessor, *Loci communi*, 575 C-D, Migne, *P.G.* (*Patrologia Graeca*) 91, Paris 1863, col. 806.—H. Schenkl, "Das Florilegium"Ἄριστον καὶ πρῶτον μάθημα, *Wiener Studien* 11, 1889, 1-42 (no. 92, p. 27). (henceforth Gn. V.) P. 31, §184:

ΞΑΝΘΙΠΠΗΣ τῷ ἀνδρὶ ἐπιτιμώσης, ὅτι λιτῶς παρεσκευάζετο ὑποδέξασθαι φίλους, 'ὦ γύναι', εἶπεν, 'εἰ μὲν γνήσιοί σου εἰσίν, οὐδὲν ἐκείνοις μελήσει· εἰ δὲ ἀλλότριοι, ἡμῖν περὶ αὐτῶν οὐδὲν μελήσει'.

—When Xanthippe censored her husband[1]) that he had prepared frugally to entertain friends,[2]) he said: "Oh woman,[3]) if they are genuine (sincere) [for you],[4]) nothing will bother them, if, however, false, nothing about them will bother us."—

For further reference: *ibid.*, #185:

Ξανθίππη ἐρωτηθεῖσα, τί μέγιστον ὑπῆρχε τῷ Σωκράτει, 'τοῦτο', ἔφη, 'ὅτι ἐπὶ ἀγαθοῖς καὶ ἐπὶ φαύλοις ἡ αὐτὴ ὄψις ἦν αὐτῷ'.

10. *Derech Erets Rabbah*. M. Goldberg, *Der talmudische Traktat Derech Erez Rabba*, Ebrslau (*sic*) 1888. Compared with the texts of: M. Higger, *Debe Rabbanan, The Treatise Derek Erez*, Brooklyn 1935. *Talmud Bavli*, Pardes, New York 1954 (Masechet Derech Erets), vol. 16, with text-critical notes of (Gaon) Eliyahu of Vilna (Hagahot). Simeon b. Tsemach Duran, *Magen Avot* on Pirke Avot, in Appendix IV, S. Schechter, *Avot de R. Nathan*, 2nd ed., repr. N.Y. 1945 (henceforth SbTD). Derech Erets Rabbah belongs to the extra-canonical tractates and is possibly cited as דרך הארץ as early as Jerusalem Talmud Shabbat 8a. In any case, all authors mentioned in it are tannaitic (before 200 C.E.) and is has a number of Baraitot (non-mishnaic but tannaitic items) in common with the Tosefta and the Talmudim. The first two chapters and the last one have been added later, and it may have gone through later recensions. (henceforth DER)

Goldberg ch. IV, p. 15. Higger, ch. IV.2, p. 200. Talmud Bavli ch. VI, p. 113 top. SbTD-Schechter, p. 175.

---

[1]) "Socrates, her husband": *P.G.*, Schenkl.
[2]) Singular in Gnomol. ined. Pal. cod. 356, see Wachsmuth, apparatus.
[3]) Cp. (ὦ) γύναι,, Plutarch, *Mor.* 507 C and E; John 2.4. *Cf.* n. 3 of 10.
[4]) Bracketed phrase missing in Gnom. ined. Pal.; *P.G.* Schenkl. All: ἡμέτεροι for γνήσιοι.

לא הבאת לנו מיד· שחה לו	היום ואין לי פרנסה	לעולם לא יהא אדם
כל המעשה· אמר לה בתי	כלום· נטלה אשתו כל	קפדן בתוך סעודתו·
אף אני לא דנתי אותך	הסעודה ונתנה לו ואחר	מעשה בהלל הזקן שעשה
לכף חובה אלא לכף וכות	כך לשה עיסה אחרת	סעודה לאדם אחד ובא עני
שכל המעשים שעשית לא	ובישלה אלפס אחר	ועמד על פתחו ואמר
עשית אלא לשם שמים·	ובאתה והניחה לפניהם·	אשה אני צריך להכניס
	אמר לה בתי מפני מה	

—Never should Man be impatient during his meal.[1]) A happening (story) with Hillel the Elder, who made a meal for a (certain) person and a pauper came and stood at his door and said to his (Hillel's) wife:[2]) "A wife[3]) I have to take (marry) today, and I have no livelihood (food) whatsoever."[4]) His wife took that entire meal and gave (it) to him and thereafter kneaded more (lit.: another) dough and cooked another dish (pie) and came and placed (it) before them. He said: "My daughter! Why have you not brought us (SbTD: to eat) immediately?" She told him the entire story (Bavli: all the events). He said to her: "I also[5]) do not judge you in the scale of guilt but in the scale of merit,[6]) for all the deeds you have done you have done only for the Name (Sake) of Heaven."[7])—

11. For further reference only: (*Arrian's Discourses of*) *Epictetus*, ed. W. A. Oldfather, vol. II, The Loeb Classical Library, Cambridge, Mass., London 1959. (henceforth Arr.)

IV. v. 33 and 35, pp. 342 and 344:

---

[1]) SbTD has ביתו, "in his house," which is too general and does not fit the context (probably dittography for בתוך).
[2]) Some mss. with Goldberg: ואמר לו רבי, "and said to him: 'Rabbi...'" This would make Hillel uncharitable.
[3]) The direct object first. So often in DER. If אשה(ה) was a vocative, we would have a chriic formulation (*cf.* n.3, above, item no. 9). But in this case we would lack a direct object. SbTD offers ... בתי, אשה אני, "and said to his wife: 'My daughter! A wife I must marry...'" It is not entirely impossible that an earlier version may have offered: לאשתו: האשה! אשה אני and that this triple use of "woman" confused the transmittors. (A younger stranger would not address the Sage's wife by "my daughter." *Cf.* the concordances).
[4]) SbTD continues: "Do you have food (פרנסה)?."
[5]) "also:" like his wife vis-a-vis the pauper or like Jehoshua b. Perachiah in Avot 1.6?
[6]) SbTD has only: "I do not judge you but on the scale of merit." Apparently terse apophthegmic finales alternate with more explicit ones just as in the Greek chriic tradition.
[7]) For an attempt at a different translation see below, under "Bon Mot."

Τούτων Σωκράτης μεμνημένος τὴν οἰκίαν τὴν αὑτοῦ ᾤκει γυναικὸς ἀνεχόμενος τραχυτάτης, υἱοῦ ἀγνώμονος. τραχεῖα γὰρ πρὸς τί ἦν; ἵν' ὕδωρ καταχέῃ τῆς κεφαλῆς ὅσον καὶ θέλει, ἵνα καταπατήσῃ τὸν πλακοῦντα·... ταῦτα τὰ δόγματα ἐν οἰκίᾳ φιλίαν ποιεῖ, ἐν πόλει ὁμόνοιαν, ἐν ἔθνεσιν εἰρήνην, πρὸς θεὸν εὐχάριστον, πανταχοῦ θαρροῦντα...

III

The major Greek items and the Hebrew unit share a general narrative structure (plot) which could be described as follows:

At the Sage's home food is to be served when owing to an emotional outburst of the Sage's wife the food cannot be consumed in time or not be consumed at all. The ensuing embarrassment to the guests (who figure in eight of the ten stories) and to the host is relieved by a bon mot of the Sage who, remaining superior to the situation, does not lose his temper.

Within this minimal framework there is a certain range of variation which makes for diversity in atmosphere and meaning. In order to understand fully the use of chriic detail in these variations of the theme, we shall call the smallest independent thematic element henceforth "moteme" and include in this category all structural and thematic detail encountered in the *chria*, such as *personae*, settings (locale), simple actions, moods, keywords, significant numbers, exclamations, segments of utterances, and within these, repetition, juxtaposition, contrast, and many others.

1. *The Setting*

	Ael.	Ath.	P.P.	P.A.	P.E.	V.Ae.	Sto.	D.L.	Gn.V.	DER
One scene	x	x	x	x				x	x	x?
Two scenes					x	x	x			

The setting is the Sage's home where the food is to be consumed. But P.E. and Sto. use two different scenes: Socrates' house and that of his friend. They thus duplicate the crucial event, probably in order to introduce the motemes of reciprocity and animal comparison (Xanthippe and the bird). In V.Ae. the destruction of the vegetables takes place earlier, the meal of one lentil (!) later, and the two localities (one is not clearly specified) seem to be the Sage's home, but a scene at the public bath is inserted. The latter, together with the lavatory, the marketplace, the games, and the temples are favorite chriic settings.[1]) DER has only one scene, but the gift will have to be consumed elsewhere as a wedding meal. This feature does not appear to be a reminiscence of the double setting but is, rather, implied in the charitable act.

2. *The Meal*

The meal is either in progress, i.e., the guest(s) is (are) seated, or the repast is otherwise anticipated, with or without express mention:

Meal	Ael.	Ath.	P.P.	P.A.	P.E.	V.Ae.	Sto.	D.L.	Gn.V.	DER
in progress			x	x	x		x			x
anticipated	x	x				x		x	x	

3. *The Food*

In four of the five stories in which the food is identified, it is made of flour: bread, (flat-)cake (πλακοῦς) and pancake or pie (אלפס, אילפס).[2]) The vegetable moteme of V.Ae. may have been transplanted here from the numerous *chriae* on vegetables[3]) in line with the usual technique of recombining chriic motemes to form new *chriae*.[4]) Significant, too, is the choice of lentils for the second meal. Lentils are popular not only in the *chria* but in Cynic literature generally, *cf.* Meleager's lost Λεκίθου καὶ φακῆς σύγκρισις, Ath. 157 B. The moteme of trampling under foot is represented in Diogenes' outrage on Plato's carpets, D.L. VI.26. The cake is also hinted at in Arr.'s mention of Socrates, *Disc.* IV.v.33 (Source #11, above).

In the other items, the food is either not identified or merely implied, because the *chria* stresses other details of the story, such as the wife's evilness and "animality," as in P.P., P.E. and Sto., or the ideal of simplicity of the Sage's diet, as in D.L. and Gn. V. This latter moteme is by no means coincidental. Lupins, lentils, and beans, often bread,

---

[1]) These localities bring the Sage in contact with the multitide, who are to be converted to the true way of life, and afford the castigation of conventional beliefs. Bathhouse or lavatory occur also in the variants of a Hillel *chria*, Lev. R. 34.3 and AdRN B, ch. 30, *cf. Cynicism*, section 15.1.

[2]) usually sweet. Loanword, from λοπάς, *cf.* S. Krauss, *Talmudische Archaeologie*, 3 vols., Leipzig 1910-1912, I 477 n. 459; II 292; III 54. Also a cooking vessel, *ibid.* I.92; Pes. 37b. Cp. the English "dish" and "casserole" for both vessel and food.

[3]) D.L. II.68; 102-103; VI.58, etc. Also on Antisthenes and Aristippus.

[4]) Demonstrated in detail in *Cynicism*, ch. IV.

salt and water, are the fare of the self-sufficient Cynic Sage. The destruction of a *sumptious* cake with Aelian may thus not merely be a product of the garrulousness of the author and his diatribic-homiletic style but a point of moralizing ("See, what happens to luxurious foods") which he picked up from the chriic tradition. τύφος, luxury, is the foremost sin and will ruin society in the view of the Cynics while πόνος, the strenuous, simple life, will re-establish it.[1])

Food	Ael.	Ath.	P.P.	P.A.	P.E.	V.Ae.	Sto.	D.L.	Gn.V.	DER.	Arr.
made of flour	x	x	x							x	x
*s*imple or *s*oiled; *u*nspecified		u		u		s	u	s	s		

Also in the Hillel item, the food is extremely simple. This should not be interpreted as a reminiscence of biblical scenes, such as the frugal meals of Elijah, 1 Ki. 17.8ff., and Elisha, 2 Ki. 4.38ff., although the existence of such stories in the biblical canon may have facilitated the acceptance of the Hellenistic item. In the Hebrew Bible, poverty is not an ideal; in the tannaitic culture it often is.[2]) By the same token, Hillel's amazing run as a servant (slave) before the carriage of the impoverished nobleman in Ketubot 67b etc. is clearly not symbolic-ecstatic-predictive as in the case of the biblical Elijah who runs before Ahab's chariot, but is in itself the fulfillment of a definite social ideal to be followed by all men. The Cynic Sage, in his bizarre (yet exemplary) actions demonstrates new ideals for all men; the biblical prophet, however, in *his* bizarre symbolism, has no such intentions. It is probable, therefore, that also the simplicity of the meal is a reflection of the cynicizing hellenist element in the pattern story.[3])

---

[1]) The *ponos* idea is represented in some aspects of tannaitic ethics in a novel positive use of the stems עמל and צער. The ethos propagated is simplicist, primitivist, (not ascetic-dualistic, as Y. F. Baer, *Yisra'el ba-'amım*, Jerusalem 1955, has suggested).—The assumption maintained by Hense, Gerhard and Dudley, that Cynicism from the third century B.C.E. on, combined with hedonistic elements (cp. the chriic Aristippus cycle, D.L. II.66-83) is less likely the reason for Aelian's description. That a cake was taboo to the Cynics is apparent from Diogenes' flinging away a πλακοῦς, which he found amongst his olives, D.L. VI.55.

[2]) Shown in detail in *Cynıcism*, 22.5f.—Jeremiah's admiration for the Rechabites, Jer. ch. 35, is not for their primitivism-nomadism but for their faithfulness to their father's command (35.14).—The simplicity of the aforementioned prophetic meals is caused by draught and famine.

[3]) Hillel's proverbial poverty is, of course, also a chriic moteme. In his case as

4. The Guests

The guest is often anonymous (the plural is not essential; the gnomological mss. vary). In all probability, the moteme of the known guest was originally introduced to explain Xanthippe's rage more realistically: it is owing to the sight of Alcibiades or a gift of his.[1]) Perhaps, the remaining *chriae* introduce the named guest on the assumption of a teacher-disciple relationship between them: the Sage demonstrates his superior wisdom or way of life before his major disciple, although Euthydemus may be a mere double for Alcibiades (more below). Pittacus, as a prototype of the early Sages, the παλαιοί, especially the Seven Sages, figures quite prominently in the *chria* (D.L. I.76-78; Sto., *passim*). It is now generally recognized that the tradition of the Seven went through a process of Cynicization.[2]) Many *chriae* originally told of other Cynic Hero-Sages were then transferred to one of the Seven and thus exist in several forms. If, however, the identification of the guest(s) is inessential to the plot, anonymity prevails as so often in the *chria*.[3])

Guest(s)	Ael.	Ath.	P.P.	P.A.	P.E.	V.Ae.	Sto.	D.L.	Gn.V.	DER
anon.	x	x		x			x	x	x
named			x		x				

5. The Sage's Wife

The wife of the Sage is mentioned by name only in the case of Socrates: it is the renowned Xanthippe. In the case of the wives of others, i.e., Pittacus, Hillel and Xanthus, we never learn of their names and

---

well as those of Crates and Cleanthes, it contradicts the opposite chriic moteme according to which the (very same) Sage is wealthy or gives his wealth away.— According to the *chria*, almost every Sage was at one time or another, a slave. See *Cynicism* 30.2ff. and 27.2ff.

[1]) This does not exclude the possibility that the Alcibiades version represents the original story. Fully treated below.

[2]) B. Snell, *Leben und Meinungen der Sieben Weisen*, 3rd. ed., Tuebingen 1952, introductions. K. Joel, *Der echte und der xenophontische Sokrates*, 3 vols., Berlin 1893-1901, II. ii, 759-809.

[3]) The anonymity of this *altera persona* may have contributed to the stereotyping of the terse *chria*:
  Asked whether... Diogenes said (or did)...
  To someone who... D. said (or did) ..
  Seeing a ... D. said (or did)... (the latter
five times in Pap. Bouriant, in E. Ziebarth, *Aus der antiken Schule*, 2nd. ed., Bonn 1913 (*Kleine Texte*...65), p. 22f.)

never hear of the former two again.¹) They remain shadow figures, merely replacing Xanthippe, i.e., they delay, question, or spoil the meal. Such shadow *personae* are legion in the *chria*. They are created for the sake of plot or contrast.²) The historicity even of the "non-chriic" Xanthippe has been doubted.³) If she is indeed a mere literary figure, the inventor can no longer be identified. In Plato's *Phaedo* she is merely womanly weak (60A), but already with Xenophon she is difficult.⁴)

In any case, Xanthippe's violence as well as the vulgarities of her description are Cynic burlesque. It may quite well be that Bion, the originator of the "spoudaiogeloiic" form of cynicizing diatribe, is the creator of these stances, and Teles his prophet, as Hense, *Teles*, p. LVIf., is inclined to think, and that the theme moves from there to Antipater of Tarsus and to Philodemus' lost περὶ τῆς ὀργῆς and others. However this may be, the institution of marriage, in its conventional form, was the object of heavy criticism by the Cynics. Crates' "cynical" marriage to Hipparchia, herself a formidable Cynic in the *chria*,⁵) Aristippus' well-educated daughter Arete (D.L. II.72; 86) and Alcibiades' patient wife Hipparete (Plutarch, *Life of Alcib.* VIII.1) seem to have represented the Cynic ideal. Xanthippe seems to be a contrastive literary portrait, illustrating the pitfalls of marriage.

In the *chria*, however, also a positive portrait of Xanthippe is found, reinforcing the suspicion that we are dealing here with non-historical characters. In one category of stories Xanthippe describes the great qualities of her husband admiringly.⁶) In one set of stories in particular,

---

¹) Of the haughty wife of the unhappy Pittacus only a brief note survives (D.L.I. 81) that may be a summary of our *chria*. Neither is Xanthus' wife known outside V.Ae., although she plays an important role in the novel. Similarly, DER offers the only appearance of Hillel's wife in all of Hebrew literature.

²) For the Hebrew *chria* cp. Hillel's brother, whose name Shevna is mentioned in an introductory statement to a *chria*-related story in Sotah 21a, never to appear again. Prof. Alan Cutler kindly informed me of a mention of Shammai as Hillel's brother in a medieval *piut*. (Could this be an improvization on the theme "both are the voice of the living God?"). In *Cynicism* 30.2ff. the possibility is discussed that the two tannaitic brothers reflect Chaerophon and Chaerecrates, if not of Xenophon (*Mem.* II.iii) so of a chriic tradition.

³) Pauly's *Realencyclopaedie*..., s.v. "Xanthippe."

⁴) *Mem.* II.ii.7,... τὴν χαλεπότητα (Adj., dat., in *Symp.* II.10)—On Karl Joel's theory of the Antisthenian origin of this material see below.

⁵) A special chapter on her in D.L. VI.96-98. A fictitious letter (no. 3) of (Ps.-) Diogenes to her in *Epistolographi Graeci*, ed. R. Hercher, Paris 1873 ("Diogenis Epistolae"), p. 235; of Ps.-Crates ("Cratis Epistolae," no. 1; nos. 28-33, p. 208, p. 214f.)

⁶) E.g., Gn.V. #185, in the appendix for further reference, above.

Xanthippe mentions Socrates' unperturbedness in the face of impending catastrophe: Cicero, *Tusc. Disp.* III.15.31 and Aelian, *V.H.* IX.7. The major part of this story was used in the item of "Hillel and the Rumor," Ber. 60a etc., with the usual adaptations but retaining all essential parts and keywords except the mention of the wife. It is not impossible, however, that tannaitic culture was once acquainted with the full version of this item and thus with a second story of the positive portrait of Xanthippe. Hillel's charitable wife in our item may thus not necessarily be a tannaitic adaptation of the shrewish wife moteme but part of the hellenistic pattern. This impression is re-inforced by the strange similarity of "Hillel and the Proselytes," Shabbat 30b etc. and a set of *chriae* in Plutarch's *Lives* (Pericles I.4f. and III-V and Alcibiades II.2.4-6 and IV-VIII). All sources involved speak of the kindness and patience of their heroes, who remain unperturbed even when rudely disturbed or the "victim" of a wager (*Cynicism* 16.5.3f.). A postscript to the Alcibiades *chriae* speaks of Hipparete's qualities. A similar postscript to the Hillel cycle speaks of "Hillel's proselytes" as if of a family. Interdependence is argued for in *Cynicism* 16.5.2ff. and n. 77, *ibid*. In other words, the Tannaim seem to have been acquainted with as many as three stories which show the Sage's wife in a positive light.

Wife of Sage	Ael.	Ath.	P.P.	P.A.	P.E.	V.Ae.	Sto.	D.L.	Gn.V.	DER
Xanthippe	x	x			x		x	x	x	
*an*on., slave(*s*)			an	ss		an+s				an

6. *The Wife's Motivation*

In our stories, Xanthippe's temper tantrum seems to be a result of her shrewish nature[1]) and she appears often as the prototype of the shrewish woman in the *chria* and beyond. This would eliminate any special motivation for her violent action. Ael. and V.Ae., however, do mention a motivation: jealousy; Ael.: "...the inflammatory gift of the lover to the loved," and, without erotic connotation, V.Ae.: "...she did not let my gift become pleasing to the master."[2]) It is thus obvious

---

[1]) So also Arr., reference text above (No. 11): ... τραχυτάτης, "roughness," "harshness."
[2]) Ael.: ὡς οὖν τὸ ἐκαυστικόν. V.Ae.: καὶ οὐκ τὸ γενέσθαι, cp. νῦν ὄψεται τίς αὐτῷ εὐνοεῖ, "and now it will be seen who is well-disposed toward him (i.e., she or Aesop)," reference text.

that the chriic imagination was acquainted with the claim repeatedly made in Greek literature that Socrates and Alcibiades entertained an erotic relationship with one another.[1]) Ancient writers who denied this had to refute this claim.[2]) There may have existed forms of our "Spoiled Meal" *chria* that were more outspoken, or periods in which one could rely on the reader's knowledge of this claim. For only with this erotic jealousy moteme is our story truly witty and Cynic-chriic. The Cynics were interested in Alcibiades not only because he was Socrates' student but also because he had become a symbol of the combination of physical beauty and moral corruption, which latter they faught violently,[3]) and they were interested in Socrates' marriage, because they condemned the traditional forms of marriage and family. However, we would have to consider Bion or his successors as the author of such a cycle, since Bion's devaluation of Socrates is well established, whereas Antisthenes is still too "Socratic." Antipater, if Ath. can be trusted, may be no more than the inventor of the cake variant or merely its transmittor. Perhaps even Stobaeus' (Bion's, Teles') item may presuppose this relationship of Socrates and Alcibiades and make Xanthippe's reaction that of jealousy, in view of the death scene of Socrates that precedes our item by a few lines. In this odd scene Socrates makes his fatal cup splash over for a toast: "Here is to the beautiful Alcibiades!" ('τουτὶ δὲ Ἀλκιβιάδῃ τῷ καλῷ'[4]).—Athenaeus discusses at great length the problem of the Socrates-Alcibiades relationship in Greek literature, 182a-b,

---

[1]) D.L. II.23; cf. Joel,... *Sokrates*..., II.ii, 719ff.

[2]) Plato, *Alcibiades* 103 A; *Symp.* 213-219 E; *Protagoras* 309 A; Xenophon, *Mem.* I.ii.15. Joel, ...*Sokrates*... II.ii, 716-728 has tried to trace the Socrates-Xanthippe cycle to an erotic symposiastic *Protreptikos* of Antisthenes (444-369). Antisthenes would also be responible for Plutarch's Alcibiades *chriae* in the *Lives*, the "thoughts" in Xenophon's *Mem.* I.iii.1-4 and parallels in Plato's *Alcibiades II* as well as the cynicization of the Seven Sages (759-810, 887ff., 996-1004). His thesis has been partially criticized by H. Gumperz, "Die deutsche Literatur ueber sokratische usw. Philosophie 1901-1904," *Archiv fuer Philosophie* 19, 1905, 234-270. Joel's rebuttal: *ibid.* 20, 1906, 1-24; 148-170. The great extension of the fictional aspects of all literary Socrates portrayals has, as a whole, been maintained by O. A. Gigon, *Sokrates*, Bern 1947; A. H. Chroust, *Socrates - Man and Myth*, London 1957; I. Bruns, *Das literarische Portraet der Griechen...*, Berlin 1896.

[3]) R. Hoistad, *Cynic Hero and Cynic King*, Uppsala 1948, p. 78f.

[4]) Hense, *Teles*, p. 17f., *ad. loc.*, is somewhat naive: "immanes errores quibus Socrates confunditur Theramene, Critiae loco Alcibiades nominatur..." In the world of the *chria* motemes are not "confounded" but wander purposely or "naturally" from hero to hero. A large number of Greek *chriae* are thus told of several sages. Similarly, the same Hebrew *chria* may be told of Hillel and Akiba, Hillel and Eliezer b. Hyrcanus, Hillel and R. Joshua, etc. These are neither "mistakes" nor scribal errors but the customary way of using the *chria*: to honor several sages and bestow upon them the distinctions of true sagehood. See *Cynicism, passim*.

continued 187c ff., but in his "Spoiled Meal" item it does not become clear how he interprets Xanthippe's behavior. Even in P.E., Euthydemus may stand for the favorite Alcibiades, since the former was the object of the ardent attention of Critias (*Mem.* I.ii.30f.) and was criticized by Plato. Xanthippe may have known him as the favorite of the philosophers, saw him brought home by her husband, and became jealous.[1])

That a tannaitic story should be the literary descendent of this type of *chria* is, of course, not extraordinary if we consider that one of the many outrightly bawdy Greek *chriae* became the basis of "Hillel and the Peace Sacrifice (Hillel and the Female Bull)," Betsah 20af. etc., which retains much of the flavor of the original pattern.[2]) The jealousy version of our "Spoiled Meal," however, is not the immediate source of our Hebrew item but a more positive form of it, as we shall presently see.

In the remaining Greek items motivation is replaced by irrational shrewishness. Finally, the delay of the meal is caused by concern on the part of the wife, as in D.L., while Gn.V. tries both, scolding and concern. The Hebrew item seems to be a further, Judaic, development of this delay-through-concern moteme: concern for the poor.

Motivation	Ael.	Ath.	P.P.	P.A.	P.E.	V.Ae.	Sto.	D.L.	Gn.V.	DER
Jealousy	x	x?			x	x?				
Concern								x	½	x

7. *The Wife's Emotion*

The description of Xanthippe's temper or that of her equivalent varies from a mere "censoring," ἐπιτιμώσης (Gn.V.) to "greatly irritated," διαγανακτήσασα (Ael.), "arrogant disdain," ἐξυβριζόμενος (Ath.), "in a rage," μετ' ὀργῆς (P.P.), "confronting (them) in a rage and scolding," μετ' ὀργῆς ἐπιστᾶσα καὶ λοιδορηθεῖσα (P.E.), "frenzy," μανία (V.Ae.), and the climactic attempt at quasi-poisoning, ὀξυρεγμίᾳ σπαράσσειν (Sto.). When no description of the wife's temper is possible,

---

[1]) A bawdy comparison to the behavior of the pig is used by Socrates regarding Euthydemus in this Xenophon passage. The pig moteme may have wandered from here to our Stobaeus item.

[2]) The basis of the Hebrew is a Diogenes *chria* on the physical aspects of the sexes and their mixup, supplemented by an item on Ariston regarding dialectics on a bi-sexual foetus. The finale comes from a Lucian-Demonax *chria* on quarrels, altars and peace. Analyzed in detail in *Cynicism* 25.11ff. ("The Female Bull").

as in the case of Arcesilaus' symposium (P.A.), the author mentions neglect, non-care (...ἀμελησάντων...) on the part of the servants. This negative emotion is replaced by positive (though misplaced) concern, i.e., a feeling of shame (αἰδουμένης) in D.L. and Gn.V., and empathy in DER. All reactions on the part of the wives have this feature in common: whether negative or positive, they are over-acted in order to effect a spoiled or delayed meal and thus put to test the Sage's self-restraint and ingenuity.

That the Greek "Vorlage" still shows through the Hebrew text could be claimed for the use of one word: On a sudden impulse Hillel's wife gives away the *entire* meal. It would have sufficed to say that she gave the meal away and began to prepare another dish. This high-pitched כל may thus be a reminiscence of the high tension prevailing in the Greek patterns. Indeed, adjectives emphasizing the momentousness of the event are found also in the Greek: "inflammatory,"... ἐκαυσ-τικὸν... (Ael.), "divine,"...θεῖον... and "treated with arrogance," ἐξυβ-ριζόμενος (Ath.).

The degree of delay or destruction—the central moteme—depends, of course, on the degree of emotion which, in turn, depends on the total concept or atmosphere of the *chria*. The effect of the women's action varies thus from a short delay to the complete spoilage of the food. Even in DER the original food completely disappears. All this contributes to the remaining chain reaction: embarrassment of guests and host and the superior act or saying of the Sage.

Emotion	Ael.	Ath.	P.P.	P.A.	P.E.	V.Ae.	Sto.	D. L.	Gn.V.	DER
negative: *s*trong; *m*edium *l*ow	s	s	m	l	s	s	s		½l	
positive:								s	½m	s

8. *Animal Comparisons*

Some measure of burlesque may make an appearance in the *chria* in order to introduce the animal comparison (analogy, simile), which is extremely popular in the cynicizing *chria*. Man refusing to use his reason resembles the senseless beast. In Cynicism, this tendency is found next to its equally popular opposite: the positive animal comparison: the animal is closer to nature, healthily "primitive," unlike man unspoiled by culture or luxury.¹) In any case, Xanthippe is a popular target of animal comparisons not only in our item but also in other *chriae*. Dealing with her resembles horsemanship.²) Her noise, but also her usefulness, are compared to the qualities of geese.³) A similar Stobaeus (-Bion? etc.) item is completely negative.⁴) Since the goose figures prominently in the *chria*, and since motemes wander from one item to the other fairly freely, it is possible to suggest that the bird in Sto. and P.E. may have been a goose, thus continuing the animal comparison above.⁵) Whereas Sto. and P.E. are merely negative in their colorful description of Xanthippe, D.L. (passage on geese) and Xenophon see in her also positive qualities. D.L.'s animal comparison represents ever so slight an improvement over the utter vulgarity of Sto., both, of his animal comparison and his "Spoiled Meal."

D.L.II.37: To Alcibiades who said that Xanthippe's scolding was intolerable he said: "Not so; I have got used to it like hearing a perma-

---

¹) In the *chria*, the sage "learns" from the animal (Diogenes and the Mouse, etc.). The animal may be replaced by the equally unspoiled child or by savages, strangers and simple people (Scythians, Indians, Persians; craftsmen, etc.). Cf. *Cynicism* 26.22ff.
It is not impossible that this contradictory evaluation of the animal stems ultimately from the purpoted origin of the general *chria*: the fable, in which animals represent both, the wise and the foolish, the virtuous and the wicked. The literary structure and the finale of the fable also resemble those of the *chria*. Cf. Wartensleben, *op. cit.*; B. E. Perry, "Fable" (*sic*), *Studium Generale* 12, 1959, 17-37; F. H. Colson, "Quintilian I.9 and the 'Chria' in Ancient Education," *Classical Review* 33, 1919, 150-154; "Phaedrus and Quintilian I.9.2," *ibid.* 35, 1921, 59-61.
²) D. L. II.37 but already Xenophon, *Symp.* II.10.
³) D. L. II.36; above, text for reference.
⁴) It precedes our "Spoiled Meal" *chria* immediatly (Hense, p. 18; text for reference above) and relates that on Critobulus' question to Socrates, how he could endure living with Xanthippe, he replied by the question how Critobulus could endure the cackling of the gesse in his (yard). Crito's reply, that nothing about them could possibly bother him, is countered by Socrates' final "Similarly, nothing about her (bothers) me. I hear her (noise) like (that) of a goose." This *chria* is structurally (dialogue) and stylistically (repletiveness) as well as through content closely related to Stobaeus' (Bion's etc.) own "Spoiled Meal" item. Note the characteristically chriic change of *personae* and the identity of the punchline:
    Sto.   τί δὲ μοι μέλει ἐκείνων
    ibid.   οὐδ' ἐμοὶ (implied) ταύτης
    D. L.   ἡμῖν   αὐτῶν οὐδὲν μελήσει
    Gn. V.   ἡμῖν   περὶ αὐτῶν οὐδὲν μελήσει
i.e., "nothing (or "what") about them (about "her") does (will) bother us (or "me").
⁵) Hense, Helmbold *et alii* suggested a chicken. It is true that the latter flies more easily but is less capable of upsetting a table. However, also the "flying" chicken is a chriic moteme: After Plato's definition of man as a featherless biped, Diogenes threw a plucked fowl (.. τίλας ἀλεκτρυόνα...) into his lecture room with the words: "Here is Plato's Man." D. L. VI.40.

nently rattling windlass. And even you," he said, "can live (are content) with shouting geese." "But they produce eggs and feathers for me," he said. "Indeed," he said, "and Xanthippe produces offspring."[1])—Far more positive, indeed a spirited defence, of Xanthippe in spite of her temper, is the dialogue between Socrates and Lamprocles, their son, in *Mem.* II.ii.1-13. Although using initially a comparison with a wild beast (!), 7f., Xenophon's Socrates shows that Xanthippe is not malicious; on the contrary, she has her children's welfare in mind and makes great sacrifices for them.[2]) Lamprocles is ungrateful and should pray to the gods for forgiveness.

Xenophon's description of Xanthippe, undoubtedly written *cum ira et studio* in defence of the Socratic family and the institution of harmonious marriage, demonstrates the elasticity of the basic "material," i.e., the motemes of the temper of the Sage's wife. It is such a more positive chriic portrayal, perhaps with a similar rhctoric-homiletic framework, that became the source of the tannaitic item.[3])

In this connection, another animal comparison deserves brief mention: a passage in Plutarch's *Apophthegmata Laconica, Mor.* 233 B,

---

[1]) Hicks, in *Loeb's Classical Library*, translates this passage more in the spirit of Xenophon-Socrates' defence of Xanthippe before their son Lamprocles: "And Xanthippe is the mother of my children." I prefer a translation closer to the Sto. item and the cynicizing *chria*.

[2]) Among others καὶ εὐχὰς ἀποδιδοῦσαν, "she proffers vows," ii.10, is fairly close to the piety expressed in our Hebrew item. —Another positive feature in the Xanthippe apology of Xenophon, which seems to be reflected in our *chriae*, is the advice to Lamprocles to take his mother lightly as actors do with one another on the stage (ῥᾳδίως φέρουσι, ii.9). This is reminiscent of our "not to be bothered" moteme, n. 43, above. However, whereas above Xanthippe should be treated as a *quantité négligeable*, the advice is here to take her lightly, because, like the actors, she is not malicious and does not mean to harm. It thus seems that some of Xenophon's Xanthippe material was used by a more radical type of *chria* (spoudaiogeloiic or burlesque) or that both drew from the same source (Antisthenes?) and reshaped it in different ways. It is also possible that Xenophon, always acceptable to the Cynics because of his own cynicizing tendencies, may have had a permanent attenuating influence in the direction of a positive picture of the Sage's wife, being widely read in the ancient world. —Xenophon uses actual *chriae* himself, but only in one section of his entire work: *Mem.* III.xiii and xiv, and these *chriae* are word (not action) *chriae* of the non-burlesque type.

[3]) To be sure, tannaitic culture did not need Xenophontian or Cynic teachings to believe in the virtue of women (although any support in countering another view, i.e., that woman is the source of non-virtue, must have been welcome). But the chriic form of this teaching offered a ready and useful illustration, and could serve the glorification of the Sage. The paucity of such stories and the persisting anonymity of the wives (Hillel's and Akiba's) indicate stimulation from outside. The story of Beruria who comforts R. Meir (*Yalkut Shimeoni* Proverbs # 964; no parallels) is also hellenistic, as I shall show elsewhere.

#18, where a Spartan refuses to repeat the feat of standing a long time on one foot and wittily refers to any goose, which would do as well.¹) In *Cynicism*, the present writer has tried to show that this moteme was influential in the tannaitic על רגל אחת, "on one foot," which makes its appearance in the famed story of "Hillel and the Proselyte," Shabbat 31a etc.²) This would be another instance that indicates that the Tannaim were acquainted with this general thematic orbit.

Animal Comparison	Ael.	Ath.	P.P.	P.A.	P.E.	V.Ae.	Sto.	D.L.	Gn.V.	DER	Xen.
"Spoiled Meal"				x		xx					
Context (cc: several)					c	cc				cc	

9. The Fate of the Meal

tr(ampled upon); up(set); ne(glected); qu(estioned); gi(ven away).

Ael.	Ath.	P.P.	P.A.	P.E.	V.Ae.	Sto.	D.L.	Gn. V.	DER	Xen.
tr	tr	up	ne	up	tr	up	qu	qu	gi	tr

10. The Gift

In some of our *chriae* the food to be consumed is a gift to the Sage: Ael., Ath., Arr. (cake), V.Ae. (vegetables). Both the banquet (which, in a way represents some kind of gift cp. Xanthippe's concern regarding its skimpiness in D.L. and Gn.V. Some of the guests are strangers) and the actual gift have this in common: they cannot be consumed. The borderlines between the meal and the gift are thus somewhat blurred. In DER the first meal becomes a charitable gift. Xenophon speaks of Xanthippe's vows on behalf of her son which must have included gifts. Such transpositions of motemes are common in the *chria*.³) It is thus not utterly impossible that the Hebrew detail of the charitable gift by the wife may still be part of the hellenistic thematic material. The centrality of a clearly ethical deed for a total stranger, however, would represent the specific Hebraic contribution.

---

¹) Sparta, in many of its aspects, is to the Cynics the ideal society. *Cf.* Dudley, Sayre, Gerhard, Hoistad, *passim*.
²) Also Horace's *pede stans in uno*, Sat. 1.4.9-10, is close to this material.
³) *Cynicism*: "Atomistic Uses of chriic elements," 10.3

11. *Embarrassment*

The embarrassment or humiliation suffered either by the host through his treatment at the hands of the wife and through his inability to be a good host or (and) by the guests through witnessing such a scene or being served spoiled food (or no food at all) is, obviously, crucial in this *chria*, since it enables the Sage to show his patience, superiority, and use of reason (bordering on ataraxy) if not his wit and his capacity to re-establish harmony. Embarrassment is therefore mentioned in one form or another in all those items in which guests are present or expected. P.A. and Sto. even wax rhetorical about it. In the Hebrew, embarrassment is expressed by the question of Hillel why the meal was not served immediately (מיד).

An interesting detail is reported in Sto. Both Alcibiades and Socrates cover their faces when ashamed and sit there in silence. Precisely the same occurs in a number of Hebrew *chriae* when Sages, including Hillel, are surprised or embarrassed by difficult questions or situations.[1])

Embarrassment	Ael.	Ath.	P.P.	P.A.	P.E.	V.Ae.	Sto.	D.L.	Gn.V.	DER
*i*mplied		x	x	x	x		x	x	i	x
*e*xpressed										

12. *The Bon Mot (Gnome, Apophthegm, Moral, Finale)*

In regard to the bon mot of the Sage four distinct motemes must be considered: 1. the bon mot is directed at all those present or only at the wife in the absence of guests; 2. the bon mot is at the expense of the wife or merely didactic when no wife is present. Even the common sense utterances of D.L. and Gn.V. are still somewhat critical of Xanthippe, because her value system is too dependent on the opinion of others. In P.P. the bon mot is half tolerant but the wife is still an "evil." DER endorses the wife's actions but, as will be shown below, in somewhat strange terms. 3. The bon mot is either (a) unitary, (b) duplex, usually in an antithetic form, or (c) tripartite.

Examples (a): "How fortunate... that the Sage is convivial." (P.A.) (b): "If they are fair... If they are mean..." (D.L.) (c): "Everyone is afflicted."-"Whoever is like me,- does well." (P.P.)

DER is tripartite but the SbTD reading is only duplex.

4. The bon mot may follow a dialogue between the Sages or between Sage and wife.

---

[1]) *Cynicism* 16.1, note c.

Bon Mot	Ael.	Ath.	P.P.	P.A.	P.E.	V.Ae.	Sto.	D.L.	Gn.V.	DER
directed to	W	W	all	all	all	all	Alc.	W	W	W
on wife	x	x	x		x	x	x	½	½	x
a, b, c,	a	a	c	a	b	b	b c+b	b	b	c(b):
di(aloguic)						di	di	di		

The Greek bon mot in our *chriae* is witty throughout. In order to guide even the meanest intelligence, Ael., Ath. and P.A. have the Sage smile! Only the Hebrew item seems to be totally serious. Hillel's words, however, offer some difficulty. He uses fairly heavy nouns: חובה, sin, guilt (legally: debt), and זכות, merit, meritorious deed (legally: privilege), reinforced by the symbolism of the scales (of justice).[1] Although the delay of the meal is irritating and embarrassing as well as unannounced and unforseen, and an infringement upon the sacred obligation of hospitality, the choice of terms, quasi-legal and quasi-theological, is disproportionate, and the whole formulation stiff if not pompous, even on the assumption that the guest was a distinguished man. To give a whole meal away needs no excuse in a Judaic setting in the light of the role played by charity. Was there not at least the mitigating circumstance of a conflict of values: charity versus hospitality.[2] Or did Hillel's wife neglect to ask for permission? Hardly—for charity,

---

[1] No non-technical, colloquial and merely metaphorical use is yet attested for these terms in pre-medieval sources, contrary to M. Jastrow's entry no. 2, which should be distributed over the remaining semantic categories in his *Dictionary...*, 2 vols. N. Y. 1943. It is therefore impossible (regrettably) to suggest that also Hillel's bon mot is witty in this fashion: "We are not going to shoot you, but will let you go this time. You were, as usual, all good intention." The suggestion to look for witticisms and double entendres in this Hebrew item is not as arbitrary as it may appear at first glance, since it is in line both with Greek and Hebrew chriic patterns. Thus "Hillel and the Peace Offering (The Female Bull)," Betsah 20af. etc., apparently does preserve a double entendre of "peace offering," i.e., for the Temple as well as for the appeasement of the opposing Shammaites, just as the Greek pattern passage of "the Altar of Mercy," vis-a-vis the quarreling Athenians and Corinthians (*Demonax* 57). The children's word to the would-be proselyte in Shabbat 31a etc. retains the oracular ambiguity of the pattern story on Pittacus (D. L. I.80, preserved in Callimachus' poem). Hebrew *chriae* can thus be illuminated through comparison with their Greek patterns, and some items may thus be understood fully for the first time. *Cf. Cynicism* 19.21 and 25.16 —On a more likely interpretation of the third part of our Hebrew gnome, see immediately below.

[2] Such a conflict of values is, of course, implicit in all those of our *chriae* that contain the simplicity moteme: simplicity versus hospitality. In the Hebrew item, however, the conflict is somehow strongly stressed, as rightly observed by the commentary *Nahlat Ya'akov* of Jacob b. Baruch Naumburg on our item (Bavli). To him the story wants to favor the poor in such a conflict situation, but also teach self-control.

on this level, is personal and Hillel is no tyrant. Or should she, nevertheless, have let her husband in on her intentions? Perhaps—but there is still no easy justification for the heavy terms of the gnome.

If the Hebrew finale indicated the principle of reciprocity, i.e., if Hillel wants to say: "I *also* do not judge you severely, etc., just as you did not judge the pauper severely (and gave him food)," the gnome would be in line with a considerable number of Hebrew *chriae* (Hillel or R. Joshua and the Skull, Avot 2.7, etc., Hillel or Akiba and the Golden Rule, Shabbat 30b) as well as hellenistic *chriae* and gnomes in which this principle of reciprocity is equally popular. However, the clue is too slim to base such an interpretation on it.

The most simple solution of the problem of the heaviness of the Hebrew formulation is that it still reflects the Greek chriic situation in which the wife is guilty, and that she must therefore be "acquitted" in the Hebrew *chria*. It is probable that in this acquittal the Hebrew author was encouraged by the moralizing rhetoric-diatribic homilies on virtues which accompanied the *chriae* and even penetrated into their text, attenuating the burlesque and showing the wife's Sage in a more positive light. The model for this tendency may have been Xenophon. But it gained momentum in the general ethicizing trend of Roman-Empire rhetorics. Thus Plutarch, too, offers a moralizing essayist context for our *chriae* or, rather, they in turn are used to illustrate a moral diatribe. P.A. and its satellite P.E., in *de cohibenda ira*, actually appear in a context on table manners, which is precisely the context of the Hebrew *chria* in DER. Plutarch explains that there is no more unpleasant meal than that at which anger prevails, servants are beaten, and the wife abused, because the food is burned, or not salted sufficiently, or too cold. And yet, in the second *chria*, the Sage's wife *is* abused! In other words, the use of a *chria* in a moralizing context may lead to incongruities, either within or without the *chria*.[1]) Similarly, Stobaeus' *chriae* on Xanthippe in their vulgarity fit only into the context if one thinks of Socrates' behavior exclusively, the context being indicated by Theodorus title "From Teles' (Work) On Independence" ('Εκ τοῦ Τέλητος περὶ αὐταρxείας, p. 5, Hense) and his own (ΠΕΡΙ ΑΡΕΤΗΣ, p. 3, W.-H.).

Most illuminating, however, is the context of the brief item in Arr. IV.5.33 (Source no. 11, above). Here, too, the continuity of the context is rather involved and probably represents a commentary on Xeno-

---

[1]) Plutarch is fully anticipated in a similar treatment of table manners and self-discipline by Seneca, *Dial.*, *de ira*, II.25f. He mentions the motemes *symposium*, *slaves*, *dumb animals*, *anger* and some others.

phon's treatment of the subject. Shortly after the mention of our *chria*[1]) he concludes: "these beliefs make for *love in the house(hold)*, *harmony* in the polis, *peace* among the nations, *gratitude toward God*..." Here, too, the *chria* is used to confirm the rhetor-philosopher's values, although some incongruity remains between the mood of the anecdote and the moral purpose of the writer. It thus seems that the Hebrew item reflects somehow reminiscences of such a diatribic moral use of our *chria*, close to Epictetus' pattern, similarly using motemes of love, forgiveness, Heaven or piety.[2])

The chriic bon mot possesses still another important characteristic: it is, in full or in part, close to the proverb owing to its terse formulation and general truth, which latter is often independent from the specific content of the *chria*. Chriic finales thus appear in other *chriae* or become independent proverbs and enter the gnomologies or daily use as, e.g., the famous "lamp at daylight" of Diogenes (D.L. VI.41 etc.). An original proverb may, vice versa, be extended into a *chria*. A chriic finale can thus be illuminated by related gnomic and chriic material.

This method suggests a solution to the problem of the third gnomic section of DER. Indeed, in Avot 2.12 (2.17) our saying in its full form, וכל מעשיך יהיו לשם שמים, "and all your deeds should be in the Name of Heaven," is attached to R. Jose,[3]) a Tanna later than Hillel (!), an indication of its chriic character (transferability to other "authors"). Its content, however, becomes clear from another originally hellenistic *chria* on Hillel that uses the same formula:[4]) the item "Everyday a Holiday," Betsah 16a etc. According to this item Hillel was wont to eat any choice food immediately without setting it aside for the Sabbath,

---

[1]) ..."that she might pour all the water she wanted over his head, that she might trample down the cake..." The former refers to another famous Xanthippe *chria*, *cf.* D. L. II.36, Ath. 219 b. Seneca, *Dial.*, *de constantia* 18.5.

[2]) A clear case of the use of rhetorical elements in connection with a *chria* is found in the simile of the statues wich Hillel uses before his students in gnomic statements on the relationship of body and soul in Lev. R. 34.3 etc. This simile of the statues is found in a rhetorical form in Seneca, *Epist.* 64.9-10! The strange ornamental adjective עליבה or עליבתא, "sad, triste," *ibid.*, has a host of parallels in the form of diminutives (ψυχάριον, etc.) in Graeco-Roman rhetorical literature of the first two centuries C. E., as demonstrated in *Cynicism* 15.11.

[3]) c. 100 C. E. The preceding R. Eliezer (b. Hycranus) and R. Joshua are also heroes of the *chria*.

[4]) We must, of course, explain chriic items by other chriic items, whether Hebrew or Greek, and not by the interpretation which later tradition gave to it. Thus לשם שמים at this stage does not yet mean that all deeds should be performed for the Sake of Heaven (glorification of God or Torah) or in the Name of Heaven (as commanded) or for their own sake (thus most often and in Avot 2.2, which is post-tannaitic).

trusting that other food would come to him somehow by divine providence. "All his deeds were for the Sake (Name) of Heaven" is here expressly called מדה אחרת יתירה, "another *special* principle," and the two opposite halakhic approaches, those of the Shammaites and Hillelites are summarized in poetic gnomic form![1])

The Graeco-Roman parallels to this item, as shown in *Cynicism* 31.6f., are told of Diogenes (Plutarch, *Mor.* 477 C)[2]) and of Crates (*ibid.* 466 E),[3]) both heroes in chriic tradition. The context speaks against "planning" for the morrow. Arr. 1.9.19, Matth. 6.25f. and possibly 6.34,[4]) *Mekhilta de R. Yishmael* on Ex. 16.4 (J.Z. Lauterbach, Philadelphia 1933, vol. II, p. 103f.) and Sotah 48b, "whosoever has a piece of bread in his basket and says 'what shall I eat tomorrow' is of little faith."[5])—all these reflect the same chriic theme. According to a major Cynic teaching, attested early, the Sage is unconcerned as to where his food comes from. This is the theme of a host of *chriae*.[6]) The Cynic ate when he had something to eat. In the Judaic and early Christian settings this unconcern of the Sage (and of the "good man" emulating him) became trust in divine providence, yet still retained the basic unconcern. To perform deeds "in the Name of Heaven" is thus to do things trustingly. Hillel's utterance in DER, spoken to his wife, but perhaps also in some small measure to the guest as an apology, could be reformulated by a modern paraphrase (disregarding the heaviness of the first two phrases which, of course, remains). It includes all hidden chriic allusions and hints at the parallels:

"I am the last one to declare you guilty but excuse you, because you acted just as I would have done: "to eat and let eat," for food will always

---

[1]) This is an unusual procedure in the Talmud and attests to the popular character of this item (the Aramaic rime is rendered freely):
—The House of Shammai say: "From the first of thy week thy Sabbath seek!" The House of Hillel say: "Praised be the Lord day by day (Ps. 68.20; [i.e., eat whenever possible!]).—

[2]) Chriic keywords italicized. "*Diogenes*, when he *saw* his *host* in *Sparta preparing* with much fuss for a certain *festival* (shades of Shammai!), said: 'Does a *good man* not consider *everyday a festival*?'"

[3]) "But *Crates*, though he had but a *wallet* and a thread-bare *cloak*, passed his (whole) life *jesting* and *laughing* as though at a *festival*."

[4]) *Cf.* F. C. Grant, *Roman Hellenism and the New Testament*, Edinburgh etc. 1962, p. 72 (on Cynic proverbs in the NT). *Cf.* also K. F. G. (also D. C. F. G.)Heinrici, "Die Bergpredigt," *Beitraege zur Geschichte und Erklaerung des Neuen Testamentes*, III.1., Leipzig 1905, 1-98, *ad. loc.*

[5]) The "author" is apparently R. Eliezer b. Hycranus ("the Great!")

[6]) Among the best known (terse formulation): D. L. VI.40: "To one who asked at what time one should dine, Diogenes said: 'If rich, when you want; if poor, when you have.'" (εἰ μὲν πλούσιος, ἔφη, ὅταν θέλῃ · εἰ δὲ πένης ὅταν ἔχῃ).

come from somewhere, I trust (and Heaven will look after us). You got me this time." (...אֲזַי וְאָ... Beruria, too, convinced Meir with his own principles).

13. *The Literary Form of the Chria*

Four different forms of the *chria* are found:
1. terse (usually not more than two sentences); (t)
2. full (but without any superfluous detail); (f)
3. elaborate (diatribic-rhetorically enlarged); (e)
4. composite (several *chriae* combined to form a new item); (c)

All four forms are used for our "Spoiled Meal." Such variety for the same item is quite common in chriic literature. DER represents a full *chria*. The remaining chriic forms are found in other Hebrew items.[1] Most "Spoiled Meal" items show light elaboration.

Form:	Ael.	Ath.	P.P.	P.A.	P.E.	V.Ae.	Sto.	D.L.	Gn.V.	DER
	f	f	f	f	f	c	e	e	t	(f-e)
(actually)	(t-e)	(t-e)	(t-e)	(t-e)	(t-e)					(f-e)

The possibility of participal constructions in Greek makes for poignant brevity that cannot be followed in the Hebrew *chria*. Still, Hebrew and Greek *chriae* in a comparative word count in *Cynicism* were still reasonably close to each other.

14. *The Context*

The Hebrew item is found in a work that could be called a collection or semi-official code of rules on mores and morals. Anecdotes are used to illustrate general norms. Similarly, Athenaeus' *Deipnosophistae*, in

---

[1] terse: "Hillel and the Skull," Avot 2.6 (or 2.7); elaborate: "Hillel on Body and Soul," Lev. R. 34.3; composite: "Hillel at the Passover," Pes. 66a etc., which combines:
1. Cleanthes sudden accession to leadership; 2. Thales forgets his learning, is publicly embarrassed; 3. Diogenes learns from simple people; 4. Diogenes at Megara comments on a device with sheep. ——Eliahu Elimelech Hallewy, in the article "Hillel mitmanneh nasi," in his fine book *Shaʿare ha-Aggadah*, Tel-Aviv 1963, 189-195, has recognized the Greek background of some Hillel stories (as did A. Kaminka throughout his works). Both are unaware, however, of the *chria* and of cynicizing tendencies. Moreover, some of the Greek pattern stories which H. quotes are not the actual patterns for the Hebrew items. The pattern for the "trick" with the Passover sheep is the story of the Megarians and not Odysseus' escape under a sheep. *Cf. Cynicism, ad loc. Cf.* also his "'Anvetanuto shel Hillel," *ibid.*, 195-202, to which the same criticism applies.

which *chriae* are used, contain substantial sections that are codifications of contemporary mores, but their symposiastic form[1]) and diatribic interludes tend to obscure this fact. Plutarch and Sto., dealing with definite moral themes, are good examples of diatribe, the latter apparently preserving its earliest form. The former, although producing "essays," is nevertheless close to what one could call a codifier of the morals and ethics of his time, as are often his predecessors Cicero and Seneca in similar essays or orations.[2]) Diogenes Laertius' work is composite: doxographic, biographic, critical, and bibliographic. His *chriae* appear almost always in accumulations. A similar tendency is found in talmudic literature, especially in Avot and Avot de R. Nathan, even in our particular DER chapter, and in the Talmudim (Shabbat, Sukkot). V.Ae. is a romance, but its central section resembles a string of narrativized cynicizing *chriae* and apophthegmata, reminiscent of the Diogenes and Aristippus sections of D.L. Gn.V. represents an example of another method of codification-collection, i.e., by "author" or hero,[3]) here, as often in gnomologies, in alphabetical order. Aelianus' work is a collection of curiosa, without much rime or reason, gossipy and moralizing.

Form is determined by function. The function of these collections is obvious: variously, the propagation or preservation of ideals and morals; entertainment, edification and comfort (the latter often the only form of "protest" possible); aid to orators and students— perhaps all: to be a didactic topical inventory for cultures that have an intense need for resource materials in a popular form. The function of the context in which *chriae* figure prominently, and their very use within this context, are thus very much the same in Graeco-Roman as well as in Hebrew surroundings.

Context	Ael.	Ath.	P.P.	P.A.	P.E.	V.Ae.	Sto.	D.L.	Gn.V.	DER	Arr.
*c*ollection-code; *r*omance; *d*iatribic-topical	c	c-d	c-d	c-d	r	c-d	c		c	c	d

[1]) *Cf.* S. Stein, "The Influence of Symposia Literature on the Literary Form of the Pesach Haggadah," *Journal of Jewish Studies* 8, 13-44, London 1957.

[2]) They, too, use *chriae* heavily and in the same fashion. Plutarch is most clearly a codifier in works such as his *Apophthegmata* (*A. Laconica*; *A. Regum et Imperatorum*; *Lacaenarum A.*) and all essays entitled "Instituta" and "Quaestiones."

[3]) *Cf.* Avot ch. 2 (but not ch. 1 which is diadochic).

15. *The System of Ethical Values*

The list of chriic-ethical values of the fullest form of our "Spoiled Meal," i.e., of an ideal "Ur"-pattern, would contain these items:

1. hospitality
2. frugality
3. self-control
4. wittiness
5. brevity of speech[1])
6. harmony
7. appeal to a higher order[2])

Count of chriic values	Ael.	Ath.	P.P.	P.A.	P.E.	V.Ae.	Sto.	D.L.	Gn.V.	DER	Arr.	Xen
1:			x	x	x	x	x	x	x	x		
2:				½*	x	½*	x	x	x			
3:	x	x	x	x	x	x	x	x	x	x		
4:	x	x	x	x	x	x	x	x	x	¼**		
5:	x	x		x				x	x			
6:		x						x	x	x	x	x
7:										x	x	x
low: 1-3½ high: 4-	1	1	1	h	1	h	1	h	h	h		

*) Soiled food replaces here the frugality (simplicity) moteme.
**) The translation of the DER gnome is designed to show more levity than the traditional interpretations of the passage, without being fully witty.

Parallels to D E R Motemes

The table p. 406 indicates, in a necessarily superficial way, the degree of relationship between the different sources. DER is closest to the episode in D.L. (9½ counts) in which the chriic burlesque is greatly attenuated, and to Gn.V. (9½ counts), its satellite. They are also chronologically close to one another, i.e., regarding the period of their codification. The highly diatribic items, whether hellenistic or Roman Imperial, are not far behind (6½-7 counts). Xenophon, although only dealing with Xanthippe's temper in general and not with the "Spoiled Meal" theme, is surprisingly close owing to the positive ethical framework of his work.

---

[1]) "brachylogy" counts often as a Cynic-Laconic value in the sources. It is occasionally Sophist. *Cf.* Plato, *Protag.* 334 E, *Gorg.* 449 C; *Euthyd.* 342 E. Antisthenes in Gn. V. # 11: ὁ αὐτὸς ἔφη τὴν ἀρετὴν βραχυλόγον εἶναι. "*Idem* said virtue to be brevity." Also newtestamental. On Laconism *cf.* Joel II.i,75.

[2]) the State, Reason, God. This occurs most often in the immediate context but in DER and perhaps also in D.L. and Gn.V. in the gnome. All other gnomes appeal to the use of reason as the highest principle implicitly.

Distribution of Motemes

	1	2	3	4	5	6	7	8	9	10	11	12	13	14	15
Ael.	1	a	f		X	J	−s		tr	x		W a	f		l
Ath.	1	a	f		X	J?	−s		tr	x		W a	f	c(-d)	l
P.P.	1	p	u	ann	an		−m		up		x	a c	f	d	l
P.A.	1	p	fs	ann	ss		−l		ne		x	a a	f	c-d	h
P.E.	2	p	s	D	X		−s	t	up	x	x	D a	f	c-d	l
V.Ae.	2	a	s	ann	an+s	J	−s		{tr / ne}		x	a b	c	r	h
Sto.	2	p	s	D	X	J?	−s	ttc	up		x	D {c+b / b / (b)} di	e	d	l
D.L.	1	a	s	rree	X	C	+s	cc	qu		x	W b	t	c	h
Gn.V.	1	a	s	e(e)	X	½C	−l+m		qu		i	W b	t	c	h
DER	1?	p	fs	an	an	C	+s		gi	(x)	x	W {c / (b)} di	f	c	h
Arr.			f		X		−s		tr	x					
Xen.					X	C	−m+s	cc		(x)				d	

1: Number of scenes;
2: Meal in progress or anticipated;
3: Food: of *f*lour; *s*imple or *s*oiled (both non-luxurious) or *u*nspecified;
4: Guests: *a*nonymous (pl.: *a*nn) or *r*ich (pl.: *rr*); *e*xpected (pl.: *ee*). Named: *D*isciple;
5: Wife: *X*anthippe; *an*on.; *s*laves instead.
6: Motivation: *J*ealousy; *C*oncern;
7: Wife's emotion: negative: −; *s*trong; *m*edium; *l*ow. Positive: +.
8: Animal comparisons: in main *t*ext (pl.: *tt*) or in *c*ontext (pl.: *cc*).
9: Fate of the meal: *tr*ampled upon; *up*set; *ne*glected; *qu*estioned; *gi*ven away.
10: Gift: to *S*age: x; to others: (x).
11: Embarrassment: expressed or implied.
12: Bon mot: directed to *W*ife or to *a*ll or to *D*isciple. / On wife: x / unitary: a; duplex: b; tripartite: c / *di*alogui*c* (prelude to gnome).
13: Form: *t*erse; *f*ull; *e*laborate; composite.
14: Context: *r*ollection-code-canon; *d*iatribic-topical; *r*omance.
15: Count of ethical values: low: 1-3½; *h*igh: 4 and more.

DER	Ael.	Ath.	P.	P.	P.	A.	P.	E.	V.	Ae.	Sto.	D.L.	Gn.V.	Arr.	Xen
1 Scene	x	x	x	x							x	x			
Meal in progress				x	x	x	(x)	x							
Food made of flour	x	x			x									x	
One guest						x		x				(ms)			
Wife central	x	x	x			x	x	x	x	x	x	x	x	x	
Concern											x	½		x	
Strong + emotion											x	½		x	
Gift from wife														x	
Embarrassment				x	x	x	x	x	x	x	x				
Bon mot to wife	x	x									x	x			
Bon mot re wife	x	x	x			x	x	x	½	½					
Tripartite (bon mot)			x					x							
Dialogue precedes									x	x	x			x	
Full chriic form	x	x	x	x	x										
Context: code	½	x			x	x					x	x			
High count ethics					x			x			x	x	x	x	
Total (16)	6½	7	7	7	7	5	7	9½	9½	3	6				

Since many specimen of our "Spoiled Meal" must be assumed lost, no certain "family tree" can be established for this item. The attenuated (less burlesque) form is hardly the result of a steadily progressing ethical refinement in the Hellenistic-Roman Age, since it seems to occur early (Xenophon) as well as late (D.L.), precisely like its burlesque sister. Neither is the attenuation necessarily a product of Stoic influence,[1]) although the Stoics did use the *chria* for the illustration of their own values whenever it lent itself to that purpose. And, finally, the rhetorical-diatribic style represents a mixture of popular philosophies to such an extent, that modern critics often speak of the Cynic-Stoic diatribe.[2]) Nevertheless, a fully Cynic burlesque *chria* was always available, not only through transmission, but also through ever new creations and variations of the moteme material in accordance with over-all chriic patterns. This abiding vitality of the *chria* is strengthened not only by the late large gnomologies that include *chriae*, such as the *Gnomologium Vaticanum*[3]) and Stobaeus, but also by the great veneration which late antiquity and, with it, patristic Christianity had for the best in Cynicism.[4]

---

[1]) Cleanthes, who retained some Cynic aspects of the philosophy of his originally Cynic teacher Zeno, the founder of Stoicism, is basically a Stoic. Hecato is the pupil of Panaetius.

[2]) P. Wendland, R. Bultmann, M. Dibelius, A. C. van Geytenbeek, and others.

[3]) ed. Leo Sternbach, "Die Gnomologia Vaticano inedito," *Wiener Studien* 9, 1887, 175-206; 10, 1888, 1-49, 211-260; 11, 1889, 43-64, 192-242. Repr. Berlin 1963.

[4]) Themistius, Libanius, the Emperor Julian (6th and 7th Orations); the Diocesan Maximus Alexandrinus and his mentor, Gregory Nazianzen (*cf.* J. Geffcken,

Roman Stoicism, in particular, with its stress on "gravitas," could not fully indulge in the more extreme situations of the burlesque *chria*. Moreover, some of the basic Cynic values were in outright clash with Stoicism, such as the extreme Cynic *philoponia* and Cynic criticism of folk religion, conventional human society, the state, patriotism, culture and athletics. To be sure, contrasting values in the Cynical *chria* can be found quite frequently, but they seem to have been produced by the inner dynamics of the movement rather than through the influence of Stoicism. There are, e.g., sudden "cynical" acceptances of Hedonism. Arrogance[1]) alternates with patience, ataraxy with concern and even *philanthropia*. The proper care of the body is at times endorsed and at other times rejected;[2]) tuition fees or donations are alternately accepted or rejected.

If in spite of the paucity of the material an evolutionary survey of the relationship of the items under discussion is demanded, the tentative picture of table p. 408 would result.

In table p. 408:

+ : positive portrayal of Sage's wife
— : negative portrayal...; = : very negative
+—: mixed (+ stronger); —+: mixed (— stronger)
Ant(isthenes); Ari(stophanes); Symp(osiastic)

IV

Adaptation in Hebrew Culture

Although the ethical level and "homey" atmosphere in DER may still reflect a chriic tradition, there are considerable instances of acculteration to the tannaitic environment in this as in almost all other Hebrew *chriae*.

1. First of all, *chriae* become "naturalized," i.e., the hero becomes a Jewish Sage, the events take place in Judaea, quite frequently in the

---

Kynika und Verwandtes, Heidelberg 1909), Asterius, Bishop of Amasea, Maximus Confessor, and the actual Cynic Sallustius (5th - 6th cts., ed. D. Nock). —They condemn, however, the theatrical and mercenary behavior of the wandering popular Cynics of the Imperial Age.

[1]) On Hillel's arrogance in the pattern of the Cynic Sage *cf.* Cynicism 16.9.

[2]) Diogenes thus frequented the bath and took good care of his body (D. L. VI *passim*). In Pap. Vienna, Croenert, *op. cit.*, IX, p. 52, however, D. never washes because he does not want to *seem* but to *be* a "dog" (i.e., Cynic, κύων).

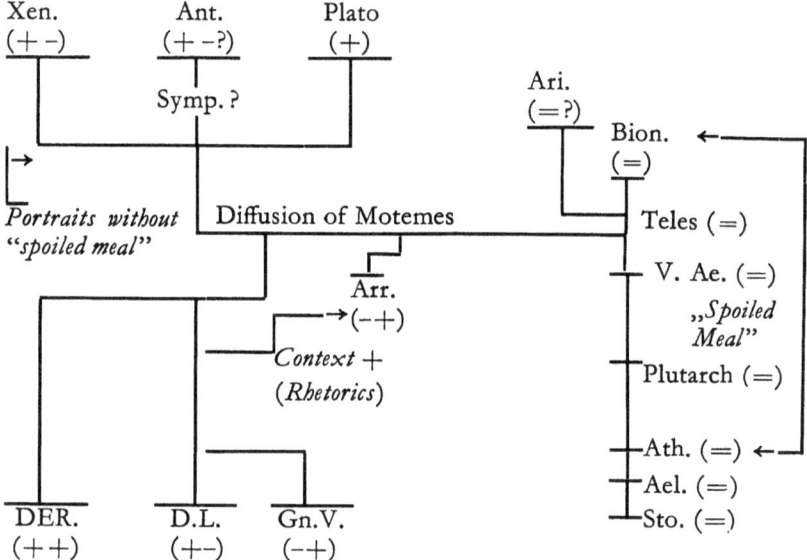

Sanctuary itself.[1]) This phenomenon is paralleled in other cultures, such as early Christianity[2]) (but not the Church Fathers) and Alexandrinian native urban opposition to Rome. With the Church Fathers, however, Latin, Greek and Syrian like, and in 'Abbassid and Mu'tazilite Islam (from 800 on), Cynic *chriae* are extremely popular in their original setting and with faithful quotation of the actual heroes or transmittors.[3]) The Romans used *chriae* for their own heroes but more often preserved the Greek *chria*, since they felt to be the successors of classical Greece. It is significant that *chriae* on Hillel the Elder and the few other tannaitic figures who are marginally affected by chriization[4]) cease after the tannaitic age and, apart from their use in the talmudic-midrashic literature, are not frequently repeated in medieval collections. Original *chriae* in their Greek setting (in contradistinction to "naturalized" items) are entirely absent in talmudic literature.

---

[1]) *Cynicism* 25.1-26.12; i.e., Greek *chriae* on Antisthenes or Diogenes in the temples are transferred to Jerusalem.

[2]) The present writer will publish elsewhere the thesis of a similar cynicizing chriic coloration of those parts of the Gospels which celebrate their central figure as a wisdom teacher and Sage.

[3]) though subject to much scribal corruption. Recently, F. Rosenthal has made accessible Islamic material which contains many *chriae*: *Das Fortleben der Antike im Islam*, Zurich 1965, (168-199) and "Sayings of the Ancients from Ibn Durayd's Kitâb al-Mujtanâ, *Orientalia* 27, 1958, 25-54, 150-183.

[4]) *Cynicism* 38.1.

2. In the Judaic culture the *chria* is, further, halakhized, i.e., seen as a legal-ethical test-case, an instance or precedent for a permanent rule (halakhah), which is often obtained only after a re-interpretation of the basic *chria* that subtly shifts its emphasis or meaning.[1]) More often a *testimonium* or μαρτύριον,[2]) i.e., a confirmatory (biblical) quotation is adduced that affects the shift of sense toward Jewish values.[3]) A sober use of *testimonia* is, of course, already customary in Greek literature; a witty use becomes frequent in the *chria*, neither sparing Homer nor Euripides (D.L. VI., *passim*). Furthermore, in this process of halakhization, original formulations which show clearly a one time happening are occasionally understood to express habit or practice. Textual variants are created by amoraic opposition to the original meaning of a *chria*, as in the story of Hillel's twofold criticism of the holiday mood at Sukkot (actually Diogenes at Olympia!), which was understood in Hebrew and Aramaic parallel versions as initial criticism and final praise (*Cynicism* 35.2ff.). Undoubtedly, a certain measure of this treatment was required also in the topical and homiletical uses of the *chria* in Graeco-Roman rhetorics. Only by this method could some of the extreme situations and values of the *chria* be incorporated into the strongly ethical atmosphere of Judaic culture. It is actually quite astonishing to see how much cynicizing burlesque was left in the Hillel cycle—but, on the other hand, chriic material was initially used to celebrate a Founder Sage who, by definition, had created new trends. Equally astonishing is the fact, established in *Cynicism*, that the gnomic parts of the Hillel *chriae* still show so many traces of the original Greek patterns. Similarly gnomic sayings could have been found in biblical sources but were rather taken from the chriic context.[4])

---

[1]) Thus, stories of Hillel's arrogance or invectives may still be subsumed under the discussion of his patience or proselytizing efforts. In one of the three parallel reports on Passover, his forgetting occurs owing to his severity with the pilgrims, but not in the other reports. His demonstration on body and soul or his heroism in the snow (Yoma 35 b) are made the basis of laws concerning the Sabbath, etc. (the actual mention of the Sabbath in the gnome of the latter is not "legal" but only a superlative endorsement of his heroism, parallel to similar endorsements in the Greek *chriae*, *cf. Cynicism* 22.9).

[2]) Cicero, *Topica* 73: "testimonium autem nunc dicimus omne quod ab alique re externa sumitur ad faciendam fidem." Also in classical culture the "canon" was used for this purpose, i.e., Homer, Hesiod, and, to a lesser degree, the great tragedians.

[3]) *Cf.* the use of the Psalm quotation in "Everyday a Holiday," above. Hillel's ataraxy is changed into confidence into the divine providence by a similar quotation from the same biblical source in "The Rumor," Berachot 60a.

[4]) In *Cynicism* 19,16-21, we try to show that this is true even in the case of the

3. In the Hebrew orbit, the *chria* is, further, "transcendentalized," i.e., brought into contact with a divine order, if not by the *testimonium*, so by the context, which, e.g., reshapes the proselytizing effort of the Cynic Sage toward the true way of life into Hillel's proselytizing effort toward Heaven, Torah and the World-to-Come. But even here, as we have seen, there are precedents of an allusion to a higher order in the hellenistic use of the Greek *chria*. In fact, some modern observers have claimed the existence of a religious tendency also in Cynicism (the Cynics were never atheists but faught superstition and convention), beginning with, or after, Crates, especially with Cercidas, the Spartan poet-statesman (*fl.c.* 255 B.C.E.), not to mention the later Peregrinus Proteus (d. 165 C.E.) and Sallustius (5th-6th ct.).[1]) Only on these grounds can some of the epithets for the Cynics, "physician of the soul," "scout of God" (Epictetus), and Cercidas' famous "Zeus-born (Dio-genes), Heavenly Hound," for Diogenes, be understood. But even in this process of transcendentalization in the Judaic context, the initial "immanent" quality of the Greek *chria* did not altogether vanish: there are no miracles in it; there is no Hillelite "mysticism," and reason prevails throughout.[2])

4. Another aspect in the adaptation of the Hebrew *chria* could be called its "humanization." Gifts to friends figure very prominently also in the Greek *chria*. Beggars, especially, abound. But the emphasis is rarely on empathy with their plight but on the arrogance of the mendicants, the wittiest way of their rejection, the riducule of the miser or the advantage to the giver.[3]) The Hebrew *chria* shows true feeling for the recipient. Invectives are rarer in the Hebrew items. The victim or butt of the Hebrew *chria* is never dealt with as sarcastically and unmercifully as in the Greek counterpart.[4])

Golden Rule, where a Hebrew formulation (Lev. 19.18) was available but a strongly hellenistic-colored form that came together with the *chria*, was preferred.

[1]) Dudley, *op. cit.* H. M. Hornsby, "The Cynicism of Peregrinus Proteus," *Hermathena* 48, 1933, 65-84. K. Joel, *Geschichte der antiken Philosophie (I)*, Tuebingen 1921, *passim*.

[2]) Partially chriic are oracles on and to the Sages: the Seven, Socrates, Diogenes and Zeno. They are paralleled by similar oracles on and to Hillel in Judaic literature. Their meaning and purposely ambiguous content are dealt with in *Cynicism* 29. 1-7. They seem to represent a variation of the "endorsement" moteme. The Greek examples are semi-witty. Important material on Jewish oracles in S. Lieberman, *Hellenism in Jewish Palestine*, N. Y. 1950, Appendix I, 194-199.

[3]) D. L. II.70; VI.7, 46, 56, 62, 66, 67; VII.14, 16, 17.

[4]) Traces of the Greek, however, always remain. Hillel's statement, in the face of a rumor of catastrophe, "I am certain that this is not my house," is rather un-

5. From its inception, the Cynic *chria* is highly political, i.e., it expresses resistance and protest, especially against tyranny. Among the most famous of all *chriae* are the encounters of Diogenes with Alexander the Great. Plato almost always, and Aristippus very frequently, are ridiculed because of their service to a tyrant. A foreign Sage, Anacharsis, is invented to castigate Greek political (and other) institutions. The Hebrew *chria*, however, is a-political. It serves exclusively socio-ethical and religious tasks. In the Judaic orbit, resistance and political protest used other literary forms of expression, such as the fable, the apocalypse,[1]) halakhah,[2]) and various midrashic forms.[3])

6. There is, perhaps, more to this Judaic reception of the *chria* than mere imitation. "Quidquid recipitur ad modum recipientis recipitur." Whereas the natural human satisfaction of repeating a good story for its own sake and the use of an effective and impressive means to honor great founders would still be imitation, the necessity of finding a tool to cope with change and an ever increasing complexity of life, is more than mere imitation. Furthermore, the new tannaitic Scholar-Sage-Bureaucrat class was in need of an ideology to set themselves off the hostile '*Am ha-arets* (while it was offering him at the same time an ideal pattern to follow) just as their Graeco-Roman counterpart set themselves off the unreasoning *hoi polloi* (while they tried at the same time to "convert" them). The renaissant *chria*, serving similar purposes in the early Roman Imperial Age offered itself at a crucial moment. The process of adaptation and the acquisition of the skill to create new effective popular *chriae* for specific socio-ethical tasks thus became the basis for a significant contribution of tannaitic culture to this vital literary form of the ancient world.

---

feeling. The same chriic background is responsible for some of the occasional harshness in the Gospels.

[1]) H. Fuchs, *Der geistige Widerstand gegen Rom in der antiken Welt*, Berlin 1938. S. K. Eddy, *The King Is Dead*, Lincoln 1961.

[2]) Recently again D. Daube, *Collaboration With Tyrants in Rabbinic Law*, London 1965.

[3]) Among these, however, there is again some Cynic material, such as the Alexander legends and the Prodicus "fable." The present writer hopes to deal with the latter within the near future.

"NOT BY MEANS OF AN ANGEL AND NOT BY MEANS OF A MESSENGER"

BY

JUDAH GOLDIN

Yale University

I

The verse being commented on by the Midrash (Sifre Deuteronomy 42, ed. L. Finkelstein, p. 88) is Deuteronomy 11:14, which reads, (If ye hearken diligently to the commandments), "then I will give the rain of your land in its season," and so on; and the Midrash interprets the verb *we-natatti*, "then I will give," as follows, "'Then I will give': I—not by means of (by the hands of) an angel and not by means of a messenger."

How does the Midrash arrive at this interpretation? R. Hillel ben Eliakim, for example, explains the Sifre exegesis this way: Since Scripture does not use the expression "I will *send* the rain of your land," but rather "I will *give*," the emphasis is on God's personal and unmediated action. As the Sifre continues, there might almost seem to be justice to R. Hillel's view. For in the commentary on the phrase "the rain of your land," the Sifre declares that such direct action is reserved for the Land of Israel only;[1]) and as prooftext quotes Job 5:10, "He *giveth* rain upon the Land, but *sendeth* waters upon the other lands."[2]) In this Job verse we see clearly that onto other lands God sends, *sholeah*, i.e., acts by means of a *shaliah*, a messenger; whereas to *the* Land, the Land of Israel, He gives, *noten*, presumably without resorting to a *shaliah*, hence directly. And the same verb, *natan*, to give, occurs in the verse we are engaged with, Deut, 11:14.

This interpretation is hardly satisfactory however, and it is not surprising that the Neṣib, that is, R. Naphtali Ṣebi Yehudah Berlin,[3]) refuses to accept it. I'm not sure I understand how the Neṣib derives the Sifre interpretation, but he is certainly explicit in stating that the source of the interpretation cannot be in the verb *we-natatti*, "then I

---

[1]) Cf. also Sifra 110d.
[2]) Naturally, I'm translating the biblical verses in accordance with the meaning given them by the Midrash.
[3]) In his '*Emeq ha-Neṣib* ad Sifre Deut., Jerusalem, 5721, p. 59.

will give." Truth to say, the Job verse is able to serve the Sifre authority in his desire to distinguish between the Land of Israel and the lands outside of Israel, because of the terms 'ereṣ and ḥuṣot, not because of the verbs in the verse (at best these offer only auxiliary support): 'ereṣ is easily understood as 'ereṣ Yiśra'el, the Land of Israel; ḥuṣot is easily equated with ḥuṣ la-'areṣ, countries outside the Holy Land.[1]) While in the Midrash it would be quite plausible to say of sholeaḥ that it is underscoring use of a messenger, and *therefore* if in the same verse in another clause noten is employed, *it* must wish to underscore action *not* by means of a shaliaḥ, hence direct on God's part, in Deut. 11:14 it would be stretching even homiletical midrash too far to insist that natan is here declaring the same thing, viz., God's personal action. As the Neṣib rightly remarks, the verb we-natatti is in no way excessive, in no way at loose ends to be picked up for special exegesis. Just as, if *shalaḥ* were by itself, one could say that God personally sends,[2]) so by the same token when *natan* appears by itself, one might press that God gives, makes a present, by means of an agent. Plenty are the gifts sent by messenger, and by itself the verb reveals neither mediated nor unmediated activity.

R. David Pardo is of no help on this point. He undertakes to reconcile the view here that it is possible for rain to be provided (to other lands) by means of an angel, with the talmudic statement (B. Ta'anit 2a) that the key to the treasure of rain is never out of God's hands. But this has nothing to do with our problem which is, to repeat, how from the expression "then I will give" does the Midrash derive, "I—not by means of an angel and not by means of a messenger"?

II

Whenever we have a problem with a text, the best thing to do is to consult other passages where a like statement or similar idiom is employed, and see whether those passages can be of assistance. Since we are dealing with a passage in the Sifre (on Deuteronomy), let us therefore first turn to another section in this treatise (325, p. 376)[3]) where we meet our troublesome clause. This time the comment is on

---

[1]) On the other hand, cf. Sifre Deut. 37, p. 70.
[2]) Note for example that in connection with the plague of 'arob (swarms of insects, or, wild beasts) Exod. 8:17 uses the verb *shalaḥ*, and in the hiph'il *noch dazu*, and yet the Midrash, Exod. R. 12:4, does not hesitate to attribute this plague (along with *deber* and *bekorot*) to God directly.
[3]) Cf. Midrash Tannaim, p. 201. See LXX on Isa. 63:9.

Deut. 32:35, "*Mine* is vengeance, and recompense;"[1]) and the Sifre says, "I personally will exact retribution from them, not by means of an angel and not by means of a messenger."

Here there is no problem at all. The order of the biblical words virtually makes the Sifre interpretation self-explanatory: *Li* naqam we-shillem, *Mine* is vengeance and recompense. If the emphasis is on *Mine*, it is not far-fetched to say that what is being taught is that the action is God's alone—He personally will reward or punish and not resort to agents to assist Him or act in His behalf. This Sifre comment is clear, but alas of no help to us in our passage.

III

Let us now follow the order of references Finkelstein furnishes in his notes. First, then, the Passover Haggadah,[2]) where we read (p. 122), "And the Lord brought us forth out of Egypt with a mighty hand, and with an outstretched arm, and in a great manifestation,[3]) and with signs, and with wonders" (Deut. 26:8). Thereupon the midrashic exegesis continues:

"'And the Lord brought us forth out of Egypt,' not by means of an angel, and not by means of a seraph, and not by means of a messenger. On the contrary, the Holy One, blessed be He, by His own glorious self (did it),[4]) as it is said (Exod. 12:12), 'For I will go through the land of Egypt in that night, and will smite all the first-born in the land of Egypt, both man and beast; and against all the gods of Egypt I will execute judgments: I the Lord.'[5])

> "'For I will go through the land of Egypt,' I, and not an angel.
> "'And will smite all the first-born,' I, and not a seraph.
> "'And against all the gods of Egypt I will execute judgments,' I, and not a messenger.
> "'I the Lord,' it is I and none other."

All editions of the Haggadah apparently[6]) carry this midrash which is not in the least difficult to follow: the emphasis attached to the

---

[1]) I am deliberately preserving the order of the Hebrew.
[2]) The edition I'm using, and to it the pagination refers, is that of E. D. Goldschmidt, Jerusalem, 1960.
[3]) So of course the midrash, and see also Goldschmidt's note 65 on p. 46.
[4]) Cf. Midrash Tannaim, p. 173.
[5]) Note how the midrash continues.
[6]) Cf. Goldschmidt, pp. 44f. and notes 60 *and* 61. See also M. Kasher, *Torah Shelemah*, XI, p. 117, note to #250.

Deuteronomy verse is "substantiated" by the Exodus prooftext, whose meaning is established by the seemingly superfluous "I the Lord" clause at the end of the verse.[1]) But this passage too is of no help to our attempt at understanding the Sifre on Deuteronomy 11:14.

IV

The next reference supplied by Finkelstein is to the Mekilta on Exodus 12:12 (ed. J. Lauterbach, I, p. 53),[2]) the details of whose terms in the Passover Haggadah we just confronted; but the Mekilta treatment differs from the one in the Haggadah. Observe: "By 'And I will smite (all the first-born in the land of Egypt)' shall I understand (that He will do this) by means of an angel or by means of a messenger? The verse (Exod. 12:29) however teaches the following:[3]) 'Now it was the Lord who smote all the first-born,' (that is,) not by means of an angel and not by means of a messenger."[4])

Note that although Exodus 12:12 concludes with the so-called superfluous words "I the Lord" which proved so useful to the Passover Haggadah, the Mekilta has ignored this opportunity altogether; instead it has sought its prooftext in a subsequent verse. But this very prooftext calls for explanation: by what right does the Mekilta impose on verse 29 of that Exodus chapter the meaning of "Now it was the Lord who smote"? Why should we not read, as the regular translations do in fact read,[5]) "(And it came to pass at midnight,) that the Lord smote all the first-born" and so on?

But, midrashic as the approach of the Mekilta may be, this is not arbitrary or carefree midrash. What is the ordinary sentence structure in the Hebrew Bible? As all the grammars will reveal,[6]) the general order of a verbal Hebrew sentence is, first the verb, *then* the subject, and then the object. To be sure, when there are two coordinate clauses and the first one is introduced by the verb in the imperfect with the

---

[1]) The question whether more than verbal exegesis is here performed, need not detain us now; but I think Goldschmidt (p. 45) has disposed of the problem too cavalierly, *Shibbole ha-Leqet* notwithstanding; cf. Kasher, *op. cit.*, XII, pp. 27f.

[2]) Notice that Mekilta R. Simeon (ed. Epstein-Melamed), p. 15 (ditto p. 227, *ibid.*) does not offer this interpretation.

[3]) Cf. Bacher, '*Erke Midrash*, pp. 135f.

[4]) Contrast *Memar Marqah* (ed. J. Macdonald) I, 9, Text, p. 23 (Translation, p. 36).

[5]) Cf. JPS; RSV (At midnight the Lord smote etc.); new JPS (In the middle of the night the Lord struck down etc.).

[6]) See for example, M. Greenberg, *Introduction to Hebrew*, pp. 129f.

waw conversive, the second clause will begin with the subject and its verb will take the perfect. *But this need not be the case.* It would make a perfectly good Hebrew sentence to read wa-yehi ba-haṣi ha-lylah, wa-yak YHWH. Compare, for example, wayehi ra'ab ba-'areṣ, wa-yered 'Abram (Gen. 12:10), "And there was a famine in the land, and Abram went down." There is nothing rare or extraordinary about this latter syntax. The Melkita is therefore entirely within its legitimate ground-rules when it decides that the order of the subject and predicate in the second clause of Exod. 12:29 may release a special meaning: we-YHWH hikkah may indeed suggest not just "And the Lord smote," but "Now it was the Lord who smote," that is to say, He personally, without recourse to any agency. And apparently the Mekilta preferred deriving its emphasis from this feature of Exodus 12:29 to the alternative proving from 12:12 itself, as the Passover Haggadah did.[1])

Here too then no special difficulty with the midrashic commentary exists. However, we are not yet done with this passage. For when we arrive at the Mekilta comment on Exod. 12:29 (I, p. 97), we discover to our amazement a virtual repetition of the passage we have just read through: "By 'Now (it was) the Lord (who) smote all the first-born' (Exod. 12-29) shall I understand (that He did this) by means of an angel or by means of a messenger? The verse (Exod. 12:12) however teaches the following: 'And I will smite all the first-born,' (that is), not by means of an angel and not by means of a messenger."

This is plainly going in circles, for Exodus 12:12 could be given its particular interpretation only by virtue of Exodus 12:29—certainly not the other way around! What shall we say therefore to this last passage? Three possibilities present themselves:

(1) The present passage is simply a mistaken repetition by copyists and should be eliminated. But this is not only the easiest way out of the difficulty, it is patently nonsense. All copyists may be fools some of the time; some copyists may be fools all the time; but that all copyists are fools all of the time is not yet an axiom in literary criticism. At all events, despite the garbled readings recorded by Horovitz-Rabin in the critical apparatus of their Mekilta edition,[2]) there is hardly justice

---

[1]) Of course I cannot say for sure why the Mekilta had this preference. Perhaps because the clause 'ani YHWH occurs in a number of contexts where the present interpretation would simply not apply. Note the formula in Leviticus 19 for example.

[2]) P. 43.

to the bland assumption that the whole passage is to be censored. See further below.

(2) It may well be that out Mekilta here in citing 12:12 as prooftext, may be referring not merely—or not at all almost—to the three words of the verse which it quotes, but to the whole of that verse, and particularly to the closing words thereof, "I the Lord," the very words which the Passover Haggadah found so profitable. Every student of midrashic-talmudic texts knows that it is far from uncommon for a verse to be adduced and the key terms that are required for the homily or exposition, the very words in fact which drive home the point, will be wanting in the text. So common indeed is this feature that it is pedantry to bring illustrations.[1]) If this be so, then we would say that the Mekilta on Exodus 12:29 enlists 12:12 for support because of its concluding clause, "I the Lord." I am not persuaded that this is the case, but the possibility is a real one.

(3) Finally there is a likelihood that originally the Mekilta on Exod. 12:29 may have simply given its interpretation of *we-YHWH hikkah* without the give-and-take that now encloses it, more or less in this fashion: "we-YHWH hikkah, not by means of an angel and not by means of a messenger"; and the present form of our Mekilta passage on 12:29 might have been adopted by someone eager to make it conform in appearance with the comment on 12:12. This is not as arbitrary or wishful a suggestion as may seem at first. In the first place, such a style would be in keeping with the style of our Sifre Deuteronomy 42 passage; it is not far off the style of the Sifre Deuteronomy 325 comment; as we shall see shortly, it would be like the reading in still another Mekilta passage. In the second place however, and more significantly, it would be in keeping with the substance of the reading we have on Exodus 12:29 in Mekilta R. Simeon,[2]) where we find in straightforward language, "'We-YHWH hikkah all the first-born in the land of Egypt,' and not by means of a messenger." No question and answer, no entertaining of an alternative to be dismissed; direct interpretation which, as our analysis above has demonstrated, may be justified by the reading we-YHWH hikkah.

The net result of this investigation of the relevant Mekilta comments on the two verses of Exodus 12 is what? The way in which subject and

---

[1]) In order not to appear grudging, let me refer to one example, and since we're discussing a Sifre Deuteronomy passage principally, let me mention the Dan. 6:11 citation in Sifre Deut. 41, p. 88. Here of course the text reads "etc." Very well then, cf. the Isa. 63:11 citation ibid., p. 86.

[2]) P. 28. But note that this is wanting in MS Antonin (ibid., p. 231).

predicate of the second clause in verse 29 are placed allows the midrashic conclusion that the action was God's own and not via some emissary. Can these Mekilta comments help us to arrive at an understanding of our Sifre statement? Perhaps. But before we explore that possibility, let us investigate one more Mekilta passage, and then still one last source.[1])

V

Commenting on the verse(s) in Exod. 31:12-13, the Mekilta (III, p. 197) says: "'And the Lord spoke unto Moses, (saying:[2]) And thou, speak unto the children of Israel),' not by means of an emissary[3]) and not by means of a messenger." Horovitz-Rabin seem to have recognized that the familiar formula was being applied this time not to God's action but to the action of Moses[4])—that is, since verse 13 says *emphatically*, "And thou, speak," the Mekilta is emphasizing that God instructed Moses himself to speak to Israel on this occasion, and not to pass on his message to them by means of some intermediary. The reading in Mekilta R. Simeon (p. 221) bears out the Horovitz-Rabin explanation,[5]) for here we have, "'And the Lord said to Moses ...[6]) And thou, speak to the children of Israel,' thou, not by means of an emissary[7]) and not by means of a messenger."

The present passage therefore tells us little of God's behavior apparently;[8]) yet it too is instructive for our purposes. As we saw in an earlier selection also, the exegesis here is determined by the special position of the subject, *we-'attah* dabber, *And thou*, speak. Indeed, in the present passage, emphasis is doubly underscored. For had one wanted merely to emphasize the *thou* element, it would have been quite sufficient to add the second person pronoun to the imperative and simply locate it, as Hebrew likes to locate its nominatives, after the verb. How, for example, does the verse (Exod. 20:19) put it when it reports

---

[1]) For other sources, based on the ones we are studying, see Kasher, *op. cit.*, XI, pp. 117ff., ≠ ≠ 250 and 251, and notes ad loc.

[2]) Cf. the reading in ed. Horovitz-Rabin, p. 340.

[3]) The word is *mal'ak* which we have been translating all along as "angel", but here such translation would be out of place. Cf. the dictionaries and Lev. R. 1:1.

[4]) See their commentary ad loc., and cf. S. Lieberman in *Kirjath Sepher*, XII, p. 65. See now also Kasher, *op. cit.*, XXI, p. 57.

[5]) Note the discussion in Kasher however.

[6]) Note also the reading in ed. Lauterbach.

[7]) Note the reading *meliṣ* in ed. Hoffmann, p. 160, and cf. the '*Efat Ṣedeq* reading quoted by Kasher in his note to ≠ 26.

[8]) And doubtless that is why in Sifre Deut. 42 Finkelstein did not bother to refer to this passage.

the demand of the Israelites that Moses and not another speak to them? *Dabber 'attah* 'immanu ... we-'al yedabber 'immanu 'Elohim, "You speak to us ... but let not God speak to us." What do we have however in Exodus 31:13? *We-'attah dabber*, the subject pronoun put first.[1]) Midrash which, if it can help it, never lets a jot or tittle of the biblical text escape its notice, would be sure to capitalize on this order: You, Moses, speak to the Israelites, you personally; don't pass it on to someone else to deliver for you: yours is the task to instruct them in the right way, as the Midrash Leqah Tob (100b)[2]) puts it.

VI

We come now to the statement in Version B of Abot de-Rabbi Natan (p. 2): "Moses received Torah from Sinai—not from the mouth of an angel and not from the mouth of a seraph,[3]) but from the mouth of the King of kings over kings, the Holy One, blessed be He, as it is said (Lev. 26:46), 'These are the statutes and ordinances and laws (which the Lord made between Him and the children of Israel in mount Sinai by the hand of Moses).'" Great indeed was Moses, as ARNB asserts at its very opening;[4]) he received his communications from God alone, no memra,[5]) no logos, no spirit, nothing intervening.

But how does the Leviticus prooftext bear this out? And why if ARNB wants to underscore that it was directly from God's mouth that Moses heard his communications, does it not quote the explicit verses of Numbers 12:6-8, "...My servant Moses...is trusted in all My house; with him do I speak mouth to mouth, and not in dark speeches," and so forth?

The latter question is not difficult, for the fact is ARNB does quote it, at the very beginning of the treatise where it proclaims the true greatness of Moses.[6]) On the other hand, the former question does demand some attention. How does the Leviticus prooftext establish that Moses received the statutes and so on directly from the mouth of

---

[1]) See also II Sam. 17:6 and cf. Driver ad loc.
[2]) See also Kasher's note.
[3]) Note that Duran on Abot 1:1 gives this as the reading of the *Mekilta*! Cf. above p. 418 n. 4 for the Lieberman reference.
[4]) P. 1.
[5]) See on the other hand the typical Targum Onkelos approach on Lev. 26:46 (cf. Tg Jonathan too).
[6]) As *Memar Marqah* (IV, 12, trans., p. 186) exclaims, "Where is there a prophet like Moses whom God has addressed mouth to mouth?"

God? Note, for example, that Version A of Abot de-Rabbi Natan (p. 1) uses this verse to prove that Moses was found worthy of serving as God's agent to Israel: in other words, all the verse really declares is that the "Torah which the Holy One, blessed be He, gave to Israel was given by none save by the hand of Moses."[1]) And so too the Sifra (ed. Weiss, 112c): "'Which the Lord made *between Him and the children of Israel*' (teaches that) Moses was found worthy of being made[2]) the messenger between Israel[3]) and their Father in heaven."

If however we will understand precisely what ARNA says, I believe we can grasp the reasoning of ARNB; and for the *precise* understanding of ARNA, a term (and reading) discovered by Louis Finkelstein sixteen years ago[4]) is particularly helpful. From Leviticus 26:46 ARNA derived that "Moses was found worthy of being the *bynyy*, the *middle-man*, between the children of Israel and God." Between Israel and God, then, there stood only one being, namely, Moses.[5]) And if it was by the hands of Moses only that the statutes and the ordinances and the laws, and lots more, as the Sifra (ibid.) insists, were given to Israel, he could have received all these only from the One Being on the other end of the line of communication. For Moses was in the middle: "'*Anoki 'omed*[6]) ben YHWH u-benekem ba-'et ha-hi', It was I standing *between the Lord and you* at that time, to declare unto you the word of the Lord" (Deut. 5:5).[7]) From none other than God, directly, did Moses receive Torah, as ARNB states. Prooftext? "Natan YHWH beno u-ben bne Yiśra'el ... be-yad Mosheh, the Lord gave by the hand of Moses who at Mount Sinai was in the middle between Him and the children of Israel."

VII

For all the instances of "neither angel nor messenger" there is an explanation. Can none of these be of assistance in the interpretation of

---

[1]) ARNA, *ibid*.
[2]) Midrash ha-Gadol, Lev., p. 680, like ARNA, reads *lihyot*, "to be."
[3]) ARNA reads, "children of Israel."
[4]) See *J. N. Epstein Jubilee Volume*, Jerusalem, 5710, p. 96, and cf. S. Lieberman, *Hellenism in Jewish Palestine*, N. Y., 1962, pp. 81f. and note 271 ad loc.
[5]) Cf. Philo, Quis ... heres, 206 (Loeb Classics, IV, p. 384), though for a different purpose: μέσος τῶν ἄρκων, ἀμφοτέροις ὁμηρεύων.
[6]) Note the order of subject and predicate.
[7]) And maybe ARNB speaks of a seraph because of Deut. 5:19 (cf. 5:5). Besides, the emphasis as we now see of "Moses merited being the *shaliah*" equals "Moses merited being the *only* shaliah." Hence the reading "*lo' 'al yede shaliah*" would be impossible.

Sifre Deuteronomy 42? I must say, I have been tempted to take a cue from the Mekilta and to some extent also from ARNB. And with that in mind, as we re-examine Deuteronomy 11, beginning with verse 13, a solution suddenly does seem to spring up. For note: "And it shall be, if ye hearken diligently unto My[1]) commandments which 'anoki meṣawweh, *I* command you this day ... then I will give the rain of your land in its season." In other words, once again the position of the subject may be the root cause of the emphasis. That this is no mean matter, or that it is something unlikely for the Midrash to pass over lightly, we have already observed. And regardless of the validity or invalidity of the midrashic interpretation, to take note of that construction is a sign of the fine sensibility of the Midrash toward the behavior of Hebrew speech. Does Scripture put the pronoun subject after a participle? In the concordance I have counted no less than fifteen examples of this with 'anoki; if therefore 'anoki precedes the participle, the Midrash would not necessarily be taking unwarranted liberties in attempting to make a stress. There are certainly times when, midrash or no midrash, subject before the participle plainly means, Read with italics. Look at Amos 7:16, for example, and then go on to the next verse. And I am virtually certain that passages like Jeremiah 1:11-12 mean something like this:

The Lord: What do *you* see, Jeremiah?
Jeremiah: What *I* see is an almond (shaqed) rod.
The Lord: You see excellently, for I'm *shoqed*[2]) to carry out My word.

And similarly with a number of other passages. "'Anoki meṣawweh" could bear this extra stress.

But "I command" is introduced by '*asher*, *which* I command. Can a clause introduced by 'asher have the subject follow the verb? Any number of times, as even a glance in the concordance will disclose.

What the concordance will not disclose—or, rather, when it does, the instances are so rare, that *these* will demand explanation[3])—is a

---

[1]) So JPS; new JPS, Pentateuch (p. 346), gets around it by translating "If, then, you obey the commandments that I enjoin upon you" etc. See however LXX, ed. Rahlfs, on the verse (P. 307).

[2]) I'm on the alert, ready to spring into action(?). At all events, in this sentence, this is the word receiving special attention, hence shoqed 'ani (and not 'ani shoqed).

[3]) II Sam. 17:13 is clearly emphatic (cf. verse 12). On Deut. 16:22 perhaps Midrash Tannaim, p. 98, is making the right emphasis. If there is a special emphasis in Job 6:4, I don't get it. Is it really possible, as Szold seems to hint (tentatively?) that a pun on *ḥamas shoteh* of Prov. 26:6 may be intended, and therefore

clause introduced by 'asher with the *participle* preceding the subject. What a dividend 'asher meṣawweh 'anoki would bring! But 'asher 'anoki meṣawweh, "which I command," is so typical a construction, I fear it cannot help us out in our present need. We are therefore back again to our problem; so I suggest we return to *we-natatti* which we may have abandoned too hastily. The truth is the solution has been lying in this verb all along, and perhaps we have overlooked what we were looking for because of overfamiliarity with the passage—sometimes it's fatal for a biblical passage to be incorporated into daily prayer: constant repetition creates the delusion that the text is intelligible, and then even the rudimentary steps of investigation are forgotten.[1])

(this Szold does not say) in the Job verse *ruḥi* is put after *shotah*? Seems fantastic to me.

As for Eccl. 8:10, cf. H. L. Ginsberg's commentary (Tel Aviv-Jerusalem, 1961), p. 94, for the meaning of *'asher* here.

Is Lam. 1:12 meant to be even more emphatic than 1:5; or is (the second) *'asher* of verse 12 like *ki* of verse 5 and 1:5 is really the more emphatic; and is the point that when YHWH strikes it's more devastating than during any other catastrophe (note 12a)?

As I Chron. 13:6 stands it is confused (cf. II Sam. 6:2 in Kittel, *Biblia Hebraica*, 1950), but see further in a moment.

Is Sifre Numbers 78 (ed. Horovitz, p. 75) in any way reacting to the structure of the clause in Ezek. 47:23? Note that there's no reference to this in Sifre Zuta (*ibid.*, p. 264); see also Midrash ha-Gadol, Numbers, ed. Fisch, p. 231. Cf. Y. Kaufmann, *Religion of Israel*, trans. M. Greenberg, p. 445.

One expression however merits special attention, "called by ... name," *niqra' shem* .... To the best of my knowledge and checking, the first time we come upon this idiom clearly (nevertheless cf. the II Sam. 6:2 reference given above), and it's in connection with Solomon's prayer after the Temple has been built, it reads, *ki* shimka niqra', "that (this house ...) is called by Thy name" (I Kings 8:43). Thereafter it's *'asher* niqra' shmi ('alaw; Jer. 7:10, 11, 14, 30; 32:34; 34:15. Cf. also the prayer in the Grace after Meals in Baer, *Seder Abodat Yisrael*, p. 556, but note also J. Heinemann, *Ha-Tefillah bi-Tequfat ha-Tannaim we-ha-Amoraim*, pp. 39f. and 48f.). Jeremiah however speaks also of the City (Jerusalem) *'asher* niqra' shmi ('aleha; Jer. 25:29; and note Dan. 9:18 too). Then in II Chron. 7:14 we hear of My People *'asher* niqra' shmi ('alehem). In these cases, it seems to me, some emphasis is certainly intended, something like an overtone suggesting that this House, this City, this People have "stamped" upon them His name—even in their destruction and desolation and dispersion. The same conception would apply to the Ark. If niqra' in Amos 9:12 is a participle, then perhaps Qimhi and Ehrlich are right in their interpretation (for Kaufmann's explanation see *Toledot*, III,i, p. 91).

Needless to say, all I am doing in this long note is speculating and raising questions. The principal point however should not be lost sight of: *'asher* introducing a clause with a participle normally brings the subject first and then the participle.

[1]) Of course the Law provides a remedy which I suppose works for half-a-dozen times half-a-dozen saints.

No one reading Deuteronomy 11:13 *et seq.* attentively can fail to be struck by the ambiguity of subject: If you obey the commandments which I command you, then I will give you rain, I will give the grass in your field. Beware lest you serve other gods, for then the anger of the Lord will be inflamed and He will hold back the rainfall, and you will perish from off the Land which the Lord gives you. So keep my words carefully in order that your days may be multiplied on the land which the Lord swore to give to your fathers.

Before these verses in the same chapter when actions of the Lord are described, He is expressly referred to and the verb is given in the third person. So too with the content from verse 22 on. However, when we read verses 13-15, the subject seems now to be Moses, now to be God. "Which I command you" in verse 13 would seem to be referring to Moses. But then in verses 14 and 15 is Moses the subject? Is it Moses who brings rain and grass? Moses who rewards for obedience? In his commentary on Deuteronomy,[1] S. R. Driver explains the shift as "the discourse of Moses passing insensibly into that of God, as very often in the prophets: so," he continues in his comment on Deut. 7:4, "11:14f., 17:3, 28:20, 29:4f." This is obviously in accordance with what the traditional Jewish commentators feel, and Rashi, for instance, even refers to that nice observation at the end of Sifre Deuteronomy 41 (p. 88): "If ye have done what is up to you to do, then I will do what is up to Me to do, 'I will give the rain of your land in its season.'"

The interpretation may well be right, but no less a fact is the ambiguity of subject in we-natatti. And that this latter fact is noticeable not only to carping grammarians is borne out by this: the Samaritan version, the Septuagint, the Vulgate—and now we know still other versions too—read not "Then I will give," but, "Then *He* will give:"[2] "If ye hearken diligently to the commandments which I command you today, to love the Lord your God and to serve Him with all your heart and with all your soul, then He will give the rain," and so forth.

We need not undertake to decide which is the correct original reading,[3] or if there was such a thing. One thing however is clear: the

---

[1] ICC, pp. 99 and 130.
[2] See M. Baillet, J. T. Milik, and R. de Vaux, *Discoveries in the Judaean Desert of Jordan*, III, Oxford, 1962, p. 159, lines 33 and 34!
[3] Cf. *Discoveries, op. cit.*, p. 151! Also, P. Benoit, J. T. Milik, and R. de Vaux, *Discoveries in the Judaean Desert*, II, Oxford, 1961, p. 84, lines 82 and 86! And see H. L. Ginsberg, "New Light on Tannaite Jewry and on the State of Israel of the Years 132-135 C.E.," in *Proceedings, Rabbinical Assembly of America*, XXV, N.Y., 1961, pp. 132ff.

reading we-natatti was not a universal reading. And if its legitimacy was to be insisted on, its use had to be defended, its form had to be justified by a particular interpretation. *We-natatti*, says the Sifre. Why we-natatti? To underline, *I* the Lord give the rain, and not by means of an angel and not by means of a messenger.

VIII

One final word. It may be of some significance that the emphasis of not by an angel and not by a messenger occurs in the following contexts: (1) God's redemption of Israel from Egyptian bondage; (2) God's punishment of Israel; (3) God's providing for Israel on its Land; (4) God's revelation of the Law to Moses at Sinai; (5) Moses's communication to Israel of the Sabbath as covenant-sign—and see Rashi's comment on Exodus 31:12, catchword *la-da'at*, as well as the Mekilta (III, p. 199) on "That I am the Lord who sanctifies you." Let the theologians make what they can of that.

FREEDOM WITHIN OBEDIENCE TO THE TORAH

BY

ROBERT M. MONTGOMERY

Ohio Wesleyan University

Erwin Goodenough was the first to give me an insight into the flexibility which has marked Judaism even before the Romans destroyed the Temple. As a non-Jewish student, I possessed a typical concept of Judaism as an unyielding structure oriented toward a Torah conceived of as static and inflexible. *By Light, Light* introduced me to that Jewish thought which adapted varied ideologies to Jewish purposes as Judaism found itself in differing cultures. We know how far Goodenough carried his interpretation. The synagogue at Dura-Europus is interpreted as the graphic expression of a Judaism which understood itself to be a Mystery. The monumental *Jewish Symbols in the Greco-Roman Period* continued his exposition of freedom within Judaism. Goodenough set forth in those volumes the evidence for the employment by Jews of symbols, non-Jewish in origin, which expressed and invoked emotions and longings which many scholars have refused to believe could be accepted by Jewish religious expression. I find myself influenced by the weight of the evidence Goodenough placed before us, but in the discussions which will go on over his, and alternative, views, I should hate to see lost his accent "on the sensitivity, keenness, and range of the Jewish mind."[1]

In this century non-Jewish study of the history of Judaism has presented perspectives which have done more justice to Judaism.
Thus Goodenough is only one of a number who enlarged the view of Jewish ideological structures. But for many of his students it was his exposition of Hellenistic Judaism which opened their eyes to the "sensitivity, keenness, and range" to be found within Judaism. The view of Judaism as a religion which possessed flexibility particularly helps us when we gaze wiftly over the history of that Judaism built on

---

[1] "Still the cult was inviolable: that lesson had been learned once and for all. But the cult could put no bounds on the sensitivity, keenness, and range of the Jewish mind." *By Light, Light*, p. 7.

the Pharisees. And the concept of flexibility and range needs eminently to be used by the non-Jewish student of Judaism. For in spite of the liberal expositions of Judaism over the last century, a stereotype can continue to linger. The student can see in the materials Goodenough interpreted, evidence of adaptability on the part of Hellenistic Jews, but he may continue to think that Pharisaic Judaism kept a consistent inflexibility. Thus we have learned to say that to describe the Pharisaic position as a legalism is to imply that the Pharisee believed that God in his mercy and benevolence had revealed unto Moses and the people of Israel his divine will for the life of man. So the notion of "benevolence" has entered; the idea of the giving of the Torah is delivered from the inference that Israel considered God an impossible taskmaster in surrounding them with law. But still the notion of the granite-like immobility of the Torah remains. The accent that persists in many non-Jewish minds probably rises from the idea that the Torah *finally* states whatever Israel must do and think, and what they should not do and not think. If the divine demands are finally stated how was it actually possible for Israel to live joyfully? How would it be possible for Israel to think that in indicating the order within which man must live and think, God had taken pity on man's disordered plight? If man considers freedom to be a prime requisite for humanity's living within changing environments, must not the Pharisee be seen as one locked within an unyielding mass of demands? The Hellenistic Jew thus makes some sense to the non-Jew in that rational considerations are supposed to provide the ground for obedience to the Jewish cult.[1]) Admittedly, the observer smiles knowingly at the rationale offered. The Jewish thinker, one says, is trying to defend an impossible loyalty. The Jewish position on his cult is impossible, so the comment continues, primarily because the dynamisms of human response cannot be confined within any body of law no matter how imaginative that body of law may be. But the Hellenistic Jew made his bow in the right direction by trying to ground obedience in the reason, as the non-Jew would see the affair.

By contrast with the Hellenistic Jew, consider the thought offered in *Midrash Genesis Rabbah* where no need is seen to provide a rational ground for the Torah. "In regard to every specific decree you order for

---

[1]) See Aristeas, 144-157 in the text of H. St. J. Thackeray as reprinted in H. G. Meecham, *The Letter of Aristeas*, 1935, pp. 5-41. Aristeas cites Right Reason as the concern of divine legislation, 161. Or see Philo, *Post.* 148 and *Agr.* 131. Josephus intended to write a volume in which he would offer the exposition of the reasons for various customs, but we do not know that he brought his project into fruition. See *J.A.*iii, 259; *A*.i, 192; and *A*.iv, 198.

men, they [the righteous] justify your righteousness and accept it in faith."[1]) In this passage, that *God* has given a sphere of obedience to Israel is considered enough. The relationship between Israel and God is evidently so secure that the faithful accept without question the burdens of response. Hence the Pharisee becomes an enigma. He, from the standpoint of the outsider, has wedded himself to fixed modes of behaviour in the life situation which demands pliability. And to make matters worse, the Pharisee does not even see a problem. Curiously enough, many did not stop to reason that if the Pharisee did not see a problem, there might not be one. At least there might not be a problem for the person who stood *within* the Pharisaic position and participated in the flesh and blood situation with respect to the Torah. So, many non-Jewish students abandoned interest in the halakah. Admittedly the haggadic speculations of the rabbis belong to the poetic ventures of man. The central devotion of the rabbis to the halakah intrudes, however, and makes it seem necessary to regard the Pharisee as the opposite to the *range* of Jewish thought Goodenough marked. Theologically, the Pharisee is lamented as bound while the Christian is considered free.[2]) Paul's contrasts between the Jew as a slave, and the convert to Christianity as a free man continue to hold the field. Yet by this time many are willing to conclude that Paul's understanding expresses authentically only the attitude toward the law which might mark a convert from Judaism. "Paul knew (even as a Christian) how the Jew *really* felt about the Law," runs the comment from which we can depart if only it turns out that obedience to the law incorporated in its own way a freedom. Was there flexibility and freedom within obedience to the law as Pharisaism developed?

As we examine the Pharisaic tradition over the centuries since Hillel and Shammai, we would have to speak of a Judaism which responded imaginatively to crises both of political repression and intellectual

---

[1]) *Mid. Gen. Rab.* 1. 7. For this Midrash I used the critical edition by J. Theodor (continued after Theodor's death by C. Albeck). For the other Midrashim Rabboth my text was published in 1923 in Wilna. English translations of the Midrashim Rabboth are those of the Soncino Press, made by various scholars under the editorship of I. Epstein, 1935 et seq. While I was aided greatly by these translations, my reconstructions of the material rest on my own interpretation except as noted.

[2]) That this picture provides a false construction of the Christian at times, as it forms an unilluminating approach to the Pharisaic position, hardly needs to be argued. The presence of moralism as a continuing historical constituent of the Protestant movement has been exposed and belabored by many. I am only pointing out here what stereotypes often influence non-Jewish students of Judaism.

pressure. For example, one can cite figures such as Saadia Gaon, Maimonides, and Moses Mendelssohn as Jews who contributed signally to formulations which brought forth new perspectives from within rabbinic loyalty to the Torah. But even if such figures were unknown, other evidence remains to be observed. Judaism flourishes though the Temple is destroyed. Judaism makes the difficult transitions from Palestine to Babylonia, to North Africa and to Spain, not to mention other areas and more recent areas. It continues to live under the uncertain mercies of Muslim and of Christian. So the inspection of the variegated cultures within which Judaism continued to live as a religion should have suggested that within obedience to the law the Jew possessed that freedom which makes for a viable faith.

That non-Jewish students failed to digest the evidence of flexibility rose in part from naivete about the life conditions within a legalism. Probably American commentators were not entitled to such innocence since legalism has marked so many religious movements in this country. Many persons are available who can recall the characteristics of life within a Christian legalism and some of those characteristics are illuminating. No corpus of decisions was collected. But decisions carried authority. For example, within a particular moralistic community no one argued that "to keep the Sabbath day holy" meant something different from avoiding work from midnight to midnight beginning Saturday night. Sunday papers could not be purchased; but Monday papers could be bought even if they were printed on Sunday. In a rural parish a farmer might be meeting the spring rush by plowing around the clock with the aid of the headlights on his tractor; nevertheless, I have seen devout farmers stop in such a time, at midnight on Saturday to resume in twenty-four hours. If anyone had kept an objective record, doubtless numerous adjustments would have been seen to be occurring. And the felt reasonableness of the decisions would remind us of rabbinic certitude. So long as the person remained within the specific community of faith, the sacrifice offered in obeying the "commandments" involved no "burden" at all. Indeed, the same spirit of joyful obedience characterized the legalistic Christian as did the Pharisee. Wedded to naivete has been the reluctance of the observer unattached to a tradition to recognize the necessary difference in perspective for those within a tradition. Outside, the data seem to lead to one interpretation; within the community of faith another interpretation may hold. The outsider looking, say, at the differences between the Jerusalem Talmud and the Babylonian Talmud sees in the modifications evidence of the imperfections in the confession that the written Torah is perfectly interpreted by the oral Torah; the insider may see the modification (if he knew it to be a modification) to be the *true* meaning the principle being applied possessed all the time. The outsider sees the system admitting its inadequacies by its changes; the insider views the changes as evidence that the system remains fixed and ever more relevant.

When, therefore, we inspect the rabbinic materials so that we may understand how the rabbis could view the Torah in such fashion that they were free to adjust its demands to the requirements of changing conditions, we cannot expect their discussions to afford us direct help. The rabbis are not going to write about their freedom and the sources from which this freedom rises, for they may not be conscious that they possess freedom in so many words. Their self-understanding tells them that the people of Israel has accepted the yoke of the law; furthermore, they may not have reflected that the yoke of the law could have been affirmed in such a way that the Torah would become an impossible burden. So our task appears to be that of analyzing diverse elements within a rabbinical tradition in which freedom as a term is unimportant. Of course, as we think about possible sources of flexibility, we recognize that certain points have come in for comment in discussions of the Pharisees.[1]) For example, the importance of the *oral* interpretation of the Torah impresses us. In fact it is so obvious that the acceptance of the validity of an oral interpretation can promote flexibility that no long discussion of its import is necessary. So long as the oral Torah remains oral new applications of old principles can slip in quite unconsciously. Further, antique provisions no longer relevant can be interpreted as involving novel and now convincing responses. A second factor, related to and supporting the oral Torah, is found in the hermeneutical rules which can aid, again unconsciously, in bringing the written Torah into touch with the changing circumstances of human society. But a less obvious source of flexibility, to which the body of my discussion turns, can be found in the conception of the process of adjudication. I am persuaded that what I take to be the principles underlying rabbinical adjudication constitute a distinctive source of vitality and "range" in Jewish legalism.

If in a word we stipulate the test which a decision must pass, the

---

[1]) See G. F. Moore, *Judaism in the First Centuries of the Christian Era*, I, pp. 256-258.

word "appropriateness" would suit rabbinical attitudes.[1]) That is to say, justice has been satisfied when all of the aspects pertinent to a situation have been considered and the judgment rendered seems appropriate to all factors. Every aspect of the human involvements relating to the persons concerned in a decision may be brought up. Whether or not litigants should be seated and if seated whether one or both, receives due attention. Whether litigants must be dressed alike so that differences in wealth will not be apparent comes within the interest of the rabbis.[2]) In fact, so numerous are the elements in the human situation which in the rabbis' opinion could distort judgment, hardly any illustration of impinging factors could represent the scope. Thus an inspection of the tractate Sanhedrin[3]) helps us to answer for the rabbis the question raised by Edmund Cahn: "...when the law of a state is infringed and someone has to be punished, is it a concept or a living person"[4]) that we condemn to death? It is clear that the rabbis are sensitive to the human condition; it is the living person to whose situation the Torah is to be applied. If first formal impediments to justice must be removed, argument about the problem for decision constitutes a second requirement. And an illuminating phrase used for the process of argument is literally "taking and giving."[5]) The import of a description of the process of adjudication as requiring "give and take" suggests that a dialectic progression through several standpoints occurred; by this means could the appropriate point of viewing the case be reached. We must remind ourselves that the give and take rests in the hands of experts. Thus the process is not understood, to put the matter in an extreme way, as desultory discussion, but as the occasion

---

[1]) The term "appropriateness" is one which I have selected. It is true that כהוגן is used when the language of Esther 2:1 is taken to mean that Ahasuerus regretted his conduct toward Vashti. It is concluded that Ahasuerus had decreed the death of Vashti and now reflects that Vashti had acted appropriately (כהוגן) while his decision was not appropriate (שלא כהוגן). I do not argue that the rabbis use "appropriate" to characterize formally the nature of a just decision.

[2]) *Mid. Deut. Rab.* V. 6. The English translation by J. Rabbinowitz, 1951, cites on p. 107 as well *Shebu'oth*, 30a. The whole discussion of whether anyone shall stand, and if so who, as well as the issue of the dress of the litigants is apposite. See the translation by A. E. Silverstone, Soncino Press, 1935, pp. 165-173.

[3]) I used the translation by Jacob Shachter and H. Freedman, Soncino Press, 1935.

[4]) *The Sense of Injustice*, 1949, p. 2.

[5]) Rabbi Jose speaks of judges' taking and giving (נושאין ונותנין) in making a decision because they are under the fear of Gehinnom. *Mid. Song of Songs Rab.* In the text the saying appears at III. 6.3., but in the Soncino translation it is found at III. 7.3.

for citing all relevant observations. Room is made for precedent, for minority opinions, for analogies, and for any element in the human situation which bears upon the matter under decision, but always under the control of specialists who at all times give judgment under the critique of their peers. True the character of rabbinical discussions as they are left to us may not strike the modern eye as restrained and orderly, but in its own way and on its own terms the material is purposive. Certainly, adjudication was not left by the rabbis to the unlearned in the Torah.

We are seeking to learn the degree to which the rabbis prized the process of argument so necessary for the correct disposition of a case. There is such a general understanding in western culture that law is a kind of fallible substitute men contrive because justice lies so far from us. Did the rabbis evaluate their process of decision in this way? The rabbis *could* conclude that the citation of evidence from the flesh and blood involvements of man are added to the statements from the Torah because men are unable to reach the lofty perspectives of God. The contrast between human fallibility and ultimate justice was certainly set forth in the ancient world and I propose to analyze one such presentation for the light it will throw upon the exposition of the rabbinical outlook. An admirable example of the radical difference conceived between ideal justice on the one hand, and the decision of human judges on the other, can be seen in Plato's presentation of the trial of Socrates.

In the *Apology*, Socrates' own expectations about Justice present the notion that it is something different from decisions reached by consulting human involvements. One might say for Socrates, responding to Edmond Cahn's question cited above, that a concept rather than a living person is in court. Socrates is a fighter for Justice, who, having been assigned to philosophy, must not desert his place in the line of battle because of a fear of death or for any other consideration.[1] In the light of our general familiarity with the metaphysical reference of Plato's thought, the conception of the issues impinging upon Socrates' trial is clear. A Universal hovers over the decision in which Socrates' judges are involved. In the light of this, Socrates chooses to defend himself by certain arguments without embarassment so long as his referent is this Universal rather than his existential situation. Nothing which will appeal to human sympathy can be allowed to intrude. Socrates can even

---

[1] *Apology* 29 A. φοβηθεὶς ἢ θάνατον ἢ ἄλλο ὁτιοῦν πρᾶγμα λίποιμι τὴν τάξιν.

dwell upon factors which may offend his judges. Presumably his clothes reflect his poverty and thus accentuate the fact that he made no charge for his conversations, unlike the other Sophists.[1]) He irritates his judges by selecting as an alternative to death, the "punishment" of being fed at public expense.[2]) Thus by selecting certain factors relating to his situation as a human being he sees to it that ameliorating data are cancelled so far as their influence upon adjudication is concerned.

Now Socrates knows that his conduct at the trial is exceptional. Another manner exists in which a defense may be conducted, and Socrates regards the other as an unworthy alternative. Socrates remarks on the expectations of his judges as to a course of conduct which they wish Socrates would pursue. Were he to follow the method usual in such circumstances, tears would have been appropriate as an instrumentality by which the judges would be affected. He would also have paraded his children before the gathering, I dare say to establish the character of his responsibilities so graphically as to make it less likely that he would be condemned to death. Socrates has three sons, one almost grown, and the other two capable by their presence alone of enlisting the sympathies of parents. There have been people, in the memory of Socrates, who in similar situations might have acted as though death were a terrible thing.[3]) Within the framework of adjudication rejected by Socrates, the full character of man's involvements becomes pertinent to the decision. Man's fear of death forms an element for the judge to consider. The degree to which other lives hang upon the life of an accused man, and the sweetness, or bitterness, of human relationships seem to be appropriate in the balances. Despite our sympathy for Socrates and our appreciation of the nobility of his stance, it is possible to recognize two differing concepts of adjudication in the *Apology*. The one sees all of the considerations rising from the environment of the litigant as irrelevant and the other understands as pertinent the conditions within which men live their lives. In the one, proceedings require that the judge be taught; in the other, one "pleads" a case before the judge.[4])

From an inspection of the Midrashim Rabboth I would conclude that the conception of adjudication as involving an impersonal appli-

---

[1]) *Ibid.*, 31 C.
[2]) *Ibid.*, 36 D, E.
[3]) *Ibid.*, 34 B-35 A.
[4]) Οὐδὲ δίκαιόν μοι δοκεῖ, εἶναι δεῖσθαι τοῦ δικαστοῦ οὐδὲ δεόμενον ἀποφευγειν, αλλὰ διδάσκειν καὶ πείθειν. *Ibid.*, 35 B, C.

cation of Justice (in the sense of a Universal) would fail to express the rabbinical ideal. If any mark of categorical decision is found, perhaps it appears in the pictures of arbitrary or tyrannical justice. In cases involving the decisions of a tyrant, no apparatus which presents contextual observations exists. Thus a man is imagined to have presented a king with a sharp sword, intending to do honor to the king. But in the illustration the king ordains that the man be beheaded with that very sword.[1] Presumably such an illustration, like many others with the same drift, conjured up to illumine a point, echoes the rabbis' acquaintance with justice dispensed without the pleading of a case by the "adversary" conception of adjudication. But rabbinical decisions do not allow for their own courts such categorical judgement which dispenses with extenuating arguments.

Fortunately for us some rabbinical material helps us to decide whether ultimately the rabbis could accept the contrast between ideal Justice on the one hand, and on the other the arena of contextual human judgements. In haggadic presentations the Heavenly Court is portrayed. Since here the imagination of the rabbis roams freely, presuppositions about the character of perfect adjudication can be revealed. If we remind ourselves that statements about Ultimate Reality exhibit poetic quality, we will not expect such sentences to preserve the same characteristics as empirical judgements. The haggadic material about heavenly judgements therefore fits into the general class of "disclosure"[2]) statements. We ought, accordingly, to regard such presentations as genuinely significant, contrary to some scholarly opinion that rabbinic presentations involving angels and the like are to be disregarded as creations of idle fancy. The stories of the Heavenly Court aid particularly in our task of trying to estimate rabbinical attitudes toward the human dispensing of justice.

Several examples of stories revolving around the Heavenly Court are needful. In one, Rabbi Jose asks how we are to envisage the functions of Michael and Samael. He replies that they are like an advocate[3]) and a prosecutor[4]) in court. In their presentation, the advocate realizes that he has argued a stronger case. The prosecutor, noting the advocate's triumphant reaction, seeks to add an argument. But the advocate

---
[1]) *Mid. Deut. Rab.* IX. 6.
[2]) A term used, for example, by Ian T. Ramsey, *Religious Language*, 1957, p. 112. At this point he is discussing the language of prophecy, but his analysis throughout his work of the idiosyncrasies of religious language has been very helpful.
[3]) סניגור equals συνήγορος Jastrow.
[4]) קטיגור equals κατήγορος, *ibid*.

quiets the prosecutor and asks that the judge be heard. So Michael and Samael stand before the Shekinah with Satan accusing Israel and Michael defending the virtues of Israel.[1]) Or, in another story rising out of the comments upon the book of Esther, Haman has devised a plan which would have led to the rejection of Israel by God. Haman invited men of Israel to a great feast, and they attended despite the counter injunctions by Mordecai. When the Jews were involved in misconduct, Satan hurried to call God's attention to the shameful spectacle. God asks what will become of the Torah were he to eliminate his people, as he is strongly tempted to do. Satan counters with the suggestion that God be content with the angels. So God signs a decree which is to bring about the end of the people of Israel. Immediately, the Torah, the angels, the sun and the moon, the patriarchs, Moses, and Elijah concern themselves with the impending tragedy. And Mordecai is prevailed upon to implore the Deity for a reconsideration of the divine intent.[2])

In the portraits of cosmic decisions a general tendency exists to emphasize the victory which the attribute of mercy in God's character wins over the attribute of justice. Thus when the angels remind God who proposes to save Hagar and her child, that the child, Ishmael, will give Israel difficulty in the future, God prefers to judge the child as he then is, in conditions of innocence.[3]) But mercy does not win out inevitably in the thinking of the rabbis. For example, all the representations made to God did not avail when God decided against Moses' entering the Promised Land before he died. Powerful considerations were presented, heavenly agents were unable to fulfill their function, and finally God himself had to remove Moses' soul. But mercy in the character of God did not save Moses from death.[4])

The daring quality in the rabbinic imagination permits the portrayal of human participation in the dialectics of divine judgement. Thus Moses is pictured as rousing the divine anger when he persists in probing the divine intentions with respect to Israel when Moses has not been successful as yet in releasing Pharoah's grip upon Israel. Moses' questions cause the Attribute of Justice to desire to strike Moses.[5]) But when God sees that Moses speaks because of the pain of

---

[1]) *Mid. Ex. Rab.* XVIII. 5.
[2]) *Mid. Esther Rab.* VII. 13. The full story may not have been given here since there is a lacuna in the text.
[3]) *Mid. Ex. Rab.* III. 2. See also the acceptance of Manasseh's repentance, *Sanhedrin* 103a.
[4]) See the translation of *Mid. Deut. Rab. op. cit.*, pp. 180-188.
[5]) *Mid. Ex. Rab.* V. 22, VI. 1, 2.

Israel, God chooses to act toward Moses in terms of the Attribute of Mercy.[1]) Such a construction seems harmonious with the portrayal of discussion as a feature of the Heavenly Court. At the same time as we explore these daring and imaginative pictures which the rabbis give, we think of the special features of religious statements which speak about the character of the unseen world. Such venturesome statements cannot be probed with the logic which applies to common-sense sentences. So we can expect a certain inconsistency in rabbinic statements as now one value is favored and then, another value is accented. Thus the Rabbis are capable of saying that God can render a verdict by himself but humans must not judge alone. Resh Lakish declares that to God by himself belong both judgment and seal.[2]) Nevertheless, when Rabbi Pappas declared that God judged alone, and no one could gainsay his judgments, Akiba corrected the statement. Akiba added that God judged completely with justice because he was surrounded with the heavenly hosts, some of whom are in favor of acquittal and some in favor of conviction.[3]) To the same need for varying the statement as different values are accented I would assign another passage in which it is said that God informs his *familia*[4]) before he speaks in order that they will be able to praise the character of his judgments.[5]) Obviously, in that comment the judgments of God have not been submitted to discussion. And the rabbis sometimes reject the idea that there could be contentiousness[6]) in the divine realm.

We return to the purpose for scanning the imaginative reconstructions of heavenly adjudication. We were not looking for formal and logically consistent statements in which the character of ideal adjudication is set forth. Rather we wished to see if any light is thrown on how the rabbis think about human adjudication. Do they consider that an imperfection by nature adheres to the discussion attendant upon the disposition of cases involving the Torah? Taking the passages about the Heavenly Court seriously, but not literally, leads me to believe that the rabbis do not drive a wedge between human justice and ideal justice. If this deduction is sound the task of the Pharisaic experts takes on dimensions of seriousness and profundity. To pay

---

[1]) *Ibid.*, VI. 1.
[2]) *Mid. Deut. Rab.*, I. 10.
[3]) *Mid. Song of Songs Rab.*, I. 9. 1.
[4]) פמליא
[5]) *Mid. Ex. Rab.*, VI. 1.
[6]) *Ibid.*, IX. 1. Jastrow corrects פלינקרא to פילוניקיא (φιλονιϰεία).

attention to formal elements which might impair justice, to encourage a give and take as considerations potentially extenuating are urged, is to participate in a *divine* process. We have found the rabbis at times able to suppose that there is no process other than debate between adversaries, even in heaven, by which an appropriate decision can be reached.

I find the concept of the ultimacy of human adjudication reinforced when I see passages in which it is suggested that judgments on earth impinge upon celestial judgments. Thus the rabbis say that decrees hold both upon heavenly as well as earthly beings and R. Joshua of Siknin corroborates adding the requirement of purity for human judges.[1]) So with respect to intercalation, God informs the angels that he and they will approve what Israel decrees.[2]) For me the strongest example of how seriously the rabbis consider their debates, appears in a lengthy story in *Baba Mezia*. In this story R. Eliezer is engaged in debate with the Sages. R. Eliezer asks that the miracle of a carobtree's being torn from its place support his version of the halakah. His opponents are not impressed by the compliance of the carobtree. In turn, a stream of water flows backward and walls of a schoolhouse start to fall, only to correct themselves in part when R. Joshua enjoins them not to interfere. Then a voice from heaven intervenes only to have celestial interference with rabbinical debate rejected. To continue the story, Elijah informed R. Nathan that God was not in the least disconcerted that the autonomy of rabbinical decision had been affirmed.[3])

If thus the rabbis are able imaginatively to construe the ultimate significance of human adjudication, a significant light is thrown upon the way in which the finality of the Torah is understood. It is affirmed by faith that the corpus of possible requirements stretching back before time and after time contains the perfect comprehension of God's expectations. But the perfect Torah must be interpreted and applied. As the oral Torah comes from God, so the serious struggles to adjudicate carry the divine majesty. Consequently, the significant adjustments in that Judaism which flowed from the Pharisees take on distinctive coloring from within the tradition. The adjustments coming from the autonomy of rabbinical decisions testify that the finality of the Torah is a conception held dynamically not statically. "Art" characterizes the way in which the Torah is held to be God's requirement for men. True it will be that the outsider may have his eye caught by types of

---

[1]) *Mid. Song of Songs Rab.*, I. 2. 5.
[2]) *Mid. Ex. Rab.*, XV. 2. See also XV. 20.
[3]) 59a, b. I used the translation by Salis Daiches and H. Freedman, pp. 352f.

responses over the century in which Judaism honors antiquity. If he fixes his eye on traditional responses, the outsider may continue to be impressed by the unyielding and static character of historical Judaism whatever the evidence may be against such a conception. But the view of the seriousness of human adjudication "disclosed" by the pictures of justice in the Heavenly Court will give the interested observer quite another idea. He will see in the Pharisees (as well as in the Hellenistic Jews) an example of the "sensitivity, keenness, and range of the Jewish mind." Certainly as we consider Pharisaism phenomenologically, refusing to force our prepossessions upon it, we would have to say that the Pharisees in their own way exhibited freedom and flexibility.

RABBIS AND COMMUNITY IN THIRD CENTURY BABYLONIA

BY

JACOB NEUSNER

Brown University

I

The Babylonian rabbis played no special role in the life of the synagogue. They exercised no sacerdotal functions. While some of them, notably Rav and Samuel, composed prayers, we have no way of knowing how widely, if at all, rabbinic liturgies were accepted in synagogues during their lifetimes. Many of these, for instance blessings to be said before eating various kinds of food, and the Grace after Meals, probably were initially recited in the school house alone, even there posing some complex difficulties for the students, as we shall see. In any event, the rabbis did not normally recite the services, read from the Torah, bless the people, or assume any other sacerdotal duties which set them apart from, and above, the people in the synagogue. While they quite naturally praised synagogue prayer, they held that *their* studies were more important. R. Ḥisda (late 3rd century), for example, explained (Ps. 87.2), "The Lord loveth the gates of Zion [ẓiyyon]" to mean that the Lord loves the gates distinguished [meẓuyan-im] through law [halakhah] *more* than synagogues and houses of study, and similarly we have the following sayings:

> Abaye said, "At first I used to study in my house and pray in the synagogue. Since I heard the saying of R. Ḥiyya b. 'Ammi in the name of 'Ulla, 'Since the day that the Temple was destroyed, the Holy One, blessed be He, has nothing in his world but the four cubits of the law alone,' I pray only in the place where I study..." Rav Sheshet used to turn his face to another side and study [during the public reading of the Torah], saying, "We with our [business], and they with theirs."
>
> (Bab. Talmud Berakhot 8a)

A contemporary of Rav Sheshet, R. Naḥman, said that he found it too much trouble to gather ten people in his home to permit him to engage in public prayer even there.[1]) The rabbis' attitude was based

---

[1]) Bab. Talmud, Berakhot 7b.

in part upon the theological presupposition, expressed many times from the first century A.D. onwards, that study of the Torah was the highest religious action, exceeding in sanctity the sacrifice of the Temple priests. Since Temple sacrifice had been replaced for the present age by synagogue worship, it was quite natural for the rabbis to regard their studies, particularly of law, as more important than synagogue prayer.

At the same time, it is quite likely that the rabbis in this period disapproved of aspects of synagogue affairs, but, possessing no power to change things to suit themselves, merely tolerated the status quo. We have a number of stories which indicate rabbinical objection to synagogue practices, not merely concerning which prayers were said at a given time, or whether the Torah was to be blessed before it was read, but more significantly, involving the presence in the synagogue of mosaics and statues. The chief sources are as follows:

> Was there not the synagogue which 'moved and settled' in Nehardea and in it was a statue [*andarta*[1])], and Rav and Samuel and Samuel's father used to go in there to pray...
> (Bab. Talmud Rosh Hashanah 24b)

> Rav happened to be in Babylonia on a public fast. The whole congregation fell on their faces, but Rav did not fall on his face. Why did Rav not fall on his face? There was a stone pavement there, and it has been taught, 'Neither shall you place any figured stone in your land to bow down upon it' (Lev. 26.1). Upon it you may *not* bow down in your land, but you may prostrate yourselves on the stones in the Temple. ...If that is the case, why is only Rav mentioned? All the rest should equally have abstained? ...
> (Bab. Talmud Megillah 22b[2])

> Rav once came to Babylonia, and noticed that they recited the Hallel on the New Moon festival. At first he thought of stopping them, but when he saw that they omitted parts of it, he remarked, 'It is clear that it is an old ancestral custom with them.'
> (Bab. Talmud Ta'anit 28b)

---

[1]) See Bab. Talmud 'Avodah Zarah 40b and Shabbat 72b (Sanhedrin 62b). In the latter discussion, bowing down to an *andarta* (carved image of a man) is not regarded as idolatry if the man did not regard it as a god. In the former, Samuel interprets the Tanna, R. Meir's prohibition of "all images" to include, quite explicitly, a royal statue. In any event, whether the rabbis permitted the placement of such a statue or not, it was clearly *not* they who instigated it, and the tenor of the Talmudic discussions leaves no doubt on that score.

[2]) Note that in the same source, it is reported Rav refrained from following the congregational practice in blessing the Torah. The geonic traditions *ad loc.*, say that later on, the synagogue floor-mosaics were covered up with dirt.

But we do not know what would have happened had Rav attempted to change their liturgy. In any event, it is possible that Rav did not approve of the mosaic, and quite clear that he would not prostrate himself upon it, but did not have the power to remove it. Despite the presence of a statue, Rav, Samuel, and Samuel's father prayed in a famous old synagogue in Nehardea, the town in which Samuel's father and, after him, Samuel himself were the rabbinical authorities. None of the three rabbis apparently had power over the synagogue's affairs. It stands to reason, therefore, that the synagogues in Sura and Nehardea were not subject to rabbinical control. And it was in these very cities that the rabbis lived, taught, and judged.

The situation in Palestine differed not at all. Sukenik long ago pointed out[1]) that pictorial representations of animals and human beings occurred with extraordinary frequency in Galilean synagogues and elsewhere:

> A theory was evolved that the synagogues found were the work of sections of Galilean Jewry which took a more liberal view of the matter than the orthodox authorities. It was realized, however, that so widespread a lack of discipline as is indicated by the number of such synagogues was rather extraordinary in Galilee, the centre of Jewish national and religious life in those times.[2])

Sukenik held that there were those who held a more lenient view of Exodus 20:4 and Deuteronomy 5:8; in such a view these verses prohibit the worshipping of images only, and the latitudinarian tendency prevailed in normal times, while in crisis, "particularistic and rigoristic views prevailed." Thus Sukenik held that "pictorial art had its ups and downs... a period of greater laxity being followed by a reaction..."[3]) Goodenough argued, however, that while the rabbis of a given period may have *permitted* one or another kind of ornament, the groups that *created* the art could not have been rabbis at all:

> Where are we to find the moving cause in the taking over of images, and with what objective were they taken over?...[4])
> Even if some rabbis tolerated such an image, the implication is that they were far from taking the initiative in introducing anything of this kind.[5])

---

[1]) E. L. Sukenik, *Ancient Synagogues in Palestine and Greece*, (London, 1934) being the Schweich Lectures of the British Academy for 1930, 61-67.
[2]) *ibid.*, 62.
[3]) *ibid.*, 63-4.
[4]) *Jewish Symbols in the Greco-Roman Period* (N.Y. 1953) IV, 10.
[5]) *ibid.*, 15.

The rabbis did not *prohibit* paintings on walls,[1]) and they did not *hinder* their contemporaries from making designs in mosaic.[2]) They were not however, the people who directed the design of murals for walls and mosaics for floors, as Goodenough said, "the decorations... express a mood and a religious attitude which rabbinic Judaism...at best only grudgingly tolerated, [but] never itself championed or advocated."[3])

The limited evidence cited above, all of which Goodenough knew, should suggest, however, that Babylonia was not so different from Palestine as he conceived.[4]) He thought that the Jews in Babylonia were dominated by the rabbis, and in some ways, as we shall see, they were. But it is quite clear that all the evidence we have, slight though it is, and tentative though is our reading of it, points in one direction: the 3rd century Babylonian rabbis controlled synagogue affairs, including their decoration, no more effectively than did Palestinian rabbis. Goodenough understood Dura to have been a representation of Judaism before the "halakhic reforms" of Rav and his colleagues. Yet these reforms took place well before the second paintings at Dura were completed in 246; Rav died, according to the Ge'onic chronology, in 247.

In fact Goodenough assumed, before he wrote volume XII of *Jewish Symbols*, a thorough-going dichotomy between Hellenistic and rabbinic Judaism. With this assumption in mind, he had to accept available descriptions of Babylonian Judaism as wholly rabbinic in the narrowest sense. Being unable to find a rabbinic center in the Greco-Roman world, he simply assumed it was, as the works he consulted said, on the other side of the Euphrates. His survey of rabbinic views of iconography[5]) should have suggested the contrary, and I think had he lived he may have revised his view of Babylonian Judaism, just as in vol. XII he modified his idea of the relationships between rabbinic and Hellenistic Judaism. He would, I think, have subscribed to the view of Professor Judah Goldin:

> This need not necessarily suggest that the Judaism reflected by midrashic-talmudic sources is unrepresentative of Judaism of the time, nor that the artifacts demonstrate the existence of a different kind of

---

[1]) Yer. Talmud 'Avodah Zarah 3.3.
[2]) Cit. by J. H. Epstein, *Tarbiz* 3, 1931, 20.
[3]) Goodenough, *Symbols*, IV, 24.
[4]) *ibid.*, I 13f.
[5]) *ibid.*, IV, 1, Ch. 2.

Judaism; but perhaps current interpretations of rabbinic sources are still too narrowly, too partially formed. Even the literary texts may reveal hitherto only partially understood details when the realities this art reflects are taken into account.[1])

An example of such a revision of the interpretation of literary texts in the light of archaeological realities will be found in Professor Morton Smith's *Image of God*.[2]) If one accepts the interpretation of the literary texts provided in *Image of God*, he must admit that the people who produced these texts might well have 'instigated' the sort of decoration found in the synagogues. Goodenough's assertion to the contrary is not completely convincing in the light of Smith's study. The texts he discusses show a very vivid verbal symbolism. Similarly, Goodenough never confronted the question of how the rabbis and their followers faced the existential issues of salvation and immortality, which the groups who made use of pictorial symbolism confronted in a mystical manner. Given the stress upon acquiring the world to come which one finds in Talmudic sayings, I find it difficult to distinguish the fundamental concerns of these groups. One cannot overstress, therefore, the importance of Goldin's statement.

Even if the texts cited above prove that the rabbis opposed synagogue decorations, as it seems to me they may indicate, they *still* have not been subjected to a form-critical study. These are, after all, sixth century collections of material about third-century rabbis. One needs to ask which traditions were preserved for what purposes, and which were purposefully, or accidentally, suppressed, lost, or revised. The notion that third-century rabbis must have disapproved of synagogue frescoes or incantation bowls is not, therefore, proven. I offer it as a working hypothesis, subject to considerable revision. I do not know how we shall achieve a history of the traditions without first composing, however tentatively, a history of the Babylonian Jews and the tendencies, issues, and ideas characteristic of each period in that history. Upon such a basis, one can isolate later tendencies which may have caused earlier traditions to be revised. A provisional history must be subjected to continual revisions, but it must, nonetheless, be attempted, if a history of the traditions is to emerge at all. So I have argued in "In Quest of the Historical Rabban Yoḥanan ben Zakkai" [*Harvard Theological Review*, Oct., 1966], and the same argument applies here.

---

[1]) Charles J. Adams, ed., *A Reader's Guide to the Great Religions* (N.Y. 1965) 209-210.
[2]) *Bulletin of the John Rylands Library* 40, 2, 1958, 473-512.

II

If the Babylonian rabbis did not play a special role in the life of the synagogue, being unable even to effect their wishes in the ornamentation of synagogue buildings, as is quite possible in Dura, Nehardea, and Sura, then what was the basis of their authority? Were they *ever* able to effect their policies? The question is not whether there was a widespread lack of discipline or not, but rather, In *which* areas of life were the Jews of Babylonia subjected to rabbinical discipline at all? And how can we know?[1])

Our only extensive source is the Babylonian Talmud, mostly a legal document, the Babylonian part of which consists mainly of discussions of the Mishnah. These discussions provide explication of Mishnaic and external traditions on given point in law, inquiry into the authorities for given laws, and, in part, comparison of the legal views of two or more authorities. None of this material can, on the face of it, be used as evidence concerning the sociology of Babylonian Jewry. Even legal questions asked in the academies do not necessarily reflect the social conditions of the time, for we have no way of knowing which questions were devised for, or emerged from, theoretical discussion, and which were actually the result of the circumstances of day-to-day life. One kind of evidence, however, is of inestimable value, the reports of cases decided in rabbinical courts, or of questions brought to the rabbis by ordinary people. Laymen cannot be supposed to have devised such inquiries for purposes of logical or rhetorical exercise, but rather asked them because they needed the answers for practical reasons. If we have no way of knowing how much of Mishnaic law, and the legal doctrines arising from it, actually influenced the life of the people, we have at least the corpus of cases and popular inquiries.

We are not helped by the language of the Talmud. I think it most likely that the rabbis used Hebrew to preserve and transmit fixed legal dicta, while Aramaic (apart from a few fixed, rhetorical forms) was most likely used for more practical matters; e.g. most of the case reports are in Aramaic. (My research, however, does not as yet justify the assertion as a fixed rule that Aramaic usage invariably connotes a practical decision.) Further, the language of the rabbis' discourse does not vary, whether the subject is theoretical or wholly practical. For example, late-third-century Babylonian rabbis held that heathens are to be

---

[1]) See my *History of the Jews in Babylon*, II. *The Early Sasanian Period* (Leiden, 1966) ch. 8, pp. 251–287.

executed for violating the seven Noachide laws;[1]) they discussed what is to be done to the layman who sacrificed the Red Heifer, a rite not carried out, quite obviously, after 70, and only a few times before then; and numerous other very serious discussions on sacrifical laws and Temple procedures took place. Further theoretical questions were considered, for instance, "How do we know that when one offers a sacrifice without proper intention, it is invalid?"[2]) Other laws, such as the following, could not have been enforced even by a vast, totalitarian government.

> Rav said, "A man who wilfully causes an erection is to be placed under the ban."
> (Bab. Talmud Niddah 13a)
> Samuel said, "The domestic and wild goose are forbidden copulation."
> (Bab. Talmud Bekhorot 8a)
> Rav said, "It is forbidden to sleep by day more than a horse's sleep."
> (Bab. Talmud Sukkah 20b)

The legal sources cannot, therefore, be used indiscriminately to provide testimony about the conditions of daily life.

The rabbis and the exilarch whom they served (see below) did not have at their disposal means of physical coercion, except in very clearly specified areas of law. The Sasanians were not at all willing for the Jews to govern themselves without imperial supervision. On the contrary, at the very outset of their rule, they made it clear that the Jewish courts would be closely watched, expected to explain their actions to the government, and required to conform to Sasanian law. Moreover, Jews could easily leave the Jewish community, and some did when confronted with rabbinic excommunication for Sabbath breaking.[3]) None of this proves that the rabbis had no authority whatever. It should indicate, however, that Goodenough's critique of the view that the Palestinian patriarchal apostles governed the whole Roman diaspora applies with equal force to the Babylonian rabbis' relationships to their community. Without armies or police, merely tolerated by the new regime, the third-century Babylonian rabbis depended, in the end, upon the actual willingness of Jews to obey the law, because it had been revealed by God to Moses on Mount Sinai and was authori-

---

[1]) Bab. Talmud Sanhedrin 57a.
[2]) Bab. Talmud Zevaḥim 46b.
[3]) See my *History of the Jews in Babylonia, I. The Parthian Period*, (Leiden 1965) 147-8.

tatively exposited and applied by them; upon the inertial force of accepted authority; and upon the willingness of the Persian government to allow them to govern some specific areas of life. The issue of rabbinic authority is therefore considerably more complicated than has been recognized.

The matter is made more difficult still by the one-sidedness of our evidence. Rabbinic sources mostly suppress or report only by indirection actions contrary to rabbinic dicta, and where such reports occur, it is only because the rabbis tell how they punished a law-violator. The two great bodies of independent archaeological evidence from Mesopotamia, the Dura synagogue and the incantation bowls, provide striking evidence that the masses of people were not living entirely in conformity to rabbinic law, but engaged in religious and magical activities which the rabbis might at best have tolerated, but which they would never in the first place have approved. When we review their sermons, moreover, we find considerable evidence that people displeased the rabbis. That, of course, is nothing new, nor can we discount the preacher's love for hyperbole. But when the rabbis preach against those who defer payment of a worker's wages, withhold wages entirely, cheat on communal taxes, behave arrogantly, and so forth, it is difficult to believe that they had the power to do more than curse the sinner and encourage penitence. Living in Babylonia were Jews who did not put on phylacteries, who did not meet the rabbis' standards for ethical economic and moral behavior, and who did not even respect the rabbis. Rav said that the blessings of the world to come are denied—a fearful threat—to anyone who insulted a scholar.[1]) We rarely, if ever, hear what those insults were, or why the rabbis were so exasperated about them. If, as we are told, an inhabitant of Naresh kisses you, count your teeth; if a Pumbeditan accompanies you, change your lodging; if thieves in Pumbedita open many casks of wine, the wine is not prohibited as it would be if it had been touched by an idolator, because the majority of thieves there are Jews.[2]) Such people as these are obviously not described by Mishnaic laws or academic discussions. And we do not know about the masses, who were neither learned academicians nor criminals.

It is hardly reasonable, moreover, to talk of the 'halakhic reforms' of Rav as if these greatly changed, in a very few years, the ancient patterns of Babylonian Jewish life. The rabbis were few in number.

---
[1]) Bab. Talmud Sanhedrin 99b.
[2]) Bab. Talmud Ḥullin 127a, 'Avodah Zarah 70a.

They were concentrated in central Babylonia itself. Elam produced students, but no teachers. Mesene was in such a state that the rabbis prohibited intermarriage between Jews from the south and those in Babylonia. Few rabbis, if any, came from Adiabene (which may by then have been Christian) and Armenia. The very instruments for the propagation and application of rabbinic laws were probably unavailable in the outlying districts. I estimate that there were from 600,000 to one million Jews in Babylonia in this period. We know the names of a handful of rabbis; certainly there were many others, but students and teachers together could not have amounted to over a thousand. Later on, the influence of the rabbis spread, as the academies grew in strength, and as large numbers of people attended their semi-annual adult-study sessions. But for the third century I have found very little evidence that the great masses of Babylonian Jewry always or even mostly conformed to Mishnaic law as expounded by the rabbis.

How then can we know which halakhic sayings affected the life of the people? As I said, minimal, but highly significant, evidence is to be derived from case reports and popular questions addressed to the rabbis. There are numerous such reports, and these are by no means scattered at random in the legal literature. Naturally, none at all exist on the laws pertaining to the Temple cult. But some of the laws did yield court cases, and while none can argue that *only* that law was enforced which produced judicial records, I think it clear that *at the very least*, here are areas of the common life which the rabbis did supervise.

Some of the laws were obeyed because the people believed that they were commanded by God. I did not expect that among these would be the laws about separating priestly gifts, and it is probable that whatever tithes were set aside, tithing ended after 260.[1]) But we have the story that Rav Ḥisda held in his possession the tithe of cattle,[2]) which suggests that some people even later gave priests their due. Samuel, moreover, fined a man for disobeying the laws on mixed seeds[3]) and Levi received a question, on 'mixed seeds' in a vineyard, asked by the citizens of Bashkar. The agricultural taboos would have been obeyed where they were explicit and well known, and held by the masses, contrary to Mishnah Qiddushin 1:9, to be valid even outside of Palestine. Hence a close study of such laws, as exposited by the rabbis, would be sociologically significant.

---

[1]) Evidence is cited in my *History*, II, chapter II.
[2]) Bab. Talmud Shabbat 10b.
[3]) Yer. Talmud'Orlah 3.7.

Those laws which were actually enforced by the rabbis mainly concerned property matters. As a general rule, one can say that wherever exchange of property was involved, as in trade, real estate dealings, torts and damages, marriage and divorce, there the rabbis exerted full and unchallenged authority. It is, moreover, quite natural to suppose that this should be the case. What the farmers did on their farms would not normally come under the supervision of the rabbis, nor what the women did in their kitchens, nor what husbands and wives did in their beds (though, as we shall see, the menstrual taboos were widely observed). Transfers of property, in *any* form, were quite another matter. They had to be regulated by public authorities; documents had to be properly written and registered, and the rabbis and their scribes were the official registrars of such documents. Transfer of property required public authorization, recognition, and confirmation. It was the rabbis, acting for the exilarchate, who supervised property transfers. When the people came to them, the rabbis had a splendid opportunity to act as they thought proper. As judges, they had no difficulty in enforcing the law. Still they did not have an entirely free hand. Practices which the people accepted, such as the writing of a *prosbul*, could not be easily changed. (Samuel said that if he could, he would abolish it.[1]) He never did.) Where transfer of property was concerned, there people could find absolutely no way to avoid the rabbinical courts.

Transfers of inheritance and the execution of wills posed numerous knotty problems. Questions were addressed from outlying parts on the matter,[2] and many cases came to the courts.[3] There is no reason to doubt that the great corpus of civil law, in the tractates Bava' Qama', Bava' Meẓi'a, and Bava' Batra', mostly contains practical, not merely theoretical, law. Moreover, the rabbis' decisions on proper acquisition of property sometimes overrode ancient custom:

> A certain lady had usufruct of a date-tree...A man came and hoed underneath it a little, and claimed ownership. He asked Levi, who confirmed title to the land. The woman complained bitterly. He said, "What can I do for you, for you did not establish your title properly?"
> (Bab. Talmud Bava' Batra' 54a).

In this case, the woman had assumed she owned the tree for thirteen years, and until someone, probably better informed than she, challenged

---

[1] Bab. Talmud Gittin 36b.
[2] Bab. Talmud Bava' Batra' 127b and 152b, to Samuel, for example.
[3] Bab. Talmud Bava' Batra' 143a.

her, no one assumed to the contrary. Hence it stands to reason that the average person identified usufruct with possession. The rabbis, (at least superficially) for exegetical reasons disagreed, and when they came to apply Mishnaic law, they were able by *force majeure* to sustain their decisions. For their part, they made great efforts to publicize the law, encouraging people to avoid purchasing lands under disputed title, publicly teaching how to acquire cattle, fields, trees, and so forth. Nonetheless, cases came before them daily,[1]) dealing with land, claims for loss and damages,[2]) and the like.

We have a number of instances, moreover, where a firm legal dictum was stated in the name of one or another of the rabbis, and challenged in dialectical argument, whereupon it was admitted that Rav or Samuel never made such a statement, but rather the disciples deduced what they *thought* was the rabbi's legal dictum on the basis of observation of an action. These cases invariably occur in matters involving transfer of property, mainly in civil and commercial law, rather than in liturgical, ritual, cultic or agricultural law. The legal sayings of the rabbis on dormant matters, such as the cult, or on theoretical issues, did not give rise to any such speculation upon the basis of an observed action. It was only where the law actually applied to daily affairs that the rabbis' actions could be subjected to close scrutiny. And these cases, for Rav and Samuel, all concerned civil law.

By contrast to the substantial number of civil suits reported by the Talmud to have been adjudicated by the rabbis, I know of not a single criminal, and certainly no capital, action reported as a precedent, described as a case at trial, or otherwise mentioned in a historically credible setting in the time of Rav and Samuel. There are two cases in which criminal action seems to be implied. In the first, a 'man wanted to show another's straw' to the government for taxation; in the second, a man had intercourse with a gentile woman. But these two cases provide no striking exceptions, for they actually involved political, and not judicial, policy, and prove (in the second case) that the Jews could not in fact freely inflict the death penalty once the Sasanians took power, although they could and did in Parthian times. (The former case entailed at best civil damages, but political circumstance transformed it into a more serious matter. This matter is fully discussed in my *History*, II. Ch. 2. i, pp. 27–35). We have many sayings on criminal law and procedure, but no cases showing that the rabbis' courts ever judged such

---

[1]) Bab. Talmud Bava' Batra' 110b.
[2]) Bab. Talmud Bava' Qama' 11a, Bava' Meẓi'a' 13b, etc.

cases. Since criminal cases must have arisen, we can best assume that the Sasanians' courts tried them for the most part.

Laws of personal status were enforced in the rabbinical courts, and I think the reason is the same as that given above: the legality of a marriage and the legitimacy (for purposes of inheritance, for instance) of offspring involved not merely private acquiescence but also public recognition, because the drawing up of documents and, frequently, property-transfers were involved. On the other hand, the rabbis' *obiter dicta* could not have meant much. For example, Rav preached that a barren marriage must be annulled after two and one-half years, but we have no case in which such a law was enforced.[1]) The rabbis did use their power to flog to enforce good public morals; they discouraged betrothal by cohabitation, or in the open street, or without previous negotation. Since they were believed to have accurate physiological and medical information, their judgments on the legitimacy of children were respected. Divorce procedures, in which property always was an issue, yielded many cases, though even here[2]) the peoples' pattern of behavior took precedence over rabbinic opinion in some matters. The rabbis' power, however, depended not upon popular acquiescence, though it was considerable, but upon the coercive capabilities of their courts, and upon the practical consequences of the decrees these might issue.

It was the Bible which shaped the religious life of the masses. The rabbis did not need to urge the people to keep biblical laws. Popular practice may have required rabbinical supervision over the ways the commandments were carried out. Where biblical laws and rabbinical interpretations were clear, well-known, and widely accepted, there the rabbis merely guided the affairs of the people, who brought them their queries. Where rabbinical injunctions were not widely accepted, there the rabbis relied upon coercion when they could, or upon public instruction in their view of the biblical requirements. The construction of *'eruvin*, for example, was in the hands of the rabbis, and the laws pertaining to Sabbath-limits were therefore enforced by them.

This is not to suggest that the greater part of the people was so meticulously observant as the rabbis would have liked. Tension between a class of religious virtuosi and the masses of their followers is certainly a common phenomenon in the history of religions. But because they knew the Bible, the Jewish masses proved amenable to

---
[1]) Bab. Talmud Yevamot 64b.
[2]) Bab. Talmud Yevamot 102a.

the guidance of the rabbis, especially when the rabbis could base their decisions upon convincing Scriptural exegesis. Three kinds of ritual law were rigorously obeyed, those dealing with slaughter of animals, menstrual separation, and the Sabbath. In all three, the rabbis were frequently consulted. The menstrual taboos were probably universally observed because the Bible is explicit about them, and the rabbis were frequently consulted about how to keep them. The Sabbath was either publicly observed, or publicly profaned, and the rabbis did not have to wait to be consulted. They aggressively punished Sabbath breaking, and the people doubtless expected them to do so, because of the well-known biblical precedents. We do not know how the Sabbath laws were kept in areas not under rabbinical influence. We have, however, numerous inquiries from distant places, and from students who would have carried the rabbis' influence far beyond the academies. By contrast, since the rabbis had no special function in synagogue affairs, and no authority over them, they had to tolerate popular practice, which was based upon very ancient, tenacious, and widely accepted traditions.

Insight into the level of popular knowledge may be derived from the questions referred to above, of the citizens of Bashkar to Levi: "What about setting a canopy on the Sabbath, what about cuscuta in a vineyard, what about a dead man on a festival?" The first was prohibited, the second permitted, and the third elicited the reply that the burial of the corpse had to be held over to a weekday. These are fairly basic matters, and the simple inquiry would suggest that the people would have been unaware of other such laws.[1]) Unless they sent an inquiry or received a pastoral visit, the rabbis could not censure them. For the rest, as we have seen, the rabbis were relatively powerless:

> Rav saw a man sowing flax on Purim, and he cursed him, so the flax would not grow.
>
> (Bab. Talmud Megillah 5b)

Doubtless the rabbis' prestige far outweighed their powers of coercion, for people believed in the rabbis' curses.

On the other hand, the rabbinical viewpoint was quite easily enforced among their own students. Such laws included mourning and burial practice, blessings before and after meals, and the like. In these,

---

[1]) Yet I am not entirely persuaded that the "men of Bashkar" were not simply the local group of rabbinical disciples, rather than the leaders of the whole community.

we have questions addressed to the rabbis *only* by students, and the single case of enforcement of burial rites involved an academician. A student of Samuel had intercourse during a period of mourning; Samuel heard and was angry, and the student died. It is likely that many would prefer to obey a rabbi than to risk his curse or some worse results.

No legal system could depend for enforcement upon the success of curses, barren flax-seeds, and the like. The many stories in which a rabbi's curse was sufficient to bring down punishment upon the head of a recalcitrant Jew—invariably cases *not* involving property-transfers —reveal that in these matters, only the curse, and *not* court action, was available for enforcing the laws. The laws the breaking of which was punished by rabbinical curses were probably, therefore, those which rabbinical courts could not otherwise have adjudicated; or which were not subject to popular inquiries addressed to the rabbis about proper observance.

Reference has been made to liturgical dicta. Within their academies the rabbinical authority was unlimited. Hence we have numerous cases, all taking place in the school house or among disciples, in which a disciple made a mistake in saying grace, in which the proper posture during a given prayer was discussed and demonstrated, or in which some detail was elucidated for a questioning disciple. But we have only one liturgical case in which a non-academician was involved:

> Benjamin the shepherd made a sandwich and said, 'Blessed be the master of this bread,' and Rav said that he had performed his oligation.
> (Bab. Talmud Berakhot 40b)

Rav's judgment was very lenient, for he did not require the normal formula of the blessing. Since the rabbis' disciples found great difficulty in understanding and carrying out the laws of saying grace (Rav's students after his funeral lamented that they still had problems with them), it stands to reason that the common people would have found it quite impossible, without the elaborate education by precept and example provided in the academies, to do precisely the right thing. If this were so in the everyday act of blessing food, one may reasonably suppose that more difficult or unusual matters were quite remote from public comprehension, let alone observance.

As the students were trained and went to their homes, and as judges were sent out from the academies to various villages and towns, the legal doctrines of the rabbis radiated into the common life. This was not a process completed in one generation, nor was the transformation of the people's life effected by a few men alone. It took many centuries before Babylonian Jewry in the mass came to approximate rabbinical ideas of how religious, social, and personal affairs should be conducted. For my part, I do not knew precisely when it was the case that rabbinical law accurately described popular conduct. But it was not in the third century. One cannot conceive that before the foundation of Babylonian rabbinical academies, in consequence of the Bar Kokhba war, Babylonian Jewry possessed neither laws nor authoritative doctrines. During the six preceding centuries, indigenous traditions of law, exegesis, and probably doctrine, were surely cultivated. It could not have been otherwise. Babylonian Jews married, bore children and educated them, divided their estates and litigated their affairs, celebrated the festivals and Sabbath, and pursued the many matters which required legal adjudication, producing a rich corpus of precedents, long before the first rabbi appeared in their midst. What is remarkable therefore is that in the third century anything changed at all, for the inertia of earlier centuries must have made the process of social and legal change painful indeed. The available cases suggest that it was mainly where the rabbis were able to apply very specific judicial-administrative pressures that matters were influenced by them.

III

If so, then one must ask, What was the basis of the rabbis' power? The later, acute tension between the rabbis and the exilarch has obscured the obvious fact that in this period, most of the rabbis were agents of the exilarch, acting under his authority, and fully respectful of his person, his office, and his prerogatives. It is true that when Rav returned to Babylonia, he got into trouble with the exilarch for refusing to enforce his decree regulating market-prices; but Rav was the *agoranomos*, or market supervisor, by virtue of exilarchic appointment, and was forced, by imprisonment, to do just as the exilarch said. Samuel, for his part, recognized the superior status of the court of Mar'Uqba, exilarch of his time,[1]) as well as its superior authority.[2]) Samuel apparently regarded his chief function, however, as instructional, while Mar'Uqba's was judicial:

---

[1]) Bab. Talmud Shabbat 55a. See my *History*, II, chapter III, pp. 92-125 and III, pp. 41-94.
[2]) Bab. Talmud Qiddushin 44b.

> When they were sitting together [at the school house] Mar'Ubqa sat before him at a distance of four cubits, and when they sat together at a judicial session, Samuel sat before him at a distance of four cubits, and a place was dug out for Mar'Uqba where he sat on a matting so that he should be heard. Every day Mar'Uqba accompanied Samuel to his house. One day he was engrossed in a law-suit, and Samuel walked behind him. When he had reached his house, Samuel said to him, 'Have you not been rather a long time at it? Now take up my case!' He realized that Samuel was angry, and submitted himself to 'reproof' for one day.
>
> (Bab. Talmud Mo'ed Qatan 16b)

Mar'Uqba cited Samuel's teachings on medicine, on judicial procedure, on the preparation of the *'eruv*, and other matters, while Samuel was guardian for the children of Mar 'Uqba after his death. The two men got on well together. Samuel taught law to the exilarch, who could not have had so extensive a legal training as the rabbi, while the exilarch honored him and submitted to his pedagogical authority. Mar 'Uqba had a good name for his generosity toward the poor, his learning, and his meticulous honesty. Rav and Samuel both explicitly stated that if a person wished to decide monetary cases without liability in case of judicial error, he *had* to obtain the sanction of the exilarch.[1] For his part, the exilarch employed Qarna, Levi, Rav, and Samuel in his administration. Apart from the difference with Rav, based upon the latter's adherence to Palestinian traditions (and, one supposes, his ordination there), there is no evidence of tension between the exilarch and rabbis, and certainly *not* with the rabbis as a group. The exilarch was not an ignorant figurehead, but a powerful, learned man. As chief judge, the exilarch was, by analogy to the *Erpatan Erpat* of the Mazdean church, certainly head of the Jewish community.

To suppose, moreover, that the sages' rulings were based not upon the authority of the exilarch, but upon their own, requires an absurd postulate. One would have to conjecture that there were two separate systems of Jewish government in the troubled times of early Sasanian Babylonia, one run by the rabbis, the other by the exilarch. There was no question in the Sasanians' mind that minority groups, including the Jews, should continue to govern their own affairs. But their supervision of the Jewish courts suggests that they would surely intervene if matters developed contrary to their will. If they approved the continuing rule of the exilarch under specified conditions, it is hardly

---

[1] Bab. Talmud Sanhedrin 5a.

likely that they would have also permitted the development of a second competing administration. Their politics required hierarchical centralization, in their own chancery, of all power, and the careful parcelling out of authority where necessary to specified bureaus and officials. It is inconceivable that they would have allowed the Jews to be subjected to competing authorities, and not to a single, hierarchical regime like their own. And, as we have seen, the actions of the rabbinical courts depended upon the willingness of the imperial regime to back up their decisions in exclusively practical cases. If the rabbi's decisions on the transfer of property were to be enforced, they must have been made with the consent of the Persian regime. If they were free of the danger of having to make restitution, it was certainly with Persian *and* exilarchic approval. The contrary would have been impossible, for the aggrieved party could simply repair to the imperial court, which, if the action was unauthorized or illegal, would doubtless reverse the decision, and probably also punish the 'judge' who made it. Moreover, the Persians collected taxes not from individuals but by millets or communities. The exilarch was responsible for collecttion of these taxes, as was the Christian *catholicus*. The sages had to collect the poll-tax in their own towns, and they must have done so as agents of the exilarch. The only Jewish judges in Babylonia whose decision could have stood, therefore, were exilarchic appointees, as Rav and Samuel explicitly stated.[1]

At the same time, the rabbis acted far more than merely as agents of the exilarch. They clearly possessed a law-code regarded by them as bearing divine sanction, and they knew how to study and exposit

---

[1] But their language is noteworthy. "If a man wishes to be free of liability for judicial error, *he should acquire permission* from the exilarch." They do not say, he should *seek appointment* (ordination). Part of the reason, of course, is that the exilarch, unlike the patriarch, did not bestow such appointment in this period, so far as we know. But it may well be that I am presenting too neat and simple a view of affairs. It is possible that in some places, a local learned man would be recognized as arbiter among the people, with or without exilarchic knowledge and permission. Such a man could issue judgments, and popular support, combined with the absence of a competing authority, would have rendered them effective. The language of the rabbis suggests that if a man does not care about possible liability for judicial error, he might as well go ahead and judge cases. Their words may well mean that such was the case. The very limitations upon the police power of the Jewish government would have made it quite feasible for local authorities to operate entirely beyond its control. The case cited below, in which a man is dissatisfied with the exilarchic court's decision, and therefore repairs elsewhere for judgment, would suggest that even in so central a settlement as Nehardea it was possible for a respected person to ignore the exilarch. But I cannot, in any case, envision the development, in this period, of a completely separate system of

the numerous traditions relating to it. Rav and Samuel were prepared to insure that the Mishnah would be the law of the Jewish courts, as in the following case:

> Once a man drowned in the swamp of Samki, and R. Shila' permitted his wife to marry again. Said Rav to Samuel, 'Come, let us place him under a ban [for he has acted against the law of the Mishnah]'. 'Let us first,' Samuel replied, 'ask for an explanation.' On sending to him their inquiry, 'If a man has fallen into limitless waters, is his wife forbidden or permitted (to remarry),' he replied, 'Forbidden.' They asked, 'Is the swamp of Samki regarded as water that has a limit or not?' 'It is regarded as water that has no limit.' 'Why then did the master act in such a manner?' 'I was really mistaken,' he replied, 'for I was of the opinion that as the water was gathered and stationary, it was to be regarded as water which has a limit, but the law is in fact not so, for owing to the prevailing waves, it might well be assumed that the waves carried the body away...'
>
> (Bab. Talmud Yevamot 121a)

This story indicates that Rav and Samuel were prepared to enforce conformity to Mishnaic law by means of the ban of excommunication. I doubt that the needs of the exilarchate impelled them to do so. If, moreover, they were acting as the exilarch's agents, they could well have used force, as did the exilarch against Rav himself. The issue was therefore, *Which* body of laws and precedents would be enforced in the Jewish courts? Rav, who had come from Palestine and was deeply committed to the enforcement of R. Judah's Mishnah, here appeared eager to demonstrate the authority of that law, even before the case was adequately clarified, but Samuel was no less anxious to enforce the same principle. Their failure to resort to an appeal to the exilarch is noteworthy. It would suggest that the latter would not have supported the rabbis' position against a judge who differed. He would rather have preferred, where the matter was not immediately relevant to his political or administrative purposes, to allow the judges themselves to decide what the law should be. In a case of family law, the exilarch was apparently prepared to stand aside, while by contrast, in a case involving economic policy, he was not. Enjoying great prestige, Rav and Samuel could denounce a dissident judge, who

---

rabbinical courts, outside of exilarchic control. The Sasanians would never have permitted it, and they *did* know what was going on in Babylonia. And the sources suggest, quite to the contrary, that Rav, Samuel, Shila', Qarna, and others were working quite closely with the exilarchate, and were officials of that institution. Given the political pressures upon the Jews exerted by the early Sasanians, who owed them nothing and regarded them with great suspicion, the Jewish leaders could not have acted prudently had they ignored or competed with one another.

seemed to them inclined to inforce the law as he saw fit. They thus apparently possessed a measure of freedom of action in some areas of law, but not in others, with moral and religious, but not political, sanctions to enforce their views about laws which the exilarch neglected.

We may, in fact, discern three kinds of law in which the exilarchate and his rabbinical judges involved themselves. The first was law which strictly concerned the Jewish religion and the inner life of the Jewish community, as in the case cited here. Here the rabbis from the very beginning probably had a completely free hand, for the exilarch, using them as judges and agents for other purposes, and respecting their learning, would have been quite content to rely upon their traditional knowledge to decide cases with no practical bearing upon public order. The second involved the economic, social, and political welfare of the community. In this area, the exilarch proved to be quite willing to intervene as he saw fit, and to impose his judgment, based upon practical necessities of his relationship to the Persians, rather than upon traditional precedents. Such a case is represented by the imprisonment of Rav for refusing to supervise the pricing of goods in the market, a refusal based upon ample precedent in Palestine. One may conjecture that the Persians would not have respected the efficiency of an administration unable to control such important matters. The third concerned the relationship between the Jews and the government, as in the collection of taxes, the regulation of land ownership, and the like. Here both the rabbis and the exilarch had to submit to Persian hegemony, but with a major difference. The exilarch was held directly responsible by the Sasanian government, and the rabbis were not, but could foster their opinions among the people without regard to, or in outright opposition against, both the needs of the exilarchate and the will of the imperial power. Therein lay the germs of their later disenchantment with one another. Samuel, for example, regretted that riparian wharfage rights were governed by Persian law, but he enforced that law.[1]) In the next generation, we find the following case:

> A certain person cut down a date tree belonging to his neighbor. When he appeared before the exilarch, the latter said to him, 'I myself saw the place. Three date trees stood close together and they were worth a hundred zuz. Go, pay thirty-three and one-third zuz.' Said the defendant, 'What have I to do with an exilarch who judges in accord with

---

[1]) Bab. Talmud Bava' Mezi'a' 108a.

Persian law?' He therefore appeared before R. Naḥman [student and heir of Samuel] who said that the valuation should be made in conjunction with sixty.

(Bab. Talmud Bava' Qama' 58b)

When Samuel decreed that the government's law is law, he did not mean to say that it must therefore take precedence in Jewish courts. After his death, the exilarchate may have gone much further than the rabbis approved in bringing into Jewish justice the precedents of Persian law, something the earliest *entente* may not have included. Hence the rabbis would have found themselves progressively more estranged from the less learned, ever more narrowly political, Jewish authority. In future research, I shall explain how it was that R. Naḥman, who was related by marriage to the exilarch, was able to act as a kind of appellate authority, if that is what the above case implies, and to ignore the exilarch's decision.[1])

IV

The bearing of these data on interpretation of the Dura synagogue art is quite obvious. The rabbis were not synagogue officials, but rather carried out wholly different political and social functions. They were teachers, judges, doctors of the law. (They were much else, but that does not concern us here.[2]) But the archisynagogus of Dura, like that of other synagogues, was not a rabbi, nor was the figure whom Goodenough called "the philosopher" of the synagogue. There was no reason why these men *should* have been rabbis. In any event, the rabbis, as we have seen, recognized a tension between their enterprise and that of the synagogue. "We with ours, they with theirs" said Rav Sheshet in explaining why he studied his traditions while the Torah was read in the synagogue. Abaye refrained from leaving his school house to attend synagogue services. Rav Naḥman did not even bother to assemble a quorum. In the earlier generation, Rav and Samuel tolerated the existence, in the synagogues of Dura and Nehardea, respectively, of a mosaic floor and a statue, though neither approved of such iconography. However much the rabbis may have wished it otherwise, they had no great role in third-century synagogue life, and

---

[1]) Compare vol. III, pp. 61-75.
[2]) Except for the sacerdotal function, they provided Jewish equivalents for the social-religious leadership of the Iranian Magi. See my *History*, II, chapter IV, pp. 126-150, and my "Rabbi and magus", *History of Religions*, 6, 2, 1966, 169-178.

the interpretation of synagogue art at Dura must take that fact into account.

If, moreover, the rabbis had wanted to assert their authority over synagogue decoration, what means of enforcement were available to them? The exilarch would surely have found their attempt troublesome, since large numbers of Jews would have been disturbed by rabbinical interference with what they doubtless believed to be ancient and honorable customs and practices. One can hardly suppose that the exilarch would have brought his influence to bear in support of his agents' interference with such delicate matters. He had no reason to do so. Indeed, if, as has been asserted, the *andarta* was a statue of the monarch, then it would surely have been contrary to the exilarchic interest to have tried to remove it from the synagogue building. For their part, the rabbis could have made use of the ban of excommunication, as they did in Parthian times against the inhabitants of a village who violated the Sabbath, and in this time as well. What could have been the result? The effectiveness of the ban depended upon popular acceptance including the virtual ostracism of the excommunicated party. But to excommunicate the Jews of a whole town would scarcely be practicable, (as R. 'Aḥai b. R. Josiah found out earlier), since they could doubtless survive by continuing their regular intercourse with one another and ignoring the rabbis' decree altogether. Its practical effectiveness would thereby have been vitiated. When it was contrary to popular desires, the ban bore no weight at all. It was precisely this fact which would have prevented rabbinical interference. Indeed, the subsequent discussions of Rav's behavior in the Sura synagogue suppose that he had a good, legal reason for refraining from issuing a decree of excommunication, but it seems more reasonable to suppose that his best "reason" was the ineffectiveness of such a decree in a synagogue-setting. During the years when Dura was in Roman hands, from ca. 165 to 256, moreover, the Babylonian rabbis could not have made use of exilarchic support even if it had been available. His power depended upon the Iranians' support. The Romans would not in any event permit its exercise within their borders, any more than the Persians would allow the Palestinian patriarch to govern their Jewish community.

As we have seen, however, it is not correct to phrase the problem in terms of communal discipline. The issue is not whether or not the rabbis had any authority over the Jews. The issue is what *kind* of authority they had and executed, and upon what basis. As I have said, their practical authority was based upon the support of the exilarchate, upon the prestige accruing to their learning, upon their power to issue decrees of excommunication, and upon the acquiesence of the people themselves. In the final analysis, it was the people who decided what they wanted to put on the walls of their synagogues, and, as Goodenough rightly pointed out, one will look in vain in rabbinical literature for proof texts upon which to hang interpretations of the Dura murals. The reason is not that we cannot find significant, relevant material, for we can. It is rather that whatever material we *do* find cannot tell us, standing by itself, which motifs and ideas were meaningful, indeed, which were even available to Dura Judaism. Goodenough has the merit of forcing us to reconsider our conceptions of Judaism in late antiquity, and especially, our view of what was normative and what was sectarian, indeed, of whether these categories even have bearing upon the social, cultural, and religious realities of Jewry and Judaism when viewed as historians must view them.[1]

---

[1] My thanks are due to the following, who offered critical comments on earlier drafts of this paper: Professors Jonathan Z. Smith, Charles Liebman, and Robin Scroggs. I am especially indebted to Professor Morton Smith for extensive criticism.

V

SYMBOLISM AND
HISTORY OF RELIGIONS

NOTES ON THE SYMBOLISM OF THE ARROW

BY

MIRCEA ELIADE
University of Chicago

A fascinating monograph could be written about the symbolism of man's tools, and especially of his oldest weapons. Contrary to what may be called "cosmic symbols"—stars, waters, the seasons, vegetation, etc.—which reveal both the structures of the Universe and the human mode of being in the world, the symbolism of tools and weapons discloses specific existential situations. For some time I have been engaged in analyzing the symbolism of the bow and arrows, as it appears in various myths, rituals and beliefs. The documentation is vast and bewildering; in this article, however, I shall discuss only certain aspects of the arrow symbolism.

To simplify our research, we may group the data according to the following main categories: I) Sickness caused by shooting darts and, consequently, magical (shamanistic) cures consisting of pulling these out or firing miniature arrows at demons; II) Shooting arrows against thunder gods; III) Arrows as symbols of fertility and luck; IV) Miraculous bows and master archers; V) The oracular function of arrows; VI) Myths of the chain of arrows and other related themes; VII) Arrows in mystical techniques and mystical imagination. I shall emphasize in particular the last two motifs, but in order for us to fully appreciate their originality a rapid review of the others is necessary.

I) The magico-medical role of the arrow has been repeatedly and competently studied. Scholars from E. B. Tylor to Lauri Honko[1]) have collected and analyzed data concerning the reputed origin of sickness as the shooting of "projectiles" (in many cases, arrows) into the body and the related cure through pulling them out or shooting in the direction of the enemy (the "magical bow," found among the Bushmen,

---

[1]) Edward B. Tylor, *Researches into the Early History of Mankind and the Development of Civilization* (London, 1865), pp. 275-277; Lauri Honko, *Krankheitsprojektile. Untersuchung uber eine urtumliche Krankheitserklarung* (FF Communications No. 178, Helsinki 1959), especially pp. 75ff.

is characteristic of all hunter cultures.[1]) This idea is widely diffused[2]) and has survived in the higher cultures: the sudden, painful ache is called "fairy dart," "Hexenschuss," "häxskott," etc.[3]) In many parts of the world demons or spirits are said to provoke sickness by shooting arrows which the healer extracts either by massage[4]) or by pulling them out.[5]) In some cases, as among the Munda-speaking Savara (Saora) and several South American tribes, the shaman shoots at the patient with a special bow and arrow.[6]) The same ritual is attested in the Atharvaveda: "with a *dārbhyuṣa* of bamboo, which has a bowstring made of black wool (and) with black arrows *(bunda-)* that have bunches of wool tied to their points, (he does) what is directed in the *mantras*..., i.e. while whispering the *mantra* he shoots after each stanza an arrow at the pustules."[7])

For similar reasons, the ritual bow and arrows are important elements in Siberian and Asiatic shamanism.[8]) During the *séance*, the shaman keeps two arrows in his right hand[9]). The Buryat shaman uses an arrow while "recalling the soul."[10]) We must also point out that in many areas (Central Asia, North Eurasia) there are myths explaining

---

[1]) H. Baumann and D. Westermann, *Les Peuples et les Civilisations de l'Afrique* (Paris, 1948), p. 103. The "pointing bone" of the Australians plays the same role.

[2]) Cf. the map #4, in Honko, *op. cit.*, p. 76.

[3]) See other examples in Rafael Karsten, *The Religion of the Samek* (Leiden, 1955), p. 43.

[4]) As, e.g., in Santa Cruz, Solomon Islands; cf. R. H. Codrington, *The Melanesians* (Oxford 1891), p. 197.

[5]) As among the Na-khi; cf. J. F. Rock, *The Na-Khi Nāga Cult and Related Ceremonies* (Roma 1952), II, p. 489.

[6]) cf. Rudolph Rahmann, "Shamanistic and Related Phenomena in Northern and Middle India" *(Anthropos* 54, 1959, pp. 681-760), p. 695; R. Karsten, *The Civilizations of the South American Indians* (London 1926), p. 159 (the medicine-man shoots into the ailing limb with a miniature bow).

[7]) Text translated by F. B. J. Kuiper, "An Austro-Asiatic Myth in the Rigveda," p. 165, quoted by Rahmann, p. 741.

[8]) See M. Eliade, *Shamanism: Archaic Techniques of Ecstasy* (translated by Willard R. Trask, New York 1964), pp. 174ff.

[9]) Cf. *ibid.*, p. 227. Carrying in his hand the golden arrow, the proof of his Apollonic origin and mission, the Hyperborean Abaris voyaged through many lands dispelling sickness and pestilence. According to a later legend, Abaris did fly through the air on his arrow, like Musaeus; cf. Rohde, K. Meuli and Dodds, quoted is *Shamanism*, p. 388.

[10]) *Ibid.*, p. 217, quoting Uno Harva, *Die religiöse Vorstellungen der altaischen Völker* (FF Communications No. 125, 1938) p. 268. A similar ritual is reported among the Tibetans and Sherpa; cf. René de Nebesky-Wojkowitz, *Oracles and Demons of Tibet* (The Hague), p. 367.

the origin of such magical arrows: they were made from a fallen branch of the Cosmic Tree.[1])

All of these ideas and beliefs reflect the demonic and ambivalent nature of the bow and arrows. The shooting of darts was probably man's first "mastery over space." The arrow's deadly flight was viewed as something "unnatural," i.e. as something to be explained by magico-religious agencies. In many parts of the world the darts were symbolically assimilated to thunderbolts. The rapidity, the suddenness, and the invisibility of the arrow could not belong to a "natural" world or an "ordinary" life. The mastery of the mysterious art of shooting darts was homologized to the meteorological prodigies of the Supernatural Beings or to the demons' power of causing illness or death.

I do not wish to imply that prehistoric and "primitive" men were not fully aware of the concrete, objective conditions and presuppositions of archery. Their mind was neither "pre-logical" nor paralyzed by a *participation mystique*. It was a fully human mind. But this also means that every significant act was validated and valorized both on the level of empirical experience and in a Universe of images, symbols and myths. No conquest of the material world was effected without a corresponding impact on human imagination and behavior. And I am inclined to add that the reflections of the objective conquests upon such imaginary Universes are perhaps even more important for the understanding of man.

II) Shooting darts against thunder clouds represents in fact a particular instance of the previous theme. The ritual is attested among various primitive tribes; it was also known in China, in Central Asia and among some ancient Thracian populations. To give only a few examples: the Thunder god of Yurakare of Bolivia is believed to throw lightning from the top of the mountains. "When Thunder was heard, men threatened to shoot him.... Whenever a storm was about to break, women and children were sent into the huts while men shot arrows and recited incantations against this 'fiery being' who threatened to destroy their houses and plantations."[2]) Likewise, during storms the Semai (Sakai) of Malacca shoot poisoned darts at the sky, while their women toss fire brands in the air and make a deafening uproar with bamboo canes.[3])

---

[1]) Cf. L. Honko, *op. cit.*, pp. 132ff.

[2]) A. Métraux, *The Native Tribes of Eastern Bolivia and Western Matto Grosso* (Bureau of American Ethnology, Bulletin 134, Washington 1942), p. 12.

[3]) G. B. Cerruti, *Nel paese dei veleni e fra i cacciatori di teste* (3rd edition, Firenze

In Asia it was the custom to shoot arrows toward the cloudy or dark sky against the demons. In China, the shooting was aimed at the "Celestial Wolf" which was considered to be the cause of the eclipses.[1]) Herodotus informs us that the Getae (IV, 94), the Calydonians (I, 172) and the Psylli (IV, 173) shot arrows to drive off the demons of the thunderstorms, and analogous practices survive in modern Bulgaria.[2]) Most probably the scenes of the Mithraic monuments which show Mithra shooting against rain clouds are to be interpreted in the same way.[3])

III) Also somehow related to the keeping away of evil spirits, but having a primarily positive role—for men, bringing luck in hunting, for women, fertility—are rituals of offering miniature bows and arrows at birth. Such bows and arrows are hung above the cradle. Gustav Ränk has abundantly shown the prevalence of this practice among the North Eurasian peoples.[4])

The offering of arrows is a well documented ritual among most Siberian tribes,[5]) in Tibet[6]) and in China.[7]) Also, when the shaman "recalls the soul" of a patient, an arrow is stuck into a vase filled with the food liked best by that patient.[8])

IV) The theme of the miraculous bow and a master archer is especially popular in the mythologies and folklores of Eastern Europe and Asia. Among the numerous motifs and incidents we need recall only two. The first presents the trial of a hero: he has to bend a giant bow and

---

1936), p. 139, quoted by R. Pettazzoni, *L'onniscienza di Dio* (Torino 1955), p. 467; cf. id. *The All-Knowing God*, trans. by H. J. Rose (London 1956), p. 317.

[1]) Marcel Granet, *Danses et légendes de la Chine ancienne* (Paris 1926), Vol. I, p. 233 n. 1, 390 n. 1, Vol. II, 538ff.

[2]) Gavril I. Kazarov, in *Klio*, XII, 1912, p. 356ff. We shall examine these rituals in a forthcoming article on Zalmoxis.

[3]) Cf. F. Saxl, *Mithras* (Berlin 1931), p. 76; Geo. Widengren, "Stand und Aufgaben der iranischen Religionsgeschichte" (*Numen*, I, 1954, pp. 16-83), p. 40; II (*Numen*, II, 1955, pp. 47-134), p. 95; id. *Die Religionen Irans* (Stuttgardt, 1965), pp. 44ff.

[4]) Gustav Rank, "The Symbolic Bow in the Birth Rites of North Eurasian Peoples" (*History of Religions*, I, 2, 1962, pp. 281-290).

[5]) Uno Harva, *Die religiösen Vorstellungen der altaischen Völker*, pp. 235, 269.

[6]) René de Nebesky-Wojkowitz, *Oracles and Demons of Tibet*, p. 543. On the erotic value of arrow-offerings in connection with the Tibetan marriage, and also on the ritual role of the arrow in promoting the fertility of the field, see S. Hummel, "Eurasiatische Traditionen in der tibetischen Bon-Religion" (*Opuscula Ethnologica Memoriae Ludovici Biró Sacra*, Budapest 1959, pp. 165-212), pp. 170f.; cf. also "Der magische Stein in Tibet" (*Intern. Archiv f. Ethnographie* XLIX, 1960, pp. 224-240), p. 237, n.l.

[7]) Marcel Granet, *Danses et Légendes de la Chine ancienne*, pp. 234, 380, 448.

[8]) Åke Ohlmarks, *Studien zur Problem des Schamanismus* (Lund 1939), p. 137.

shoot an arrow through a number of obstacles (shield, trees, etc.). The ritual, surviving as a literary motif in the *Odyssey* (XXI), *Mahābhārata, Rāmāyāna* and the *Lalitavistara*, was probably related to the ceremony of royal installation.[1]) Gabriel Germain considers it to be of Indo-European origin. But in the *Rig Veda* we have a similar myth whose Austro-Asiatic origin has been substantiated by F. B. J. Kuiper: Indra shoots an arrow that passes through a mountain and kills the boar guarding a treasure (a dish of rice) on the farther side of it. The words for the bow *(drumbhulī)*, the arrow *(bunda)*, the dish of rice *(odaná)* and the name of the boar *(Emuṣá)* are of Mūṇda origin.[2])

The initiatory character of all these tests is evident: the victorious hero conquers a "treasure," a wife or a kingdom. An analogous theme, surviving primarily in folklore, narrates the spectacular shooting of a fabulous bird or a dragon who defends or steals miraculous (golden) apples, etc.[3]) The interest of all these myths and tales consists principally in their insistence upon the *apparent impossibility of attaining the goal*. Only a hero, a king or a Bodhisattva is capable of emerging victorious from a test that surpasses human possibilities.

As we shall see later on, the theme of the "miraculous shooting of an arrow" can be integrated into the symbolism of the thread and thus can come to convey, in certain cultures, a purely metaphysical meaning. Such is the case, for example, in an episode from the *Sarabhanga Jātaka* (V, 130) "where the Bodhisattva Jotipāla (the 'Keeper of Light'), standing at the center of a field, attaches a thread to the neck of his arrow and with one shot penetrates all four posts, the arrow passing a second time through the first post and then returning to his hand; thus, indeed, he 'sews' all things to himself by means of a single thread."[4])

---

[1]) Gabriel Germain, *Genèse de l'Odyssée* (Paris, 1954), pp. 11-54. On the Chinese parallels cf. *ibid.*, pp. 45ff.

[2]) F. B. J. "An Austroasiatic Myth in the Rig-Veda" (*Mededelingen der Koninklyke Nederlandse Academie van Wetenschappen*, XIII, 7, 1950, pp. 163-82). Cf. M. Eliade, *Yoga. Immortality and Freedom* (New York 1958), p. 352.

[3]) K. von Spiess, "Schuss nach dem Vogel" (in: *Marksteine der Volkskunst*, Bd. I, Berlin 1937, pp. 288ff.). The Chinese materials have been discussed by E. Erkess, "Chinesishe-amerikanischen Mythenparallelen" (*Toung Pao*, 24, 1926, pp. 32ff.). For the Romanian and Caucasian parallels, cf. Octavian Buhociu, "Thèmes Mythiques Carpato-Caucasiens et des Régions riveraines de la Mer Noire" (*Ogam*, VIII, 1956, pp. 259-278).

[4]) Ananda Coomaraswamy. "The Iconography of Durer's 'Knots' and Leonardo's 'Concatenation'" (*The Art Quarterly*, Spring 1944, pp. 109-128), p. 121. On the symbolism of shooting darts toward each cardinal point, see Marcel

V) Shooting darts for oracular purposes is attested among the Tibetans[1]) (cf. the so-called *mda'dar* or "divination-arrow," used frequently in the rites of the Bon magicians and Buddhist lamas), among the Ostyak[2]) and the Buryat.[3]) Martti Räsänen has proven that the ritual was also known by the Turks.[4]) The original meaning of the oracular shooting of darts seems to be related to the ideas of conquering, organizing or "re-creating" a territory and of "fixing" the destiny of a certain period of time.

VI) The myths and tales narrating the ascent to heaven by means of a chain of arrows have been discussed by Wilhelm Wundt, Raffaele Pettazzoni and Gutmund Hatt.[5]) The story can be summarized as follows: a hero "hurls darts; one embeds itself in the celestial vault, then another embeds itself exactly in the notch of the first, a third in the second, and so on until they form a long chain of arrows upon which the hero mounts as upon a ladder to heaven."[6]) This mythological theme is popular in North America (especially in the Western regions) and has also been found in South America, Melanesia and Australia. It seems to be absent in Africa, Polynesia and, according to Ehrenreich,[7]) also in Asia; but G. Hatt quotes some similar myths from Koryak, Chukchee and Ainu sources.[8]) The problem of the

---

Granet, *Danses et Légendes de la Chine ancienne*, pp. 233 n.2, 234, 380, etc.; R.-A. Stein, *Recherches sur l'Epopée et le Barde au Tibet* (Paris, 1959, p. 278).

[1]) Nebesky-Wojkowitz, *Oracles and Demons of Tibet*, p. 543. On the shooting of arrows at the occasion of the Tibetan New Year (the Tibetan State Oracle) cf. *ibid.*, p. 510.

[2]) K. F. Karjalainen, *Die Religion der Jugra-Völker*, vol. III (Helsinki 1927), pp. 568, 596, 597.

[3]) Georje Nioradze, *Der Schamanismus bei den sibirischen Völker* (Stuttgart 1925), p. 95.

[4]) Martti Räsänen, "Wahrsagung und Verlosung mit Pfeil und Bogen" (*Symbolae in Honorem Z.V. Togan*, Istanbul, 1950-55, pp. 273-277), p. 275ff.

[5]) W. Wundt, *Völkerpsychologie: Mythus und Religion* (Leipzig 1909), vol. II, pp. 218ff.; R. Pettazzoni, "The Chain of Arrows: the Diffusion of a Mythical Motif" (*Folk-Lore*, XXXV, 1924, pp. 151-165); G. Hatt, *Asiatic Influences in American Folklore* (Coppenhagen 1949), pp. 40-48. R. Pettazzoni published a more complete version of his article in Italian, in *Saggi di storia delle religioni e di mitologia* (Roma 1946), pp. 63-79; but we shall refer exclusively to the article in *Folk-Lore*.

[6]) R. Pettazzoni, "The Chain of Arrows", pp. 156-57.

[7]) P. Ehrenreich, "Ueber die Verbreitung und Wanderung der Mythen bei den Naturvölkern Sudamerikas" (*XIV International Amerikanisten-Kongress*, Stuttgart 1906), p. 676. Cf. also Stith Thompson, *Tales of the North American Indians* (Cambridge, Mass. 1929), pp. 131f., 333, note 202-203, on the distribution of the myth among the North American tribes.

[8]) G. Hatt, *op. cit.*, p. 42.

distribution and probable routes of diffusion of this myth will not detain us here.¹)

None of the three authors cited above has tried to analyze the causes prompting the hero's ascent on his arrow-chain. The most frequent seem to be the following: a) a Supernatural Being retires to Heaven after the creation of the Earth or the civilization of the tribe; b) a hero climbs to Heaven to bring fire to the Earth; c) or to bring back his wife and children who have either been abducted by a celestial being or have gone of their own accord (the Swan motif); d) the ascent to Heaven occurs as the result of an incestuous love between brother and sister; e) or of a love affair with a brother's wife; f) or in order to prove the full possession of magic powers; g) or to wage war on Heaven; h) or in order to meet the gods.

A few examples will illustrate each of the foregoing motifs:

a) The Indian Coos (Kusun family) have this myth: after completing the creation, the Two Brothers "shoot arrows at the heaven, each of which strikes the staff of the preceding one, and thus is formed a ladder by which the two climb to heaven."²)

b) Among the natives of Lake Condah, a Primordial Being, in order to bring fire from the sky, ascended to Heaven by means of a lance with a line, thrown and stuck in the vault.³) Both of these themes, a and b, are related to the well-known myth of the withdrawal of Supernatural Beings at the end of the "primordial" epoch.

c) In a Chukchee myth, the hero goes out in search of his abducted wife, a polar bear. He shoots arrows out into the open sea, and land arises where the arrows fall.⁴) In an island of the New Hebrides (Logana), a hero abandoned by his wife and son, who have flown to heaven, shoots a hundred darts in succession; the last touches earth

---

¹) Pettazzoni and Hatt insist on diffusion. F. Boas inclines to accept a polygenesis; cf. "Mythology and Folk-Tales of the North American Indians" (*Journal of American Folklore*, XXVII, 1914, pp. 374-410), p. 384; G. Hatt, *op. cit.*, p. 48.

²) Pettazzoni, *op. cit.*, p. 158, quoting H. B. Alexander, *The Mythology of All Races*, Vol. X (North America), Boston 1916, p. 221. A similar myth was known by the Australian Tribes of the Adelaide and Encounter Bay: Monana, a Primordial Being, climbs to heaven by a chain of lances (Pettazzoni, pp. 162-63). The bow being unknown in Australia, the place of the darts is taken by lances.

³) "The myth continues with an account of how all human beings later on ascended to the sky in the same manner, except one man who became the ancestor of all the earth's now living inhabitants"; G. Hatt, p. 46, summarizing R. Brough Smyth, *The Aborigines of Victoria* (London 1878), I, p. 462. On the meaning of this type of Australian myths, cf. M. Eliade, "Australian Religions: An Introduction" (*History of Religions*, VI, 1966), p. 129.

⁴) G. Hatt, pp. 41-42, after Bogoras, *Chukchee Mythology* (1910), pp. 112ff.

and the hero ascends the chain and recovers the lady with her son.[1])

d) Among an Indian tribe of the Rio Jamundá there is the following myth: a woman "fell in love with her brother and visited him unknown at night. The brother felt suspicion and put marks in her face. In the morning when she saw her image in the water she felt ashamed because she was recognized. She took then her bow and arrows and shot up in the sky, forming a chain of arrows by which she climbed up and became the moon."[2])

e) The motif of climbing to Heaven as a result of a love affair with the brother's wife is attested in myths from New Guinea and Australia. Among the Jabin and Tami of New Guinea, the hero, pursued by his brother, shoots into the sky to form an arrow-chain and then escapes by means of it. In some versions he takes along the brother's wife and all of his household—and they become the Pleiades.[3]) In the Australian (Narrinyeri) myth, the hero pursues his brother and his two unfaithful wives; the brother hurls towards heaven a barbed lance with a line attached and mounts it with the two women behind him. Finally all are turned into stars.[4])

f) A Tupi-Guarayú myth tells how the god Tamoi demanded proof of their magical powers from his two sons; they shot arrows upwards, one into the butt of another, and climbed the arrow chain until they reached the sky. There they became the Sun and the Moon.[5])

g) Franz Boas recorded a myth of the Ntlakyapamug in which the birds declare war on Heaven. "After various unfruitful attempts, the bird Tcituć succeeds in forming a chain of darts which reaches to

---

[1]) R. Pettazzoni, p. 160, quoting P. J. Bt. Suas, "Mythes et légendes des Nouvelles Hébrides" (*Anthropos*, VII, 1912), pp. 57ff. The same myth, from another source, was published by Frazer, *Anthologia Anthropologica*, I, p. 221. Cf. also Pettazzoni, *op. cit.*, p. 158, a similar myth of the Quinault Indians.

[2]) G. Hatt, pp. 42-43, after Ehrenreich, *Die Mythen und Legenden der Süd-amerikanischen Urvölker* (Berlin 1905), pp. 37, 49.

[3]) G. Hatt, p. 44.

[4]) Pettazzoni, p. 162. Subsequently the hero also mounts to heaven by the same means; one can still see his canoe floating in the Milky Way. The same myth was recorded among the Euahlayi, with this difference: the hero forms a continuous chain of javelins; G. Hatt, pp. 46-47, after K. L. Parker, *More Australian legendary tales*, p. 11. Among the Palikur Indians at Rio Uaça in Brazilian Guiana there is a similar myth: in conflict with his brother-in-law, a hero climbed to the sky by means of an arrow-chain, and there became the constellation of Orion (Hatt, p. 43, after Curt Nimuendajú).

[5]) A. Métraux, *The Native Tribes of Eastern Bolivia and Western Matto Grosso*, p. 95; cf. Pettazzoni, p. 159, quoting other source.

earth, and on this climb the birds; then they re-descend; but only a few had touched the earth again when the chain broke, and the others remained in the air."[1]) In this example the arrow-chain motif has been adapted into an aetiological myth about the origin of birds.

h) There are also journeys to Heaven undertaken in order to prove shamanistic powers or to meet the celestial gods. "Kumana shamans claimed to be able to climb to the sky on an arrow chain made by shooting each arrow into the butt of the one previously shot. Upon reaching the sky the shamans were welcomed by Narmakon, the Lord of the sky."[2])

In reviewing the foregoing myths once again, one can say that the personages attempting—and succeeding—to climb to Heaven by an arrow-chain are gods and cultural heroes at the close of their creative period; primordial beings who, as a result of breaking a taboo (incestuous love) mount to heaven and become astral bodies; mythical heroes climbing to heaven to bring back fire or to recover their wives; shamans and magicians ascending for mystical reasons. In all of these myths the symbolism of the arrow emphasizes not the "magic of flight" (rapidity, instantaneousness, invisibility, etc.), but the communication obtained through a "paradox": the transformation of an eminently fragile and flying object—the arrow—into a solid chain. The "paradox" illustrated by this plastic *coincidentia oppositorum* belongs to the well-known class of "impossibilities rendered possible": symplegades, razor bridges, passing through rocks or mountains, "dying and ressurecting," etc.[3]) We shall presently see how such "paradoxical" images and symbols came to be integrated in mystical techniques and theologies. For the moment, it is important for us to notice that already at a very archaic level of culture, the "imaginary Universes" which had evolved around the art of archery allowed the human mind to reach a perspective from which the "impossibilities" could be resolved. One may see in such "paradoxes" the prehistory of some *aporiai* that haunted the beginnings of Greek philosophy (for example, Achilles and the tortoise).

Through the paradoxical transformation of flying arrows into a stable and solid chain, a new means of communication between Earth and Heaven has been obtained, comparable to the Cosmic Tree, the Mountain, the Ladder, and so on. As was already surmised by Pettaz-

---

[1]) Pettazzoni, p. 157, summarizing Boas.
[2]) A. Métraux, *op. cit.*, pp. 94-95.
[3]) Cf. M. Eliade, *Birth and Rebirth* (New York, 1968), pp. 61ff. and *passim*.

zoni and Hatt, the absence of the "chain of arrows" theme in some areas may be accounted for through the substitution of other means of communication: the Sky-Tree, the Mountain, the Sky-rope, the Ladder, etc. We have elsewhere studied the symbolism of the *Axis Mundi*,[1]) and we do not need to take up this problem again. We might point out, however, that the chain of arrows motif represents the creation of a hunting culture. In other words, the myth of a primordial communication with Heaven and of its catastrophic interruption was already familiar in an archaic stage of culture. The implicit idea is that, in the beginning, the Sky was fairly close to the Earth, and climbing to Heaven was an easy and "natural" thing. The raising of the sky or the withdrawal of Gods and Cultural Heroes marked the end of the primordial epoch.

VI) In a previous article I have briefly presented some pre-Buddhist (Bon) Tibetan traditions of the mythical rope that originally bound Earth to Heaven. "The first king of Tibet was said to have come down from Heaven by a rope. The first Tibetan kings did not die; they mounted again into Heaven. But since the rope has been cut, only souls can ascend to Heaven; the bodies remain on Earth."[2]) Two Tibetan texts give a precise description of the way the Mythical Kings reascended to Heaven by means of a rainbow. According to a *bonpo* chronicle, the first kings "avaient tous a leur sinciput une corde *mu* de lumière, corde lointaine (ou tendue), couleur jaune pâle (ou brune). Au moment de leur mort, ils se dissolvaient (comme un arc-en-ciel) à partir de leurs pieds et se fondaient dans la corde *mu* du sinciput. La corde *mu* de lumière, à son tour, se fondait dans le ciel.' Une variante très proche, dont nous ne connaissons malheureusement que la version mongole, précise: 'quand venait le moment de transmigrer, ils se dissolvaient vers le haut à partir des pieds et, par le chemin de lumière appelé Corde-de-Sainteté qui sortait de leur tête, ils partaient en devenant un arc-en-ciel dans le ciel.' "[3])

What happened to the kings of mythical times *in concreto* now

---

[1]) Cf. *The Myth of the Eternal Return*, pp. 12ff.; *Patterns in Comparative Religion*, pp. 367ff.; *Images and Symbols*, pp. 27ff.; *Shamanism*, pp. 259ff.

[2]) M. Eliade, *Méphistophélès et l'Androgyne* (Paris 1962), p. 206; *Mephistopheles and the Androgyne* [= *The Two and the One*], trans. by J. M. Cohen (London-New York, 1966), p. 166, after H. Hoffmann and Mathias Hermanns. Cf. also Siegbert Hummel, "Der Motiv der Nabelschnur in Tibet" (*Antaios*, IV, 1963, pp. 572-580).

[3]) R. A. Stein, *La civilisation tibétaine* (Paris 1962), pp. 189-190. Cf. for some Australian parallels *Méphistophélès et l'Androgyne*, pp. 231ff.; *Mephistopheles and the Androgyne*, pp. 184ff.

happens to the "soul" of the human being. Through specific yogic practices, the "soul" (i.e. the conscious principle) is let free at the moment of death by way of *brahmarandhra* (the "hole" at the summit of the skull, i.e. of the sinciput) and it is transferred to a certain heaven. The images used to suggest this "transferral" are primarily that of the flying bird, the shooting star or the shooting arrow. In the biography of Milarepa the soul of the departed master is seen as "a bird which takes off through a open hole of the roof."[1]) Finally, the soul is seen penetrating through the "hole in the roof" of Heaven as a shooting arrow.[2]) For the non-initiates, the lama accomplishes the "transfer to Heaven" by opening a hole on the skull (i.e. the sinciput) of the dying one. Now it is significant that this operation is called "shooting an arrow by the Hole of the Roof" or "Opening of the Gate of Heaven":

"A la mort d'une personne l'âme s'en va par le trou du sinciput ('trou du Brahmā,' Brahmarandhara, Chans-pa; bu-ga). L'opération ('pho-ba) faite pour libérer l'âme en la faisant sortir du corps par ce trou est appelée 'tirer une flèche par l'Ouverture du Toit' (skar-khun mda'-'phans). Cette flèche est lumineuse: on l'imagine comme une étoile filante. S'élançant hors de l'*Ouverture du Toit' de la tete, elle atteint au loin le Trou de Fumeé du Ciel où elle disparaît. Aussi, ce rite du lancement de la flèche-étoile ou de l'âme par le trou du sinciput s'appelle-t-il encore 'ouverture de la Porte du Ciel' (nam-mkka'sgo-'byed)."[3])

One can see from these examples how the symbolism of the flying arrow rejoins that of ascending to Heaven, i.e. the vast and archaic mythology of the communication between Earth and Heaven.[4]) The equivalences between rope, rainbow, light-rope, flying bird, shooting star and shooting arrow emphasize the essential meaning of all these images and symbols: the possibility of ascending to Heaven. Moreover, one can decipher in the Tibetan traditions the remembrance of a precedent, mythical epoch when the ascension to Heaven was carried out *in concreto*; in other words, the "spiritual condition" of the present man

---

[1]) R. A. Stein, *op. cit.*, p. 190.
[2]) *Ibid.*
[3]) R. A. Stein, "Architecture et pensée religieuse en Extrême-Orient" (*Arts Asiatiques*, IV, 1957, pp. 163-186), p. 184.
[4]) The same idea is implicit in the symbolic usage of the bow and arrows in the Upanishads. The understanding of Brahman is compared to the exact shooting of an arrow: "Taking as the bow the great weapon of the Upanishad, one should place in it the arrow sharpened by meditation. Drawing it with a mind engaged in the contemplation of That (Brahman), O beloved, know that imperishable Brahman as the target." (*Muṇḍaka Upaniṣad*, II, 2,3. Trans. Radhakrishnan).

is the result of a primordial "fall." In the beginning the separation between "body" and "spirit" did not exist. It is of consequence to stress this aspect of the archaic symbolism, because it reveals a rather profound nostalgia for human completeness and totality.

This is not the place for us to elaborate on these notes. Furthermore, we shall have an opportunity to take up the subject again in a forthcoming work devoted to the symbolism of habitations, sanctuaries and cities. But we must recall a methodological presupposition which underlies all of these studies; our conviction, namely, that the "documents" collected and studied by ethnologists, archaeologists and folklorists exercise the same claims within the history of the human mind as do the written texts of the poets, the mystics, the theologians and philosophers of the Great Traditions. This means that human creativity and, ultimately, the history of human culture is more directly related to what man has dreamt, believed and thought of his specific mode of being in the world than to the works which he has undertaken in order to promote and validate this mode of being.

If this methodological presupposition is accepted, then the exegesis of an "obsolete" symbolism—let us say, that of the arrow—should play a role in the understanding of archaic man which is comparable to the study of the Greek poets and philosophers in the understanding of Western culture. Such a hermeneutical approach overcomes the gap between the "prehistoric" and "primitive" on the one hand, and men belonging to the high cultures, on the other. There is, of course, a radical difference between the levels of these two types of creations, but the act of spiritual creation is the same. This principle is implicitly accepted when the art historian homologizes the ephemeral beauty of, for example, a nomad's hut or a sand-painting to the corresponding perennial forms in architecture and painting. The "primitive" *oeuvres* have an epiphanic nature: the essential thing is that they *came into being*, even if only for a season or a night. Likewise, the different and innumerable "epiphanies" of a given symbolism in a certain type of culture (hunters, planters, pastoralists, etc.) are to be studied and interpreted in their constantly changing contexts. As a matter of fact, each new epiphany of a given symbolism is to be analyzed with the same accuracy and understanding as, let us say, the symbolism of Christos Cosmokrator, such as it unfolds itself in so many and such different ways from its first expression in Byzantium to the splendour of the Western cathedrals or the provincial and rural reinterpretations attested in Russia and the Balkans. The creativity of "primitive," traditional and "popular" spiritualities is accessible to us primarily through such epiphanic *oeuvres*, so hard for us to appreciate with our present historiographical criteria. As is well known, these historiographical criteria were elaborated with an end to collecting, chronologically classifying and interpreting non-ephemeral and mainly written documents. In the study of archaic symbolism, chronology and the temporal dimension in general is of less importance. On the contrary, the "creative variations," the reinterpretations and revalorizations of a given symbolism, merit a greater attention than they have attracted until now. On the horizon of archaic and popular spirituality these "creative variations" play an analogous role to, let us say, the personal reinterpretations of the Graeco-Roman models by the European writers from Corneille and Racine to Shakespeare, Goethe and Hölderlin. If the history of Western literature from the Renaissance to Goethe is, ultimately, a series of creative reinterpretations of the classical and Biblical heritage, the "history" of "primitive" and traditional cultures is constituted by their selective assimilation and creative revalorizations of the primordial symbolism.[1])

---

[1]) I am grateful to my former student, Miss Nancy Auer, for her care in correcting and stylistically improving this text.

THE "SIGNIFICANCE" OF SYMBOLS

A HYPOTHESIS TESTED WITH RELATION TO EGYPTIAN SYMBOLS

BY

BEATRICE L. GOFF

Yale University

Thirty-one years ago I was first introduced to the study of symbols by Professor Goodenough when he brought me to Yale to assist in his work on *Jewish Symbols in the Greco-Roman World*. At first I was his research assistant, then I undertook my own investigation of symbols that are basic to the Jewish and Christian faiths. Whatever new avenues I may have followed, however, I am constantly in his debt. Thus I am happy to contribute this article to the volume in memory of Professor Erwin R. Goodenough, pioneering scholar, guide, and friend.

Whenever a person asks the meaning of a symbol he usually interprets the word "meaning" as implying the possibility of a simple answer in words.[1]) In my book *Symbols of Prehistoric Mesopotamia* I discovered that the "meaning" of the art forms in ancient Mesopotamia rested on three levels: 1. where the symbols provided reassurance and no words were necessary to explain their meaning; 2. where a few words were sometimes used but they were very general and could be applied to a large number of art forms; 3. where more words were used that sometimes were elaborated in a myth, but the art and the myth were independent symbols that reinforced the values of each other. I strongly suspect that these three levels are found very widely in the use of symbols, and it is my purpose here to test this hypothesis with relation to Egyptian symbols of the Twenty-first Dynasty, a period that stands just at the brink of a general renaissance of culture in the eastern Mediterranean. The Egyptian rulers of this period were those with whom Saul, David, and Solomon might have had contact.

---

[1]) This article was written during the winter of 1965-66 at Chicago House, Luxor, United Arab Republic. I wish to express my appreciation to Professor Charles Francis Nims, director of the headquarters in Egypt of the Oriental Institute of the University of Chicago and to his staff for the assistance they gave me at many points during its preparation.

If the Hebrew aristocracy were inspired by the luxury of their Egyptian neighbors, they would have found the art of the Egyptian court being used in ways some of which are about to be described.

Much of the Egyptian ornament of the Twenty-first Dynasty falls in the class of symbols used for reassurance without verbal explanation, although always it must be recognized that from one person to another the amount of verbal explanation associated with a group of symbols presumably varied greatly. Artists covered the sarcophagi with a multiplicity of symbolic forms. They abhorred empty spaces. Whereas in earlier periods the covers and boxes had been divided by bands simulating the bands around the mummies and only a few designs had been placed in the spaces created by these bands, on most of the coffins of the Twenty-first Dynasty all available spaces were filled with symbols. Many of these seem to have served for reassurance without any verbal explanation. This may be seen especially on the sarcophagus of $3\check{s}$.t-m-$3\underline{h}$-bi.t, where many "pseudo-texts" demonstrate that little need was felt to supplement the symbolic forms by words.[1]) Similarly on such a papyrus as that of B3.w-Mw.t-r-n$\underline{h}$t.w "incomprehensible" signs stand in several scenes.[2]) One wonders how often the corrupt texts often noted in this period come from the ignorance or carelessness of the scribe and how often the scribe felt that the text itself was inherently potent apart from any comprehensible meaning. The mumbo-jumbo of medicine men is a well known parallel.

So widespread in America in the twentieth century is the feeling that there is something lucky or unlucky in abstract numbers that hotel managers consider it unwise to number one of the floors in their hotels 13. In Mesopotamia investigation discovered a great concern for abstract numbers. This concern appears also in Egypt in the Twenty-first Dynasty. Numbers are used in Egypt in ways that illustrate how variable is the amount of verbal significance associated with them. Often no words at all define their significance. Again, accompanying the designs are very general words that are applicable to a great variety of Egyptian symbols. In a few instances a specific application of the number is given. Of primary importance is the number two. This appears repeatedly as a pattern in which a central figure is flanked

---

[1]) Georges Daressy, *Cercueils des cachettes royales*, Catalogue général des antiquités égyptiennes du Musée du Caire (Cairo, Imprimerie de l'Institut français. 1909), pp. 134-171. [Abbreviated: Daressy, *Cercueils*.]

[2]) *Mythological Papyri*, translated by Alexandre Piankoff, Bollingen Series, 40, 3 (New York, Pantheon Books, 1957), No. 13, pp. 128f. Cf. also Nos. 19, p. 159; 28, p. 200. [Abbreviated: *Myth. Pap.*]

by a pair of figures, whether, for example, a scarab is flanked by falcons, a disk by cobras, a pectoral by presentation scenes, a divinity by other divinities, a lion's couch by goddesses, or the deceased by divinities. Many other illustrations could be given of the importance of antithetical arrangements as an artistic form.

Symbols may be simply set in pairs. In a presentation scene a goddess very often stands behind the god who is being worshiped, and the deceased who makes the offerings is frequently preceded or followed by a god. A duplicate pair of goddesses may precede a central scarab in the solar bark (fig. 1).[1] On one papyrus a solar bark is followed by a pair of cobras, a pair of eyes, a pair of *nfr* signs, and a pair of Gold signs.[2]

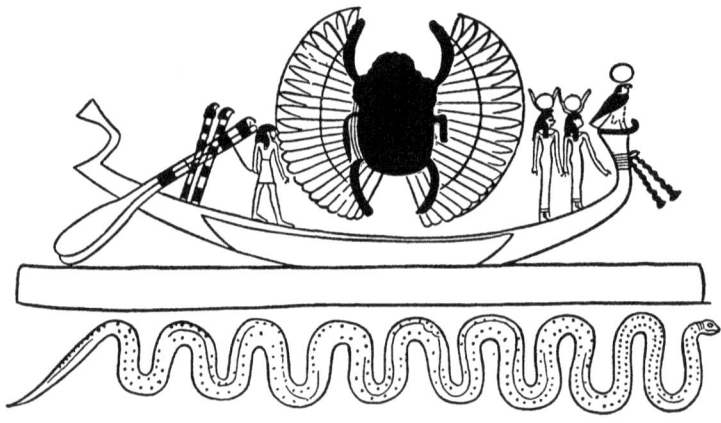

Fig. 1

Not only does Egyptian art in this period use pairs of duplicates. Sometimes the same figure appears in slightly different ways, as when a falcon-headed god is both the central god in the bark and his first companion, standing behind.[3] Most commonly a pair of goddesses that are dressed alike and performing the same function are given different names, as, for example, Isis and Nephthys (fig. 2).[4] From the cones on the heads of the figures in the illustration shown one may infer that the deceased thought of both these goddesses as identified with his wife, though because of the conventional design shown twice.

---

[1] From *ibid.*, fig. 55; cf. No. 5, Scene 2.
[2] *Ibid.*, No. 7, Scene 6.
[3] *Ibid.*, No. 2, Scene 1.
[4] From *ibid.*, fig. 34; cf. No. 17, Scene 6.

THE "SIGNIFICANCE" OF SYMBOLS 479

Fig. 2

At another time the pair might be labeled as goddesses of the South and the North, though a Red Crown (of the North) is on the head of each.[1]) In this series of designs the pairing conception appears to represent different aspects of a single figure. The same is true when the deceased appears twice in the same scene, as frequently in representations of the deceased coming to judgment (fig. 3).[2]) The first appearance is intended to show him before, the second after judgment.

Fig. 3

When a divinity is given two different heads the significance of the form once more seems to be that a god has more than one function. At times the two heads may be identical, and then one may suspect that the double head suggests an increase in the god's power. The

---

[1]) *Ibid.*, No. 9, Scene 8; cf. also No. 16, Scene 3.
[2]) From *ibid.*, No. 17, Scene 3; line drawing by Michael John Barnwell.

pairing concept thus has no single interpretation, and such attempts as have just been made to suggest interpretations doubtless are oversimplifications that do violence to the comprehensive values of each design.

Since the popularity of the number two as an abstract form is seen to be so great, one may consider other appearances of this form with fresh insight. The phrases "King of Upper and Lower Egypt," "Lord of the Two Lands," the sign for Union of the Two Lands, the Red and White Crowns that sometimes appear separately as the crowns of Upper and Lower Egypt and sometimes appear as a single Double Crown, all are familiar examples of the Egyptian use of the number two. For many years historians explored the possibility that the origin of these phrases and designs lay in a historical period when the land was divided and an early king succeeded in uniting the two sections of the country. Frankfort, however, pointed out how homogeneous the Nile Valley has been even from the most distant past.[1]) This homogeneity is true both of physical and cultural factors, and extended from Nubia on the South to the Delta in the North, from the Red Sea in the East well into Libya on the West. While there were times when the country passed through periods of instability, there was always an "underlying community of beliefs." He concluded, then, that "the dualistic forms of Egyptian kingship did not result from historical incidents. They embody the peculiarly Egyptian thought that a totality comprises opposites.... It is important to realize that the dual monarchy had no historical foundation; it was not as if an Upper Egyptian king had been confronted with a united but antagonistic Delta over which he assumed sovereignty in addition to his rule of Upper Egypt. The political structure of pre-dynastic Egypt had been amorphous to a degree ...; if the geographical configuration suggested a division of the country into Delta and Nile Valley, there is no reason to believe that these were any more thought of as political entities than the equally obvious divisions of desert and arable soil, the 'Red Land' and the 'Black Land.' "[2]) Frankfort thus brilliantly recognized that the basis for these and other dualistic phrases lies in an underlying symbolism. But when he said that the significance of the symbols consists of a totality comprising opposites he was being too precise. While that indeed probably was one significance often seen in the forms, if they

---

[1]) Henri Frankfort, *Kingship and the Gods* (Chicago, University of Chicago Press, 1948), pp. 16-23.
[2]) *Ibid.*, pp. 19f.

are considered in the light of the Egyptians' continued interest in abstract numbers and in the number two as only one of the numbers considered significant, then that the forms had many interpretations, some of which were on a level where words were inadequate and unsought-for, will be seen to be nearer the truth.

While two was the most important of the abstract numbers in Egyptian symbolism, the number four appears as a close second. Like the number two it was used in many ways and was applicable to many forms. The solar bark is sometimes drawn by four figures, whether by jackals, or both jackals and cobras, or divinities in human shape.[1]) Of course, since the Egyptians disliked using any symbol mechanically, sometimes three jackals and three animate cobras appear.[2]) The number three is also an important abstract number, as we shall see. Again, four divinities in human form conduct not a solar bark but a bearded, winged serpent.[3]) In another design four cobras are divided into pairs, set on either side of a wine—press above which stand four Fire signs. On the same papyrus four animate cobras are arranged two on each side of a Horizon sign enclosing the word for Soul.[4]) Four rams, four libation vases, four divinities with different heads, sitting under arcs, and four cows tended by the deceased in the Yaru Fields, all appear in different scenes on another papyrus.[5]) The number four recurs as an especially important form on a papyrus that contains many unique and thus perplexing forms. First, the solar bark is preceded by four cows and followed by four snakes above small vases. Again, there are four chapel signs; four male figures carry sacred objects. Behind them four gods with different heads sit in the coils of a snake biting its tail. These are followed by four mummies with different heads. Farther on four more gods with different heads sit within the coils of a serpent. Behind them are four Fire signs, four winged jackals, and four women standing by a canal or lake, each holding a jar, a *s3* sign of magic or protection before each. In subsequent scenes one sees four mummiform figures with Fire signs for heads, four others with West signs for heads, these preceded by Fire signs, another serpent biting its tail within whose coils are four headless mummies, their bearded severed heads beside them, and four soul-birds full face,

---

[1]) Jackals: *Myth. Pap.*, No. 21, Scene 1. Jackals and cobras: No. 2, Scene 1. Divinities in human shape: No. 26, Scenes 1, 3.
[2]) Jackals: *ibid.*, No. 6, Scene 2. Animate cobras: No. 26, Scene 2.
[3]) *Ibid.*, No. 23, Scene 3.
[4]) *Ibid.*, No. 21, Scenes 1, 2.
[5]) *Ibid.*, No. 15.

with a Fire sign above each. Within the coils of another serpent are four seated, human-headed gods, each with a ♀ sign before him, while above are four divinities—two goddesses in profile, two gods facing front. The next figures are what Piankoff doubtfully calls four "Osiris-headed jars(?)," since they wear Atef Crowns and carry ḥḳ3 scepters and flagellums. Farther on there are four open doors, four more seated gods, four standing gods, the familiar set of four oars, and finally four torch-bearers about to extinguish their torches in four clay troughs with "the milk of a white cow," this last scene referring to Chapter 137 or 145 of the *Book of the Dead*.[1]) Since, then, symbols are grouped in fours so often, and so many different kinds of symbols are arranged in groups of four, one will hesitate to attribute a single interpretation to the number.

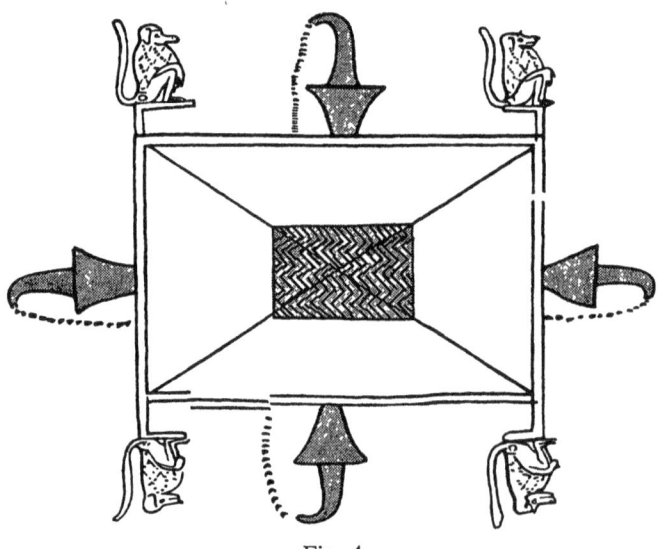

Fig. 4

When the scene reflects Chapter 126 of the *Book of the Dead*, the Lake of Fire is pictured with many variations. Most simply a baboon is placed at each corner, and a Fire sign at the center of each side (fig. 4).[2]) In a variant version, a baboon is at each corner, but four Fire

---

[1]) *Ibid.*, No. 22. Cf. Siegfried Schott, "Das Löschen von Fackeln in Milch," *Zeitschrift für ägyptische Sprache* [Abbreviated: *AZ*], 73 (1937), 6-10.

[2]) From Édouard Naville, *Papyrus funéraires de la xxie dynastie* (Paris, Leroux.

signs are set two on a side, on opposite sides of the lake.¹) On other papyri the four baboons may sit, one at each corner while a pair of Fire signs is set on each side;²) the four baboons may sit one in the middle of each side, flanked by Fire signs;³) there may be no baboons but four Fire signs on opposite sides of the lake;⁴) or the four baboons may apear at the corners but six Fire signs may be set on opposite sides of the lake.⁵) No verbal significance is given to the number four in any of these scenes, and no tradition derived from Chapter 126 of the *Book of the Dead* may be supposed to interpret the number. The chapter is concerned with the baboons' ability to meet the needs of the deceased in the Netherworld:

> O ye 4 baboons who sit at the prow of the bark of Re, who cause truth to ascend to the Lord of the Universe, who judge between the needy and the rich, who gladden the gods with the scorching breath of their mouths, who give divine offerings to the gods and mortuary offerings to the blessed, who live on truth and sip of truth, who lie not and whose abomination is sin, may ye remove all evil from me, may ye blot out my sins, for no foulness attaches to you. May ye let me penetrate the underworld and enter into Rosetau and pass through the secret portals of the west. Then shall ye give me a cake and a loaf like these blessed ones who go in and out of Rosetau.⁶)

Such words would be suitable for use with many other symbolic forms. These four baboons may also be shown in adoration of the sun.⁷)

Just as the number of the baboons and of the Fire signs of the preceding design is seen to have its importance in the abstract number, so it is prescribed in Chapter 140 of the *Book of the Dead* that offerings

---

1912, 1914), Vol. 1, pl. xxix [Nś-Ḫnś.w]; line drawing by Michael John Barnwell. Cf. also 2, pl. LIV [GЭw.t-sśśn.w].

¹) *Myth. Pap.*, No. 8, Scene 13.
²) *Ibid.*, No. 9, Scene 7; Piankoff, "The Funerary Papyrus of Tent-Amon," *Egyptian Religion*, 4 (1936), fig. 4 at p. 62.
³) *Myth. Pap.*, No. 15, Scene 7.
⁴) *Ibid.*, No. 12, Scene 4.
⁵) *Ibid.*, No. 25, Scene 8. The Lake of Fire appears also on the unpublished box of the inner coffin of 'Imn-m-pr-Mw.t usurped by PЭ-di-'Imn (Cairo Museum, No. 6153), and on the unpublished papyrus of Ḥn.wt-tЭ.wy, daughter of Pinedjem, found by the Metropolitan Museum in Deir el-Bahri, Tomb 60, Chamber, Coffin No. 6, now in Cairo (Nos. 51948, 51949).
⁶) *The Egyptian Book of the Dead*, edited by Thomas George Allen, Oriental Institute Publications, 82 (Chicago, University of Chicago Press, 1960), 208. [Abbreviated: Allen, *BD*.]
⁷) *Myth. Pap.*, No. 11, Scene 4.

be made on four altars, and in Chapter 141 that the spell be repeated four times.[1]) In all such cases the number itself mysteriously enhances the potency of a symbol apart from any verbal explanation.

The Four Sons of Osiris, in earlier periods named the Four Sons of Horus, are probably the most common group of four. On the sarcophagi they recur in many places and in several functions. They stand before tables on the exterior of the boxes, and the deceased is shown presenting offerings to them.[2]) They may be on the inner walls of these boxes,[3]) and in offering scenes on the covers above the legs.[4]) They may also appear in a series of divinities on the forearms,[5]) or, divided into pairs, on either side of the lion's couch on which the deceased is stretched as Osiris.[6]) Again, they may be shown emerging from a lotus in a scene in which the other principal figures are Horus and Isis standing antithetically beside a fetish of Abydos.[7])

In the tomb of Psusennes at Tanis the Four Sons of Osiris occur not only on the rose granite sarcophagus he borrowed from Merneptah but in both series of Netherworld deities that he drew on the wall, following the example of the sarcophagus.[8]) Inscriptions on the four canopic vases made for Wn-ḏbꜣ.w-n-ḏd and for himself show that the vases represented these deities. Those belonging to Wn-ḏbꜣ.w-n-ḏd had human heads, those to Psusennes the human, cynocephalous, jackal, and falcon heads traditional for these figures.[9]) On the gold plaque placed above the embalming wound on the mummy of Psusennes the four divinities stand two on either side of a central eye. The same design was used for the plaque on the mummy of Ḥn.wt-

---

[1]) Allen, *BD*, pp. 224, 226. See also pp. 105, 125, 196.

[2]) E.g., Daressy, *Cercueils*, No. 61,027, pl. xxxvii, pp. 72f. On the right side of the box there are not only the four funerary gods but two others labeled by the texts that precede as Geb and Anubis but in titles beside them as second figures of Hapy and Duamutef. Such errors seem to me less a result of the ignorance of the scribe than of a carelessness born from a feeling that the figures were potent apart from any particular explanation.

[3]) E.g., *ibid.*, No. 61,025, p. 58.

[4]) E.g., *ibid.*, No. 61,027, pp. 68f.

[5]) *Ibid.*, p. 66.

[6]) *Ibid.*, No. 61,032, pp. 186, 192.

[7]) Émile Chassinat, *La Seconde Trouvaille de Deir el Bahari*, Catalogue général des antiquités égyptiennes du Musée du Caire (Cairo, Imprimerie de l'Institut français, 1909), No. 6008, p. 28, fig. 25. [Abbreviated: Chassinat, *La Seconde Trouvaille*.]

[8]) Pierre Montet, *Les Constructions et le tombeau de Psousennès à Tanis*, La Nécropole royale de Tanis, 2 (Paris, 1951), 33, 115, 121; pls. xi, xc, xcii. [Abbreviated: Montet, *Psousennès*.]

[9]) *Ibid.*, pp. 86, 93, pls. lvii, lx, lxi.

t3.wy.[1]) An inscription on a winged scarab lists these divinities among a series of gods to whom Psusennes looks for protection:

> Words said by Anubis, first of the divine booth: O Imsety, Hapy, Duamutef, and Qebehsenuf, He Who Sees his Father, He Who is Under His Moringa Tree, Horus-Ḫnty-'Ir.ty, venger of his father, He Who Named Himself,[2]) be protectors of the Oriris king '3-Ḫpr-Rᶜ stp-n-'Imn, Lord of diadems, Psusennes, when he joins the necropolis. The Eater of Corpses has no power at all over him. The North wind will come to his nostrils. He will never die again. His soul lives before the gods. He escorts Re on his marches. The Osiris king Psusennes.[3])

It seems clear that to Psusennes the role of the four funerary divinities was to provide reassurance, but of a nebulous nature that could be offered by many other deities as well.

On the funerary papyri the group frequently appears, recognizable sometimes by their characteristic heads,[4]) sometimes because their names are also given.[5]) It is interesting that sometimes the names are given only very inadequately. On the papyrus of T3-šd.t-Ḫnś.w only three names are set beside the four figures. On that of B3.w-Mw.t-r-nḫt.w four names are provided, though they are very faulty, one is given twice, and furthermore, on the bearded human head of the first divinity, usually named Imsety but here called Hapy in spite of the fact that the name is used again, are a cone and lotus such as are conventional on the head of the deceased. The artist who made this papyrus seems to have been less concerned with the individuals who comprised the group than he was to identify the deceased as one of the famous four, standing within the protective coils of a poison-spitting serpent. The divinities on the papyrus of Ḥry.t-wbḫ.t also stand within such coils, though there the serpent is shown as a saving figure bringing the dead Osiris to life. In a more schematized scene on the papyrus of T3-n.t-Mw.t the deceased makes offerings before these figures as they stand below a canopy consisting of the coils of a serpent. The text that accompanies this scene shows that, as on the

---

[1]) *Ibid.*, p. 148, pl. cxii; G. Elliot Smith, *The Royal Mummies*, Catalogue général des antiquités égyptiennes du Musée du Caire (Cairo, Imprimerie de l'Institut français, 1912), pl. lxxvi, 2.

[2]) Cf. Allen, *BD*, pp. 228, 230, n.bg.

[3]) Montet, *Psousennès*, p. 145, No. 508, fig. 53, pl. cxvi.

[4]) *Myth. Pap.*, Nos. 2, Scene 3 (Ḥry.t-wbḫ.t); 7, Scene 3 (T3-n.t-Mw.t); 18, Scene 7.

[5]) *Ibid.*, Nos. 3, Scene 3; 13, Scene 2 (B3.w-Mw.t-r-nḫt.w); 14, Scene 2 (T3-šd.t-Ḫnś.w); 17, Scene 6; 18, Scene 3.

preceding papyrus, the deceased wishes for resurrection, but also has many other aspirations:

> Come to me, rays of the Western One, the entrance of (my) tomb is anointed with his rays. Let my soul come out toward heaven like the soul of Re. (May) the Netherworld be for my body like (? for) the soul of Osiris. May the gifts presented to Ptah be given to me, pure bread from the altar of Horus. May I come out from the sky toward earth, may I enter the Netherworld, assuming all the forms I like, while being like the complete soul of Re-Osiris, the Great God, He at the Head of the West in Abydos, Unen-nefer residing in Coptos(?).[1]

We have seen that in the Twenty-first Dynasty the four funerary divinities were associated with the canopic jars and thus with the embalming ceremonies. Such ideas can be seen in the *Pyramid Texts* in which it is these four who "Open the Mouth" of the deceased and accomplish his resurrection.[2] In these early texts, however, the deceased is also protected by the funerary deities, kept from hunger, and identified with them.[3] In other words, if any myth was associated with these figures it was subordinated to their practical functions, and these functions were diverse and, insofar as the texts indicate, not associated with a philosophical interpretation of the number four. Chapter 17 of the *Book of the Dead* assigns to the four divinities an astronomical meaning interpreted by Allen as identifying them with the constellation Leo. "As for the 'Council around Osiris,' these are Imset, Hapi, Duamutef, and Qebehsenuf, who are back of the Great Bear in the northern sky." While Allen's text is late, this section is confirmed in New Kingdom texts.[4] If in the New Kingdom they were identified as a constellation, however, this by no means warrants our supposing that when they were set on the corners of sarcophagi in the Middle Kingdom they represented the four corners of the earth, as Bonnet supposes.[5] Thus the evidence seems to indicate that at the

---

[1] *Ibid.*, p. 89.
[2] *Pyramid Texts*, §§ 1983, 734. The ceremony of "Opening the Mouth" was part of the funeral rites.
[3] *Ibid.*, §§ 1333, 552, 149.
[4] Allen, *BD*, pp. 89, 98, n. x; cf. *Urkunden*, 5, 42.
[5] Hans Bonnet, *Reallexikon der ägyptischen Religionsgeschichte* (Berlin, Walter de Gruyter, 1952), p. 315. É. Chassinat, *Une Campagne de fouilles dans la nécropole d'Assiout*, Mémoires ... de l'Institut français d'archéologie orientale du Caire, 24 (Cairo, Imprimerie de l'Institut français, 1911), 13 and passim. Heinrich Schafer, *Priestergräbe ... vom Totentempel des Ne-User-Rê* (Leipzig, Hinrichs, 1908), pp. 23, 32-35. For a comprehensive treatment of the funerary divinities cf. Kurt Sethe, "Zur

time of the Twenty-first Dynasty the role of the Four Sons of Osiris was varied, and the number four enhanced their potency as effective symbols but contributed no specific interpretation.

Fig. 5

A scene of "Hoeing the Earth" occurs on funerary papyri and a few sarcophagi of the Twenty-first Dynasty (fig. 5).[1]) Whether it occurs also in other periods I do not know. In its usual form two goddesses stand one on either side of a large disk, pouring fluid that encircles the disk. Two small disks at top and bottom within the larger disk are connected by dotted lines that presumably represent solar rays. At either side four small human figures wield hoes. Above this design is set a collection of resurrection symbols that differ with each appearance of the scene. None of these designs is accompanied by a text that offers interpretation. It may be that a festival of hoeing the earth *(ḫbś t3)*

Geschichte der Einbalsamierung bei den Ägyptern und einiger damit verbundener Bräuche," *Sitzungsberichte der Preussischen Akademie der Wissenschaften*, phil.-hist. Klasse, 13 (1934), 211-239.

[1]) From *Myth. Pap.*, fig. 59; cf. Nos. 8, Scene 2; 9, Scene 5; 16, Scene 3. For a further bibliography cf. p. 95, n. 3; and Piankoff, "The Funerary Papyrus of Tent-Amon," p. 66, n. 1. See also the box of the unpublished outer sarcophagus in the Cairo Museum belonging to P3-ḫr.y (the Syrian), J.E. 29670, mentioned by Daressy in *Annales*, 8 (1907), 11, No. 115 and by Hermann Kees, "Der sogenannte Vorlesepriester," *AZ* 87 (1962), 135.

such as possibly underlies Chapter 1 of the *Book of the Dead*,[1]) is reflected in this scene. In *Pyramid Texts* hoeing the earth for the benefit of the deceased is mentioned several times as an activity performed for one wishing resurrection but denied to the evil man.[2]) It is clear, then, that as an art form this is an appropriate resurrection scene whether or not the act had been incorporated in a rite. One must always remember that a rite is in itself a symbol, comparable to both art and myth, and often accompanying either one or both. What is important for our purpose at the moment, however, is that there is no suggestion that the four figures at either side reflected a particular group of divinities or suggested any mythological interpretation. Once again the number four may have made the scene seem more effective.

A rather different situation appears with the four oars and eyes that by convention illustrate Chapter 148 of the *Book of the Dead*. In this case the texts of the *Book of the Dead* and also of the mythological papyri of the Twenty-first Dynasty specifically interpret the number four as a reference to the four corners of the sky. Thus the oars on the papyrus of Nś-t3-nb.t-t3.wy are named: "Beautiful rudder of the Southern Sky. Beautiful rudder of the Northern Sky. Beautiful rudder of the Western Sky. Beautiful rudder of the Eastern Sky."[3]) While the number four here has an unmistakable philosophical interpretation, significant variations appear in some cases. The chapter is commonly illustrated by not only the four oars and eyes but also by seven cows and a bull, as will be seen when the number seven is discussed. In variant forms four oars alone may appear,[4]) or four cows with four crudely drawn oars above them,[5]) two oars, two eyes, and two cows,[6]) or two oars alone.[7]) In none of these cases is there any accompanying text. In one case an ⌐⌐ sign and what at first glance appears to be

---

[1]) Allen, *BD*, p. 69; cf. Chapter 18, 8, p. 102. See H. Kees, "Gottinger Totenbuchstudien," *AZ*, 65 (1930), 68f.
[2]) *Pyramid Texts*, §§ 817, 818; 978; 1120, 1121; 1138; 1323; 1325f.; 1394f.; 1561.
[3]) *Myth. Pap.*, No. 8, Scene 9. Cf. also Nos. 17, Scene 1; 3, Scene 6; and Naville, *Papyrus funéraires de la xxie Dynastie*, Vol. 1, pl. VI [M3c.t-k3-Rc]. On the papyrus of T3-n.t-'Imn texts attribute cosmic significance to the four torch-bearers who at least in some appearances of this scene are about to extinguish their torches in the milk of a white cow. Piankoff, "The Funerary Papyrus of Tent-Amon," p. 60; Schott in *AZ*, 73 (1937), 1-25.
[4]) *Myth. Pap.*, No. 22, Vignette 14.
[5]) *Ibid.*, No. 11, Scene 4.
[6]) *Ibid.*, No. 6, Scene 8.
[7]) *Ibid.*, No. 7, Scene 8; in Scene 12 the four oars appear in a conventional way but with no text.

words accompany four oars and four eyes. These words on close examination appear to be the name of Isis repeated four times without ascertainable attachment to any symbol and three incomprehensible groups of signs that again are not clearly to be associated with particular symbols.[1]) One thinks of the way Christians sometimes use the name of Jesus or Mary in adoration but without fully formulating the content of their prayers. The words "Isis" may be comparable. The goddess, famed as the faithful wife, seems to have been one of the chief divinities to whom the Egyptians turned for comfort and protection. It is in this role that her name stands here, and it is as symbols of comfort that the four oars stand on this papyrus. The suspicion arises, then, that though sometimes the oars and eyes were interpreted as cosmic symbols that represented the four corners of the universe, at other times these symbols brought to mind without detailed reflection the comforting spell in this chapter of the *Book of the Dead*, which is said to enable the deceased to be received by Osiris so that his body should remain sound forever.[2])

The Father-Mother-Son relationship of Egyptian gods is the most prominent use of the number three. Osiris, Isis, and Horus, Amun, Mut, and Khonsu are the two triads most prominent in the Twenty-first Dynasty. Most commonly they appear in scenes showing the deceased standing in the presence of the gods or perhaps presented by the son to the Father-Mother combination of gods. The triad may be shown standing, as the Four Sons of Osiris did, in the coils of a serpent, with ram's head, lion's head, and jackal's head respectively.[3]) Sometimes, however, the group of three represents only three famous gods, without any thought of a filial connection. So on the sarcophagus of Pȝ-ndm II three gods stand in the coils of a snake, and they have the same heads as in the preceding example, but the first is named Re, the second Isis, and the third Anubis.[4]) The same design is repeated on the opposite side of the box, and on the right side exterior and interior of the box of the inner sarcophagus of Nś-Ḥnś.w, but each time without naming the figures.[5]) Another variation appears on the inner sarcophagus of Tȝ.w.-ḥry.t, where the same three gods are found

---

[1]) *Ibid.*, No. 13, Scene 3.
[2]) Allen, *BD*, p. 255.
[3]) Chassinat, *La Seconde Trouvaille*, No. 6009, p. 33. In Nos. 6008, pp. 30f. and 6010, p. 34 the scene is the same but the jackal-headed god is unnamed.
[4]) Daressy, *Cercueils*, No. 61,029, p. 98.
[5]) *Ibid.*, pp. 99, 128, 131f.

but the ram-headed god is named "Soul of Ṯhn.t, Great in the Netherworld," the lion-headed god "Divine Isis," and the jackal-headed god "Horus great of forms, ruler of the West."[1]) What the "Soul of Ṯhn.t" may signify is obscure. The word Ṯhn.w is known elsewhere only in *Pyramid Text* §427, where scholars have been at a loss to translate it.[2]) Possibly this phrase is an epithet of Osiris, but except as most gods may basically be thought to fall in that category this need not be true. The philosophical ideas of the Egyptians were pragmatic, as will be shown in my discussion of symbols of the Twenty-first Dynasty, and they were developed in accordance with the wishes of the individual for as comprehensive a role as possible for himself as a god. Thus the deceased could say in Chapter 69 of the *Book of the Dead*, "I am Osiris, lord of the living. ... I am Orion, who reaches his two lands. ... I am Anubis on the day of the Centipede; I am the bull presiding over his fields. I am truly Osiris."[3]) If the Egyptians had followed such ideas to a logical conclusion, all gods were one and the deceased was identified with them. But the Egyptians of the Twenty-first Dynasty did not follow their ideas to a conclusion. They kept, as it suited their needs, both the distinction between their gods and the identification of one with another. The amount of distinction between gods and identification of one with another was very variable. Thus this name need no more be assigned to Osiris than any of the figures seen on another sarcophagus on which the heads are a Fire sign, an ass's head in front view, and a feather.[4]) No name is given to any of these.

While, then, the groups of three sometimes signify a Father-Mother-Son relationship, it is clear that the number is important apart from that particular signification. This view is confirmed by other groups of three on both the sarcophagi and the papyri. On the interior of the inner sarcophagus of ꜣś.t-m-ꜣḫ-bi.t there are groups of three gods and goddesses on the walls.[5]) The solar bark is drawn by three jackals on two papyri (fig. 6).[6]) On the second of these papyri, in the lower register, groups of three stars precede a row of six goddesses riding on snakes. In the preceding scene of this papyrus what are probably the

---

[1]) *Ibid.*, p. 188.
[2]) Erman-Grapow, *Wörterbuch*, 5, 389; cf. Kurt Sethe, *Übersetzung und Kommentar zu den altägyptischen Pyramexidentten*, 2 (Hamburg, Augustin, 1936), 199.
[3]) Allen, *BD*, p. 144.
[4]) Daressy, *Cercueils*, p. 131.
[5]) *Ibid.*, p. 168.
[6]) From *Myth. Pap.*, No. 19, Scene 4; line drawing by Michael John Barnwell. Cf. also No. 6, Scene 2.

familiar funerary divinities emerge from a lotus, only this time not four but three figures are shown. To this artist three seems to have been a more potent number than four. On other papyri there is a group of three ships,[1]) groups of three bearded human-headed gods on either side of a pair of raised arms,[2]) a group of three enigmatic signs that usually accompany representations of the Sed Festival, and three divinities with a Bes head, a donkey's head, and a human head facing backwards respectively.[3]) Again, a group of three divinities crowned with feathers (two with snake's heads, the one between with the head of a cobra) precedes the creation scene in which Shu supports the arched body of the goddess Nut.[4]) Before a large poison-spitting serpent is a vertical group of three animals, two cows reclining on mats with a calf set between them.[5]) Another scene is devoted to three divinities crouching on a support. The first has a bearded snake's head crowned with a disk and it holds a feather. The second has the head of a cobra and it holds a knife. The third has a vulture's head and it holds a coiled serpent.[6]) Before an assemblage of Netherworld deities on another papyrus are three coiled snakes, and concluding the papyrus the houses where the Netherworld gods are supposed to dwell, represented as three in number, with a snake emerging from each one. These houses refer to the *Book of the Dead*, Chapters 149, 150, but there the "abodes" are usually fourteen in number. This artist preferred the number three.[7]) Again, in a unique version of the creation scene in which the arched body of Nut gives birth to the new day, one of the solar barks bears a poison-spitting snake and a winged deity with a disk as head. This bark is towed by three cobras with human legs and arms.[8]) Further, the unique papyrus that was earlier seen to exhibit a fondness for groups of four, also in some cases presents groups of three. There are three gods seated on looped serpents, the first with a hippopotamus' head, the second a jackal's head, and the third the head of an ass facing front. Again, three gods with heads of a lion, ram, and jackal stand in the coils of a serpent. A text names them "Lords of the Netherworld." Among the gods that follow a

---

[1]) *Ibid.*, No. 13, Scene 4.
[2]) *Ibid.*, No. 29, Lower register, Scene 2.
[3]) *Ibid.* No. 17, Scenes 4, 5.
[4]) *Ibid.*, No. 11, Scene 7.
[5]) *Ibid.*, No. 14, Scene 6.
[6]) *Ibid.*, No. 7, Scene 4.
[7]) *Ibid.*, No. 5, Scenes 3-5.
[8]) *Ibid.*, No. 26, Scene 2.

solar bark are three that sit on the loops of a serpent. They are baboonheaded and hold lizards. It will be remembered that often baboons are arranged in groups of four. Clearly there was no fixed interpretation for the baboons that required the use of a specific number. Both the numbers three and four were considered potent. In subsequent scenes three men are shown at work on a building; three eyes, each with hand uplifted in adoration, precede the solar bark; and four groups of three gods, each with distinctive heads (ibises, jackals, falcons, and phoenixes), represent the royal ancestors of famous cities, for example—Hermopolis, Nekhen, Pe, and Heliopolis. Such vignettes accompany Chapters 107, 111-116 of the *Book of the Dead*.[1])

In evaluating the uses of groups of three and four it may, then, be said that the variety of figures set in combination precludes any particular significance attaching to the form while it demonstrates the value attached to the number. Both numbers enhance the effectiveness of a design without specific interpretation.

The situation is the same with the number seven. One can find instances in which a text accompanies a group of seven figures, but in many cases no words are associated with such groups. Most common are the seven cows with a bull that illustrate Chapter 148 of the *Book of the Dead*. The seven cows are sometimes, but not always, given names,[2]) as, for example, above the first, "Lady of the House of Exaltation," above the second and third, "Ladies of the West," above the fourth and fifth, "Ladies of the East," above the sixth and seventh, "Ladies of the Holy Land." Above the bull in this instance is written, "The Holy Bull, Chief of the Beautiful Ones."[3]) There is, then, interpretation, but not of the sort to employ the number seven. Indeed, since only four titles are ascribed to the seven figures one might suspect that the accompanying four oars that also are conventional illustrations of this chapter, as has been said, are lessening the force of the seven. In fact only four cows are presented with the four oars on one papyrus, and on another two cows and two oars.[4]) In papyri of the *Book of the Dead* seven distinct names are often given, but in no instance with which I am familiar is an interpretation of the number offered.[5])

---

[1]) *Ibid.*, No. 22.
[2]) For cows without names cf. Naville, *Papyrus...de la xxi^e Dynastie*, Vol. 2, pl. xlix [G3w.t-sššn.w]; *Myth. Pap.*, Nos. 9, Scene 9; 17, Scene 1.
[3]) *Ibid.*, No. 8, Scene 9.
[4]) *Ibid.*, Nos. 11, Scene 4; 6, Scene 8.
[5]) Naville, *Papyrus...de la xxi^{e}Dynastie*, Vol. 1, pl. v.i. [M3c.t-k3-Rc]. Allen, *BD*,

As the numbers two, three, and four appear with different associations so does the number seven. Chapters 145 and 146 of the *Book of the Dead* present spells to be said as one passes through the portals of the house of Osiris. By convention the portals are twenty-one in number. In the papyrus of Nś-Ḥnś.w there are only seven.[1]) A second papyrus of this woman groups together seven Netherworld deities. Since on this papyrus groups of three figures are also prominent, one may guess that to her three and seven seemed the most lucky numbers.[2]) The final scene on the papyrus of Ḏḥwty-mśy(.w) dramatically juxtaposes the birth of a soul in the new sun on the horizon and the concept of Darkness. A text before the scene ("Words spoken by Darkness, Lady of the West") personifies Darkness as a woman. Instead of picturing her as a goddess, however, Darkness is suggested by seven mounds on top of which sit black, headless goddesses, with a serpent placed above each.[3]) In this instance the number, although presumably potent, would seem to incorporate the idea of terror. Finally it may be noted that while three or four gods may stand within the coils of a serpent, seven gods may stand within its coils. On one papyrus on which such a form appears a solar bark is drawn not by three or four but by seven soul-birds.[4])

Thus the favorite numbers of the Egyptians of the Twenty-first Dynasty were two, three, four, and seven.[5]) The evidence has shown how many different figures were arranged in groups of one or another of these numbers. The numbers themselves seem to have been more important than any particular interpretation, and often there seems to have been no interpretation in words. That, however, was not always the case. Sometimes words were associated with the designs. Often they were suitable for a variety of designs, but, as in the case of the four oars that illustrate Chapter 148 of the *Book of the Dead*, they could have a specific meaning, in this case as a reference to the Four Corners of the Sky. It is clear, then, that the Egyptians' use of abstract numbers illustrates that there were three levels in their use of symbols.

---

pp. 255 f. E. Naville, *The Funeral Papyrus of Iouiya* (London, Constable, 1908), pl. xii (an Eighteenth Dynasty papyrus).

[1]) *Myth. Pap.*, No. 4, Scene 2.
[2]) *Ibid.*, No. 5, Scene 4.
[3]) *Ibid.*, No. 21, Scene 2.
[4]) *Ibid.*, No. 29, Upper register, Scene 2, Middle register, Scene 1. Cf. also the seven soul-birds towing a bark on No. 30, Middle register.
[5]) Sethe recognized that the numbers 4, 7, and 9 were sacred numbers: Sethe, "Zur Geschichte der Einbalsamierung," p. 217.

Much the same situation can be observed from a study of the objects associated with burials in the Twenty-first Dynasty. Both designs and inscriptions were placed on the linen wrapped around the mummies. Often on the shroud was painted a figure of a bearded Osiris, wearing an Atef Crown and carrying a flagellum and ḥkȝ scepter. Sometimes he was set before a table of offerings. When to this picture the name and titles of the deceased were added it becomes clear that the deceased identified himself with the god.[1] That such a shroud was expected to confer material blessings appears when a picture of offerings or a spell for invocation offerings is added.[2]

Some of the linen used for wrappings and the leather "braces" crossed on the breast were marked with figures or names of gods other than Osiris, as, for example, Mut, Montu, Min, and Amun.[3] Such markings apparently invoked aid from the deities.

Especially common were markings with the name and titles of a king or high priest. Most famous among them are the inscriptions on linen wrappings around the royal mummies of the New Kingdom. In the Twenty-first Dynasty many of the mummies of earlier dynasties were desecrated by tomb robbers. The rulers of the period were deeply concerned and had the mummies rewrapped in cloths on which were inscribed the names of the officials that undertook the rewrapping and the date on which it was completed.[4] Such names and dates have been the prime source for reconstructing the history of the Twenty-first Dynasty, but their importance to their contemporaries was not as a historical record. To evaluate the role of these inscriptions in their own day one must place them alongside the markings previously described invoking the aid of deities and also beside other markings on linen used to wrap lesser officials who died during the Twenty-first Dynasty. For these lesser officials sought to use linen, leather "braces," and pendants inscribed with the name of a king or high priest,[5] or

---

[1] G. Daressy, "Les cercueils des prêtres d'Ammon," *Annales*, 8 (1907), 22-38, Nos. 10, 11, 30, 33, 38, 42, 49, 64, 106, 107, 108, 114, 119, 133, 139, 150.

[2] *Ibid.*, Nos. 15, 43, 66, 114, 120.

[3] *Ibid.*, Nos. 7, 33, 60, 64, 66, 81, 91, 113, 148. G. Maspero, "Les Momies royales de Déir el-Baharî," *Mémoires...de la Mission archéologique française au Caire* (Paris, Leroux, 1887), p. 576.

[4] *Ibid.*, pp. 520-583.

[5] Daressy, Nos. 2, 11, 12, 13, 17, 24, 26, 30, 32, 38, 43, 48, 58, 61, 64, 65, 66, 81, 82, 83, 91, 96, 98, 105, 109, 113, 114, 115, 116, 119, 120, 124, 125, 127, 130, 132, 133, 135, 139, 143, 148, 151, 152. For the use of leather "braces" cf. Caroline Ransom Williams, "The Egyptian Collection in the Museum of Art at Cleveland, Ohio." *JEA*, 5 (1918), 275-277.

marked as coming from the estate of Amun,¹) or Khonsu.²) One or two eyes,³) or a seated goddess were sometimes painted as "magical" signs on the cloth.

These inscriptions do not serve as precise definitions of the "meaning" of a symbol in terms that are usually expected when a definition is sought. Rather, they are symbols themselves, as are the cloths and "braces" on which they are found. Their role may be comprehended more adequately if one considers the added values a Roman Catholic finds in a crucifix or rosary blessed by the pope than in one unblessed. Of this nature were the values of a mummy wrapped in materials made and dedicated in a workshop of the king or high priest. Both of these officials, by virtue of their offices, were in a position to give divine protection and benediction.

A large number of potent objects were associated with the mummies. We have already noted that a gold plaque incised with an eye flanked by the four funerary divinities was found above the embalming wound of both Psusennes and Ḥn.wt-t3.wy.⁴) A simpler form of this plaque in wide use was made at times of wax, copper, bronze (sometimes gilded), or gilded wood, and decorated with a single eye.⁵) To none of the latter was an inscription added.

It was very common to place small figurines of the Four Sons of Osiris inside the body with the viscera. Sometimes these were made of wax, sometimes of clay or resin covered with wax. Usually there were several bundles of viscera and one of the divinities was wrapped with each, though there was no tradition linking a divinity with a particular organ. Thus in unpublished mummies found by excavators of the Metropolitan Museum at Deir el-Bahri the liver was once protected by the falcon-headed divinity, at other times by the human-headed figure.⁶) With the lungs were found a cynocephalous- or jackal-

---

¹) Daressy, Nos. 26, 33, 38, 48, 82.
²) *Ibid.*, No. 133.
³) *Ibid.*, Nos. 74, 150. Metropolitan Museum. Excavations at Deir el-Bahri, the unpublished mummy of Ḥn.wt-t3.wy, Tomb 59.
⁴) Pp. 484f.
⁵) Daressy, Nos. 12, 17, 33, 39, 45, 54, 58, 71, 91, 98, 114, 125, 141, 144, 148. See also Metropolitan Museum, unpublished excavations at Deir el-Bahri, Tomb 60, Pit, Coffin Nos. 3 (Ty); 4 (G3w.t-sššn.w).
⁶) Falcon-headed: Tomb No. 60, Pit, Coffin No. 4 (G3w.t-sššn.w). Human-headed: Chamber, Coffin Nos. 1 (Nś-3ś.t); 4 (Ḥn.wt-t3.wy, daughter of 3ś.t-m-3ḫ-bi.t); 5 (Ḍd-Mw.t-iw=s-ʿnḫ).

headed figure.¹) With the intestines came a jackal-headed figure, human-headed figure, a falcon-headed figure, and in one case two figures, one jackal-headed, the other falcon-headed.²) The stomach was wrapped around a cynocephalous figure in one mummy.³) In the upper part of the abdominal cavity of another mummy figures of the four funerary divinities were laid in loosely, and along with them were packages of imitation guts, one in the shape of the liver, another with imitation intestines.⁴)

Amulets were found sometimes loose with the mummy, at other times tied to a finger with a piece of string to simulate a ring, or perhaps strung together as necklaces, bracelets, or girdles. They might consist of simple stone beads or pebbles, or of a familiar symbol. Among the latter were Ankhs, Wadj signs, Djed pillars, hearts, eyes, falcons, vultures, cobras, serpents, figures of Isis, Thoth, Shu, the Horus child, Hapy, the phoenix, the solar bark, and sistra.⁵) Often these objects were strung together with knotted string, and the knots contributed to the potency of the group. Similar objects were found by Maspero with the royal mummies. To the list given he adds a Hathor figure, a fan, a serpent's head, and lotus flower.⁶) With the mummies from Deir el-Bahri the excavators of the Metropolitan Museum found also an amulet consisting of the Aker lions back to back, cynocephalous figures, figures of the god Thoueris, a crocodile, and a *stp* sign.⁷) It was common to wrap the mummy in garlands.⁸)

When the amulets consisted of simple pebbles or beads, obviously they served for reassurance apart from words, as lucky stones or blue beads are used in many parts of the world today. How often the amulets shaped like the popular contemporaneous symbols were used as lucky pieces without verbal interpretations one cannot say. They are of the same nature as the signs used on sarcophagi and papyri sometimes in positions of prominence, sometimes as space-fillers. The

---

¹) *Ibid.*, cynocephalous-headed: Chamber, Coffin No. 5; Pit, Coffin No. 3. Jackal-headed: Chamber, Coffin No. 4.

²) *Ibid.*, Pit, Coffin No. 4; Chamber, Coffin No. 1; Pit, Coffin No. 3 and Chamber, Coffin Nos. 4; 5.

³) *Ibid.*, Chamber, Coffin No. 1.

⁴) *Ibid.*, Pit, Coffin No. 1 (name illegible).

⁵) Daressy, pp. 22-38.

⁶) Maspero, pp. 572 f.

⁷) Metropolitan Museum, Tomb Nos. 59; 60, Chamber, Coffin No. 4, Pit, Coffin Nos. 3, 4.

⁸) Daressy, Nos. 66, 72, 77, 82, 127, 148, 151. Maspero, p. 546. Metropolitan Museum, Tomb Nos. 7; 60, Chamber, Coffin Nos. 1, 3, 4; 65.

Ankh sign is used as a sign in writing to signify "Life." Presumably it always bore that significance whenever it appeared, although what was meant by "Life" must have been as varied as the needs of the individuals who employed it. At the same time the Ankh sign is by no means the only sign whose significance should be defined as a "Life" sign. Among other symbols that bore that meaning are Tyet (𓎬) signs and the lotus. One might illustrate the fluctuation in meaning of all the symbols listed. For example, the Djed is the sign for "Eternity," but often it suggests the god Osiris who is viewed as "the Lord of Eternity." On the sarcophagus of T₃.w-ḥry.t a West sign accompanied by a falcon is grouped surprisingly among the gods of the East and is named "He Who is in the Place of the Sunrise."[1]) Apparently to this artist the West sign and falcon represented the Netherworld that was the place of both sunset and sunrise, that is, the place of both death and new life. In my book on the symbols of this period a more detailed analysis of the meaning of some of the symbols will be undertaken, in an attempt to show the wide scope of values each embraces and at the same time the essential similarity in significance of one with another. Whatever words may have been used offered no precise meaning.

Scarabs were among the most prominent type of amulet. They were made of paste, enamel, basalt, feldspar, limestone, soapstone, schist, granite, wax, or wood. Often rather large scarabs were placed on the breast, where they might be accompanied by a heart or falcon. These are usually known as heart scarabs. Scarabs often with other amulets were found also on many other parts of the body, as, for example, on the neck, the arm, the finger, or the abdomen. Often they were uninscribed and seem to have served as inherently lucky objects. At times, however, they bore an individual's name, who might be the owner himself,[2]) but not necessarily so. One scarab was inscribed with the name of the scribe P₃-w₃ḥ.[3]) This was not the name of the owner of the coffin in which it was found, but there is no way of knowing whether or not P₃-w₃ḥ was a member of the family. In a few cases the name inscribed on the scarab was that of a famous contemporaneous person. With Ḥn.wt-t₃.wy in Tomb 59 at Deir el-Bahri the excavators found a scarab inscribed with the name of the princess

---

[1]) Daressy, *Cercueils*, pl. lvi, p. 185.
[2]) Daressy, "Les Cercueils des prêtres d'Ammon," No. 65.
[3]) *Ibid.*, No. 32.

Maat-ka-Re. Daressy reports the finding of one with the name of the queen *3š.t-m-3ḫ-bi.t*.¹) In a coffin that belonged to an unknown person was a scarab inscribed with the name S3-'Imn,²) who possibly was the well-known king. If, as seems likely, lesser officials were seeking amulets inscribed with famous names, one may reasonably infer that to them the names increased the amulets' effectiveness.

On the larger scarabs, whether with or without wings, a more elaborate inscription was often found. Some of these were designed both to protect the heart of the deceased and at the same time to prevent the heart from testifying about the man's evil deeds when he came to judgment. The spell most suited to accomplish this was Chapter 30 B of the *Book of the Dead*, which was sometimes engraved on the base of the scarabs. A version offered by Allen, though from a later papyrus, represents fairly what was common in the Twenty-first Dynasty:

> Spell for not keeping away a man's heart.
> My heart of my mother, my heart of my mother, my breast of my being, rise not against me as witness, oppose me not in the Council. Weigh not heavy against me before the keeper of the balance. Thou art my spirit that is in my body, Khnum who preserves...³)

While this is substantially the text of two scarabs in the tomb of Psusennes and his courtiers,⁴) a variant clearly based on this chapter but with alterations to make it accomplish a different result appears on another of Psusennes' scarabs:

> The heart of the Osiris king, Lord of the Two Lands, *c3-ḫpr-Rc mri-'Imn*, Son of Re, Psusennes, beloved of Amun, he says: My heart is the heart of Re. The heart of Re is my heart. My heart is mine as a reality. It is mine, my heart. My heart rests in me. My soul goes forth with the Ennead of the gods. It goes forth to whatever place it pleases. I enter into Heaven in the morning, in Heliopolis.⁵)

In this spell the deceased, as before, desires to establish that his heart shall remain his own, but instead of concentrating on his sense of sin that, contrary to all protestations of innocence, seems to have weighed heavily on the Egyptians, he is seeking to ensure that he shall have freedom of movement and a place after death among the gods. Thus

---

¹) *Ibid.*, No. 58.
²) *Ibid.*, No. 130.
³) Allen, *BD*, p. 115.
⁴) Montet, *Psousennès*, pp. 146, ,No. 510; 169, No. 647.
⁵) *Ibid.*, pp. 145 f., No. 507, fig. 53.

this spell is by no means the one that has come to be known as Chapter 30 in the *Book of the Dead*, but it is related to it. Whoever composed it felt free to utilize some of the phraseology of the familiar spell while he developed a spell to suit his altered purpose.

Similarly, Chapter 126 of the *Book of the Dead*, already quoted in our discussion of the abstract number four,[1] formed the basis of a spell inscribed on another of Psusennes' scarabs:

> Homage to you, O gods who sit at the prow of the bark of Re, who cause truth to ascend to the universal lord, who judge the weak and the strong, and appease the gods by the flame of their mouth, you chase away evil. There is no enemy against the goods(?) of the Osiris king Psusennes.[2]

This version is not only abbreviated to permit it to fit on the scarab's limited surface, but its announced purpose differs from that of the other text. Psusennes' scarab seeks protection for the king and his property. The version quoted by Allen, however, seeks access to Heaven and satisfaction of hunger in the heavenly abode. This variation in phraseology is due not simply to a difference in the date of the spells, though Allen's text is later. Rather it demonstrates that the Egyptians of this period, and at other times too, were not bound by a sense of canonicity. A familiar spell might be varied in accordance with the particular needs of the moment. On another of Psusennes' scarabs quoted above[3] a spell calls upon a series of gods to protect the king and ensure him breath and continuous existence with the gods in the after life.

While, then, the scarabs seem often to have been uninscribed and to have served as potent objects, clearly when their significance was put into words those words could be as varied as the needs of the owner. When the name of the owner was inscribed upon it, presumably the scarab was expected to offer protection. When the name of a famous person other than the owner was placed upon it, the power of that person was seen as reinforcing the power of the scarab. When a spell was placed upon it, that too reinforced the power of the scarab and gave it particular direction. But the spell could and often did appear in other situations than on the scarab. When associated with each other the spell and the scarab reinforced the effect of each. The

---

[1] P. 483.
[2] Montet, *Psousennès*, p. 146, No. 509, fig. 53.
[3] P. 485.

spells were not canonized in a single form. Like the scarabs the text of the spells could be varied to meet the particular needs of individuals.

Artists who made the mythological papyri of the Twenty-first Dynasty and those who decorated the sarcophagi also used their designs in varied ways. Often the designs stood alone, the scene reflecting the artist's purpose with no formulation in words. On the papyrus of Nś-Ḫnś.w Netherworld deities are arranged in groups of three, nine, and seven, the abstract numbers contributing to the potency of the design.[1]) A basket before one group shows a preoccupation with providing food in the Netherworld. Presumably also the gods represent the beings to whose company the deceased wished to belong. There are no texts, but their absence contributed to the adaptability of the papyrus for various purposes.

Texts are lacking also with the concluding scene of this papyrus, which consists of snakes emerging from three House signs. This design, however, is adapted from a conventional series of designs generally accompanying Chapters 149 and 150 of the *Book of the Dead*. On the papyri and sarcophagi are many such standardized designs. For example, a human head rising out of a lotus reflects Chapter 81 of the *Book of the Dead*, a bearded serpent with two human legs Chapter 87, a falcon Chapters 77 and 78, a ram Chapters 9 or 85; the seven cows and bull, and the four oars Chapter 148, the Lake of Fire Chapter 126. Whenever these and other traditional designs are used no texts are necessary, though at times a few words may be given. The design in itself is expected to evoke the power of the spell apart from the words.

In many cases words supplement the designs. These may be very simple, as when the deceased stands before a god and beside him are set his name and titles. The name and titles serve various purposes. They may give him prestige when he stands in the god's awesome presence. They may assure him of the power inherent in his rightful name; and they may ensure that this papyrus will be effective for him and not diverted to the aid of another. Other texts identify the gods, their role in the life of the deceased after death, and the activity of the deceased in their presence. Sometimes a hymn of adoration is sung by the deceased. In all of these cases the artists were free to vary design and words in accordance with their sense of fitness.

Sometimes they utilized an adaptation of a traditional scene and

---

[1]) *Myth. Pap.*, No. 5.

added to it a portion of the spell with which it was customarily associated. Thus on the papyrus of Nś-p3-ḳ3y-šw.ty behind the lotus from which emerges a human head are the words: "I am the pure lotus which comes out of Re."[1] One version of Chapter 81 of the *Book of the Dead*, from which this is derived, reads: "I am the pure lotus which came forth from the Sunshine and is at the nose of Re and at the nose of Hathor. I accomplished the mission; I seek it for Horus. I am the pure lotus which came forth from the fields of Re."[2] The abbreviated version on the mythological papyrus is perhaps a title evoking the power of the longer spell and reinforcing the power of the design to transform the deceased into a lotus.

Fig. 6

At other times the purpose of a design might be established not by utilizing words derived from a single text but by assembling a composite text from several sources. On the papyrus of Ḏd-Ḥnś.w-iw=f-'nḫ the Sun-god is shown sailing in his bark, while the deceased stands before an offering table in adoration (fig. 6). The significance of this scene is established by a composite text derived from Chapters 136 and 149 of the *Book of the Dead*:

> Chapter of Sailing in the Barge of Re.
> Behold, you stars in Babylon, the Great God is being born!
> Words to be spoken:
> I am well provided in the Yaru fields. These Yaru fields, their walls

---

[1] *Ibid.*, No. 9, Scene 7.
[2] Allen, *BD*, p. 156.

are of copper, the height of their wheat is 8 cubits, the ears 3(?) cubits long, and their stalks 8 cubits. The spirits, 8 cubits in height, reap (it) by the side of Horus of the Horizon. I know the door which is in the center of the Yaru fields by which Re comes out in the East.¹)

The design reflects Chapter 136, and the first two lines of the text are adapted from that chapter, the parallel sections of which, far more prolix than the version of the Twenty-first Dynasty, are as follows:

Another, to be used on the 6th day feast, the day of sailing in the bark of Re.
To be said by Osiris N.:
Behold indeed the Starry Host in Heliopolis, the sun-folk in Kheraha, the offspring of 1000 gods. O god who has bound on his band and grasped his steering oar, Osiris N. has been assigned with them to the rigging lofts and shipyards of the gods. Osiris N. takes therefrom the bark recurved at its ends, that he may ascend therewith to the Sky. When they sail therein with Re, he (N.) sails as the monkey who wards off the surf that covers that district of Nut to that stairway of Sebeg.²)

The remainder of the text of the mythological papyrus is derived from Chapter 149:

To be said by Osiris N.:
O great of possessions in that field of rushes, whose wall is of metal, the height of whose barley is 7 cubits, its ears 2 cubits, its stalks 3 cubits. It is a blessed one 7 cubits tall who reaps it alongside Harakhte. I know the gate of the Field of Rushes through which Re comes forth in the east of the Sky.³)

In the papyrus of the *Book of the Dead* that accompanied the body of Maat-ka-Re, closely appended to the text of this chapter was a design showing the deceased harvesting tall grain in the Yaru Fields, a design that traditionally accompanies Chapter 110.⁴) Such a design does not appear in the papyrus of Ḏd-Ḫnś.w-iw=f-ʿnḫ. It has only one picture and a single text. The opening two lines of the text conform to the picture. This scene, we are told, will bring the deceased as a god into the bark of Re and therewith to a new birth after death. The concluding lines go right along to create a unit as they provide the deceased with prosperity in the heavenly realm and the knowledge that gives him access to the aforesaid bark of the Sun-god. Thus the artist

---

¹) *Myth. Pap.*, p. 159.
²) Allen, *BD*, p. 220.
³) *Ibid.*, p. 258.
⁴) Naville, *Papyrus...de la xxiᵉ Dynastie*, Vol. 1, pl. x [M3c.t-k3-Rc].

of the Twenty-first Dynasty showed himself a masterful workman in unifying, abbreviating, and sharpening the focus of his sources.

Skill in the use of sources is exhibited with material derived not only from the *Book of the Dead* but from other books. An anonymous papyrus turns to the *Book of Gates* for some of its scenes. In Scene 1 six mummies are shown reclining on couches, a disk upon the chest of each.[1]) In the parallel scene in the Fifth Division of the *Book of Gates* twelve mummies recline on couches along the top of which lies the body of a large serpent.[2]) There are no disks on their chests. The text that accompanies this scene in the anonymous papyrus is focused on preserving the body of the deceased, keeping him in health, and providing for his food and drink in the Netherworld:

> The gods who are in the Netherworld, the reclining ones in their caverns. You are ... You are not weary. Your members belong to you, they do not perish. Your flesh is yours, it is not injured. Your heads are attached, your arms are gathered, your bones thrive for you continually. You live again, eternally. Your members are fresh, your limbs are complete. Your bread is for you, consisting of cakes. You possess your bread, you possess your refreshment. Your bread does not leave(?) you, you know the way to your refreshment. You quench your thirst with water, your heart is pleased with your bread, you enjoy your limbs, you are not in pain. Your members are in good health on your couches. Your hearts are refreshed. There is no heat(?) for these reclining ones who are in the Netherworld.

By contrast with this text the parallel in the tomb of Ramesses VI is diffuse:

> O you gods who preside over the Netherworld, you among whom is the Regent of the West. Those who are stretched out on their sides, who repose in their place of rest. Take up your flesh, collect your bones for yourselves, join your members for yourselves, put together your members for yourselves. (May) sweet winds be for your nostrils, looseness be for your swathings, removal for your kerchiefs! May light be for your divine eyes so that by them you may see the rays. Rise from your lassitude, take hold of your fields in the Field of the Lady of Offerings. There are fields for you in this field, and the water thereof is for you. You are satisfied with me (in) the fields (of) the Lady of Offerings.
>
> Their refreshment is water, the serpent Nehep guards their bodies while their souls pass on to the Fields of Yaru that they may receive

---

[1]) *Myth. Pap.*, No. 28, Scene 1, p. 194.
[2]) A. Piankoff, *The Tomb of Ramesses VI*, Bollingen Series, 40, 1 (New York, Pantheon Books, 1954), 176, fig. 42. (Abbreviated: Ramesses *VI*.]

their libations. The Protector of the Earth reckons for them their flesh.
Their gifts are bread, their beer is *Djesert*, their refreshment is water. They receive offerings upon earth as the Noble One, He who rests upon his seat.

A comparison of the picture and text of the two versions reveals that by words in the tomb of Ramesses VI provision was made for light instead of darkness, while in the anonymous papyrus this was accomplished by a disk on the chest of each mummy. In both the picture and text of the Ramesses VI version the serpent on which the mummies lie provided added assurance of protection and provision for material benefits. By eliminating this figure entirely the Twenty-first Dynasty artist created a more direct and forceful presentation.

Similarly on the sarcophagus of 3š.t-m-3ḫ-bi.t when the designs are derived from the *Book of Gates* or the *Book of What is in the Netherworld* the texts are either independent of the version of Ramesses VI or only loosely derived from it. Whereas the gods who carry a snake from which three heads emerge appear also in the Fifth Division of the *Book of Gates*, the text on the sarcophagus stands independently:

> The gods who are in the following of Re in the Heaven, they are the ones who tow, tow, tow this bark. They are the ones who receive Re in Heaven for the Mysterious Netherworld, the foremost of Re with... (?), who give the M'nd.t bark to the Western mountains.[1]

The decorator of the sarcophagus was concerned with the gods who often haul the bark of Re by a serpent-rope. By inference he saw them ready to haul the deceased along with Re. The decorator of the tomb of Ramesses VI viewed this scene as an example of gods overcoming the serpent Apophis and the enemies of Re.[2]

The four goddesses who precede the solar bark on the box of this same sarcophagus are described in words somewhat closer to the parallel figures on the tomb:

> The great goddesses tow, tow, tow to that Mysterious Netherworld, together with Re, Lord of the Mysterious Netherworld.[3]

The parallel text from the tomb of Ramesses VI reads:

> They are like this. It is they who receive the *Nefert*-rope of the barge of Re when he comes out of the backbone of the serpent, Life of the

---

[1]) Daressy, *Cercueils*, pp. 145 f., pl. li.
[2]) *Ramesses VI*, p. 174, fig. 46.
[3]) Daressy, *Cercueils*, p. 141, pl. li.

Gods. It is they who tow this Great God in the sky and conduct him to the roads on high. It is they who cause to arise in the sky the winds and calmness, the storm and the rain. What they decree among the living is what the Great Barge does in the sky.[1])

Once again the Twenty-first Dynasty artist has given a simplified and abbreviated form.

If the skill of the artists of the Twenty-first Dynasty appears from these examples to be great, as I think it does, one must not suppose that they stood alone in the history of Egyptian art and literature. We are concerned here to give a fair appraisal of this period and not necessarily to imply that it was unique in Egyptian history. If, as I suspect, in many cases Egyptian artists used their designs and texts in this way, this study will appear all the more useful since it will have a wider application. To be conservative in our inferences it may be concluded that at least in the Twenty-first Dynasty the symbols in every medium were used with great freedom and with no sense of being bound by a canonical tradition. At times the designs stood alone to make their own impact on the minds of the viewers. At other times they were supplemented by a few words. At still other times a longer text was added that might be the artist's own composition or an adaptation from traditional sources. Such texts, however, were not necessarily companions of the designs. Like the designs, they were often capable of accomplishing their purpose quite independently.

---

[1]) *Ramesses VI* p. 316, fig. 87.

THE WATERS OF LIFE

Some Reflections on Zionist Water Symbolism

BY

V. W. TURNER
Cornell University

Erwin Goodenough[1]) has quoted, to some effect, in his massively scholarly account of Jewish symbols, Ovid's comment in the *Heroides* on the nature of the symbol:

Crede mihi; plus est, quam quod videatur, imago (Heroides, Epist. XIII, 155*)*
"Believe me; an image (or representation) is more than it appears to be."

He then paraphrases Ovid's understatement as follows: "a symbol is an object or a pattern which, whatever the reason may be, operates upon men, and causes effects in them, beyond mere recognition of what is literally presented in the given form." *(Jewish Symbols in the Greco-Roman Period,* Vol. 4, p. 28). In various papers I have attempted to explore the realms of denotative and connotative thinking that lie beyond the *imagines* of certain religious symbols in Central African tribal cultures. More ambitiously, and perhaps rashly this time, I am going to follow Sundkler's example and consider a set of so-called "syncretistic" symbols found in the practices of the *modern* Zulu Zionist Churches *(Bantu Prophets in South Africa,* London: O.U.P. (1961) Second Edition). These symbols, especially, as we shall see, water and whiteness, derive from confluent Christian and traditional Zulu sources. I shall not be content, however, to leave the matter at that, but will pursue these symbols back through time into the ancient world of the Mediterranean and the Fertile Crescent. This will raise questions about the constancy of certain values expressed in symbols and about the nature of selective borrowing. I hope, too, to relate my

---

[1]) This paper was first read at a Conference on Modern African Religious Movements, convened by Professor John Middleton and the author and sponsored by the Institute of African Studies, at Northwestern University in April, 1965. It is in large measure the fruit of the author's first encounter with Erwin Goodenough's work.

findings to what I have previously written about the properties of the liminal (or marginal) period in life-crisis ritual.

Sundkler, it will be recalled, characterized the Zulu Zionists as a type of independent Church which has its roots historically in Zion City, Illinois; claims ideologically to emanate from the Mount of Zion in Jerusalem; and is theologically today a syncretistic Bantu movement with healing, speaking with tongues, purification rites, and taboos as the main expressions of its faith (Sundkler: 54). Though there are numberless Zionist sub-groups, their pattern of beliefs and ritual practices "show an amazing uniformity, caused no doubt", Sundkler writes (p. 55), "by certain fundamental needs and aspirations in the broad masses of these Churches, which needs and aspirations find their satisfaction in the behaviour patterns of the movement."

Let me take as example one characteristic "behaviour pattern" and investigate its symbolism. At the beginning of a chapter entitled significantly "New Wine in Old Wineskins" Sundkler describes an encounter in Natal, shortly before sunrise, between a traditional Zulu *isangoma* diviner and her novices and the prophet Elliot Butelezi of the Sabbath Zionist Church and his followers, reputedly Christians. They confront one another from opposite sides of a stream. Sundkler stresses the parallelism of the rites they subsequently perform: first the diviner and her party, then the prophet and his.

The sequence of symbolic activities, in the diviner's rites, runs as follows:

(1) Songs are sung to the ancestral spirits:
   "I know my father
   who made me
   I know the spirit
   who made me."
(2) The party drink from calabashes, a mixture of water from the stream and *ubulawo*-medicine (which I will discuss shortly), stirred until froth is formed;
(3) After drinking they vomit;
(4) The diviner finds white clay and smears it upon herself and the novices;
(5) The group runs back to her kraal while the diviner dances round them in joy, beating them with twigs.

Now consider the sequence of Zionist ritual activities:

(1) The prophet's followers circle him singing,
   "God Father, I have erred,
   and have gone astray from home."
(2) The prophet asserts that because there is *running* water the diviners have not defiled it by their rites;

(3) He sings a hymn and blesses the water, by stirring in the stream with his index finger, and with his eyes on heaven says a short prayer to the Lord of the Living Waters that the stream may be cleansed from vile things.
(4) Next a patient is brought to him. With both hands he scoops water into her mouth, at the same time shouting: "In the name of the Father and of the Son and of the Holy Ghost. This blessed water will take away the illness from this sick person. Drink!"
(5) The prophet then takes the patient with him into the middle of the stream and makes her stoop until the water goes over her head.
(6) He places his hands upon her head and in the same moment becomes filled with the Holy Spirit. His whole body shakes, and he shouts, first slowly, but soon faster and faster: "Hhayi, hhayi, hhayi, hhe, hhe, hhe!"
(7) The patient drinks repeatedly from the water, praying in the intervals: "Descend, Spirit, descend like a dove!" Soon she also gets the Spirit, begins to shake and to speak with tongues: "Di-di-di-di-didi!"
(8) While this is happening, the faithful on the banks sing a hymn. The sick woman comes up from the stream and begins to vomit on the rocks.
(9) Other patients follow her into the water and go through the same process ending with vomiting.
(10) One of the Church Elders is suddenly possessed by the Spirit. He dashes round the group in his long white gown, beating the air with a long white cross; he sings, shouts, and speaks with tongues.
(11) After the "water and vomiting" ceremony, the Prophet takes white ashes and mixes them with water. He smears the patients' faces and shoulders with this mixture.
(12) To complete the cure, green sashes are tied round their shoulders.
(13) The Zionists than return to the prophet's home. He leads the procession for a while, but when he is again possessed by the Spirit, he circles round the others in the group, singing and dancing. The older Zionists soon follow him, dancing round the remaining group of patients.

Let us now compare these two sets of ritual activities. It is clear that they are not really homologous, since the diviner's rites seem to represent part of her instruction of the novices in divining *gnosis* and techniques, while the prophet's rites are manifestly curative, though they are initiatory at the same time, as is common in African ritual. Nevertheless, they share certain symbolic motifs, and the debt of Zionism to *isangoma* divination is obvious, though its debt to Christianity is equally patent. What do they, then, share?

(1) Songs to spiritual beings—in both cases, masculine and paternal—plural in the pagan and singular in the Christian instance;
(2) A stress on the importance of water as a purificatory medium;[1]

---

[1] p. 260. Rivers. Callaway p. 321, 322.

(3) An emphasis on white symbolism: in the case of the diviners, *ubulawo*-medicine (p. 142-143, p. 272, "cleansing"), froth[1]) and white clay;[2]) in that of the Zionists, white garments,[3]) a "long white cross", white ashes, and (possibly) the "dove" symbolism of the Holy Spirit;
(4) An acknowledgement of the ritual efficacy of drinking from the sacred stream then vomiting;
(5) Circling of adepts round novices or followers on return to the leader's home.

To this list might be added, from Sundkler, Callaway, Bryant and other sources, a common belief in the importance of dreams as an indication of religious vocation, in the possession of adepts by supernatural beings and in the divining and curative powers of adepts, assisted thereto by supernatural entities.

On the other hand, significant differences emerge. The Zionists use the Biblical phraseology of God the Father, the baptismal formula of the Trinity and become possessed by the Holy Spirit. They wear long white robes with green sashes and carry crosses. The diviner, for her part, beats her novices with twigs.

What is interesting and theoretically provocative, however, is that certain of the symbols shared by diviners and Zionists are widely used in Christian worship. These include songs to spiritual beings, the ritual use of water, and the liturgical use of white symbolism. Furthermore, these very same clusters of symbols are found not only in early Christian worship but in Jewish and pagan religious practices in the ancient societies of Europe and Hither Asia.

To focus the analysis more sharply I am going to examine in detail two motifs only, whiteness and water, first in traditional Zulu religion, then in the ancient world. I will refer to other motifs at appropriate points in the discussion.

A. *Whiteness*

(1) In Zulu Religion

a. *Ubulawo*-medicine. According to Callaway *(The Religious System of the Amazulu*, London: Tribner and Co. (1870), pp. 142-144, p. 272), there are two kinds of *ubulawo* medicine—black *ubulawo* and white *ubulawo*. Since only white *ubulawo* is used in connection with divination

---

[1]) Froth-madness, akin to ecstacy.
[2]) White *impepo* p. 261, to produce distinct and clear vision. *Kcakcambisa*, to make white.
[3]) Green clothes are 'dress of the Spirit' (*izingubo zika Moya*) p. 214.

and ancestral spirits, the reference in Sundkler's account is clearly to this type. Callaway describes this class of medicines as "used for cleansing and brightening, with the view of removing from the system something that causes dislike and introducing into it something that will cause love." White *ubulawo* is in fact often used as a love-medicine. Callaway describes how it is used by youths rejected by their lovers or persons wishing to win favours from great men. Some of its significance may be erotic—and this factor will play an important part in our later argument. For example, it is regarded as indispensible to churn *ubulawo* into a "high froth" before it is drunk or splashed on the head and body. In kindred Ndembu symbolism the foam of a waterfall used in love medicine may be compared with that of orgasm. Froth may also be connected—as by Ndembu— with madness, for the "white *Itongo*", as the diviner's possessing spirit is called, produces in him symptoms that are at first mistaken for madness and also commands him to dig up roots to churn into the frothy "cleansing *ubulawo*". The *Itongo* spirit is called "white" because it enables the diviner "to see clearly" and help others (Callaway: p. 271).

This theme of "seeing clearly" or "truthfully" is exemplified in another class of "white" medicines taken by novice diviners. This is "white *impepo*", of which one of Callaway's informants spoke in the following terms: "*Impepo* means true knowledge *(ukwazi impela)*...(it) means especially that clearness of perception which a diviner possesses; nothing is too hard for him; but he sees a difficult thing at once" (Callaway: p. 321). The term Callaway translates as "clearness of perception" *(kukcakcamba)* means literally "to be white". Here as elsewhere the Zulu ritual vocabulary is closely similar to that of the Ndembu (see for example my articles in *Essays in the Ritual of Social Relations* and *African Systems of Thought*, and my *Chihamba the White Spirit*).

The medicine-possession syndrome would here appear to indicate that the diviner, partly through a call from an ancestral spirit, partly through drinking medicines, imbibes mystical power, vomits out impurities, and falls into an ecstacy, comparable to that of a lunatic or a lover, and in this state "sees a difficult thing at once", perceives matters clearly. Let me anticipate and say that the theme of a neophyte drinking or sucking a white fluid, receiving into the body a white spirit, and being successively purified and possessed, will recur quite often in this account.

b. Other White Symbols. Sundkler (p. 22) gives additional data on white symbols connected with divination. He mentions how a novice-diviner adorns her body with white strips *(imigwambo)* from the skin of a sacrificial goat. "White", he says, "is the diviner's colour. The purification rites and the whiteness of the dress are all part of the same process to 'make the initiate see,' to give her a clear vision, and to cause her to become totally possessed by the spirit." The use of white clay, mentioned by Callaway, Sundkler and others, is an expression of the same theme. Again, in stereotyped pagan dreams the goddess of fertility, Nomkubulwana, appeared dressed in white (Gluckman, "Zulu Women in Hoecultural Ritual," *Bantu Studies*, 1935, p. 263).

(2) In Zionism

The major white symbols in Zulu Zionism are *white garments*, variously described by Sundkler as "gowns", "veils" (p. 249), "uniforms" (p. 268), "baptismal robes" (p. 268) and "robes". Persons in white robes are stock elements in the dreams of Zionist converts, and, indeed, if a non-Zionist dreams of white garments Zionists regard the dream as a sign of election to their faith. Such men in "shining cloths" (p. 267) or white clothes (p. 268) are usually represented in the stereotyped dream symbolism as being in some way connected with streams or pools. The whiteness of a patient's veil given after immersion rites is thought "through its whiteness to attract a host of healing angels" (p. 214).

"White ashes are connected with most purification rites of the Zionists, as indeed was the case in traditional pagan Zulu purification rites" (p. 212). Sometimes the ashes are smeared on the body, as in the episode related earlier. "When the Zionist neophyte realizes that he has received heavenly inspiration for the first time," says Sundkler (p. 212), he will ask...his Zulu friends to cover his body with ashes, "because I have been filled with the Holy Spirit." Any self-respecting Zionist congregation now has a special holy "Vessel of Ashes" set aside in the church house as a receptacle for its holy ashes. Sometimes the ashes are used, mixed with water, to induce vomiting or as a purgative, not as a sign but an agency of purification. Zionists believe that vomiting rids one of spiritual defilement as well as physical illness. A prophet keeps pure and holy by vomiting in a stream every day at dawn.

Other white symbols such as crosses, flags, doves, light, and white "holy sticks" (p. 214)[1]) share these notions of purity, purification and the washing away of defilement *(imikhokha)*.

(3) In Ancient Religion

Of course, there is plenty of Biblical precedent for Zionist white garb. According to S. Krauss *(Talmudische Archaeologie*, 1910: "Kleidung und Schmuck," I, 127-207; see also H. Riesenfeld, *Jésus Transfiguré*, 1947, 115-129 *(Acta Seminarii Neotestamentici Upsaliensis*, XVI)[2]) Jews, in old Testament times, distinguished between "white" and "coloured" garments. White was the garb of joy, of purity, and of social dignity. God Himself, Daniel had said, is clothed in a garment white as snow (Dan. VII, 9), while a Psalm says, "Thou coverest thyself with light as with a garment." Throughout the ancient world in fact, as Erwin Goodenough has shown us in great detail (Vol. 9, pp. 165-169), whiteness was connected with light and blackness with darkness. The Essenes gave a white robe to each new member as a mark of his final entry into the order—that is, upon his initiation—and thereafter he wore white always. Herein, writes Goodenough, "the Qumran Community probably resembled the Essenes, for members of the community called themselves "sons of light" in anticipation of heaven where, in a life of eternity, they would wear "a crown of glory" and a "raiment of majesty in everlasting light." The community could also have had no more fitting mark of their dedication and hope than to wear white robes in this life" (p. 169). In early Jewish, as in New Testament tradition, angels wore white, as is witnessed in the *Testament of Levi* (VIII,2). The convention of the sanctity of the white-robed figure may have been very old. We read in Exodus XXVIII,4, and Leviticus, XVI,4, of the high priest who took off his official garments on the Day of Atonement and went into the Holy of Holies wearing only a white linen ephod, "a garment that seems to have been the robe of light, at least in later interpretation" (Goodenough *ibid.*, p. 169). Samuel as a boy wore a "linen ephod," as did David when he danced before the ark (II Sam. VI,14), in both cases probably the same garment the high priest wore when he entered the Holy of Holies.

In the New Testament, of course, white symbolism proliferates, especially in the Gospel narrative of the Transfiguration, when Christ's face "shone like the sun, and his garments became white like light," and of the Resurrection, where the angel's appearance was "like

---

[1]) Reminiscent of Moses' "rod".
[2]) Cited by Goodenough, op. cit., p. 165.

lightning and his raiment white as snow" (Matthew, XXVIII,2f.). "Revelation makes so many references to white that even the white horse and the white throne seem likewise to be this supernal light" (Goodenough, *ibid.*, p. 167). Then there is the vesture, "made white in the blood of the Lamb," worn by the victors in Christ, mentioned in Revelation. "St. Paul spoke directly of this change of vesture on two occasions, and made it specifically our changing the garment or tent of flesh in which we now dwell to don a new garment. In the new garment we shall not be "naked," but will be clothed with incorruptibility *(aphtharsia)* or immortality *(athanasia)*, two terms for deification, one from philosophy, the other from popular religious parlance. "Behold I tell you a mystery," says Paul as he gets into the heart of this conception," and Goodenough surmises that the figure was much closer to the symbolism of the new robes in Greek and Asian mystery religions than we can ever document (Goodenough, *ibid.*, p. 167).

In ancient Greece "white" or "light" garments also had religious significance and we find Plato saying that a piece of white *(leukos)*. cloth was a most suitable votive offering to the Gods (Plato, *Laws*, XII, 956A). According to Plutarch *(The Roman Questions*, XXVI, as trs. by H. J. Rose, 1924, 131) white dresses and kerchiefs were worn by women as a sign of mourning, because "natural white is pure and unmixed, neither stained nor imitable by dyes; it is therefore peculiarly fitting to the dead at burial. For a dead man is become simple, unmixed, pure, in short freed from the ingrained dye of the body." This is curiously reminiscent of the Zulu, and indeed, general Bantu belief that ancestral spirits are "white" in colour.

In the mysteries of Isis in Roman times, Apuleius tells us, the young men in the procession wore robes that were "snowy and festal," *candore puro luminosi*, "pure shining white" (Metamorphoses, XI, 10). According to Goodenough, "it is the shining, light effect that was the real meaning of the garments—this effect was related to the rising after death of Osiris or Serapis, the sun deity."

It is, indeed, a constant theme of ancient religion that light and water are identified as cleansing, and even deifying, agencies, and that both are associated with white symbolism.

B. *Water*

(1) In Zulu Religion

Water is an important symbol in traditional Zulu sacred lore. Callaway, for example, cites an informant as saying of the origin of man, that "We came out of the water, from a bed of reeds, by the sea" (Callaway, *op. cit.*, p. 88) and later that "all things came out of the water, dogs and cattle" (p. 90). Yet another informant described the Zulu creator being Unkulunkulu as sitting "in a hole somewhere near the Umtshezi, a river in Zululand, appearing with his body only above the ground, and thus sitting moulded all things" (p. 90). Other accounts appear to indicate that men first appeared out of a "pool of water" (p. 36). Once again, then, we meet with a set of ideas that relate man's origin or birth to water or generalized fluid and at least one account which connects flowing water (the Umtshezi river) with the creative work of a male (father) figure. We have seen earlier, how in divination training a running stream was connected with the first light, with the ancestors, with white symbolism and with purgation and cleansing.

(2) In Zionism

Sundkler makes specific reference to the importance of "river cults" in traditional African religion, quoting Herskovits and Willoughby in support of his view that "the propensity of the Zulu Zionist to total immersion is intimately linked up with traditional Zulu practices in streams and pools" (Sundkler, p. 201). "These tendencies" (he goes on) "have been strengthened by the Biblical teaching of the Zionist churches on baptism...The Zulu Jordan is, as it were, the River of Life which like an artesian well springs to the surface in the various purification rites of the Zionist Church."

Since we have already considered in some detail a Zionist curative rite with total immersion as a main feature, we need only consider Zionist water beliefs and practices briefly. The expressed aim of baptism and subsequent washings, drinkings and immersions is to rid people of *imikhokha*, the results of breaking a taboo or moral norm. The bad luck of *imikhokha* indicates that a person is "unclean" or "inauspicious". The Zulu term for "unclean" is *ukoba nesinyama*, literally "to have blackness on," i.e. to be in the opposite state to "whiteness." It refers to people passing through life-crises, as, for example, menstruating women, people who have recently handled a dead body, and so forth. It may also refer to possession by malevolent spirits—"demons" as the Zionists call them.

It is important in Zionism that the water used in baptism or some other purification should be *blessed*, "prepared by prayer in order to make it efficacious" (Sundkler, p. 206). In other words the water must be sacralized, informed by mystical or divine power and at the same time exorcised, for "demoniac monsters" are thought to haunt the pools of Zionist baptism. Here there may be detected an echo of the Catholic blessing of the baptismal waters at the great "liminal" Mass of Holy Saturday that signalizes the end of the penitential season of Lent. But there is more here than mere borrowing, as we shall see presently. The notion that water, when blessed, represents an emission of mystical power, a divine primordial fluid from which persons are reborn or regenerated is of very ancient provenience.

(3) In Ancient Religion

It is to Erwin Goodenough's patient researches that we owe much of our knowledge of the importance of what he calls "the divine fluid" in the ancient religions of Mesopotamia, Syria, Egypt, Greece, Greco-Roman Egypt, Gnosticism, Jewish cult and observance and in early Christianity. "The divine fluid" takes many forms—water, blood, milk, wine, semen are the most prominent—but here I have only time to discuss the symbolism of water. My own findings during anthropological fieldwork among the Ndembu incidentally are rather remarkably confirmed by Goodenough's researches. His major interest is in the Jewish symbolism of wine but he finds (Vol. 6, p. 112) that "the earliest drinking symbols... seem to refer to water or the seminal fluid. Only much later does wine take over and become the Sacramental fluid, or the means of imparting divine life, par excellence. Even in Christianity wine never displaced water completely as a spiritual vehicle. It is said that blood, another of the fluids, and water both flowed from Jesus on the cross, and the water of baptism and holy water still vividly witness the survival of symbolic water. While neither of these is drunk, holy water is a direct means of spiritual blessing or increment, and the water of baptism is the sacramental means of spiritual birth. That the desire for rebirth in more primitive and direct ages should have expressed itself in symbols of the fluid of the god's semen is not only what we should expect but what we shall abundantly find was true. Similarly, in feminine terms, the desire was for milk from the divine breasts, for here also was life for the infant which, before the gods, man always was. The desire for deity in the form of fluid naturally had its counterpart in the need for rain, or the great rising of the Nile (often expressed in ithyphallic imagery), to give life to the crops. It was just as inevitable that the symbol in desert countries should often have been the drinking of cool water.

"Much less to be expected but still everywhere encountered is the identification of this fluid of life with quite another fluid, the flow of light from the sun. The phrase 'flow of light' is about all we have left of the ancient notion that light itself is a fluid. So the water of life and light of life become interchangeable figures in a way entirely natural to the ancient mind though it seems strange to us."

In this passage Goodenough summarizes, with perfect accuracy and probity, a mass of evidence, documentary and archaeological, which requires twelve massive volumes to present.

Analysis

This comparison of the motifs of whiteness and water in Zulu religion, Zionism and ancient religion points up a remarkable constancy in the basic values ascribed to the symbolism. Some of my own articles on the Ndembu symbolism of whiteness and the relationship between colour symbolism and bodily fluids would suggest that fuller information on Zulu religion would make the resemblance between it and ancient religion even closer.

The material poses a number of problems. Let me mention three only.

(1) Why is it that whiteness which represents, inter alia, purity and purification, also has connections with sexual and bodily fluids, such as semen and maternal 'waters'?

(2) What connection, if any, does ritual symbolism maintain with social structure?

(3) What is the nature of the relationship between clusters of symbols used in traditional religious systems in stable societies and similar clusters in new religious movements in societies undergoing rapid change?

All three of these questions are closely related, even if they appear at first to be quite disparate. To answer the first we must rid ourselves of the widely distributed Western preconception that sexuality is in itself impure. But it is recognized in many cultures that sexuality may give rise to social conflict, even when it is domesticated in the institution of marriage, for every marriage involves not only the marital pair but a number of corporate groups who may be drawn into opposition over many aspects of the marriage—quarrels between the spouses, quarrels over the filiation of the children, quarrels over bridewealth, and so forth. Again sexuality leads to adultery, murder and feud. These things are well recognized in ancient and primitive society. But the act of sex itself is not necessarily impure or sinful. Moreover, when the varied religious symbolism clearly indicates sexual relations between an invisible one this is regarded as the acme of immaculateness or purity, not its obverse. It was William James who often stressed that it is "not the indecency of our roots but the sublime possibility that our simplest organic cravings can transmute themselves into guides to man's most exalted experiences." And Goodenough has expanded this to argue that "in the early age of frankness about bodily functions which will probably never return, these emotions could still be overt and sublime; one's emotions could still find true access to the Logos, as Plutarch did, in the frank worship of the heavenly phallus... Salvation began with an open desire for the new birth in water and spirit, through Dionysus the phallic wine god who was Osiris the phallic water and sun god. This new birth was effected by a fertilization of the mystic with fluid and fire, until reborn, he could rise in his new power to become himself identified with God, or the Logos, and so immortal."

Who can doubt that much of this applies also today, not only to the Lingayats of India, but also to both traditional and Zionist Zulu? The impregnation by foaming sacralized water, consecrated to a spiritual "father", the vomiting (as in pregnancy) of the recipient, the rebirth or regeneration out of sacred waters of the neophyte who is now identified with the white life and light giver—this is not too fanciful an interpretation for the Zulu procedures. In this, as in many other religious systems sexuality is utilized as a matrix of symbols for what is felt by the believers to be trans-sexual, that is, sociologically speaking, above or beyond that domain of social life where multiplicity, differentiation, conflict, opposition, quarrelling, hence witchcraft and murder prevail. What is sought is unity, not the unity which represents a sum of fractions and is susceptible of division and subtraction, but an indivisible unity, "white", "pure", "primary", "seamless", expressed in such symbols as the basic generative and nurturant fluids such as semen and milk, as "running water," as "dawn", as "light", and as "whiteness". Homogeneity is sought, instead of heterogeneity. The members of the religious community are to be regarded, at least in rite and symbol, as a simple unit, not as a sum of segments or the ultimate product of some mode of the social division of labor. They are impregnated by unity, as it were, and purified from divisiveness and plurality. The impure and sinful is the sundered, the divided. The pure is the integer, the indivisible.

This brings me to my last question: what is the relationship, on the one hand, between such symbols of homogeneous unity between gods or spirits, men—and I would add, the non-human setting in traditional religions—and, on the other, similar symbols in modern religious movements. The main point I would like to make here is that such symbols in stable societies form critical components of *rites de passage*, especially life-crisis rites, while in rapidly changing societies they sometimes tend, in the early stages at least, to become the whole content of the religious praxis. In other words, the entire life of the convert or believer is regarded in much the same way as the transient, liminal or marginal period in a traditional *rite de passage*, or rather an initiation rite. In such liminal periods, I have argued elsewhere, a novice, in passing from the incumbency of one structural position to another, is for a time in an inter-structural limbo to which the normal categories of social thought do not strictly apply. In this condition he is often described, portrayed or symbolized as a creature of paradox —as androgynous, as neither living nor dead, as theranthropic, as a companion of ancestral spirits, as alternately female and male, etc. He learns about *sacra*, or holy objects, in terms of myths or riddles which often relate strikingly to what I have said about the divine or sacred fluids and their regenerative power. Novices are often treated as a homogeneous anonymous group without personal or status differences—they either go naked or wear identical costumes or "uniforms". But, eventually, in traditional societies, the novices are removed from this homogeneous community and are inducted into new statuses— roles which, as it were, eternally precede and await them. What is similar to all this in religious movements of the types we are considering at this conference is the breakdown of antecedent social structure. Yet here not merely a given age or sex group but the whole community experiences a destructuring of its crucial relationships, and this not in an orderly and expectable fashion but in a disorderly and unprecedented way. Society itself is felt to be in a liminal phase but like the Unfinished Symphony it has only a beginning... No end is foreseeable in culturally familiar terms. Such societies are peculiarly liable, on exposure to the written apocalyptic symbolism of such religions as Christianity and Islam, (which were themselves born in times of rapid cultural change) to blend these with crucial elements of the symbolisms of their own traditional *rites de passage*. In the new syncretism, life on earth is now seen as "liminal" and heaven is seen as the state to which funerary rites constitute the rites of incorporation, or even of re-aggregation, in the "Golden Age" or "Platonic" types of belief.

In both liminal rites and the ritual of modern sects and cults there is often an emphasis on release from the bonds of norm and moral obligation and a proliferation of sexual imagery, notably imagery connoting the flow of bodily emissions which indicate the presence of powerful emotions. Autonomic rhythms and regularities, in fact, replace the broken or disturbed cultural ones. In religions of pronouncedly mystical cast the physiological imagery is regarded as itself a symbol of union with the mystical or divine source of everything. In these cases exuberantly sexual symbolism and verbal imagery may accompany considerable restraints on sexual behaviour—the stress is on ecstatic union with the source of unity not with specific persons. In other religions, promiscuity in behaviour may itself be seen as means of obtaining, as well as symbolizing, a structureless, homogeneous community that has all things in common. In both cases, what is sought is escape or liberation from, standing outside of (i.e. ecstacy) the structured order of society which by its very nature is full of conflict, evil and sin, the disintegration of which is not only a source of anxiety and insecurity but is also the hope and instrument of a "truer", "whiter", "clearer", more "godly" community of the saved.

BIBLIOGRAPHY

1870 Callaway, H. *The Religious System of the Amazulu*, London: Trubner and Co.
1935 Gluckman, M. "Zulu Women in Hoecultural Ritual", *Bantu Studies*, Vol. IX, pp. 255-71
1953 f. Goodenough, Erwin *Jewish Symbols in the Greco-Roman Period*, New York: Pantheon Books i-xii.
1961 Sundkler, B. *Bantu Prophets in South Africa*. London: Oxford University Press (Second Edition)
1962 Turner, Victor "Three Symbols of *Passage* in Ndembu Circumcision Ritual" in M. Gluckman, ed., *Essays on the Ritual of Social Relations*, Manchester University Press

1963 — *Chihamba the White Spirit: A Ritual Drama of the Ndembu*, Rhodes-Livingstone Paper No. 33, Manchester University Press
1965 — "Ritual Symbolism, Morality and Social Structure" in M. Fortes and G. Dieterlen, eds, *African Systems of Thought*, London: Oxford University Press for the International African Institute

ΝΟΜΟΣ ΦΥΣΕΩΣ
THE CONCEPT OF NATURAL LAW IN GREEK THOUGHT

BY

HELMUT KOESTER
Harvard University

I

It is widely assumed that the concept of "natural law" is of Greek origin. In treatments of a more general, albeit scholarly, character, one may find statements such as these:

> The early Greek philosophers of natural law had no difficulty in finding an answer on the basis of their pantheistic philosophy... Stoic philosophy, because of its belief in a well ordered Cosmos, attempted to revive the original idea of natural law. Still the Stoics had to admit that human laws... are but imperfect ... realizations of the law of Nature. The idea of a dual order has formed the basis of most natural law speculation ever since ... The [Greek] dualistic theory of law fitted in with the Christian dogma of the Fall of Man and was, therefore, made part of the Christian system of natural law.[1]

Established and dignified assumptions are not easily challenged. Furthermore, there can be little doubt that Early Christian, Medieval and Modern concepts of natural law include basic elements which ultimately are of Greek origin. My concern in this paper is specifically with the term "law" as it occurs as a component of the legal and moral concept "Law of Nature."[2] Insofar as this conception also appears under the term "Natural Rights,"[3] this inquiry is relevant only inasmuch as such natural rights are said to derive from a universal *law* of nature which stands against over codified or positive law.

---

[1]) Kessler, Theoretic Bases of Natural Law, *The University of Chicago Law Review* 9 (1941/42), p. 100 f.; for a substantially similar, although more detailed, presentation of the same view see J. L. Adams, "The Law of Nature in Greco-Roman Thought, *"Journal of Religion* 25 (1945), 97-118.

[2]) For "law of nature" as a term of natural sciences in antiquity see Robert M. Grant, *Miracle and Natural Law in Graeco-Roman and Early Christion Thought*, Amsterdam 1952.

[3]) Cf. the German *Naturrecht* which, however, is largely equivalent to Natural Law=*lex naturalis* or *naturae*.

It is questionable whether the assumption that Greek thought ever conceived of the basic moral and legal principles inherent in nature as a universal natural *law* can be justified. There is, in fact, very little evidence for the occurrence of the term "law of nature" (νόμος φύσεως) in classical Greek texts. The term never appears in any of the fragments of the pre-Socratic philosophers, nor among the Sophists. It is also absent from the extant fragments and writings of the Greek Stoics (with a few exceptions which will be discussed below). There is still the possibility that the Pythagoreans and, with quite different connotations, the Epicureans might have used the term; but the scanty sources which are left to us do not permit any firm conclusions.

For the first time in Greek literature the term "law of nature" is liberally employed in the writings of Philo of Alexandria. The question arises, thus, whether the thought of this Jewish philosopher from the first century A.D. was the melting pot in which the Greek concept of Nature as a universal power and the Jewish belief in the universal validity of the divine Law coalesced and were amalgamated into the new concept of a "Law of Nature."

It is necessary, however, to note that the Latin equivalent *lex naturalis* occurs even before Philo, and seems to have arisen independently of the formulation of the Greek term νόμος φύσεως.[1])

Since this paper is concerned primarily with Philo of Alexandria, it seems to be appropriate to dedicate it to the memory of Erwin Goodenough, whose work has contributed so much to Philo scholarship.[2])

II

In pre-Socratic Greek thought the law of the Polis was understood to exist by divine sanction and to be derived from the one and only divine law which sustains the existence of all men.[3]) What one does not find here, however, is the appeal to nature as the source of law. Although the particularity of the existing laws and constitutions is recognized quite early (at least in the fifth century, B.C.), the conflicts which arise are not seen as the antagonism of particular laws and a "law of nature," but rather as conflicts between the law of the polis

---

[1]) On the occurrence of *lex naturae* in Cicero, see below, p. 529.

[2]) The paper was read on December 4, 1965, at the Harvard History of Religions Club of which Erwin Goodenough was a member during the last years of his life.

[3]) Cf. e.g. Heraclitus fragment 114; see further W. Gutbrod, νόμος, in: *Theologisches Wörterbuch zum NT* IV (1942), p. 1018 ff. and the literature given on p. 1016f. See also my forthcoming article φύσις, in: *Theologisches Wörterbuch zum NT* VIII.

and the law of the Gods[1]) or between written and unwritten law.[2])

In the famous Pindar fragment 169 κατὰ φύσιν νόμος πάντων βασιλεύς, the words κατὰ φύσιν are not a part of the quotation. A correlation between law and nature is not yet developed. The term "law of nature" is extremely rare, even in the following centuries. The two earliest occurrences are in Plato[3]) and in Theophrastus.

In Plato's Gorgias 483 e, Callicles says about the right of the stronger one that it exists κατὰ νόμον τὸν τῆς φύσεως. There is no doubt that the phrase here has to be understood, as Leisegang says, as "a paradoxon, in which the two antonymus terms have been forced together."[4])

Theophrastus, fragment 152, says that he who does not give due respect to the Divine, but is neglectful τῶν τε τῆς φύσεως τῶν τε τῆς πόλεως νόμων has trangressed the two due requirements of righteousness. Obviously the desire to find an all-encompassing formulation and a parallelism with the traditional "laws of the Polis" has caused this unusual expression.

But even for the two last pre-Christian centuries it is possible to list only two more occurrences of the term νόμος τῆς φύσεως; once in the pseudipigraphical work On Nature under the name of Ocellus Lucanus[5]) (49, 23, 8 ed. Harder) that has to be dated ca. 150 B.C., and the second time in a passage in Dionysius of Halicarnassus III 11, 3.[6])

[1]) Cf. R. Bultmann, Polis und Hades in der Antigone des Sophokles, *Glauben und Verstehen* II (4th ed. 1965), p. 20 ff.

[2]) R. Hirzel, ΑΓΡΑΦΟΣ ΝΟΜΟΣ, in: *Abhandlungen der Sächsischen Akademie der Wissenschaft* 20 (1900), p. 65 ff.

[3]) A second occurrence in Plato would be Tim 83e where disease is said to be παρὰ τοὺς τῆς φύσεως... νόμους. Here, however, the term refers to the normal and natural functioning of the body. But even the use of this term for the physical laws of nature is unique. The only other early example is Aristotle's statement that the Pythagoreans speak of numbers as if they had received them παρὰ τῆς φύσεως... ὥσπερ νόμους ἐκείνης De Caelo I 1, p. 268 a 13; Aristotle himself prefers to use the simple term "nature". On the physical law of nature see further R. M. Grant, *Miracle and Natural Law in Graeco-Roman and Early Christian Thought* (1952), p. 19-28.

[4]) H. Leisegang, Physis, in: *Pauly-Wissowa* XX, p. 1144; cf. R. M. Grant *op. cit.* p. 20.

[5]) Ocellus is known as a Pythagorean, but this work is certainly spurious and its orientation is peripathetic. The occurrence of this term in "Ocellus", however, is of some interest, since Philo is using "Ocellus" in his De aeternitate mundi. Yet, although Philo shares the view of "Ocellus" that it is "against (the law of) nature" to marry a barren woman (Spec. Leg. III 34. 36), there is no indication that he is deriving either this view or the terminology from "Ocellus".

[6]) On the question of the use of this term in the Stoa see below. An interesting occurrence of the term "law of nature" in the first century A.D. is Dio Chrys. Or. 80,5; here the law of nature that has been forsaken by men is contrasted with written laws and rules engraved in stone.

III

As the words φύσις and νόμος are terminologically developed and brought into correlation with each other in Greek thought before Plato, they designate two realms of human experience that are quite different in scope and character. They may supplement each other, but more often they are opposed to each other. Φύσις is the realm of self-sustained "natural" things and events, a realm which is not called into being and not ordered by human activity. Νόμος, on the other hand, does not designate just any law or rule one might find somewhere; but νόμος also is a realm, the world of men and their activities, customs, morality, and deliberate efforts of ordering.

It was probably in the Greek Ethnography that the two terms were brought together for the first time.[1]) Herodotus uses φύσις frequently for the "character" of a country (φύσις τῆς χώρης Herod. 2,5),[2]) and, in one instance, also of men side by side with the term νόμος: "The Greeks who say this seem to me to be without any knowledge τῆς Αἰγυπτίων φύσιος καὶ τῶν νόμων" (2,45). But neither this passage nor Sophocles Ajax 548f., which speaks about the habits of life (νόμοι) and the character (φύσις) of Ajax, are sufficient evidence to show that the two terms were used antithetically before the Sophists.

A parallel to such an antithetical usage has been seen in Parmenides' antithesis δόξα-ἀλήθεια.[3]) But this shows a terminological difference, even if in one instance Parmenides can use νενόμισται = "it is an accepted convention" (fr. B 6,8) in contrast to "truth".[4]) Any other evidence for the antithesis from pre-Socratic philosophy is even less conclusive. If genuine, Philolaus fragment B 9 φύσει καὶ οὐ νόμῳ would be an early witness; nothing of the context, however, is preserved. Diogenes Laertius II 16 reports as doctrine of Archelaus, Socrates'

---

[1]) For a detailed study of the origin of the combination and antithesis of the terms see F. Heinimann, *Nomos und Physis*, (Schweizerische Beiträge zur Altertumswissenschaft I, 1945); cf. further M. Pohlenz, Nomos und Physis, *Hermes* 81 (1953), p. 418-438.

[2]) See further 2,19.35.68.71. Possibly Herodotus had learned this usage of the term from Hecataeus; cf. F. Heinimann, *op. cit.* p. 106f. It is doubtful, however, whether this would also prove that the antithesis Nomos-Physis had its origin in Ionic Natural Philosophy, as Heinimann (p. 40,107f.) believes; cf. M. Pohlenz, *op. cit.* p. 425.

[3]) Cf. K. Reinhardt, *Parmenides und die Geschichte der griechischen Philosophie* (2nd ed. 1959), p. 81-88.

[4]) W. Jaeger, *Theology of the Early Greek Thinkers* (1947), note X 69, believes that here we have a prefiguration of the later antithesis Nomos-Physis. For νόμος = "convention" in contrast to "truth" cf. F. Heinimann, *op. cit.*, 85-89.

teacher, who is said to have introduced Ionic philosophy to Athens, "that the good and the bad is not by nature, but by law" (οὐ φύσει, ἀλλὰ νόμῳ); yet, this sharply antithethical formulation probably does not represent Archelaus' own wording but that of the doxographer.[1]

The terminological juxtaposition of Nomos and Physis is firmly established in one of the oldest writings of the Hippocratic Corpus, De Aere Aquis Locis (ca. 430 B.C.): The author wants to discuss only those nations which differ widely both in their nature and in their conventions: ἢ φύσει ἢ νόμῳ (14). Quite different from the use of these terms in ethnography, "law" and "nature" here are not understood as descriptive but as causal categories. They are the ultimate reasons for the development of different features in the character of various people. At the same time, Physis and Nomos are clearly distinguished as factors of quite different properties. They can also be seen in conflict with each other, e.g. in the description of the courage of the Asian people (De Aere Aquis Locis 16): If someone is by nature (φύσει πέφυκεν) courageous and noble, his character will soon be changed through the laws (ὑπὸ τῶν νόμων).

The further elaboration of this contrast into a real antithesis was achieved by the *Sophists*, resulting in the creation of the first formulated doctrines of natural rights of men (not, however, of natural law!). Not only is there no evidence for the term "law of nature" in the extant fragments of the Greek Sophists, but such a concept could not have found any place whatever in their teachings. Law and Nature are mutually exclusive. The best extant example is the Antiphon fragment Pap. Oxyrh. XI 1364 (fr. B 44 A in Diels). The contrast is between "that which pertains to the laws" (τὰ τῶν νόμων) and "that which pertains to nature" (τὰ τῆς φύσεως). Even when the transgression of the laws and its consequences are contrasted to the violation of the things pertaining to nature, Antiphon never conceives of the latter as if they were something like laws in their own right, albeit of a different order. On the contrary, what pertains to nature does not have the character of "law". Nature's ways are "of necessity" (ἀναγκαῖα, not ἐπίθετα); they have come about "through natural growth" (φύντα, not ὁμολογηθέντα), are "ingrown in human nature" (ξύμφυτα) and their violation implies disaster as a natural consequence, i.e. laws regulating punishment would be superfluous for nature's trials. Of course, nature requires that men should give to their lives a not uncertain direction.

---

[1] Cf. F. Heinimann, *op. cit.* p. 110-114; M. Pohlenz, *op. cit.* p. 432f.

This, however, is not identical with the recognition of any laws, whatever their character may be, but is rather the insight into the true conditions of human nature, namely that by nature we are all equal (πάντα πάντες ὁμοίως πεφύκαμεν),—since all men are breathing with nose and mouth—and thus we can recognize the things which are by nature necessary for all men (τὰ τῶν φύσει ὄντων ἀναγκαίων πᾶσιν ἀνθρώποις).[1])

It seems to me that the limited intention and function of these teachings of the Sophists are often overlooked. What they have said, of course, implies nothing less than the discovery of the one and common nature of all men. Consequently they fight against artificially established political and social distinctions which are controlled by the laws which give specific rights to certain classes, cities, and nations, and deny the same rights to others. But they do not speak of nature as if it were a divine lawgiver. In their concept of education, the Sophists share with earlier philosophers—and elaborate even further—the threefold schema of φύσις, ἄσκησις and διδασκαλία (cf. Protagoras, fragments B 3 and B 10), and men like Plato have no quarrel with the Sophists at this point.[2]) Furthermore, Plato's and Aristotle's criticism of the Sophists never implies that their nature doctrines lead to dangerous consequences for legislation, but rather that any concept of nature is completely mute with respect to legislation. The Sophists, Plato and Aristotle agree that anything like a law of nature would be absurd. Plato and Aristotle differ from the Sophists in their rejection of the concept of a κατὰ φύσιν ὀρθὸς βίος (Plato, Leges X 890a) and in their emphasis upon the necessity of law for the education (paideia) of men. Law, however, has its origin not in nature, but in the νοῦς or λόγος: law originates from the νοῦς κατὰ ὀρθὸν λόγον (Plato, Leges 890d).

Aristotle emphasizes that no virtues for moral and political action can be derived from nature: οὐδεμία τῶν ἠθικῶν ἀρετῶν φύσει ἡμῖν ἐγγίνεται (Eth. Nic II 1, p. 1103 a 19). Virtue and vice are independent of nature: δυνατοὶ μέν ἐσμεν φύσει, ἀγαθοὶ δὲ ἢ κακοὶ οὐ γινόμεθα φύσει (Eth. Nic II 4, p. 1106 a 9f.). Although one may speak of a δίκαιον φυσικόν (to which e.g. belongs love between husband and wife, cf. Eth. Nic V 10, p. 1134b), the knowledge of virtue belongs to the Logos which Nature has given to men for this purpose (Polit I 2, p. 1253 a 9ff.). To be sure, it was Nature who endowed man with the Logos,

---

[1]) The characterization of the Sophists' teaching about nature in the statement of Hippias in Plato's Protagoras 337 c-d is essentially the same.
[2]) Cf. e.g. Plato, Respublica II 374 e; but also Aristotle, Polit. VII 13 p. 1332a 39f

and, thus, man is φύσει πολιτικὸν ζῷον (Polit I 2, p. 1253 a 2f.). But far from drawing from Nature any criteria or laws, Logos and Nous as the true sources of law and art (τέχνη) are rather the fulfillment of Nature's purpose (τῆς φύσεως τέλος Polit VII 15, p. 1334 b 14f.).

IV

The goal of *Stoic Philosophy* was to overcome the split between Physis and Logos. This certainly had to include reconciliation of Physis and τέχνη (the human ability to create things through his mind and his skill): Nature is the master technician whom man imitates. Whether such a view also implied the reconciliation of Physis and Nomos is more than doubtful. Nomos is a social and political category. Concerns in this realm, for the Stoics, were only preliminary and without ultimate value. The real concern for the truly wise man was with the positive correlation of reason and nature (λόγος and φύσις), whereas the relation of law and nature was still seen as an irreconcilable antithesis.

It is necessary to emphasize here that the oldest form of the Stoic Telos formula in Zeno does not contain the term φύσις, but was simply: τέλος... τὸ ὁμολογουμένως ζῆν,[1]) and is to be translated "to live in agreement with the Logos."[2]) Zeno's aim was to express the agreement with man's essential self, i.e. the Logos. The intention of the formula, thus, is to express harmony qua harmony and not agreement with something else outside, as e.g. with certain laws of nature. It was Cleanthes who added to Zeno's formula the term φύσις, thereby eliminating the awkwardness of Zeno's impossible etymology of ὁμολογουμένως and creating what was to become the classical form of the Telos formula: τέλος ἐστὶ τὸ ὁμολογουμένως τῇ φύσει ζῆν.[3]) Through this alteration the divine nature of all things, rather than the specific nature of man (the Logos), became the ultimate criterion for man's moral decision. The divine nature of all things, however, is by no means identical with the external world of natural appearances. As

---

[1]) vArnim I 54, 24; cf. for the history and interpretation of the Telos formula M. Pohlenz, Die Stoa I (1948), p. 116; II (2nd ed. 1955), p. 67f.; G. Bornkamm, ʽΟΜΟΛΟΓΙΑ, *Hermes* 71 (1936), p. 338-393; H. Jonas, *Augustin und das paulinische Freiheitsproblem* (2nd ed. 1965), 27-29. A useful compilation of the various forms of the τέλος formula is given by Clem. Alex. Strom II 129, lff.

[2]) It is known that Zeno understood the word ὁμολογουμένως (= conformably, admittedly) to express the thought "conforming with the logos", or he may have understood the word to mean simply "to live consistently".

[3]) Cleanthes fragment 552, vArnim I, p. 125, 18ff.

the further development of the Telos formula demonstrates, "according to nature" means "according to man's nature which is reason"; cf. e.g. Panaetius: "to live according to the inclinations which are given to us by nature" (ἐκ φύσεως ἀφορμαί)[1]) similarly in Epictetus where "to live according to nature" is understood as "to live λογικῶς" = "after the manner of the Logos" (Diss. III 1, 25). The Logos which man has received from nature and which thereby is his true "nature" enables him to the right use of the perceptions (χρῆσις τῶν φαντασιῶν, Diss. I 28, 12) and thus to find his moral purpose (προαίρεσις Diss. I 4,18). Consequently, man finds his true nature in the agreement with internalized reason.

At the same time, moral decision is primarily characterized in its form, but not in its content, according to an explicit code of moral values. The question as to the content of the life "according to nature" is answered by the statement that it is righteousness which comes from God and out of the "common nature" (κοινὴ φύσις).[2]) If the goal is "to do everything in our power, continuously and steadfastly, in order to achieve what is principally according to [our] nature" (τῶν προηγουμένων κατὰ φύσιν),[3]) then the goal is found in man's acting according to nature as such and in the development of his own nature, but not in the things that are according to nature in the manner of independent or external laws of moral values.[4]) Following this maxim, man does not transcend his own self through an encounter with a greater challenge, but only becomes what he already is.

It is not surprising to find that Stoicism would not attempt to produce any independent set of moral values and would not establish the claim to possess the knowledge of the law of nature in any way whatsoever. It is "according to nature" that a man accept his social and political role, whatever that may happen to be (general, husband, father, etc.), i.e. Stoicism accepts any existing order, and only requires that man in such state behaves "according to nature" (ἐν ταύτῃ τῇ ὕλῃ κατὰ φύσιν ἔχοντα αὑτὸν τηρεῖν Epict. Diss. IV, 5,6). And to say that it

---

[1]) Quoted in Clem. Alex. Strom. II 129; cf. also: "All men by nature have inclinations towards virtue" Cleanthes fragment 566 (vArnim I 129, 18f.).

[2]) Chrysippus fragment 68 (vArnim II 17, 4-7); fr 326 (vArnim III, 80, 34-36). Cf. also the frequent identification of τὸ κατὰ φύσιν ζῆν with τὸ καλῶς ζῆν, τὸ καλὸν κἀγαθόν, ἀρετὴ καὶ τὸ μέτοχον ἀρετῆς, e.g. vArnim II 6,16ff.; 6,7ff.

[3]) Antipater fr. 57 (vArnim III 252, 39-253, 1.

[4]) The moral orientation according to the appearances of external nature are only τὰ πρῶτα κατὰ φύσιν (like health, strenght, etc.), and thus only a preliminary stage towards the things which are truly according to nature, i.e. τὰ περὶ τὴν ψυχὴν κατὰ φύσιν ὄντα. Cf. vArnim III, 34, 14-18; 33, 14-16.

is against nature (παρὰ φύσιν), if a man goes to bed with his neighbor's wife and destroys his marriage,[1]) does not require recourse to any doctrine of natural law—and no Stoic believed that it did.

The term "natural law" is, thus, almost totally absent from Stoic writings. It is quite certain that Zeno never used this term. He, as well as Chrysippus, would rather speak of the λόγος ὀρθός or the νόμος κοινός,[2]) although Chrysippus could say that the δίκαιον does not exist on the basis of arbitrary determination (θέσει) but on the basis of nature (φύσει), as do the Nomos and the ὀρθὸς λόγος.[3]) There is only one passage which approaches the term "law of nature": "The world is the city of Gods and men, since they share the followship of the Logos which is law by nature" (ὅς ἐστι φύσει νόμος). This passage, however, is of a somewhat doubtful origin; it is quoted by Eusebius praep. ev. XV 15 from Arius Didymus, a first century B.C. doxographer, although it is commonly ascribed to Chrysippus.[4])

All evidence for the concept "natural law" in Stoicism comes from Cicero or from Philo. Cicero de nat. deor. I 36 says: *Zeno naturalem legem divinam esse censet eamque vim obtinere recta imperantem prohibitenque contraria.*[5]) It has already been observed that other Latin sources for the same sentence of Zeno, Lactantius, Instit. div. I 5, and Minucius Felix, Octav. 19,10, are dependent upon Cicero and, thus, have no value as independent witnesses.[6]) This quote from Cicero is obviously a translation of the frequently quoted Stoic sentence about the "constitution" (νόμος) of the universe which is said to be the λόγος ὀρθός or λόγος φύσεως προστακτικὸς μὲν ὧν πρακτέον, ἀπαγορευτικὸς δὲ ὧν οὐ ποιητέον[7]) which otherwise, even in Cicero, is translated with: *lex est ratio summa*, or: *recta ratio*.[8]) In particular the Greek phrase λόγος φύσεως apparently has given rise to the Latin *lex naturalis*, since the precise translation *ratio naturae* seems to be absent in Latin Stoic sources. Thus, what actually corresponds to the Latin *lex* in the term *lex naturalis* is not the Greek term νόμος, but the Greek λόγος.

---

[1]) Zeno fragment 244 (vArnim I 58, 13-15).
[2]) There is overwhelming evidence for the technical use of these two terms in Stoic writings; cf. vArnim I 43, 1f.; III 4, 2f.; 81, 23f.; 158, 10f. 18-20.
[3]) Fragment 308 (vArnim III 76, 4f.).
[4]) vArnim II 169, 26-29.
[5]) Cf. vArnim I 42 35-37.
[6]) Cf. R. M. Grant, *op. cit.* p. 21.
[7]) Stobaeus, Ecloge II 7 (Wachsmuth p. 96=vArnim III 158, 11-13); Philo de Josepho 29 (=vArnim III 79, 38-41); cf. Clem. Alex. Strom. I 166,5 where Clem. refers to those who identify the λόγος ὀρθός with the law of the Old Testament.
[8]) Cicero de legibus I 6, 18; 15, 42 (=vArnim III 78, 2-4; 79, 9).

There are, in fact, two occurrences of the Greek νόμος φύσεως in Epictetus, Diss. I 29,19 and II 17,6. In both instances Epictetus quotes as a Law of Nature the same proverbial triviality, namely that the one who has something has more than the one who has nothing (τὸν κρείττονα τοῦ χείρονος πλέον ἔχειν). This confirms the fact that even in Stoic thought, the concept of a "law of nature" which is the superior guide and criterion for morality and institutional law does not exist.

It is true that on occasion νόμος can be used to designate the constitution of the universe and the rule through which Zeus governs all things, as e.g. in the famous Zeus Hymn of Cleanthes: Ζεῦ, φύσεως ἀρχηγέ, νόμου μέτα πάντα κυβερνῶν[1]) ("Zeus, the beginning of the world of nature is from you; and with law you rule over all things"). But with respect to moral values, Stoicism has not overcome the deep-rooted Greek antithesis of Nomos and Physis. Neither does nature, although of divine dignity in Stoicism, ever have the status of a divine legislator; nor could law lose its connotation of existing by "thesis" (i.e. by enacted agreement and contract), and, thus, it does not quite agree with all things which exist by "physis".

V

Compared to the rare and problematic occurrences of the term "law of nature" in Greek literature (not even half a dozen in all extant Greek literature of pre-Christian times) the evidence from Philo of Alexandria is overwhelming: there are at least thirty occurrences of νόμος φύσεως in his works; in addition there a numerous equivalent formulations such as θεσμοὶ φύσεως, διάταγμα φύσεως, νόμιμα φύσεως.

As we have seen, it is not possible to posit a Greek background for Philo's frequent use of the term "law of nature,"[2]) and it seems more advisable to understand this term as a fruit of Philo's efforts to unite basic elements of Jewish tradition with the inheritance of Greek thought. Does the formulation of the concept "law of nature" have its origin in this process of amalgamation of Greek and Jewish thought? In order to answer this question it is convenient to begin with a few remarks about the term "nature" in Philo's writings.

---

[1]) vArnim I p. 121, 35.
[2]) It is very unlikely that Philo should have developed his concept of the law of nature on the basis of any of the very rare occurrences of this term in older Greek literature, even if he knew "Ocellus" who uses the term once in a way very similar to Philo's usage; cf. above p. 523, note 5.

As is well known, the word φύσις has no Hebrew equivalent in the Old Testament. The word occurs more or less occasionally only in such books of the LXX which were composed originally in Greek (Wisdom of Solomon, 3 and 4 Maccabees). It is also used in a few passages of the Testaments of the Twelve Patriarchs, notably in Test. Naphth. 3,4f. which says that the order of nature (τάξις φύσεως) has been perverted by the guardians of Gen. 6:1-6 and by the Sodomites. It is quite typical that this refers to sexual perversion which is perhaps the only violation of a moral value that, ever since Plato, has been characterized consistently as "against nature" (παρὰ φύσιν).[1])

Philo is the first Jewish writer who uses the word φύσις more frequently and more specifically. In fact, φύσις is one of the most regularly employed terms throughout his writings. In this usage it is also apparent that Philo has directly borrowed a number of specific meanings and particular connotations from Greek philosophical conceptions of nature, notably from Aristotle.[2]) Nevertheless, the Greek concept of nature in the process of this adaption has been re-evaluated. In Philo, the Aristotelian conception of the *natura creatrix* was combined with the Jewish belief in the Creator God. Thus, the Greek view of the universe as an impersonal yet harmonious and inventive nature was merged with the Old Testament doctrine of creation.

Erwin Goodenough has shown[3]) that there are numerous occasions where Philo's discourse about nature, almost unnoticed, passes over into speaking about God, and vice versa. One example must suffice: "Nature gives a thousand gifts to men, although she has no part in them; she is unborn, yet gives birth, etc. ... [she gives] a happy old age and a happy death, and yet in neither has nature any share... Even the phrase "as a man" (Deut. 1,31) is not used of God in the literal sense... Separate, therefore, my soul, all that is created, mortal, mutable, profane, from thy conception of God, the uncreated, the immutable, the immortal" (Sacr. Abel et Cain 98ff.).[4])

Thus, the predicates which are alloted to God can also be given to nature and the terms God and Nature are often interchangeable. Traditional statements about the divine creation and preservation of

---

[1]) Against homosexual intercourse Plato Leges VIII 836c; cf. II 636b; Josephus c. Ap. II 273; Athenaeus 13, p. 605d; and more often.

[2]) On the use of the term φύσις in Philo cf. especially E. Goodenough, *By Light Light* (1932), p. 50ff. and passim; H. A. Wolfson *Philo* I (1948), p. 332-347; II (1947), p. 165-200.

[3]) *Op. cit.* p. 51.

[4]) Other instances are Rer. Div. Her. 114-116; Fuga 170-172; Spec. Leg. II 172f.

the world, regardless of their Greek or Jewish provenience are sometimes assigned to nature, sometimes to God. The creation of the world by God is interpreted in terms of Aristotle's description of the *natura creatrix*,[1]) and about the creation of man Philo can say that Nature created all men free (Vit Cont. 70),—a clear reflection of a sophistic tenet. On the other hand, statements about God's ordering of the world by means of legislation (before and through Moses) can now be described as activities of "Nature".[2])

In this syncretistic process of adaptation of Greek concepts the notions of a divine legislator and of a divinely sanctioned law are apparently a genuinely Jewish contribution. This can be observed in the adjustments which Philo makes in his reproductions of Stoic concepts.

In Jos. 29-31 Philo reproduces the well known Stoic topic about the world, the Megalopolis of Gods and Men. He repeats the traditional statement that the (ὀρθὸς) λόγος φύσεως is the constitution and law (πολιτεία and νόμος) of this city. But then he introduces the term θεσμοὶ φύσεως when he speaks about the rejection of the laws of the universe by men and their replacement by man-made laws. The use of θεσμός in this context is striking, since it is an archaic word that denotes the act of divine or human legislation (e.g. by Solon, or in such terms as θεσμοὶ ἀρχαῖοι, πάτριοι θεσμοί).[3]) It was not a word in ordinary usage in Hellenistic Greek,[4]) and the older Stoics did not use it.[5]) This is not surprising since θεσμός refers to an act of legislation and implies the notion of a lawgiver which would not accord with the Stoic concept of the ὀρθὸς λόγος φύσεως; cf. also Chrysippus' statement φύσει τε τὸ δίκαιον εἶναι καὶ μὴ θέσει.[6])

In another passage, Opif. Mund. 143, Philo is even more explicit. After the mention of the φύσεως ὀρθὸς λόγος as the constitution of the

---

[1]) Cf. E. Goodenough, *op. cit.* 51.

[2]) There is a conflicting concept in Philo where he sees "nature" as subject to God, limited and inferior. But this is not our concern here.

[3]) Cf. Liddell-Scott sv.

[4]) F. Preisigke, *Wörterbuch der griechischen Papyrusurkunden* (1925) lists only an occurrence of the word in a Byzantine Papyrus.

[5]) vArnim, Vet. Stoic. Fr. lists two occurrences; one of them (vol. III, p. 82,32) is a passage from Philo (op. Mund. 143, see below); the second is Dio Chrysostom's reproduction of the above Stoic topic (vArnim, vol. III, p. 82,18) where θεσμὸς is used parallel to νόμος. This writer, who flourished half a century after Philo, is also the first pagan writer to use the term "law of nature" in a pregnant sense (although there is only one occurrence of the term in his writings; see above p. 523, note 6).

[6]) vArnim Vet. Stoic. Fr. III 76, 4f.

universe, he adds: "this should be more properly called an ordinance (θεσμός), since it is a divine law (νόμος θεῖος ὤν), in accordance with which there was duly apportioned to all existences that which falls to them severally." It is unmistakable that Philo prefers the terms νόμος and θεσμός as also that his concept in these passages is quite un-Stoic. E. Goodenough has already observed, commenting on Opif. Mund. 143, that nature here is not the nature of things, but it is the nature of God who stands in direct opposition to the world of existing things and imposes his law upon them.[1]) The law of nature is not an immanent law, but it is the law of the transcendent creator who rules his creation φύσεως νόμοις καὶ θεσμοῖς (Opif. Mund. 171).[2])

If Philo can speak of "following nature" (φύσει ἕπεσθαι, ἀκολουθία φύσεως) as the truly right way of life, distinguished from those things which often people suppose to be right (Spec. Leg. IV 46), he is simply quoting a common Stoic thought. However, instead of juxtaposing the everchanging laws of the nations with nature,[3]) Philo also contrasts these human laws with the laws (νόμιμα)[4]) of Moses "which stand firm, unshaken... stamped with the seals of nature herself." (Vit. Mos. II 13f.).

There can be no doubt that for Philo the law of nature is the Torah, and that the new term "law of nature" was designed to express a new concept which did not exist before in the Hellenistic world: "that the Father and Maker of the world was in the truest sense also its Law-giver (νομοθέτης)" and "that he who would observe the laws (νόμοι = law of Moses) will accept gladly the duty of following nature and live in accordance with the ordering of the universe" (Vit. Mos. II 48).[5]) Only if the impact of Jewish belief in the Law of Moses is considered, it can be explained that the earliest formulation of natural law in Greek literature can find its appropriate expression in a sentence that

---

[1]) Op. cit., p. 51f.
[2]) Cf. Praem. Poen. 42; Spec. Leg. III 189; also the fragment quoted by Eusebius, Praep. Ev. VIII 14,3.
[3]) Cf. Jos. 29-31.
[4]) The term τὰ νόμιμα is again (see above on θεσμός p. 532) an archaizing term which was not part of the Stoic vocabulary. It was used in particular as an equivalent of νόμοι in the meaning of "customs", "practices", (cf. the title of Aristotle's treatise "Barbarian Customs"), and is, thus, a precise parallel to νόμος in contrast to φύσις in the terminology of the Greek Physicians (see above p. 525). The term, however, is frequent in the LXX, usually in the singular as translation of חֹק and חֻקָּה (especially in the phrase νόμιμον αἰώνιον Ex. 12,14.17; 27,21 etc.), a few times in the plural for תּוֹרָה (Gen. 26,5; Jer. 33,4; Ez. 43,11; 44,5.24 etc.).
[5]) Translation by F. H. Colson in Loeb Classical Library.

is a monstrosity within the Greek concepts of law and nature: "For law is an invention of nature, not of men" (νόμος γάρ ἐστι φύσεως εὕρημα ἀλλ' οὐκ ἀνθρώπων) Quaest. in Gen. IV 90.[1])

The fundamental Greek antithesis of law and nature is overcome here by virtue of the Jewish belief in the universality of the Law of God. The new antithesis has now become that of the "law of nature" and the numerous laws of men; this is exemplified in many instances of Philo's writings. He who looks up to semblance (τὸ δοκεῖν) writes up laws which are in opposition to those of nature (νόμους ἐναντίους τοῖς τῆς φύσεως - about Jethro as distinct from Moses) Ebrietas 37; cf. about Laban ὃς τοὺς ἀληθεῖς τῆς φύσεως νόμους οὐ κατιδὼν ψευδογραφεῖ τοὺς παρὰ ἀνθρώπους Ebrietas 47. In these passages, the traditional Greek contrast between written and unwritten law is renewed; that the Law of Moses, the representative of the true law of nature, is also written is only for the benefit of later generations. In the true sense, it is written on the "tables of nature" (Spec. Leg. I 31; cf. Abr. 60).

On the other hand, the contrast to the obedience to the law of nature can also be described in traditional Jewish terms of sin and disobedience (cf. Somn. II 174) or as παρανομία (Spec. Leg. I 155).[2]) Fulfillment of the law is at the same time understood as harmony with nature. But although Philo uses the Stoic term ὀρθὸς λόγος τῆς φύσεως in this context, he does not intend to suggest the Stoic thought of harmony with one's own true self. The logos of nature is that which pours out ablutions into the souls of those who love him (Spec. Leg. I 191); thus harmony is agreement with the divinely ordained νόμοι καὶ θεσμοί τῆς φύσεως in a life truly blameless with respect to the law of God (Spec. Leg. I 202).

When Philo speaks about the life that follows nature, the men of old are his primary examples, especially Abraham, whose life and obedience is often described in well known Greek terms. When "Abraham journeys, even as the Lord spoke to him," he follows the aim extolled

---

[1]) On the other hand, Philo is fully aware of the traditional Greek distinctions. He employs them, e.g., in the interpretation of the words προστάγματα, ἐντολαί, δικαιώματα, νόμιμα Gen. 26,5, where he says that "the δικαιώματα exist φύσει, but the νόμιμα exist θέσει, thus, since things existing by nature are older than those existing by convention, that which is right (τὸ δίκαιον) is older than the law." (Quaest. in Gen. IV 184).

[2]) When Philo says here that παρανομεῖν carries its punishment in itself, he repeats a Sophistic sentence about the violation of the things of nature; see above, p. 525.

by the best philosophers: τὸ ἀκολούθως τῇ φύσει ζῆν (Migr. Abr. 127f.).[1]) But this does not mean that Abraham is subject to a guide other than the Torah, even though he sojourned before Moses gave the law. It is precisely the Torah as the divine law of nature that is his guide: the ἄγραφος νόμος..., ὃν ἡ φύσις ἔθηκε (Abr. 16). The Greek notion of an unwritten law is strangely altered in this formulation, since it is presented as the result of a divine legislation which includes all laws and commands (i.e. of the Torah), albeit unwritten. Thus Abraham is characterized by a passage that recalls typical Greek phrases but actually describes an exemplary observer of the Law of the Old Testament. Moses confirms that "this man did the divine law and all the divine commands" (τὸν θεῖον νόμον καὶ τὰ θεῖα προστάγματα πάντα); he was not taught by written words, but by unwritten nature (ἀλλ' ἀγράφῳ τῇ φύσει...); he was law-abiding (νόμιμος) being himself law and unwritten statute (νόμος αὐτὸς ὢν καὶ θεσμὸς ἄγραφος), Abr. 275f.

However, this theory about the unwritten Torah being available to the men of old before the legislation of Moses does not serve as merely a convenient stopgap for that period in history between Creation and Moses. The theory has much wider ramifications and consequences for the understanding of law and of a truly law abiding life. It produces the extremely momentous insight that a true law of nature is in fact an ultimately superior criterion for the life of the truly wise man. Thus, Philo's aim is to show that such a divine law is recognizable, if only one can synthesize the (Greek) concept of nature's right reason and the (Jewish) knowledge of the Torah of God—those two seen as one: the "law of nature."

Such a synthesis is present and personified in the men of old who lived κατὰ νόμον, τὸν ὀρθὸν φύσεως λόγον (Quod Omn. Prob. Lib. 62). Especially Philo's introduction to his treatise on Abraham sets forth the principles of this concept (Abr. 3-6): The more universal (καθολικώτεροι) laws are those which existed before the written legislation of Moses. They are the originals (ἀρχέτυποι) of the particular laws given through Moses, which Philo calls their copies (εἰκόνες). Since the men of old have followed the archetypal unwritten legislation (ἄγραφος νομοθεσία), holding that nature itself was the most ancient statute (τὴν φυσὶν αὐτὴν...πρεσβύτατον θεσμὸν εἶναι), these men are ἔμψυχοι καὶ λογικοὶ νόμοι. The particular and written legislation of Moses appears

---

[1]) The same sentence is quoted with explicit reference to Zeno in Quod Omn. Prob. Lib. 160; cf. Plant 49. Furthermore cf. Vt. Mos. I 48 about Moses who had set before himself the ὀρθὸς τῆς φύσεως λόγος, the only source and fountain of virtues.

as that which is "not inconsistent with nature" (τὰ τεθειμένα διατάγματα τῆς φύσεως οὐκ ἀπᾴδει).

But this particular legislation did not preclude the possibility of direct access to the laws of nature; on the contrary, it is the immediate representative of nature's law and leads the wise man into the following of nature; cf. e.g. Philo's conclusion about the meaning of the first commandment: God gave this commandment to lead the human race "that following nature (ἕπεσθαι τῇ φύσει) they might win the best of goals (τέλος!), knowledge of him that truly is" (Decal. 81; cf. Poster. Cain. 185). A righteous man is one who follows nature and her ordinances (Spec. Leg. II 42). The law abiding true citizen of the world regulates his doings by the will of nature (βούλημα τῆς φύσεως Opif. Mund. 3).

There is perhaps one particular reason for the designation of the Torah as the law of nature. Since this is the archetypal law it is part of the world of reason as distinct from the sphere of sense perception. In this respect Philo's concept of the law of nature is an integral part of the Platonic (not Stoic!) structure of his philosophy. It is, therefore, specifically the mind (νοῦς) which is taught by the law of nature and, therefore, enabled to guide the soul (Agric. 66). Obedience to the laws of nature is identical with pruning away the superfluous passions from the mind (ἡγεμονικόν Spec. Leg. I 305f., cf. I 191).

But on the whole, this Philonic identification of Torah, divine order, and nature's law is rooted in his understanding of the unity of all realms of human experience. The Greek concept of the world assigned fundamentally different qualities to the two realms of human experience, to the realm of man's activity—the law—on the one hand, and to the world of nature on the other; and even the monistic system of the Stoics was unable to overcome this dichotomy, or, rather: the Stoics sacrificed large portions of the realm of law, since they declared that the region of political and social involvement was ultimately irrelevant. Philo, on the contrary, knows only one realm of human experience, which can be variously characterized either through his concept of God, or through the investigation of nature, or through the interpretation of the legislation of Moses. But in every case, the one and only unifying principle remains the Torah, the law par excellence.[1]

---

[1] On this Jewish apologetic concept of the Torah in which the "basic identity of the understanding of God, world, and human existence is defined" see G. Bornkamm, Die Offenbarung des Zornes Gottes, in: *Das Ende des Gesetzes* (2nd

A final problem that has to concern us is the question of the particular content of specific laws of nature, or specific implications of the law of nature, to which Philo refers on many occasions. That there will be any individual sets of commandments which are law or laws of nature in particular, seems to be quite unlikely.[1]

That the law of nature is understood as the law of number may reveal Pythagorean influence upon Philo.[2] According to the laws of nature, the number 6 is most suitable for productivity; thus, the creation of the world in six days (Opif. Mund. 13). Since six is three times two (= male and female), "these two were the source of origin κατὰ φύσεως θεσμοὺς ἀκινήτους" (Spec. Leg. II 58).[3] The celebration of the seventh day, accordingly, was ordered by Moses for all who were inscribed on his holy roll of citizenship (of the universe) and who followed the θεσμοὶ φύσεως (Vit. Mos. II 211).

Specific structures in the functioning of the world or in the life of men are often called law of nature. Sometimes such structures are part of Philo's philosophical and theological tenets, and not necessarily the result of his observation of nature.[4] Thus, sense perception appears as the handmaiden of reason "by the laws of nature" (Vit. Mos. II 81).[5]

---

ed. 1958), p. 14f.—E. Goodenough, *op. cit.*, p. 49 has emphasized that nature and its laws sometimes seem to be placed above the Torah and the world, and, on occasion, even above God; but it appears to me that these observations only describe inconsistencies of secondary importance and functional distinctions; this is the case, e.g. when the relation of the archetypal law to the legislation of Moses is seen in terms of a Platonic schema.

[1] About the relationship of Philo's laws of nature to the so called Noachite laws, cf. Wolfson, *op. cit.*, II, p. 183-187. Although a certain similarity cannot be denied, the scope of Philo's term is much wider. One might also ask whether the Rabbinic concept of the Noachite laws is related to Philo insofar as both depend upon the tradition of Jewish apologetics.

[2] E. Goodenough, *op. cit.*, p. 52f. has pointed out that this challenges the sovereignty of God, since even God, in his work of creation, is subject to the superior rule of certain numerical laws. This consequence is, of course, not intended by Philo.

[3] Cf. also on the male-female principle Spec. Leg. II 29f.; Ebriet. 33f.

[4] There are also some general rules which Philo calls "law of nature", e.g. that the place of creation is in all respects lower than the creator, since that which is made is later than its maker (Plant. 132); or: "the wise man by the law of nature has all fools in subjection." (Quod. Omn. Prob. Lib. 30). These rules are similar to the law about superiority and inferiority which is called a law of nature in Epictetus (see above, p. 530). In those instances Philo is perhaps reflecting a proverbial usage of the term; cf. also the quote of the people's excuse for the suicide of Tiberius Gemellus forced by Gaius: "Sovereignty cannot be shared; that is a θεσμὸς φύσεως ἀκίνητος." (Leg. Gaj. 68).

[5] Cf. also the reference to the Virgin Charites (representing the four faculties

That the creator cares for the creation since this is necessary because of nature's laws and ordinances (Opif. Mund. 171; Praem. Poen. 42)[1]) is primarily a theological sentence, even if it is supported by the reference to parents who normally care for their children.[2])

But usually the common sense observation of the natural order is the main point of reference, e.g. in the statement about the firmly established seasons for fruits and crops, which Philo calls φύσεως προθεσμία (Spec. Leg. IV 208), φύσεως νόμιμα (ibid. 212), or φύσεως θεσμοί (ibid. 215).

Here, as well as in the following instances, the reference to the laws of nature purports to argue that certain laws given by Moses are absolutely necessary and indispensible. In the interpretation of Ex. 23:26a ("There shall not be in thee anyone infertile or barren") Philo relates Moses' and nature's law in a very characteristic way which, again, expresses the harmony of his understanding of law, nature and man: For those who keep the divine writing of the law, God grants as a prize the more ancient law of immortal nature (παρέχει τὸν ἀρχαιότερον νόμον τῆς ἀθανάτου φύσεως), i.e. the begetting of sons and the perpetuity of the race (Quaest. Ex. II 19). At the same time, the injunction to produce children is called a "law of nature" (Praem. Poen 108; cf. Abr. 249; Spec. Leg. II 233).[3])

Other laws that are based on the law of nature in a similar way are: the law of inheritance, from parents to children and not vice versa, since children do not naturally die before their parents (Vit. Mos. II 245; cf. Migr. Abr. 94).[4]) The law against killing infants at birth is given, since to do this would tear down what nature builds up, and this violates the laws of nature (Virtut. 132; Spec. Leg. III 112). A similar argument appears with respect to the general law against killing (Decal. 132).

---

of king, lawgiver, high priest, and prophet, as they are combined in Moses) "which an immovable law of nature forbids to be separated" (Vit. Mos. II 7).

[1]) Different is Spec. Leg. III 189 where Philo speaks of the Creator's care for his creation by means of the law of nature; cf. the fragment in Eusebius, Praep. Ev. VIII 14,3.

[2]) That "his creation is itself necessitated by a Law of Nature which seems to antecede it, at least logically" (Goodenough, op. cit., 53), is, of course, quite right; but this statement only emphasizes the harmony which is part of Philo's unity of the understanding of God, world and law.

[3]) See also the reason for the law against touching a woman when the menstrual issue occurs, since the seed would be wasted; thus this law was given in order to respect the law of nature (Spec. Leg. III 32).

[4]) Cf. also the use of the term νόμος φύσεως opposed to the ἀνομία among men, in the allegory about the right of the firstborn who represents virtue, Sobr. 25.

There are a great number of instances where Philo uses the traditional Greek phrases κατὰ φύσιν and παρὰ φύσιν in his discussion of the laws given by Moses, although it is not possible to discuss these passages in detail in this context. These two terms in Philo became precise equivalents of "lawful" (νόμιμος etc.) and "unlawful" (ἄνομος etc.). It is remarkable, however, that in Philo the use of κατὰ/παρὰ/φύσιν in the moral sense is not limited to sexual matters as is normally the case in Greek literature.[1]) However, this is one of the three topics, in which Philo continues the traditional Greek reference to nature. The other two are arguments against the breeding of animals of different species, and, finally, the argument against slavery. But in these cases as well, the use of the term "law of nature" is specifically Philonic.[2])

With the designation of the sin of the Sodomites as a violation of the law of nature Philo repeats a traditional argument of Jewish apologetics (Abr. 135).[3]) Similarly, the passions of love between man and woman are described as the fulfillment of the laws of nature; the opposite is homosexuality (Vit. Cont. 59.).[4])

Philo also calls it a law of nature that unequal animals should not be yoked together (Spec. Leg. IV 204; cf. Dt. 22:10). But he goes further than the Mosaic law suggests when he not only repeats the injunction against breeding different kinds of animals (Lev. 19:19), since it is against a δόγμα φύσεως to do so (Spec. Leg. III 46), but also applies this specifically to the breeding of mules (Spec. Leg. III 47). In this specification of the law, Philo perhaps depends upon Greek tradition, since Aristotle had already pointed out that it is against nature for a horse to beget a mule.[5])

Also the interpretation of the law against slavery reveals Greek influence upon Philo. That nature has borne and reared all men alike

---

[1]) Cf. e.g. Diod. Sic. 32, 10, 4; Athenaeus 13 p. 605d; also Josephus c. Ap. II 273.

[2]) See the different terms in a corresponding usage in one instance in Plato with respect to sexual morality: to introduce a law against homosexuality ἀκολουθῶν τῇ φύσει Plato Leg. VIII 836c.

[3]) Cf. Test. Naphth. 3,4f.; see above p. 530.

[4]) In another instance Philo says that men who belie their sex are affected with effeminateness, since they debase "the currency of nature" (τὸ νόμισμα φύσεως Spec. Leg. I 325; cf. III 38). The same term is used parallel to θεσμὸς φύσεως and ἕπεσθαι τοῖς τῆς φύσεως βουλήμασι in an argument against the beholding of the nakedness of the other sex (Spec. Leg. III 176). This argument is, of course, as convincing as St. Paul's argument from nature for the short hair of men and the long hair of women (1 Cor. 11:14f.).

[5]) Aristotle, Metaph. VII 8, p. 1033b 32f.

as brothers is an old Sophistic statement[1]) which Philo echoes when he describes the Essenes who denounce slaveholders, since they violate the equality of all men and act against an ordinance of nature (θεσμὸς φύσεως, Quod. Omn. Prob. Lib. 79).[2])

VI

It seems that there can be little doubt that Philo has to be considered as the crucial and most important contributor to the development of the theory of natural law. Most probably, Philo was its creator, at least insofar as the evidence from the Greek literature is in question. Only a philosophical and theological setting in which the Greek concept of nature was fused with the belief in a divine legislator and with a doctrine of the most perfect (written!) law could produce such a theory, and only here could the Greek dichotomy of the two realms of law and nature be overcome. All these conditions are fulfilled in Philo, and the evidence for the development of this theory of the law of nature in Philo is impressive.

The still unanswered problem is the Roman concept of *lex naturalis* which is apparently developed independently by a productive misunderstanding and mistranslation of a Greek Stoic concept. That this Roman *lex naturalis* later has influenced especially the Latin church as well as Roman and Western Law cannot be doubted. I believe, however, that for the further development of the concept of law of nature in the Early Church, beginning with Clement of Alexandria and Origen, the Philonic doctrine was the most vital element. To show this, of course, would require a fresh analysis of the pertinent texts.[3]) A detailed investigation of the history of Philo's doctrine of the law of nature in the early church is urgently called for, and as far as I can see, it would most probably confirm the results of this study.[4])

---

[1]) Cf. the Antiphon fragment, Pap. Oxyrh. XI 1364 (see above p. 525); see also Philemo Comicus 95, 2-6 (C.A.F. vol. II, p. 502).

[2]) In a similar context (Quod. Omn. Prob. Lib. 37), Philo speaks of the νόμοι φύσεως in contrast to the "laws of the lower world."

[3]) See, however, M. Pohlenz, Stoa II, 218, 222; R. M. Grant, *op. cit.*, passim.

[4]) Even a superficial review of the material in question (now more easily accessible through Lampe's Patristic Lexicon) shows a surprisingly great number of echoes from Philonic passages; examples are frequently drawn from the figures of the Old Testament before Moses; and a number of terms which have been reintroduced into the technical vocabulary by Philo, such as θεσμός and νόμιμα (the latter from LXX), are used very often in these contexts, although they continue to be rare in pagan sources.

Furthermore, the study of the re-evaluation of Greek concepts of nature in the light of Philo's doctrine of the law of nature by the Church Fathers (and also in later pagan writers?)[1]) should be a most rewarding task.

---

[1]) In this connection it would be most important to evaluate the context and origin of the unique and striking reference to the "law of nature which men have forsaken to follow written laws", in Dio Chrys., Or. 80,5 (referred to above, p. 523, n. 6). Is Dio Chrys. dependent upon Philo and Jewish apologetics and propaganda? Or is he influenced by Cicero and Latin Stoic terminology? Or does he just reflect the general temperament of his time?

A SABAZIOS INSCRIPTION FROM SARDIS

BY

SHERMAN E. JOHNSON
Church Divinity School of the Pacific

I

In the summer of 1958, during its first season, the expedition sponsored by Harvard and Cornell Universities and the American Schools of Oriental Research discovered an inscription referring to the god Sabazios.

The inscription is registered in the Sardis catalogue as IN 58.11. It is a fragment of a marble slab, 0.47 m. high, 0.32 wide at its widest point, and 0.15 thick. The inscription consists of parts of six lines. The letters in the first five lines are 0.015 to 0.025 m. high, and the larger letters in the sixth line 0.035 and 0.04 high. The stone was discovered by John Washeba and Halil Akyar, at the western village of Sart Mustafa, House No. 41, in the northwest part of the village, and it was in use as a doorstep toward the courtyard in the back (west) of the house.

The style of lettering of this inscription is very similar to that of one which Buckler and Robinson dated to the time of Eumenes II (197-159 B.C.).[1])

Μη]νοφιλος Μηνοφ [ιλου
φυλ]ης Ευμενηιδος ιε[ρευς
Διος]Σαυαζιου εν τωι γ[αωι
βασι]ληι Ευμενηιδι τον βω[μον
αι θεας

Part of the restorations above were suggested by Prof. George M. A. Hanfmann and the late Prof. A. D. Nock.

II

As background for a discussion of this inscription it seems well to summarize the present state of our knowledge of the Sabazios cult,

---

[1]) W. H. Buckler and D. M. Robinson, *Sardis*, VII, 1 (Leiden, 1932), No. 88.

and it is particularly fitting to do this in a volume dedicated to the memory of Professor Erwin R. Goodenough.

The name of the god takes various forms. The most common is Sabazios (Σαβάζιος, Lat. Sabazius; gen. Sabazis, dat. Sabazi). This occurs in inscriptions found in a cluster of villages in Lydia, surrounding Kula (Koloë) and the Gygaean lake, in Pergamum, Bithynia, Mylasa, various points in Thrace and Moesia, in Rome and Mainz in Germany. It is also the usual form in literary sources. Eisele is no doubt correct in understanding the Greek form as an adjective. The god's native name was probably Sawazis or Savazis, the w-v consonant being represented in Greek by a beta. This accounts for the variant forms Σαουάζιος, Σαυάζιος, Σαοάζος, Σαυάδα and Σαάζιος. Σανβά-[τιος, found in one inscription from a place near Bursa, indicates a shift to the b consonant.[1]) The form Σαβαθικός, however, suggests confusion with the Hebrew *shabbath* or *ṣebaôth*.[2]) Sabadius is also attested in Latin inscriptions and in Apuleius,[3]) and there are variants Sebadius, etc.

The cult of Sabazios was very widespread in antiquity, stretching from central Asia Minor to Thrace, Moesia, the Greek mainland, Italy, and as far as Switzerland, Mainz in the Rhineland, and Belgium.[4]) It is most strongly attested, however, in Phrygia and Lydia, in Thrace and Moesia, and in the region of Rome. The chief Phrygian sites are Blaundos and various places near the Pisidian border, and the evidence of coins indicates Laodiceia on the Lycus, Apameia and Synnada. In Lydia the principal centres are Kula (Koloë), Santal, Üşümüş, Menye (Maeonia), Gölde, Bebekli, and Alaşehir (Philadelphia). Sabazios is known to have been worshipped in Mylasa and Yaikin in Caria, Gebze in Bithynia, and probably at Attaleia in Pamphylia. It has been conjectured that Soatra in Lycaonia was named for the god. The Sabbatistai of Cilicia, to be mentioned later, are not so certainly worshippers of this deity.

---

[1]) Eisele, *s.v.* "Sabazios," in W. H. Roscher (ed.), *Ausfuhrliches Lexikon der griechischen und römischen Mythologie* (Leipzig, 1884-1937), IV, 232-64.
[2]) Μουσεῖον, III (1880), p. 167, No. τλη.
[3]) Apuleius *Metamorphoses* viii. 25.
[4]) The most important treatments consist of Eisele's article, referred to above; Schaefer, *s.v.* "Sabazios," Pauly-Wissowa, *Realencyclopädie*, 2. Reihe, I A, cols. 1540-51; M. P. Nilsson, *Geschichte der griechischen Religion*, 2nd ed. II (Munich, 1961), pp. 621, 658-67; W. O. E. Oesterley in S. H. Hooke (ed.), *The Labyrinth* (London, 1935), pp. 115-58; Nilsson, *Opuscula Selecta*, III (Lund, 1960), 297-303 = *Eranos*, LIV (1956), 167-73. For more recently studied inscriptions, see J. and L. Robert, *Hellenica*, VI (1948), 111-13; VII (1949), 45f.; IX (1950), 7-25; L. Robert, *Anatolia*, III (1958), 112ff.

Popularity of Sabazios worship in Lydia was probably due to the fact that it was an official cult of the Pergamene kings. An important inscription, consisting of a letter of Attalus III to the *boule* and *demos* of Pergamon, B.C. 135-4, indicates that his mother Stratonice, consort of Eumenes II, brought the cult from her homeland, Cappadocia. Here Sabazios is identified with Zeus.[1]) It has been conjectured that Sabazios was the god of the royal family cult of Cappadocia, and corresponded to Dionysos Kathegemon, the family god of the Attalids.

References in Aristophanes show that Sabazios was known in Athens as early as the late fifth century B.C., and was identified with Dionysos.[2]) Greek literature indicates that the cult continued to be popular through the Hellenistic and imperial periods. There is inscriptional evidence from Thera, Sikinos and Delos in the Greek islands, and in an inscription from the Asclepion in Epidaurus there is a dedication by the πυροφορήσας Menophilos in A.D. 186. Most of the references in ancient literature, summarized by Eisele, equate Sabazios and Dionysos, but in Lydia Zeus Sabazios is the common identification. Here he is associated with the mother goddess, Meter Hipta or Artemis Anaïtis, and at Ağlan-köi in Phrygia with Demeter.[3]) The obscure last line on the Sardis inscription mentions a goddess.

III

In art there are two main types of Sabazios. Of these perhaps the Phrygian is the more common. The god is in Phrygian dress and bearded, frequently the hand is raised in the so-called *benedictio latina*, and at times he holds a lance or a pine-cone. He is often pictured with animal figures and various symbols and cult-objects. Many bronze Sabazios hands have been preserved, often covered with these objects. In the other type, Sabazios has the traits of Zeus or Jupiter, for example in reliefs from Blaundos in Phrygia and Nea Aule and the Κολοηνῶν κατοικία in Lydia.

In this connection, an equestrian statue of Zeus, published by Vermeule, is particularly significant.[4]) Here the god has the dis-

---

[1]) M. Fränkel, *Die Inschriften von Pergamon* (Berlin, 1890), No. 248.
[2]) Aristophanes *Wasps* 8f.; *Lysistrata* 388.
[3]) Cf. J. Keil, "Die Kulte Lydiens," in W. H. Buckler and W. M. Calder (eds.), *Anatolian Studies Presented to Sir William Mitchell Ramsay* (Manchester, 1923), pp. 239-67.
[4]) C. Vermeule, "An Equestrian Statue of Zeus," *Bulletin, Museum of Fine Arts, Boston*, LVI, No. 304 (1958), 69-76.

PLATE I

The Sabazios Inscription from Sardis (Photograph by the Author)

tinctive features that are associated with the Phrygian god Mên—the torch, the bovine head under the horse's hoof, the rectangular altar. But whereas in most reliefs, and on many imperial coins. Mên is beardless and wears (like Attis) the pointed Phrygian cap, in the statue being discussed he is bareheaded and is bearded like Zeus, Sarapis and Asklepios. The fact that the god is mounted on horseback suggests Zeus. Evidence, e.g. from a relief studied by Buckler, leads Vermeule to conjecture that this is actually a statue of Zeus Sabazios. The important point to note is that this statue, which might be dated A.D. 160-260, represents a coalescence of two types.

What is known of the cult of Sabazios shows continual syncretism and variation.[1] The earliest full account, that of Demosthenes *de Corona* 259f., indicates that the *thiasos*, adorned with crowns, was led by a priest who carried snakes in his hands.[2] The worshippers called on the name of the god, played Phrygian music, and their dances were similar to those in the cult of the great Mother. There were purifications with clay and meal, and a representation of the hand of the god was used to bless the worshippers.[3] The myth, as recounted by Clement of Alexandria and others, tells of a theogony in which Zeus in the form of a bull mates with the Mother, and afterward in the form of a snake begets on their offspring Kore the god Dionysos-Zagreus-Sabazios. This myth evidently attempts to systematize the connections of Sabazios with Zeus on the one hand and with Dionysos on the other. The snake is a constant element in both cult and myth; for example, Theophratus *Characters* xxviii indicates that the snake is an incarnation or manifestation of the god. While at times in the history of religion the snake can have phallic significance,[4] this can be exaggerated. As Nilsson says, the ceremony of drawing the snake through the bosom of the initiate does not demand the notion of a sacred marriage; the essential point may be simply blessing through direct contact with the god.

The centrality of the serpent in the Sabazios cult must have led to

---

[1] Nilsson, *op. cit.*, II, 658-67. Cf. also Macrobius *Saturnalia* i. 18. 12-15; 23.22. Buckler, *BSA*, XXI (1914-16), 171, quotes an Orphic hymn referring to Samazios, son of Kronos.

[2] Cf. Nilsson, *Opuscula Selecta*, II (Lund, 1952), 531; Sir W. M. Ramsay, *Cities and Bishoprics of Phrygia* (Oxford, 1895-97), I, 290.

[3] For Sabazios hands, cf. Ch. Blinkenberg, *Archäologische Studien* (Copenhagen, 1904), pp. 66ff.; H. Seyrig, *BCH*, LI (1927), 210-14. On the reliefs generally, cf. also E. Will, *Le relief cultuel gréco-romain* (Paris, 1955).

[4] E. R. Goodenough, *Jewish Symbols in the Graeco-Roman Period* (New York, 1953-65), VI, 16f.

connections between Sabazios and other snake deities. It may have been a primary factor in his identification with Zeus, who was often represented as a snake; at the same time his similarity to Mên and association with the great Mother made him the principal male god and therefore this was another factor in equating him with Zeus. Leisegang discusses a singular alabaster bowl, now in New York, and sometimes claimed to be a forgery, in the centre of which is a winged snake twined around an egg-shaped omphalos. From the base of this arise petals or flames and out of these come sixteen male and female figures. The inscription, which is garbled, is from an Orphic poem, and identifies the serpent as Helios-Dionysos-Phanes, who "turns forever the radiant sphere of distant motion that runs around the celestial vortices." Leisegang compares this with the Sabazios relief from Koloë and notes that half of the sixteen worshippers pictured in it hold their right hands on their breasts, as on this bowl, while for reasons of symmetry the others so place their left hands.[1]) Leisegang interprets the sixteen as mystai who "having ascended into heaven and soared over the starry sphere in the ecstasy of their mystery cult, are re-enacting their experience in ritual."[2]) What began as a rather primitive Anatolian cult has now become a highly sophisticated mystery with a cosmology and philosophical, perhaps Gnostic, traits.

If Sabazios became a cosmic deity, it was natural that he should also be connected with the orderly procession of the months and seasons. Goodenough understands the hymn to Month in the Phrygian mysteries of Sabazios as perhaps referring to unmoved and timeless nature.[3]) One element that may enter into this is the character of Mên as a moon-god.

On the other hand, the frescoes in the tomb of Vincentius and Vibia in the catacomb of Praetextatus exhibit quite a different aspect of Sabazios worship in the imperial period. Sabazios and his priests are here obviously Anatolian, clothed in the Phrygian cap, with the chlamys fastened with a brooch, and a belted under-tunic and long tight-fitting trousers. One fresco pictures a banquet in which fish,

---

[1]) H. Leisegang, "The Mystery of the Serpent," in J. Campbell (ed.), *Pagan and Christian Mysteries* (New York, 1963), pp. 3-69 (reprint of a translation of this paper from *Eranos-Jahrbuch*, VII [1939], 151-250).
[2]) *Ibid.*, p. 42.
[3]) Goodenough, *op. cit.*, VIII, 192; cf. G. M. A. Hanfmann, *The Season Sarcophagus in Dumbarton Oaks* (Cambridge, Mass., 1951), I, 142-310. Proclus, the principal authority for the idea, is of course late.

roast fowl and hare are in dishes on the table. The fish had quasi-sacramental meaning in Phrygian religion, and the hare suggests the dismembered Dionysos. Goodenough conjectured that the meal was eaten sacramentally in anticipation of the ultimate banquet.[1]) Here enters in the element of life after death, no doubt connected with the revival of vegetation in the spring. Nilsson believes that it was in Ionia, by identification with such local gods as Sabazios, that Dionysos —originally known in Thrace and Athens as a god of ecstasy—became the more sober deity celebrated in the first century as the child in the basket, the god who rose from the dead in the spring.[2])

IV

Very little of the foregoing helps to explain the tantalizing identifications of Sabazios with Yahweh, the God of the Hebrews and the Jews. Yet evidence for this exists as early as the second century B.C. Valerius Maximus i. 3.2 tells of the charge of the praetor Hispalus (139 B.C.) against *Iudaeos qui Sabazi Iovis cultu Romanos inficere mores conati erant.* Plutarch speculated that the Jewish Sabbath had some relation to Bacchus, because the Bacchi are sometimes called σάβοι, and the Jews drink wine on the Sabbath, often to the point of drunkenness.[3]) Cumont has called attention to the representations of Noah's ark on the coins of Apameia, and Johannes Lydus' identification of Sabaoth and Iao with Dionysos-Sabazios.[4]) It is probable, however, that the earliest identification was with Sabbath rather than Sabaoth.

One wonders how much Plutarch and most other pagans actually knew about the Jews, apart from their abstention from pork, loyalty to their other food laws, and their celebration of the Sabbath.[5]) There is nothing to suggest that the Sabbatistai of Elaiussa in Cilicia were worshippers of a syncretized Yahweh-Sabazios, but why do they not describe themselves as Jews, and why is their god called τὸν θεὸν τὸν Σαββατιστήν? The fact that Yahweh was the supreme God, plus Sabbath worship, might have been sufficient to lead pagans to identify him with Zeus Sabazios.[6])

---

[1]) Goodenough, *op. cit.*, II, 47f.; VIII, 88.
[2]) Nilsson, *op. cit.*, I, 545-50.
[3]) Plutarch *Quaest. conv.* iv. 6.
[4]) F. Cumont, *CRAI*, 1906, pp. 63-79; see also Nilsson, *op. cit.*, II, 662, 664-67, and literature there cited.
[5]) Juvenal iii. 14; vi. 544-47.
[6]) E. L. Hicks, *JHS*, XII (1891), 233f.

Unquestionably there was some Jewish-Sabazian syncretism. Goodenough, for example, calls attention to an amulet with the label Iao Sabaoth, on which the various animals are of the sort one finds on Sabazios hands.¹) While such an object might have been made by a pagan rather than by a Jew, the rabbis warned against making the image of a separate hand or foot.²) Nock suggests that the domestic altar from Pergamon, published by Nilsson, may have been used by a Jew to burn incense, though Delling considers the dedicator to be a "God-fearer."³) The danger of assimilation to paganism was always present. Goodenough is, however, careful not to claim too much. In discussing the tomb of Vincentius and Vibia, he sees no reason to connect the scenes pictured there with Judaism or Christianity.⁴) What is significant is that Jewish art in the Graeco-Roman period often employs the same symbols that one finds in the cults of Dionysos, Mithra, Osiris, the Etruscan gods, Sabazios and Attis.⁵) These were part of a symbolic language used and understood everywhere.

Connections between the God of Israel and θεὸς ὕψιστος have often been discussed. Very little needs to be added to the important article of Roberts, Skeat and Nock on this subject.⁶) Their conclusion was that it was quite natural for pagans to regard any principal deity as the Most High God, and that while both Jews and pagans used the term in referring to the God of Israel, Jewish influence was a contributory, not a decisive, factor.

While dedications to Zeus Hypsistos are very common, in only one known instance is Sabazios called *theos hypsistos*, and this is in a dedication from Sardica set up by a θίασος Σεβαζιανός.⁷) In view of the fact that Theos Hypsistos is found in Lydia, e.g. at Kula, it may be that here also Sabazios was given this honorific. A group of frequently discussed inscriptions uses the terms ἄγγελος or θεῖος ἀγγελικός to

---

¹) Goodenough, *op. cit.*, II, 267.
²) *Ibid.*, IV, 16.
³) Nock, *Gnomon*, XXIX (1957), 524, n. 1; Nilsson, *Eranos*, LIV (1956), 167-73 = *Opuscula Selecta*, III, 297-303; G. Delling, "Die Altarinschrift eines Gottesfürchtigen in Pergamon," *Novum Testamentum*, VII (1964/65), 13-80; E. Bickerman, "The Altar of Gentiles: A Note on the Jewish 'ius sacrum'," "*Revue Internationale des Droits de l'Antiquité,* "3rd Series, V (1958), 137-64.
⁴) Goodenough, *op. cit.*, II, 45-50.
⁵) *Ibid.*, IV, 36f.
⁶) C. Roberts, T. C. Skeat and A. D. Nock, "The Gild of Zeus Hypsistos," *HTR*, XXIX (1936), 39-88.
⁷) A. von Domaszewski, *Archaeologisch-epigraphische Mittheilungen aus Oesterreich-Ungarn*, X (1886), 238f.

refer to Theos Hypsistos. Here there is at least a tenuous contact with Judaism. But, as Sokolowski has shown, the epithets are applied to Zeus, Hecate-Artemis and Hermes. In many cases one cannot tell whether the document using ἄγγελος is pagan, Christian or Jewish. Nevertheless there is a distinct increase in the interest in angelology when Judaism comes in contact with the pagan world.[1])

In the Sardica inscription, Sabazios is called θεὸς ἐπήκοος ὕψιστος. As Nock noted, ἐπήκοος is an attribute of Zeus Hypsistos in the bilingual Palmyrene inscriptions, and in Syria Zeus Hypsistos and Theos Hypsistos are used regularly to refer to the local Baal. An inscription from Ptolemais-Accho in Palestine, published by Avi-Yonah, and dating probably from the second or first century B.C., describes Hadad and Atargatis as θεοὶ ἐπήκοοι.[2])

V

The Sabazios inscription from Sardis almost certainly comes from the time of Eumenes II, at the height of glory of the kingdom of Pergamum, when the great altar of Zeus was built. The dedication suggests that for whatever reason—loyalty to the state or because of religious propaganda—the cult of Zeus in his Sabazios form has spread to Lydia. Here he is no doubt associated with the great Mother, known in Sardis as Cybele or Artemis.

The conjectural restoration in line 2 presumes a tribe Eumeneis, but no such tribe is known from Sabazios inscriptions previously published. If the reading is correct, it must have received its name from Eumenes II. The end of the inscription is even more problematical. There may be a reference to the tribe or to the monarch, but not enough of the text is preserved to give any sense of certainty. Still another possibility is that Zeus Eumenes is mentioned. Zeus in this form was worshipped at Philadelphia in the first century B.C., together with a number of other divinities, in the private sanctuary of a certain Dionysios.[3]) Both freemen and slaves were invited to worship here.

---

[1]) F. Sokolowski, *HTR*, LIII (1960), 225-29. Cf. L. Robert, *Anatolia*, III (1958), 112ff., for an improved edition of the most famous inscription.
[2]) M. Avi-Yonah, *Israel Exploration Journal*, IX (1959), 1-12. The article gives a particularly good bibliography of this epithet, which does not appear in the New Testament.
[3]) W. Dittenberger, *Sylloge inscriptionum graecarum*[3], No. 985.

Menophilos is evidently the person who dedicated the altar.[1]) It is interesting that this name should appear again in connection with the Sabazios cult in Epidaurus in the second century A.D. Perhaps the only significance of this is that it is an Anatolian name.

Nothing in the inscriptions from Sardis and other places in Lydia suggests involvement of Jews or Judaism in the Sabazios cult. It is well known that the Jews of Asia Minor, who were settled there by Zeuxis in great numbers, were loyal to the Seleucids. No doubt they readily transferred their allegiance to the Attalids. The Jews of Apameia may perhaps have conformed their religion to the Dionysiac cult. But, although the royal road connected their city with Sardis, there is no evidence that it was the Jews of the latter city who worshipped Sabazios.

---

[1]) For another dedication of an altar at Sardis, cf. Buckler, *Sardis*, VII, 1, No. 98. An altar was dedicated κατὰ προφητείαν θεοῦ Σαυ[αζίο]υ at Yaikin, 12 km. south-, west of Aphrodisias in Caria; cf. *JHS*, XX (1900), 75, n.4 = *BCH*, XIV (1890), 610, n.5. For another dedication of an altar to Sabazios, cf. an inscription from Pandik, *CIG*, No. 3791; also Domaszewski, *AEM*, X (1886), 241, No. 6. A Menophilos is mentioned in another inscription found at Sardis, IN 58.3 (=NOEX 58.18) in the expedition's catalogue. The name is known from *Sardis*, VII, 1, Nos. 5:8, 23; 120; 123; 126; 153; 166; and from coins of Sardis, *BMC Lydia*, p. xcix; Mionnet, IV, 119, No. 669.

For suggestions and corrections I am indebted to Prof. George M. A. Haufmann and Mr. A. Thomas Kraabel.

HEAVENLY ENTHRONEMENT AND BAPTISM
STUDIES IN MANDAEAN BAPTISM

BY

GEO WIDENGREN

Uppsala University

I. In the so-called Naassene Sermon and the Book of Baruch, written by the gnostic Justin, there is in the description of the lustration of the ascending saviour one detail that calls for notice.[1]) It is related how the saviour when entering into the presence of the highest deity, the Good One, is baptised in "the living water" from which he also drinks, Hippolytos, Philosophoumena V 27, 1-3.[2]) His water of baptism accordingly at the same time is a bath in which he—and all pneumatics after him—is purified, and an element of communion of which he—and all pneumatics—participate. This remarkable circumstance at once directs our thoughts to the Mandaean baptism. After the great—in some respects perhaps somewhat exaggerated-importance ascribed to it by Reitzenstein[3]) there was a strong reaction, leading to a still more exaggerated opinion according to which the Mandaean baptism, being derived from the Nestorian Christian rite, hardly possessed any importance at all, except of course for its position within the small and insignificant Mandaean community. This attitude of which Hans Lietzmann was the chief representative may be said to find no advocates to-day.[4]) Recent research represented by Eric Segelberg has clearly demonstrated the independent origin of Mandaean baptism.[5]) For this reason it is obvious that Reitzenstein was

---

[1]) For this description cf. Widengren, Baptism and Enthronement in some Jewish-Christian Gnostic Documents, *The Saviour God*, E. O. James Volume, ed. S. G. F. Brandon, Manchester 1963, pp. 205-217, esp. pp. 206-212.

[2]) Cf. Widengren, *op. cit.*, p. 208 where other passages are quoted too.

[3]) Cf. above all his book *Die Vorgeschichte der christlichen Taufe*, Leipzig 1929.

[4]) Cf. his short monograph Ein Beitrag zur Mandäerfrage, *SPAW* Phil.-Hist. Kl. 1930.

[5]) Cf. E. Segelberg, *Maṣbūtā. Studies in the Ritual of the Mandaean Baptism*, Uppsala 1958, esp. pp. 155ff. Lietzmann was criticized from more general points of view—quite correctly—by R. Bultmann, *ThLZ* 56-1931, col. 577-580 as well as by H. Schlier, *ThR* NF 5-1933.

right in ascribing a great importance to this baptismal rite, and this both from the phenomenological and historical point of view. But his method was faulty in so far as he didn't try to place it in its historical context, but tried to connect it exclusively with Indo-Iranian mythical ideas and ritual ceremonies.[1]) In spite of the fact that Zimmern at the beginning of this century pointed out some striking similarities between Mandaean baptism and Mesopotamian water-purification ceremonies[2]) this line of research was entirely left out of consideration in Reitzenstein's investigations.

In the following we shall try to follow up this Mesopotamian approach to the problems offered by Mandaean baptism, at the same time linking up this treatment with some earlier investigations of ours where we have tried to establish a connection between baptismal and coronation ceremonies.[3])

In order to get a clear conception of the structure of Mandaean baptism we start by giving an analysis of it dictated by the comparative point of view. First of all we should note that at the baptismal ceremony the priest appears dressed in the holy garment which is made up of seven different parts, *ML* pp. 232-239 = *CP* pp. 162-166; *Šarḥ ḏQabin ḏŠišlam Rba* pp. 44-47. The number seven reminds us of the fact that at the heavenly enthronement of Levi, as it is described in Test. Levi, seven men hand over to him various emblems and articles of dress.[4]) In the survival of the number of 7 we presumably have to see a heritage from an original ritual of enthronement in ancient Mesopotamia where everyone of the 7 planetary deities handed over to the newly enthroned king one single emblem or article of dress.[5]) Highly significant in this respect is the text of the marriage-

---

[1]) Cf. Reitzenstein, *op. cit.*, pp. 35ff., 44ff., 249ff., 348ff. (contribution by L. Troje).

[2]) Cf. H. Zimmern, Das vermutlich babylonische Vorbild des Pehta und Mambuha der Mandäer, *Orientalische Studien Th. Nöldeke ... gewidmet*, Giessen 1906. pp. 959-967.

[3]) Cf. our contribution to the E. O. James Volume (quoted above n. 1) and our article in *RoB* 5-1946, pp. 28-61. The present article is a revised and much enlarged English version of one part of this Swedish article of mine, cf. pp. 38-50.

[4]) Cf. Widengren, Royal Ideology and the Testaments of the Twelve Patriarchs, *Promise and Fulfilment*, Hooke Volume, Edinburgh 1963, ed. F. F. Bruce.

[5]) Cf. *Promise and Fulfilment*, p. 206 n. 19 where references were given to Witzel, *Keilinschriftliche Studien*, V-VII, pp. 57ff.; Meissner-Rost, *Bauinschriften Asarhaddons* CCXXXII, pp. 52ff. and to the great rock-reliefs of Maltai. As I said in the place indicated: "Every deity actually hands over to the ruler a special gift according with its own special character." The same holds true of the Mandaean text referred to in the following

ceremony, part III, where the seven planets bring their gifts to the bridal pair, the six gods Sun, Moon, Mars, Mercury, Jupiter, Saturn handing over to the bridegroom *their* gifts, while Venus gives her gifts to the bride, *Šarḥ dQabin dŠišlam Rba*, p. 57-59 (transl.), 15 : 220-26 : 270 (text). The planetary deities of whom the names are given as Šamiš, Sin, Nirig, Nbu, Bel, Kaiwan and Libat are clearly depicted as benevolent—something quite exceptional in Mandaean religion, a fact testifying to the survival not only of their Babylonian names,[1]) but also of their positive function at the coronation of the ruler.[2])

The priest who underwent a baptism at the occasion of his own consecration[3]) accordingly appears dressed in a garment which is a late correspondence to that given to the enthroned ruler in ancient Mesopotamia, with a typical deviation caused by the Iranian influence of which we will speak in what follows. Many poems in the Mandaean liturgies actually describe these various parts of the priestly ritual dress.[4]) In the order in which they are mentioned they comprise the following emblems and articles of dress:

1.	Garment	*lbuša*
2.	Girdle	*himiana*
3.	Covering (shirt)	*ksuia*
4.	Stole	*naṣifa*
5.	Crown	*taga*
6.	Drawers	*šaruala*
7.	Staff	*margna*

In a text describing the marriage-ceremony there is an enumeration of the bridegroom's emblems and articles of dress, *Šarḥ dQabin dŠišlam Rba* p. 56. Here are missing the drawers (which he actually is wearing) and the stole (ditto), and instead of the crown, *taga*, we meet with the wreath, *klila*. In the passage describing the gifts handed over by the planetary deities we find that Sin gives to the bridegroom crown *and* wreath, *taga uklila*, Bel brings him his vestment, *lbuša*, and Kaiwan his shirt ("smock" translates Lady Drower) while Nirig hands

---

[1]) For the Mandaean names of the planets cf. Furlani, I Pianeti e lo Zodiaco nella religione dei Mandei, *MANL* Ser. 8d. scienze mor. stor. e filol., Vol. 2, pp. 119-187, Rome 1948; K. Rudolph, *Die Mandaer*, I, Göttingen 1960, p. 207.

[2]) We should compare the altogether negative attitude to their gifts in *Ginzā*, transl. Lidzbarski, p. 28 : 25-29 :16.

[3]) Cf. E. S. Drower, *The Mandaeans of Iraq & Iran*, Oxford and London 1937, pp. 148ff.

[4]) Already Reitzenstein, *op. cit.*, p. 168 referred to these poems.

over to him his armour, *zaina*. This last article appears rather misplaced in this peaceful context where only the battles of Venus could be spoken of. If we examine somewhat closer this ritual dress, to-day called *rasta*, and composed of the parts already indicated,[1]) we will find that besides the true Semitic words *lbuša, ksuia, naṣifa* and *klila*, we also meet with some Iranian loanwords: *himiana*, girdle, *šaruala*, drawers, and *margna*, staff, to which should be added the word for armour, *zaina*,[2]) It is possible that another Iranian loanword, the *burzinqa*, a kind of turban, also belonged to the original dress, but this surmise is indeed rather uncertain.[3])

Without any doubt the trousers and the girdle as being typically Iranian articles of dress must have been borrowed by the Mandaeans from the Iranian culture area,[4]) but if directly or indirectly we must leave undecided.[5]) A direct Iranian influence is at any rate difficult to state with the aid of *these* loanwords.[6]) But the use of such a typical Iranian riding dress as trousers as part of the Mandaean ritual dress is very striking indeed. In case we assume an Iranian direct influence we

---

[1]) Cf. M. N. Siouffi, *Études sur la religion des Soubbas ou Sabéens*, Paris 1 880, pp 121ff.; Drower, *op. cit.*, p. 30f. where also another enumeration with two more parts is given. As Rudolph. *op. cit.*, II, p. 51 n. 1 rightly observes the texts do not speak of *rasta* but of '*uṣtla*, '*ṣtla* (< Greek στόλη, a loanword in Aramaic in general). The term *rasta* is therefore of a younger date. It is kept as a technical term for the ritual dress in my article for the sake of convenience. Segelberg, *op. cit.*, p. 116 takes '*uṣtla* as a synonymous word of *lbuša*, which it certainly is, but only in the general sense of the word and not as a technical term. This is clear from the passages registered by Segelberg where '*uṣtla* and *klila* very often are mentioned together.

[2]) For the Iranian loanwords among these terms cf. Widengren, *Iranisch-semitische Kulturbegegnung in parthischer Zeit*, Köln-Opladen 1960, pp. 94 *(himiana)*, 107 *(šaruala*, cf. also *RoB* 5-1946, p. 39 n. 7), 102 *(taga)*, 194 *(zaina)*, 94f. *(margna)*.

[3]) For this Iranian loanword cf. Widengren, *Kulturbegegnung*, p. 91f. This term is not included in the enumeration of the articles belonging to the ritual dress and is actually seldom mentioned in the texts (but cf. *CP* p. 160 No. 178) except in ritual directions. The tentative derivation of this word from Akkadian *paršigu* (cf. in the last instance Macuch, *A Handbook of Classical and Modern Mandaic*, Berlin 1965, p. 117 :10) is impossible (for reasons indicated by me *op. cit.*).

[4]) For the girdle cf. Widengren, *Le symbolisme de la ceinture* (to be published shortly). For belt and trousers as articles of dress cf. Widengren, Some Remarks on Riding Costume and Articles of Dress among Iranian Peoples in Antiquity, *Studia Ethnographica Upsaliensia* XI-1956.

[5]) Already Josephus, Antiquitates III 7,2 knows the word for girdle. All the three terms *šaruala, himiana* and *taga* are found in the other two dialects of Eastern Aramaic, i.e. Syriac and Babylonian Talmudic. The same holds true also of *zaina* and *burzenqa*. Not only the nobles of Palmyra but also some of their gods were dressed *à la parthe*.

[6]) This sentence is reproduced *verbatim* from my article *RoB* 5-1946, p. 40 in order to show that my position in these problems is unchanged.

could presume that the old Mesopotamian 7-fold sacral vestment had been taken over by a religious community, later exposed to Iranian influence, thanks to which these Iranian articles of dress were added to the older ritual dress. Such a development would agree with the picture we are able to form of the syncretistic character of the Mandaean community. On the other hand it would be equally simple to suppose that the original Mandaeans had accepted as theirs a ritual dress already composed of both Mesopotamian and Iranian elements. At any rate it should be emphasized that the phenomenon we meet with here is anything but isolated, for we find such Mandaean terms as *pandama*, the mouth-covering, the Iranian *padām*,[1]) and the "banner", *drabša*, used in the baptismal ceremonies, the Iranian *drafša* mir. *drafš*,[2]) as well as *gauaza*, the staff, used in the ritual,[3]) as well as the bridegroom's baton of camelthorn, *aštargan*,⟨mir. *uštrgān*.[4])

The list of articles of dress or implements, used in the cult, that have names derived from the Iranian language, is then the following:[5])

      burzenqā = turban
      tāgā = crown
      hemyānā = girdle
      šalvār = trousers
      aštargān = the bridegroom's staff
      margnā = staff
      gawwāzā = staff
      drabša = "banner"

It is important to note that all these loanwords *could* be of Parthian origin. Accordingly they are all of them of a rather remote date.

It is of great interest to note that on the day of his wedding the bridegroom is invested with this ritual dress as we already observed. This is done in connection with the baptism he has to receive at this occasion.[6]) If he is a priest he is then called "a king."[7])

---

[1]) Cf. Widengren, *Kulturbegegnung*, p. 96f.; Rudolph, *op. cit.*, II, p. 54 n. 1 (with my corrections *JSS* XII-1965, p. 295f.).

[2]) Cf. Widengren, *op. cit.*, p. 92.

[3]) Cf. Widengren, *op. cit.*, p. 93. What Rudolph, *op. cit.*, p. 35 n. 6 has to say against *gauaza* being an Iranian loanword is based upon a confusion of two words: *gᵉwāzā* and *gawwāzā* (adaptation in Aramaic to the qaṭṭāl-nouns), cf. my corrections *JSS* XII-1965, p. 294.

[4]) Cf. Widengren, *Kulturbegegnung*, p. 90.

[5]) Cf. Widengren, *op. cit.*, p. 107 where this list is reproduced.

[6]) Cf. Siouffi, *op. cit.*, p. 167; Drower, *The Mandaeans*, p. 62; Rudolph *op. cit.*, II, p. 311. The bridegroom shall be clothed in the five ritual garments, cf. *Šarḥ dQabin*, p. 33.

[7]) Cf. Drower, *Šarḥ dQabin dSislam Rba*, p. 40 n. 3.

2. Leaving aside such passages where only one or two articles of the ritual dress are mentioned we shall pay attention to the context in which the ritual dress appears in the texts.

First of all it calls for notice that several of these articles are mentioned at the occasion when the human soul leaves its earthly existence and is met by "the guide," "the helper," or "the companion," the Mandaic terms being *mdabrana*, *ahed eda*, or *adyaura*, and *paruanqa*. Of these terms two are Iranian loanwords, *adyaura* (〈mir. *adyāvar*[1])) and *paruanqa* (〈mir. *parvānak*[2])), while *ahed eda* exactly corresponds to mir. *dastgīr*[3]) and therefore could be classified as a loan-translation. All these names are designations of the saviour who in the moment of death brings the soul back to its heavenly home:

> The Man who brought me hither,
>   brought me a beautiful robe.
> He put on me a robe of splendour,
>   in a turban of light he covered me.
> He set on me a wreath of ether,
>   and of what the Great bestoweth on the Uthras.
> He set me up amongst the Uthras,
>   and raised me up amidst the perfect.
>   *ML* p. 164:5-8 = *Ginzā* p. 516:14-19 = *CP* p. 100.[4])

The articles of dress mentioned in this passage are only *uṣṭla*, *ṭarṭabuna* and *klila*.

In another passage, found in Ginzā only, there is a more complete enumeration of the various parts of the dress. Here the soul addressing its body when leaving it for the House of Life exclaims:

> If thou, my body, wert a garment of splendour and light,
>   that I might put thee on,
>   thou wouldst ascend with me to the House of Life.
> If thou wert a girdle of splendour and light,
>   that thou wert bound around my hips,
>   thou wouldst ascend with me to the House of Life.
> If thou wert a wreath of splendour and light,
>   that thou wert placed on my head,

---

[1]) Cf. Widengren, *op. cit.*, p. 89 and *The Great Vohu Manah*, Uppsala 1945, p. 79.

[2]) Cf. Widengren, *op. cit.*, p. 98 and *The Great Vohu Manah*, p. 79.

[3]) The Mandaic expression *ahed eda* means "he who seizes the hand," the same meaning as *dastgīr*.

[4]) My translation in this case as in several other passages is more in accordance with that of Lidzbarski than with Lady Drower's, but the deviations are rather insignificant, except in a few cases where she has edited texts not accessible to Lidzbarski.

thou wouldst ascend with me to the House of Life.
If thou wert a staff of splendour and light,
  that I might hold thee,
    thou wouldst ascend with me to the House of Life.
If thou wert shoes of splendour and light,
  that thou wert put around my feet,
    thou wouldst ascend with me to the House of Life.
      Lidzbarski, *Ginzā* p. 537 : 4-18 = Petermann, *Left Ginzā* p. 97 : 13-20

The parts of the ritual dress enumerated in this passage are the garment, the girdle, *himiana*, the wreath, the staff, *gauaza*, and the shoes (or perhaps better: sandals).[1]) This last mentioned article could hardly be said to be part of the Mandaean ritual dress. Presumably they have been added to make the dress as complete as possible.[2])

What is of importance in the passage just quoted is the fact that both girdle and staff are mentioned in this place and that both of them are given their Iranian designations. Both of them accordingly belong to the emblems that are handed over to the soul at its ascension to the House of Life. The basic mythic conception therefore must be that the soul *before* its ascension is invested with the holy vestments and emblems. With this mythic conception corresponds from a cultic point of view that the deceased before his heavenly ascent is wrapped up in the ritual dress, *rasta*, at which occasion a wreath of myrtle is placed on his head and the knot of the girdle completed in the very moment of his passing away.[3]) Before his investment baptismal ceremonies are undertaken with him and after his burial a *massiqtā*-ceremony takes place and a cultic meal is celebrated. Three main parts in the ritual of the *massiqtā* are thus easily discernible:

1. Water purification of a baptismal character
2. Investment with the ritual dress
3. Celebration of a cultic meal

All these ceremonies are placed within the framework of the recital of a great many prayers belonging to the *massiqtā*-ceremonies but we are not concerned here with them nor with the obvious accretions of this ritual in more recent times.[4]) That the ritual dress is possessed of a royal character is obvious because of such emblems as crown and

---

[1]) However, Macuch, *Handbook*, p. 190 : 3 renders *msana* with "shoe", "boot".
[2]) Or do the shoes indicate an original more northern home?
[3]) Cf. Drower, *The Mandaeans*, p. 179; Segelberg, *op. cit.*, p. 123f.; Rudolph, *op. cit.*, II, p. 262f.
[4]) Segelberg, *op. cit.*, pp. 122ff. discusses at length the relevant problems. That the massiqtā-ceremony has been considerably expanded, thereby losing something of its original character has been rightly emphasized by Rudolph, *op. cit.*, II, p. 269.

staff. But we encounter a difficulty here because we find both wreath and crown used as parts of the ritual dress, one, the wreath, called by the Semitic name of *klila*, the other, the crown, receiving as its appellation the Iranian loanword *taga*. Dr. Segelberg tried to solve this difficulty by assuming that the myrtle wreath, *klila*, originally was used in the coronation ceremonies mentioned in our texts but later replaced by the *taga* and relegated to a more humble position. This solution would seem to be acceptable because the rubrics of the Mandaean ritual texts speak of the crown, *taga*, or the turban, *burzinqa*, but the prayers themselves only mention the *klila*.[1]) It should however be emphasized that in the *massiqtā*-hymns the ascending soul receives "a great crown of splendour," *taga rba dziwa*, Petermann, *Left Ginzā* p. 101:12 = Lidzbarski, *Ginzā* p. 542:25. It may be that from the outset only the priest is the possessor of the royal emblems but that a process of democratization set in, so that every ascending soul at its ascension to the House of Life was held to be a recipient of the royal vestments. Moreover, it should not be left out of consideration that the ascent of the soul reaches its end in a ceremony of enthronement when the Deity receives the ascending soul. Dr. Segelberg has indicated the existence of a problem here when saying: "The result of this investigation is that a liturgical development is clearly distinguishable, although its date is uncertain."[2]) Is it possible to solve this problem? At any rate it is possible to find a text of Jewish origin where in a similar ritual context (water-purification and investment) both a turban (or a diadem) *and* a crown are handed over to the recipient in a kind of enthronization ritual. In Test. Levi, analyzed at previous occasions,[3]) in a scene of heavenly enthronement Levi is given a crown and the diadem of priesthood, as well as the staff of judgment and a branch of rich olive, an ephod, and a girdle, Test. Levi VIII 1-12. The double series of emblems indicates that "Levi is invested with a holy garment of a character at the same time priestly and royal."[4]) Thus the combination of *taga* and *klila* may indicate that in Mandaean religion there was a tendency to stress the both royal and priestly character of the garment with which the priest is invested. We are reminded of the

---

[1]) Cf. Segelberg, *op. cit.*, p. 113.

[2]) Segelberg, *op. cit.*, p. 115.

[3]) Cf. Widengren, *HS* I 3-1947, pp. 1-12; *Sakrales Königtum im Alten Testament und im Judentum*, Stuttgart 1955, pp. 49-53; H. Ludin Jansen, *La regalita sacra-The Sacral Kingship*, Leiden 1959, pp. 356-365, and finally Widengren, *Promise and Fulfilment*, pp. 202-212, cf. above n. 9.

[4]) Widengren, *Promise and Fulfilment*, p. 206.

fact that the priest also is called *malka*, king.¹) Lady Drower observes rightly that the crown when born by the priest is a symbol of his position as a both spiritual and secular leader. In this connection she quotes a Mandaean writing saying:²)

> Crown and kingship are put on his head,
> and he is made perfect in them.

When the priest is ordained it is indeed remarkable to what extent his royal character is emphasized in the prayers recited or the sayings addressed to him. It would carry us too far to quote all the relevant passages so it must suffice in this place to give a few quotations and references. Here a special importance must be ascribed to the following passage from a hymn addressed to the man who is ordained, the so-called "postulant," *šualia*:

> The king took the first myrtle
> from the hand of the new king,
> who had learnt from him the wondrous "treasure".
> He twined for him a wreath,
> and at the Jordan bestowed on him victory.
> The king was confirmed by the myrtle,
> and the Jordan was circulating in the king.

Drower, *The Coronation of the Great Šislam*, p. 7 (transl.), 40:21-24 (text)³)

---

¹) Cf. Drower, *The Mandaeans*, p. 31 and above p. 553.
²) Cf. Drower, *op. cit.*, p. 34.
³) The indefatigable editor and translator Lady Drower (to whose labour we all are indebted) doesn't always facilitate the task of her readers. There is sometimes rather difficult to check the text she makes accessible, because no crossreferences are given between text and translation. For the benefit of other readers I therefore give such references when I assume that they are useful. For the convenience of the reader I also sometimes transcribe the text—which in this writing is badly written and reproduced on a very small scale.

מאלכא נסיב אסא בוכרא
מן עדא דמאלכא הדתא
דגינזא שאניא סבאר מינה
גדאלה כלילא
וליארדנא זאכותא עהאבלה
מאלכא תקן באסא
ויארדנא במאלכא מיתכאראך

There are some deviations in my translation. Here and elsewhere I have rendered *zakuta* with "victory" and refer to what Lidzbarski has said so well *Johannesbuch*, II, p. 1f. Lady Drower renders *bmalka mitkarak* as "was crowned by the king" but I doubt that the verb *krak* can have this meaning. Actually ethpa'al of ܟܪܟ in Syriac means "to go hither and thither, to circulate, to linger," cf. the passages

Likewise the high priest, *rba*, says:
I have constructed thrones ...
And have instructed the Uthras who sit on them.

Drower, *The Coronation of the Great Šišlam*, p. 12 (transl.), 41 : 7f. from below (text)[1]

At that moment of the ritual "they put a throne, *kursia*, for the postulant and bid him sit upon it." The correspondence between recital and action, between myth and ritual, is accordingly quite perfect here.

Further on, when the following words are recited:

Then that Lord of Lofty Greatness
took a circlet of radiance, light and glory,
and set it upon my head,

a crown is placed upon his head, Drower, *The Coronation*, p. 13 (transl.).

In the sequel of the ritual "the priests respond this antiphonal hymn":

In the name of the Great Life.
Thou art a king, our father, a son of kings.
And thou wilt crown kings,
thou wilt set a crown upon kings.

Drower, *The Coronation of the Great Šišlam*, p. 16 (transl.), 42 : 3-2 from below (text)

The logical conclusion of the coronation is reached when the *rba* recites:

And King Manhirel conferred the signation upon him,
and reached out to him splendid *kušṭa*,
Made him ascend, set him up in the House of Perfection,
for ever and always.

Drower, *The Coronation of the Great Šišlam*, p. 17 (transl.), 43 : 6-8 (text)[2]

---

quoted in *Theasurus Syriacus* s.v. and Brockelmann, *Lex. Syr*. The meaning must be that the water of the Jordan was mingled with the king at his baptism because of his drinking the baptismal water. Perhaps we could simply translate "embrace" as Drower-Macuch, *Dictionary*, s.v. KRK does in some cases, cf. *op. cit.*, p. 223b.

[1] This text is given in full in *CP* p. 203 No. 246.
[2] I reproduce the text here:

ומאנהיריעיל מאלכא רושומא עהאבלה
ופשאטלה כושטא יאקרא
ואסיק תירצה בית תושלימא
מן ריש בריש

(corrected after *CP* No. 309)
In *CP* No. 309 p. 222 Lady Drower translates wrongly "House of the Perfected"

We can see in this passage how the postulant is given the signation, *rušma*, and how *kušta* then is conferred upon him,¹) further how he is caused to make the heavenly ascent after which he enters the House of Perfection, *bit tušlima*, where he is "set up" or "erected" *(traṣ)*. This is in accordance with the ritual practice as it is prescribed in the liturgies. To mention but one instance we may compare as illustration the following passage:

> Read these three prayers ... upon the oil and sign the souls thou hast baptised, when they ascend from the Jordan ... Three times sign them and read out *kušta* to them.   *ML* p. 40:1ff. = *CP* p.21

Here the same technical expressions recur, for we meet with the verb *pšaṭ* with *kušta* as object, and *ršam*, to sign. Note the phrase: *tlata zibnia ršum upšuṭ kušta minaiin*, which corresponds to *rušuma ehablḫ upšaṭlḫ kušta* in the passage just quoted from the Coronation.²)

The ascension and "erection" mark the logical end of the ritual action and correspond in this regard with the ritual of baptism as it is actually performed.³)

3. We left the ritual action when the mythical correspondence said that Šišlam-Rba had received the signation and *kušta* and was "erected" in the House of Perfection. This locality corresponds evidently to the *škinta* where this part of the ritual takes place, *Coronation*, p. 12:1ff. Some ritual actions of no great significance are further undertaken, looking very much like accretions of later times. But one important act has to be mentioned. After his enthronement when he is "set up" in the House of Perfection (according to the mythical pattern) the postulant partakes of the communion, taking the *pihta* and *mambuha* and drinking the *halalta*, implying the rinsing of his mouth.⁴) This is an important point to which we shall return.

---

but in *The Coronation*, p. 17 she has the correct translation "House of Perfection." For *tušlima* cf. Nöldeke, *MG*, p. 133 §112 and Macuch, *Handbook*, p. 191 §139. The afʻel *asiq (⟨slq)* if possible should always be translated with "made ascend" or "caused to ascend" to guard the connection with the *masiqta*, "ascension". The idiomatic expression *pšat kušta* is difficult to render in a satisfactory way. It implies that the hand is reached out to give *kušta*, the ritual handclasp. We should compare the Syriac expression ܡܘܫܛ ܐܝܕܐ, to reach out the hand to give.

¹) It looks as if Lady Drower hasn't quite understood the passage for she puts the word "insignia?" in a parenthesis after "sign". But *rušma* denotes "signation", the ritual act following the immersion at baptism.

²) Cf. also *ML* p. 57:10, 12f. = *CP* p. 30 where we have the same series of actions *urišmh tlata ... upšat kušta*.

³) Cf. Segelberg, *op. cit.*, pp. 89-91. He says rightly p. 90: "Logically the end of the rite should also be here."

⁴) Segelberg has not devoted much space to *halalta*, only pointing out p. 59 n. 2

We have already observed the fact that in the ordination text the postulant was placed on a throne while a text was being recited, alluding to the heavenly thrones on which the Uthras are seated. But every soul actually has the same heavenly privilege, for it is emphasized repeatedly that a throne is prepared for the soul in the dwelling of Life:

> Thy place is the Place of Life,
>   thy home the Everlasting Abode.
> For thee a throne of rest is set up
>   in which there is no heat and wrath.
> For thee is kept a girdle
>   in which there is no trouble or fault.
>   ML p. 158:7-9 = CP p.96[1]

This theme of the throne erected in the heavenly abode recurs also in other passages in Ginzā, cf. Lidzbarski, *Ginzā*, pp. 456:3ff., 473:28ff. That the soul here receives the same destiny as the deity who is enthroned on his divine seat in power and splendour is quite obvious. It is also interesting to compare the rehabilitation given to Yoshamin —who was once hurled down from his heavenly glory. The messenger who is sent to him from the highest godhead, the Great Life, gives the following announcement to him:

> Thy throne is firmly erected as it was,
>   and thou wilt be called a king in thy *škina*.
>   Lidzbarski, *Das Johannesbuch*, p. 40 (transl.), 36:7-8 text)

We meet in this passage with the idea that every deity is possessed of a special dwelling, a *škina*, with a throne erected *(tris)* in it. In Mandaean literature the word *škina* has kept its original meaning of "abode," "dwelling,"[2]) But every ascending soul too has a similar privilege. It is always said that the soul after its ascension will be "erected" in the House of Perfection which we shall illustrate by quoting some typical passages. The first one shows the result of this ascension:

> In the splendour of my Father I am standing,
>   and in the glory of the Man, my Creator.

---

that it should not be confused with the drinking of water at the occasion of baptism. Rudolph, *op. cit.*, II, p. 87 n. 6 has somewhat more to say on this point with a valuable reference to the *bit rimki* ritual, for which cf. below p. 575f.

[1]) The riddle of the term *asga* which puzzled Lidzbarski, cf. *op. cit.*, p. 158 n. 1 has been happily solved by Lady Drower, *op. cit.*, p. 96 n. 4.

[2]) Cf. Rudolph, *op. cit.*, II, p. 21.

In the splendour of my Father I am standing,
and in the House of Perfection I am erected.
ML p. 205 : 7-8 = *CP* p. 127[1]

Another passage mentions the action of erecting as being itself an eschatological action:

My measure was full and my number complete,
then there went and came to me a helper.
He took me away from their midst,
made me ascend and erected me in the House of Perfection.
Petermann, *Left Ginzā*, p. 45 :10-12 = Lidzbarski, *Ginzā*, p. 463 :15-18[2])

At the moment of ascending the human soul receives a garment of splendour, a wreath and a throne. The following exhortation to the soul is therefore a normal one:

Hurry on, put on thy garment of splendour,
and take on thy exulting wreath.
Sit on thy throne of splendour
which Life has set up in the Place of Light.
ML p. 160 XCIV 4-5 = *CP* p. 97 = Petermann, *Left Ginzā*, p. 78 : 25-79 : 2
Lidzbarski, *Ginzā*[3], p. 511 : 26-2

As we have seen already a throne has been prepared for the soul, set up in the Place of Life which is also called the Place of Light. To set up, to erect a throne for the soul in order that it may take place on it, and to set, to erect the soul itself obviously are synonymous expressions for the same ritual action, with that qualification that the throne beforehand is set up for the soul, it is already prepared there.

A striking variation, however, is that the garment of the soul in this connection can change place with the soul itself, for it is said by the Saviour to his elect ones:

---

[1]) Lady Drower renders here *tarṣina* with "I am upright," I use consistently for *traṣ* "erect", for reasons that will be clear from the following discussion.

[2]) Perhaps we should translate "the Helper" because this word indicates the Saviour.

[3]) Lidzbarski consistently translates *klila rauzia* with "ein prunkender Kranz" which seems to me better than the various expressions used by Lady Drower: mostly "fresh" (which she also uses for *hadta*) e.g. *CP* p. 51 "fresh and living," p. 97 only "living". The verb *ruaz* is a denominative verb from the Iranian loan-word *ruaza* for which cf. Widengren, *Kulturbegegnung*, p. 100, meaning "jubilation", "exultation". Macuch, *Handbook*, p. 391 :2f. renders *rauzia* with "exulting" which seems to me the best translation. The imper. *paṣ* here has the same meaning as the Syriac ܦܘܫ ܠܟ. Nöldeke, *MG*, p. 240 renders "schuttle dich," Lidzbarski "rege dich" and Macuch, *Handbook*, p. 292 : 24 "jump up," "hurry" which I have adopted.

> For he that entereth in me and carrieth me,
> his garment is erected in the House of Perfection.
>
> *ML* p. 153:9 = *CP* p. 93)¹

Here in the usual gnostic symbolical way the garment is seen as the higher *ego* of the soul and therefore held to be the figure that in reality is "erected."²) But what does this action of "erecting" really imply? It is indeed difficult to form an opinion about the concrete situation described by means of the verb *traṣ*, erect. But it is probably possible to get a better understanding of the ritual context by analyzing somewhat closer a passage already referred to:

> In the splendour of my Father I am standing,
> and in the House of Perfection I am erected.

In this passage we come across the expressions "I am standing," *qaiimna*, and "I am erected," *tarṣina*.³) The purpose of "erecting" is the "standing". With this observation we are placed in a better position, for here we are in contact with a religious term the technical significance of which is approximately clear. While the verb *qaiim* (pa'el) in Mandaic has as its basic meaning "to confirm, to make firm, to make standing, to raise up" its derivative meaning is to be a synonymous expression for "to baptise". This was shown by Lidzbarski in one of his excellent introductions to his editions and translations.⁴) If we take our starting point in one of the passages of the liturgies to which Lidzbarski refers his readers we will easily understand how this derivative meaning of *qaiim* was possible from the Mandaean point of view. The soul describes the baptism that its Father made the soul undergo. It is said in this text which is one of the classical Mandaean baptismal texts:

---

¹) I have followed Lidzbarski here for the translation given by Lady Drower must be wrong, owing to the fact that she has missed the technical meaning of *mitriṣ*, "is erected", and not understood the mystic identity between the Saviour and his worshippers. They are in fact one and the same, the worshipper both entering the Saviour ("he that entereth me," not "if" as Lady Drower has for *datilbia*) and carrying him upwards *(udaralia)*. For the partic. pe. *dara* cf. Macuch, *Handbook*, p. 285:15, and above all Nöldeke, *MG*, p. 237 n. 3.

²) That the garment in this passage is the highest principle of the human soul was rightly observed by Lady Drower, cf. *CP*, p. 93 n. 3 (though I cannot find that there is any wordplay here).

³) For the difficult form *tarṣina* cf. Nöldeke, *MG*, p. 231f. and Macuch, *Handbook*, p. 277:23ff. Nöldeke mistook it, however, for an active instead of a passive partic.

⁴) Cf. *ML* p. XXIII.

"What did thy Father do for thee, Soul.
   the great day on which thou wast made firm?"
He brought me down in the Jordan, planted me,
   and he made me ascend to its bank, made me standing.
He prepared and gave me *pihta*,
   praised the cup and gave me to drink.
He placed me before him,[1])
   and pronounced over me the name of the Mighty.
                                   ML p. 46:7-10 = CP p. 25

If we leave aside here the symbol of plantation which belongs to a special circle of ideas[2]) we may understand from this passage how the meaning of "baptise" has developed from *qaiim*. Actually the verb *qaiim* denotes a special action, a part of the complete ritual of baptism.[3]) After the baptism the baptizand is made to ascend, *sliq*, to the bank of the river, the Jordan, where he is raised up, *qum*. When—as we were in a position to state—it is spoken of an "erecting" of the soul, resulting in its "standing", or being raised up, in the House of Life, also called House of Perfection, this then would seem to mean that the soul has to receive a baptism before its entrance there. We know that from the ritual point of view this baptism is given to the departing and ascending soul in the *massiqtā*-ceremony. We should await therefore to meet with the term *qaiim* in the preserved eschatological *massiqtā*-hymns. This is however not the case. But we possess a sufficient substitute in the song ML XLVII = CP p. 132 = Lidzbarski, *Ginzā*, p. 527. Only the context of Ginzā, however, makes it clear that we have to do with an eschatological setting in life, cf. Lidzbarski, *Ginzā*, p. 528:13ff.:

Ye are erected and made firm,
   by the word of truth which hath come to you ...
To the place which is all Life
   your souls are called and invited.
   Petermann, *Left Ginzā*, p. 91:11ff. = Lidzbarski, *Ginzā*, p. 529:5-6, 9-10)[4]

---

[1]) For this translation of *autban binia burkh* cf. Schaeder, *Gnomon* 5-1929, p. 357. In case this interpretation is correct there can be no idea here of an adoption ceremony. This problem was briefly discussed by Segelberg, *Masbūtā*, p. 91f. (who didn't follow Schaeder).

[2]) Cf. Widengren *RoB* 2-1943, p. 57.

[3]) Cf. Segelberg, *op. cit.*, pp. 89-91.

[4]) In this passage Lady Drower has "Ye are uplifted and fortified," a translation I find somewhat misleading. Lidzbarski: "Ihr wurdet aufgerichtet und gefestigt," but I prefer with Lady Drower the conception of the perf. as the result achieved of the action in question.

4. Still more impressive are the psalms in which the ascension of Hibil-Ziwa is depicted, the ascension of the Saviour, who is a pattern of the individual soul. In these poems it is related how he takes part in a baptism at his entrance into heaven, and this in a way perfectly corresponding with the "erecting" and "raising up" or "confirmation":

> Uthras rose up from their throne,
>   baptised me with their baptism,
>   and made me firm with their wondrous voice.
> Shitil-Uthra went forward
>   and addressed me, Hibil-Ziwa:
> He said:
> "Thy garment be shining and thy figure honoured
>   with thy Father, the Lord of Greatness."
> He twined for me a pure wreath,
>   preserving me from everything detestable.
> It made me take place in its *škina*,
>   where it itself already was.

Petermann, *Right Ginzā*, p. 352:20-353:1= Lidzbarski, *Ginzā*, p. 370:5-15

Accordingly Hibil-Ziwa is baptised, "confirmed", "made firm", given a wreath, and made to take place in the dwelling of the highest deity, in his *škina*. The ceremony of enthronement thus follows in this passage after baptism and "raising up", confirmation. We are again brought back to the fundamental fact that baptism, confirmation (the "erecting") in the dwelling of God, and enthronement with investiture belong together.

The baptism of Hibil-Ziwa is described at some length in an obviously late and in places rather confused and corrupt text where however some fragments of older and more correct texts are found.[1] At least two important details are expressed in this text in a very clear way. The first one is a fact very often overlooked in the discussion of the Mandaean baptism, its theological implications. Mandaean baptism provides forgiving of sins and creates a new moral status.[2]

Thus when Hibil-Ziwa is baptised all the Uthras cry out:

---

[1] This text has been edited and translated by Lady Drower in her publication *The Haran-Gawaita and the Baptism of Hibil-Ziwa*, Città del Vaticano 1953. I know from personal communications that owing to difficult circumstances the editor and translator couldn't devote herself wholeheartedly to her task. In the following I give a few proposals which I hope will be found acceptable.

[2] It is to the credit of Prof. Rudolph that he has devoted some space to this aspect of baptism, cf. *op. cit.*, II, pp. 240-243 (here also in connection with the *massiqtā*).

> Health and victory and forgiving of sins
> > be there for this the soul of Hibil-Ziwa son of Manda ḏHayyē,
> > that descendeth to the Jordan
> > and is baptised and receiveth the pure sign.
> > > Drower, *The Baptism of Hibil-Ziwa*, p. 51 with parallel passage p. 55[1]

The expression "forgiving of sins" is in Mandaic *šabiq haṭaiia* which was taken by Nöldeke in its literal sense of "a forgiver of sins."[2] This interpretation, though correct from the formal point of view and accepted by Lidzbarski and Rudolph, has to be rejected.[3] Lady Drower translates "forgiving of sins," and so does Macuch, who points out correctly that there has been a semantic development here from "forgiver of sins" to "forgiving of sins."[4] If we look at the passages where *šabiq haṭaiia* is asked for we will see at once that this expression is mentioned together with a series of abstract nouns.[5] For this reason I think that in such a series it cannot possibly be translated otherwise than by "forgiving of sins."

The second detail is also very clearly expressed here when Hibil-Ziwa is made to say:

> Every one that is baptised with my baptism, Hibil-Ziwa's,
> > shall be erected with me,
> > and shall be like me
> > and be a dweller in my world, Hibil-Ziwa's.
> > > Drower, *The Baptism of Hibil-Ziwa*, p. 59[6]

---

[1]) In order to be able to give references to the text I have numbered each fold of the facsimile text which is added to the translation in a folder. These section numbers are given in Roman numerals from I to XXI. The text quoted above is found VIII 14-16 with the parallel passage XI 7-9 and runs as follows:

אסותא וזאכותא ושאביק האטאייא
ניהוילה להאזא נישימתא דהיביל זיוא ברא דמאנדא דהייא
דנאהית ליארדנא ומיצטבא ומקאביל דאכיא רושומא

In VIII 16 it is written *urušuma* but XI 9 has the correct text *rušuma*, without a waw before the word.

[2]) Cf. Nöldeke, *MG*, p. 310 with n. 3.
[3]) Cf. Rudolph, *op. cit.*, II, p. 239.
[4]) Cf. Macuch, *Handbook*, p. 181 : 9, 390 : 28.
[5]) Such expressions will be discussed in the following, cf. section 6, p. 576 below.
[6]) The text quoted above is found XIII 9-11 and runs as follows:

כולמאן דבהאזין מאצבותא דיליא היביל זיוא מיצטבא
לואתאי דיליא מיתריץ
ובאדמותאי נידאמיא
ובאלמאי דיליא היביל זיוא דאיאר

It should be noted that the word *daiar* is exactly the same as Syriac ܕܐܝܪ. The name of Hibil-Ziwa has probably been added to the poem and should be blotted out—*metri causa*.

In this passage it is clearly stated that every believer shares the lot of the Saviour who is his real model—as we have seen above.¹) The believer who takes the baptism with which the Saviour was baptised shall be a dweller in his *alma*, his aion, be like him, and be "erected" with him. They are in a way identical.²)

In view of the importance attached to the wreath of myrtle we may in this place as a kind of supplement refer to a few passages where the myrtle is spoken of.

The first passage says:

> On the day that a root of fresh myrtle was set before the king,
>   and the king stretched out his right hand for it,
>   and took it, giving it to the Uthras, the "arrangers",
>   and said to them: "Take from me the fresh myrtle,
>   and bless the *škinata* with a blessing,
>   pronounce a benediction upon the *škinata*."
>   Drower, *The Baptism of Hibil-Ziwa*, p. 61 (transl.)³

A second equally interesting passage is the following:

> On the day that Hibil(-Ziwa) went towards Yawar,
>   myrtle he multiplied with them and for Yawar.
>   Into his right hand he placed it and said to him:
>   "Receive from me fresh myrtle,
>   and bless the *škinata* with a blessing."
>   Drower, *The Baptism of Hibil-Ziwa*, p. 65 (transl.)⁴

---

¹) Cf. above p. 564.

²) In Mandaean religion there are texts speaking of the dwelling of the deity in the worshipper, cf. the passages quoted by W. Bauer, *Das Johannesevangelium*, 2. ed. 1925, p. 181 and H. Becker, *Die Reden des Johannesevangeliums und der Stil der gnostischen Offenbarungsrede*, Gottingen 1956, p. 108 n. 1.

³) The text quoted above is found XV 10-19. The Uthras are called *msadrania* "arrangers", because assisting at the baptism.

⁴) The text quoted above is found XIX 1-7 and runs as follows:

ביומא דאסגיא היביל ‹זיוא› לואת יאואר
אסא אסגיא לואתאיהון ועל יאואר
ביאמינה עהאבלה ואמרלה
ניסיב מינאי אסא האדתא
ובריכתא בשכינאתא ברוך

There is a marked difficulty here in the second *asgia*. Lady Drower translates "he brought", adding in n. 4 "Literally went." For obvious grammatical reasons it is impossible to translate the intrans. verb *asgia* as a trans. verb unless we make a slight emendation, reading ⟨b⟩*asa asgia*, "he went with the myrtle," meaning he brought it. This is a regular Semitic construction very often found in the Arabic. But I would rather prefer to think of a word-play here, a phenomenon very popular in all Semitic poetry, assuming the poet to use in the second place the af'el *asgia* of *sga*, "be many, much." This verb is actually used also in Mandaic, cf. Macuch, *Handbook*. p. 333 : 26 and Drower-Macuch, *Dictionary*, p. 317b.

In view of the following discussion I attach some weight to the fact that from these two passages it is perfectly clear that the deity, considered as the enthroned royal ruler, holds in his right hand the fresh myrtle which he then twines as a pure wreath, Lidzbarski, *Ginzā*, p. 370 :12-13. We shall return later to this point.

5. There is another way in which we are able to shed light on the concrete context of the terms "confirmation" (or "raising up") and "erecting". A Greek alchemistic text, evidently possessed of a Syrian background, is of great importance in this connection.[1]) This writing presupposes a mystery ritual, concluded by an act of divinization, consisting in the erecting of the *mysta* as an image of an astral deity. The relevant passage of the text runs as follows:

> "The mystery was perfected and the dwelling sealed, and a statue erected, full of light and divinity."[2]

In this text there meet such expressions as the "erecting", the "dwelling", the "sealing" and the statue, *andriás*, which is made up of light and divinity. As Reitzenstein who edited this text rightly observed: "Eine ähnliche Vorstellung mögen die Mandäer gehabt haben. Den Schluss der Himmelswanderung bildet fast immer die Angabe, dass der göttliche Führer den Emporgeführten in seiner Shkina aufrichtet "[3])

We already had ample opportunities of confirming the correctness of this statement. The "erecting" in the *škina* concluded the ascension

---

[1]) Reitzenstein has edited this text in *NGGW* 1919, pp. 1ff. The editor himself refers to the fact that the priest who communicated the revelation is called *Komarios* which is nothing but the designation of "priest" in Aramaic-Syriac: *kumar*, stat. det. *kumrā*. Reitzenstein has repeated his observation in *Das iranische Erlösungsmysterium*, Bonn 1921, p. 167.

[2]) The text is:
ἐτελειώθη τὸ μυστήριον καὶ ἐσφραγίσθη ὁ οἶκος καὶ ἐστάθη ἀνδριὰς πλήρης φωτὸς καὶ θεότητος

We are reminded here of the somewhat enigmatic use of the term *andriás* in the Manichaean texts where this name is applied to the eschatological macrocosmic representation of the rescued souls, cf. the passages registered by Puech, *Le manichéisme*, Paris 1949, p. 177 n. 353. But it would seem that the connections in Manichaeism rather point to India than to Mesopotamia. This cannot be demonstrated here. We are on firmer ground as far as the term στηρίζειν is concerned for it recurs in the baptismal formula used by the Marcosian gnostics as is well known: ἐστήριγμαι καὶ λελύτρωμαι says the initiated, Irenaeus, Adv. haereses I, XXI 3. Segelberg, *OrSuec* VIII-1959, pp. 31-34 also pointed out the similarities between the Odes of Solomon, the Evangelium Veritatis and the Mandaean writings as far as the expressions for "erecting" and "standing" are concerned.

[3]) *Das iranische Erlösungsmysterium*, p. 167 n. 5.

of the soul, constituting its logical end. But the term "erecting" receives further illustration, if with Reitzenstein we refer to the well-known passage where Apuleius relates the circumstances of his initiation in the Isis mysteries. He says in his somewhat veiled description that he went forward, sanctified by means of 12 garments and took his place on a tribune of wood before the image of the goddess. In his hand he was holding a burning torch, on his head he had a wreath of palm-leaves, protuding from his head as rays of the sun. The initiated *mystae* called this robe the *Stola Olympiaca*. Apuleius himself says that he was adorned like an image of the Sungod and set up as a kind of a statue. Accordingly the *mysta* thanks to his initiation (which actually meant not only a *descensus ad inferos* but also a heavenly ascent —*deos inferos et deos superos accessi coram et adoravi de proxumo*) was transformed into a deity of solar character, and "erected" as an image of the Sungod, like his cult-statue, he received the worship of the believing community, assembled to give him their acclamation.[1]) We should note the detail that he has in his hand a burning torch. This trait also characterizes him as a deity of light, a most characteristic detail which must have been typical of the Syrian cults, because it recurs even in the description given by Afrem of the newly baptised, cf. *Hymni et Sermones*, ed. Lamy, I, p. 65 : 9[2])

In general, however, the enthroned deity has some symbol of fertility, a bunch of grapes, some sheaves, or a branch, in his right hand. In Syria and its neighbour parts of Asia Minor and Mesopotamia we are provided with good illustrations of this iconographic detail.[3]) For

---

[1] The text of the relevant passages Metamorphos. XXIII 7, XXIV 1-6:
Accessi confinium mortis et calcato Proserpinae limine per omnia uectus elementa remeaui, nocte media uidi solem coruscantem lumine, deos inferos et deos superos accessi coram et adoraui de proxumo.
Mane factum est, et perfectis sollemnibus processi duodecim sacratus stolis, habitu quidem religioso satis ... Namque in ipso aedis sacrae meditullio ante deae simulacrum constitutum tribunal ligneum iussus superstiti byssina quidem, sed floride depicta ueste conspicuus. Et umeris dependebat pone tergum talorum tenus pretiosa chlamida. Quaqua tamen uiseres, colore uario circumnotatis insignabar animalibus: hinc dracones Indici, inde gripes Hyperborei, quos in speciem pinnatae alitis generat mundus alter. Hanc Olympiacam stolam sacrati nuncupant. At manu dextera gerebam flammis adultam facem et caput decore corona cinxerat palmae candidae foliis in modum radiorum prositentibus. Sic ad instar Solis exornato me et in uicem simulacri constituto, repente uelis reductis, in aspectum populus errabat.
[2] In another connection I hope to discuss some related aspects of Christian baptism, for the time being cf. my article RoB V/1946, pp. 51-60.
[3] For general references cf. O. Eissfeldt, *Tempel und Kulte syrischer Städte in hellenistisch-römischer Zeit*, Leipzig 1941, pp. 47-49, 123, 126, 134 with Pl. V i, XI 3, XII 1, XIV 2.

geographical reasons we may refer here to Dura-Europos.¹) As to Asia Minor it will be sufficient to refer to the Attis-mysteries where the high priest as the representative of the young god is depicted as holding a branch of olives in his hand.²)

The crown of rays on the other hand, put on the head of the initiated to symbolize his identification with the sungod, is found on several monuments of Syria. We may refer here to the wellknown representations from Palmyra³) and Dura-Europos.⁴)

From Mesopotamia I am not in a position to give any illustrations of this kind, but on the other hand we have funeral representations showing the deceased, dressed in Parthian costume, holding a palmleaf in his right hand.⁵) This is a way of representing the dead which agrees with the figure of the priest in the Gad relief of Dura. On that relief moreover, a wreath is placed by the attendant Seleucus Nicator on the deity's head.⁶) Much the same scene is found on the representation of Atargatis as the Gad of Palmyra, but there it is a Nike, holding in left hand a palm-leaf, that with her right hand reaches out the wreath to place it on the enthroned deity's head.⁷) This is a representation very well known from the Parthian coins where the enthroned king is attended by a Nike in exactly the same way.⁸)

Before leaving this topic we may refer to a passage in a gnostic text, originally written in Syriac and preserving much ancient Syrian and Mesopotamian material beside gnostic ideas of Iranian origin, viz. The Apocryphal Acts of Thomas.⁹) The scene depicted is from a marriage where the Apostle has been invited:

---

¹ Cf. *The Excavations at Dura-Europos, Prelim. Report of the Seventh and Eight Seasons of Work*, New Haven 1939, pp. 296 with Pl. XXXVII (=Eissfeldt XIV 2). C. Hopkins thinks p. 296 of a Hittite tradition. In view of existant Mesopotamian material this would seem somewhat uncertain. The relief of Gad is discussed pp. 258f. and reproduced pl. XXXIII.

² Cf. the monument in the museum of Ostia, reproduced in *Handbuch der Orientalistik* VIII 2 Pl. IV, Widengren, Synkretistische Religionen.

³ Cf. Eissfeldt, *op. cit.*, p. 83.

⁴ Cf. F. Cumont, *Fouilles de Doura-Europos*, Paris 1926, Pl. L; Eissfeldt, *op. cit.*, p. 137 with Pl. XV 1.

⁵ Cf. Sarre, *Die Kunst des alten Persien*, Berlin 1925, p. 29 with fig. 5 p. 27.

⁶ Cf. *Prelim. Report, Dura*, p. 258 f. with Pl. XXXIII, Eissfeldt. *op. cit.*, p. 126 with Pl. XII 1.

⁷ Cf. *Prelim. Report, Dura*, p. 260 f. with Pl. XXXIV; Eissfeldt, *op. cit.*, p. 126 with Pl. XIII 1.

⁸ Many illustrations in W. Wroth, *Catalogue of the Coins of Parthia*, London 1903.

⁹ Cf. Widengren, *Mesopotamian Elements in Manichaeism*, Uppsala 1946, p. 123 ff.

And when they had eaten and drunk both oil and dried fruits were brought in to them, and they took. Some were anointing their faces, other their beards, and other other places. But Judas was praising God, and sealing the middle of his head; and he moistened his nostrils with a little, and put in his ears, and signed his heart, And a wreath of myrtle was placed on his head, and he was holding a reed-branch in his hand.
Wright, *Apocryphal Acts of the Apostles*, II, p. 150 (trans.), I, ܡܢ f. (text[1])

We see how the Apostle Judas Thomas in connection with the ceremony of anointing takes a wreath of myrtle on his head and a branch of reed in his hand. This ritual behaviour most probably continues an age-old Mesopotamian custom, probably found also in Syria.[2]

While Hellenistic—and behind them Greek—ideas certainly have played a role in connection with the representations with which we are occupied it is nevertheless of fundamental importance to observe that the Mandaean texts agree in a twofold way with the material adduced here from Syria and Mesopotamia. They are in accordance with both cultic ceremonies—as attested in the Isismysteries ("erecting" as a deified figure, an image of the deity with a wreath placed on his head)—and with cultic representations in art—as attested in the cult-reliefs of above all Dura and Palmyra (enthroned deity being crowned with a garland, holding in its hand a symbol of growth and fertility)-but also with funerary representations of the deceased (standing with a palm-leaf in his hand in a kind of *aedicula*). This agreement shows that the Mandaean cultic ceremonies and mythical ideas are possessed of a very real background in contemporary Syrian and Mesopotamian religion. This observation of course does not exclude the possibility that the Mandaeans in their ritual practice continue some Jewish gnostic traditions which may in their turn then, be dependent on the Syrian ideas and ceremonies indicated. But the agreement shows that we, more than has been done, should devote our attention to Syrian religion as a possible source of some traits in Mandaean religion, the more so as Lidzbarski undoubtedly was right when pointing to some quite obvious Palmyrene influences. There are certainly very important aspects in Syrian religion that have so far not been given due attention, mostly perhaps because of the widely scattered material. It is to the credit of the great scholar Franz Cumont

---

[1] Some insignificant changes have been made in the translation in order to present a consistent usage of technical terms.

[2] Cf. Widengren, *The King and the Tree of Life*, p. 17 n. 1; 38 n. 1.

that in his classical book on the oriental religions within the Roman empire he, in another connection than that with which we are occupied, mentioned such traits, perhaps without insisting on them to the extent they really deserve.

First of all Cumont underlines the fact that Palmyrene religion distinguishes clearly between the highest god, who is called Bel, and the Sungod, his visible representative and agent.[1]) This fact is demonstrated *inter alia* by a circumstance recorded by Zosimos I 61, viz. that Aurelian brought to Rome the cultstatues of *both* Bel and Helios (i.e. Šamaš). As deified the initiated is therefore identified with the subordinate young god, probably thought of as the son of the highest deity. Cumont further points out that the Sungod in Syrian religion acts as a kind of psychopomp, conducting the righteous believer after death to heaven. He refers *inter alia* to the inscription Le Bas-Waddington No. 2442:

> O King and Lord, be gracious and give to us all a pure health, good actions and a happy end of life.

In this connection Cumont also draws attention to the inscription Kaibel, *IG* XIV 2462 = Epigrammata Graeca No. 650, where the deceased says that he has found a god as his conductor or guide, ἡγεμονεύς. For the eschatological conceptions in Syrian religion it is further of considerable interest to note the presence also of the idea of an ascension through the celestial spheres, guarded as they are by the so-called "archontes", or of a passing beyond frontiers where the souls are examined by the so-called "custom-officers" τελώνια.[2]) These ideas have been investigated by me in a book, published 20 years ago, where I was interested in demonstrating that there is a common technical language in Manichaean, Mandaean, and Syrian Christian religion of a certain Gnostic tinge, and that behind it we in most cases are able to discover the original Mesopotamian religion.[3])

6. Mesopotamian, and quite especially Babylonian, influence represents, beside Jewish and Iranian components, the third main

---

[1]) Cf. also Eissfeldt, *op. cit.*, p. 83, and 90 f.; J. Starcky, *Palmyre*, Paris 1952, pp. 90ff.

[2]) Cf. F. Cumont, *Die orientalischen Religionen im römischen Heidentum*, 3. ed. Leipzig-Berlin 1931, p. 270f.=French ed. *Les religions orientales dans le paganisme romain*, Paris 1929, pp. 263-265. The text of Le Bas Waddington, No. 2442 runs: Βασιλεῦ δέσποτα ἵλαθι καὶ δίδου πᾶσιν ἡμῖν ὑγίην καθαρὰν, πρῆξις ἀγαθὰς καὶ βίου τέλος ἐσθλόν.

[3]) *Mesopotamian Elements in Manichaeism*, Uppsala 1946.

stream of influence in Mandaean religion. It has been observed that in the Mandaic dialect more than 80 words are Akkadian loanwords, some of them ultimately derived from Sumerian.[1] A few of the religious terms of Mesopotamian origin will be mentioned in the following.

Because our preceding investigation has carried us back to the Mesopotamian royal ritual I propose to say here a few words about the *bīt rimki* ritual the importance of which in connection with the development of baptismal ceremonies has been emphasized.[2]

In the *bīt rimki* ritual there are seven houses, *bītu*, into which the king enters accompanied by the priest called *mašmašu*,[3] whereupon "in each of the seven 'houses' the mašmašu recites (*imannū* ...) a Sumerian incantation ... whereupon the king 'says' *(idabbub)* ... an Accadian incantation."[4]

In the Mandaean ritual there is a more simple ritual to be found at the initiation of the "postulant", but nevertheless of considerable interest for a comparison. We find there two houses, the *andiruna* and the *škinta*. There are—as in the *bīt rimki*—two chief actors: the high priest, *rba*, and the postulant, *šuiala*. One special detail calls for mention because it is characteristic of all Mandaean ritual texts, as far as it has been possible to check the relevant passages at least: there is in Mandaean ritual directions always a distinction between two verbs, *qra*, "recite", "read", and *emar*, "say", the former reserved for the recital of longer prayers, the latter used for the saying of shorter formulas. This usage can be illustrated from the language of the Liturgies:

> If you are baptising one soul (only) say, *amur*, "my body, I go down before this the soul of N." If you are baptising several souls, read as written," *qria kd dktib, ML* p. 20:12-13 = *CP* p. 10. Then read, *haiẓak qria*, "In the name of Life. Let every man etc. When you are signing them, say, *amur*: "N. son of N! Thou art signed with the Sign of Life" etc. *ML* p. 26:13; 27:6 = *CP* p. 13f.[5]

---

[1] Cf. W. Baumgartner, Zur Mandaerfrage, *HUCA* XXIII 1/1950-15, p. 58.
[2] Cf. Widengren, *Religionens vàrld*, 2. ed. Stockholm 1953, p. 179; German ed. *Die Welt der Religion*, Topelmann-De Gruyter, Berlin, 1968, Chapt. 7.
[3] This is a loanword from Sumerian *maš-maš*. He is always said to be an incantation-priest, but it would be more correct to call him a purification-priest, because *maš-maš=mullillu*, purifier, cf. Deimel, *Sumerisches Lexikon*, 2:1, p. 161:200.
[4] Cf. Laessoe, *Studies on the Assyrian Ritual and Series bit rimki*, Copenhagen 1955, p. 32. Laessoe has established this distinction between *manū* and *dabābu* in this series which stimulated me to pursue this line of investigation.
[5] As far as I can see Lidzbarski is consistent in his usage: "lies" and "sprich"

There is, however, also another verb used in these ritual directions, for we find e.g. *ML* p. 29:1 the following direction: "Then utter the antiphon", *uhaizak rmia 'niana*: "At the waterhead I went forth," = *CP* p. 15, where Lady Drower translates "and recite the hymn". Presumably, however, the usage is consistent in similar cases for *ML* p. 149:6-8 the same direction is given together with the same technical expression, and that for the very same ritual occasion: *haizak 'niana rmia.*

The use of the verbs *qra* and *emar* is selfevident and doesn't need any commentary. It agrees very well with the use in *bīt rimki* of *manū* and *dabābu*. As to the use of the verb *rma* it should be pointed out that this verb is used in Syriac too in connection with liturgical expressions, for we have in Syriac both ܐܡܪ ܩܠܐ and ܐܡܪ ܐܘܢܝܬܐ, meaning "to utter lament."[1] It calls for notice that in a few cases we meet with a fourth verb, *draš*.[2] This verb in Mandaic has developed a rather general meaning, "to expound", but also "to read, to recite." As an illustration we may quote *ML* p. 34 = *CP* p. 18 No. 21: *hazin draša druš abatar brikit tira baraia*, "Read this hymn after 'Blessed be thou, outer Door'".

The variation of expression is well illustrated by a reference to *ML* p. 49f. with its manifold ritual directions for recitation and reading of hymns and prayers. Here we meet with the following expressions: *truṣ drašia, rmia 'niania, druš drašia, qria* and finally p. 50:5, 9. *amur.* Cf. also *CP* p. 26.[3]

This highly differentiated usage in liturgical language corresponds to the variations found in Mesopotamian ritual texts. We already had occasion to mention the use in the *bīt rimki* series of both *manū* and *dabābu*, where however according to Laessøe these two verbs are distributed, *manū* on the priest, and *dabābu* on the king. But we have in the ritual for the *kalu*-priest three different verbs, obviously used in connection with the recitation of three various categories of prayers or formulas: *manū*, "recite", *qabū*, "say", and *zamāru*, "to sing."[4]

---

whereas Lady Drower has "recite" or "read" (or in this case "cry") but consistently "say".

[1] Cf. *Thesaurus Syriacus*, II, 3293, 3296. It calls for notice that a part of the Psalms is called ܡܐܡܪܬܐ, thus a noun formed from this verb.

[2] It would seem, however, that this verb is seldom used.

[3] Lidzbarski translates - correctly in my opinion - "trage die Hymnen recht vor" whereas Lady Drower, *CP*, p. 26 has "Set up (*recite?*) the hymns". In Syriac *turrāsā* is the correctness of language, e.g. ܬܘܪܨ ܡܡܠܠܐ, the right reading. The term *turrāsā* therefore denotes "grammar".

[4] Cf. F. Thureau-Dangin, *Rituels accadiens*, Paris 1921, p. 16:23; 22:1f. ;32:23; 34:6, 13f., etc.

Interesting is the command: *ana šarri tušadbab*, "thou shalt cause to be recited for the king," *Rituels Accadiens*, p. 36:24; 38:19. The king on his side shall say his confession in a loud voice: *šarru šigū išassi*, *op. cit.*, p. 38:24. Without being able to carry out a more thorough investigation I risk the statement that the usage has been rich and differentiated. In a ritual tablet, used for a nocturnal ceremony in the Anu-temple of Uruk there is e.g. another expression: *naqbīt iqabbī*, "he shall say a formula," *op. cit.*, p. 119:32; 120:2, and with the plural: *iqabbū*, *op. cit.*, p. 120:17, 24. The same usage is most probably found in the famous New Year festival ritual at Babylon, but here in some decisive passages the text is unfortunately broken.

In the ritual directions attached to the *šu-illa*-category of psalms we have the same usage, for there we find both *manū* and *qabū*, e.g. *minūtam (annītam) tamannū*, cf. Ebeling, *Die akkadische Gebetsserie "Handerhebung,"* p. 24:10; 74:45, and: *3-šu taqabbī*, p. 82:99 (p. 40:51 *iqabbī*). On p. 82:103, however, we find: *kīma annam 3-šu tamnū* used of the same direction, which seems somewhat puzzling. On the other hand we have p. 82:104 *ki'ām taqabbī* followed by the direction: *kīma annam ... taqtabū* p. 84:115, which is the regular usage which we should expect also in the other place.

It is clear that various priestly schools may have used various expressions. What calls for notice is the fact that clear distinctions were made as to the manner of recitation of ritual formulas and prayers.

That such a specialized technical liturgical language hardly could be developed except in priestly colleges, possessed of long training and age-long traditions would seem self-evident. When we meet with the same phenomenon in Mandaean writings we presumably have to see in this variegated ritual language an illustration of the practice of a very long priestly training, perhaps inherited—partly at least—from Mesopotamia. Everyone reading the ritual directions accompanying the Mandaean liturgies recalls the corresponding ritual directions in the various series of Mesopotamian ritual tablets.

In the Mandaean writings we often meet with a special formula of blessing which shows a few variations but of which a standard version runs as follows:

> Health and victory, strength and firmness, speaking and hearing, joy of heart and forgiving of sins be there for me.
>
> *ML* p. 3:5f. = *CP* p. 1; *ML* p. 125:1f. = *ML* p. 251:2f. (a shortened formula)

In Mandaic:

> asuta uzakuta uhaila ušrara u'mra ušima
> uhaduat liba ušabiq haṭaiia nihuilia.

This formula corresponds to some Akkadian formulas, often used in the prayers, such as: *qabū u šemū* or: *qabū šemū u magāru*, "speaking and hearing (and favour),"[1]
and on the other hand:

> *ṭūb šēri u ḫūd libbi*, "Health and joy of heart".

It further calls for notice that the Mandaic *asuta uzakuta* corresponds exactly with the two Akkadian words *asūtu*, healing, and *zakūtu, purity*, but also immunity,[2] often found in the texts, though I am not in a positon to find them united in a formula of blessing.

The similarities found between Mandaean and Babylonian religion, as demonstrated here and in previous investigations,[3] do not concern only formal aspects but also ideas of far-reaching consequences. Because the Mandaean baptism is in the focus of our interest it is imperative to compare more closely the *bīt rimki* series, our starting point. This series comprises seven separate ritual actions implying water purifications of the king's person. The formulas recited in the *bīt rimki* most probably were conceived of as a juridical action by means of which the demons attacking the king (leading to sin, disease, political misfortunes) are cited for the judgement of the divine judge, the Sungod *Šamaš*. It stands to reason that such water purifications as those found in the *bīt rimki* series cannot be isolated from water purifications in other series such as *bīt salāmē, mis pī*, and *pit pī*. As we already mentioned it was Zimmern who pointed out the probable historical connections between these purification series and the Mandaean baptism. Here it was noted that both etymological and phenomenological reasons speak for an immediate connection between akkadian *tēliltu* and Mandaean *halalta*.[4]

"Bathing of the dead was part of the funeral ritual at least during the Neo-Assyrian period," says Laessøe,[5] who refers to the text *CT* XV 47:47f., where directions are given for the water purifications of

---

[1] Cf. C. J. Mullo Weir, *A Lexicon of Accadian Prayers*, Oxford-London 1934, s.v. II *kabu*, p. 163. The correspondence was pointed out in Widengren, *The Ascension of the Apostle and the Heavenly Book*, Uppsala 1950, p. 53 n. 2.
[2] For the meaning "immunity" cf. *CAD* Vol. 21, p. 21b.
[3] Cf. Widengren, *Mesopotamian Elements* and *The Ascension of the Apostle*.
[4] Cf. also Lidzbarski, *ML*, p. XXIII n. 2.
[5] Cf. Laessoe, *op. cit.*, p. 13. Translation after L.

Tammuz, i.e. the image of the god, as he was lying in the state of a dead:

> Tammuz, the husband of her youth,
> bathe with pure water, anoint with fine oil,
> clothe him in a bright red garment!

Here we find three essential ritual actions: bathing in water, anointing with oil and clothing in a garment. This is precisely three of the central actions in Mandaean baptism. The whole funeral ritual therefore corresponds to the Mandaean *massiqtā*-ceremony.

It should further be observed that the *bīt rimki* was no permanent structure, but a building "erected for the occasion," quite possibly made from perishable material such as straw or rush."[1] This temporary character corresponds with the structure of the Mandaean cult-hut as Lady Drower has described and fotographed it.[2] There is, however, also an ideological aspect to note. A sufferer who according to general Babylonian opinion had been exposed to an evil spell might be released, if taken to a *bīt rimki*. But this ceremony also possessed a more positive aspect. "The assumption does not seem wholly unjustified that a kind of 'rebirth' was attained through the *bīt rimki* ceremonies (for this concept note the association of *rimku* and *tēdištu*, 'renewal, innovation'), says Laessøe.[3] This corresponds well to the Mandaean idea that the baptizand acquires a new life after baptism, cf. the famous liturgy *ML* No. XXX.

"With Shamash presiding as the divine judge ... the king ... wins his case, i.e. is freed from the influence of evil powers."[4] The king accordingly is the "victor" and this corresponds to the "victory" attained by the Mandaean baptizand, his *zakuta*. It is possible that *zakūtu* in some places in the prayers has a shade of this meaning, and not only means "purity" as it is always understood. In the *bīt rimki* prayers addressed to the Sungod Šamaš there is an important passage which gives us valuable information about the ideas attached to the king's purification in the House of Washing.

> The lofty gods of heaven and earth are standing by him,
>   In the great chapels of heaven and earth they are standing by him.
> Their designs are pure, clean,

---

[1] Cf. Laessoe, *op. cit.*, p. 17.
[2] Cf. Drower, *The Mandaeans*, pp. 124ff.
[3] Cf. Laessoe, *op. cit.*, p. 86. For the deliverance from evil cf. p. 18.
[4] Cf. Laessoe, *op. cit.*, p. 87.

> With their pure, clean water
> The Anunnaki, the great gods themselves purify him,
> Before them he will be clean.
> The counsellor of the pure things of Eridu,
> The lord Isimu, the clean inspector of Eridu ...
> Incantation-priest of the Freshwater Deep, magnificently fitted out,
>   dressed in linen from Eridu, magnificently fitted out,
> In the House of Washing they are standing by Ea's king.
>
> Command of Šamaš, the great lord in heaven and earth:
>   "Life, joy of heart I shall give him as a gift"!
> "King, calf of the Pure Cow,
>   When thou approachest to the House of Washing,
> [daily (?)] may Marduk of the Freshwater Deep [purify thee (?)],
>   daily may Šamaš make thee bright!
> In the garment of kingship may he dress thee!
>   When thou sittest on the throneseat,
> daily may he bestow joy of heart!...
>   Marduk, the prince of heaven and earth,
> Life of the soul for distant time [may he command (?)]!"
> Schollmeyer, *Sumerisch-babylonische Hymnen und Gebete an Šamaš*, p. 35f.[1]

This very important text cannot be given in this place the commentary it really deserves. It must be sufficient to point out some striking features. First of all the cosmic perspective calls for notice: the great gods of heaven and earth take place near the king in the House of Washing. He is then purified and dressed in his royal garment. Purification in water and investment with the royal garment are the two most important ritual actions undertaken. It is further clearly seen how this water-purification is attached to the cult of Ea in Eridu, a fact testifying to its high antiquity, but that the two Semitic gods Marduk and Šamaš have become associated with these ceremonies.

As to the water purification ceremonies it should be pointed out that Ištar was recalled to life in the nether world by being sprinkled with the Water of Life, *mē balāṭi*, cf. *CT* XV 47:34, 38.[2])

Also the oil, in some passages at least, is said to be the oil of Life,

---

[1] The deviations from the translation given by Schollmeyer are insignificant and mostly due to the fact that some technical expressions are better known to-day. That *uṣurāti* e.g. must be "designs" in this passage is rather self-evident, cf. in the prayers the expressions *uṣurāt balāṭi esēru* (in II) and *bēl ṣimāti u uṣurāti* which shows that *uṣurtu* has about the same meaning as *šīmtu*. I read *mēšu⟨nu⟩*, corresponding to *a-bi-ta* in the Sumerian text (Prof. Åke Sjöberg endorses this emendation).

[2] Cf. Widengren, *The King and the Tree of Life*, p. 33f.

cf. *Maqlū* VII 31ff. where in the very interesting invocation to the oil it is called Oil of Life, *šaman balāṭi*:

> I made thee drip from the oil of healing
> which Ea has given to health,
> I have anointed thee with the oil of Life.
> *Maqlū* VII 35-37[1]

Here again we find the ritual action closely associated with the Ea-Eridu-cult and get the supplementary detail that this purification also included an anointing with oil., the Oil of Life. This anointing had as its consequences that the demons of sickness were chased away from the body of the supplicant.

When Adapa ascended to heaven he was offered there both the Water of Life and the Plant (or Bread) of Life, *Epic of Adapa* vv. 60ff.[2]) Moreover he was also given oil, with which he anointed himself, and a garment which he put on. Accordingly we have here a scene in heaven with three ritual actions referred to:[3]) anointing with oil, investment with a garment, and partaking of food of immortality and water of immortality—probably for purification. This looks very much like the three ritual actions undertaken in the Mandaean *massiqtā*-ceremonies.[4]) It is further essential to note that the temple Esagila in Babylon was looked upon as the House of Life, *bīt balāṭi*, cf. IV R 59 No. 2 Rev. 25.[5]) This is not at all an isolated case, for other designations of the same or a similar character are e.g. Dwelling of Life, *šubat balāṭi*, also said of Babylon, or Place of Life, *ašar balāṭi*, said of a holy shrine, cf. *BIN* 2, 22 :146f.[6]) Here we accordingly find the correspondences of the Mandaean expressions "House of Life" and "Place of Life."

That these Accadian expressions are no merely conventional names

---

[1]) Why *CAD* Vol 2, p. 49b renders *mē balāṭi* and *šam balāṭi* as Water of Life and Plant of Life, but *šaman balāṭi* as "health-bringing oil" is difficult to understand. The entry *balātu* shows many such inconsequential renderings.

[2]) For a discussion of the term *u-nam-ti-la*, the Sumerian correspondence of *akal balāṭi* cf. Widengren, *op. cit.*, p. 33 and 35. It calls for notice that the Sumerian version of the Descent of Inanna into the Nether World mentions also the Plant of Life (or Food of Life), cf. above p. 579, n. 2.

[3]) That Adapa actually declined the offer of immortality doesn't change anything in the ritual pattern of course.

[4]) Cf. above p. 578.

[5]) This penitential psalm has been treated several times, cf. S. Langdon, Babylonian Wisdom, in *Babyloniaca* 192, p. 139 n. 4.

[6]) Cf. *CAD* Vol. 2, p. 46a.

is shown by the fact that when a Babylonian sufferer has entered the House of Life and passed into the Gate of Life he was given "life", *balāṭu*, there.[1]) The cultic Babylonian background in this case is perfectly clear.

From the mythical primeval king Adapa we descend in time to a real historical figure, king Lipit-Ištar, fifth ruler of Isin. Several royal hymns glorify his divine kingship, among them a text describing his heavenly enthronization in the Chamber of Destiny, Sumerian *ki-nam-tar-ri-da*, Akkadian *parak šīmāti*, the place where the great gods, the Annunaki assemble, a fact well suited to illustrate the cosmic aspect of the just quoted *bīt rimki* text. At this occasion the Highgod Anu says in his solemn proclamation:

> In the temple of Nippur, in Duranki, he is standing with elevated head.
> Zimmern, *König Lipit-Ištar's Vergòttlichung*, p. 18:50[2]

The Sumerian term *gub*, used here to denote the "standing", corresponds to the Akkadian verbs *nazāzu*, to stand, and *uzzuzu*, to make standing, to erect, as well as to *ašābu*, to dwell.[3]) Its significance is thus conform to the Mandaic *traṣ* and *qaiim*. The enthroned ruler, the divine Uraš, is moreover said to be "standing like the Sungod, *ᵈBabbar-gim gub-ba*, Zimmern, *op. cit.*, p. 16:46. This again is no isolated case for it is said in a bilingual poem addressed to a deity of Tammuz character that he is:

> standing in the sanctuary of the Freshwater Deep, the adorned,
> purified with sparkling lustration.
> *AnOr* 10, p. 214:2-6[4]

Here again the term *gub* is used for "standing".

The deity's or the king's "standing" in the sanctuary has its ritual background in the well-known fact that at the enthronement festival (or at another occasion) his statue was placed in the sanctuary. In a very real sense he was "standing" there, the cultic representation of his mythical "standing" in the heavenly *parak šīmāti*, the Chamber of Destinies.

We must break off here, leaving many details without any discussion. But we think that enough has already been said to demon-

---

[1]) Cf. *Ludlul bēl nīmēqi*, *KAR* 10+11 Rev. 7, W. G. Lambert, *Babylonian Wisdom Literature*, Oxford 1960, p. 60:82.
[2]) Sumerian text: *éš En-lílki Dur-an-ki-ka sag-íl-la gub-ni*.
[3]) Cf. A. Deimel, *Sumerisches Lexikon*, 3:1, p. 49.
[4]) Cf. the discussion of this text in Widengren, *op. cit.*, p. 8f

strate that Mandaean baptism continues above all some Syrian-Mesopotamian ritual traditions, intimately associated with the king's person and having their centre in certain water-purifications with which were connected also the rite of anointing with oil and the investment with the royal garment. These purification ceremonies originally came from the Ea cult in Eridu, near the Persian Ocean, where the Fresh Water Deep was held to be found and where the Water of Life and the Plant of Life had their place in the Sumerian Garden of Paradise. In that way the Mandaeans, living in the same part of Mesopotamia and constructing their cult-hut after the same manner as the Sumerians, have been true to a venerable cultic tradition. However, other cults than the Ea religion incorporated such baptismal rites. Above all Babylon with its cult of Marduk must have propagated it, as well as the *bīt rimki* ceremonies under the protection of the Sungod Šamaš. In that way baptismal ceremonies already existing in Syria may have been greatly stimulated. But we are not able to fill the gap here, and above all—we are not able to say how gnostic sects came to adopt these baptismal rites, a process which may have taken place in the West. Anyhow, such an adoption of water purifications ultimately led to such a baptism as e.g. the Mandaean baptismal rites where Iranian and gnostic ideas have been intimately bound up with the ancient Mesopotamian myth and ritual pattern.

ABBREVIATIONS

AnOr = Analecta Orientalia
BIN = Babylonian Inscriptions in the collection of Nies
CAD = Chicago, Assyrian Dictionary
CP = E. S. Drower, The Canoncial Prayerbook of the Mandaeans
CT = Cuneiform Texts
HS = Horae Soederblomianae
HUCA = Hebrew Union College Annual
JSS = Journal of Semitic Studies
MANL = Memorie dell'Accademia Nazionale dei Lincei
MG = Th. Noldeke, Mandaische Grammatik
ML = M. Lidzbarski, Mandaische Liturgien
NGGW = Nachrichten der Gesellschaft der Wissenschaften, Göttingen
OrSuec = Orientalia Suecana
RoB = Religion och Bibel, Nathan Söderblomsallskapets Årsbok
SPAW = Sitzungsberichte des preussischen Akademie der Wissenschaften
ThLZ = Theologische Literaturzeitung
ThR = Theologische Rundschau

PROBLEMS IN THE STUDY OF IRANIAN RELIGIONS

BY

RICHARD N. FRYE

Harvard University

One is accustomed to speak of the religion of the ancient Greeks, the religion of the Hebrews, or the religion of the Iranians. One merit of the late Erwin Goodenough's work was to show the error of assuming a unique, fixed, "normative" Judaism in the first few centuries of our era as the only Judaism then in existence. This could be paralleled in the Iranian field, for prior to the Sasanian dynasty it would be difficult to find an organized Zoroastrian "church", hence an "orthodox" Zoroastrianism. On the other hand, it would be equally unwise to assume an open field of countless movements, mysticism, gnosticism, whatever one would like, or rather what a scholar might need to fit his particular theory. As a result of the lack of data, we find religions, sects, and great movements in religion, constructed on the basis of one or two passages, or even words, in our sources. One must guard against a monolithic, direct linear descent of Zoroastrianism from the time of the prophet to the present. Likewise, a scholar should hesitate to accept the other extreme of a proliferation of various religions and sects about which we know very little or nothing at all. The present paper is concerned with some of the problems or pitfalls in the study of religion in ancient Iran.

The problems of the date and locality of Zoroaster are by no means solved, at least to everyone's satisfaction, but the concensus among scholars today is that he flourished in eastern Iran about the time of the rise of Cyrus the Great in Fars (Persis) in western Iran. Such was the opinion of some scholars almost a century ago and nothing has changed that opinion. Others still argue that the *Gathas*, the words of Zoroaster, must be much older than the sixth century B.C. to parallel the language of the Vedas, but we know that in some parts of a large linguistic area, a language or dialect can be more conservative, or archaic, than elsewhere, so the argument *ad linguam* is not particularly convincing. The absence of relevant data prevents us from further delineating the history of Zoroaster, for the Avesta is no more a book of history than are the Psalms in Hebrew.[1]) It would be the height of folly, in my opinion, to seek Gnostic elements, a mystery religion, or the like, in the Avesta. Perhaps an overall glance at the question of how the West learned about Zoroastrianism might help at least to clarify the difficulties a scholar in the Iranian field faces.

For the history of Zoroastrianism one may use the figure of an artichoke, which must be peeled layer by layer to reach the heart of the vegetable. The Parsis in Bombay are the most important group of living Zoroastrians, and they were the first source of information for European scholars. But the first leaf of the artichoke was the contact of the Parsis with European ideas which shaped the interpretation of their own religion, consciously or unconsciously. Then a second layer had to be removed, the six hundred odd years in which the Parsis had lived in an Indian milieu. Some may protest that neither the European connections of the Parsis nor their living in India influenced their religion or their interpretation of it. To measure such influences would be very difficult, but to absolutely deny their existence would be unwise.

The next layer to remove is the period when Iran was under Muslim domination, over four hundred years before followers of Zoroaster left Iran for India. Then we arrive at the Sasanian era which is the only one where our sources even approach adequacy. But even here influences from Christianity, Manichaeism and from the Roman, followed by the Byzantine, empire cannot be ignored. In the Parthian and Seleucid periods of history Hellenistic influences on the culture of Iran were massive, not to mention Buddhist and Central Asian contacts. Finally, in Achaemenid times the impact of the ancient Near East, with age-old traditions of Assyria and Babylonia, was sufficient to influence the rapid development of a highly inflected Old Persian language to a Middle Persian stage where grammatical categories had been simplified almost to the stage of New Persian, just to mention one minor aspect of change. In short, to recover the religion of Zoroaster as it existed shortly after the death of the prophet is an almost impossible task beset with many difficulties and pitfalls. On the other hand, the Sasanian state church did develop from a pre-Sasanian Zoroastrianism which traced its origin back to the prophet. There was a continuity, however twisted and wandering, otherwise there would

---

[1]) For a survey of work in Avestan see J. Duchésne-Guillemin, "L'étude de l'iranien ancien au XXème siècle," *Kratylos*, 7 (1962) 1-45, and B. Schlerath, "Die Gathas des Zarathustra," OLZ. 57 (1962) 565-590.

have been no Sasanian church. I believe that all studies of Zoroastrianism should take their departure from the Sasanian state church, for with it we have sources which can be studied, and also analyzed for a picture of what existed previously.

The historical setting must be kept in mind, otherwise it is too easy to construct elaborate theories on the meagre data relating to religion. This is not to say that the phenomenologist has no place in the study of Iranian religions, but rather the historical situation should be the *basis* of study rather than a pattern of religious development derived from other fields. At the outset, in my opinion, belief in magic, amulets, or what might be called "popular religion" should be distinguished from literary, theologic, or "formal religion". The discovery of a statue in Iran with elements of the zodiac, or talismanic representations on it should not cause one to postulate a new religion or cult in Iran. Undoubtedly the religious history of Iran was complicated, but we should be on our guard not to further complicate it with our own pet theories. For example, the statement of Geo Widengren that Zurvanism was, "als eine lebendige Religion mit wirklichen Opferriten, für die parthische Periode gut bezeugt,"[1]) must be examined critically. As evidence for this position, Widengren brings the following data: 1) the mention of χρόνος ἄπειρος "unending time" in the inscription of Mithradates Kallinikos of Commagene;[2]) 2) the name Zurvāndāt in the Shapur Kaʿbah of Zoroaster inscription (Parthian, line 28, M.P. line 35); 3) the position of time *(zurvan)* as over both Ohrmazd and Ahriman in several non-Zoroastrian writings.[3]) Other data, such as the word *zurvan* in the Avesta, are not significant for the reconstruction of a religion. It is not the existence of a god of time in Iran, similar to Greek Kronos (= Xronos), which is under discussion, but the flourishing of a living religion with rites, priesthood, etc., which religion according to Widengren is well attested. I must confess to an inability to see where it is well attested. Or are we in the realm of faith? For my part, until concrete evidence for an established religion of Zurvanism is forthcoming, it is simpler to accept Zurvanism as time speculation inside Zoroastrianism. If Widengren were to answer that Zurvanism was the Iranian form of western Mithraism, then he becomes even more difficult to follow.[4])

---

[1]) Geo Widengren, *Die Religionen Irans* (Stuttgart 1965) 219.
[2]) F. K. Dörner, *Arsameia am Nymphaios* (Berlin, 1963) 44.
[3]) Cf. the discussion in Widengren, 219-222.
[4]) See my review of Widengren's book in *The Journal for the Scientific Study of Religion* 1966.

To repeat, the springboard for the study of Iranian religions must be history, as reconstructed from archaeology, inscriptions and notices of Classical authors. Religious texts must be fitted into the historical pattern and not vice-versa. One must also proceed systematically from the known to the unknown. Simple statements to be sure, but how often forgotten in the study of Iran! Such sentiments need not force one to the statement of resignation, "I do not know" (unfortunately rarely, if ever, heard in the Iranian field), for one should make reasonable inferences, even on the basis of meagre information. Take the problem of Mithraism as an example.

The salient historical facts about Mithra and Mithraism in Sasanian Iran can be briefly summarized since they are so few. So far no traces of a mithraeum have been found in Iran, and the characteristics of a temple of Mithraism are very distinctive.[1]) This can have at least two meanings, either Mithraism, as we know it from many shrines discovered throughout the Roman Empire but especially where the legions were stationed, did not exist in Sasanian Iran, or it did exist, but then was uprooted and destroyed so that no traces have survived. Further, from seals and seal impressions we know that theophoric names with Mithra continued to be popular, although apparently not as widespread or important as during the Parthian period.[2]) We should distinguish between the cult of Mithra, or "the mysteries of Mithra", and a general reverence for Mithra, which latter, from names in Sasanian Iran, seems to have been widespread. The cult of Mithra, with priests or magi, flourished in Asia Minor and existed in the Roman frontier garrison of Dura Europos, but did the cult, or a proto-cult of "the mysteries of Mithra" ever exist in Iran? At the outset one could say that it would be simpler to trace the origins of "the mysteries of Mithra" back to Iran than to assume that even a proto-cult of the "mysteries" never existed in Iran. I stress the word "proto-cult" because, to repeat, there is no evidence for the "Roman" cult of Mithra in Iran.

Once the hypothesis is proposed then one must search for possible evidence for a "proto-cult" of Mithra. There is no direct evidence since the theophoric names, the Mithra Yašt of the Avesta, and the

---

[1]) The mithraeum of Uruk-Warka *has no Mithraic relief*, contrary to G. Widengren, *op. cit.*, 229, where a bibliography is given. The form of the building caused the excavator to speculate that the structure might have been a mithraeum.

[2]) I. M. Dyakonov and V. A. Livshits, *Dokumenty iz Nisy* (Moscow 1960) 24. Further examination of more ostraca in Leningrad in November 1965 showed even more theophoric names with Mithra.

like, merely provide a good background for a cult and little more. The Mithraism of the Roman Empire was primarily a cult for soldiers, so we might expect a counterpart in Iran among the soldiers. We do have references to Iranian reverence for Mithra in Classical sources and the god is portrayed on a bas-relief at Taq-i Bustan, but this is not enough. What we should seek is evidence for a special cult, and such evidence might be forthcoming in archaeological excavations. At Persepolis, probably from the time of Xerxes and Artaxerxes, we have almost a hundred mortars and pestles in green chert, many with Aramaic inscriptions in black ink.[1]) The inscriptions give many names of priests, or '*bd hvn* lit. "servant of the mortar," of treasurers *gnzbr*', and sub-treasurers '*pgnzbr*', and Mithra is present in some compound names.[2]) Since troops of the royal garrison seem to have been the chief occupants of the terrace of Persepolis, one might tentatively connect whatever cult was attached to the mortars and pestles with the soldiers. Another question which must be raised is the fruit, grain, or plant pressed in the mortar. It would hardly be grapes to make wine since the mortars are too small for the purpose and unsatisfactory being of stone. The natural supposition would be that *haoma* (Indian *soma*) was pressed in the mortars, whatever *haoma* was, a flower, weed, or even a mushroom. Regardless of the answer to that question, we can make a further assumption that the cult practiced by the troops at Persepolis was a cult involving the use of *haoma*. If this was a proto-Mithraic cult, then we must assume that for *haoma* wine was substituted later. So we may have had a cult of soldiers in Iran dedicated to Mithra, which passed to Mesopotamia and then to Anatolia, finally to spread throughout the Roman Empire, with changes in the cult all along the way.

The main trouble with the above reconstruction is that it is based on one hypothesis after another in lieu of any concrete evidence of Mithraism. On the other hand, compared for example to the interesting theories of Geo Widengren, the reconstruction above is a model of sobriety and conservatism. Widengren may be completely correct, and future archaeology or the discovery of new written sources may support his views, but at the present they are primarily a matter of imagination and faith.

Another problem in any reconstruction of religion in Iran is the role

---

[1]) Eric Schmidt, *Persepolis* II (Chicago 1957) plate 23 and *passim* in text.
[2]) The inscriptions are unpublished but will be published by R. Bowman of the University of Chicago. Cf. Schmidt, *op. cit.*

of Mesopotamia, which was considered an integral part of Iran, the lowlands, by the Sasanian Iranians. The capital of the Parthians and then of the Sasanians was located in the land between the two rivers, and Babylonia was a great center of culture in antiquity. What happened in Babylonia from the time of Xerxes to Muhammad? Obviously in such an important area much must have happened. Later we know of Manichaeism and Mandaeanism, both of which arose in Mesopotamia. But during and after the decline of the ancient cults in the Hellenistic age, what took their places? Schaeder spoke of a "Babylonian-Iranian syncretism, the existence of which could be inferred only hypothetically from the history of its influences."[1]) Bidez and Cumont wrote extensively about *les mages hellénisés* but we still have no clear picture of Mesopotamia in the Seleucid, Parthian and Sasanian periods.[2]) In my opinion the key to many problems in contacts between Iran and the Mediterranean world lies underground in Mesopotamia. If archaeologists would become concerned with the Parthian and Sasanian strata in their excavations in Iraq, rather than cutting through these levels to reach virgin soil, then we might have a better picture of the land between the two rivers in this period.

In regard to the external relations of Iran, contacts between Judaism and Zoroastrianism have roused great interest over a long period of time with extensive writings. I have dealt with these relations elsewhere, but a few remarks here may not be amiss.[3]) I postulated a continuous influence of Iranian law on Judaism from the time of the Achaemenids (e.g. *dat* "law" in Deut. Daniel and Esther 11.3, *datobar* "judge" in Daniel 3.2) to the Sasanians.[4]) The influence of Sasanian law on the Talmud is revealed in a number of Iranian legal terms in the Talmud, good evidence for a borrowing.[5]) Other borrowings are less evident while a third class would represent possible borrowings for which there is no evidence. In the second category would be the

---

[1]) H. H. Schaeder, article "Parsismus und Judentum", *Die Religion in Geschichte und Gegenwart* (2. Auflage), IV (Tübingen, 1930), 1085.

[2]) *Les mages hellénisés*, 2 vols. (Paris, 1938).

[3]) "Iran und Israel", *Festschrift für Wilhelm Eilers* (in press).

[4]) In the Babylonian Talmud one finds מוהרקי ואבריגני (Erubīm 62) which is Middle Persian *muhrak-i vāvartyan* "an authentic, or credible, document of agreement". Cf. B. Geiger in the *Additamenta ad Librum Aruch Completum*, ed. A. Kohut (New York, 1955) *sub* מהרק. *Muhrāq* also occurs in the Muʻallaqa of an Arab poet; cf. *al-Muʻarab* of al-Jawālīqī, ed. Ahmad Shakīr (Cairo, 1361/1942), 304.

[5]) For example פרסשמנו in Aruch, *op. cit.*, 343, which is MP *pursišnnāmay*, "a record of judicial investigation." See also L. Ginzberg in his introductory essay to the Palestinian Talmud. (New York 1941).

question of the Iranian origin of the demon Ašmdai of the Talmud and Asmodaios of the Book of Tobit, which question is still unresolved. This demon was often identified with the Zoroastrian demon of wrath *aēšma daēva*, whereas some scholars derived the name from the Semitic root *šmd*. An argument against the Iranian etymology is that the Iranian word (Avestan *daēva*, Old Persian *daiva*) probably would have been written *devā* in Aramaic, and the variant forms of the name, from one codex of Tobit, Ἀσμοδαυς does not help us. On the other hand, the nature of the demon Asmodaios, which L. Ginsberg has described fully, does correspond in several aspects to the Iranian demon of wrath.[1]) Unfortunately, I fail to see what one would do with the identification, if true, for this could not be used to demonstrate an influence of Zoroastrianism on Judaism.

In the first category I would place the two Iranian words found in the Dead Sea Scrolls, *nhšyr* "cosmic battle" and *raz* "mystery", about which much has been written.[2]) The latter is the most significant word of the two for it has led to a supposition that it implies the influence of an Iranian mystery religion on the Dead Sea sect.[3]) Regardless whether *raz* is to be traced to Avestan *razah* "loneliness", Sanskrit *ráhah* "solitude", an open question which presents problems, an Iranian mystery religion created on the basis of this word is most unwise.

It is evident that the study of Iranian religions is beset with many problems. What has been briefly mentioned above may give an indication of the nature of such problems and emphasize the need of field work to recover inscriptions and other archaeological pieces of evidence.

---

[1]) *The Jewish Encyclopedia*, II (New York 1902) 217 *sub* Asmodeus.
[2]) Cf. J. De Menasce, "Iranian naxčir," *Vetus Testamentum*, 6 (1956), 213.
[3]) K. Kuhn, "Die Sektenschrift und die iranische Religion," *Zeitschrift für Theologie und Kirche*, 49 (1952), 296-316.

RELIGIONSWISSENSCHAFT REVISITED

BY

WILLARD GURDON OXTOBY
Yale University

I

As late as 1959, the history-of-religions field in America seemed a sideline, even a dead end, peripheral to the main stream of scholarship in the study of religion. A scant eight years later, the field is prospering in American universities and colleges. These paragraphs will attempt to see what has changed and what, despite change, is still with us.

I choose 1959 as a moment for comparison from the recent past because it is the year of Erwin Goodenough's methodological essay "Religionswissenschaft."[1]) In this paper he stated why he felt the turn of the century's ambitious dreams for the history-of-religions field had not materialized, and went on to articulate his own vision of the scientific spirit and its potential for comprehending the religious aspirations of modern as well as ancient men. Goodenough was addressing a gathering of some thirty historians of religions from American universities, who had met to mull over the state of their discipline. That as late as 1959 the outlook was bleak is evident from his reference to the group as a "remnant."[2])

World War I and its aftermath had smothered the earlier Religionswissenschaft, demoting human goodness and progress from the status of an accepted fact to that of a wistful Eden. The scientifically oriented study of religions all but expired in the theological atmosphere of "Paul Barth" which "taught man the complete sovereignty of God [and] the pusillanimity of man,"[3]) and the scholars who might in more favorable times have studied man in the capacity of Religionswissenschaftler had identified themselves with other fields. Moreover, the related disciplines, particularly the social sciences, had turned away

---

[1]) E[rwin] R[amsdell] Goodenough, "Religionswissenschaft," *ACLS Newsletter*, X, 6 (1959), pp. 5-19. Reprinted in *Numen*, VI, 2 (1959), pp. 77-95. Further references to this article will cite both printings, in the order ACLS/Numen.
[2]) *Ibid.*, p. 9/82.
[3]) *Ibid.*, p. 8/81.

from analysis of religious material to data more readily quantified. Religionswissenschaft as a discipline, then, was in disarray partly because it was off limits to theologians as being far too scientific, and off limits to science as being not scientific enough.

To the second half of the address, stating Goodenough's hopes for reviving the discipline through a reconciliation of science and religion, we shall return at the close of this essay, after some remarks about academic disciplines and an examination of certain current methodological alternatives.

The term 'discipline' in the jargon of the past decade means one of the segments of the academic spectrum, one of the fields in which a self-respecting university might consider maintaining a department. The use of this term has been motivated in part by a desire to assert that it is the rigorous method, rather than the content, of one's field which differentiates it from others, particularly in the social sciences: thus one may avoid ruling any facet of human behavior out of his study, and may claim total applicability for his theories, and yet restrict to a manageable number the types of questions he asks in pursuing his research. Speaking of disciplines implies also the compartmentalization of scholarship: disciplines function for scholarly activity as a whole in a way analogous to the department within an individual institution, in that a man is lost without proper credentials in at least one of them, and also in that conversation within them is facilitated and conversation between them impeded. Resistance to the term, or to what it stands for, has come from those who decry compartmentalization of scholarship, those who argue that the proper business of academe is content rather than method, and those who feel that the career loyalties of ambitious scholars are diverted from their rightful object in the university and its departments to a will-o'-the-wisp-like chase after greater prestige in some overarching, therefore uncontrollable, and therefore sinister scale beyond. "The discipline" is in fact a powerful factor in many decisions a department is called upon to make, and perception of the values of "the disciplines" does, I feel, motivate the professional training and activity of most scholars. In many fields an increase in strength of centers of graduate study, relative to undergraduate colleges, has in recent years brought this situation into sharp focus, but the problem itself is by no means new. Goodenough in his article did not use the term "discipline"; he said "field." But clearly he was commenting on the condition of Religionswissenschaft as a discipline, or as a major sub-field of one, and if he were addressing the same subject today he might well speak in the term now current.¹)

Without attempting to resolve the ambiguity of whether any individual sub-field is or is not sufficiently independent to qualify as a discipline in its own right, I propose to characterize the features of an academic discipline. A discipline is: 1) a field of subject matter which 2) is studied with the conscious of a method or methods by 3) a community of scholars. If this is so, then the false choice between method and content dissolves, for both are essential; and adequate attention can be given also to those professional influences—possibly impure but nonetheless real—on a scholar in a discipline which derive neither from pure data nor pure theory.

Let us consider in these terms the status of Religionswissenschaft in 1959. 1) The field was already vast, incredibly so; as Goodenough saw it, "No field of human activity, really, can be thought irrelevant."²) "If analysis of our particular data takes us into strange fields, we go out into them." The limits to this are "the limits of human capacity and length of life."³) But breadth of subject matter, as I have claimed, does not in itself disqualify Religionswissenschaft from status as a discipline.⁴) 2) On the subject of method, however, there was less clarity. Goodenough sought a scientific attitude, "a really objective approach to the value of the myths and practices of religions,"⁵) which he felt had been denied by the theologians of his generation and largely ignored by the scientists. To the extent that his findings ought to be compatible with those of the general historian, the historian of religions has a guideline—in effect, one looks to man for the causes of human experience. A claim of divine intervention may be part of the data one is studying, but the likelihood—even the remote possibility— of divine intervention is highly suspect as a methodological assumption. Goodenough was here speaking for himself; whether he spoke, or speaks, for all in the discipline remains for us to see. 3) As a community of scholars, American Religionswissenschaft in 1959 was in disarray, and it was toward focusing its energies that the meeting had

---

¹) For an instance of the term ten years ago, see below at note 14.
²) Goodenough, "Religionswissenschaft," p. 16/92.
³) *Ibid.*, p. 17/92.
⁴) Mircea Eliade has in fact berated historians of religions for not being broad enough; they have shied away from the comprehensive creative syntheses by which their work could "contribute to the elaboration of a universal type of culture." Eliade, "Crisis and Renewal in History of Religions," *History of Religions*, V, 1 (1965), esp. pp. 5 and 15.
⁵) Goodenough, "Religionswissenschaft," p. 14/89.

been called. There was no regular learned society specifically devoted to the field in America, and the scholars who might have composed one had their principal contacts in related disciplines. There were only a meager handful of graduate students training in the history of religions. While courses in perhaps hundreds of colleges were being given by faculty with training in other fields, the number of full-time teaching positions in the field where trained scholars might anticipate placement seemed pitifully small. Theological schools were hostile; "it is precisely Religionswissenschaft in any meaningful sense that the religious leaders of our generation have rejected."[1])

What has happened in only eight years to transform the picture is an about-face on this third factor, that is, the crystallization of a community of scholars active in the field, in an atmosphere that is now encouraging. Professional-society developments include the American Society for the Study of Religion, dating from the 1959 gathering, with Goodenough as its first president; the creation of the Society for the Scientific Study of Religion, with membership spanning the social sciences; the holding for the first time in America of a congress of the International Association for the History of Religions in 1965, and the National Association of Biblical Instructors' change of its name to the American Academy of Religion, representing a recognition of broader scope in college departments of religion. As colleges have added to their religion departments, and as tax-supported schools in particular have established new programs, the religious traditions of the non-Western world have been a prime area for development; American global involvements of recent decades have helped to pull interest in this direction, while at the same time the sensitivity of college administrators to avoid preferential treatment of Christian or even Judeo-Christian topics has often provided a helping push toward a broader range of comparison.[2]) Employment opportunities for his-

---

[1]) *Ibid.*, p. 9/82. A recent account of the discipline portrays the odium of this period not so much in theological terms as in academic; the blame isplaced on the poor level of history-of-religions scholarship as such. Philip H[arrison] Ashby, "The History of Religions," in [Robert] Paul Ramsey, *ed.*, *Religion* (Englewood Cliffs: Prentice-Hall, 1965), pp. 6, 16.

[2]) It was not characteristic for area-studies programs established ten to fifteen years ago to incorporate "non-Western religions" into their organizational structure; the area-studies pattern was being shaped by the departmental structure of state (i.e., secular) universities, which did not as a rule have departments of religion. To newly-established religion departments in such institutions, area studies represent an existing pattern into which they can fit. For some implications of including "religion" among area-studies fields see Wilfred Cantwell Smith, "Non-

torians of religions, formerly scarce, now far exceed the supply of trained scholars. An important graduate program at Harvard in world religions has gained momentum since 1959 to rival Chicago's formerly undisputed primacy in the field, and with any further increase in the number of first-rate applicants other institutions are bound to prosper too.

The dominance of theologians, which Goodenough lamented in 1959, has yielded to a new pluralism in religious scholarship. Many of the more recently established departments are removed from the centers of traditional theological endeavor and reflect other needs in their educational philosophies. Thus, for example, Robert Michaelsen, now the chairman of such a department in the University of California (Santa Barbara campus), wrote an analysis of religion scholarship presenting the history of religions as a principal alternative on equal status with theological studies.[1]) The distinctions he draws are relevant to established centers as well: most scholars in religion still take their professional training at older institutions where a theological faculty is close to the graduate program if not directly responsible for it, but such centers are increasingly alert to the differences in outlook between the scholarly study of religion and the professional training of the clergy. A reorganization affecting the doctorate in religious studies at Yale in 1963 made this point explicit, and it is safe to expect similar developments at some other leading universities.[2]) And the number of theologians alerting their students to the history-of-religions field may signify a liberalizing and more pluralistic trend—a new humanism[3])— in present-day theology itself.

Whatever the causes, American Religionswissenschaft today boasts besides its engrossing data a still small but growing community of scholars prospering in a hospitable environment. It remains to consider some of the methods proposed for this would-be discipline.

Western Studies: the Religious Approach," in *A Report on an Invitational Conference on the Study of Religion in the State University* (New Haven: The Society for Religion in Higher Education, [1965]), pp. 50-62.

[1]) Robert [Slocumb] Michalesen, *The Scholarly Study of Religion in College and University* (New Haven: The Society for Religion in Higher Education, [1964]), esp. pp. 17-24.

[2]) James M[oody] Gustafson and Robert C[lyde] Johnson, "The Study of Religion at Yale," *Reflection*, LXIII. 1 (1965), pp. 1-3.

[3]) For the phrase see Mircea Eliade, "History of Religions and a New Humanism," *History of Religions*, I, 1 (1961), pp. 1-8.

II

What cohesiveness the American history-of-religions scholarly community possesses is not notably due to agreement on method. Divergence of view is nothing new; rival theories of the nature of religion kept the field lively during the last century and the early part of this one. But discussion in the past decade has differed in focusing not so much on the nature of religion as on the nature of the discipline, not so much on the findings of a "science" as on whether any scientific principles are operative at all. We still wish, as did our predecessors, to know how religions have developed; but the feeling is strong in many quarters that any really useful knowledge is available only when the assumptions on which it rests have been clearly labeled. Joseph Kitagawa, one of the more persistent in the quest for explicit methodological statement, in describing Chicago's program ten years ago sought to embrace the contrast between such relevant disciplines as theology and anthropology: "the History of Religions is neither a normative discipline nor solely a descriptive discipline, even though it is related to both."[1]) And it is this question of the extent to which the variegated hues of Religionswissenschaft can be sorted into primary colors—detached, hortatory, derogatory, antiquarian—which has left the status of the discipline as a "science" open to debate in spoken and written symposia in the decade since.

One approach which has gained considerable vogue during recent years is the phenomenological. The term 'phenomenology' has had a long and intricate history in continental philosophy, and the approach in the study of religion is traced back eighty years to P.D. Chantepie de la Saussaye; but as a major methodological option on this side of the Atlantic it is still something of a novelty. Gerardus van der Leeuw has been available in English since 1938,[2]) Mircea Eliade's *Patterns* since 1958,[3]) and Brede Kristensen since 1960.[4]) Since the death of

---

[1]) Joseph M[itsuo] Kitagawa, "The Nature and Program of the History of Religions Field," *Divinity School News* (November, 1957), p. 17. Repeated in "The History of Religions in America," in *The History of Religions: Essays in Methodology*, ed. Mircea Eliade and Joseph M[itsuo] Kitagawa (Chicago: University of Chicago Press, 1959), p. 19.

[2]) Gerardus van der Leeuw, *Religion in Essence and Manifestation*, trans. J[ohn] E[van] Turner (Sir Halley Stewart Publications, V) (London: Allen and Unwin, 1938).

[3]) Mircea Eliade, *Patterns in Comparative Religion*, trans. Rosemary Sheed (New York: Sheed and Ward, 1958).

[4]) W[illiam] Brede Kristensen, *The Meaning of Religion: Lectures in the Phenomenology of Religion*, trans. John B[raisted] Carman (The Hague: Nijhoff, 1960).

Joachim Wach, the complicated ontological and epistemological baggage of philosophical phenomenology has been left far behind, and the philosophically non-technical masses are fair game for initiation into the rites of the phenomenology of religion. For we shall see that, as practiced, phenomenology is a stance with respect to certain of this century's religious questions in the evaluation of religion.

What is set forth in phenomenological treatments is the generality of religion. Patterns are delineated: persons and places, times and things which are infused with religious meaning are phenomena whose meaning is carefully to be explicated. The phenomenologist characteristically concentrates his interest on those patterns which seem most general, most persistent, most nearly universal. It is the timeless quality of the religious response, its inherent and inevitable domicile in human behavior and expression, which is planted as seed in the assumption and develops to full bloom in the finished treatment of the material. Thus it is not surprising that the religious behavior of primitive societies and the now abandoned practices of pagan antiquity should be fully as deserving of phenomenological study as the religious conceptions of modern civilization; for in the primitive and in antiquity are seen often in simplest, most readily distilled form, the patterns held to be still present in our own culture. Through this emphasis on continuity the primitive in all of us is brought to the surface. Moreover, what is studied is, while not exclusively, certainly dominantly, behavioral. The contemporary findings of the social sciences provide a treasury of data to supplement what can be gained by a reading of classical religious texts. An aim of phenomenology appears to be to find in such data the typical religious response, the representative pattern; for while in the generality of religion it remains to be shown that all men think, there is no doubt that all men behave.

What, then, is man's religiousness? To the phenomenological school it is a response—a response at whatever level of consciousness to a stimulus commonly called "the sacred." Too many problems would arise in an attempt to locate this stimulus within or without the individual or the society, and agreement among scholars on its locus would be probably as undesirable as it is impossible; for, in deciding this, the phenomenologist might cut himself off as he does not wish to do from much of traditional religion. Most of the time "the sacred" is treated as external to human initiative, and basically man responds. If an individual phenomenologist wishes to go so far as to say that all of religion is human, this is a grace-less position to which he commits himself without, as it were, the blessings of the school. Religion—which one might understand in this context as the patterns of faith in something external to man called the sacred—is treated as true.

Two basic methodological principles of the phenomenology of religion have been discerned and frequently stated.[1]) The names of both are inherited from the philosophical writings of Husserl: *epoché* and "the eidetic vision." *Epoché* is the suspension of judgment concerning truth or value, a conscious open-mindedness toward the pattern under study, a willingness to "bracket" or set aside in parentheses one's critical reaction to a religious practice or teaching in which one does not participate, in order to let the data under study manifest themselves unhindered. Kristensen is quoted on this point:

> Let us not forget that there is no other religious reality than the faith of the believers...Not only our own religion, but every religion is, according to the faith of the believers an absolute entity and can only be understood under this aspect.[2])

Thus having set aside the procrustean beds of preconceived critical notions, the phenomenologist applies to his subject "the eidetic vision," a grasp of a religious configuration in its totality. Analogous in a sense to Gestalt psychology, the eidetic vision constitutes a confident, self-validating sense that the pattern which one has distilled represents the real essentials of the data. *Epoché* and eidetic vision are neither critical nor objective in the commonly understood sense of critical objectivity. Just as *epoché* suspends criticism, eidetic vision suspends objectivity. There is nothing outside one's intuitive grasp of a pattern which validates that pattern. The phenomenologist is obliged simply to set forth his understanding as a whole, trusting that his reader will enter into it. But there is no procedure stated by which he can compel a second phenomenologist to agree with the adequacy and incontrovertibility of his analysis, unless the second phenomenologist's eidetic vision happens to be the same as the first's. For this reason phenomenological expositions of religion are in fact very personal appreciations of it, akin more to certain forms of literary and aesthetic criticism than to the natural or even the social sciences. As

---

[1]) See, for example, C[laas] Jouco Bleeker, "The Phenomenological Method," *Numen*, VI, 2 (1959), pp. 98-99. Reprinted in his *The Sacred Bridge: Researches into the Nature and Structure of Religion* (Studies in the History of Religions, Supplements to *Numen*, VII), p. 3.

[2]) W[illiam] Brede Kristensen, *Inleiding tot de godsdienstgeschiedenis* (Arnhem: Slaterus, 1955), pp. 22-23. Quoted by C[laas] Jouco Bleeker, *opp. citt.*, pp. 106-107; p. 11.

an approach phenomenology can be characterized, and yet when it is used for presenting phenomena there appear to be as many phenomenologies as there are phenomenologists, each proceeding from a particular background of religious experience and academic training unique to the individual.

What are the motives of phenomenologists? Unscientific though I find it, the paradox is that phenomenology shares the central aim of descriptive science.[1]) For it moves from data to hypothesis by the inductive principle and, up to a point, holds that the personal commitment of the observer is irrelevant to fact. But why, one is entitled to ask, should a student of religion be interested in being disinterested? The history of the discipline in this century offers ample explanation. The critical history-of-religions school which had its heyday prior to World War I had insisted, among other things, on the primacy of the human, which could be observed by the secular historian and depended not one whit on participation in the revelatory claims of the religious tradition under study. In the West, the theological reaction had limited its ground of truth to precisely those revelatory claims. The use of phenomenology marks an attempt to break this dilemma, by refusing to deny the claims of the participant and at the same time upholding the principles of description and generalization characteristic of the inductive method in science. It is not without significance, I feel, that many of the American scholars who associate themselves with phenomenology come from the circles of theological concern rather than from an academic background in the social sciences. The social sciences study man as man, and assumption of a force such as the sacred is not methodologically necessary; but phenomenologists, in conferring approval in principle on the faith of others, preserve it for their own tradition as well. Scholarship is kept from contradicting evangelism. Phenomenology's chief potential clientele is among religiously committed persons as an appreciation of religious commitment.[2]) This is primarily individual (rather than corporate, and

---

[1]) I use "science" here in its English-language sense, referring to the natural and social sciences. I find phenomenology "unscientific" as the humanities (Geisteswissenschaften) are in general, in that the scholar's (open) sympathy and creativity bear on his findings. I so not mean to say that he vitiates his findings by forcing his (closed) sympathies on them; were that the case, I should choose to say "unscholarly" (unwissenschaftlich),

[2]) Van der Leeuw as participant is described by John B[raisted] Carman. "The Theology of a Phenomenologist: an Introduction to the Theology of Gerardus van der Leeuw," *Harvard Divinity Bulletin*, XXIX, 3 (1965), pp. 13-42. On being

certainly not cultic): each student of primitives enters sympathetically into primitive religious patterns, and discovers the primitive in himself; each student of mythology and symbolism enters into ancient myths with a recognition of the myth-maker in himself. The individual scholar enters into a reverent extension of knowledge which strengthens his own private or shared attitudes toward a transcendent reality. In phenomenology, the science of religions has in effect become a religious exercise itself.

III

If "the faith of the believer" is a rallying point for phenomenologists, it is also a central concern of a second approach which in recent years has been influential in North America. It lacks a commonly agreed-on name, being in America often identified with an individual scholar, but I have heard Europeans refer to "the American approach." I propose to refer to it as the dialogic approach. For, while phenomenology asks that the believer pose, as it were, for the portrait the observer draws, the dialogic approach asks him to do some of the drawing. This too, we shall see, is a stand in respect to some of this century's basic issues of evaluation.

What is set forth in the dialogic treatments, especially Wilfred Smith's, is the particularity of religion. One prefers to talk of one religion, or one interreligious contact, at a time; if "response to the sacred" is important, the *diversity* of response to the sacred must be an equally salient point. Insofar as the study of history stresses the particularity of individual developments, this approach welcomes history in contrast with phenomenology's persistent categories; for to Smith, Islam, Christianity, and the rest, are new every day—different from each other, from their own earlier forms, different even from one Muslim or Christian to the next.[1]) For an analysis of what has made religions different from each other one turns not to mass man in his totality nor to an archetypal figure as a paradigm, but to the actions, ambitions, and ideas of the leading individuals who have in fact left their mark on mankind in the course of events. The intellectual is the

---

"theologically conditioned" see also Bernard E[ugene] Meland, "Theology and the Historian of Religions," *Journal of Religion*, XLI, 4 (1961), p. 267.

[1]) Wilfred Cantwell Smith, "The Comparative Study of Religion: Reflections on the Possibility and Purpose of a Religious Science," *McGill University Faculty of Divinity Inaugural Lectures* (Montreal: McGill University, 1950), p. 51.

key to religion. Ideas shape practices, so one concentrates on the elite in preference to the masses, the conceptual in preference to the cultic. Even primitive men, insofar as they are treated at all, are considered as reflective. The dialogic approach would thus appear to side with the humanities, but relevance is social. Concern for the pressing contemporary implications of religious diversity characterizes the position to such an extent that despite Smith's historical and philological bent a British historian of religions described his approach as sociological.[1]) The dialogic school does indeed contrast with earlier conceptions of the work of Religionswissenschaft by lending its imprimatur to the view that the religious traditions worth studying are a handful of "great" (intellectualized),[2]) "living," "world" faiths not far exceeding half a dozen.[3]) The religious history of the ancient Mediterranean, Near East, and Iran tends to attract interest only as it illuminates the identity of the major contemporary faiths.[4]) (And the minor living faiths are not commonly party to the world dialogue). Paradoxically, a scholar working in the history of ancient Egyptian religion might more readily find an audience among the phenomenologists than among professed historians of the dialogic school. For the discipline takes on the characteristics of applied research, rather than pure.

What, then, is religion? Smith explores some of the presuppositions and prejudgments that have been implicit in talking about such a thing as religion at all.[5]) For "religion" is not a thing, nor is it, as some in the West have thought, the generic term for a series of separate things called "religions." He proposes to replace the noun "religion" (the adjective "religious," which does not beg the ontological ques-

---

[1]) [Samuel George Frederick Brandon], "Americans Pioneer New Trend in Study of Religion," *The Times* (London), September 20, 1965, p. 9.

[2]) See the preface of Charles J[oseph] Adams, *ed., A Reader's Guide to the Great Religions* (New York: Free Press, 1965). Adams confesses his discomfort with the wording of his title: "there is reason for challenging the use of the adjective 'great' in the title in view of the inclusion of a chapter on primitive religions" (p. xiv).

[3]) See, for example, Huston [Cummings] Smith, *The Religions of Man* (New York: Harper, 1958); Wilfred Cantwell Smith, *The Faith of Other Men* (Toronto: Canadian Broadcasting Corporation, 1962; expanded version New York: New American Library, 1963); and particularly the selection implicit in the series of Kenneth W[illiam] Morgan, *ed., The Religion of the Hindus* (New York: Ronald, 1953), *The Path of the Buddha: Buddhism Interpreted by Buddhists* (New York: Ronald, 1956), and *Islam—the Straight Path: Islam Interpreted by Muslims* (New York: Ronald, 1958).

[4]) Note the virtual absence of these ancient religions from Adams, *ed., op. cit.*

[5]) Wilfred Cantwell Smith, *The Meaning and End of Religion* (New York: Macmillan, 1963).

tion, remains admissible) by speaking of "tradition" or of "faith" or of the combination of the two, depending on the context of discussion. Tradition is the cumulative deposit of religious communication; it is overt and consists of observable particulars. And there is a diversity of traditions, so that the noun may have a plural. But faith, *sensu stricto*, does not take a plural. Faith is the activity of man's religiousness which is always personal, always properly understood only in terms of its believing subject, always particular—but yet at the same time universal. Smith, ready at other points to challenge essences and categories, here commits himself to a constant common denominator of religion, and he follows it with the expectation that the recognition of its common quality can serve as the basis for interreligious understanding.

With characteristic skepticism, Smith has professed to be impatient with methodological formulations and has claimed no commitment to a methodological program, preferring to be what I have called a methodological program, preferring to be what I have called a "methodological pluralist." By this he appears to intend an eclectic reading of the findings of various approaches, postponing decision at least until more data are in hand—a cautious echo, in a sense, of Kitagawa's ideal of interdisciplinary catholicity. One could hardly set forth the tradition-faith dichotomy or the universality of human faith as methodological principles of the dialogic school. In the first place, though I see them ultimately as assumptions, Smith treats them in *The Meaning and End of Religion* as though they were conclusions following from his historical analysis of word usage. In the second, no "school" consensus has rallied about the dichotomy. But I do discern two points which are close to status as accepted "dialogic" principles. The first is *the mutuality of scholarly statement*. Since what Western scholars now say about Asian faiths is no longer limited to a Western public but may at once be challenged by adherents of the tradition described, scholarship should be a joint effort on the part of participant and non-participant. Any attempt to represent the faith, say, of Muslims must be not only recognizable to Muslims but should be a step toward "our" understanding of Ourselves (Muslims and non-Muslims together) as scholars and as religious men simultaneously.[1]) In the case of religion, the desired scholarly understanding

---

[1]) Wilfred Cantwell Smith, "Comparative Religion: Whither—and Why?" in *The History of Religions: Essays in Methodology*, ed. Mircea Eliade and Joseph M[itsuo] Kitagawa (Chicago: University of Chicago Press, 1959), p. 34.

entails not a passive subject matter but is an involvement with other persons as persons. Note the generous assumption underlying this process: that Religionswissenschaft is not limited to observation and description; the advanced stages call for the observer-describer to speak as a religious man. Note further the even more generous assumption that academic discourse of this sort is, or can be made, so nearly intercultural that the *religious* man of the tradition being described can enter into the academic frame of mind to serve as the court of authority in testing the description. That such understanding is highly desirable is one proposition; that it is, or will soon be,[1]) realized on any adequate scale is quite another.

Distinctions between observer and participant are to wither away also in the second "dialogic" principle, *the manipulability of religious history*. Process, for Smith, is the nature of things. Change is to be looked for in the past; it is the acid test of all rigid formulations, and one delights in finding how something now taken for granted was not always so. But even more importantly, change is to be expected in the future, and future change is largely within the possibility of man's conscious control. The future history of religions depends on what religious men decide, and the discipline is thus applied toward mutuality in an increasingly cramped world.[2]) By the moral imperative for scholarship to foster world community the religious leader in the capacity of historian of religions can judge the partisan revelatory claims of his own tradition to be insufficiently inclusive.[3]) By this moral imperative, the historian of religions in the capacity of religious leader can influence his community toward change. The dialogic school hopes, as the saying goes, to eat its cake and still have it too, in expecting the individual scholar-leader to identify publicly with his tradition and at the same time to modify it. Change has been effected by religious leaders in the past, but they have not characteristically been historians of religions; the charismatic Religionswissenschaftler may turn out to be as elusive as the philosopher-king.

What are the motives of the dialogic approach? Whereas phenome-

---

[1]) Even in 150 years, the length of time for which Smith proposes that the effort be sustained. Wilfred Cantwell Smith, "Mankind's Religiously Divided History Approaches Self-Consciousness," *Harvard Divinity Bulletin*, XXIX,1 (1964), p. 9.

[2]) *Ibid.*, pp. 1-5.

[3]) Wilfred Cantwell Smith, "The Christian in a Religiously Plural World," in the expanded edition of *The Faith of Other Men* (New York: New American Library, 1963).

nology is more or less comfortable with theological orthodoxy, I see among the dialogic school more frequently a sharp struggle with such orthodoxy, in some cases as a survival of the older liberal Protestant theology, in the case of younger scholars particularly a dissatisfaction with exclusive truth-claims. Asian travel is frequently an influence, and may include frustration with an embarrassingly isolationist Christian mission enterprise. The tradition-faith dichotomy may be rooted in part in the pietistic strand of historic Protestantism, with its distaste for institutional, ceremonial religion. At all events, the hoped-for result is a change in Christian theology rather than either to jettison it or archivally to preserve it, family-album fashion, in the brackets of *epoché*.[1]) The dialogic approach may stress the particular in its data but it seeks a corporate experience of shared faith. In this the science of religions is once again a religious exercise itself.

IV

Having examined the phenomenological and the dialogic approaches as stemming from classical Religionswissenschaft in their descriptive concern but departing from it in their religious sympathy and theological motivation, let us now return to the parent discipline. The family of offspring from the turn-of-the-century Religionswissenschaft includes also what one might call the scientific humanists. This emphasis continues the older Religionswissenschaft alongside the others, in America as well as in Europe. Though historically a product of Western culture, it claims universal validity and at least in theory admits into the company of scientists any non-Westerner who masters its use.

What is held central by the scientific humanists is that religious experience and behavior are a human activity, and that the scholar's inference of any value or transcendent truth from his material is beyond the strict limits of the science of religion as such. The commitment of the observer to any religious view, or to none, is irrelevant, and the presence or absence of adherents of the tradition he is describing is likewise irrelevant, because the scientist uses exclusively data which are public, external, and observable to all. No theological, practical, or humanitarian concerns, in short, are to have any bearing

---

[1]) Certainly this is my intent in "The Post-Ecumenical Era," *Theology Today*, XXIII, 3 (1966), pp. 374-385.

on the method of pure scholarship. Zwi Werblowsky in 1960 stated the consequences of this empiricism as follows:

> It [Religionswissenschaft] is an anthropological discipline, studying the religious phenomenon as a creation, feature, and aspect of human culture. The common ground on which students of religion *qua* students of religion meet is the realization that the awareness of the numinous or the experience of transcendence (where these happen to exist in religions) are—whatever else they may be—undoubtedly empirical facts of human existence and history, to be studied like all human facts, by the appropriate methods... On the other hand the discussion of the absolute value of religion is excluded by definition, although it may have its legitimate place in other, completely independent disciplines such as e.g. theology and philosophy of religion.[1])

Seemingly dispassionate, this strict view has been championed in heated discussions in recent years, notably in questions of the membership and program of international history-of-religions congresses. In attendance at Tokyo (1958), Marburg (1960), and Claremont (1965) were adherents of religious traditions that Western scholarship had once been content to study from the outside; and with their presence came assorted theological, practical, and humanitarian concerns. Werblowsky wrote concerning the Marburg congress:

> Very frequently papers are presented that testify to the good will and moral endeavour of certain religions and/or certain scholars, but they can hardly be said to be relevant to the work which the IAHR was meant to do. Their rightful place would be at conferences convened for the purpose of promoting international and interreligious peace and understanding.[2])

And at Claremont, the same essential stand was taken in the presidential remarks of Geo Widengren.

From this point of view, it may be irrelevant to ask concerning the secular humanist's motives. In the simple classical model of a science, the interest of the observer, and the uses to which his discovery might be put, are not part of the data. But one is tempted to speculate nonetheless, and I venture the suggestion that there are two chief incentives toward secular-humanist Religionswissenschaft: some such as Werblowsky (who are not Christians) understandably deplore the

---

[1]) Quoted by Annemarie Schimmel, "Summary of the Discussion" [at Marburg] *Numen*, VIII, 2-3 (1960), pp. 236-237. See also R[aphael] J[ehudah] Zwi Werblowsky, "Revelation, Natural Theology and Comparative Religion," *Hibbert Journal* LV,3 (1957), pp. 278-284.

[2]) R[aphael] J[ehudah] Zwi Werblowsky, "Marburg—and After?" *Numen*. VIII,2-3 (1960), p. 217.

importation of theological concerns because such concerns when imported have been dominantly Christian; others, such as Morton Smith, include Christians by background who through their own past frustration with obscurantist conservative theologians have come to resist theological concerns.[1])

We return now to the remainder of Goodenough's essay outlining his hopes for reviving the scientific study of religion in America. Goodenough sided unquestionably with the scientific humanists in background and outlook, and yet there is a searching openness in his proposals which goes beyond the sterile isolationism and externalism of Werblowsky's Marburg platform.[2])

Goodenough modifies the characterization of science by including, after all, the motivation of the scientist and his quest as a human being. "Historians of Religions, that is, must include in their study, and in their sympathy, the new religion of science, or of scientists, along with the religions and thoughtways they have hitherto considered."[3]) We cannot ultimately compartmentalize the religious in man any more than we can prevent biochemists, psychologists, or economists from seeing ramifications of their study everywhere.

> But all these approaches blend so inextricably that to define the character and compass of any one aspect invades the boundaries of every other. If we do not recognize this we limit to the point of petty distortion the aspect we try to define... we must resort to description which moves from an essential center indefinitely outward, rather than fabricate definitions that work from borders inward.[4])

Religion, for Goodenough, is man's attempt to adjust himself to life in the presence of the "tremendum," the great unknown, the overwhelmingly uncontrollable and anxiety-producing universe around him. No matter how much he knows, man is anxious; most men therefore screen themselves from the source of anxiety by accepting the myths, rites, codes, and explanations of their society, while

---

[1]) Morton Smith has set forth a systematic statement of his position in a paper, "Historical Method as Used in the Study of Religion," at the American Society for the Study of Religion, New York, April 23, 1966.

[2]) Let this not be interpreted as unfair to Werblowsky, for he says as much himself: "Of course 'comprehension' by itself [i.e., as distinct from *mutual* understanding] is a purely academic virtue and as such in a way sterile. And that is what it ought to be; it would be disastrous for scholarship if it were otherwise," R[aphael] J[ehudah] Zwi Werblowsky, "On the Role of Comparative Religion in Promoting Mutual Understanding," *Hibbert Journal*, LVIII,1 (1959), p. 34.

[3]) Goodenough, "Religionswissenschaft," p. 11/85.

[4]) *Ibid.*, p. 12/86.

a few venture to formulate new explanations which are then available for others to accept as screens. Religionswissenschaft is not merely the cataloguing of the things we do not believe which others have thought of the tremendum, nor is it a Jungian rummaging through the catalogue for parallels to what we do believe; for Goodenough it is not data but hypothesis, a search for inherent principles, "a really objective approach to *the value of* the myths and practices of religions" (italics mine).[1]) The ideal religious man is one who "keeps his integrity, his dignity, as an ignorant but seeking human being."[2]) That religion is a human quest is Goodenough's starting point which he finds corroborated constantly in his examination of human quests, and for contemporary man scientific exploration is the form which that quest takes. "Creative scientists, like creative painters and musicians, advance into the tremendum as they try methods never used, join the hitherto unconnected, break all rules as they seem inadequate, even though earlier men had found those rules useful."[3]) The fate of creative scholarship in Religionswissenschaft is thus like that of religious "loners" and innovators in all ages: it means going against what one's society accepts as revelation concerning the tremendum. But by Goodenough's standards this act, impious in the eyes of the traditionalist, is a truly religious act: "For if we still have to kill the old dream that religion is a matter of revelation, through Religionswissenschaft we may discover that the scalpel itself has become a sacramental instrument."[4])

What seems to have motivated Goodenough toward this position, apart from his own lifelong stance as an outspoken critic of traditional theology, is a concern to add to the critical-historical equipment of the older Religionswissenschaft the insights of psychology. Psychology was, he felt, America's distinctive contribution to the discipline. One does not only read texts; the motivation of the scholar is a particularly interesting and accessible sort of data. Religionswissenschaft as Goodenough conceived and practiced it was often a lonely venture, affording psychological satisfactions in some ways akin to the phenomenologist's, more often than it led to the sociological results the dialogic school seeks. But the self-understanding which Goodenough saw as the fruit of Religionswissenschaft differs in a salient respect

---

[1]) *Ibid.*, p. 15/89.
[2]) *Ibid.*, p. 16/91.
[3]) *Ibid.*, p. 17/93.
[4]) *Ibid.*, p. 18/94–95.

from that of phenomenology: it is in principle transferable to others, objectively, as scientific knowledge, because it has been scientifically arrived at. One's judgment is part of the data, and no gymnastics are required to keep it bracketed. In Goodenough's version of scientific humanism, the science of religions is a religious exercise, and science and true religion have become one and the same.

It is doubtful that any very large following will come in the foreseeable future to agree with Goodenough's presentation of science as a religious exercise; "religious" is a word the revision of whose public connotations would be a monumental undertaking. Majority sentiment among American scholars in the discipline, moreover, seems sympathetic to the idea that religions are by nature traditional religions, while Goodenough's proposal is traditional neither by religious nor by academic standards. Then, too, most American scholars identify, however contentedly or restlessly, with one of the traditional religious bodies, and in consequence tend to give more emphasis to religious community than the psychological-philosophical interest of his essay makes a place for. But an appreciation of his influence does not stand or fall on the success of one daring thesis. I wish to single out three implications of his work which seem to me not only widely acceptable but imperative for the future health and balance of the discipline.

1) The scholarly study of religion cannot set theoretical limits to the type or range of its data. Specialization is, by contrast, a *practical* necessity; each scholar must master "a philology," as Eliade says. We must, to be sure, see that patient hours are spent in the exegesis of traditional texts, but the analysis of other data by other techniques must not be overlooked in the process.[1]) Consider, for example, what is added to a conception of ancient Judaism by Goodenough's research on symbols.

2) Nor may we set chronological limits: a "dead" religion is just as inherently worthy of study as is a living one. To restrict the study of religions to a politically significant handful potentially reduces the range of human experience available to the student of religion. In the face of the popularity of chronologically provincial area-studies and social-science emphases on the American academic scene, there is a value in asserting a non-pragmatic cosmopolitanism of religious study. More could be done, as along the lines of this memorial volume, to

---

[1]) *Ibid.*, pp. 16-17/92 and the passage quoted from p. 12/86.

bring together in the history-of-religions enterprise the scattering of American students and scholars in ancient religions who see themselves as belonging still in linguistic and historical disciplines.

3) An outsider to a tradition can have as much to say as its participant. To offset the past Protestant bias of departments of religion by hiring as teachers Buddhists or Catholics (or agnostics) *because* they are Buddhists or Catholics (or agnostics) is a case of righting one wrong with another. Such a policy, while perhaps politically expedient, mistakes the criteria of scholarship; such individuals, even possibly the same individuals, ought to be employed because they are scholars and for no other reason. Party commitment as contrasted with academic competence is no criterion of scholarship in any responsible department of political science; why should it be otherwise in the study of religion? Christian observers of Asian religions, and of Judaism, have committed grievous errors of interpretation in the past, it is true; but why should the careful scholar of today suffer for their sins? Religionswissenschaft rightly conceived is not the religious indoctrination of the young, nor a bland, laudatory interfaith panel, but a quest for new descriptive formulations in which the trained outsider might—just might—have something to say. These three goals for Religionswissenschaft, then, are each a little closer to realization through the work of Erwin Goodenough.

The article "Religionswissenschaft" stands, therefore, as a very personal credo, even a spiritual autobiography, coming in the fullness of Goodenough's career. We see him, in his categories, as an unorthodox but profoundly religious man. Looking back at his essay from the perspective of the present, we see it also as one of the important statements in the history of the discipline. It remains a provocative critique of the mood of traditional theology, and in readable language enshrines points with which any discussion of scientific attitude in the study of religion must come to terms. It is, as it were, an oracle which we shall do well to visit now and again.

ON THE UNIVERSALITY OF SYMBOLS

BY

PAUL FRIEDMAN M.D., Ph. D.
New York City

In a letter to me of January 3, 1964, Goodenough mused: "I have written myself out of all but a very few readers, and my work will be used as a quarry as the medieval people used the Greek temples unless I do this last [referring to Volume XII which is a summary and review of the preceding volumes]. I have no objection to its use as a quarry, so long as its thesis is not forgotten."

And forgotten it will never be. For Goodenough's monumental contribution to our understanding of symbolism will endure as a source of inspiration for many years to come, primarily for the psychological researcher. I have pointed out elsewhere[1]) that among all the theories advanced to explain how the breach of the Jewish prohibition against image-making became possible, the psychoanalytic approach might prove the most appropriate. Goodenough's belief that the motifs and pictorial representations gleaned from paganistic cultures were not intended to serve merely as a decorative appeal but had an active symbolic meaning finds ready acceptance by modern psychology. The religious symbol "is a thing of power or value operating upon us to inspire, to release tensions, to arouse guilt or to bring a sense of forgiveness and reconciliation."

Goodenough was able to demonstrate how symbols could pass from one religion to another because they did not carry literal meanings. By taking over some special symbols while rejecting others along with the myths of the pagans, Jews and Christians sustained the continuity of religious experience. For instance, both Judaism and Christianity rejected Dionysus "with horror," but they preserved his symbols. Thus, there is a definite meaning inherent in religious symbols which to the devout is as expressive and as direct as a verbal language. The *lingua franca* in the history of religious symbols consists primarily of abstract signs and not of mythological scenes. The borrowed motifs

---
[1]) Jewish Symbols in the Greco-Roman Period. *The Psychoanalytic Quarterly*, Vol. XXIX: 254-263, 1960.

held real meaning for the Jews as symbols the value of which they had thoroughly Judaicized. Had they failed to do so, had they used them in pagan ways with pagan meanings, the Jews would not have been able to remain Jews.

In my comments on the symbols presented in Goodenough's volumes published between 1953 and 1956, I stressed the point that the themes which found access to and became an integral part of Jewish religious belief and practice were irresistible because of their universal validity—they expressed the fundamental yearnings and strivings of all mankind, namely, for fertility and immortality.

It is, indeed, gratifying to see that the theologian and historian of today arrive at the same interpretations which the psychoanalyst only yesterday advanced with diffidence. A case in point is the following citation from Professor Bickerman: "The perennity of symbols, which survive their various and passing explanations, is conditioned by the perennity of man's condition, who, as the Greeks knew, is tormented by the two grimmest tyrants: Hope and Fear."[1]

Although Goodenough claimed to have remained eclectic in his psychological evaluation of the symbols, nonetheless he tended to rely considerably upon classical psychoanalytic concepts. It is true that he rejected the concept of libido replacing it by a more general philosophic life urge reminiscent of the Bergsonian *elan vital*.

His views on the psychology of religion definitely reflected the psychoanalytic theory of infantile development although he did not subscribe to the ubiquitous presence of the oedipus complex. Paralleling the evolution of religion to the maturation of the individual he explained the *unio mystica* as the identification with the mother; he sees the formation of the superego as submission to the father, that is, to God. Thus, in Judaism, the human being is rewarded in both life and the hereafter "strictly on the basis of obedience."

However, in spite of Goodenough's attempt to construct a conceptual framework more appropriate perhaps, in his view, for a history of religion than the concept of libido, he found himself "driven with relentless regularity to identical explanations, and to ascribing identical values to all the symbols—driven not by my predilections but by the evidence itself. The basic value... appeared definitely an erotic one. This was the major element all the symbols had in common." Indeed, his reluctance to accept the libido theory may

---

[1] Symbolism in the Dura Synagogue. *The Harvard Theological Review*, 58, No. 1, 1965.

be due only to insufficient familiarity with its clinical applications. This would also explain his misunderstanding and rejection of the concept of sublimation.

At this point we must consider the problem of transmission of symbols from ancient times to modern life, a question still replete with enigmas, although it cannot be examined in detail in this paper. Freud and some of his disciples (Ferenczi, Rank and Sachs) believed in an inheritance of so-called memory traces. Jones adhered "to the view that symbolism has to be re-created fresh out of individual material and that the stereotypy is due to the uniformity of the human mind in regard to the particular tendencies that furnish the source of the symbolism, i.e., to the uniformity of the fundamental and perennial interests of mankind."[1]) It must be stressed here that Jung's assumption of inherited archetypes independent of individual experience which have their source in the collective unconscious is clinically untenable. To Jung, archetypal images appear phenomenally as entities of an external existence rather than as part of the self.

Perhaps a few ideas on the general theory of symbolism should be mentioned. Symbols may have a multiplicity of simultaneous meanings and with some exceptions are expressible in ideational or verbal terms. The psychoanalyst does not accept dream symbols as having *a priori* meaning. Even those regarded as of universal occurrence must be analyzed against the background of an individual's psychological constellation. For the same symbol, in its condensed latent structure, may vary in its meaning from individual to individual.

The two universal symbols which would seem to represent a perfect continuity between the mythological fantasies, fears and anxieties of primtive times and the dreams and phobias of our patients of today are the ladder and the bridge. In actuality, these are two different aspects of the nostalgic yearning inherent in man: the *unio mystica*, a concept so much cherished by Professor Goodenough.

The symbols of the ladder which figured so prominently among the relics in the Dura Synagogue were widely represented in the ancient Egyptian, Syrian, and Greek cultures. According to Goodenough, for the Egyptians the ladder meant the ascent to heaven or to the glorious hereafter; for the Syrians, the ascent to Astarte; and for the Greeks, to Adonis or, according to Plato, to Beauty by the ladder of love. To the Jews the ladder meant to lift oneself to God, to Jehovah.

---

[1]) The Theory of Symbolism. In *Papers on Psychoanalysis*. London: *Bailliere, Tindall & Cox*, 1948.

Jacob's dream of the ladder is perhaps the most eloquent fulfillment of the fantasy nurtured by man. According to the Biblical story, Jacob dreamed of a ladder reaching up to heaven; he saw angels ascending and descending on the rungs. He awakened with a start and in awe exclaimed: "This is the place of God."

At one level the meaning of ladder symbolism in this dream is easily discernible: the ladder represents a connection between God and man and the dream represents the hallucinatory wish fulfillment of a union with God. The angels are the intermediaries between God and man. While this mystical symbolization is readily accepted and reconciled with all the traditional Jewish concepts there is another level of interpretation which is less easily fathomed, namely, the psychoanalytic concept of the underlying erotic and sexual connotation of the symbol as seen in the dreams of our patients. The ladder stands for the phallus, for sexual intercourse (angels going up and down).[1] Although angels are conceived of as sexless creations, in many painting of the Sixteenth and Seventeenth Centuries, especially in that of Feti,[2] they are undisguised female forms.

The symbolism of the ladder as such has not greatly preoccupied the psychoanalyst;[3][4] more clinical studies have been devoted to bridge symbolism. In my own study[5] I aimed to show that the same ambivalence which we observe today in the neurotic's attitude toward the bridge and his fear of the other shore must have existed in the human mind since the dawn of civilization; an ambivalence which reflects nothing else but the longing to reunite what has been divided by the act of creation.

The mythologies of many cultures contain the concept that creation is a disruption of the sexual act; thus in the Egyptian theogony the earth and sky were not separated until the god Shu lifted up the sky and thereby severed the sexual union of the sky goddess and the earth

---

[1] Dr. William G. Niederland devoted a special study to Jacob's Dream in which he examined this complex and highly condensed symbol and elaborated on the events preceding the dream. *Journal of the Hillside Hospital.* Vol. III, No. 2, 1954.

[2] *The Ladder of Jacob.* Domenico Feti (1589?-1623), Wien Kunsthistorisches Museum.

[3] According to psychoanalytic experience the equivalents of the ladder may be a staircase, steps, shafts, elevators, etc.

[4] *The Anchor Bible Genesis,* New York, 1964, pp. 217-218. E. A. Speiser translates ladder as ramp or solid stairway.

[5] The Bridge: A Study in Symbolism. *The Psychoanalytic Quarterly,* Vol. XXI: 49-80, 1952.

god. This act of division is depicted in Egyptian grave pictures which unmistakably show the phallic link.[1])

In the Sudan similar representations were found, but with the position reversed: the natives there spontaneously described the male as "sky" and the female as "earth." This variant is paralleled in Greek mythology; Uranos (the sky) forbids his children by Gaia (the earth) to be born (come forth into the light); Kronos, the youngest son, attacks and castrates the father at night as he rests upon the earth, thus separating the sky god from the earth goddess.

Small wonder, then, that in the lore of so many cultures we find the dream of reuniting by magic, by supernatural bridges, what had been divided: earth and sky — heaven and earth. It is clearly represented, for example, in the rainbow bridges of the Nordic and the Jewish mythologies. In the Edda the link between heaven and earth takes the form of a rainbow joining the earth to Valhalla, the heavenly dwelling of Odin; over this bridge the Valkyries transported the heroic warriors killed in batlle. In the Old Testament the rainbow appears as a symbol of the covenant between God and man.

The recurring symbols in these images of magical bridges reflect cultural fantasies in which the process of elaboration is subtler and more obscure than in the neurotic symptom. However, they can easily be elucidated by the methods of dream interpretation. In West Africa the bridge between heaven and earth was thought to be formed by a stream of arrows — certainly the least disguised of all phallic symbols — shooting rapidly into the air. It does not require analytic acumen to discern the phallic symbolism in the "sword bridge" of Arthurian romance, over which the hero had to pass before he could claim his lady; nor to understand the second ordeal awaiting him on the other shore, the ferocious lions that had to be killed before he could penetrate the fortress in which the heroine was imprisoned.

Even more striking, perhaps, are the underlying wishes and fantasies about the connection between this world and the other world: the world of the living and that of the dead. A typical legend has the devil wrestling with God for the soul of man on the "Bridge of Judgment" which links this world to the afterworld; the righteous make the passage successfully while the wicked fall into the raging waters of hell below. In the Greek myth, the river Styx lying between earth and

---

[1]) *The Gods of the Egyptians*. Wallis Budge, E. A. London: Metheun & Co., Vol. II, 1904.

Hades was bridged by the ferry of Charon, to whom the spirits of the departed had to pay a toll before they could cross.[1][2]

Special reference should be made here to Roheim's work where passage to the other world is believed to lead over a gulf "which has to be crossed by the soul on a bridge...and passage is obstructed by a demon or animal...The demon who obstructs the road and all the other dangers of the passage represent anxiety derived from the oedipus and castration complex...Sacrifice is a substitute for castration, for to those who are dilligent in sacrificing it is promised that the funeral pyre will not burn their genital organs..."[3]

The theme of sacrifice recurs again and again in our own culture in innumerable legends and tales dealing with bridges that span rivers or chasms, linking territory to territory. These legends seem to imply acts of defiance which aroused feelings of guilt, thus providing the motivation for sacrificial atonement.

Folklore abounds in stories about the "bridge sacrifice" without which the bridge could not be built, which alone could make safe its foundations. Some of the medieval legends had the master builder, desperate after a long series of mishaps and frustrations, enter into a pact with the devil, who would help erect the bridge and in return receive the soul of the first creature that crossed it. Sometimes the builder outwitted the devil by sending an animal across the bridge first; but more often he "gave the devil his due." Many bridges in in Europe still bear the name of Devil's Bridge and there are some that even today are believed to have the victim's body built into the foundation.[4]

These are but a few examples from religion and mythology. They show that recurrent themes of anxiety, fear, awe, sin, and atonement are associated in the popular imagination with bridges, even as they are in the dreams and fantasies of neurotics. Indeed, it is not surprising that the bridge assumed the significance it has had from antiquity to

---

[1]) Charon and the Obolos. Roheim, Geza. *The Psychiatric Quarterly Supplement*, XX, 2, 1946.

[2]) Another group of legends about the bridge to the other world exists in the Indian folklore of North America. One of these, reported by Wilbur J. Watson, presents a remarkable resemblance to the Greek myth: "Like Cerberus by the river Styx, the Hurons have a dog guarding a tree trunk (notice the primitive form of the bridge) which spans the river Death." *Bridges in History and Legend*. Watson and Sara Ruth. Cleveland: J. H. Hansen, 1937.

[3]) Animism and Religion. Roheim, Geza. *The Psychoanalytic Quarterly*, I, 1932.

[4]) Cf. Watson: Op. cit.; also: Bridge, in *Encyclopedia of Religion and Ethics*, Vol. II, New York: Charles Scribner's Sons, 1910.

the present. In ancient Rome the most important priesthood was the *Collegium of the Pontifices*, charged with the administration of the *jus divinum*, that part of the civil law which governed the relations of the community with the state deities. The *pontifices* were the builders and guardians of bridges; it was their task to pacify the river spirits and make the structure of the bridges secure.

The word *pontifex* clearly derives from *pons* (bridge) and *facere* (to make), literally bridgemaker. This institution was later incorporated in the Catholic Church, and *Pontifex Maximus*, the title borne by the Roman emperor as the head of the *Collegium of the Pontifices*, was assumed by the Pope as head of the Church of Rome. Nor was this merely a formal title; the actual control of bridges also passed to the Church and bridgebuilding became, officially and in fact, a religious enterprise and a work of notable piety. In 1189 the religious order of the *Fratres Pontifices* was created in France and chapels were attached to the bridges built by these priests, some of them erected upon the bridge's span.[1])

But whether in mythology or religion, we always find an underlying guilt associated with bridge symbolism. A source of this guilt is suggested in the following passage from the ancient Hindu epic, the *Ramayana*:

> O'er the deep sea where monsters play
> A bridge, O Rama, will I lay;
> For sharer of my father's skill
> Mine is the power, and mine the will.[2]

"Sharer of my father's skill" is the motif of myth, romance, and neurotic drive alike. Whether it be a bridge to the forbidden shore, to the omnipotent god, or to the inviolate heroine, the same primitive, incestuous drive is apparent. And it is this common element which illuminates the progression from myth to romance. The sacrifice, in all bridge myths, is the abstention from instinctual gratification involving a renunciation by the individual for the greater good of the community. This gave to the bridge its "holy" character and made of it a sacred monument. The primitive rebellion is personified in the hero of romance, the defiant adventurer ever seeking new exploits by which to assert his manhood. What is an awesome object to the devout

---

[1]) It is believed that the *Pont St. Cloud* in France was called *"un pont maudet"* because it was not built by or under the supervision of the clergy. (Watson: *Op. cit.*)

[2]) Watson, *Op. cit.*

exercises a compulsive—an "unholy"—attraction for the hero. He flaunts his potency: "Mine is the power, and mine the will."

In the evolution from tribal myth and anonymous romance to the highly differentiated expressions of modern thinking, the symbol of the bridge has acquired new overtones without losing its original meaning.

Space does not permit mention of more than a few literary products in which the bridge motif plays an important part. One such product is a story by Goethe, "Das Märchen," which is an elaborate political allegory of the internal division and chaos in Germany at that time couched in terms of a fairy tale. In this tale a serpent, sacrificing himself for the good of the community, turns into a bridge as a symbol of love linking the "ugly" (pre-revolutionary) world and the "ideal" (post-revolutionary) world across the abyss of ruthless asceticism and irresponsible politics. The entire story, with its involved action and symbolism, would be deserving of detailed analytic examination which cannot be attempted here. The most significant point is that Goethe chose two phallic symbols and transformed one into the other: the serpent into the bridge.

This symbol also provides the central image of Thornton Wilder's novel, *The Bridge of San Luis Rey*.[1]) The last sentence of the novel reads: "There is a land of the living and a land of the dead, and the bridge is love, the only survival, the only meaning." The book ends on this apparently hopeful note. In a wicked world five good people have died and will be forgotten but the love that was in them will suffice to give meaning to their lives and to confute the nihilistic suspicion that life has no meaning, that their lives and loves were in vain. Such is the ostensible (though not entirely explicit) message of the book. Yet the theme itself, with its profoundly tragic implications, belies the moderate optimism of its conclusion; the inescapable fact is that the Bridge of San Luis Rey breaks. Love had failed the lovers because it was inherently incapable of giving or recieving satisfaction.

That the theme is not the miracle of love but its failure is apparent in the final scene. Brother Juniper, intent upon demonstrating in the the lives of the victims the ultimate wisdom and righteousness of a God who confounds the wicked and saves the good, is rewarded for his pains by being pronounced a heretic and burned at the stake. His death is the crowning monument to imperfect faith and love.

---

[1]) New York: Albert & Charles Boni, Inc., 1927.

The incapacity to love, as symbolized by the collapse of a bridge, is most daringly pictured by Franz Kafka in his shortest story, "The Bridge," in which the author completely identifies himself with the bridge. "If was stiff and cold," the story opens. "I was a bridge, I lay over a ravine." No tourist had yet approached his impassable height over the icy stream and he was not yet recorded on any map. Nevertheless, he was indubitably a bridge, he reassured himself; for "without falling, no bridge, once spanned, can cease to be a bridge."

One evening above the roar of the stream below he heard the sound of a human step. "Straighten yourself, bridge," he told himself, "make ready, railless beams, to hold up the passenger entrusted to you. If his steps are uncertain, steady him unobtrusively, but if he stumbles show what you are made of and like a mountain god hurl him across to land." The man advanced, tapped the bridge with the iron point of his walking stick, plunged the stick into "my bushy hair," and then jumped suddenly and violently with both feet. "I shuddered with wild pain, not knowing what was happening. Who was it? A child? A dream? A wayfarer? A suicide? A destroyer? And I turned round so as to see him. A bridge to turn round! I had not yet quite turned round when I already began to fall. I fell and in a moment I was torn and transpierced by the the sharp rocks which had always gazed up at me so peacefully from the rushing water."[1])

To the psychoanalyst, Kafka's personification of himself as a bridge indicates a deep-seated, overwhelming fear of failure in sexual intercourse: the bridge (phallus) bends, loses its rigidity, falls onto the piercing rocks in the water below.

Elsewhere, while meditating on the activities of life and work, Kafka again likened himself to a bridge: "...A delicate task, a walking on tip-toe over a brittle plank that serves as a bridge; having nothing under one's feet, with one's feet raking together a plank to walk on; walking on nothing but one's own reflection seen in the water below, while holding the world with one's feet so that it doesn't fall apart; clenching one's hands in mid-air merely to help one bear the strain."[2])

The most famous treatment of a bridge in contemporary litarature is Hart Crane's poem, "The Bridge," immortalizing Brooklyn Bridge.[3])

---

[1]) *The Great Wall of China and Other Pieces*. Trans. by Willa and Edwin Muir. London: Martin Secker Ltd., 1933.

[2]) *A Franz Kafka Miscellany*. Second edition. New York: Twice A Year Press, 1946.

[3]) *The Collected Poems of Hart Crane*. Edited with an Introduction by Waldo Frank. New York: Liveright Publishing Corp., 1946.

It not only epitomizes the tragic struggle of the poet but is also an example of a work of creative imagination which thwarts the intentions of its author. Crane intended the bridge to stand as a multiple symbol denoting the union of finite and infinite, matter and spirit, physical and spiritual love (Eros and Agape), past and present, being and becoming. "Very roughly," he explained, "it concerns a mystical synthesis of 'America'..."[1]) The bridge is meant to synthesize the temporal world of chaos and bring man to the state of order which his soul craves; the machinery itself is the benevolent instrument for the expanding consciousness of man, the thrust into an absolute and eternal, beyond time and space.

This, then, was the bridge that Crane had intended to represent in in his poem. To him, love — the bridge of love — was as much a prerequisite of poetic creation as of physical creation. But normal heterosexual love lay beyond his capacity. "Sterility," he once wrote, "is the only decadence I recognize"[2]) — and his was the sterility of the homosexual.

Crane's biographers and critics have made much of the poet's unhappy family constellation: the deep attachment to the mother; the divorce of the parents ("the curse of sundered parentage," he called it in "The Bridge"); but above all, the image of a strong, successful, virile father, contemptuous of the son's poetic leaning and effeminate ways (the parallel with Kafka is striking) and the "ricochet of antagonism and attraction," as Waldo Frank[3]) characterizes this son's relationship to his father. This strong ambivalence appears to be the underlying principle of his poetry. When the twenty-one-year-old Crane finally broke away from his father he seemed elated. "The best thing is that the cloud of my father is beginning to move from the horizon now," he wrote to a friend.[4]) In the same breath, he rhapsodized over this severance of the parental tie as the "bridges burn't behind." But these were the very bridges he was attempting to construct and reestablish.

One year after the death of his father Hart Crane committed suicide. He could not erect the bridge of love.

---

[1]) In a letter to Gorham B. Munson, quoted in Weber, Brom: *Hart Crane. A Biographical and Critical Study*. New York: The Bodley Press, 1948.
[2]) In a letter to The Little Review. Weber: *Op. cit*.
[3]) Frank: *Op. cit*.
[4]) Weber: *Op. cit*.

VI
BIBLIOGRAPHY

A BIBLIOGRAPHY OF THE WRITINGS OF ERWIN RAMSDELL GOODENOUGH

BY

A. THOMAS KRAABEL

University of Minnesota

Introductory note

Within each year, the following order is used: First, books; second, sections of, or articles in, books, annuals, Festschriften, etc.; third, articles and review-articles in periodicals, listed chronologically; fourth, book reviews, listed alphabetically by author.

The 23 entries marked with an asterisk are those Professor Goodenough considered "my more important articles," according to a list drawn up in 1961 and last revised in 1964. Some substantial articles do not appear on the list, probably because they were incorporated into later publications, e.g. parts of *The Psychology of Religious Experiences* (1965) had their beginnings in the paper, "Religion and Psychology" (1947).

Abbreviations often used: H.T.R. for *Harvard Theological Review* and J.B.L. for *Journal of Biblical Literature*.

1915

"Christianity and the War" (The Sixtieth Clark Prize Oration), *Hamilton Literary Magazine* XLIX (1915) 344-48. (Published with a picture of the author in the year of his graduation from Hamilton College; other undergraduate writings have been omitted from this bibliography—A. T. K.).

1923

The Theology of Justin Martyr, Jena, Verlag Frommannsche Buchhandlung, 1923.

1925

* "The Pseudo-Justinian 'Oratio ad Graecos'," *H.T.R.* XVIII (1925), 187-200.

1926

"Philo and Public Life," *The Journal of Egyptian Archaeology*, XII (1926), 77-79.

1928

* "The Political Philosophy of Hellenistic Kingship," *Yale Classical Studies*, I (1928), 55-102.

1929

The Jurisprudence of the Jewish Courts in Egypt. Legal Administration by the Jews under the Early Roman Empire as Described by Philo Judaeus, New Haven, Yale University Press, 1929.
"Paul and Onesimus," *H.T.R.* XXII (1929), 181-83.
* "Kingship in Early Israel," *J.B.L.* XLVIII (1929), 169-205.

1931

The Church in the Roman Empire (The Berkshire Studies in European History), New York, Henry Holt and Company, 1931.

1932

* "A Neo-Pythagorean Source in Philo Judaeus," *Yale Classical Studies*, III (1932), 115-64.

Review of:

H. Schneider, *The History of World Civilization from Prehistoric Times to the Middle Ages*, New York, 1931, 2 vols. In: *The Saturday Review of Literature* VIII, no. 40 (April 23, 1932), 690.

1933

"Introduction" to Stewart Means, *Faith: An Historical Study*, New York, The Macmillan Company, 1933, xi-xiii.
"Philo's Exposition of the Law and his *de vita Mosis*," *H.T.R.* XXVII (1933), 109-25.

Review of:

I. Heinemann, *Philons griechische und jüdische Bildung*, Breslau, 1932. In: *The Journal of Religion*, XIII (1933), 93-95.

1935

By Light, Light. The Mystic Gospel of Hellenistic Judaism, New Haven, Yale University Press, 1935.

1936

"Archaeology and Jewish History," *J.B.L.* LV (1936), 211-20

(Review-article on J.-B. Frey, *Corpus Inscriptionum Iudaicarum, IIIe siècle avont J-.C. au VIIe siècle de notre ère* (volume I), Rome-Paris, 1936).

Review of:

S. Belkin, *The Alexandrian Halakah in Apologetic Literature of the First Century C.E.*, Philadelphia, 1936. In: *J.B.L.* LV (1936), 319f.

E. Eyre, *European Civilization: Its Origin and Development*, New York, 1935, Vols. I-III. In: *The Saturday Review of Literature*, XIII, no. 15 (Feb. 8, 1936), 16f.

Philon von Alexandrien *Von den Machterweisen Gottes: Eine zeitgenössische Darstellung der Judenverfolgungen unter dem Kaiser Caligula*, uber. H. Lewy, Berlin, 1935. In: *J.B.L.* LV (1936), 245f.

R. Schütz, *Les idées eschatologiques du Livre de la Sagesse*, Paris, 1935. In: *J.B.L.* LV (1936), 318f.

1937

Religious Tradition and Myth, New Haven, Yale University Press, 1937.

* "Literal Mystery in Hellenistic Judaism," in *Quantulacumque: Studies Presented to Kirsopp Lake by Pupils, Colleagues and Friends*, eds. R. P. Casey, S. Lake and A. K. Lake, London, Christophers, 1937, 227-41.

"New Light on Hellenistic Judaism," *Journal of Bible and Religion*, V (1937), 18-28.

"Symbolism in Hellenistic Jewish Art: The Problem of Method," *J.B.L.* LVI (1937), 103-14.

Review of:

W. Schubart, *Die religiöse Haltung des frühen Hellenismus* ("Der Alte Orient, XXXV, 2"), Leipzig, 1937. In: *J.B.L.* LVI (1937), 279f.

1938

The Politics of Philo Judaeus, Practice and Theory, with a General Bibliography of Philo by H. L. Goodhart and E. R. Goodenough, New Haven, Yale University Press, 1938.

Review of:

P. Boyancé, *Le Culte des Muses chez les philosophers grecs: Études d'histoire et de psychologie religieuses*. ("Bibliothèque des Écoles Françaises d'Athènes et de Rome, 141"), Paris, 1937. In: *American Journal of Philology*, LIX (1938), 487-90.

J. R. Marcus and A. Bilgray, *An Index to Jewish Festschriften*, Cincinnati, 1937. In: *J.B.L.* LVII (1938), 106f.

W. O. E. Oesterley and H. Loewe, eds. *Judaism and Christianity*, London-New York, 1937, 2 vols. In: *J.B.L.* LVII (1938), 345-48.

A. Parrot, *Le "Refrigerium" dans l'au-delà*, Paris, 1937. In: *J.B.L.* LVII (1938), 104-06.

1939

"Problems of Method in Studying Philo Judaeus," *J.B.L.* LVIII (1939), 51-58. Review-article on W. Volker, *Fortschritt und Vollendung bei Philo von Alexandrien: eine Studie zur Geschichte der Frömmigkeit*, Leipzig, 1938).

Review of:

T. Arvedson, *Das Mysterium Christi: Eine Studie zu Mt. 11 : 25-30* ("Arbeiten und Mitteilungen aus dem NT Seminar zu Uppsala, VII") Leipzig-Uppsala, 1937. In: *J.B.L.* LVIII (1939), 303-06.

M. Braun, *History and Romance in Graeco-Oriental Literature*, Oxford, 1938. In: *J.B.L.* LVIII (1939), 64f.

1940

An Introduction to Philo Judaeus, New Haven, Yale University Press, 1940.

* "The Fundamental Motif of Christianity," *The Journal of Religion*, XX (1940), 1-14. (Review-article on A. Nygren, *Agape and Eros*, London, 1938).

Review of:

R. O. Ballou et al., eds. *The Bible of the World*, New York, 1939. In: *J.B.L.* LIX (1940), 316.

S. Belkin, *Philo and the Oral Law: The Philonic Interpretation of Biblical Law in Relation to the Palestinian Halakah* ("Harvard Semitic Series, XI"), Cambridge, 1940. In: *J.B.L.* LIX (1940), 413-19.

A. Bertholet, *Über kultische Motivverschiebungen* (Reprint from the Sitzungsberichte der preus. Akademie der Wissenschaften, phil-.hist. Kl., XVIII, 1938, 164-84), Berlin, 1938. *J.B.L.* LIX (1940), 83.

C. Clemen, *Lukians Schrift über die syrische Göttin* ("Der Alte Orient, XXXVII, 3-4"), Leipzig, 1938. In: *American Journal of Philology*, LXI (1940), 250.

T. Klauser and A. Rucker, eds., *Pisciculi: Studien zur Religion und Kultur des Altertums, F. J. Dölger dargeboten* ("Antike und Christentum, Ergänzungsband I"), Münster, 1939. In: *The Journal of Religion* XX (1940), 403-07.

Comte Robert du Mesnil du Buisson, *Les peintures de la synagogue de Doura-Europas, 245-256 après J.-C.* („Scripta Pontificii Instituti Biblici, LXXXVI"), Rome, 1939. In: *J.B.L.* LIX (1940), 420-23.

Philo, with an English Translation, by F. H. Colson ("The Loeb Classical Library"), Cambridge, 1939, vol. VIII. In: *J.B.L.* LIX (1940), 57-59.

Philonis Alexandrini, In Flaccum, ed. and tr. H. Box, London, 1939. In: *J.B.L.* LIX (1940), 59f.

1941

Review of:

S. W. Baron, *Bibliography of Jewish Social Studies, 1938-39*, New York, 1941. In: *J.B.L.* LX (1941), 446f.

M. P. Nilsson, *Greek Popular Religion*, New York, 1940. In: *J.B.L.* LX (1941), 345-48.

H. M. Orlinsky, *An Indexed Bibliography of the Writings of W. F. Albright*, New Haven, 1941. In: *J.B.L.* LX (1941), 447.

A. Reifenberg, *Ancient Jewish Coins*, Jerusalem, 1940. In: *J.B.L.* LX (1941), 445f.

1942

* "Scientific Living," *The Humanist*, II (1942), 8-10.

Review of:

Philo, with an English Translation, by F. H. Colson ("The Loeb Classical Library"), Cambridge, 1941, vol. IX. In: *J.B.L.* LXI (1942), 305f.

1943

"Early Christian and Jewish Art," *The Jewish Quarterly Review* XXXIII 1942-43 (1943), 403-18. (Review-article on C. R. Morey, *Early Christian Art: An Outline of the Evolution of Style and Iconography in Sculpture and Painting from Antiquity to the Eighth Century*, Princeton, 1942).

1945

* "John a Primitive Gospel," *J.B.L.* LXIV (1945), 145-82.

"A Reply (to R. P. Casey, "Professor Goodenough and the Fourth Gospel," *J.B.L.* LXIV (1945), 535-42)", *J.B.L.* LXIV (1945), 543f.

* "The Mystical Value of Scholarship," *Crozer Quarterly* XXII (1945), 221-25.
* "Make-Believe," *The Deke Quarterly*, October 1945, 97f.

Review of:

W. L. Knox, *Some Hellenistic Elements in Primitive Christianity* ("Schweich Lectures on Biblical Archaeology, 1942"), London, 1944. In: *The Journal of Religion* XXV (1945), 297f.

1946

* "Philo on Immortality," *H.T.R.* XXXIX (1946), 85-108.

"The Crown of Victory in Judaism," *The Art Bulletin* XXVIII (1946), 139-59.

1947

"Religion and Psychology" (A seminar conducted at Columbia University, New York City, in 1947), mimeographed.

"The Old Conditioning" *in:* "Jewish Culture in this Time and Place, a Symposium," *Commentary* IV (1947), 431.

1948

* "Needed: Scientific Study of Religion. How Long Will Free Inquiry Neglect This Basic Field?" *Commentary* V (1948), 272-77.

"Wolfson's Philo," *J.B.L.* LXVII (1948), 87-109 (Review-article on H. A. Wolfson, *Philo: Foundations of Religious Philosophy in Judaism, Christianity and Islam*, Cambridge, 1947, 2 vols.).

Review of:

Norman Brown, *Hermes the Thief*, Madison, 1947. In: *Crozer Quarterly* XXV (1948), 181f.

1949

Review of:

L. Delatte, *Les Traités de la royauté d'Ecphante, Diotogène et Sthenidas* ("Bibliothèque de la faculté de philosophie et lettres de l'Université de Liège, fasc. 97"), Paris, 1942. In: *Classical Philology* XLIV (1949), 129-31.

1950

Review of:

A. J. Festugière, *L'Hermètisme* ("K. Humanistiska Vetenskapssamfundets i Lund, Arsberättelse 1947-48, I"), Lund, 1948. In: *The Review of Religion* XIV (1949/50), 423f.

1951

"The Menorah among Jews of the Roman World," *The Hebrew Union College Annual* XXIII, 1950-51, part 2, (1951), 449-92.

"The Place of Religion in the Treatment of the Mentally Deficient," *Crozer Quarterly* XXVIII (1951), 120-26.

Review of:

C. Bonner, *Studies in Magical Amulets, chiefly Graeco-Egyptian*, ("University of Michigan Studies, Humanistic Series, XLIX") Ann Arbor, 1950. In: *American Journal of Philology* LXXII (1951), 308-16.

G. Kisch, ed. *Pseudo-Philo's Liber Antiquitatum Biblicarum* ("Publications in Mediaeval Studies, The University of Notre Dame, X"), Notre Dame, 1949. In: *Speculum* XXVI (1951), 394f.

1952

"The Evaluation of Symbols Recurrent in Time, as Illustrated in Judaism," *Eranos-Jahrbuch* XX, 1951 (1952), 285-319.

* "The Inspiration of New Testament Research," (Presidential Address, Society of Biblical Literature and Exegesis), *J.B.L.* LXXI (1952), 1-9.

Review of:

M. Bodkin, *Studies of Type-Images in Poetry, Religion and Philosophy*, London, 1951. In: *The Review of Religion* XVII (1952), 69-71.

W. Wolff, *Changing Concepts of the Bible: a Psychological Analysis of Its Words, Symbols and Beliefs*, New York, 1951. In: *The Review of Religion* XVII (1952), 71-73.

1953

Jewish Symbols in the Greco-Roman Period ("Bollingen Series XXXVII"), New York, Pantheon Books, 1953, vol. 1-3: *The Archaeological Evidence from Palestine and the Diaspora*.

* "Religious Aspirations," in *The Age of Diocletian: A Symposium, 1951*, New York, 1953, 37-48.

* "The Crown of Acanthus (?)," (with C. B. Welles), *H.T.R.* XLVI (1953), 241f.

Review of:

S. Aalen, *Die Begriffe ,Licht' und ,Finsternis' im Alten Testament, im Spätjudentum und im Rabbinismus* ("Skrifter utgitt av det Norske

Videnskaps-Akademi i Oslo, II, Hist.-Filos. Klasse, 1951, No. 1")
Oslo, 1951. In: *Journal of Theological Studies*, N.S. IV (1953), 63-68.
S. A. B. Mercer, *The Pyramid Texts in Translation and Commentary*, New York, 1952, 4 vols. In: *Yale Review* XLII (1953), 440f.

1954

Jewish Symbols in the Greco-Roman Period ("Bollingen Series XXXVII"), New York, Pantheon Books, 1954, vol. 4: *The Problem of Method; Symbols from Jewish Cult*.

Review of:

Philo, Supplement I: Questions and Answers on Genesis and Exodus translated from the Ancient Armenian Version of the Original Greek, by R. Marcus ("The Loeb Classical Library"), London-Cambridge, 1953. In: *J.B.L.* LXXIII (1954), 169-71.

1955

Toward a Mature Faith, New York, Prentice-Hall, Inc., 1955 (reissued as a Yale Paperbound, Yale University Press, 1961).
"Our Faith and Doctor Freud," *The Saturday Review* XXXVIII, no. 20 (May 14, 1955) 9f, 40f.

Review of:

H. I. Bell, *Cults and Creeds in Graeco-Roman Egypt*, New York, 1953. In: *Jewish Social Studies* XVII (1955), 335.
G. Dix, *Jew and Greek: A Study in the Primitive Church*, New York, 1952. In: *Jewish Social Studies* XVII (1955), 334.

1956

Jewish Symbols in the Greco-Roman Period ("Bollingen Series XXXVII"), New York, Pantheon Books, 1956, vol. 5-6: *Fish, Bread and Wine*.
"New Light from Stones," *America-Israel Bulletin*, Vol. I, no. 2, Dec. 1, 1956, 3f.

1957

"Pagan Symbols in Jewish Antiquity. The Vine, the Eagle, the Lion," *Commentary* XXIII (1957), 74-80.
* "The Bosporus Inscription to the Most High God," *The Jewish Quarterly Review* XLVII 1956-57, (1957), 221-44.

1958

Jewish Symbols in the Greco-Roman Period ("Bollingen Series XXXVII"), New York, Pantheon Books, 1958, vol. 7-8: *Pagan Symbols in Judaism*.

"The Paintings of the Dura-Europos Synagogue, Method and an Application," *Israel Exploration Journal* VIII (1958), 69-79.

* "A Jewish-Gnostic Amulet of the Roman Period," *Greek and Byzantine Studies* I, (1958), 71-80.

"Communication" (Reply to H. Strauss' review of *Jewish Symbols in the Greco-Roman Period*, vol. 4-6, in *Judaism* VII (1958), 81-85), *Judaism* VII (1958), 177-79.

Review of:

C. H. Kraeling, *The Synagogue*, with contributions by C. C. Torrey, C. B. Welles and B. Geiger ("The Excavations at Dura-Europos conducted by Yale University and the French Academy of Inscriptions and Letters. Final Report, VIII, pt. 1"), New Haven, 1956. In: *American Journal of Archaeology* LXII (1958), 248-51.

1959

"Philo of Alexandria" in *Great Jewish Personalities in Ancient and Medieval Times*, S. Noveck, ed. (B'nai B'rith Great Books Series, I), New York, Farrar, Straus and Cudahy, 1959, 102-19.

* "Honest Doubt," *Yale Alumni Review* XXII, no. 7 (April, 1959), 19-21.

"Religionswissenschaft," *ACLS Newsletter* X, no. 6 (June, 1959), 5-19; also printed in *Numen* VI (1959), 77-95.

"Philo of Alexandria," *Jewish Heritage* I, no. 4 (Winter, 1959), 19-22 (reprinted in *Jewish Heritage Reader*, selected, with introduction by Morris Adler, New York, Taplinger Publishing Co., 1965, 173-77).

"Opening Remarks by the President," *Transactions of the Connecticut Academy of Arts and Sciences* XXXVIII (1959), 154f.

"The Orpheus in the Synagogue of Dura-Europos: A Correction" (Reply to H. Stern's article in *Journal of the Warburg and Courtauld Institutes* XXI (1958), 1-6), *Journal of the Warburg and Courtauld Institutes* XXII (1959), 372.

1960

* "The Bible as Product of the Ancient World," in *Five Essays on the Bible*, Papers Read at the 1960 Meeting of the American Council of Learned Societies, New York, Published by the ACLS, 1960, 1-19.
* "A Yale Professor and Groton Parent Looks at the School," in *Views from the Circle: Seventy-five Years of Groton School*, Groton, Massachusetts, Published by the Trustees of Groton School, 1960, 335-46.
* "The Evaluation of Symbols in History," 519-25, and
"The Characteristics of Western Culture," 675-79, in *Proceedings of the IXth International Congress for the History of Religions, Tokyo and Kyoto, 1958*, Tokyo, 1960.

Review of:

M. Eliade and J. M. Kitagawa, eds. *The History of Religions: Essays in Methodology*, Chicago, 1959. In: *Ethics* LXX (1960), 343f.

V. Tcherikover, *Hellenistic Civilization and the Jews*. Philadelphia-Jerusalem, 1959. In: *Jewish Social Studies* XXII (1960), 105-08.

1961

"The Rabbis and Jewish Art in the Greco-Roman Period," *Hebrew Union College Annual* XXXII (1961), 269-79 (Julian Morgenstern Festschrift).

"Judaism at Dura-Europas," *Israel Exploration Journal* XI, (1961), 161-70.

1962

An Introduction to Philo Judaeus (second edition, revised), Oxford, Basil Blackwell, 1962; New York, Barnes and Noble, 1963 (sic).

"Philo Judaeus," in *The Interpreter's Dictionary of the Bible*, eds, G. A. Buttrick *et al.*, New York-Nashville, 1962, vol. 3, 796-99.

"The Scientific Study of Religion," Fourth Centennial Lecture, University of Denver Centennial, April 24, 1962 (mimeographed).

"A Rhyme on My Retirement," *The Spider's Web* XXVII, no. 2 (February, 1962), 5 (This issue of this publication of Jonathan Edwards College, Yale University was dedicated to the author at his retirement.)

* "Myths and Symbols for Children," (with Evelyn W. Goodenough), *Religious Education* LVII (1962), 172-77, 236.

"Catacomb Art," *J.B.L.* LXXXI (1962), 113-42 (Review-article on A. Ferrua, *Le Pitture della Nuova Catacomba di Via Latina*, Città del Vaticane, 1960 (Monumenti di antichita cristiana, Ser. 2, Vol. 8).)

"The New Synagogue at Woonsocket, Rhode Island," *Art International* VI, no. 10, (December 20, 1962) 26-29.

Review of:

Werner Jaeger, *Early Christianity and Greek Paideia*, Cambridge, 1961. In: *American Historical Review* LXVII (1962), 760.

1963

"Symbols as Historical Evidence," *Diogenes* XLIV (1963), 19-32; also printed in the French edition as "Les symboles et les preuves en histoire," (tr. M-.A. Béra), *Diogène* XLIV, 21-37.

Review of:

M. Avi-Yonah and E. G. Kraeling, *Our Living Bible*, New York, 1962. In: *J.B.L.* LXXXII (1963), 140f.

H. Rahner, *Greek Myths and Christian Mystery*, New York, 1963. In: *J.B.L.* LXXXII (1963), 444-48.

1964

Jewish Symbols in the Greco-Roman Period ("Bollingen Series XXXVII"), New York, Pantheon Books, 1964, vol. 9-11: *Symbolism in the Dura Synagogue.*

* "Religionswissenschaft," in *Religion Ponders Science*, ed. E. P. Booth, New York, Appelton-Century-Crofts, Inc., 1964, 63-84.

"An Early Christian Bread Stamp," *H.T.R.* LVII (1964), 133-37.

1965

The Psychology of Religious Experiences, New York, Basic Books, 1965.

Jewish Symbols in the Greco-Roman Period ("Bollingen Series XXXVII"), New York, Pantheon Books, 1965, vol. 12: *Summary and Conclusions* (vol. 13: General Index, with Maps, is in preparation).

1966

"Early Christianity in Acts," in *Studies in Luke-Acts, Essays Presented in Honor of Paul Schubert*, eds. L. E. Keck and J. L. Martyn, Nashville, 1966: Abingdon Press, 51-59.

"The Greek Garments on Jewish Heroes in The Dura Synagogue," Philip W. Lown Institute of Advanced Judaic Studies, Brandeis University, *Studies and Texts*: Volume III, Biblical Motifs, ed. Alexander Altmann, Cambridge, Harvard University Press, 1966, 221-37.

1967

"A Historian of Religion Tries To Define Religion," *Zygon* 2 (1967) 7-22.

1968

"Life Purpose in View of the Past," in *Studies in Honor of Rudolph Willard*, ed. A. A. Hill, 1968.

"Paul and the Hellenization of Christianity," with A. Thomas Kraabel, in the present volume.

BIBLICAL INDEX[1]

I. Biblical Passages
II. Apocrypha and Pseudepigrapha
III. Babylonian Talmud
IV. Palestinian Talmud
V. Midrashim
VI. Mishnah

I. BIBLICAL PASSAGES

Genesis	p	Genesis	p	Genesis	p
1.1	324	12.10	416	48	255, 256
1.26	324, 362	14.17	213	48.18	255
1.27	364	15.6	48	49	255, 256
1.28	324	23	190	50	256
2.10	339	24	161	50.5	256
2.11	339	25.9	190	50.13	190
2.13	340	25.22-26	274	50.25	256
3.1	340	25.23	275		
3.16	344	25.26	275	Exodus	
3.17	341, 345	25.29-34	274	2.12	337
3.22	317	27	275, 276	3.6	191, 360
4.2	346	27.36	275	3.12	190
4.3	346	28	79	3.15	191
4.4	346	28.10-27	284	4.17	356
4.7	324	28.12	161, 285	4.22	268
4.16	326	28.13	285	7.1	355-57, 358
4.17	350	29.29-32	190	9.9	321
4.22	350	30.37-38	337	12.1	143
5.6	351	32	265, 270, 281, 291	12.12	414, 415, 416, 414-418
6.4	352	32.20	265		
6.5	352	32.24, 255	255, 276	12.12-13	418
6.1-6	531	32.26-27	280	12.29	415-418
9.5	323	32.29	264, 276	15	74
9.6	319, 323	32.30	270	16.4	401
10.29	340	36.1	275	16.7	59
11.26	191	36.8	275	17.6	85
11.32	191	36.9	275	17.7	85
12.1	191	36.43	275	20	192
12.4	191	38	337	20.4	440

[1] Indices were prepared by Mr. Arthur Woodman, Canaan, New Hampshire, under a grant from the Dartmouth College Comparative Studies Center and Committee on Research. The editor is very grateful for this additional support.

BIBLICAL INDEX

Exodus	p
20.19	418
20.19-26	79
20.21	355
23.26	538
24.12	360
24.16	146
25.9	218
25.40	218
28.2	321
28.4	512
30.2	323
31.12	424
31.13	419
32	337, 186, 337
32.1	85
33.20	145
34.9	85
34.29	356, 361
34.30	362

Leviticus	p
16.4	512
16.17	211
18.5	321
19.19	539
23	92
26.1	439
26.46	419, 420

Numbers	p
10.1-2, 355	355
12	337
12.6	369
12-6-8	419
14.13-16	77, 78
14.42	77
14.44	77
19.14	323
20.10-12	337
21.4-9	337
22.7	80
22.38	80
23.3-4	80
23.13	80
23.15-16	80
23.34	80
24.1	80
28	94
29	94
31.40	321, 323

Deuteronomy	p
1.31	531
2.5	192
5.5	414
5.8	440
6.4-9	116
7.4	423
11.13	421, 423
11.13-15	423
11.14	412, 413, 415, 423
11.22	423
17.3	423
18.15	192
18.18	192
22.10	539
26.8	414, 415
28.20	423
29.4	423
30.15	116
32	74, 368
32.35	414
33.1	357, 361, 362
33.2	74, 588
33.5	356, 357, 367
34.7	363, 364
34.10	366

Judges	p
5.4-5	74
6	76
6.13	76
18.30	324
19	121
20	121
21	121

1 Samuel	p
4.3	77, 78
7.3	77, 78
11.13	164
12.2	161
14.6	117

2 Samuel	p
2.4-7	164
6.14	512
7.19	321
22.17	73

1 Kings	p
1.9-10	167
1.11-12	167
2.8	180
8.12-13	81
17.1-6	167-169
17.8-16	167
17.17-24	167, 170
17.22	356
18.1-40	167
18.36	171

2 Kings	p
2.1	170
2.6-15	171
2.9-12	167
2.11	356
2.14	167, 170
2.15-18	171
2.17	171
2.19-20	168
2.19-23	167
2.23-24	167
3.13-20	167, 168
4.1-7	167, 168
4.8-17	167
4.18-37	167, 170
4.27	170
4.38-41	167, 168
4.42-44	167, 169
5.-1-14	167, 169
5.3	171
5.13	171
5.19-27	167
6.1-7	167, 170
6.12	171
6.15-19	167
9.4	171
13.21	167, 170
16	164
17	164
20.22	171
22	91
23	91

1 Chronicles	p
29.23	356

2 Chronicles	p
11.13	163

Ezra	p
4	368

BIBLICAL INDEX 635

	p
Nehemiah	
7.73-9.38	91
9	92
10	92
Job	
5.10	412, 413
13.15	117
25.2	280
28.28	325
Psalms	
2.7	210
15	83
18.17	73
21.6	356
24	83
24.7	356
32.1	48
42	83
42.6	83
46	81
46.2-6	82
46.6	84
46.35-36	82
47.6-9	356
49.21	364
50.3	318
63.3	84
63.7	83, 84
63.8	83
65.1-2	84
65.10	84
65.12	84
68.8-9	74
68.36	84
74.11,12	75
84.2-13	84
84.5-6	85
87.2	438
89.27	268
104.1	356
110	212, 214
115.16	321, 322
118	97-106
118.1-4	97
118.5	98
118.5-21	99
118.6	321
118.22	101
118.24-27	101
118.29	102

	p
Psalms	
132.13	188
139.7-9	72
139.8	118
145.18	71
Proverbs	
31.29	364
Ecclesiastes	
1.4	324
Isaiah	
2.2-4	90, 93
3	121
12.6	87
43.7	361
49.3	285
56	93
60	90
63	121
66.1	188
Jeremiah	
1.11,12	421
7.3	81
14.8,9	87
17.9	275
31.31-34	94
32.20	321
Ezekiel	
8	86
8.12	86
10.4,5	86
11.16	86
34.31	322, 323, 325
36.22-32	94
38	90
39	90
Daniel	
2.45	308
3.2	588
7	299-302, 308
7.9	512
8.11	269
12.1	269
12.1-3	118
Hosea	
3.4	164
12.3	275

	p
Amos	
4.13	75
5.25-27	186, 190
7.16	421
Obadiah	
1.18	278
Jonah	
4.11	321, 323
Micah	
1.3,4	75
3.11	81
4.1-4	90
Nahum	
1.3	356
Haggai	
2.3	328
Zechariah	
9	88
10	88
11	88
12	88
13	88
14	88
14.1-15	93
14.2-5	88, 89
14.6-11	89
14.8	88
14.9	88, 91, 95
14.12	88, 89
14.13,14	89
14.15	89
14.16-21	88-96
14.21	94
Matthew	
1.18-25	113
5.3-12	119
5.19	177
5.21	65
5.27	65
5.38	65
6.25	401
6.34	401
7.21-23	177
7.22	206
10.5	161, 177

BIBLICAL INDEX

Matthew	p	John	p	John	p
10.5,6	166	1	162	5.36	142
10.6	161	1-20	122	6.1	172
10.23	236	1.1	146	6.4-14	168, 169
10.24	140	1.2	158	6.5-7	174
11.27	113	1.3	228	6.14	174
13.24-30	248	1.7	158	6.16-21	168, 170
13.24-31	247	1.7,8	161	6.27	233
13.29	248	1.11	166	6.38	140
13.30	248	1.14	146	6.39	141
13.54	165	1.18	145	6.42	160
13.57	165	1.25	171	6.44	142
16.17-19	113	1.29-34	171	6.46	145
16.18	174	1.29-37	161	6.53	233
18.20	124	1.37	171	6.62	233
21.9	160	1.43-38	174	6.66-71	114
24.27	236	1.45	160	7.1-9	165
24.30	236	1.47	159, 166	7.16	141
24.37	236	1.47-51	146, 161	7.34	171
28.2	513	1.49	159	7.35	155
28.19	178	1.51	233, 286	7.41	166
		2.1-11	167, 168	7.41, 42	160
		3.1-2	158, 159	7.53	172
Mark		3.3-5	159	8.11	172
6.1	165	3.3-13	146	8.16-18	147
6.4	165	3.5	164	8.26	141
7	202	3.10	158, 159	8.28	233
7.1-23	178, 181	3.13	233	8.28	141
7.15	178	3.14	233	8.29	140, 141
7.19	178	3.16, 18	146	8.31-41	165
8.35	118	3.30	171	8.42	141
8.36	118	3.34	141	8.48	165, 161, 165
11.9,10	160	4	196, 197	8.49	161
13	205	4.5	161	9.1-7	168, 169
13.2	206	4.7-28	161	9.16	161
14.58	181, 206	4.9	165, 166	9.22-26	161
		4.19	171, 197	9.31	161
		4.21-23	196	9.35-38	233
Luke		4.22	165	10.13	165
1.1-4	110	4.25	197	10.22-24	165
1.18	113	4.26	197	10.30	139
1.26-38	113	4.29	197	10.36-38	139
4.16	165	4.34	142	10.40	165
6.21-23	119	4.35	166	11.1-44	168, 170
6.40	140	4.39	166	11.7	165
12.8	235	4.44	165	11.8	165
17.24	236	4.46-54	168, 169	11.32	170
17.26	236	4.54	166	11.54	165
17.30	236	5.1	172	12.13	160
18.8	236	5.2-9	168, 169	12.21, 22	174
21.36	236	5.23	139	12.23	233
22.69	236	5.27	233	12.31,32	141-143

BIBLICAL INDEX 637

John	p	Acts	p	Acts	p
12.34	233	7.11	181	26	27
12.44	138	7.13	181	26.5	28
12.45	139, 145	7.16	189, 190		
12.49	141	7.20	184	Romans	
13	142	7.22	184	1	35-39
13.3	143	7.23-25	194	1.1	35
13.16	140, 143	7.25	184, 185	1.3	35, 160
13.20	138, 143	7.31	185	1.4	35
13.31	233	7.32	191	1.5	35
13.33	165	7.34	184	1.7	35
13.35	165	7.35-38	184, 194	1.16	35
14.8	174	7.37	196	1.17	37, 120
14.9	139, 174	7.38	195	1.18	38
14.10,11	139	7.39	185	1.20	38
14.19	119	7.39-41	186	1.23	39
14.22	165	7.42	185, 186, 190	2	39-43
14.24	141	7.44-50	187	2.6	39
15.19-37	161	7.46	188	2.9	39, 43
15.23	139	7.47	187	2.10	42, 47
17	143	7.48	206	2.12	40
17.4	142, 143	7.50	188	2.13	43
17.6	141	7.51-53	183, 185	2.14	39
17.16	143	7.54-60	181	2.15	39, 43
17.20-23	139	8	197, 199	2.17	40
17.21	143	8.1	180	2.25	40, 47
18.33	159, 165	8.4	180	2.29	40
18.37	159	8.5	198	3	43-48
19.19	159	8.5-40	174	3.1	43
19.20-22	159	8.14-17	175	3.2	43, 44
19.30	142, 143	8.14-25	198	3.3	44
20.21	143	8.40	199	3.20	43, 44
20.23	110	9.26-30	29	3.21	44, 47
20.30	172	10.1	199	3.22	44, 45
21	122, 123	11	199	3.23	44
21.24	123	11.1-18	199	3.24	44
21.25	110	11.19	199, 202	3.25	44
		11.22	199	3.26	44, 45
Acts		15.11	30	3.27	47
6	199, 204	15.5	30	3.28	47
6.1	179	15.28	32	3.29	47
6.5	174	16.1-3	30	3.31	47
6.8	180	19.25	199	4	48-50
6.8-15	181	20.18-35	110	4.4,6,8,9	48
6.14	206	21	201	4.11	49
7	193, 196, 197, 199-201	21.8	199	4.13	49
7.1-50	196	21.20	181	4.17	49
7.2-53	181	22	27	4.19	49
7.4	191	22.3	29	4.21	49
7.5	192	22.25	32	4.22	49
7.6	190	23.6	28	4.23	49
7.8	185	25.9-12	32	4.24	49

Romans	p
4.25	49
5	50-53, 232
5.2,8,9	50
5.12	50, 51, 53
5.14	64
5.17	65
5.20	66
6	53-54
6.1	53
6.1-11	51
6.2,4,5	53
6.13	54
7	54-60
7.1-3	54
7.4	54
7.7	32, 54, 55
7.10	55
7.12	55
7.14-20	55
7.21, 22, 23, 25	56
8	35, 60-62
8.1	60
8.2	62
8.3, 4,9	60
8.11	61
8.12	61
8.13	61
8.17	61
8.19-22	61
8.23	61
8.26	61
9-11	61-64
9.6-8	62
9.9-13	62
9.14	62
9.20-23	62
9.24	62
10.3	63
10.8	63
10.9	33
10.13	63
10.14	63
11.1	64
11.17	64
11.21	64
12-15	67
1 Corinthians	
1.26	111
7.18,19	173

1 Corinthians	p
8.6	228
9.19-22	34
10.1-4	59
11.2	110
11.23-26	114
2 Corinthians	
12.1-10	114
Galatians	
1.13-5	26
1.16	26
1.18-24	29
2.1	30
2.1-10	31
2.7-9	173, 174
2.11-21	32
2.12	174
5.6	173
6.15	173
Philippians	
3.4-6	26, 28
Colossians	
1.2	175
1.15	268
1.16	228
1.17	268
2.1	175
3.11	173
4.12-17	175
1 Thessalonians	
	33, 34
2.14	34
3.5-10	34
3.13	34
4.13	34
5.11	34
5.23	34
2 Thessalonians	
2.15	110
3.6	110
1 Timothy	
1.3	110
2 Timothy	
3.16	109

Hebrews	p
1	223
1.1	228
1.2	212, 215, 222
1.3	210, 215, 223, 224
1.5	210
2.1	207
2.10	222
2.14	223, 224
3.1-6	208
3.12	207
4.15	223
5.7	223
5.11	217
6.1	110, 224
6.2	110, 224
7.3	212
7.25	223
7.27	224
8.1	224
8.2	215
8.5	215
8.34	223
9	215
9.5	217
9.8	215, 220, 225
9.11	215
9.12	224
9.24	215, 218, 224
9.26	224
9.28	224
10	220
10.1	91, 224
10.10	224
10.12	224
10.21	220
10.23	207
10.32	220
10.35	220
11	183, 220, 221
11.10	217
11.13-16	217
11.32	221
12.1	226
12.2	224
12.22	217, 219
13.14	217
13.23	225
13.24	225
1 Peter	
3.21	218

Jude	p		Jude	p
3	110		17	110

II. APOCRYPHA AND PSEUDEPIGRAPHA

IV *Ezra*			IV *Ezra*			2 *Enoch*	
5.6	310		13.13-24	304, 305			308
5.41	300		13.25	305		22.6	311
6.25	298, 312		13.25-53	305		33.10	311
6.58	310		13.26	309, 311		*3 Enoch*	
7.26-44	311		13.27	305		10.3-4	290
7.27	300		13.28	306		48c	290
7.28	295, 296, 300, 303, 304, 310, 312		13.29-35	306		*Testament of Levi*	
7.29	295, 311		13.32	296, 307, 311		8.1-12	558
7.37	300		13.36	306		8.2	512
7.75	300		13.37	296, 307, 309, 311		*Test. of Naphthali*	
7.11-3	298		13.38	309		3.4	531
11	296, 298, 301, 308-312		13.48	305, 306		*Apoc. Baruch*	
11.37	295, 296		13.49	309		3.37	283
11.38	309		13.50	309, 310		30.1	295
11.38-43	301		13.51	305		39	310
11.38-45	296		13.52	296, 306, 309-311		39.5	301
11.39-46	298		14.9	296, 310, 311		39-40	301
11.45	298, 301		25-52	296		*Syrian Baruch*	
11.46	298, 299, 301, 311		26	304		4.2-7	369
12	296, 298, 301, 307-312		29-33	304		*3 Baruch*	
12.1	295		36	304		11.1	269
12.1-3	296, 297, 301		40.1	301		*Prayer of Joseph*	
12.11	301, 302		40.3	301		2	265, 268
12.31-34	295		48	304		3	260, 264
12.32	296, 297, 309, 311		52	304		4	264, 268
12.33	296, 301		*Judith*			5	268
12.34	296-299, 304, 311		8.11-27	118		10	276
13	303, 308, 311, 312		*Jubilees*			11	278
13.1-13	305		3.28	340		15	268
13.3-13	296		6.17,18	93		17	271
13.4	306						
13.7	308		*1 Enoch*				
13.13	309			295, 301, 307			

III. BABYLONIAN TALMUD

Berakhot			*'Eruvin*			*Sukkah*	
8a	214, 444		31b-32a	140		20b	444
40b	451						
47a	326		*Rosh Hashanah*			*Ta'anit*	
			24b	439		2a	413
						28b	439

Megillah	p	Qiddushin	p	Sanhedrin	p
5b	450	41a	143	57a	323
22b	439	43a	139	59a	321
25a-b	338			72b	323
		Bava' Qama'		104b	322
Mo'ed Qatan		58b	457		
16b	453	70a	141, 142	*'Avodah Zarah*	
				3a	321
Hagigah		*Bava Mezi'a'*			
12b	269	114b	326	*Hullin*	
				91b	263, 326
Nedarim		*Bava' Batra'*			
32a	322	54a	447	*Keritot*	
				6b	323, 326
Gittin		*Sanhedrin*			
47a	322	46b	320	*Niddah*	
				13a	444

IV. PALESTINIAN TALMUD

Terumoth		*Shabbat*		*Qiddushin*	
4.4	140	2.7	322	2.4	140
Bikkurim				*Sanhedrin*	
1.4	325			4.5	325

V. MIDRASHIM

Genesis Rabbah		*Exodus Rabbah*		*Deuteronomy Rabbah*	
8.11	324	30.16	325	4.4	318
8.12	324	40.1	325		
21.1	317			*Deuteronomy Targum*	
21.2	317	*Exodus Targum*		10.1	360
21.5	317	7.1	360	33.5	367
34.14	323				
39.4	326	*Leviticus Rabbah*		*Mekhilta*	
77.3	277	34.3	319	Beshallah	
78	140			7.73	317
78.3	278	*Numbers Rabbah*			
		16.15	317	*Sifré Zuta*	
		16.24	317	8.2	363

VI. MISHNAH

Qiddushin		*Avot*		*Middot*	
1.9	446	2.12	400	2.3	332
		2.17	400	4.1	333
Avot		3.14	317	4.2	335
2.7	399				

GENERAL INDEX

Aaron 186, 212, 214, 357
—— Challenged to produce deity 85
—— Lower Mystery 209
Aaronites, Psalm 118, 97, 105
Abaye 438, 457
Abbassid 408
Abel 214, 221, 346-348
Abot de Rabbi Nathan 323, 419, 420
—— ed. Goldin 325
—— ed. Schechter 319
Abraham, 44, 47-50, 62, 173, 182, 184, 185, 190, 191, 193, 214, 217, 256, 283, 322, 338, 534, 535
—— Faith of 45
—— Sealed covenant 332
Abram 416
Abydos 482, 484
Archaemenid era, Iranian religious history 584, 588
Achaia, Christ meaning to church, 118
Achilles
—— Horse 340
—— Saul likened 338
—— Tortoise, arrow symbol 471
Actium 134
Acts 119
—— Hellenistic influences on Christianity 176-206
—— Paul, Hellenization of Christianity 23-68
—— Tradition in scripture 110
Acusilaus 342
Adam 341, 345, 351, 361, 363
Adam-Christ typology 232
—— Decline of civilization 339
—— Envy of Satan 278
—— Lost glory returned at Mt. Sinai 364, 365, 371
—— Man 315-326
—— Serpent, Ophites 238
—— Symbol of Israel or man 51-53
Adapa, Epic of 580
Adapa, Lipit-Istar 581
Adiabene 446
—— Queen Helena 333
Adonis, ladder symbol 611
Adriatic, Roman influence 128
Adultery, woman taken in adultery, St. Augustine 120
Aegean sea, Roman influence 126
Aelian, 376, 385-388, 390, 392, 393, 396-398, 402-406, 408
—— Chria 378
—— *Varia Historia* 377

Aeropagus, Paul 183
Aesop 380
—— Fables 340
Aesopica 376, 379, 385-388, 390, 392, 393, 396-398, 402-406, 408
Aesopus, 374
Aetna 341, 344
Afrem 570
Africa, Hippo 120
—— Symbols 506
—— Roman influence 126
—— Water symbolism 514
African Systems of Thought 510
Agada 339, 344
Against Verres 136
Agamemnon 345
Agape and Eros 618
Age of science, Bible, catechism 115
Agency of god, principle 138
Agent
—— God's agent, Gospel of John 148
—— Heavenly 144-158
Ağlan-Koi 544
Agrippa 132
Aharoni, Yoḥanan 103
Aḥaz 164
Aḥriman 585
Ainu, arrow symbol 468
Aker lions 494
Akiba 317, 402, 435
—— Golden Rule 399
Akkadian, word structure 574-577
Akyar, Halil 542
Alasehir (Philadelphia) 543, 549
Albright, W. 154
Alcinous 341
Alcibiades 377, 378, 381, 382, 394, 397
Alexander Janneus, *see* Janneus
Alexander the Great 133, 411
—— Psalm 118 98
—— Inspired 102
Alexandra, widow of Alexander Janneus 129-131
Alexandria
—— Christ, meaning to Church 118
—— Influence on Epistle to the Hebrews 218
—— Origin of Gospel of St. John 149, 154, 173
—— Philo of, *see* Philo
Allegory of the Cave 54
Allen 162, 484, 496, 497
American Academy of Religion 593
American Society for the Study of Religion 593
Amonites, Psalm 118 105
Amoraim 285
Amores 344, 349

Amos 166, 190, 193, 195
—— Image of God portrayed 75
—— Of Tekoa 108
Amun 487, 492, 496
Anacharsis 374, 411
Analecta Orientalia 581
Anatolia 546, 550
—— Mithraism 587
Angelican Prayer Book, Epistle for Monday in Holy Weeks 121
Ankh 494
Antioch 149, 151, 17, 174
—— Christ, meaning to Church 118
—— Paul 30
—— Spread of Christianity 176, 177
—— Stephen's mission 199, 202
Antiochus 130
Antiochus Asiaticus (Antiochus XIII) 130, 131
—— Resistence 112
Antiochus Epiphanes 202
Antiochus the Great 126
Antipas 125
Antipater 132, 134
"Antipater of Tarsus" 378
Antiphon, *Pap. Oxyrh.* 525
Antiquitates Judaicae 336
Antiquities 336, 338, 343, 352
Antisthenes 374
Antonius 127
Antony, Mark 134, 135
Anu, High god 581
Anubis 483, 487, 488
Anuntample of Uruk 576
Apameia 543, 550
—— Coins 543, 547
Aphek 77
Aphraates 244, 249
Apion 363
Apocalpse 156, 157
Apocalypse of Abraham 279, 280
Apocalyptic literature
—— Feast of Booths 89, 92, 95, 96
—— Universal kingdom 96
Apocryphal Acts of Thomas 571
Apophethegmata Laconica 395
Apopis 501
Apostles, authority in scripture 115
Apostolic age, Biblical interpretation 111
Apostolic Constitutions 214, 221, 222
Apuleius 543, 570
—— White symbolism 513
Aquinas, St. Thomas, Catholic dogma 111
Arubia, Paul 29

Arad, Tel, see Tel Arad
Arafel 358
Aramaio 115
Aratus, *Phaenomena* 347
Arcesilaus, Plutarch 379
Archaeological excavations, Tel Arad 104
Archelaus 128, 129, 136, 524, 525
Archontikoi 273
Ariarathes 127
Aristin of Chois, Chria 376
Aristippus 374, 403, 411
Aristobulus 131
Aristophanes 381, 544
Aristotle 343, 374
—— *Ethics* 351
—— Natural law 526, 531, 532, 539
—— *Politics* 526, 527
Arius Didymus 529
Ark 77, 116
—— Of the Covenant, Herod's Temple 330, 332
Armenia 129, 130, 132, 446
—— Tigranes of 129, 130
Armillos 161
Arrian-Epictetus 376
—— Discourses 384-388, 390, 392, 396-399, 401
Arrows, bridge symbolism 613
—— Symbolism 463-475
Ars Poetica 337
Art, Egyptian symbols 476-478
Artaxerxes 587
Artemis 549
Artemis Anaitis 544
Artemis, Hecate 548
Arthurian romance, sword bridge, symbolism 613
Asenath 256
Asia,
—— Arrow symbols 464
—— History of religions 601, 608
—— Deification, symbols 570, 571
—— Paul 31
—— Roman influence 126-146
—— Sabazios 543
—— Thunder clouds, symbols 465, 466
—— White symbolism 509
Asclepion 544
Asklepios 545
Ašmedai 589
Asmodaios 589
Assyria
—— Astrological myths 218
—— Exile 190
—— Hebrew history and tradition 107
—— Iranian religious history 584

—— Temple 218
Astarte, ladder symbol 611
Atargatis 549, 571
Atef Crowns, Egyptian symbols 481
Atharvaveda 464
Athenaeus 376, 378, 385-388, 390, 392, 393, 396-398, 402-406, 408
—— *Deipmosophistae* 378, 402
Athens
—— Natural law, Ionic philosophy, 525
—— Paul's speech, 25
—— Roman influence, 128, 129
—— Sabazios, 544, 547
Atonement Day of 92
Atreus 345
Attaleia 543
Attalids 544, 550
Attalus III of Pergamum 126, 129, 544
Attis 545, 548, 549
Augustus (Octavian) 135, 136
Aulus Gabinius *see* Gabinius
Aurelian 573
Australia, arrow symbol 468, 470
Avesta 583-586, 589
Avi-Yonah, M. 549
Avot de R. Nathan 403
Ax head, floating 170
Axis Mundi, arrow symbol 472
Azov sea 127

Baal 549
Babylon 156, 158
—— Astrological myths 218
—— Esagila temple 580
—— Exile 190
—— Hebrew history and tradition 107
—— Inscriptions in the collection of Nies 580
—— Iranian religious history 584, 588
—— Judaism, transition to 428
—— New Year Festival 576
—— Property transfer and probate 447
—— Rabbis and the community 438-59
—— Talmud 428
Bacchus 547
Bach, B. W. 122
Bacon, B. W. 152, 185, 203, 204
Bainton, Roland, *Horizon History of Christianity* 122
Baka valley 83
Balaam 352
—— Attracting deity 79, 80
Baldensperger, Wilhelm 300
Balkans, arrow symbol 474
Bantu. 507, 513
Bantu Prophets in South Africa 506

Bantu Studies 511
Baptism 551-582
—— Coronation ceremonies, compared 552
—— Indo-Iranian 552
—— Mandean 551-582
Baptism of Hibil-Ziwa, the 568
Barak 221, 222
Bar Kochba 327-331, 335
—— War 452
Barnabas 29-31
Barrett, C. K. 137, 152, 162
Barsauma 244
Barth, Paul 590
Baruch 263, 302, 551
—— Syriac 301
Bashkar 446, 450
Basilideas, Gnostic system 238
Bas-Wadington 573
Battle Hymn of the Republic 121
Beatitudes 119
Bebekli 543
Beersheva 103
Beethoven, *Unfinished Symphony* 519
Beginnings of Christianity, the 24
Bel 553, 573
Belgium, Sabazios 543
—— Temple at Palmyra, 329, 330, 335
bene'adam 321
Benjamin 159, 161, 451
—— Paul's heritage 28
Ben Sirach 182
Bergson, H. 610
Bernard, J. H. 151
Bernlef, Frisian monk 246, 249
Beroea 249
Beruria 402
Bethany, raising of Lazarus 165
Bethel
—— Jacob's experience 79
—— Jacob's vision 161, 284, 287
Beth Shearim, archaeological discoveries 331
—— Cemetery 362
Betsah 387, 400
Bible
—— Age of science 115
—— Ethical and theological interpretation 120
—— Interpretations and difficulties 111
—— Luther 120
Biblicarum antiquitatum 255
Bickerman, E. J. 610
Bidez, J. 588
Bion, Chria 376, 394
Birmingham, England 121

Bithynia 127, 129, 131, 132, 543
—— Nicomedes 128, 129
"Black land" Egyptian symbol 479
Blaundos 543, 544
Boas, Franz 470
Bodhisattva Jotipala 467
Bolivia, Thunder God of Yurakare 465
Bombay, Parsis 584
Bon, arrow symbol 468, 472
Bonnet, Hans 485
Book of Gates 500
Book of Jubilees 255
—— Divine dealings with Israel 109
—— Moses theophany 367
Book of the Dead 481, 482, 484-491, 496, 498-500
Book of What is in the Netherworld 501
Book of Tobit 588
Booths, Feast of 88-96
Borgen, P. 144
Bousset, W. 214, 221, 240
Box, G. H. 280, 296-300, 303-309
Brandon, S. G. F. 154
Braude, W. 325
Braun, F-M. 152
Brazen serpent 337
Bread, symbolism 124
"Bridge of Judgment," symbolism 613
Bridge of San Luis Rey, the, symbolism 616
Bridge symbol 612, 613
—— Sacrifice 614
—— Sword bridge 613
"Bridge, the" 617, 618
Brooklyn Bridge 617
Buber, M. 280
Buckler, W. H. 542, 545
Buddists
—— Arrow symbols 468, 472
—— History of religions, study 608
—— Iranian religious history 584
Bulgaria, arrow symbol 466
Bultman, R. 120, 137, 144, 148, 152, 153, 162, 172, 223, 224, 231
—— "Kerygma of the Hellenistic Church Aside from Paul, the" 223
Burch, V. 271-273
Burney, C. F. 150
Bursa 543
Buryat, arrow symbol 464, 468
Bushmen, "musical bow" 463
Butelezi, Elliot 507
Buttenweiser, M. 99, 102
By Light, Light 40, 57, 59, 259, 425
Bythos 238
Byzantine Age, Chria 373
Byzantine empire, Iranian religious history 584

Byzantium, arrow symbol 474

Caedmon, inspired *Heliand* 245
Caesar 32
—— Claudius 132
—— Julius 349
Caesarea 125
Caesarea Philippi 113, 123
Cahn, Edmund 430, 431
Cain 326, 345-350
Caird, Edward 208
Caleb 214
Callaway, H. 509-511, 514
—— *Religious System of the Amazulu*, the 509
Callicles 523
Calvin 244
Calvinist churches, predestinarians 63
Calydonians, arrow symbol 466
Cana, wedding miracle 168
Canaan 191
—— Entry of Israelites 107
—— Feast of booths 94
—— Jacob's visit 276
—— Psalm 118, 98
—— Warriors repulsed 77
Capernaum synagogue 330
Cappadocia 127, 132, 544
Caria 127, 543
Carlyle, worship of sorrow or suffering 122
Carnival of blood, Palestine 126
Carroll, K. L. 154
Case, Shirley Jackson 111
Cassuto, U. 346
Catechism, age of science 115
Catholics
—— Biblical interpretations 111
—— History of religions, study 608
—— Symbolism 615
Cato 134
"Celestial wolf," thunder clouds, symbolism 466
Centurion's son 169
Cephas, *see* Peter
Cercidas, the Spartan 410
Corinthus, Christ 287
Chaeronea 129
Chaos 239
Chamber of Destiny 581
Chantepie de la Saussaye, P. D. 595
Characters 545
Charlemagne 249
Charles, R. H. 271, 272
Charon, symbolism 614
Cherubim 264, 279

Cheyne, T. K. 102
Chihamba the White Spirit 510
Children of Noah 318, 323
China
—— Christianity 245
—— Thunder clouds, arrow symbol 465, 466
Chria, transformation 372-411
Christ, *see* Jesus Christ
Christian, Judaism co-existence 428
Christianity 119
—— History of Religions 599
—— Iranian religious history 584
Christologie des N. T. 231
Christos Cosmokrator 474
Chronicles 108
Chrysippus 528, 532
Chrysostom, Dio of Prusa 376
Chukchee, arrow symbol 468, 469
Cicero 128, 131, 134, 343
—— *Against Verres* 136
—— Natural law 529
—— *Optimo Genere Oratorum, de* 337
—— *Tusc. Disput.* 376
Cilicia 127, 131, 132, 543, 547
—— Paul 28, 29
—— Pirates 131
Circumcision celebration 102
Circumcision
—— Requirement for salvation 30
Citadel, Song of the Citadel 97-106
Claremont, history of religions congress 604
Claudius 132
Claudius Caesar 132
Cleanthes 374, 376, 527
Clearchus 352
Clement of Alexandria 155, 216, 545
—— Natural law 540
Clementine Homilies, the 150
Clementines, pseudo 186
Cleopatra 134
Clytemnestra 345
Code, see Torah
Codex Fuldensis 245, 246
Coins, markings 327-331, 335
Collegium of the Pontifices, symbolism 615
Colorbaseans 240
Colossae 175
Colwell, E. C. 162
Commagene, Mithradates Kallinikos of 585
Commandments, Noachite 321
Commentary on John 281, 282
Condah, Lake, arrow symbol 469
Confusione linguarum, de 267, 340

Contra Celsum 288
Conselmann, Ernst 181
Conzelmann, H. 120
Coos (Indian), arrow symbol 469
Coptic Codex II 264
Coptos 484
Corinth, disloyalty 124
Corneille, Pierre 475
Cornell University, Sabazios inscriptions **542**
Cornerstone proverb 101
Coronation of the Great Sislam, the 559-561
Cosmic tree, arrow symbol 465, 471
Cosmos 211
Cotta 129
Council of Trent, Catholic dogma 111
Covenant
—— Adam to Christ 109
—— Day of Pentecost 93
—— Foreign nations 93
—— House of David 91
—— Jeremiah's 94
—— Noah 93, 95
—— Rainbow as symbol 613
—— Renewal 90-96
Crane, Hart, "The Bridge" 617, 618
Crassus 133
Crates, Chria 374, 401, 410
Crimea 132
Criticism of Bible 112
Croenert, W., *Kolotes und Menedemos* 377
—— Vienna Papyrus, ed. 376
Cross, Frank 154
Crucifix, psychological effects 121
Cullmann, Oscar 150, 153, 163, 228
—— *Christologie des N. T.* 231
Cuming, G. J. 163
Cumont, F. 547, 572, 573, 588
Cuneiform Texts 577-579
Cup, symbolism 123, 124
Curetonianus 247
Cybele 549
Cyclopes 342
Cynicism, ancient Near East 372-375
Cynicism 396, 401, 409
Cynic *philoponia* 407
Cyorian, *Testimonia adversus Indaeos* 273
Cyprus, Stephen's mission 199
Cyrus 116
—— The Great in Fars 583

Dahl, N. A. 144
Damascus 198, 202
—— Exile beyond 190

—— Paul 29
Daniel 115
—— Book of 118
Danielou, J. 271, 273
Danube Valley, cannibals 121
Das Jonannesbuch 562
"Das Marchen" 616
David 115, 117, 160, 161, 163, 356, 476
—— Jesus descended from 35
—— White symbolism 512
Davidic Descent 297, 304, 311
Davidic Messiah 296
Day of Atonement 92
Dead, raising 170
Dead Sea
—— Approach of God 73
—— Discoveries, Prayer of Joseph 253-292
—— Scrolls 149, 153, 154, 589
"De Aere Aquis Locis" 525
Debe Rabbanan, the Treatise Derek Erez 383
Decalogue 192, 194
Decorations, mosaics 438-459
de Corona 545
Deipmosophistae 378, 402
Deir el Behri, Metropolitan Museum 493-495
Delilah 345
Delitzsch, Franz 102
Delos 128, 131, 544
Demeter 544
Demetrius of Phalerum, Chria 376
Demonax, Lucian 376
Demosthenes, *de Corona* 545
Derbe 132
—— Paul 30
Derekh Eretz Rabbah 377, 385-388, 390, 392, 393, 396-408
Desert-Hekhal, King Solomon's Temple, excavations 104
De Specialibus Legibus 65
Devil's Bridge, symbolism 614
de Virtute 65-67
de Swaanm 150
Diaspora 109, 153
—— Judaism 111
Diatessaron 245-249
Dibelius, Martin 113, 120
Didache 124
Diels 525
Diodorus 339
Diodorus Siculus 343
Diogenes 411
—— At Olympia 409
—— Chria 374, 400, 401
—— Heavenly Hound 410
—— Laertius 376

—— Laertius II 524
Diogeni Lertii Vitae Philosophorum 382, 385-388, 392-394, 396-398, 400, 402-406, 408
Dionysius 156, 157, 546-549
—— of Halicarnassus 350
—— of Halicarnassus III 523
Dionysos Kathegemon 544
Dionysos-Zagreus-Sabazios 545
Dionysus, symbolism 517, 609
Dio of Prusa (Chrysostom) 376
Divorce, third century Babylonia 449
Doctrine of Grace 120
Dodd, C. H. 137, 152, 162, 222-224
Dogma, Biblical interpretation and difficulties 111
Domitian 156
Donation of Constantine 122
Doresse, J. 147
Dositheus 287
Doxographoi 373
Driver, S. R. 423
Drower, E. S.
—— *Baptism of Hibıl-Zıwa, the* 567
—— *Cononical Prayerbook of the Mandaeans* 552, 556, 561-565, 574, 575
—— *Coronation of the Great Sislam, the* 559
Druids 121
Dualism 58
Duamutef 483, 485
Duhm, B. 102
Dummelow, J. R. 99
Dura-Europos 250, 586
—— Cult reliefs 572
—— Deification, symbols 570, 571
—— Gad relief 571
—— Synagogue 59, 289, 290, 330, 425, 441, 443, 445, 457-459, 611
Duranki, Temple of Nippur 581
Dynamis 239

Ea, cult in Eridu 579, 580, 582
Eagle vision 293-303, 309, 310
Easter, Christology, turning point 229
Eater of Corpses 483
Ebeling, H. 576
"Ebionite" Judaisers 155
Ebrietas 534
Eclogues 343, 349
Ecphantus 210
Edda, symbolism 613
Eden, Okeanos river 339
Edessa (Syrian) 248
Edom 275
—— Approach of God 73, 74
—— Excavations 103
—— Psalm 118, 105

Edwards, R. A. 152
Egypt 156, 185
—— Art and symbols 476-478
—— Attendance on Feast of Booths 89
—— "Black Land" symbols 479
—— Eater of Corpses 483
—— Fire signs 480, 482
—— Great Bear constellation 485
—— History of religions 600
—— Israel's deliverance 112, 116
—— "King of Upper and Lower Egypt" 479
—— Lake of Fire 481
—— Leo Constellation 484, 485
—— "Lord of the Two Lands" 479
—— Moses, general 338
—— Red Crown 478, 479
—— "Red Land" symbols 479
—— Symbols 611-613
—— Twenty First dynasty, symbols 476-478, 484-488, 491, 492, 496, 497, 499, 500, 502
—— Water symbols 515
—— White Crown 479
—— Yaru Fields 480
Eisele 543, 544
Elaiussa 547
Elam 446
Eleazar the Priest 329
Eliade, Mircea, *Patterns* 595, 607
Eliezer, R. 436
Elijah 434, 436, 166, 356, 434, 436
—— Comparisons with Christ and Elisha 166-175
—— Miracles 167, 170-172
Eliot, T. S. 111
Elisha 166
—— Comparisons with Christ and Elijah 166-175
—— Miracles 167, 169, 170-172
'Elyon, Jerusalem cult 213
Ennead 496
Enoch 214, 290, 358, 368
—— Similitudes 300, 301, 307
Enoch, Slavonic 290, 291
Enos 41, 214
Epaphras 175
Ephesus 149-152, 154-158, 173
—— Paul's life 110
Ephraim 159, 161, 165, 255
Ephron the Hittite 190
Epic of Adapa 580
Epictetus 376, 384-388, 390, 392, 396-401
—— Natural law 528, 530
Epicureans 343
—— Natural law 522
Epidaurus 454, 550

Epigrammata Graeca 573
Epistle to Hebrews, Hellenistic patterns 207-226
Epoche 597, 603
Eridu, cult of Ea 579, 580, 582
Eros and Agape 618
Esagila Temple, Babylon 580
Esau 62, 192, 274-276, 281, 291
Eschatology
—— Feast of Booths 89, 92
Essays in the Ritual of Social Relations 510
Essen, *Heliand* 246
Essenes, Natural law 540
—— Origin, gospel of St. John 153
—— Paul 28
—— White symbolism 512
Esther, Book of 434
—— Hellenistic motifs 338
Ethics 351
Ethiopia
—— Gods 341
—— *Narrative of St. Clement* 273
Etruscan gods 548
Eucharist, psychological study 114, 115, 124
Eumenes II 542, 543, 549
Eupator, Nicomedes, *see* Nicomedes
Euphrates 126, 131, 441
Eupolemos 203
Euripedes 409
Europe
—— Symbols 614
—— White symbolism 509
Eusebius 174, 202, 529
Eustathius 350
Euthydemus 379, 385-388, 390, 392-394, 396-399, 402-406, 408
Eve 344
—— Decline of civilization 339
Ewald, G. H. 102
Exilarchate and law 456
"Exodus, the," Ezekiel 359
Exodus
—— Theophany 360
Exposition of the Law 65
Ezekiel, "The Exodus" 359
—— Presence of God at Jerusalem 87
—— Vision 86
Ezra 91, 92, 160, 164
—— Memoirs 108
—— Rededication of Temple 102

False Decretals 122
Fars, Cyrus the Great 583
Fearer of the Lord, see Yirei Adonai

Feasts
—— Booths 88-96
—— New Years 88-96
—— Tabernacles 102, 165
Fertile Crescent 506
Festivals
—— New Moon 439
—— New Year, Babylon 576
—— Nikanor Day 102
—— Royal Zion 90
—— Sed 488
—— Succoth 101, 105
Feti, Domenico 612
Finkelstein, Louis 412, 414, 415
Fire signs, Egyptian symbols 480-482
First revolt, Jerusalem 329
First Triumvirate 133
Fischel, Henry A., *Cynicism* 396, 401, 409
"Florilegium, Das" 383
Foreigner from Galileo, (Jesus) 244
Foreign worshippers, Feast of Booths 93
"Former Prophets," compared 108
Fortress Sanctuary, King Solomon's Temple 104
Four Empires, vision 302
Four-fold Gospel Canon 122
Four Sons of Horus 482
Four Sons of Osiris 482, 485, 487, 493
Fourth Gospel 286
—— Agency of God 137-148
—— Prologue 282
Frank, Waldo 618
Frankfort, Henri 479
Fratres Pontifices, symbolism 615
Freud
—— Id 55
—— Symbols 611
Friedlander, M. 213
Friedman, M.
—— Pesiqta Rabbati, ed. 318
—— Sifre Deuteronomy, ed. 318
Fritsch, Charles T. 217-219
Fr. Papyrus Hibeh, Chria 376
Fr. Papyrus Reinach, Chria 376
Fulda, *Heliand* 245-246
Funerary divinities, Egyptian symbols 484, 485

Gabinius, Aulus 131
Gabriel 270, 271-273, 280
Gad Relief 571
Gaia, symbolism 613
Gaius Gracchus, *see* Gracchus
Galatia 132
—— Retaken by Mithradates 128

Galatians (Gauls) 126
—— Paul's warning to Hebrews 208
Galilee 123, 153, 161, 165, 166, 174
—— Early Christian Church 178
—— Hellenistic influences 176, 198, 200
—— Mark's Gospel 178
—— Roman influences 125-136
—— Sea 125, 172
—— Synagogue 440
Gamaliel 28, 29
Ganges River 339
Garden of Eden 344
Gathas 583
Gauls (Galatians) 126
—— Druids 121
Gebze 543
Gedichten 74
Gedulat Mosheh 369
Gemini 280
Genesis
—— Tradition in of scriptures 107
—— Truth 115
Genesis Apocryphon" 255
Gentiles, contact with Christianity 177
Georgics 343, 344, 349
Gerizim, *see* Mt. Gerizim
Germain, Gabriel 467
Germany
—— *Diatessaron* 246
—— Mainz, Sabazios inscription 543
—— Symbolism 616
Gesenius, H. S. W. 98
Getae, arrow symbol 466
Gideon 221, 222
—— Encounter with angel 76
—— Presence and absence of God 78
Gihon River 340
Ginzberg, L. 340, 589
Ginza 556-558, 562, 563, 565-567, 569
Glabrio 130, 131
Gluckman, M.
—— *Bantu Studies* 511
Gnomologium Vindonense 377, 383, 385-388, 390, 392, 393, 396-398, 402-406, 408
Gnosticism 116, 119
—— Christian 213
Goddess of North and of South 478
Goethe, Johann Wolfgang von 475
—— "Das Marchen" 616
Goff, Beatrice L.
—— *Symbols of Prehistoric Mesopotamia* 476
Goguel, M. 205
Goldberg, M., *Talmudische Traktat Derech Erez Rabba, der* 383
Golden Age 339, 341-343, 347-349, 352

Golden calf 186, 187, 192, 337
Golden Rule, Akiba 399
Goldin, Judah 441, 442
—— Abot de Rabbi Nathan, ed. 325
Goodenough, Erwin, R. 71, 227
—— American Society for the Study of Religion 593
—— Biblical interpretation advanced 111
—— *By Light, Light* 259, 289, 290
—— Cynicism and ancient Near East culture 372
—— Dating Gospel of St. John 149, 150
—— Flexibility of Judaism 425
—— Iranian studies 583
—— Jewish symbols 244, 227, 244, 315, 316, 441
—— *Jewish Symbols in the Greco-Roman Period* 109, 119, 124, 259, 441, 476, 506, 512, 513, 515-517
—— Judaism 176
—— Moses' kingship 355
—— Mystical Judaism 144
—— Natural law 531, 533
—— Paul, book concerning 244
—— Philo of Alexandria 148
—— Philo's *Life of Moses* 354
—— Philo's scholarship 522
—— Prayer of Joseph 253, 283
—— Rabbis and art 440-442, 444, 457, 459
—— "Religionswissenschaft" 590-592
—— Religious scholarship 594, 605-608
—— Sabazios inscription 543, 546-548
—— Scriptural interpretation 327
—— Studies of Philo (Epistles to Hebrews) 208, 209, 211, 213, 214, 218
—— Symbolism 123
—— Syncretism 354, 371
—— Symbols, contributions to universality cited 609-611
—— *Toward a Mature Faith* 112
—— Waters of Life 506
Gorgias 523
Gospel, see specific Gospel
—— Historic truth 119
Gospel of the Hebrews 248, 249
Gospel of the Nazorees 248, 249
Gospel of Thomas 245, 247-249
Grace, doctrine of Grace 120
Gracchus, Caius 127
Gracchus, Tiberius 126, 132
Grant, Frederick C.
—— *Rome and Reunion* 135
—— *Translating the Bible* 109
Grant, R. 155, 271, 273
Grasser, F. 162
Great Bear, constellation, Egyptian symbol 485
"Great Man," *see* Pompey
"Great" Mithradatic War 129
Great Sufferer, *see* Job

Greco-Roman areas, influences on early church 178
Greece 176
—— Roman civil wars 372
—— Roman influences 126, 129
—— Sabazios 543
—— Tradition in literature 108
—— Water symbolism 515
Greek
—— Christians 244
—— New Testament 246
—— Symbols 610, 611, 613
—— Telchines 350
Green-Armytage, A. H. N. 152
Gregory, school at Utrecht 246
Gunkel, Herman 99, 103, 219, 304
Gygaean lake 543

Hadad 549
Hades, symbolism 614
Hadrian 328
—— Temple of Jupiter Capitolinus 328
Haenchen, Ernst 201
Hagar 434
Haggadah, Passover 414-417
Halakhah
—— Christology parallels 137-148
Hallel 439
Hallevi, A. 325
Ḥama b. R. Ḥanina, R. 277
Haman 434
Hamor, sons 190
Hanfmann, George M. 542
Ḥanina, R. 324
Hapi 435
Hapy 483, 484, 494
Harakhte 499
Ḥaran 191
Harder 523
Harris, J. Rendel 282
Harvard, graduate study of history of religions 594
Harvard University, Sabazios inscription 542
Hasmonean kings 366
Hastings, J. 98
Hathor 494, 498
Hatt, Gutmund 468, 472
Haupt, Paul 102, 117
Halīẓah 439, 440
Heavenly Justice 425-437
Hebrew Bible 72
Hebrews, Epistle
—— Hellenistic patterns 207-226
—— Luther Bible 120
—— Philo Judaeus compared 207

Hebrews, Gospel of 248, 249
Hebron 190
Hecate-Artemis 548
Hecato of Rhodes 376
Hedonism 407
Hekhaloth Rabbati 261, 285
Helen of Troy 345
Heliand, Jewish influences 244-250
Heliopolis 490, 496, 499
Helios-Dionysos-Phanes 546
Helios-Samas 573, 577-579, 582
Heller, C. 193
Helmbold, W. C. 378
Hennecke-Schneemelcher, *Neutestamentliche Apokryphen* 253
Hense, O. 399
—— *Ionnis Stobael Anthologium*, ed. 380
—— *Teletis Reliquiae* 380, 381
Heracles, Philicretes 123
Heraclitus 352
Hercher, R., *Varia Historia*, ed. 377
Hercules, savior 58
Hermes 548
Hermopolis 490
Herod 125, 132, 134
—— Temple 327-335
—— The Idumean 275
Herodotus 339, 340
—— Arrow symbol 466
—— Natural law 524
Hesiod 341, 342, 347
—— *Works and Days* 341
Hexateuch, tradition of scripture 107
—— Truth 115
Hezekiah 97, 104
Hibil-Ziwa 566, 567
Hierapolis 175
Higger, M., Debe Rabbanan, the Treatise Derekh Erez 383
Higher Mystery of Moses 209, 220
Hillel 319, 427
"Hillel and the Proselyte" 396
Hillel ben Eliakim, R. 412
Hillel the Elder, Chria, 375, 376, 384, 393, 397-399, 401, 408-410
Hillelites 400, 401
Hindu, symbolism 615
Hinnom Valley 333
Hippo 120
Hippocrates, *De Aere Aquis Locis* 525
Hippolytus, Phaedra 338
Hippolytos 551
Hisda, R. 438, 446
Hispalus 547
History of Religions 590-608

Ḥiwi al-Balkhi 345
Ḥiyya, R. 285
Ḥiyya b. 'Ammi, R. 438
"Hoeing the Earth", Egyptian symbolism 485
Holderlin, Friedrich 475
Holland 246
Holscher, G. 352
Holtzmann, Beer-Holtzmann 325
Homer 245, 339, 342, 349, 409
—— Odyssey 341, 345
Honko, Lauri 463
Horace, *Ars Poetica* 337
Horizon History of Christianity 123
Horovitz-Rabin 416, 318
Horus 484, 487, 489, 498, 499
—— Four Sons 482
Hosea 163, 166, 174
Household of Israel 97
House of Life, Mandaean rites 557, 558, 565
House of Perfection 560-565
House of Washing 578, 579
Huna, R. 278
Husser, L., Epoche 597, 603
Hymn to Month 546
Hvmni et Sermones 570
Hypsistos, Zeus 458, 549
Hyrcanus II 131, 132, 134

Iambulus 343
Iao 547, 548
Id 55
Idumea, Roman influence 215-136
Iliad 340
Image of God 442
—— Notes on the Hellenization of Judaism 315, 319, 320
Imago Dei 315
Imsety 483, 484, 485
Incantation bowls 445
Incarceration Theory, Hans Schmidt 106
Incarnation, symbolism 113
India
—— Christianity 245
—— Josephus identifications 339
—— Lingayats 517
—— Persis 584
—— Tradition in literature 108
Indians (Coos), arrow symbol 469
Indra, arrow symbol 467
International Association for the History of Religions 593, 604
Ionia 547
—— Natural law 525
Ionnais Stobaei Anthologium 380, 385-388, 390 , 392-394, 396-398, 402-406, 408

Iran
—— History of religions 600
—— Religious studies, problems 583-589
—— Rites, Mandaean influences 553, 554
Irenaeus 151, 155-157, 240
—— Ophites 238
Iron Age, Hesiod 342, 347
Isaac 62, 190, 214, 256, 276, 283
—— Sacrifice depicted 331
Isaiah 115
—— Resident deity 87
—— Tradition in scripture 108
Ishmael 424
Isin, Lipit-Istar 581
Isis 513
—— Mysteries 570, 572
—— Savior 58
—— Symbols 478, 486, 487, 494
Islam
—— History of religions 599
—— Mu'tazilite 408
Israel
—— Angel of God 262-265
—— Deliverance 112
—— Divine dealings, Book of Jubilee 109
—— Election and enslavement in Egypt 107
—— Kings, chronicles compared with prophets 108
—— Land of Israel 412, 413
—— "Last stand" of faith 118
—— Law 316, 317
—— Man who has seen God 146
—— Paganism 116
—— Post-exile restoration 112
—— Rejection of Christ 52-64
—— Trial before Shekhinah 424, 425
Israelites
—— Battle with Philistines 77
—— Challenge authority of Moses 85
—— Culture 88-96
—— God's nearness 76
—— Horses, suspicions 93
—— Goodenough studies 71
—— Image of God 315-326
—— Mispah, battle 77
—— Motivations, religious 72
—— Origins of St. John's Gospel 158
—— Sanctuary, excavations 104
—— Worship 105
Istar 579
Istrael 262
Italy
—— *Diatessaron* 246
—— *Epistle to the Hebrews* 225
—— Sabazios 543

Jabbok River 276, 280, 281
Jabesh-gileadites 164
Jabin, arrow symbol 470
Jackson, Foakes, The Beginnings of Christianity 24
Jacob 62, 84, 159, 161, 189, 190, 214
—— Dream, ladder symbol 612
—— Experience at Bethel 79
—— House of 367
—— Laban's flock 337
—— Ladder vision 284, 286, 287, 291
—— Prayer of Joseph 255, 256, 258, 260, 272, 275-277, 284
—— Uriel conflict 259, 265, 270-272, 274-276, 278, 280, 281, 291
—— Vision and Israel 145, 146
—— Vision at Bethel 161
Jaldabaoth 239
Jamanda Rio, arrow symbol 470
James 157, 173-175
—— Christ and salvation 24
—— Luther Bible 120
—— Paul, association 29, 31, 33
—— Prominence in church 123
James, M. R. 255, 271, 272, 281
James, William 517
Janneus, Alexander 130, 136
Jaoel 279, 280
Japheth, settlement 340
Jebusite 213
Jephtha 221, 222
Jeremiah 212
—— Law observance 116
—— New covenant 94
—— Prophecy 87
—— Warns Royal Cult 81
Jericho, excavations 331
Jeroboam 97, 104, 173
Jerusalem 113, 213, 217-219, 309
—— Destruction 117
—— Fear God leaving Temple 85
—— Feast of Booths 88-96
—— First revolt 329
—— Hellenistic influences 176, 177, 180, 198-201, 204
—— Origin of St. John's Gospel 149, 153, 157, 163, 172, 173
—— Paul 29-31
—— Poverty after fall 118
—— Post-resurrection message 119
—— Roman influences 125-136
—— Royal cult, warnings 81
—— Second revolt 329
—— Temple 186, 195, 196, 327-335, 368
—— Temple cult 209, 213, 225
Jervell, J. 316-320, 322-326, 363
—— *Imago Dei* 315
Jesus Christ 121-123, 181, 182, 196, 197, 201, 202, 205, 206-208, 210, 212, 215,

—— 220-224, 226, 259, 272, 273, 291, 486
—— Adam to Christ, covenant 109
—— Adam-Christ typology 232
—— Agent for God 137-148
—— Cerinthus 287
—— Comparisons with Elisha and Elijah 166-175
—— Descended from David 35
—— Faith in resurrection 33
—— Faith of 45
—— Foreigner from Galilee 245
—— Galilean ministry 113
—— Gnostic Christology 227-243
—— Israel's rejection 62-64
—— Liberals, Biblical interpretation 111
—— Life history, difficulty 110
—— Logion 178
—— Meaning of ministry 118
—— Post-resurrection choice of leaders 123
—— St. John's Gospel 149, 159, 160, 163
—— Signs compared with miracles 167-173
—— Son of God related to Old Testament 137
—— Titles bestowed 229
—— White symbolism 512
Jesus Transfiguré 512
Jethro 534
Jewish Symbols in the Greco-Roman Period 109, 119, 124, 227, 259, 425, 441, 476, 506, 512, 513, 515-517
Jewish Targum 192, 193
Job 214
—— Truth 117, 118
John 115, 123, 196, 239, 287
—— Author of Gospel 149-175
—— Gospel of 112, 113, 197
—— God's agent 137-148
—— Philo parallels 146
—— Prominence in Church 123
—— Revelation to, deplored 120
—— Truth in Gospel 119
John Hyrcanus 164, 196
John Mark 157
John of Ephesus 151
John the Baptist 161, 171, 172, 256
Johnson, A. R. 213
Jonathan 164
Jones, Ernest 611
Jordan River 125, 171
—— Bathing miracle 169
—— Elijah and Elisha 171
—— Miracles 170
Jose, R. 400, 433
Joseph 184, 185, 190, 214
—— Prayer of Joseph 253-292
—— Tribe of Northern Kingdom 159-161

Josephus 164, 198, 201, 202, 216, 329, 363
—— *Antiquities* 336, 338, 352
—— Portrayal of man's decline 336-353
—— *Republic* 342
Joshua 91, 214
—— Extracts in Chronicles of Kings 108
Joshua, R., the skull, Chria 399
Joshua of Siknin, R. 436
Josiah 91, 104
Jubel 350
Judah 153, 160, 162-166, 190, 195
—— Chronicles of Kings compared with prophets 108
Judah, R. 455
Judah, Tamar 337
Judaism 119
—— Diaspora Judaism 111
—— God's presence, post-Biblical influence 87
—— History of religious study 607, 608
—— Justice 425-437
—— Mystery 425
—— Transitions 428
Judas Thomas 572
Jude, Luther Bible 120
Judea 162
—— Chria 407
—— Early Christian church 178, 190, 193, 198, 202
—— God's presence, departed 86
—— Roman influence 125-136
Judah 89, 90, 93
Judges 108
Jugurtha 128
Julia, daughter of Caesar 133
Julian the Apostate 345
Julius Caesar 121, 133-135
Julius, Suetonius 133
Jung, C. G. 242
—— History of religions 606
—— Symbols 611
Juniper, brother symbol 616
Jupiter Capitolinus, Temple 328
Jupiter, Mandaean rites 553
—— Sabazios traits 544
Justice
—— Heavenly Justice 425-437
—— Socrates' *Apology* 431
Justin Martyr 41, 109, 157, 193, 272, 551
—— *Baruch* 263

Kadesh, Ribeboth Kadesh 74
—— Approach of God 73
Kafka, Franz, "The Bridge" 617, 618
Kahle, Paul 190-192, 202
Kaibel, inscription 573

Kaiwan 553
Kasemann, Ernst 177, 178
Keulers, J. 296, 297
Kheraha 499
Khnum 496
Khonsu 487, 492
King Solomon's Temple, excavations 104
Kirkpatrick 102
Kiriath-arba 190
Kitagawa, Joseph 595, 601
Koester, Helmut 248
Koloe 543, 546, 548
Kolotes und Mendemos 377
Konig Lipit-Istar's Vergottlichung 581
Kore 545
Koryak, arrow symbol 478
Kraus, Hans-Joachim 90, 99, 103
Kraus, S., *Talmudische Archaeologie* 512
Kronos 585
—— Symbolism 613
Kristensen, Brede 595, 597
Kuiper, F. B. J., arrow symbol 467
Kula (Koloe) 543, 546, 548
Kumana, arrow symbol 471
Kusun family, arrow symbol 469
Kuthim 161

Laban 276, 534
—— Flocks 337
Lactantius Institute 529
Ladder, arrow symbol 471
—— Symbol 611, 612
Laessoe 575
—— *Cuneiform Texts* 577
Lake Condah, arrow symbol 469
Lake Kirsopp, *Beginnings of Christianity, The* 24
Lake of Fire, Egyptian symbol 481
Lalitavistara, arrow symbol 467
Lamprocles 395
Lamy, *Hymni et Sermones* 570
Land of Israel 412, 413
Laodiceia 543
Last Supper, Passover connection 114
Latin Christianity 244
Latter prophets, tradition in scripture 108
Lauterbach, J. Z. 317, 401, 415
Law
—— *Manilian law* 128
—— Moses 35, 47, 63
—— Nature, stoics 41
—— Prophets 116
Laws 347, 351, 513
Lazarus 165

Leah 190
Left Ginza 557, 558, 563, 565
Leges 526
Leisegang, H. 523, 546
Leo constellation, funerary divinities 484, 485
Leodicia 175
Leslie, Elmer A. 99, 102
Levi 212, 446, 450, 453
—— Enthronement 552, 558
Levi, R. 323
Levitical priesthood 212, 216
Lewis the Pious 245, 249
Libat 553
Liber Graduum 249
Libya, symbols 479
Lidsbarski 567, 572
—— *Das Johannesbuch* 562
—— Ginza 557
—— *Mandaische Liturgien* 552, 556, 561-565, 574, 575, 578
Lietzmann, H. 240, 551
Life of Moses 354
Lightfoot, J. B. 162, 163
Lingayats 517
Lion vision 296
Lipit-Istar 581
Liudger, Frisian missionary 246
Loci communi 383
Logana, arrow symbol 469
Logos 37, 59, 62, 63, 146, 210-212, 215, 259, 265, 267, 268, 272, 291, 517, 527, 529
—— Socrates and Plato incarnations 41
—— Son of man, relation 230-243
Lohmeyer, Ernst 178
Long, H. S., ed. *Diogeni Laertii Vitae Philosophorum* 382
Longinus 339
"Lord of the Two Lands," Egypt 479
Lower Mystery of Aaron 209, 216, 220, 225
Lucian (*Demonax*) 376
Lucretius 343, 346, 347, 350
Lucullus 129-131, 133
Luke 118, 149, 150
—— Compared with Matthew 119
—— Speech of Stephen 183
—— Stephen's mission 197-200
—— Tradition in scripture 110
Luther, Martin
—— Bible 120
—— James, Epistle of 120
—— *Neue Testament Deutsch* 120
—— Psalm 118, 99
—— Weimar-Ausgabe 120
LXX, *see* Septuagint
Lycainia 127, 543
Lycia 132

Lycus 543
Lydia 127
—— Sabazios inscription 543, 544, 548-550
Lydus, Johannes 547
Lystra 30, 132

Maat-ka-Re, princess 495, 499
Maccabees 328, 531
—— Martyrs 221
—— Restoration of Temple 102
—— Revolt 164
—— Samaritan 202
Macuch, R. 567
MacDonald, John 193-195
Macedon, Philip V 126
MacGregor, G. H. C. 151
Machpelah 190
Maeonia 543
Magdeburg, *Heliand* 245
Magen Avot 383
"Magical bow," bushmen 463
Magnesia 126
Mahabharata, arrow symbol 467
Maimonides 428
Mainz 543
Makiri 325
Malacca, Thunder Gods 465
Malachi, tradition in scripture 108
Mamre 190
Manasseh 161, 255
Manda dḤayye 567
Mandaeans 242
—— Baptism 551-582
—— Dialects 573, 574
—— Iranian religious history 588
—— Literature 137, 148
Manicheans 240, 241, 260
—— Dualism 58
—— Iranian religious history 588
Manilian law 128
Manilius 131
Marburg, History of Religions Congress 604, 605
Marchen, Das, symbolism 616
Marcus Aurelius 352
Marduk 579, 582
Marius 128, 129
Mark 118, 149, 160, 177
—— Divergent church, 206
—— Early church history 200
—— Gentile mission 202
—— Gospel, where composed 178
—— Tradition in scripture 110
Mark Antony, see Antony

Markus, gnostic system 240
Marqah 104
Marriage
—— Mandaean rites 552
—— Third century Babylonia 449
Mars, Mandaean rites 553
Marshall, J. T. 271, 272
Martyr, *see* Justin Martyr
Mary
—— Mother of Christ 486
—— Sister of Lazarus 170
Marxsen, Willi 178, 235
Matthew 115, 118, 119, 154, 160
—— Gentile mission 202
—— Gospel 174, 249
—— Revision of Mark 118
Maximus Confessor 383
Meaning and End of Religion, The 601
Mediteranean
—— History of religions 600
—— Truth of Gospels 119
—— Water symbols 506
Me'ir, R. 320, 321
Mekhilta 317, 415-418, 421, 424
Mekhilta de R. Yishmael 401
Mekhilta R. Simon 417, 418
Melanesia, arrow symbol 468
Melchisedek 297, 346
Melschzedek 212-214, 221
Memar 194, 195
Memar Marqah 160, 164, 360, 361, 362, 369
Men, Phrygian God 545, 546, 549
Menander 287
Mendelssohn, Moses 428
Menophilos 544, 549
Menye 543
Mercury, Mandaean rites 553
Merkabah 260, 264, 270, 279, 281, 284-286, 288, 289, 292
—— Mysticism 144, 147
—— Traditions 148
Merneptah 483
Merx, A. 366
Merzbacher, E. 332
Mesene 446
Mesopotamia 130, 246, 248, 249
—— Archaeological evidence 445
—— Baptismal rites 552, 554, 555, 570
—— Deification, symbols 570
—— Iranian religious history 588
—— Mithraism 587
—— Pre-Israelite religious traditions 73
—— Symbols 476, 477
—— Syrian 256

—— Water symbolism 515
Messalinianism 244
Metamorphoses 343, 348, 350, 352, 513
Metatron 259, 260, 263, 270, 271, 277, 279, 286, 291
Meter Hipta 544
Metrocles, Chria 376
Metropolitan Museum at Deir el-Bahri 494, 495
Meyer, H. A. 151
Micah
—— Image of God portrayed 75
—— Jerusalem Royal cult, reminders 81
Michael 259, 263, 265, 269, 270, 275, 277, 280, 291, 433, 434
Michaelson, Robert 594
Middle Kingdom, Egyptian symbols 485
Midianites 76
Midrash 412, 413, 419, 420
Migne, C-D. 383
Milarepa, arrow symbol 473
Mithra, arrow symbol 466
Min 492
Minucius, Felix Octav 529
Miracles
—— Elijah 167, 170-172
—— Elisha 167, 169, 170-172
—— Nature 170
—— Signs of Jesus 167
Miriam, leprosy 337
Mishnah 116, 325, 329, 377, 443, 455
—— Image of God 321
Mishnaic law 446
Mispah, battle 77
Mithra 548
—— Arrow symbol 466
—— Tag-i Bustan 587
Mithra Yast 586
Mithradates Kallinikos of Commagene 585
Mithradates of Pontus 127-131, 136
Mithradatic Wars 129
Mithraism 585-587
M'nd.t 501
Moabites 105
Moesia 543
Moloch 187
Month, Hymn to 546
Montu 492
Moon, Mandaean rites 553
Moralia 378, 379, 385-388, 390, 392, 393, 396-399, 401-406, 408
Moral Theology 120
Mordecai 424
Mosaic law 58
Mosaics, decoration 438-459
Moses 41, 59, 115, 181, 184-189, 192-197, 208, 210, 211, 214, 215, 219, 220, 224, 226, 418-420, 423, 426, 434, 435

—— And name of God 359-361
—— As God and King 354-371
—— Authority challenged 85
—— Brazen serpent cure 337
—— Code 56, 59
—— Crown of Light 361-365
—— Enthronement 354-359
—— Face of God 145, 146
—— General, against Ethiopians 338
—— Higher Mystery 209
—— Image of God 361-365
—— Mt. Sinai 444
—— Natural law 532-535, 537-539
—— Slaying Egyptians 337
—— Torah 43
—— Tradition in scripture 108
—— Warning, approaching Canaan 77
—— Water from rock 337
Mountain, arrow symbol 471
Mt. Gerezim 190, 193, 196, 197
—— Temple 161, 162
Mt. Horeb 360
Mount of Olives 89
Mt. Paran 74
Mt. Sinai 116, 190, 209-211, 217, 219, 317
—— Moses' Theophany 355, 357-360, 364, 367, 368, 371
—— Moses' revelation 444
—— Torah 351
Mt. Zion 217, 219
—— Zulu Zionists 507
Mowinckel, S. 98, 102
Muehsam, Alice 332
Muhammad 588
Multiplication of loaves 169
Munda, arrow symbol 467
Murena 129, 135
Muslim, history of religions 599, 601
—— Iranian religious history 584
—— Judaism, co-existence 428
Mut 487, 492
Mu'tazilite Islam 408
Mylasa 543
Mysia 127
Mystery of Israel 260
Myth, St. Sylvester 122

Naaman, miracle of Jesus 169
Naassene Sermon 551
Nachmanides 346
Nag Hammadi 147, 148
—— Prayer of Joseph 253-264
Nahman, R. 438, 457
Naphtali Sebi Yehudah Berlin, R. 412

Narsh 445
Narmakon, arrow symbol 471
Narrative of St. Clement 273
Narrinyeri, arrow symbol 470
Natal, Zulu Zionism 507
Nathan, R. 268, 436
—— Avot 403
Nathaniel 146, 159, 161, 162
National Association of Biblical Instructors 593
Nativity 112
Natural law 521-541
Nature, miracles 170
Nausicaa 341
Nazorees, Gospel of 248, 249
Nbu 553
Ndembu, symbolism 510, 515, 516
Nea Aule 544
Nebiim and Torah 116
Negev 73
—— Excavations 104, 105
Nehardea 439, 440, 443, 457
Nehemiah 164
—— Memoirs 108
Nehep 501
Nekhen 490
Neo-cynics 372
Neo-stoics 372
Nephthys, symbols 478
Nesib 412, 413
Nestorians 244
—— Baptism 551
Neue Testament Deutsch 120
Neutestamentliche Apokryphen 253
New Guinea, arrow symbol 470
New Hebrides, arrow symbol 469
New Kingdom texts, Egyptian symbols 485
New Moon Festival 439
New Year Festival 576
Nicephorus, *Stichometry* 254
Nicodemus 158, 159
Nicomedes Eupator 129
Nicomedes III of Bithynia 128
Nies, Babylonian inscriptions 580
Nikanor Day 102
Nike, Gad relief 571
Nile River 340
Nile Valley, symbols 479
Nillson, M. P. 545, 547, 548
Nippur Temple 581
Nirig 553
Noah 214, 318, 323, 326
—— Covenant 93, 95
Noachide laws 444

Noachite commandments 321
—— Paul's teachings 30
Noah's Ark, Apameian coins 547
Nock, A. D. 542, 548, 549
Noldeke, Th. 567
Nomkubulwana, goddess of fertility 511
Nomos 525, 527, 529, 530
Norden 184
Nordic symbols, bridge or ladder 613
Northern Kingdom 158, 159, 161, 164
Ntlakyapamug, arrow symbol 470
Nubia, symbols 479
Numbers, abstract superstitions 477
Numbers, Book of 77
Nunn, A. P. V. 152
Nut (goddess) 489, 499

Ocellus Lucanus 523
Octavia 348, 349
Octavian Caesar 134, 135
Odeberg, H. 144
Ode to Thanksgiving, Psalm 97
Odin, symbolism 613
Odysseus 341, 345
Odyssey 341, 345
—— Arrow symbol 467
Oedipus 347
—— Solomon likened 338
Oesterly, W. 97, 103
Ogdoad 147
Ohrmazd 585
Okeanos River 339
Old Covenant, titles given Christ 229
Oldfather, W. A. 384
Ophite 213
—— Gnostic system 238
Optimo Genere Oratorum 337
Origen 157
—— *Commentary on John* 254, 256, 281, 282
—— *Contra Celsum* 288
—— *Philocalia* 254, 258, 281, 284, 286, 291
—— *Prayer of Joseph, The* 253, 254, 271-273, 287
Orion 488
Orpheus 289
Orphics 57
Osiris 484, 487, 488, 490-492, 494, 499, 513, 517, 548
—— Four Sons 482, 485, 487, 493
—— O-headed jars 481
Ostyak, arrow symbol 468
Otzen, Benedikt 89
Ovid 343, 348, 349
—— *Amores* 344, 349
—— *Heroides* 507

—— *Metamorphoses* 343, 350, 352

Padan-aram 276
Palaioi, Seven Sages 374
Palestine 149, 190, 200, 225, 245
—— Carnival of blood 126
—— Gentiles, land acquisition 322
—— Hellenistic culture 176
—— Judaism 318, 428
—— Matthew's Gospel 178
—— Rabbis in third century 440, 441, 444
—— Roman influence 125-136
Pappas, R. 435
Palmyra 549
—— Cult relief 572
—— Deification symbols 431
—— Gad 571
—— Temple of Bel 329, 330, 335
Pamphylia 127, 543
Panaitios 528
Papias 110
Parable of the Wheat, *Heliand* 247, 248
Paran 73
Pardes, scriptural interpretation 327
Pardo, R. David 413
Parmenides 524
Parousia 61
Parsis 584
Parthian
—— Coin symbols 571
—— Iranian religious history 584, 588
—— Mandaean rites, terminology 555
Passion art 122
Passover Haggadah 414-417
—— Haggadah 414-417
—— Last Supper, connection 114
Patrologia Graeca 383
Patterns 595
Paul 115, 118, 136, 149, 157, 173, 175, 223, 427
—— Arrest 201
—— Doctrine of Grace 120
—— Exceptional author 112
—— Hellenistic influences 177, 179, 183, 198-200, 202, 206
—— Hellenization of Christianity 23, -68
—— Liberals, Biblical interpretation 111
—— Reversion to Judaism 207
—— Visions and revelations 114
—— Vision, Damascus Road 26, 29, 68
Parker, P. 152
Pe 490
Peniel 270
Pentateuch 78
Pentecost 93

—— Biblical style 112
Peretian 238
Perea 125
Pergamum 127, 131, 543, 544, 548, 549
—— Attalus III 126
Peregrinus Proteus 410
Perry, B. E.
—— *Aesopi* 379
—— *Vita Lolliniana* 379
Persepolis 587
Persians, dualism 58
Peshat 327
Peter 30, 33, 157, 174, 175, 273
—— Christ and salvation 24
—— Paul in Arabia 29
—— Post-resurrection commission 114
—— Promise 113
—— Restoration 122, 123
—— Stephen's mission 198, 199
Peterman
—— *Left Ginza* 557
—— *Right Ginza* 566
Petra 335
Pettazzoni, Raffaele 468, 471
Phaeacians 341
Phaedra 348, 349
—— Hippolytus 338
Phaedrus 57
Phaenomena 347
Phaethon 352
Phanes 546
Pharnaces 132
Pharaoh 434
Pharsalia 134
Philadelphia (Alasehir) 543, 549
Philanthropia 407
Philemon 342
Philip 174
—— Samaritan mission 180, 197-199
Philip V of Macedon 126, 129
Philip, son of Herod the Great 125
Philippi 134
Philistines
—— Aphek, battle 77
—— Mispah, battle 77
Philo 109, 144, 185, 191, 193, 203, 231, 235, 236, 240, 260, 265-267, 270, 272, 275 282, 291
—— And law 40-43, 58, 59, 62-68
—— Chria 376
—— *De confusione linguarum* 267, 340
——— *De Specialibus Legibus* 65
—— *De Virtute* 65-67
—— *Exposition of the law* 65

—— Influence, Epistle to Hebrews 207-212, 214-220, 222, 224, 225
—— John, parallels 146
—— *Leg. all.* 145, 146
—— *Life of Moses* 354, 355, 357, 359, 360, 364, 369
—— Natural law 522, 529-541
—— Prayer of Joseph 259
—— *Quaestiones in Genesin* 213
—— Romans, Epistle compared 23-68
—— *Sacrificiis Abelis et Caini,* de 345, 346
—— Specific laws 32, 35, 38, 50, 51
—— *Vit. Cont.* 532
Philocalia 254, 258, 281, 286, 291
Philoctetes, Heracles 123
Philolaos 524
Philoponia 49, 407
Philosopher, Chria 373
Philosophoumena 551
Phineas 214
Phoenicia, Stephen's mission 199
Phrygia 127, 128, 543-547
Physis 525, 527, 530
Piankoff, Alexander 481
Pilate, Pontius 159
Pindar 523
Pirke Avot 383
Pirke Hekhaloth 264, 280
Pishon River 339
Pisidia 127, 543
Pittacus, Plutarch 378, 379, 385-388, 390, 392, 393, 396-398, 402-406, 408
Plato 41, 42, 54, 58, 231, 337, 342, 349, 411, 431
—— *Allegory of the Cave* 54
—— *Gorgias* 523
—— Influence on Epistle to Hebrews 218
—— Ladder symbol 611
—— *Laws* 347, 351, 513
—— *Leges* 526
—— *Phaedrus* 57
—— Psalm 118, 99
—— Salvation 232
—— *Statesman* 340, 342
—— *Timaeus* 352
—— White symbolism 513
Pleiades, arrow symbol 470
Pliny 340
Plutarch 376, 399, 403, 547
—— *Apophthegmata Laconica* 395
—— *Ancesilaus* 379
—— *Moralia* 378, 379, 385-388, 390, 392, 393, 396-399, 401-406, 408
—— *On Euthydemus* 379, 385-388, 390, 392-394, 396-399, 402-406, 408
—— *On Socrates* 379
—— *Pittacus* 378, 385-388, 390, 392, 393, 396-398, 402-406, 408
—— *Roman Questions, The* 513
—— White symbolism 513, 517

Pneuma, Corinthian letters 232, 239
Polis 522, 523
Politics 526, 527
Polycarp 228
Pompey 127-133, 135
Pontifex Maximus, symbolism 615
Pontius Pilate 136
Pontus, Mithradates of 127
Pontus
—— Roman influence 125-136
Pope, title, symbolism 615
Pool of Siloam 169
Poseidon 341
Potiphar, wife 338
Praetextatus, tomb frescoes 546
Prayerbooks, pagan Rome 244
Predestinarians 63
Preuss, Theo 137, 138
Priam 351
Prologue to the Fourth Gospel 282
Prophets, law and the prophets 116
Protagoras 526
Protestants
—— Biblical interpretations 111
—— History of religion, study 608
Prounikos 239
Proverbs, tradition in scripture 108
Psalm 118
—— Alexander the Great inspiration 102
—— Circumcision celebration, time of 102
—— Corner stone proverb 101
—— Feast of Tabernacles 102
—— History unsettled 97
—— Incarceration theory, Hans Schmidt 106
—— Masoretic text, analysis 97-106
—— Nikanor-Day 102
—— Restoration of the Temple 102
—— Song of the Citadel 97-106
—— Succoth festival 105
—— Tradition in scripture 108
Pseudo-cynic letters 376
Pseudo-Seneca, *Octavia* 348, 349
Psychology, interpretation of Bible 107-124
Psylli, arrow symbol 466
Psysennes 483, 493, 496, 497
—— Tomb at Tanis 482
Ptah 484
Ptolemais 130
Ptolemais-Accho 549
Ptolemeans 240
Ptolemy 32
Pumbedita 445
Punic War, third 126

Pyramid Texts 484, 485, 487
Pythagoreans, natural law 522, 537

Qarna 453
Qebehsenuf 483, 485
Queen Helena of Adiabene 333
Quispel 144
Qumran 116, 154, 368
—— Community, white symbolism 512

Ra, *see* Re
Rabbis, role in Babylonia 438-459
Rachel at the well 161
Racine, Jean Baptiste 475
Rainbow, symbolism 613
Raising the dead 170
Ramayana 615
—— Arrow symbolism 467
Ramesses VI 500-502
Raney, W. H. 150
Rank, Gustav 466
Rank, O. H. 611
Rappaport 339, 351
Rasanen, Martti 468
Rashi 423, 424
Rav 438-441, 444, 445, 448-455, 457
Rav Sheshet 438, 457
Re, Egyptian symbols 481, 483, 484, 487, 496, 498, 499, 501, 2 502
Real 42
Rebekah 190, 274
Red Crown 478, 479
Red Heifer sacrifice 444
"Red Land," Egypt, symbols 479
Red Sea, baptism into Moses 59
—— Symbols 479
Reformation, Biblical study 120
Rehoboam 163
Reitzenstein 551, 552, 569, 570
Religionswissenschaft 590-608
Religious studies 590-608
Religious System of the Amazulu, The 509
Remez 327
Remus 350
Rengstorf, K. H. 137
Rephan, star 187
Republic 342
Resh Lakish 269, 435
Resurrection
—— Appointment, church leadership 123
—— Biblical style 112
Restoration
—— Peter 122, 123
—— Temple 103

Reuben 160
Revelation
—— Book of 156, 157
—— Deplored 120
—— Inacceptability 121
—— Luther Bible 120
Rhodes 126, 127, 350
Ribeboth Kadesh 74
Riesenfeld, H., *Jesus Transfiguré* 512
Right Ginza 566
Rig Veda, arrow symbol 467
Rio Jamunda, arrow symbol 470
Ritschlians 109
Ritual law, third century Babylonia 450
Roberts, C. 548
Robinson, D. M. 542
Robinson, J. A. T. 153, 163
Robinson, W. 102
Roman civil wars 372
Roman Empire
—— Mithraism 587
—— Vision in IV Ezra 296-300, 302, 304, 305
Romans, Epistle, compared to Philo's writings 23-68
Roman Questions, The 513
Rome 156, 161, 176, 275, 350
—— Christ and meaning to church 131
—— Eastern development 125-136
—— Iranian religious history 584
—— Latin Christianity 244
—— Pagan prayerbooks 244
—— Paul 32
—— Sabazios inscription 543
—— "Social war" 127
—— Symbolism 615
Rome and Reunion 122
Romulus 350
Rose, H. J. 513
Royal Citadel of Arad 104
Rubicon 134
Rudolph, K. 567
Russia, arrow symbol 474
—— Mithradates of Pontus 127

Saadia, Gaon 428
Sabaoth 147, 264, 547
Sabazios inscription 541-550
Sabbath, laws of 399, 401, 403
Sabbath Zionist Church 507
Sabbatistai of Cilicia 543, 547
Sacred Blood 114
Sacrifice of Isaac, depicted 331
Sacrificiis Abelis et Caini, De 345, 346
Sadducees, Paul 28

Sage-Philosopher, Chria 373
St. Augustine, woman taken in adultery 120
St. Boniface
—— *Codex Fuldensis* 245
—— *Heliand* 245
St. Sylvester 122
Sallustius 410
Samael 433, 434
Samaria 190, 198, 199
—— Elisha 171
—— Feast of Booths 94
—— Prophets 166-173
—— St. John's Gospel, origins 149-175
—— Spread of Christianity 177, 178, 198-200, 202
—— Targum 191, 193
Samaritans
—— Mission of Christianity 177, 178
—— Pentateuch 191, 192-194, 196, 202
Samas (Helios) 573, 577, 579, 582
Samis 553
Samki 455
Sammael 275
Samson 338
Samuel 221, 438-440, 446-448, 450-457
—— Defects at Aphek 77
—— Extracts on Chronicles of Kings 108
—— White symbolism 512
Sanctuary, fortress, excavations 104
Sanday, W. 151
Sanhedrin 430
—— In Judea 133
—— Stephen summossed 180
Sarabhanga Jataka, arrow symbol 467
Sarah, wife of Abraham 49, 190
Sarapis 545
Sarcophagus, symbols 477
Sardica 548, 549
Sardis, Sabazios inscription 542-550
Sasanians 444, 448, 449
—— Iranian religious history 584
Satan, envy of Adam 278
Saturn 344
—— Mandaean rites 553
Saturnian Age 343, 349
Saul 171, 174, 213
—— Depicted by Josephus 338
Saussaye, Chantepie de la 595
Savara (Saora) 464
Savazis 543
Saxony, *Heliand* 249
Schaeder, H. H. 588
Schalit, A. 350
Schechter, S. 325

—— *Avot de R. Nathan* 383, 319, 383
Schlatter, A. 150
Schenkel, H. 383
Schmidt, Hans, Incarceration Theory 106
—— Psalm 118 103
Schneemelcher, Hennecke, *Neutestamentliche Apokryphen* 253
Scholem, G. G. 144, 279
—— *Jewish Gnosticism, Merkabah Mysticism and Talmudic Tradition* 319
Schollmeyer, *Sumerisch-babylonische Hymnen und Gebete an Samas* 579
Schoolmen, Catholic dogma 111
Schubert, Kurt 154
Science age, Bible, Catechism 115
Scripture
—— Second Vatican Council debate 107
Sebeg 479
Second birth 146
Second Revolt, Jerusalem 329
Sed, festival 488
Sedek 213
Seechem 190, 193
Sefer Raziel 262
Segekberg, Eric 551, 558
Seir 275
—— Approach of God 73, 74
Seleucids 550
—— Iranian religious history 584
—— Kingdom 129-132
Seleucus 133
Seleucus Nicator 571
Semai, arrow symbol 465
Seneca 344, 376, 403
—— *Phaedra* 348, 349
Septuagint 99, 101, 158, 190-193, 338, 339, 345, 423
Seraphim 264
Serapis 513
Serpent, Adam, Ophites 238
Sertorius 131
Seth 214, 350, 351
Sethians, Gnostic system 238
Seven, importance in Mandaean rites 552
Seven Sages (*Palaioi*) 374
Sextilis 135
Shakespeare, William 475
Shamanism 463, 464
Shamash 578
Shammai 427
—— School 321
Shammaites 401
Shekhinah 434
—— Wisdom 282
Shila, R. 455
Shiloh
—— Israelites carry Ark to Aphek 77

―― Micah and Jeremiah cite fall to Royal Cult at Jerusalem 81
Shitil-Uthra 566
Shi'ur Qomah 319
Shu 489, 494
―― Symbolism 612
Shutt, R. J. H. 350
Siberia, arrow symbol 464, 466
Signs of Jesus 167-173
"Signs Sources" 153
Sikinos 544
Siloam, healing at pool 169
Silver Age 347
Simeon 160
Simeon b. Lakish, R. 285, 289
Simon 287
Simon Bar Kosiba 327
Simon b. Tsemach Duran, *Magen Avot* 383
Simon Magus 152
―― Stephen's mission 188
Simon, Marcel 177, 186-188
Simon ben Yoḥai, R. 322
Sinnai, see Mt. Sinai
Sinaiticus 247
Sirach, tradition in scripture 108
Sislam-Rba 561
Skeat, T. C. 548
Smith, C. W. F. 154, 341
Smith, Morton 287, 605
―― "Image of God: Notes on the Hellenization of Judaism, The" 315, 319, 320, 442
  Moses theophany 361-363
Smith, Wilfred C. 599, 600, 601, 602
―― *Meaning and End of Religion, The* 601
Smith, T. V. 120
Snape, H. C. 154
Soatra 543
"Social War", Rome 127
Socrates 41, 58, 432
―― *Apology* 431, 432
―― Chria 374, 337-379, 395, 397, 399
―― Plutarch on 379, 385-388, 390, 392-394, 396-399, 402-406, 408
Society for the Scientific Study of Religion 593
Sod 327
Sodomites 531, 439
Sokolowski, F. 548
Solomon 182, 187, 195, 476
―― Depicted by Josephus 338
―― Temple of 330
Solon 351, 532
Song of the Citadel, Psalm 11 97-106
Son of Man, concept of Messiah, IV Ezra 295-312
―― Logos relation 230-243
Sontheimer, W. 377

Sophia 59, 232, 239, 282-284
Sophists 432
—— Natural law 522, 524-526, 540
Sophocles Ajax 524
Soteriology 230, 232, 237, 240
"Soul of Thn't, Great in the Netherworld" 487
South America, arrow symbol 464, 468
Southern Kingdom 159
Spain
—— Judaism, transition to 428
—— Roman influence 131, 133
Sparta, Roman influence 129
"Spoiled Meal, The", Chria 375, 394, 402, 406
Statesman 340, 342
Stations of the Cross, psychological effects 121
Stephen
—— Blasphemous remarks 181
—— Hellenistic Christianity 176-206
—— Hostility toward Temple 177
—— Mission 197-200
—— Speech 182-197
—— Trial and death 181
Stichometry 254
Stobaeus 210, 352, 377, 378, 394, 399, 403, 406
Stoicism 374
Stoics
—— Law of nature 41
—— Natural law 521-541
Stoicorum Veterum Fragmenta 378
Strabo 339, 350
—— Psalm 118 99
Stratonice 544
Styx, symbolism 613
Succoth festival 101, 105
Sudan, symbols 613
Suetonius 132, 133
—— *Claudius* 132
—— *Julius* 133
Sulla 128-130, 132
Sulpician riots 128
Sulpicius 128
Sumerian word structure 574
Sumerisch-babylonische Hymmen und Gebet Samas 579
Sun, Mandaean rites 553
Sundkler, B. 506, 507, 509-511, 514, 515
—— *Bantu Prophets in South Africa* 506
Sura synagogue 440, 443, 458
Suzanna 158
Swan motif, arrow symbol 469
Switzerland, Sabazios 543
Sword bridge, symbolism 613
Symbolism 107-124
—— Catholic Church 615

GENERAL INDEX 683

—— Collegium of the Pontifices 615
—— Psychological study of Bible 107-124
Symbols
—— Ancient to modern times 611
—— Bridge of arrows 613
—— "Bridge sacrifice" 614
—— Christianity 609
—— Deification 570
—— Dionysus 609
—— Dream 611
—— Greeks 610
—— Hades 614
—— Judaism 609
—— Ladder and bridge 611
—— Prehistoric Mesopotamia 476
—— Sword bridge 613
—— Universality, contributions by Goodenough 609
Synnada 543
Synoptic Gospels 376
Syria
—— Christians 244, 245
—— Paul 29
—— Roman influence 129-132
—— Symbols 570
—— Hellenistic influences 176, 198-200
—— Matthew's Gospel 178
—— Origin of St. John's Gospel 150, 164, 174
—— Paul 29
—— Roman influences 129-132
—— Symbols 570, 611
—— Water symbols 515
Syro-Palestinian Semite Christianity 244

Taheb 195, 197
Talmud 428
—— Babylonia 443
Talmud Bavli 383
Talmudim 383, 403
Talmudısche Archaeologie 512
Talmudısche Traktat Derech Erez Rabba, Der 383
Tamar, Judag 337
Tami, arrow symbol 470
Tammuz 578, 581
Tamoi, arrow symbol 470
Tanḥuma, Bereshit 280
—— Buber, ed. 318
Tanhuma, R. 355, 357-359
Tanis, Psusennes' tomb 482
Tannaitic Hillel, *Chriae* 376
Taq-i Bustan Mithra 587
Targum Jonathan on Genesis 317
Targumim 284
Tarsus 28, 29

Tatian 245, 246, 248, 249
Taurus 280
Taylor, E. B. 463
Tcitue, arrow symbol 470
Teaching of Marqah 194
Teeple, H. M. 154, 162
Tel Arad, excavations 103, 104, 106
Telchines 350
Teles 376, 399
Teletis Reliquiae 380, 385-388, 390, 392-394, 396-398, 402-406, 408
Telos 527, 528
Teman 74
Temple
—— Ark of the Covenant, Herod's Temple 330, 332
—— Assyrian 218
—— Babylon, Esagila Temple 580
—— Cult 154
—— Herod's 327-335
—— Jerusalem 186, 195, 196, 327-335, 368
—— Jupiter Capitolinus 328
—— Liturgy 97, 99
—— Motivations 78
—— Nippur 581
Temple-Gate Liturgies 103
Temple of Bel, Palmyra 329, 330, 335
Temple of Solomon 330
Terah 191
Testimonia adversus Iudaeos 273
Teutons 128
Thackery, H. St. J. 350
Thanksgiving, Ode to, Psalm 118 97
Theicritus of Chios, Chria 276
Theodorus, Chria 376, 381, 399
Theophratus, *Characters* 545
—— Natural law 523
Theos Hypistos 548, 549
Thera 544
Third Session of the Vatican Council 114
Thomas, Gospel of 245-249
Thoth 494
Thoueris 494
Thrace 543, 547
—— Arrow symbol 465
Thucydides 351
Thunder clouds, symbols 465, 466
Tiber 125
Tiberius 125
Tiberius Gracchus, *see* Gracchus
Tibet, arrow symbol 466, 468, 472, 473
Tibullus 349
Tiglathpileser 164
Tigranes of Armenia 129, 130, 132, 136
Timaeius 352

Timothy 30, 31
Titus 31
Tobit, Book of 589
Tokyo, history of religions congress 604
Torah 40, 41, 65, 116-118, 178, 182, 186-188, 196, 197, 201, 209, 310, 351, 420, 438, 439
—— And Moses 43
—— Nation's learning 92
—— Natural law 533, 535, 536
—— Nebiim 116
—— Obediance and freedom 425-437
—— Relation to community 92
—— Sophia 283
—— Wisdom-Torah 283
Torrey, C. C. 150
Toward a Mature Faith 112
Tradition
—— New Testament 110
—— Old Testament 107
—— Protestant-Catholic controversy 115
—— Psychological study of Bible 107-124
—— Second Vatican Council debate 107
Trajan 151
Transjordan 165
Translating the Bible 109
Troeltsch, Ernst 119
Tubal-Cain 350
Tupi-Cuarayu, arrow symbol 470
Turks, arrow symbol 468
Turner, V. W.
—— *African Systems of Thought* 510
—— *Chihamba the White Spirit* 510
—— *Essays in the Ritual of Social Relations* 510
Twenty first dynasty, Egyptian symbols, 476-478, 484-488, 492, 492, 496, 497, 499, 500, 502

Ugaritic literature 73
'Ulla 438
'Ukba, Mar 452, 453
Umtsgezi River 514
Unen-nefer 484
Unfinished Symphony 517
University of Chicago, religious studies 594, 595
Unkulunkulu 514
Uranos, symbolism 613
Ur, pattern in Chria 404
Uras 581
Uriel 256, 258, 265, 270-278, 280, 281, 291
—— Jacob-Israel conflict 258, 260, 265, 270-272, 274-276, 278, 280, 281, 291
Urmensch-Redeemer 231, 233, 234, 236
Usumus 543
Uthra 560, 562, 566, 568
Utrecht 246

Valentinians 240, 241
Van Unnik 155, 156
Valerius Maximus 547
Valhalla, symbolism 613
Valkyries, symbolism 613
Van der Leeuw, Gerardus 595
Varia Historia 377
Vatican Council
—— Second session 107
—— Third session 114
Vedas 583
Venus, Mandaean rites 553, 554
Vermeule, C. 544, 545
"Vessel of Ashes," Zulu Zionism 511
Vetus Latina 247
Vibia, tomb frescoes 546, 548
Vienna Papyrus, ed. Croenert 376
Vincentius, tomb frescoes 546, 548
Virgil 343, 349
—— *Eclogues* 343, 349
—— *Georgics* 343, 344, 349
Virgin birth, symbolism 113
Virtue, de 65-67
Visions 297-302, 304, 305
—— Eagle vision 296
—— Lion 296-303
Vita Aesppi 376, 379, 385-388, 390, 392, 393, 396-398, 402-406, 408
Vita Lolliniana 376, 379, 385-388, 390, 392, 393, 396-398, 402-406, 408
Volz, P. 307
von Dobschutz, E. 151
von Rad 90
"Vorlage" 393
Vulgate 346, 247, 423

Wach, Joachim 596
Wachsmuth, C.
—— *Weiner Apophthegmensammlung* 383
—— *Gnomologium Vindobonense* 383
—— *Ioannis Stobaei Anthologium* 380
Wadj, signs 494
Washeba, John 542
Water, symbolism 514-516
Wedding at Cana 168
Weimar-Ausgabe 120
Weiser, Artur 90, 98, 99
Wellhausen, Graf von 102
Wendt, H. H. 151
Werden, *Heliand* 246, 249
West Africa, symbols 613
Western religious history 119
Wheat parable, *Heliand* 248
White Crown, Egyptian symbol 479

Whiteness, symbolism 509-513
Widengren, Geo 287, 587, 604
—— Zurvanism 585
Wiener Apophthegmensammlung 377, 383, 385-388, 390, 392, 393, 396-398, 402-406, 408
Wilcox, Max 191-193
Wilder, Thornton, *Bridge of San Luis Rey, The* 616
Wilkens, W. 152, 153
Willoughby, R. 514
Windisch, Hans 212, 219
Wisdom Books
—— Tradition in scripture 108
Wisdom literature 272
Wisdom of Ben-Sira, The 282, 283
Wisdom of Solomon 182
Wisdom-Shekinah 282
Wisdom-theology 270
Wisdom-Torah 283
Woman taken in adultery, St. Augustine 120
Works and Days 341
Wright, Apocryphal Acts of the Apostles, The 572
Wundt, Wilhelm 468

Xanthippe 377-379, 381-383, 394-397, 399, 404
Xanthus 380
Xenophon 396, 395, 396, 399, 400, 404, 406
Xerxes 587, 588
Xronos 585

Yaikin 543
Yale, religious studies 594
Yalkut Reubeni 276
Yannai, R. 285, 286
Yaru Fields, Egyptian symbols 480, 499, 501
Yawar 568
Yirei Adonai 97, 105
Yoshamin 562
Yurakare, Bolivian thunder god 465

Zagreus 545
Zealots 116
Zebedee 152, 156, 157
Zechariah 113
Zeigler, K. 377
Zeitgeist 120
Zeitz, H. 377
Zeno 374, 527, 529
Zeus 345, 352, 410
—— Hymn of Cleanthes 530
—— Sabazios identity 544-549
Zeuxis 550
Zimmern, H. 552, 577
—— Konig Lipit-Istar's Vergottlichung 581

Zion
—— Pilgrimage of nations 89, 90, 95
Zion City, Illinois, Zulu Zionists 507
Zoroastrianism 583-589
Zosimos I 573
Zululand 514
Zulu religion, whiteness as symbol 509-511
Zulu Zionism 506-520
Zurvandat 585
Zurvanism 585
Zwi Werblowsky, Raphael Jehudah 604, 605

www.ingramcontent.com/pod-product-compliance
Lightning Source LLC
Chambersburg PA
CBHW050514020526
44111CB00052B/1551